THE WAITE GROUP®

Falcon 3.0: The Complete Handbook

Joel Powell
and
Tom Basham

WAITE GROUP PRESS™

Editorial Director: *Scott Calamar*
Development Editor: *Mitchell Waite*
Managing Editor: *John Crudo*
Content Editor: *Heidi Brumbaugh*
Technical Reviewer: *Rob Heittman*
Design and Production: *Rogondino & Associates*
Illustrations: *Pat Rogondino*
Cover Design: *Michael Rogondino*
Production Manager: *Julianne Ososke*

Published by Waite Group Press, 200 Tamal Plaza, Corte Madera, CA 94925.

Waite Group Press is distributed to bookstores and book wholesalers by Publishers Group West, Box 8843, Emeryville, CA 94662, 1-800-788-3123 (in California 1-510-658-3453).

Printed in the United States of America
92 93 94 95 • 10 9 8 7 6 5 4 3 2 1

Powell, Joel.
Falcon 3 : the complete handbook / Joel Powell and Tom Basham
p. cm.
Includes bibliographical references and index.
ISBN: 1-878739-29-8 : $34.95 ($44.95 Can.)
1. Falcon (Computer program) 2. Computer war games. 3. Fighter plane combat—Computer simulation. 4. Flight simulators. 5. Air interdiction—Computer simulation. 6. F-16 (Jet fighter plane—Computer simulation. I. Basham. Tom. II. Title.
U310.p69 1992
793.9'2—dc20

92-32808
CIP

Dedication

To Lori.
- *Joel Powell*

To Sara.
- *Tom Basham*

Introduction

Your heart is pounding, hands sweating as the hangar doors slide open revealing the moonless Arabian sky. Slowly your F-16 stalks its way to runway 27. The Pratt & Whitney turbofan whines in anticipation as you release the wheel brake marking the start of your mission. Racing down the runway you kick in the afterburner lifting off and up into a twenty degree climb. A mile away, an American journalist reports via satellite that something is unusual about your takeoff tonight. You bank toward the north heading for the southern border of Iraq. You know something the journalist only suspects...this is not a drill...this is not a training mission...Desert Storm has begun! Are YOU ready for this challenge? With ***Falcon 3: The Complete Handbook*** at your side, you will be!!!

The Popularity of the Flight Simulator

Flight simulators have been very popular since the introduction of the personal computer. Enthusiasts from all walks of life have spent countless hours flying these digital aircraft. In the early stages there was only one major player in the flight simulation market. This has changed remarkably in the past few years. Improvements in computer performance and graphics technology provide programmers with the platform for creating simulators that approach realism. Today you can experience the thrill of actually sitting in the cockpit of any aircraft from a Piper Cub to a Fighting Falcon. All it takes is a visit to your local software store and a few dollars to get started. You will find simulators ranging from mild to challenging.

Falcon 3.0—A Leap Forward in Simulation

In the fall of 1991, Spectrum Holobyte released a product that has changed the standards of the flight simulator: *Falcon 3.0*. The product evolved from the original *Falcon* released in 1985. Subsequent versions have taken advantage of the leading-edge technology to get the most out of today's computers. The high-speed 80386 processor and VGA graphics are the platform for Falcon 3.0. These features, coupled with sound boards (such as the Creative Labs Soundblaster), present the most realistic challenges ever seen on a home computer. You truly feel like you are part of the action at all times.

Not Just a Flight Simulator At first glance, Falcon 3.0 appears to be a high-tech flight simulator or just another arcade-style game. While such comparisons may be valid, it is also a campaign simulator. Not only does the software call on your piloting skills, it also requires you to be a military strategist. You are squadron commander of eighteen F-16 Falcons and thirty pilots. Your decisions and tactics will affect the outcome of conflicts in Kuwait, Panama, or Israel. Of course you can use the *Instant Action* mode if arcade action is your game. But the real fun starts in training for and successfully completing a Falcon 3.0 campaign.

Continuing Improvement of Falcon 3.0 Because Falcon 3.0 is on the leading edge of simulator technology, it was bound to contain a glitch here and there. Spectrum Holobyte has revised the original package to fix problems they have discovered. Every time you start Falcon 3.0, the version is listed in the lower right hand corner of the copyright screen. As of this publication date, the current release version is 3.0D, and 3.0E has been prepared in conjunction with the release of Operation: Fighting Tiger. This book is based on these latest versions. If you do not have either version D or E, refer to Appendix E, Falcon 3.0 Upgrade Information for information on obtaining the latest patch from Spectrum Holobyte free of charge.

Who This Book Is For

Falcon 3.0 appears to be very complex at first glance. Virtually all of the keys on the keyboard, as well as the joystick, are used during flight. This book provides a building approach that presents one feature at a time. For example, the book takes you on a mission devoted to using the *padlock view* (a feature unique to Falcon 3.0); only the keys necessary to complete the mission are discussed during that lesson. You also have the advantage of flying missions with no enemy aircraft or ground troops. This lets you concentrate on your lesson's objectives during your flight.

Eventually you will face the enemy in Falcon 3.0. We have designed custom missions to help you face your first combat mission with confidence. One-on-one confrontations as well as multiple enemy engagements are covered. A separate lesson for each weapon is included, along with a mission designed to increase your skill with each specific type of ordnance.

This book covers a wide audience. If you have never flown a simulator aircraft, this book will guide you each step of the way. If you have dabbled with flight simulators, or Falcon 3.0 itself, this book will give you the edge to make you a successful pilot and strategist. If you consider yourself a

Falcon 3.0 authority and want to win campaigns, this book has the inside information to take you to that next level.

How This Book Is Structured

Falcon 3: The Complete Handbook is carefully organized to help you get the most out of Falcon 3.0. Each chapter contains lessons to help build up the skills you will need to successfully complete the missions, and ultimately the campaigns.

The first chapter introduces the Falcon 3.0 demonstration and provides a starting point for new pilots. Chapter 2, *Introduction to Falcon 3.0* gives you a tour of the software menus and system configuration. Chapters 3 through 5 are designed to help you build up your basic skills necessary to be a successful pilot. Chapter 6, *Introduction to Red Flag* helps you get the most out of the training ground as well as teaching you how to create your own missions. Chapter 7, *Introduction to the Campaigns* gives you the basic steps to participating in a Falcon 3.0 campaign. At this point, you should be a fairly successful pilots. Now it's time to reach for the next level.

To be truly called a Falcon expert, you must master the High-Fidelity Radar. The entire content of Chapter 8 is devoted to this complex radar mode. Chapter 9 is full of detailed Red Flag training missions with tips on how to get you and your wingmen home alive. Chapter 10 provides tactics for the strategist that is looking for the edge in mission planning. Chapter 11 gives you the inside hints and tips that will make your friends (and foes) wonder where you learned them! Chapter 12 addresses the exciting Falcon 3.0 upgrade package from Spectrum Holobyte, *Operation: Fighting Tiger.*

The Falcon 3 Flight Disk

This book also includes the Falcon 3 Flight Disk. This disk contains a demonstration from Spectrum Holobyte, superb Falcon 3.0 utilities, and a host of custom missions to be used with the text. The demonstration is a version of Falcon 3.0 with limited functionality. It lets you take Falcon 3.0 for a test drive before making the decision to buy. The utilities let you customize the Falcon 3.0 software. You make the decision where the Red Flag training sessions take place. The custom missions are used with the lessons in this book. The lessons start in Chapter 3, *Learning to Fly.* Be sure to install the missions before starting Chapter 3.

Installing the Flight Disk files Appendix A, *The Falcon 3 Flight Disk* provides instructions for installing files from the flight disk. There are separate installation procedures for the demonstration, the utilities, and the custom missions. Refer to Appendix A, *The Falcon 3 Flight Disk* for complete installation information.

The Sky Is the Limit

Climb into the cockpit and master the greatest simulator of all time: Falcon 3.0. Any time you run into trouble, you can always turn to the chapter that covers the subject. For example, if you are having trouble delivering iron-bombs, you can turn to Chapter 5, *Using Weapons* and find a lesson to help develop your skills. Keep ***Falcon 3: The Complete Handbook*** by your side, and you will bring yourself and your squadron home safely, mission after mission!

Acknowledgments

The authors would like to thank Mitchell Waite for the inspiration and ideas that got this book off the ground. Special thanks to Scott Calamar and John Crudo for keeping the project moving, answering questions, and resolving difficulties. Thanks to Heidi Brumbaugh for an excellent editing job and many great suggestions. Thanks to Julianne Ososke for putting the whole thing together.

Thanks to Rob Heittman, Greg Prete, and Steve Kramp for generously providing the Falcon 3.0 utilities. Additional thanks to Rob Heittman for his technical review of this book, and to Tom Byron of Spectrum Holobyte for his valuable assistance.

Joel Powell would like to thank Pete Thorsen and Bill Heptig for their support, ideas, and interest throughout the project.

Tom Basham would like to thank Gary Stottlemyer, Michael Mancuso, and Marisa Ong at Spectrum Holobyte for the wealth of information they provided during many phone calls. Thanks to Mike "Moondawg" Weksler for helping me understand the world of publishing. A special thanks to Sara Abate for her support and encouragement. Lastly, thanks to my family and friends (especially Russell "Q" Keating) for encouragement along the way.

About the Authors

Joel Powell is a technical writer and educator. He currently writes user, technical, and training documentation for industrial and commercial graphic imaging equipment. He has also written several training documents for the United States Air Force on ground radar technology. His area of radar specialization was the IFF/SIF feature used to identify friendly/enemy aircraft (the same IFF used in Falcon 3.0). He has provided training for over 3000 students from the U.S.A.F. , vocational schools, and private companies. Over 25 countries are represented by his former students. Joel is an avid C programmer and enjoys games involving strategy. Joel can be reached at his CompuServe address: 72067,3360.

Tom Basham is a former defense contractor with experience maintaining and flying US Army helicopter simulators. He currently is an Electronics Engineer for a leading R&D firm. In his spare time he beta tests flight simulators for Spectrum Holobyte and spends time on CompuServe's Flight Simulation Forum. Besides being involved in post-release testing of Flight of the Intruder, Tom was actively involved in the entire Falcon 3.0 beta test program, and has an in-depth knowledge of the simulation. Tom can be reached via email at his CompuServe address: 73760,1251.

Dear Reader:

When I was 10, I created a two-kid, walk-in, P-51 Mustang plane entirely in my garage from cardboard boxes. Working constantly, two old ironing boards became our wings, a W.W.II surplus radio the control panel, a broom handle the joystick, water balloons our cluster bombs, and a Windex sprayer our cannons. A flashlight behind the control panel gave us stealth capability.

Thirty-five years later I found myself rummaging through the shelves of a Software Etc. store. My eyes fell on the game called Falcon 3, a powerful flight simulator for the IBM PC. I recalled those imaginative days in the garage, and wondered what flight simulations looked like today on the PC. So I bought Falcon 3, installed it on my 386 and disappeared for the next two days.

I had no idea that game technology had advanced so far. Within a few seconds I was blasting sidewinders at enemy aircraft, dive-bombing bridges, tanks, and trucks so realistic looking that it made my palms sweat. I quickly discovered how to change the viewpoint to be the trailing edge of my fired missile so I literally rode it into the enemy aircraft like Dr Stranglove. Spectrum Holobyte got every detail right in this simulation—from the whine of the engine as it revs up, to the static filled radio messages from my wingmen—all of it added up to one incredible adrenaline burning, heart pounding experience.

WAITE GROUP PRESS™

I soon discovered that Falcon 3 was not just a shoot-em-up game, but was capable of letting you organize complex, realistic, strategies and tactics for a real battle. I quickly realized that many grown-ups like myself would love to know about this hot game and how to use it.

It didn't take long in the Spectrum Holobyte forum on Compuserve to find two experts, Tom Basham and Joel Powell. I asked them to write a book for grown-up beginners who didn't know a lot about flight simulators and to make the book graphic and friendly. We arranged with Spectrum Holobyte to include a demo of Falcon 3 so someone who did not have the game could experience it. I think you will find that this book goes way beyond similar titles on the market. If you have any suggestions or opinions about this book please fill out the Reader Satisfaction Card, or send me email on Compuserve: 75146,3515.

Sincerely,

Mitchell Waite

Mitchell Waite
Publisher

200 Tamal Plaza Corte Madera California 94925 415-924-2575 FAX 145-924-2576

Table of Contents

Contents

1

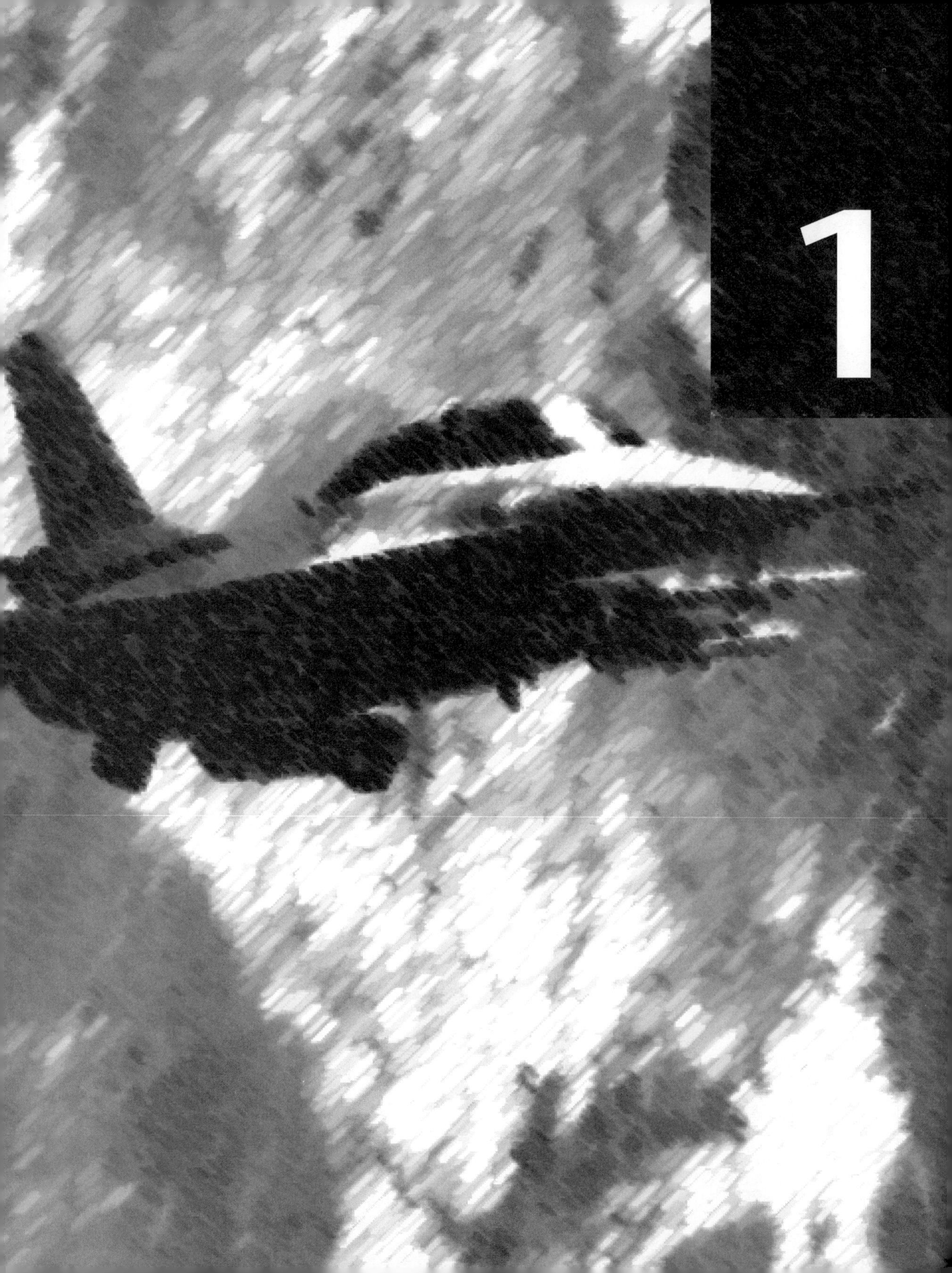

CHAPTER 1

The Falcon 3 Demonstration

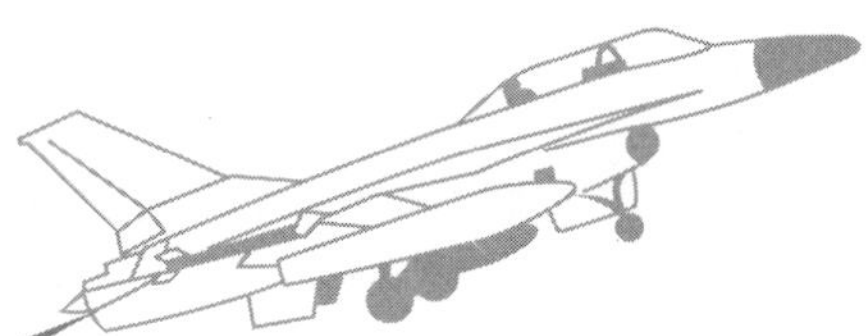

Falcon 3: The Complete Handbook includes a utility disk loaded with missions to be used with Spectrum Holobyte's Falcon 3.0. Also included on the disk is a demonstration of what Falcon 3.0 has to offer. You and your lone wingman will be thrust into the air at 3,500 feet. The two of you will have plenty of enemy activity with which to deal. You have enough fuel for approximately 10 minutes of flight. . . that is if you can make it 10 minutes without getting shot down! This chapter is designed to help you get the most of the Falcon 3.0 demonstration program. Although the demo is intended for those who have not yet purchased Falcon 3.0, it provides a challenge to experienced pilots. This chapter is designed to get you flying and fighting quickly. You will learn the basics of maneuvering, using the views/radar, and attacking the enemy. The details are beyond the scope of this chapter. However, all of the Falcon 3.0 features will be covered in the subsequent chapters.

Loading the Demonstration

You can install the demonstration program on a hard disk or run it directly from a floppy. A hard disk is recommended. Be sure to make a backup copy of the demo disk before proceeding with the installation program.

This section tells you how to install and run the Falcon 3 demo, included on the disk in this book. See Appendix A, The Falcon 3.0 Flight Disk, for instructions on installing the additional utilities and missions on the disk.

Installing to a Hard Disk

> WARNING: If you already have installed the retail package of Falcon 3.0, it will be located in the C:\FALCON3 subdirectory. Installing the demo to the same directory will copy over files with the same name including Falcon 3.0 itself! If you have already installed Falcon 3.0, change the demo install subdirectory to C:\FALDEMO.

The demonstration program requires at least 1.2 megabytes of free disk space. Ensure that you have adequate free space before proceeding. Use the following steps to install the Falcon 3.0 demo.

1. Place the flight disk in a floppy drive, type the drive letter of a 3.5-inch disk drive followed by a colon (A: or B:) and press ENTER.
2. Type DEMO followed by the hard drive specifier and the subdirectory on which you want to install the demo, and press ENTER (DEMO C:\FALDEMO). The installation process begins.
3. If you receive an error message before the installation begins, it will likely be due to one of the following errors:
    - No subdirectory specification.
    - Setting the subdirectory to C:\FALCON3.
4. If you receive an error while the demonstration files are decompressing, it will most likely be due to lack of disk space. The Falcon 3.0 demonstration requires over 1.2 megabytes of free disk space. Free up space on the hard drive and retry.
5. The files will be copied to the appropriate subdirectory and a message will be displayed upon a successful install.

Installing to a Floppy

To install the Falcon 3.0 demonstration program to a floppy, use one of the following methods:

- Install to a hard disk and copy the files to a 1.44M, 3.5-inch disk, OR
- Use the hard disk installation procedure and substitute the hard drive and subdirectory specifier for the 3.5-inch drive.

Starting the Demonstration

The Falcon 3.0 demonstration is a limited version of the retail package. However, it is full of features and requires a large amount of your computer's resources. The processor must be a 286 or higher. You must have at least 560K of free RAM to run the demonstration. You can find out the amount of free RAM by typing MEM. Note that free conventional memory must be over 560K (573,440 bytes). Keeping memory-resident programs to a minimum will increase available memory. Your system must also be capable of displaying VGA graphics.

From a Floppy To run the demonstration from the floppy disk:

- Insert the disk and type the appropriate drive specifier (A: or B:).
- Type FALCON3 and press ENTER.
- Enter a selection to indicate your type of sound device.

  After several seconds the demonstration will begin. Note that running the program from a floppy will cause the program to experience delays due to disk access time. This is why we recommend that you install to a hard drive.

From a Hard Disk To run the demonstration from the hard disk:

- Change to the drive on which the demonstration was installed.
- Change to the Falcon Demo directory by typing CD\FALDEMO.
- Type FALCON3 and press ENTER.
- Enter a selection to indicate your type of sound device.

Using the Demonstration

The demonstration begins. A few introductory screens are displayed including an animation sequence of an F-16 taxiing, then you are placed in the cockpit view. As soon as the cockpit screen appears, press ESC to bring up the menu bar. The menu bar allows you to configure the Falcon demonstration. Under FILE you can exit to DOS, restart the mission, or continue with the current mission. Under CONTROL you can set the demo for keyboard or joystick operation. Under OPTIONS you can set World Detail, Terrain, or Change Scale. The World Detail setting affects the detail level of the screen graphics. Slower machines may get better overall screen performance by selecting the medium or lower detail setting. The Terrain setting enables or disables the 3-D terrain. Changing the scale will result in other aircraft being displayed larger than true scale so that it becomes much easier to see enemy aircraft; however, it reduces realism significantly.

The Falcon 3.0 demonstration offers an infinite number of challenges. Each time you fly you can find different objects (ground targets and other planes) to attack. . . and some objects that may attack you! When the demo starts, you are at a low altitude (3,500 feet) and you are over enemy territory. The enemy is equipped with anti-aircraft artillery (AAA) along with surface-to-air missiles (SAM). You may even hear the blasts from below you.

Before getting into the details of artillery, missiles, and attacks, let's look at the cockpit of the F-16 and some of the keyboard controls. Reacting quickly and understanding how to use the different views and controls is important if you want to be a successful pilot! Click on RETURN TO GAME in the FILE menu to continue the demonstration.

Flying the F-16

The Cockpit As soon as the cockpit view appears, press the P key to pause the demonstration. Refer to Figure 1-1 and Table 1-1 for information regarding the F-16 cockpit.

Flight Controls You must be very familiar with the numeric keypad when flying without a joystick or ThrustMaster. Using the numeric keypad gives you access to the most controls without much hand movement. This is especially needed in a dogfight. Not only can you control direction, you also can drop chaff or flares, control the throttle, and control some of the views. Figure 1-2 shows the effects of joystick and keyboard controls.

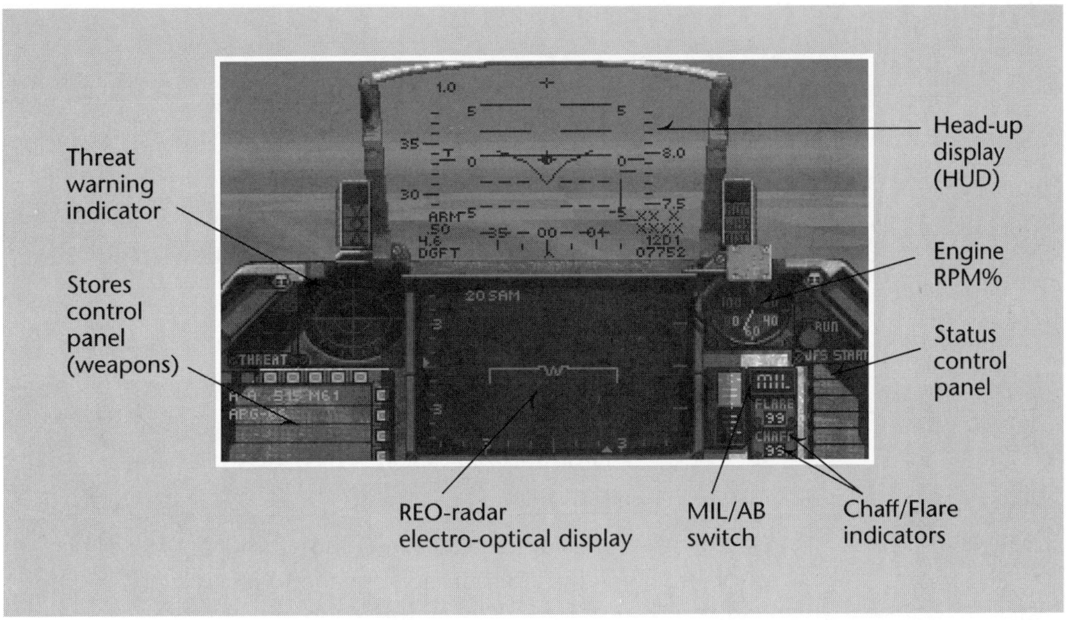

Figure 1-1 F-16 Falcon Cockpit View

It's Time to Fly!!! Once you feel familiar with the controls, it's time to put them into action. Remember, you can press P at any time to stop and examine all of the head-up display (HUD) information. This is very useful when learning to fly. There is no place to land in the demonstration, so flying and surviving are the mission goals. Read the following suggestions before taking the demonstration off pause. If you crash or are shot down, the demonstration will cycle back through the introduction screens and back to the start of the mission.

- Notice there are two aircraft passing in front of your F-16 as the demonstration begins. Start to bank to the left to turn toward the enemy aircraft. You will identify these aircraft as enemy An-12 Cubs later in this chapter.

- Try climbing and diving, note the airspeed indicator on the left-hand side of the HUD. The altitude indicator is on the right side. You are subjected to more attacks from the ground when you are at a low altitude.

Feature	Purpose
Head-Up Display	Allows you to maintain visual contact with the enemy while obtaining vital information. Altitude, airspeed, target tracking, and waypoint information are available without having to lose sight of the enemy.
Engine RPM %	Displays the percentage of engine power. This gauge will read 100% at full throttle and in afterburner mode.
Status Control Panel	Displays the status of wheel brakes, air brakes, flaps, landing gear, and autopilot.
Chaff/Flares	Displays the number of remaining chaff cartridges or flares. Chaff is used to decoy or distract radar-guided missiles, while flares are used against infrared missiles.
MIL/AB Indicator	Displays the status of the afterburner. AB1 through AB5 will be displayed when the afterburner is engaged. MIL (military or stan dard power) is displayed when the afterburner is off.
REO (Radar)	Used to track targets within the range of your radar. You can obtain target altitude and speed information from the REO.
Stores Control Panel	Displays the currently selected weapon and the quantity loaded. You have an unlimited amount of ammunition in the demo. Remember, however, that fuel is limited.
Threat Warning Panel	The circular display indicates the relative *azimuth* (direction) of the incoming threats. The top half of the circle represents the threats in front of the F-16, and the lower half of the circle represents threats to the rear. The Threat Panel also may display LCK or LNH. LCK indicates that an enemy aircraft has locked on your aircraft. LNH indicates an enemy missile has been launched.

Table 1-1 F-16 Cockpit Features

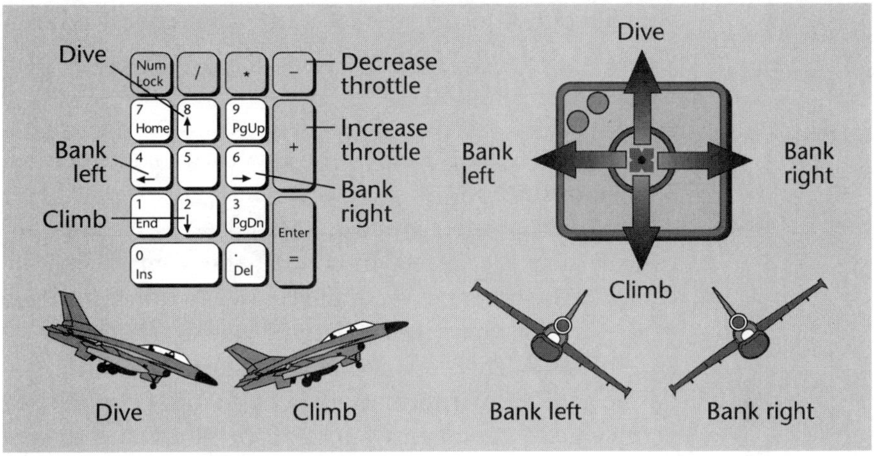

Figure 1-2 Keyboard and Joystick Controls

Use the throttle to increase and decrease engine RPM%. Try engaging the afterburner. Engaging the afterburner dumps fuel directly into the exhaust of the F-16, providing additional thrust. Notice that the engine RPM increases to 100% when the afterburner is engaged. You must manually decrease it from 100% by pressing the [-] key after disengaging the afterburner.

Take the demonstration off pause by pressing [P] and give it a try! Concentrate on maintaining control of the F-16. You will notice that banking the aircraft left or right causes a decrease in altitude unless the banking is offset by additional throttle or pulling back on the stick slightly.

Views and Navigation

It is important to keep track of your surroundings during your flight; hostile forces could be anywhere. There are two methods of tracking threats surrounding you. Aircraft within visual range can be tracked using the padlock view. Aircraft beyond visual range must be tracked using the F-16 radar. Let's look at the views and radar of Falcon 3.0.

Checking Out the Views The Falcon demonstration is well equipped with different views. Four in-cockpit views are available, as well as numerous outside angles. Some views are useful in combat, while others should only be used while sightseeing. One view is designed with true air combat in mind, the *padlock* view. The padlock view allows you to see 360° around your aircraft. Knowing the location of the enemy is essential to winning a dogfight. Although you are not able to defend yourself yet, you will soon learn how to seek out the enemy and go on the attack. Keep in mind that you are in hostile territory. The demonstration will restart if you crash or are shot down. Figure 1-3 shows the keys used for different views in the Falcon 3.0 demonstration.

Note that the zoom and rotate keys only function when an out-of-cockpit view is selected. In combat the primary views will be Front and Padlock. The other views should be used in noncombat situations. Try each of the various views. Use the right view to check out the Falcon damage control panel. The left view has a compass and the fuel gauge. The rear view has no additional information, but you may want to switch to this view to verify whether an enemy aircraft is behind you. Having an enemy in this position is very undesirable.

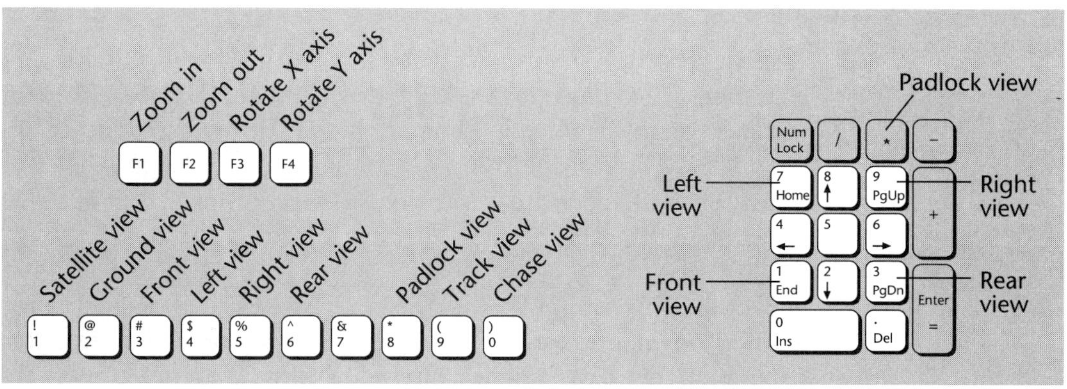

Figure 1-3 View Keys

Padlock View The view that is the most useful in air-to-air combat is the padlock view. This view allows you to keep your eye on the enemy in a dogfight. Even if he gets directly behind you, you will have the ability to see him. This helps simulate the environment of the real F-16, where the pilot can see almost 360°. Figure 1-4 illustrates the padlock view tracking an An-12 Cub within visual range.

The padlock screen is divided into four regions: status information, 360° window, orientation window, and main window. The status window (upper left) provides information such as

TARGET The type of target being tracked

ALT The altitude of *your* aircraft

YAW The movement of your F-16 in the vertical axis

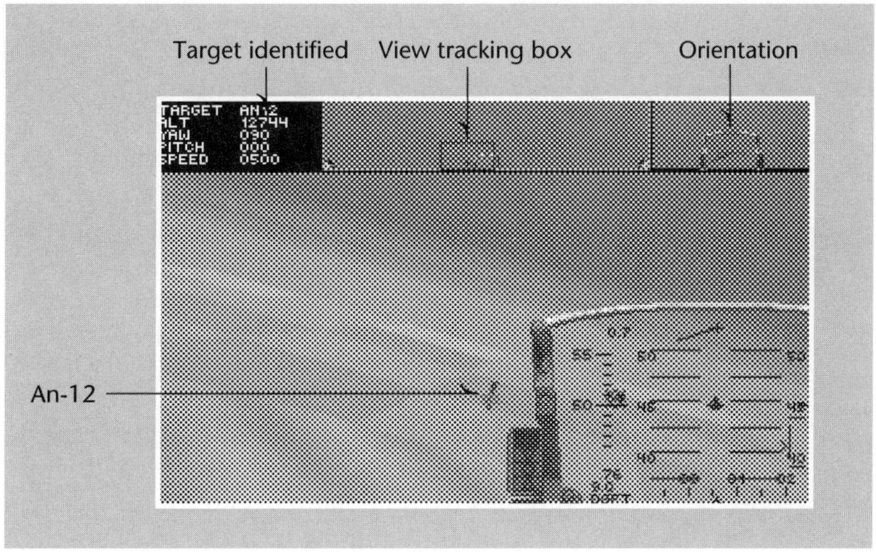

Figure 1-4 Padlock View Tracking the Enemy

PITCH	The angle of your aircraft relative to the ground (diving results in a negative angle)
SPEED	The speed of your F-16 in knots.

The 360° window (upper center) allows you to see a target that would not be seen from the front view. Note the small representation of the head-up display (HUD) in the center of the window. The center indicates straight ahead (12 o'clock). The extreme right edge of the window represents the view over the pilot's right shoulder. The view tracking box automatically follows the target being tracked. The contents of the view tracking box are displayed in the main window. The tracking box in Figure 1-4 shows the target to the left of the HUD. Note that a portion of the HUD is visible in the main window.

The orientation window (upper right) performs two functions. It helps you maintain control of the F-16 when engaged in a heated dogfight. You can quickly determine the orientation of your aircraft by checking the *waterline* in this window. The waterline is a line with two small lines extending from the ends. It is very easy to become disoriented in padlock view and the waterline helps you get an idea of the position of your F-16.

The main window displays (in a larger perspective) the contents of the view tracking box in the 360° window. Use this window when the target is directly in front of the HUD, after gaining a position to successfully use air-to-air weapons. In padlock view you usually will be monitoring the 360° window. Only aircraft within visual range can be seen in padlock view.

At this point, you should be able to fly the F-16 and maintain level flight. You should also be able to locate enemies within visual range. However, it is usually better to know about an enemy target *before* visual identification. You do not want the enemy to see you first! The F-16's radar is essential in locating enemy aircraft.

Radar Detecting the enemy before being detected is a great advantage in the air. The absolute worst position to find yourself in is having an enemy aircraft directly behind you (on your 6 o'clock!) You are vulnerable in more than one way when this occurs. First, it is easier for the enemy pilot to anticipate and react to your next move. Second, you are exposing the hottest portion of your aircraft to him. A heat-seeking (infrared) missile would have no problem finding such a target. If you see the enemy before he sees you, it allows you to get on his "six" (rear) before he even knows you're there. Radar is the answer. Figure 1-5 shows the Falcon REO (Radar/Electro-Optical) display tracking a target.

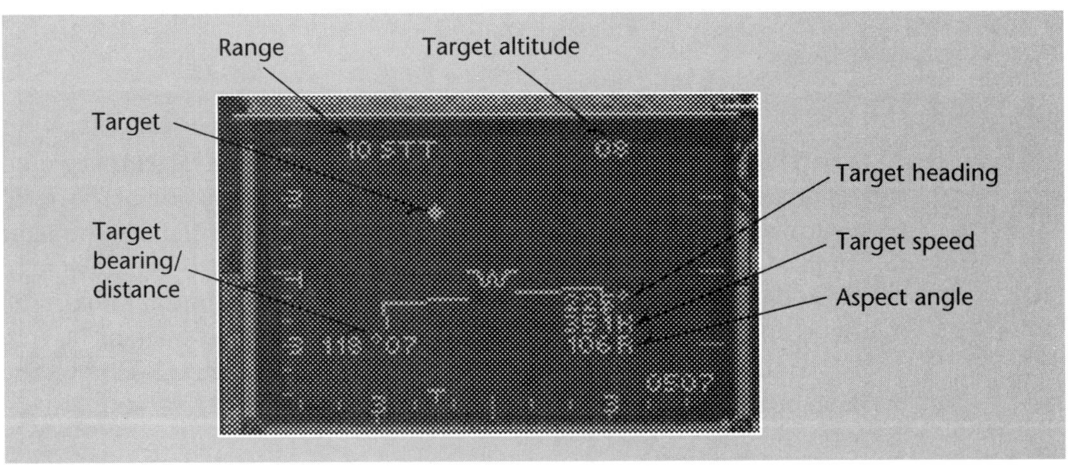

Figure 1-5 F-16 REO (Radar/Electro-Optical) Display Tracking a Target

Only targets that are in front of the aircraft will be displayed on the radar. The range indicates that the current range of the radar is 10 miles. This range switches automatically in the demonstration, depending on the location of targets. The nose of your F-16 is represented at the bottom center of the radar display, facing up. For example, if a target was in the center of the radar display, it would be at a distance of five miles and directly in front of you. The radar provides a considerable amount of target information. You have the target altitude, distance, bearing, heading, speed, and aspect angle. Aspect angle is the angle between your F-16's nose and the tail of the target. The lower the aspect angle is, the better the attack position you will have on the enemy. Getting the angle down to zero would place you directly on the enemy's tail.

Start the demonstration again and observe the radar. You may have to bank to the left to keep the two An-12 Cubs on the radar display. Notice that these targets are on the bottom of the radar display due to the close range. Fly around the area to locate other aircraft. If you spot any targets closer than five or six miles, switch to the padlock view to identify the aircraft type. Keep in mind that aircraft to the rear of your F-16 will not be detected by your radar.

Attacking the Enemy

You probably have already noticed that the demonstration drops you off suddenly in an unfriendly region. Your job is to survive for the 10 minute fuel limit. This is hard to accomplish by soaring around and ignoring the enemy. Successfully attacking the enemy aircraft will increase your chances for making it to the time limit. If you destroy an enemy fighter, there will be one less opponent with whom to deal.

Aircraft are not the only targets to attack in this simulation. There are several targets on the ground for target practice as well. The demonstration sets you up with unlimited air-to-air and air-to-ground weapons, so fire at will. Let's take a look at the available weapons and how and when to use them.

The Keys to Combat In addition to view keys, there are four keys used during air-to-air and air-to-ground combat. The (T) key selects a target to lock up (if more than one target exists). Locking up the target means that the weapon computer system can locate the target. When the weapon is fired, it follows this lock unless something distracts it. The (ENTER) key cycles through the air-to-air weapons. The (BACKSPACE) key cycles through the air-to-ground weapons. The (SPACEBAR) fires the selected weapon. The selected weapon will be displayed on the stores control panel on the lower left side of the cockpit.

Air-to-Air Weapons Your F-16 is equipped with four types of air-to-air weapons. The AIM-9M and the AIM-9P "Sidewinder" infrared missiles, the AIM-120 AMRAAM radar missile, and the M61A1 cannon. The HUD will be slightly different for the four weapons. The three missile types each have a distinct situation in which to choose them.

The M61A1 cannon can be used at very close range during a dogfight. The HUD will display a *funnel* to use for aiming purposes. This funnel will change based on the current motion of your F-16. Try climbing, diving, and banking while observing the aiming funnel. If the target is between the funnel and in range (1–2 miles), the cannon can be very effective. The funnel will always display where the 20mm bullets would have hit had you fired it a few seconds before. Gunsights of this nature are referred to as *historical* gunsights.

The AIM-9M and AIM-9P Sidewinders are very similar in appearance. Both missiles are infrared (heat seeking) and can successfully hit targets within a range of 10 miles. The -9P is less effective because it must be fired at the rear of the enemy aircraft to achieve a hit. The -9M can be fired from any angle around the target. The primary difference you see in the HUD is the size of the aiming *reticle* (aiming circle on the HUD). The goal is to place the target in the reticle before firing these weapons. The reticle is largest with the AIM-120 and smallest with the AIM-9P. The -9M's reticle is larger than the -9P's, making it easier to achieve a position to lock on the target. It also has a wandering target locator (diamond). This locator will stop over the target when it is locked on.

The AIM-120 is a radar-guided missile. The 20-to-25 mile range is much longer than the infrared missiles'. You can lock on the target before you can visually identify it. Don't worry about shooting down a friendly aircraft from this range. All aircraft in this demonstration (except for your wingman) are the enemy.

Figure 1-6 shows a target locked up for the radar-guided AIM-120 missile. Notice that the target is slightly out of the reticle. Firing the missile at this point would not bring about guaranteed success. You could increase the odds by gaining a better position on the enemy before firing the missile. Achieving a hit on an enemy aircraft will require you to maneuver into a position that places the intended target in the aiming reticle. The chances for a successful hit are high if the target is within the reticle and within effective range for the type of missile. The AIM-120 and AIM-9M display a diamond on the HUD that will indicate a target lock-on by following the target. The -9P will display the same diamond, but it will be fixed in the center of the HUD.

You will run across several different types of enemy aircraft while flying your F-16. Some aircraft may be easy to dogfight while others may give you more than you can handle. Remember to switch to padlock view (the * key) to get aircraft identification. You will find a new assortment of air-to-air challenges every time you run the demonstration. If you can destroy or avoid the air threats, the ground targets become fair game!

Figure 1-6 A target is locked up. Ready to fire the AIM-120?

Air-to-Gound Weapons Three air-to-ground weapons are loaded on the demonstration Falcon. The M61A1, the same cannon used for air-to-air combat, is also used for *strafing*. Strafing is a method of firing your cannon at ground targets as you pass low over the target. The AGM-65B (Air-Ground Missile) Maverick is a "fire and forget" missile. This means that it is not necessary to maintain the target lock after firing the weapon. The missile will be responsible for finding the target after it is released. The GBU-15 (Guided Bomb Unit) is a bomb guided by fins to the designated target. Observe the firing of the various types of weapons from the out-of-cockpit views. The methods for delivering both the AGM-65B and the GBU-15 are virtually the same.

Figure 1-7 shows a target lock-on for the AGM-65B Maverick. The crosshairs on the HUD indicate the target lock-on. These crosshairs normally will remain in the center of the HUD when there is no target to lock on. Notice that a representation of the target is displayed on the REO. There is a very high chance of success when firing under these conditions.

There are several ground targets located throughout the demonstration region. If you are not engaged with an enemy aircraft, try locating these ground targets. Start by flying level and switching to the chase view or track view, then rotate the view and look for dark patches or spots on the ground. If you spot a target, note its relative location to your aircraft, switch back to cockpit view, and start to turn in the direction of the target. Try to place the target in the center of your head up display to *lock on*. You must be in range of the weapon to lock on. You will notice the target lock on when the

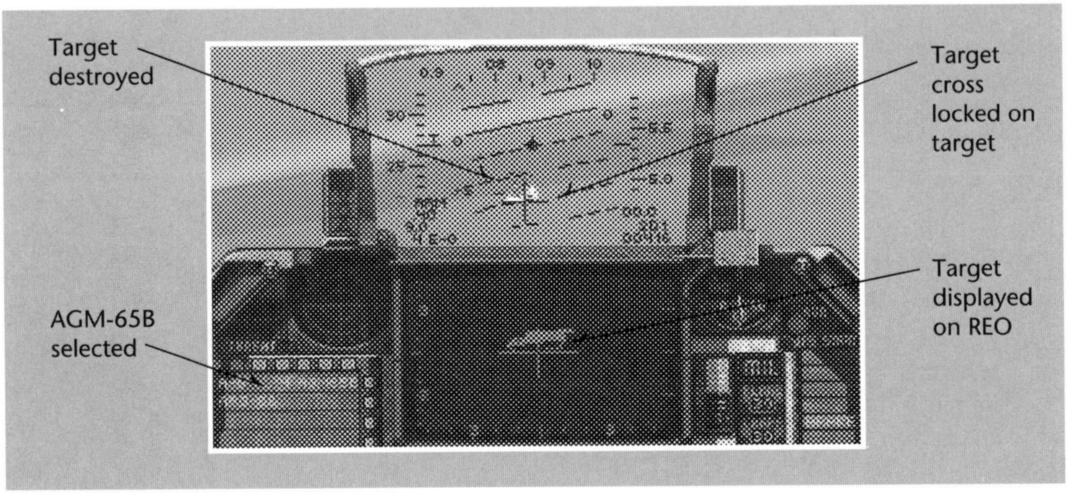

Figure 1-7 An AGM-65B radar-guided missile finds the target!

crosshairs on the HUD start following (tracking) the target. A graphical representation of the target will be displayed on the radar/electro-optical display.

When you press the SPACEBAR to fire the weapon, you will hear the missile being launched and seconds later you will see the missile on its way to the target (assuming you are in the cockpit view). You should be able to observe the target being hit and the missile explosion. The demonstration version of Falcon 3.0 does not display damaged targets. Even if you score a direct hit, the target will appear to remain intact. The released version will show damaged targets for successful hits.

When delivering powerful weapons such as the Maverick and the GBU, be careful not to fly into the blast when the missile strikes the target. Severe damage to the aircraft will result. You can experiment to see how close you can actually get to the exploding weapon without damaging your aircraft. Approach the demonstration as the training ground for the real thing!

Other Keys The majority of the keyboard is used to control the aircraft and its weapons systems. There are a few keys that you may want you employ while running the demonstration. Table 1-2 provides a summary of the remaining keys and their functions.

Key	Purpose
A	Toggle the autopilot status, permitting the computer to control the aircraft.
B	Toggle the speedbrakes, this will cause the aircraft to decelerate quickly.
G	Lowers and raises the landing gear. There is no landing strip in the demonstration. You can land the F-16 on any level land. Do not lower the gear at high speeds!
P	Pauses the simulation. Press P again to resume.
S	Toggles the sound on and off.
ESC	Pauses the game and displays the menu bar.
F5	Toggles engine sounds only.
F6	Toggles missile sounds only.
CTRL - R	Restarts mission (after introductory screens).
CTRL-C	Exits to DOS (you can also select QUIT TO DOS from the FILE menu on the menu bar).

Table 1-2 Noncombat Keys Used with the Falcon 3.0 Demonstration.

Winning the Demonstration Battle

Your goal in this demonstration program is to survive over the battlefield until your fuel runs out. This will take approximately 10 minutes, depending on what maneuvers were made during the mission. For example, the length of the demonstration will significantly decrease when you engage the afterburner for long periods of time. The word FUEL will be displayed in the center of all displays when your fuel has run out. You should eject from the aircraft using CTRL-E if this occurs. There is no way to save the aircraft, but you can save the pilot's life. Use the following advice to increase your success rate. The following includes information for autopilot flight, avoiding enemy weapons, air-air combat, and air-ground combat.

Autopilot Flight The autopilot can be engaged at any time by pressing the A key. This is very beneficial to new pilots. The Falcon 3.0 autopilot will not only fly the F-16 for you; it will also track down enemy aircraft or ground targets and perform maneuvers to avoid incoming missiles and anti-aircraft artillery (AAA). You may notice the AAA fire when you are flying relatively low in a hostile area. You can hear and see the AAA explosions at a low altitude.

Start a new mission and switch to autopilot. You can now look at any view without being concerned with flying the aircraft. The track view always provides an interesting perspective when the aircraft is hunting down the enemy and firing missiles. In the normal cockpit view, you can view the instruments to examine the methods the "computer" pilot is using. If the F-16 is shot down or crashes, the demonstration will restart.

Avoiding Enemy Weapons It is difficult to become an effective pilot if you cannot avoid the enemy weapons being launched in your direction. Although being hit does not always render your F-16 useless, it usually causes enough damage to cause a premature end of the mission. The longer you can avoid the enemy's advances, the longer you can plan and execute your own attack on the enemy. You have four tools to aid you in avoiding the incoming missiles: chaff, flares, jinking (hard maneuvering), and the threat warning indicator (TWI).

The first tool is chaff. Chaff is a cartridge of foil strips that can be dropped from your F-16 by pressing the DEL key. These foil strips may distract or confuse an enemy radar-guided missile. The radar-guided missiles depend on electro-magnetic reflections off of the target (your aircraft). A number of additional reflections are generated by dumping chaff into the air. This makes it more difficult (but not impossible) for the incoming missile to determine if the reflection is your aircraft or the chaff. In effect, the chaff blinds the incoming missile. The enemy missile will not always be misdirected by chaff. It may *find* you again and cause great harm to your F-16.

Another tool is the flare. Flares can be dropped from your F-16 by pressing the INS key. The flare is used to distract infrared (I-R) missiles. All I-R missiles require heat to maintain a lock on the target. By firing a flare, the missile may temporarily or permanently follow (lock on) the flare. Like chaff, the success of the flare depends on several variables. The location of the rear of your aircraft, the location of the I-R missile, and the position of the flare all play a part in whether or not the missile will find your aircraft or the flare.

Jinking an incoming missile refers to making hard turns with the F-16 to avoid the missile. This also enables you to possibly break the missile lock, causing the missile to wander aimlessly until it runs out of power. Using these sudden maneuvers along with chaff and flares can significantly reduce the chances of being hit by a missile. You may notice the autopilot performing these maneuvers when a missile has been fired and is locked on the F-16.

One of the most important devices in avoiding enemy missiles is the threat warning indicator (TWI). The TWI can spot incoming missiles when they are launched. The top half of the TWI circle indicates missiles in front of your F-16, while the bottom indicates missiles to the rear. You may be able to escape some missiles by *out turning* them (turning faster than the missile) as they close in. The demonstration TWI displays all incoming missiles as small blips. The retail version of Falcon 3.0 displays additional information in this display, such as the type of radar detected (pulse/doppler). The individual radar modes are discussed in Chapter 4, Radar and Enemy Identification.

You may be asking the question, "How do I know whether to release chaff or flares? I don't have any idea if the missile is infrared or radar-guided!" The answer is: Do not analyze the missile type when the LCK or LNH is lit. Drop both chaff and flares and start your moves! You have an unlimited supply of chaff and flares in the demonstration so you don't have to worry about releasing too much.

Air-to-Air Combat One of the most exciting and difficult actions you will experience in Falcon 3.0 is air-to-air combat and dogfighting. It is a great challenge for you and your wingman to go head-to-head against enemy aircraft. You must be very proficient at controlling your aircraft, reading the HUD and the instruments, switching views, and selecting weapons before pursuing an air-to-air engagement with an enemy fighter. After a few hours of practice you will be able to fly and fight without looking down at the keyboard. The numeric keypad is very useful for dogfighting. All of the basic views and controls are available to one hand, as well as chaff and flares, to fend off an incoming missile!

There are primarily two key objectives when in an air-to-air engagement. The first is *sight*. Losing sight of the enemy can be fatal in a dogfight. Chances are when you find the enemy again, he will be right behind you firing a missile at your tail! The padlock view is designed to help you maintain sight of the enemy. The only time you will not be able to locate the enemy in the padlock view is when the target is out of visual range or when the target is below you.

The other key objective in the dogfight is *position*. It is wise to gain and maintain an advantageous position on the enemy. The best possible position is directly behind and slightly above the enemy aircraft. The worst position would be the exact opposite of this. Having an altitude edge was very important before the days of the jet engine. The power of today's aircraft can overcome the altitude difference easily.

"What happens if there are more than one enemy aircraft?" you may ask. Although different situations require different actions, the best action is to continue engaging one aircraft at a time. Use the padlock view to make sure another enemy is not sneaking up on your tail, however. If an enemy is on your tail, bank left or right to 90° and pull back hard on the stick. Depending on your airspeed (and the enemy's airspeed and direction), you will come around to a position with the enemy in front of you! Take advantage of this position by firing your guns (if you are at close range) or a missile (at greater than two miles). Remember you must be directly on the enemy's tail to make a successful hit with an AIM-9P. Always keep an eye on the aspect angle caret and the aspect angle reading on the REO. Figure 1-8 shows the proper position and conditions for firing the -9P.

The aspect angle in Figure 1-8 is 005R. This indicates that the F-16 nose is only five degrees off angle from the enemy aircraft's tail. Firing the -9P under these conditions will usually result in a successful hit. Note the position of the aspect angle caret on the HUD. This indicates the current direction of the target lock-on. This is one of the best positions to be in against an airborne enemy.

Air-to-Ground Combat Although it is not essential to attack ground targets to endure the demonstration time limit, it does provide training for Falcon 3.0 beginners. The three-dimensional world con-

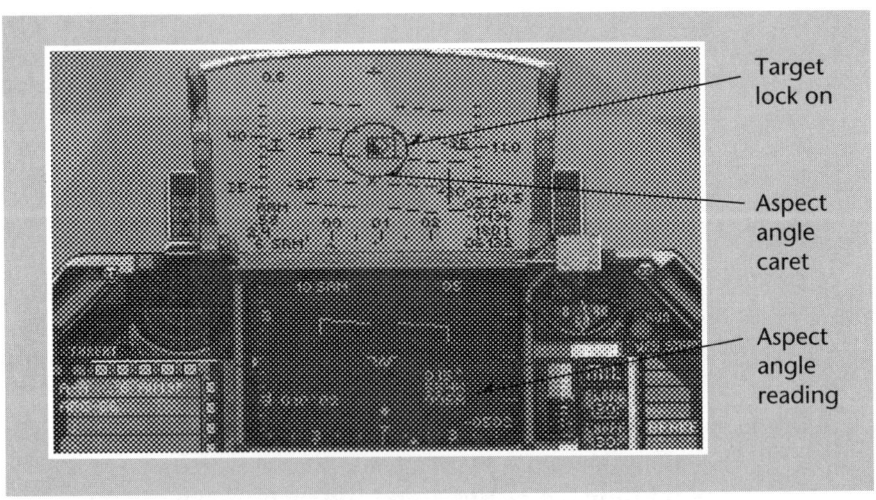

Figure 1-8 Optimum Firing Conditions for the AIM-9P Sidewinder

tains several ground targets. The best method for ground attack is to take care of the air-to-air confrontations first, then go after the tanks and other targets.

The Falcon 3.0 retail version has several additional air-ground missiles and air-ground bombs. The demonstration is limited to two air-to-ground weapons. The AGM-65B Maverick is a missile, while the GBU-15 is a free-fall bomb that is guided by computer controlled fins which actually *fly* the bomb into the target. Both the AGM-65B and the GBU-15 appear to function identically in the demonstration. In reality (and in the complete retail version of Falcon 3.0), they react quite differently.

Summary

The Falcon demonstration is designed to give you an intensive introduction to one of the finest flight/battle simulations ever constructed, Falcon 3.0. Although the functionality is limited somewhat, the demo offers a challenge to the new *first time* pilot through the veteran Falcon 3.0 driver. Most of the aspects of flight are available in the demonstration. This chapter introduced you to the fundamentals required to keep the F-16 in the air and flying level. The retail version of Falcon 3.0 takes the challenge several steps further.

The remainder of this book provides all of the details of the Falcon 3.0 features. Although some of the material will work with the demonstration, the major portion is devoted to the complete package. If you are already familiar with using the retail version, you may wish to skip Chapter 2, Introduction to Falcon 3. Chapter 2 introduces the new user to the Falcon 3.0 menu structure and configuration.

2

Introduction to Falcon 3.0

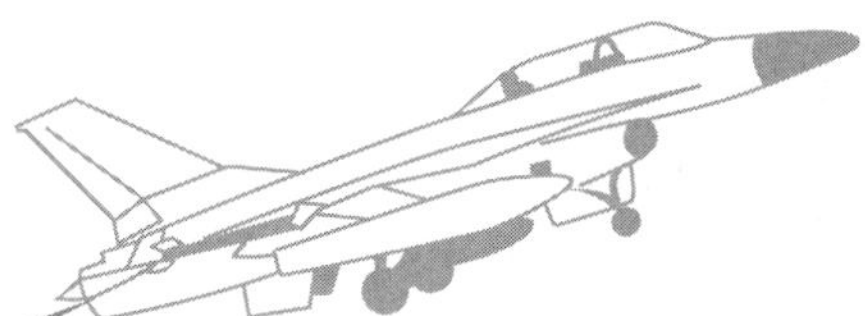

Falcon 3.0 is one of the most realistic challenges ever offered by a computer simulation. You are in control of a squadron of F-16 Falcon pilots with varying skill levels. You are responsible for conducting the training that will increase these skill levels. Having a properly trained squadron is your goal as you enter a *campaign* in one of three regions in the world: Israel, Panama, or Kuwait. What is your ultimate goal in Falcon 3.0? Coming home victorious after a successful campaign with a minimum number of friendly casualties is your primary mission.

The Falcon 3.0 software has virtually hundreds of configuration possibilities. You select a squadron to fly and fight. After this selection, several other options become available. You can configure the difficulty of the simulation over a wide range to match your skills at a given time. In addition, you can set up Falcon to work with different types of hardware such as joysticks, sound cards, etc. You can record missions or portions of a mission to play back later so you can analyze your strengths and weaknesses. For a taste of the arcade-style simulation you can visit *Instant Action*. This places you among as many enemies as you can possibly handle at one time . . . and you will be alone in the battle! No friendly aircraft will be found in Instant Action. You can also invite a friend to go head-to-head, each of you controlling your own Falcon. The *Comm* mode allows two systems running Falcon 3.0 to connect via modem, direct serial port, or network connection. If you have never used Falcon 3.0 before, this chapter will introduce you to the main features and controls available.

Starting Falcon 3.0

If you have not installed the Falcon software yet, do so now. Refer to the documentation provided with Falcon 3.0 for installation instructions. After a successful installation, you can start the program by changing to the chosen install directory and typing FALCON3. A startup sequence appears.

The Startup Sequence

Although you can bypass the startup sequence by pressing any key, it is definitely worth more than a passing glance. After the Sphere logo, a quiet landscape scene appears. The quiet is quickly brought to an end as a Soviet-built MiG-29 appears on the horizon, headed in your direction. Hot on the tail of the MiG is the star of this Spectrum Holobyte simulation—The F-16 Fighting Falcon. The scene pans to the left as it follows the two aircraft. You may overhear the pilot's radio squawk, *"Fox Two. Fox Two,"* indicating that he has just fired an AIM-9P heat-seeking missile. The F-16 banks to the right as the missile locates the red hot tail of the MiG and scores a direct hit! A wingman of the victorious Falcon pilot responds, *"Good Kill. Good Kill."* By using *Falcon 3: The Complete Handbook* and with a little practice, you will find yourself on the tail of many such enemies.

The War Room

After the startup screens, you will come to the *War Room*. You can access nearly all areas of the simulation from this screen. Several simulated television screens are located in the War Room. Think of each of these screens as a gateway to another area of the program. Figure 2-1 shows the War Room screen and its features.

After you form a squadron and assign it to a *theater* (region), the world map in the top center of the screen will display your selection and highlight the campaign region. A flashing red light will appear next to the lower screens indicating that you may access them. For example, if no squadron is selected, there is no flashing light below the Red Flag screen. If you attempt to select a screen while the light is not flashing, the program displays a message on the world map indicating that you must select a squadron before proceeding.

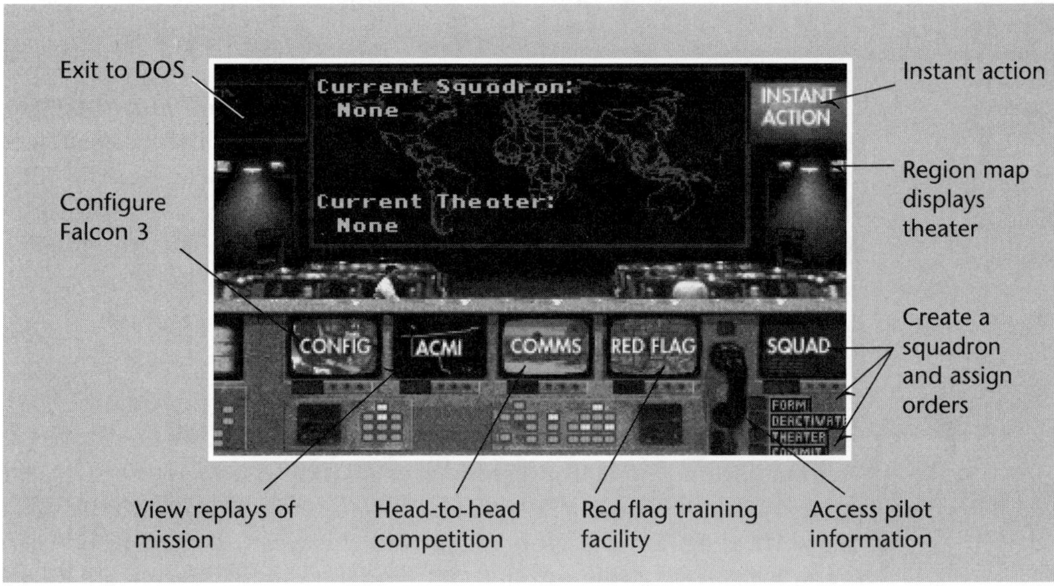

Figure 2-1 The War Room

Mice, Keyboards, and Joysticks The method for selecting menus and menu options varies depending on the type of input device you are using. It is generally easier to use the mouse or joystick for accessing the different screen items. You can use the keyboard instead of a mouse; however, using the keyboard is more difficult when moving the cursor (graphic arrow) and making selections. Pressing TAB and BACKSPACE moves the cursor to different areas of the screen. Pressing the ↑, ↓, ←, or → moves the cursor between selections. Pressing ENTER accepts the selection that the cursor is on. Pressing ESC accesses the previous screen.

In flight, either a joystick or the keyboard may be used. You can use the mouse for menu selection only, not when flying the F-16. The joystick must be calibrated once a mission or flight has begun. The calibration routine will be discussed during your first flight. One particular brand of joystick, the ThrustMaster, must be selected in the configuration screen. Configuration is covered later in this chapter.

This book assumes you will be making menu selection with a mouse. For example, to access the Red Flag area, our instructions read, "Click on the Red Flag screen." We assume that if you are a keyboard user, you will use the keys listed above to select the option. Specific instructions will be given for special instances.

A Tour of Falcon 3.0

There are many screens accessible in Falcon 3.0. We start off with a brief tour to examine the features available. Many of the screens will be accessed again later in the book, so don't worry about remembering details at this time. Try to get a feel for what is available and how to get there. We will visit the configuration area last. Be sure to visit this area and follow the configuration instructions at the end of this chapter. The learning missions in the following chapters require your system to be configured properly. To make sure that all screens are accessible, let's start by forming a squadron.

The Squadron Utilities

You must form a squadron before participating in training or campaign missions. Initially, thirty pilots are assigned to your control. The skills of the pilots will range from beginner to seasoned veteran. You are responsible for training the beginners from the ground up, and maintaining the sharp abilities of the veterans.

The FORM light (located below the SQUAD screen) should be flashing. This indicates that you are able to form a squadron. You can form more than one squadron; however, only one squadron can be *active* (current) at a time. The world map will display the name of the current squadron. Each squadron has its own set of records. Forming and activating a squadron consists of three steps.

1. Click on the FORM light. This will display a squadron insignia in the SQUAD screen along with scroll arrows.
2. Click on the scroll arrows to cycle through the available squadrons. The scroll arrow will change to red when the end of the squadron list is reached.
3. When SQUAD screen displays the desired squadron insignia, click directly on the screen. You have formed and activated a squadron.

You can repeat this process to form up to six squadrons. When you form the sixth squadron, the form light will stop flashing, indicating that the maximum has been reached. Note, however, that you can have only one squadron active at a time. The active squadron is indicated by the SQUAD screen and the world map.

When multiple squadrons are formed, you can cycle through the squadrons by clicking directly on the SQUAD screen. The world map displays the name of the squadrons as you do this. To take part in the training that is presented in this book, you only need to select one squadron.

Now that the selection process is over, several other options become available on the War Room screen (indicated by the flashing red lights). For instance, a light flashes above the telephone (located beside the SQUAD screen). This phone allows you to access the *Squadron Ready Room*. Click on the light or the telephone.

The Squadron Ready Room The Squadron Ready Room provides a gateway to information on the current status of your squadron's pilots. Figure 2-2 shows the ready room and the four additional screens that you can access. The screens are: Sierra Hotel, Pilot Information, Pilot Transfer, and Squadron Records. Click on the appropriate section of the Ready Room screen to go to a new screen. Pressing (ESC) will return you to the ready room from any of the four screens.

Figure 2-2 The Squadron Ready Room

Sierra Hotel Figure 2-3 shows the Sierra Hotel screen. You can access Sierra Hotel by clicking on the back wall area of the Ready Room. Sierra Hotel provides a list of the top pilots in the active squadron. This screen lists the number of missions flown (sorties) along with the number of confirmed enemy kills for each pilot. Status information is also available for pilots who are missing in action or who are temporarily out of action due to injury. No pilots are listed in Sierra Hotel until the active squadron has flown a mission. Pressing (ESC) will return you to the Ready Room.

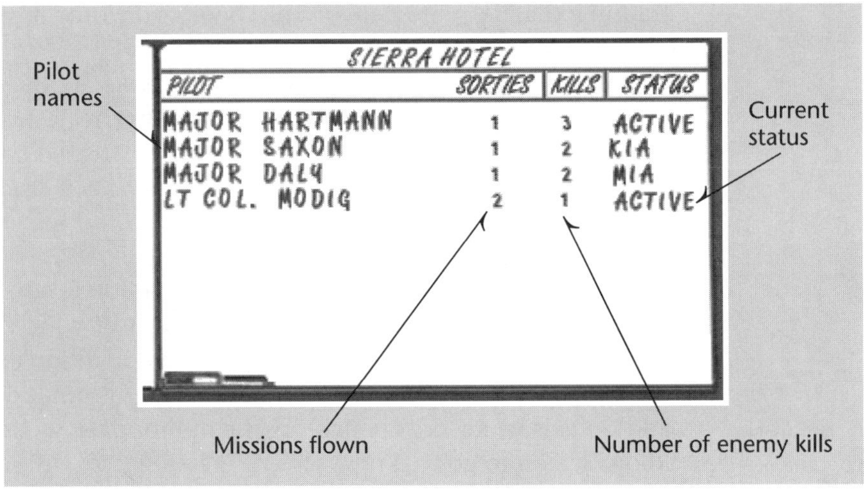

Figure 2-3 Sierra Hotel

Pilot Information Pilot Information provides detailed data on the active squadron pilots. Click on the back row of seated pilots to access the Pilot Information screen. Figure 2-4 shows the Pilot Information screen. This screen displays the selected pilot's photo, callsign (nickname), and status (Active, MIA, etc.) at the top of the screen. The pilots are listed in order of rank on the simulated screen in the upperright portion of the screen. The commander of the squadron is always at the top of the pilot list. You can display more pilots by clicking on the scroll arrows. Thirty pilots are initially available. In a campaign, this number will go down if a pilot is killed. The number will go up when the squadron receives replacements.

Pilot abilities are provided for three different skill areas. The overall fatigue value affects each of these values. Each ability rating is given with two numbers. The first number indicates the current ability state of the pilot with fatigue factored in. The second number is the maximum ability for the pilot (without additional training). For example, a pilot that has a dogfighting ability of 75/86 would indicate that the pilot would have an 86 rating *if* the fatigue value is 100 (fully rested). However, the 75 indicates that the pilot is suffering somewhat from fatigue. In this case, you may be better off assigning a different pilot if dogfighting ability is a priority for the mission. This is assuming you are sending pilots to do battle in *Campaign* mode.

If the mission were being flown in Red Flag (training), you would assign the lower ability pilots to help them develop their skills and subsequently increase their ability ratings. This does not affect fatigue;

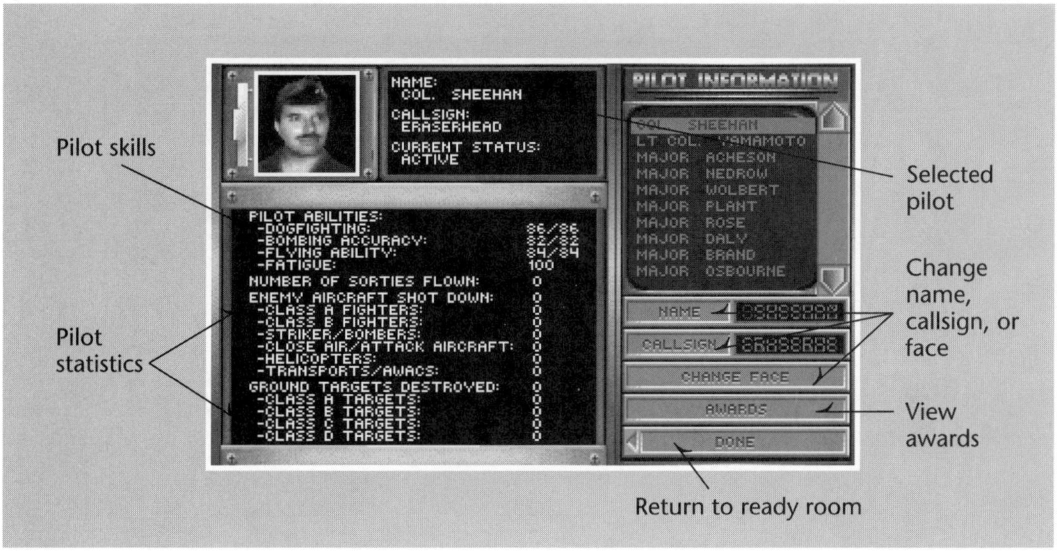

Figure 2-4 Pilot Information

however, it will increase the maximum skill value the pilot can attain. In the above example, the pilot has a dogfighting rating of 86. If the pilot successfully completes a dogfighting mission in Red Flag, the rating will increase.

Detailed statistics are available for each pilot based on prior missions. The number of sorties (missions) is given along with the number of air-to-air and air-to-ground targets destroyed. Creating a new squadron will reset all statistics to 0 and set the fatigue to 100 (fully rested).

You can change the name of any pilot by clicking the NAME button, typing the new name, and then pressing (ENTER). The callsign can also be changed using the CALLSIGN. The photograph can also be changed by clicking on the CHANGE FACE button. Changing this information has no effect on the performance of a pilot or the active squadron as a whole. However, it can be helpful to rename your pilots using names and callsigns that you recognize (family names, friend's names, etc.). This allows you to keep track of pilots easier.

NOTE: The utility FALCNR, described in Appendix C, Skunk Works Utilities, simplifies these modifications. FALCNR is included on the Falcon 3.0 Flight Disk.

Clicking on the AWARDS button displays the ribbons that the selected pilot has earned. Pilots can earn these awards for exceptional

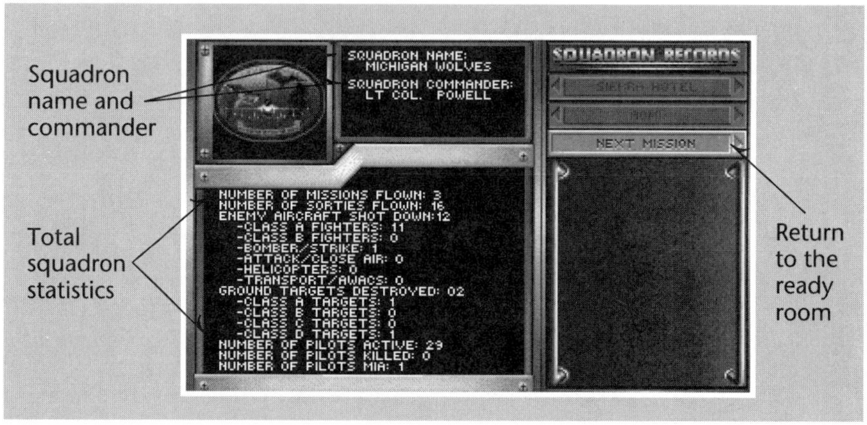

Figure 2-5 Squadron Records

performance in a campaign. Several awards are available ranging from the Air Medal through the Air Force Medal of Honor. Pressing (ESC) returns you to the Pilot Information screen. Pressing (ESC) again returns you to the Ready Room.

Squadron Records Click on the Squadron Records area located on the right wall of the Ready Room. The Squadron Records screen provides information on the overall status of the selected squadron. Figure 2-5 shows the Squadron Records screen. The squadron name and the commander's name are at the top of this screen. The data provided here is very similar to the individual pilot information except it is a summary of the entire squadron. The screen also provides the total number of active, killed, and missing in action (MIA) pilots. Click on NEXT MISSION to return to the Ready Room.

Pilot Transfer Click on the Pilot Transfer area of the Ready Room (the file cabinet in the lower left portion of the screen). You use the Pilot Transfer screen to exchange pilots between different squadrons. Figure 2-6 shows the Pilot Transfer screen. The small screen on the right half of the screen displays a list of pilots from the active squadron. The left half of the display shows another Falcon 3.0 squadron and provides a list of pilots. To exchange pilots, first select the pilot you want to give up by clicking on his name. Click on the pilot name you want to assign to the active squadron. The pilots exchange places. Clicking on SQUADRON accesses other squadrons. You must, however, create another squadron before selecting it.

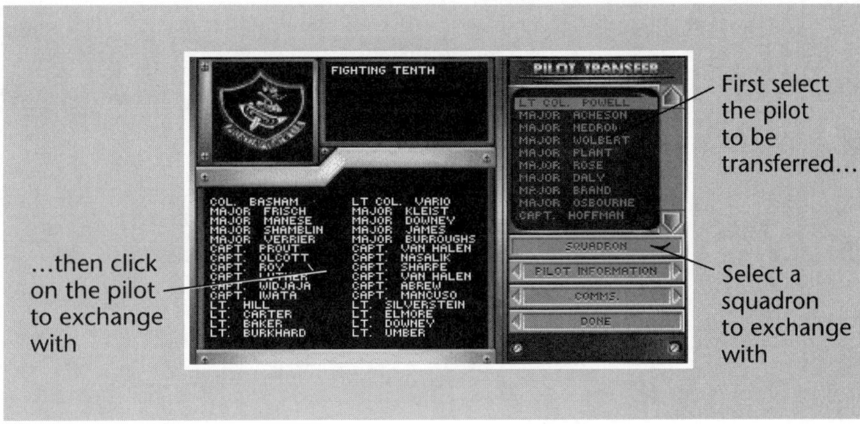

Figure 2-6 Pilot Transfer

Notice that PILOT INFORMATION is also available from the transfer screen. Clicking on the COMMS controls accesses the head-to-head communications area of Falcon 3.0. Refer to COMMS later in this chapter for more information. Click on DONE to return to the Ready Room. Click on the telephone setting on the file cabinet to return to the War Room.

Some screens in Falcon 3.0 are accessible from more than one place. For instance, you can select PILOT INFORMATION from the Transfer Screen, Ready Room, or during a campaign or Red Flag mission.

Below the FORM light in the War Room there are other selections that are used for campaigns. *Do not select any of these controls at this time.* The THEATER selection cycles through the available campaign regions. The area of conflict is highlighted by a box on the world map. The COMMIT control will send the active squadron off to battle in the selected region. The DEACTIVATE control will pull the active squadron from the region, sending it back home. You will be notified that deactivating the squadron causes all progress in the campaign and squadron records to be discarded.

Red Flag—The Training Ground

Click on the Red Flag screen to give the active squadron orders to report for training. Figure 2-7 shows the initial screen of Red Flag. Many different screens are available when using this training facility. All of the screens are discussed in detail in Chapter 6, *Introduction to Red Flag*. In reality, Red Flag is an exercise that is held at Nellis Air Force Base, Nevada. Many of the top pilots in U.S. Armed Forces hone their skills in the desert near Las Vegas.

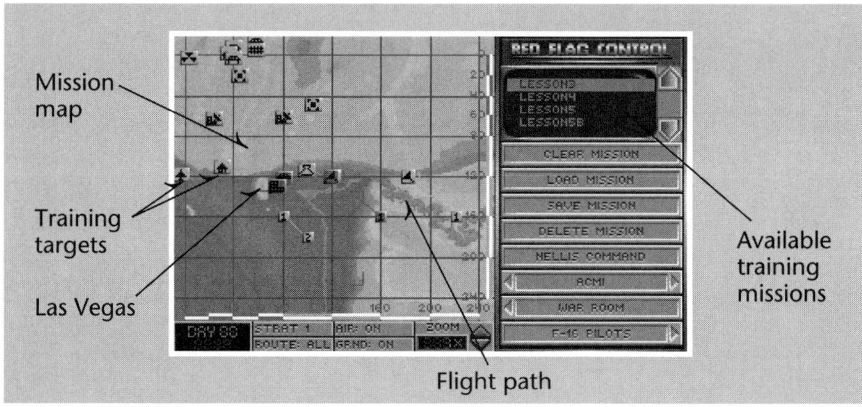

Figure 2-7 Red Flag—Your Squadron Training Facility

Much of the detail of this area is available in the 3-dimensional world of Falcon 3.0—Red Flag.

Here you will create your own custom missions designed to improve your pilot's ability ratings. For example, if Captain Peabody had a bombing rating of 65, this would indicate a need for some bombing training. Red Flag gives you the tools to create a bombing mission and assign the Captain to carry it out. If the pilot successfully carries out the bombing mission, his ratings will increase as a result. All 30 pilots in your unit are able to get the specific training they need to prepare for the ultimate challenge—The Campaign. You are in control of the training!

Falcon 3: The Complete Handbook contains several missions for the Red Flag area. Here you will learn to take off, fly, attack the enemy, avoid enemy attack, and safely land. For now, click on WAR ROOM to return.

COMMS—For Head-to-Head Action

One thing that sets Falcon 3.0 apart from the competition is the flexible capability of the communications mode. You and a friend can team up and take out the enemy together, or compare your skills in a head-to-head confrontation! This can be done by direct connection between two PC serial ports, via modem (2400 baud or greater), or over a Novell compatible network connection. You must commit the current squadron to a theater in order for the COMMS screen to be accessible. Click on the COMMS screen in the War Room to access the communications area. The PILOT TRANSFER screen appears. Select a pilot from the display on the right side of the screen by clicking on the name. More pilot names can be accessed by using the scroll arrows. Pilot names are used for identification purposes in COMMS mode. No pilot ability ratings apply. Click on COMMS to access the communications screen.

> **WARNING:** Each computer involved in the communications battle must have the same version or revision of the Falcon 3.0 software. Falcon 3.0 displays the revision level (3.0A, 3.0C, etc.) in the lower right corner of the copyright screen when you start the program.

Setting Up Communications Figure 2-8 shows the COMMS screen. Head-to-head communications requires a small amount of setup in order to properly establish communications. The left half of the setup screen is used for modem-modem hookup. The position of the MODE button determines whether the system is initiating the call or receiving. The PORT setting determines whether the modem (or direct connect) is using the COM1: or COM2: serial port. The LINE TYPE is set for the type of dialing used, TONE or PULSE. If yours is the calling system, enter the phone number of the receiving system by clicking on TELEPHONE, then type the phone number and press ENTER.

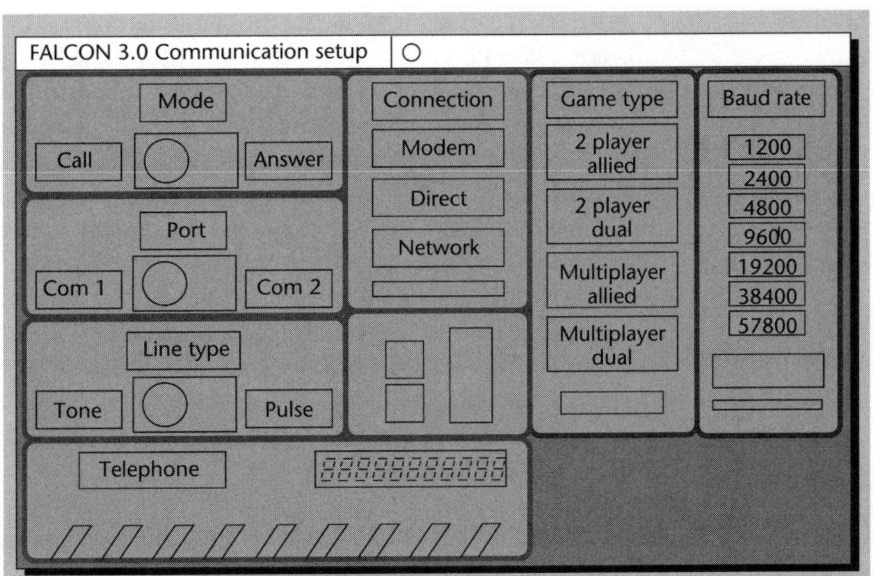

Figure 2-8 The COMMS Setup Screen

The CONNECTION selection must match the type of connection the systems are using. MODEM indicates that the connection will be made via phone lines. The BAUD setting establishes the rate that data is transferred between the systems. At least 2400 baud modems must be used on both ends of a comm connection. A baud rate of 1200 is not supported, even though the screen has a 1200 baud option. DIRECT indicates that the systems are connected directly, serial port to serial port. This requires a *null modem* cable to work properly. The direct connection can usually support up to 57600 baud (transmission speed). Higher transmission speeds permit more information to be exchanged in a shorter period of time. The NETWORK selection is for systems that are connected via a Novell compatible network system (IPX compatible). A network setup will allow up to six Falcon pilots to fly simultaneously.

WARNING: Because Falcon 3.0 requires a high amount of RAM, all network drivers must be loaded into high memory for Falcon to run properly. Consult your operating system and network documentation for information on loading drivers into high memory.

The GAME TYPE setting determines whether the pilots will be competing against each other or acting together as a team. The TWO PLAYER ALLIED setting allows two pilots to fly together in a campaign. The calling player is responsible for selecting the campaign region before initiating the call. The TWO PLAYER DUEL allows the players to battle each other until one of the aircraft is destroyed. Both of the two player settings will work with the modem, direct, and network settings. The MULTI PLAYER ALLIED mode allows up to six players to engage in a campaign. The MULTI PLAYER DUEL places up to six players in the air in a free for all. This mode will continue until all but one aircraft is destroyed. Note that multiplayer modes require the network connection. In network configurations, one player is the caller while all other participants must be set to answer.

Once the settings are established, click on SAVE SETTINGS to save the parameters (this will also start the first COMMS session). This will save you from having to reconfigure the settings on your next mission. In subsequent sessions, clicking ACCEPT starts a game using the previously saved settings. Clicking CANCEL returns you to the War Room.

Keys Used in COMMS Mode The following keys are used in communications mode:

- ALT-Q ends the current mission (caller only).
- ALT-A aborts the current mission.

- (ALT)-(X) exits to DOS and aborts mission.
- (P) pauses the simulation (caller only).
- (') allows radio message to be typed.
- (ENTER) sends radio message.

If a player other than the caller aborts the mission, that player's aircraft will continue to *fly* without control. It is recommended for the caller to end the mission. Click on CANCEL to return to the War Room now.

Air Combat Maneuvering Instrumentation (ACMI)

One of the most useful and interesting features in Falcon 3.0 is Air Combat Maneuvering Instrumentation. ACMI permits you to record a mission or parts of a mission. This information can be played back at a later time. This gives you the ability to analyze the results and improve as a pilot. You will be able to view the replay in the normal view (like a VCR tape) or in a 3-dimensional wire-frame mode. In addition, several perspectives from outside the aircraft are available.

ACMI closely resembles the system that the trainers and trainees in the actual Red Flag exercises employ. Several sensors are distributed throughout *Redland*, a fictional country in the desert sands of Nevada. These sensors record the positions of aircraft throughout the day and night while the pilots fly their missions. All of this sensor information provides input to a central computer. This computer uses the data to generate a recreation of the day's events. This allows the pilots to view and analyze their movements from past missions. This provides valuable information for the pilot to improve his skills while flying in a controlled environment.

Using ACMI consists of two steps: recording the mission and playing back the mission. You can install two ACMI recordings from the companion disk. Refer to Appendix A, *The Falcon 3 Flight Disk*, for instructions on loading the missions. The ACMI recordings are installed when the missions are installed. Two sample recorded missions are included. CANYON1 and CANYON2 are recordings of the F-16 maneuvering through the Grand Canyon and following the Colorado river. We will use these sample files to demonstrate the features of ACMI.

> **WARNING:** Recordings of missions can only be played back on the same revision level of Falcon 3.0. If you do not have revision D of the Falcon 3.0 software, the ACMI system will display WRONG VERSION

(Continued)

when attempting to load the replay. In this case, refer to Chapter 3, *Learning to Fly*. Then return to the ACMI demonstration after recording a mission and saving it to disk. Replace CANYON1 or CANYON2 with the name of the recording you choose for the remainder of this example. CANYON1 and CANYON2 were generated using Falcon 3.0D.

Accessing ACMI Although we will access ACMI through the War Room, you can actually access the flight recorder for playback from four different locations: The War Room, the menu bar (REPLAY) during flight, the Red Flag debriefing screen, and the Campaign debriefing screen. Using ACMI from the menu bar limits you to the current recording only. You cannot load a different recording using this method. The menu bar is discussed in Chapter 3, *Learning to Fly*. Click on the ACMI monitor in the War Room and let's take a look at the recorded tour of the canyon run. The control panel for the recorder appears.

Loading a Replay The load/save control panel for the Airborne Video Tape Recorder (AVTR) is very simple to use. The existing recordings are shown on the left side of the panel. The right side of the panel lists the available functions. This panel also appears at the end of any mission during which the AVTR was turned on, so you can use the SAVE feature. However, you will need to type a valid DOS filename in the box at the top of the control panel before selecting SAVE. To load a recording, first click the name of the desired recording, then click on the LOAD button. A graphic bar at the bottom of the panel indicates that the file is being loaded. As soon as the file is completely loaded, the first frame of the tape is displayed along with the playback controls. Figure 2-9 shows the AVTR display. Try loading the CANYON1 file now and experiment with each of the controls as they are discussed.

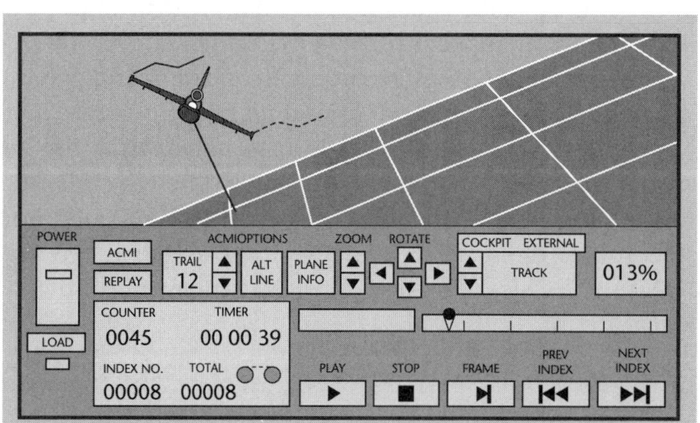

Figure 2-9 ACMI Video Tape Playback

ACMI vs Replay You can choose between two viewing modes when playing back a recording, *ACMI* and *Replay*. Replay is more like watching a videotape in that the screens are displayed like the original mission. The ACMI setting displays the aircraft and the terrain in wireframe and closely resembles the system used during the actual Red Flag exercises.

There are several controls on your simulated tape player. Some controls are restricted to ACMI only, while others are available depending on the view (cockpit/external). To select a control, just click on it. Table 2-1

Control	Purpose	Valid Mode	Key
POWER	Return to calling screen	All modes	ESC
LOAD	Displays load/save screen	All modes	L
COUNTER RESET	Resets tape counter	All modes	C
ACMI/REPLAY	Toggles between modes	All modes	TAB
ZOOM	Display view magnification	External	F1-F2
ROTATE	Display view rotation	External	F3-F4 (L/R)
			F5-F6 (Up/Dn)
SCALE	Displays tape position	All modes	P then ; and '
TRAIL	Displays trails on wingtips	ACMI	[and]
ALT LINE	Displays line from aircraft	ACMI	F7
PLANE INFO	Displays aircraft information	ACMI	F8
HIDE CONTROLS	Hides the tape player controls	All modes	ENTER on num. keypad
PLAY	Starts the tape	All modes	V
STOP	Stops the tape	All modes	B
FRAME	Advances one frame	All modes	N
FAST FORWARD	Fast advance of tape	All modes	M
PREV INDEX	Rewinds to previous index	All modes	<
NEXT INDEX	Fast advance to next index	All modes	>

Table 2-1 Controls for Video Tape Player

lists the available keys (for non-mouse users) for the tape player and the modes in which they are active. You may want to start the tape before trying the controls. Click on PLAY or press the V key. You can return the tape to the beginning at any time by dragging the scale indicator (circle with pointer) to the far left and releasing, or by pressing the < key and then pressing V to start the tape again. For controls that require other views, click on the view control (the arrows located beneath COCKPIT). You can also click directly on the words COCKPIT and EXTERNAL to switch between the different sets of views.

The cockpit and external views each have several perspectives: Satellite, Enemy View, Front View, Left View, Rear View, Right View, Wingman View, Missile View, Track View, and Independent View. Some of these views are only available under certain conditions. For example, the wingman view is useful only when you have a wingman assigned to the recorded mission. Table 2-2 shows the keystrokes to control the views in ACMI.

The Independent View allows you to view the area from any fixed point on the battlefield. The arrow keys and the PGUP, PGDN keys change the point of reference for this view. This view can be set up to produce very interesting results. For example, if you have recorded a bombing mission, set this view to show a close up of the target. You can watch the incoming missiles or bombs destroy the target from a close-up perspective. You can locate the target by first watching from the cockpit or external-track view. When you see the target, switch to external-independent view and use the keys listed above to position the target in the center of the display. Also, you can press ENTER to temporarily remove the video tape control panel from the bottom of the display.

The best way to become familiar with the ACMI features is to load a tape and try each of the controls. Also, check out each of the views available. The independent view provides an interesting perspective on the battlefield, especially when there is a lot of activity. Press ESC now to return to the War Room.

View	Valid Mode	Key
Satellite	External	1
Enemy	External	2
Front	Cockpit	3
Left	Cockpit	4
Rear	Cockpit	5
Right	Cockpit	6
Wingman	External	7
Missile	External	8
Track	External	9
Independent	External	0

Table 2-2 ACMI View Keys

Instant Action—An Arcade Style Battle

If you like the action of battling the enemy without the details of mission planning, Instant Action mode is for you. You are instantly dropped in the air with nothing but enemy activity all around and beneath you. The goal in Instant Action is simple: try to destroy as many enemies as possible without being destroyed yourself!

Start the Fight!!! To start the battle, click the Instant Action screen located in the upper right corner of the War Room. The view starts from above your F-16 and zooms down quickly. The cockpit view appears. You are instantly in the air; no takeoff is needed. A full explanation of weapons and techniques of fighting with your F-16 is beyond the scope of this short section. There are, however, a few keys to get you started. The arrow keys or the joystick control the aircraft directional movement. To climb, pull back on the stick or press the ↓. To dive, push the stick forward or press the ↑. Bank the F-16 to the left or right using the stick or ←/→ keys. Select a weapon by pressing ENTER and fire at the enemy by pressing ↑, ↓, ←, or →. There is an unlimited supply of weapons in Instant Action. You may be able to hunt down and destroy a few enemies, but you will soon find there is a lot to learn about flying and fighting with the F-16 Falcon. If you are hit, you can press CTRL-E three times in succession to eject from the aircraft. You will watch as the pilot punches out of the canopy, opens his parachute, and floats softly to the earth.

After you are destroyed in Instant Action, and if you have qualified with a high score, the program will prompt you for your name to add to a list of Falcon 3.0 Instant Action aces. You will also see a graphical representation of the enemy kills. Revision C or above of Falcon 3.0 will also display the number of weapons fired in the Instant Action battle. The score you are given is based on a ratio of kills to weapons used. Higher numbers of kills will increase the score, while using a high number of weapons will decrease the score. Pressing any key will return you to the War Room.

Ending the Battle Early If you wish to end the battle before being destroyed, press ESC to bring up the menu bar. Select FILE from the bar, then select END MISSION. The menu bar has several options to choose from. For more information on the menu bar, refer to Chapter 3, *Learning to Fly*.

Configuration and Setup

Two screens are available to set up Falcon 3.0 for your system and ability level. The first screen sets the difficulty levels of the simulation. This allows you to select a setting that reflects your current ability. There are predefined setups to make the selection process easier and a custom setup mode with virtually hundreds of possibilities. The second screen matches your computer system to the simulation. Settings for input devices, graphics detail, expanded memory usage, and sound are available on this screen. Click on CONFIG in the War Room to access the difficulty level screen.

The settings on both setup screens can be changed by clicking on the desired item. Also, clicking on the category will cycle through the available settings for that particular category. Keyboard users can use the (TAB) key to select a category, use the (↑), (↓), (←), or (→) keys to select a setting, and then press (ENTER) to accept the new setting.

Difficulty Levels

The difficulty levels can be changed at any time. As your expertise at flying and attacking the enemy increases, you can alter the skill level settings to increase the difficulty of the missions. Each setting affects an overall realism rating. This realism rating is a number that is displayed directly above the SKILL LEVEL settings. The more difficult the settings, the higher the realism number. The maximum realism value is 100. Let's take a look at the individual difficulty settings and what they affect.

Skill Level The skill level setting affects all other settings on the difficulty screen. Each setting represents *groups* of other settings. For example, selecting BEGINNER will automatically set ENEMY LOGIC LEVEL to TRAINEE, FLIGHT MODEL to SIMPLIFIED, etc. Falcon 3.0 defaults to BEGINNER upon install. Leave it at this setting as you start to learn to fly in Chapter 3, *Learning to Fly*. You will be instructed to change to the INTERMEDIATE level after the first flight.

The ADVANCED setting should be used only after mastering flying and using weapons effectively. This setting will automatically select the RADAR type of HFR. HFR (High Fidelity Radar) is covered in Chapter 8, *Using High Fidelity Radar*, and is used for the remainder of the book. The CUSTOM setting will light when any other selection is chosen on the difficulty screen. This lets you know that you are no longer using a predefined group of settings.

Enemy Logic Level This setting affects both individual flights and campaign mode. Each setting progressively increases the enemy's ability and effectiveness. Individual flights are affected because the enemy pilot's ability to fight is based on this selection. Campaigns require planning on your part; the enemy must make strategic decisions as well. The lower settings (TRAINEE and CADET) will result in second-rate enemy flying and fighting ability as well as planning and tactical errors on the battlefield. The higher settings are more challenging because the enemy will rarely make mistakes, either in flight or in mission planning.

Flight Model The flight model selection affects the way the F-16 reacts during flight. Several factors affect the overall performance of the aircraft. Physical parameters such as *lift* and *drag* directly impact the way your aircraft will respond when it performs maneuvers. Higher settings increase these effects. The SIMPLIFIED setting allows you to fly without taking these parameters into consideration and it is the least realistic. The COMPLEX setting is the most difficult and requires you to consider these parameters during flight. For example, if the F-16 is loaded with several heavy iron bombs, the way the aircraft responds will be impacted by the additional weight. The HI FIDELITY setting can only be used if you have a numeric coprocessor installed in your system. The HI FIDELITY setting provides the most realistic flight simulation possible using an actual Air Force flight model.

Weapon Effectiveness This selection refers to how effective your weapons are when you deliver them. The HIGH setting requires the weapon to explode within 40 feet of the target to be considered a successful hit. The MEDIUM selection alters the effective area to 20 feet surrounding the target area. The LOW setting requires solid contact with the target or a miss will result.

SAMS—AAA You will soon find out that enemy aircraft is not the only thing to worry about on your missions. The enemy may also be located on the ground with weapons aimed to bring you down in flames. You will need to be concerned with two basic enemy ground weapons: Anti-aircraft Artillery (AAA) and Surface-to-Air Missiles (SAM). This setting affects how accurate and how often the enemy will fire at you. The NONE setting prohibits the enemy from firing at any time during your mission. You will, however, be able to fire weapons at the ground units and destroy them. This is useful for weapons practice. The remaining settings become increasingly troublesome as the enemy will fire more often and avoiding the bullets and missiles will be more difficult. Keep this setting low until you have learned enemy weaponry avoidance techniques (covered in Chapter 4, *Radar and Enemy Identification*).

HUD There are two basic HUD models: A and C. The F-16C HUD is much easier to use and read, and it has less information displayed. The F-16C selection includes detailed target information and scales for altitude, heading, and speed. The following chapter starts with the BEGINNER skill level which includes the C-model HUD. However, the majority of this book will use the A HUD which is covered in detail in Chapter 3, *Learning to Fly*. The A-model HUD is the more realistic of the two.

Limited Fuel You can fly with an infinite amount of fuel by setting this option to OFF. Normally, you will want this setting ON for the realism factor. Additional fuel can be loaded on the wings or centerline (under the center of the aircraft) for longer flights. Keep in mind that more fuel will mean more weight. This will affect the handling of the Falcon if the flight model is set to MODERATE or above. This setting will deduct a minimum of 20 points from the realism value if set to OFF.

Limited Armament This option allows you to fly with an unlimited number of weapons. The stores control panel will display the available number of weapons as 99 if this option is set to OFF. Once again, it is more realistic to turn this switch ON. You will be responsible for loading weapons at the start of each mission. Once you run out of weapons you must return to base and end the mission. This setting will deduct a minimum of 40 points from the realism value if set to OFF.

Limited Chaff—Flares Chaff and Flares are used to decoy or distract enemy missiles that are fired in your direction. Chaff is an exploding cartridge of metal strips that confuses radar guided missiles. Flares are used to confuse the infrared (heat seeking) missiles that rely on the exhaust of your aircraft to work properly. You will soon learn procedures to avoid these incoming missiles—and dispensing chaff and flares is a big part of it. Setting this option to OFF will give you an infinite supply of chaff and flares. The indicators on the control panel will indicate 99 if the setting is OFF. When this option is set to ON, you will be limited to 30 each. Keep this in mind during your flight, especially if you run out.

Radar Three types of radar are available on the Falcon 3.0 F-16. Although each of them is based on the Westinghouse APG-66 pulse-Doppler radar, only the High Fidelity Radar (HFR) represents the actual radar closely. The SAD (Situation Awareness Display) is the easiest radar to use, and as a result, it is also the least versatile. The SAD displays targets from 360° around the aircraft (very unrealistic for fighter aircraft radar). The relative altitude of the targets is also color coded in the SAD mode. Targets are also *locked on* (selected) automatically.

The SAM mode is more realistic than the SAD mode. The radar will display only targets that are within a 45° cone of the front of the F-16. The range of the SAM is greater than the SAD; range settings and target selection occur automatically.

The closest you can get to the real thing is the High Fidelity Radar (HFR). The HFR requires you to select the range of the radar and where the radar is scanning (horizontally and vertically). Also, targets must be locked on manually using this radar. Learn how to fly and use all of your weapons effectively before attempting to master HFR. Chapter 8, *Using High Fidelity Radar*, is designed to transform you into an HFR expert.

Collisions Occasionally, you may fly very close to other aircraft in the simulation. There are times when the skies become very busy with both friendly and enemy aircraft. This setting will disable the detection of an air-to-air collision by setting it to OFF. You will appear to fly through the other aircraft by using this setting. You can also fly through buildings and structures on the ground when the selection is OFF. This setting will not, however, save you from colliding with the ground.

Redout-Blackout Force created by acceleration (G-forces or Gs) has an undesirable effect on the human body when they become excessive. Positive Gs (more than the normal force of gravity) can cause the blood to run out of your head and toward your feet. This affects your vision, causing it to turn all white and subsequently to black. The opposite of this is negative Gs which cause the blood to rise to your head which in effect turns your vision red. The human body tolerates positive Gs better than negative Gs.

Setting this option to ON will cause Falcon 3.0 to simulate these conditions by fading the screen to solid white for positive Gs and solid red for negative Gs. Extending these forces for more than a few seconds will result in the screen going blank.

Intelligence Intelligence is gathered during a conflict to determine locations of enemy forces and permits you to plan missions based on the information received. The amount of information made available to you is based on this setting. Setting the option to PER (perfect) will display every target and ground unit you will encounter on your mission. This scenario is not very realistic. The STD (standard) setting will permit most of the ground forces and units to be displayed, resulting in a more realistic form of intelligence. The LIM (limited) setting provides you with limited information. Reconnaissance data is not easy to come by in an actual battlefield situation, therefore, the LIM setting is the most realistic.

Exiting and Saving the Difficulty Settings After setting the difficulty options to the desired values, you can accept the changes by selecting either the DONE or SYSTEM SETUP button in the upper right corner of the screen. The DONE button accepts the values and returns to the War Room while the SYSTEM SETUP button accepts the values and displays the system setup screen. If you want to discard all changes, select CANCEL. The RESTORE button will discard the changes and remain in the Difficulty Settings screen. This will return to the War Room without saving any changes.

We must prepare the Falcon software for our initial lessons in Chapter 3, *Learning to Fly*. Click on the BEGINNER skill level selection and then the SYSTEM SETUP button.

Configuring Falcon 3.0 for Your Computer System

Not only is the Falcon 3.0 simulation one of the most realistic today, it also supports several different computer configurations. The system setup screen is used to match the Falcon 3.0 software with your computer hardware. Various options for input device, expanded memory, and sound boards are available. The installation program sets most of the options on this screen. However, you may want to change some of the settings from time to time. For example, if you install a SoundBlaster card in your system after you install Falcon 3.0, you can change the settings here to enable the new hardware.

Flight Control This option selects the type of input device you are using with Falcon 3.0. You can control the aircraft movements and fire weapons with the keyboard, a standard joystick, or the ThrustMaster. The ThrustMaster is a particular brand of joystick designed for flight simulators. The keyboard is used in addition to the joystick and ThrustMaster for other controls such as selecting views, enabling autopilot, lowering/raising landing gear, etc. The buttons on the joystick select and fire weapons. If you are using the ThrustMaster, you will have to calibrate it at this screen. If you are using a standard joystick, you will need to configure it with the menu bar, which can be accessed only during a flight.

Detail Level This option determines the detail level of the graphics. Slower machines may achieve better overall results by choosing a lower level of detail. Always choose the highest setting that works properly on your system. Four settings are available. MINIMUM provides the lowest level of detail. This mode will not display clouds or 3-dimensional terrain. The gradient horizon is also disabled. The MEDIUM mode adds a small, local area of 3-dimensional terrain. The HIGH mode adds clouds and gradient horizon as well as expanding the 3-D terrain. The MAXIMUM setting provides the greatest level of detail and the largest 3-D viewing area. You should have at least an 80386 system to select the MAXIMUM setting.

Background Sound The background sound controls the engine and sidewinder (air-to-air missile) noises. Selecting OFF will disable both sounds. ENGINE will send only the engine noise to the speaker or sound board. SIDEWINDER will send the rumbling sound of the missile to the speaker/ sound board; no engine noise will be heard. ENGINE-SIDEWINDER will enable both engine and sidewinder noises. Some systems sound distorted when selecting ENGINE-SIDEWINDER. Eliminate one of the sounds to resolve the problem.

Radio Messages To hear digitized speech through the internal PC speaker or SoundBlaster, you must have a minimum of 2MB of RAM. If the Ad Lib card is selected for radio messages, it cannot be selected for sound and music. The SoundBlaster can be used for messages and sound/music simultaneously. You can disable radio messages entirely by selecting NONE.

Sound and Music You can disable the sound and music by selecting NONE, or by assigning the sound to the PC speaker, an Ad Lib card, a SoundBlaster card, or a Roland LAPC-1/MT-32 card. The PC speaker can provide sounds but is not capable of music. The Ad Lib card can provide sound and music *if* it is not being used for radio messages. The Roland card is capable of music and sound.

Expanded Memory Settings The EMS settings allow you to put data into expanded memory (if it exists). This can significantly reduce the amount of time the program has to access the disk for the data. An expanded memory manager, such as EMM386 or QEMM, must be installed to use this setting. The altitude data places information on the shape of the terrain into high memory. The object data places ground objects (radars, tanks, etc.) in high memory. If properly enabled, the program can quickly access the data from EMS instead of the slower disk access method. Keep in mind that replay for Air Combat Maneuvering Instrumentation (ACMI) requires EMS. Using EMS for altitude and object data reduces the maximum time for replays in ACMI.

Music and Animation The music that is played during menu selection and the animation sequences that are displayed before and after missions can be enabled or disabled. Setting the music option to OFF will disable the music regardless of any of the above settings. After seeing the animation sequences a few times, you may wish to set the animation option to OFF to speed the start up and ending portions of the mission.

Save the Settings Select DONE to save and return to the War Room. Select DIFFICULTY LEVELS to save and return to the Difficulty Level selection screen. Select CANCEL to discard any changes and return to the War Room.

Summary

This concludes the tour of Falcon 3.0. There are many screens and functions that are available to you as the system user, pilot, and squadron commander. The screens are more manageable when broken down into the following major areas:

- War Room—The main menu and central headquarters of Falcon 3.0.
- Squadron Ready Room—Examine squadron and pilot records, commit the active squadron to a region, and transfer pilots to and from other squadrons.
- Red Flag—Train the active squadron pilots; increase pilot abilities in flying, fighting, and bombing. Create your own custom missions to improve your skills and those of your pilots.
- Comms—Establish communications with other Falcon users via direct serial port, modem, or network connections.
- Air Combat Maneuvering Instrumentation (ACMI)—View replays recorded while performing training and campaign missions.
- Instant Action—Find out your ability as a fighter pilot instantly as you are tossed into the fray with nothing but enemy confrontations with which to deal. Arcade-style action.

- Config—Set up the difficulty levels of the simulation to match your ability. Configure Falcon 3.0 to match your PC and associated hardware.

This has been an overview of what Falcon 3.0 has to offer. You will access many of the screens discussed in this chapter throughout the book. Most of the following activities in *Falcon 3: The Complete Handbook* require selection of a squadron before proceeding. The Red Flag area will be used to load the sample missions that were provided on the companion disk. You will start to create your own missions in Chapter 6, *Introduction to Red Flag*.

Now it's time to get down to business and learn to fly! If you have never flown any kind of flight simulator before, or if you are an experienced pilot who needs to brush up on your skills, Chapter 3, *Learning to Fly,* is for you.

3

Learning to Fly

3 CHAPTER

Although Falcon 3.0 is a battlefield simulation, it is also a first rate F-16 flight simulator. It takes a high level of skill to hunt down and attack the enemy successfully. Without a solid understanding of basic flight, all other aspects of the game become more difficult. You will undoubtedly end up in a situation with enemy missiles headed in your direction, anti-aircraft guns tossing metal up at you from the ground, or an enemy aircraft that you just can't seem to get off your tail. Safely escaping from any of these positions requires you to fly and maneuver at an instinctive level. Use this chapter to learn how to fly or improve your piloting skills. Even if you have never flown a simulator before, you will be tearing up the skies after using the lessons in this chapter.

You will use the training missions supplied on the flight disk. If you haven't installed the training missions, install them now using the instructions in Appendix A, *The Falcon 3 Flight Disk*. No enemy activity is present on the following training missions. Their absence allows you to concentrate only on learning to fly. If you are proficient with flight simulators and with the F-16 Falcon, you may want to skip to the advanced flight maneuvers toward the end of this chapter.

This chapter starts with the fundamentals of flight. These basics will not qualify you for aircraft design, but they will help you understand how you get into and out of certain situations. After this brief introduction, you will slide into the cockpit and take your first training flight.

Four Forces of Flight

There are four forces to consider when keeping twelve tons of aircraft, fuel, and weapons in the air: lift, weight, thrust, and drag. All four of these forces can be your friend or your enemy. It all depends on your current situation. Factors such as your altitude, your attitude (the position of your aircraft with respect to the horizon), and many others determine the effect of each of the forces we are about to discuss. Figure 3-1 illustrates the basic effects of the four forces of flight.

Lift

The first force is *lift*. Without lift your F-16 (and any other airplane) would never make it off the ground. The design of the wing and movement through the air at a high rate of speed causes an air pressure differential between the top and bottom of the wing. The wing design and motion cause high air pressure under the wing and low air pressure on top the wing. This difference in pressure is *lift*. The aircraft is able to takeoff when the pressure difference is greater than the force of gravity. Put simply, lift and gravity are opposing forces.

Weight

The second force is *weight*. We are all familiar with effects of gravity; we see them in our everyday lives. **Closely associated with gravity is *weight*.** The weight of the F-16 Falcon can vary significantly depending on the load it is carrying. For instance, air-to-air weapons add little weight to the aircraft, while heavy iron bombs significantly increase the overall weight. Overcoming the effects of gravity with the latter will be clearly more difficult. You will notice this difference in Falcon 3.0 based on your difficulty level setting for FLIGHT MODEL.

Thrust

The F-16 is very capable when it comes to *thrust*. The single Pratt and Whitney F-100 Turbofan is the source of power or thrust for the Falcon. The measurement of thrust is pounds. This power plant can generate in excess of 20,000 pounds of thrust when enabling the *afterburner*. The afterburner mode consists of injecting fuel directly into the exhaust of the jet engine. The Falcon has five stages of afterburner, each progressively dumping more

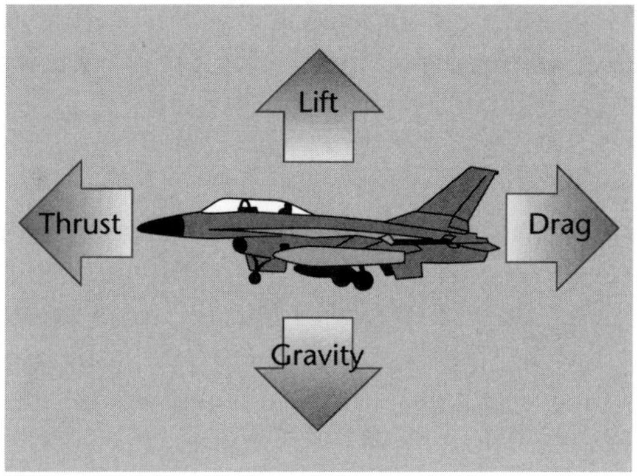

Figure 3-1 Four Forces of Flight

and more fuel into the tailpipe. All of the extra thrust does not come without a cost, however. Using the afterburner consumes fuel at a much higher rate than standard or *military power*.

Drag

Some automobile advertisements refer to aerodynamic design. Usually this refers to a design that reduces the amount of *drag*. Drag is basically resistance or friction and is the converse of thrust. A certain amount of drag exists on all aircraft, regardless of the design. In fact, without some amount of drag, you could not have the lift. Loading weapons and other devices that have a large surface area will increase the amount of drag on your aircraft. Once again, the large iron bombs are the culprit. Not only do they increase the weight of the aircraft, they increase drag.

Putting the Forces Together

Not one of the four forces listed above exists in a vacuum. All four have some kind of effect the entire time your Falcon is in the air. It is not necessary to concentrate on any particular one (you will soon have plenty of other things to worry about!), but it pays to understand what makes your aircraft fly. You will understand why the response becomes more sluggish when loaded to the gills with heavy armament and why it may be necessary to *jettison* (drop prematurely) this armament to quickly escape an enemy attack.

Other Factors

There are other factors to consider as you roam around the countryside in your multi-million dollar aircraft. One factor is the *angle of attack*, or AoA. Figure 3-2 shows the effects that the angle of attack has on lift and drag. Increasing the AoA by pulling back on the stick gives you additional lift, but also increases drag. A severe AoA, without the thrust to overcome it, results in a *stall*, or loss of lift. You can recover from most stalls by pointing your nose toward the ground and increasing your airspeed. You trade altitude for lift. This brings up an important point. Don't stall at a low altitude! You may crash into the ground before you can recover.

What exactly causes the stall? An excessive angle of attack creates a stall; there is not enough lift to counteract the aircraft's weight. Air density has a significant impact on lift. For example, the air at ground level and the air at 50,000 feet above ground level are very different. Higher altitudes have thinner air which reduces lift; reduced lift increases an aircraft's *stall speed.* The stall speed is the airspeed at which the wings lose sufficient lift. Eventually you will reach an altitude where the stall speed is equal to the cruise speed. For the Falcon, this is somewhere between 50,000 and 60,000 feet above ground level, even with the afterburners blazing! To counteract a loss of lift, get air flowing smoothly over your wings again by decreasing your AoA (i.e. put your nose down).

What Does All This Mean?

You may be asking this question. The answer is . . . not much until you start to gain practical experience. You have to get your hands on the controls of the aircraft and feel the results of your own actions. There are many maneuvers you can pull off in your F-16 and you will learn some of them by utilizing the lessons in this chapter. Learning to fly the F-16 is about 10% reading and 90% actual air time. Each lesson in designed to give you another building block towards becoming an ace at Falcon 3.0. Before we start the first lesson, let's take a look at the format of the lessons.

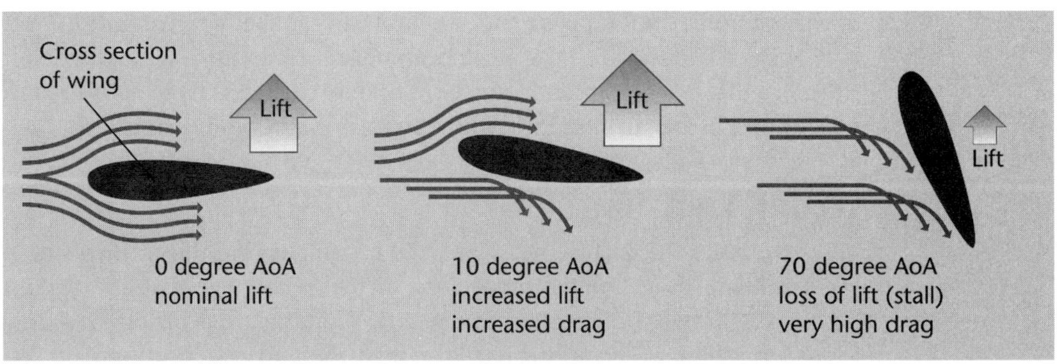

Figure 3-2 Effects of Angle of Attack (AoA) on Lift and Drag

Falcon 3.0—Lessons in Flight

Each of the lessons in this chapter builds both your knowledge and your skills when flying the F-16 Flying Falcon. We discuss *passive* flight in the lessons. No enemies to attack or attack you and no weapons loaded. These lessons intend to teach you to takeoff, fly around and navigate the sands of southern Nevada, and land safely back at Nellis AFB. In doing so, you learn about cockpit instrumentation, different views, and several different maneuvers.

The lessons are in a logical order starting with the basic and moving towards the complex. It is best to take the lessons in sequence. By the end of this chapter, you will have mastered the basics that enable you to fly, perform impressive maneuvers, and land your F-16. You learn to fly at a location where many pilots have received countless hours of training. The emphasis is on learning here, so don't worry about making mistakes. By spending the time now to master the basics, you will enjoy this great simulation that much more.

The Lesson Format

Each lesson uses the same approach. You load the mission and receive your ground school instruction. In ground school, you start with a list of lesson objectives and keys used, along with an overview of what you will see and do during the lesson. Then, using step-by-step instruction, you perform the mission. At the end of each mission you receive a debriefing (review) to analyze your results. If you have not performed a lesson to your satisfaction, you can try the mission again. Fly the missions as many times as you need, until you feel comfortable with the outcome of the lesson.

Loading Lessons All of the lessons supplied with *The Complete Handbook* are available in Red Flag. In Falcon 3.0, you use Red Flag to create custom missions to serve any purpose. You learn how to create your own missions in Chapter 6, *Introduction to Red Flag*. For now, you will be loading RFM (Red Flag Mission) files and carrying out the orders given in this chapter. Let's load our first lesson now.

Start the Falcon 3.0 program by changing to the install subdirectory, typing FALCON3, and pressing ENTER. You can press any key during program startup to bypass the introductory screens. You first enter the War Room. Select your squadron by clicking on the SQUAD display, then click on RED FLAG to enter the training facility.

The simulated display on the right side of the screen lists the filenames of available training missions. Highlight the filename TAKEOFF by clicking on it. It may be necessary to use the scroll arrows to display additional files. After highlighting TAKEOFF, click on LOAD MISSION to load the takeoff lesson. The prompt ARE YOU SURE? (Y/N) appears. Answer the prompt by pressing (Y). This loads your first mission . . . *The Takeoff.*

Getting to the Runway The procedure for getting to the runway is the same for all lessons. From the Red Flag Control screen, click on F-16 PILOTS. At the pilot selection screen, click on F-16 ARMAMENT and at the armament screen click on TAKEOFF. This places you on the runway, ready to perform the preflight checklist. Chapter 5, Using Weapons, and Chapter 7, Introduction to the Campaigns, examine pilot assignment and armament respectively. For now, think of these screens as the path to the runway.

You can load the remaining lessons in the same manner. If you exit Falcon 3.0, you can always return to your training by the following steps:

- Select your squadron.
- Select Red Flag.
- Load a lesson.
- Head for the runway.

If you crash or end the mission early, you can always use the preceding steps to reload the mission and start again.

The Menu Bar Just one last item before we start our first excursion. Press the (ESC) key to bring up the *menu bar*. You can use this menu to exit any of the lessons or missions in this book. The menu bar has three main selections: FILE, CONTROL, and OPTIONS. Choosing each of these selections displays additional choices.

Click on the FILE selection. This first selection on the file menu is RETURN TO THE GAME, which closes the menu bar and continues the simulation. The END MISSION selection ends the simulation and brings up the debriefing. The ABORT MISSION option aborts any progress you may have made and returns you to the War Room. The REPLAY selection allows you to play back a replay if you have recorded a flight. Chapter 2, *Introduction to Falcon 3*, has additional information on using ACMI and recording missions. Note that this option is dark gray indicating a disabled selection. The QUIT TO DOS selection is the same as aborting except it exits the Falcon 3.0 software entirely.

Press (ESC) to close the FILE menu and select the CONTROL menu. The control menu selects the KEYBOARD or JOYSTICK for flight control. If you select joystick, you have to calibrate the joystick before continuing. Note that several keys on the computer keyboard perform functions regardless of the type of flight controls selected. For example, the joystick does not provide a way to lower the landing gear, so the (G) key accomplishes this for keyboard and joystick users. An X indicates the current selection.

Press (ESC) to close the CONTROL menu and select the OPTIONS menu. The Options menu contains selections for sound, graphics, and collision detection options. Some of these settings are also available in the system setup screen in the CONFIG section of the software. The menu bar settings have priority; however, they only affect the current mission. The WORLD DETAIL, TERRAIN, CLOUDS, and HORIZON selections affect the overall appearance of the graphics display. Slower machines may have a difficult time displaying the more complex settings. The SCALE selection sets the relative size of other objects in the simulation. The 1X setting is the most realistic, while the 8X setting is the easiest for visually spotting aircraft. The SOUND selection allows you to enable engine sounds, missile sounds, both, or none. Press (ESC) to close the OPTIONS menu and select FILE and RETURN TO GAME.

Flight Lesson #1: The Takeoff

Our first lesson helps you practice taking off. You should have the difficulty level set to BEGINNER. Refer to Chapter 2, *Introduction to Falcon 3*, for setting difficulty levels. Using this mode, taking off is relatively easy. The weight and drag for this setting have virtually no effect on the lift of the aircraft. After you have finished the lesson, you will set the difficulty level to INTERMEDIATE to demonstrate the effects of the weight of a fully loaded aircraft.

Lesson Objectives In this lesson you:

- Learn the basic aircraft controls.
- Perform a standard takeoff.
- Achieve level flight.
- Perform basic maneuvers.
- Use the five stages of the afterburner.

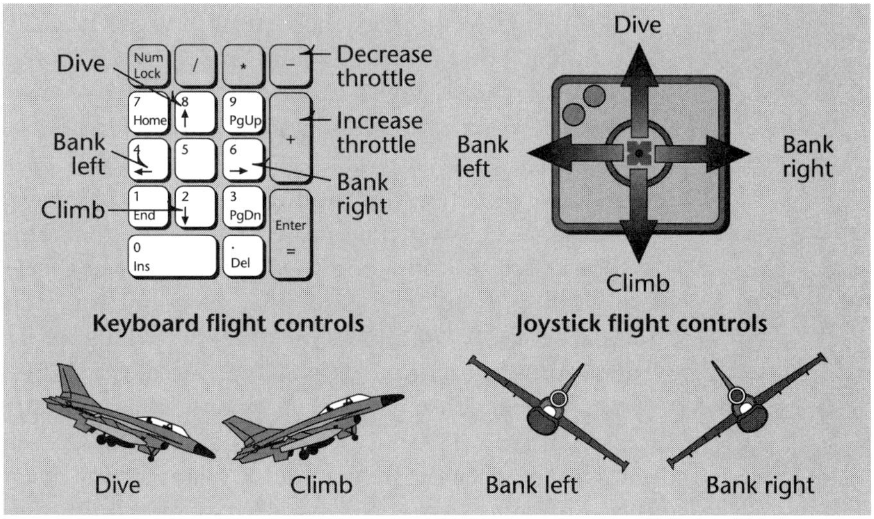

Figure 3-3 Flight Controls for the F-16 Flying Falcon

Ground School Before we take to the skies, let's take a look at the flight controls you will use in this lesson. Figure 3-3 shows the keyboard and joystick controls for the F-16 Falcon. These are the only controls necessary for this initial flight. You will also be using the pause control by pressing the P key on the keyboard. All instruction for flight control refer to joystick operation. Keyboard users can substitute the appropriate commands. For example, when our instruction reads *pull back on the stick*, keyboard users substitute the ↓ key.

The Cockpit If you have loaded the mission and made your way to the runway, you should be looking out of the *head-up display*, or HUD as we refer to it. As the name implies, the HUD keeps the pilot's head up and eyes looking out the front of the aircraft. The HUD displays important information such as your current airspeed, altitude, and heading. The version of the HUD you are looking at is the *C-model* HUD. This version is much easier to use than the *A-model* HUD. We will switch our configuration to the A model after this flight. The remaining flight lessons assume you're a using the A model. Figure 3-4 illustrates the C-model head-up display.

Although the HUD also displays information about other aircraft and weapons status, for now we will concentrate on the items that are essential to flying the aircraft. Your airspeed, measured in nautical miles per hour (knots), is on the left side of the HUD under the label SPD. The altitude of

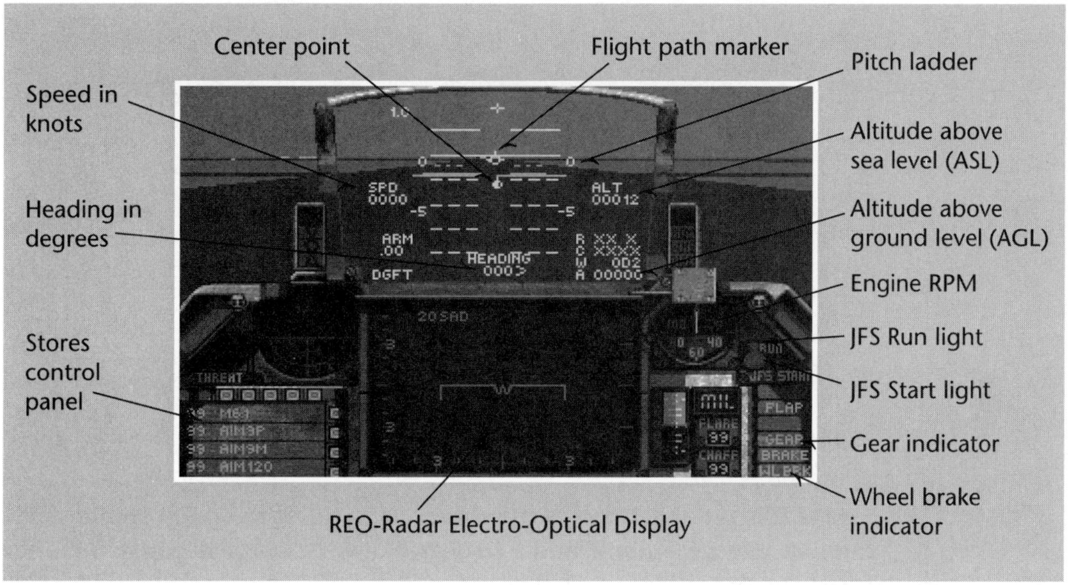

Figure 3-4 The Cockpit Control Panel and the C-Model Head-Up Display

the aircraft is on the right side of the HUD, under the label ALT. Note that this value reflects your altitude *above sea level*, or ASL. Your altitude for *above ground level*, or AGL, is in the lower right corner of the HUD after the character A. If you are flying close to the ground, this is the more important figure to keep an eye on. The direction indicator for your F-16 is in the lower center of the HUD under the label HEADING. The heading value is in degrees with 0 indicating due north, 90 is east, 180 is south, and 270 is west.

The HUD also has two items designed to help keep your bearing while in flight. They are especially useful when the Falcon is in an awkward position, such as upside down. The first is the center point. The center point helps maintain awareness of the center of the HUD. The second is the flight path marker. This marker provides some representation of the direction of the aircraft. Stick movement causes this marker to move, indicating a change in direction of the nose of the aircraft.

The pitch ladder is also part of the HUD display. This indicates the angle of your climb or descent in degrees. Notice the 0 and –5 degree lines are visible with the aircraft sitting on the runway. You can determine the current angle by viewing the pitch ladder as it lines up with the top of the SPD and ALT characters on the HUD. If you are climbing straight up, the ladder indicates 90°. Likewise, heading straight towards the earth would

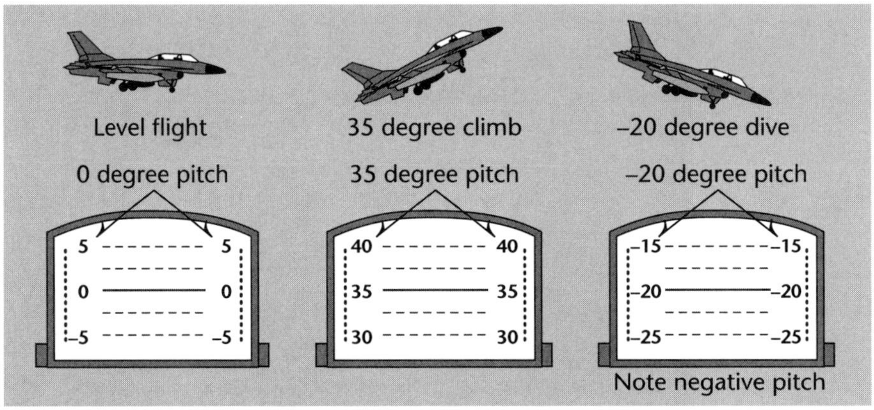

Figure 3-5 Pitch Ladder (Level, Climb, and Dive)

read –90°. Figure 3-5 shows the three examples of the pitch ladder: level flight, a 35 degree climb, and a 20 degree dive. Note the negative numbers on the pitch ladder for the dive.

The JFS run and start lights are indicators for the *Jet Fuel Starter* system. The start light turns red as soon as you crank up the engine and turns green when it is ready for takeoff. The run light glows red as long as the engine is in operation. The JFS run light turns green if the engine is damaged

The large screen in the center of the cockpit control panel is the *radar electro-optical display* or REO. This is a dual-function screen. As a radar, it tracks air activity. As an electro-optical display, it can display a photo of a designated target. The lower left corner is the stores control panel. *Stores* refer to weapons and other materials you load onto the F-16. The quantity available for each weapon on this mission is 99. This indicates an unlimited number of weapons. This, however, is a pleasure flight. The mission requires no weapons.

You now have the basic information on controls and the head-up display. Now is your chance to put your newfound knowledge to work. Let's get in the air! Try to get comfortable with the controls and indicators while you are in flight. You may want to read through the next few paragraphs before taking off. Remember to press (P) at any time to pause the simulation. Pressing (P) again resumes action.

Start Your Engine! Perform the following steps to start the engine and takeoff:

- Set the wheel brake by pressing the (W) key. Note the wheel brake indicator illuminates on the lower right status panel in the cockpit. This prevents the aircraft from rolling during the JFS start sequence.

- Press the + key once to start the engine. The RPM indicator rises to approximately 60% and the JFS start indicator turns green.
- Release the wheel brake by pressing W again. At this point, you start to roll down the runway. You should see the airspeed indicator start to rise.
- Continue the acceleration by pressing the + until the engine RPM is at 100%. Keep an eye on the speed indicator.
- When the speed reaches 150 knots, start to pull back on the stick slightly. This should pull the nose up and you should notice the altimeter value increasing, indicating you are rising above the ground. Raise the landing gear by pressing the G key to prevent damage.

> **WARNING:** If a second joystick is used as a throttle, make sure it is set at least in the center position (50%) before starting the JFS. If it is not, the engine will die immediately following the JFS sequence.

Recall that the ALT indicator denotes above sea level or ASL. It registers 12 feet when on the ground at Nellis AFB. *If you do not pull up before reaching 200–210 knots, you will damage the gear and your flight will be over!* It is also necessary to takeoff before you reach the end of the runway, which should be no problem for the Falcon.

You're In the Air!

- Continue to pull back on the stick until the pitch ladder indicates a climb of 10 to 20 degrees.
- Continue to climb until you reach approximately 9,000 feet. As you reach and pass this altitude, start to press the stick forward to stop your ascent.
- Try to bring the pitch ladder back to an indication of 0. You have now achieved level flight.
- Fly along level for a moment and note your airspeed. You should be traveling at approximately 550 knots.
- Cut back on the throttle a bit by pressing the − key 3 or 4 times.

The AWACS (Airborne Warning and Control System) will report across the top of the screen periodically during the missions (the word "waypoint" is also spoken if Radio Messages is enabled in configuration).

This occurs when you stray off the designated course for the mission. You can force this message at any time by pressing SHIFT-N. Disregard the messages for the first three lessons. You will learn how to utilize these messages in Lesson 4, *Waypoints*.

Three things happen when you decrease throttle. The engine RPM will decrease to around 80%, your airspeed starts to drop, and you may start to lose a small amount of altitude. You have reduced *thrust* which in turn decreases your lift. You can offset the loss in lift by pulling back on the stick a small amount.

Try climbing and diving by pulling back and pushing forward on the control stick. Note the changes in airspeed and altitude as you make the moves. Try climbing to 20,000 feet and leveling off, then return to 10,000 feet and level off once more. Are you getting the hang of it?

Kick In the Afterburner! Make sure you are flying level at approximately 10,000 feet. Now it is time to break the sound barrier!

- Engage the afterburner by pressing the / key. Try to use the / key on the numeric keypad if you are controlling the aircraft with a keyboard. This allows you to select the afterburner *and* control the aircraft with the right hand only.

Notice the afterburner indicator indicates AB1. This is the first stage of the afterburner. You are now dispensing jet fuel directly into your exhaust. Depending on your sound settings and sound hardware, you may hear a pop or a small explosion. Your airspeed should be increasing and the engine RPM should indicate 100%.

- Now switch to the next stage of afterburner by pressing the > key. The afterburner indicator displays AB2.

Do this with your left hand. It is better to have your right hand over the controls (the numeric keypad) at all times. Note that you do not have to press the SHIFT key when pressing >. Keep an eye on your airspeed as it increases even more.

- Press the > key three more times until the afterburner indicates AB5. This is the final stage of afterburner.

You are burning a significant amount of fuel in this stage. Don't worry about running out, however. The BEGINNER setting provides an unlimited fuel supply. Your display should resemble Figure 3-6.

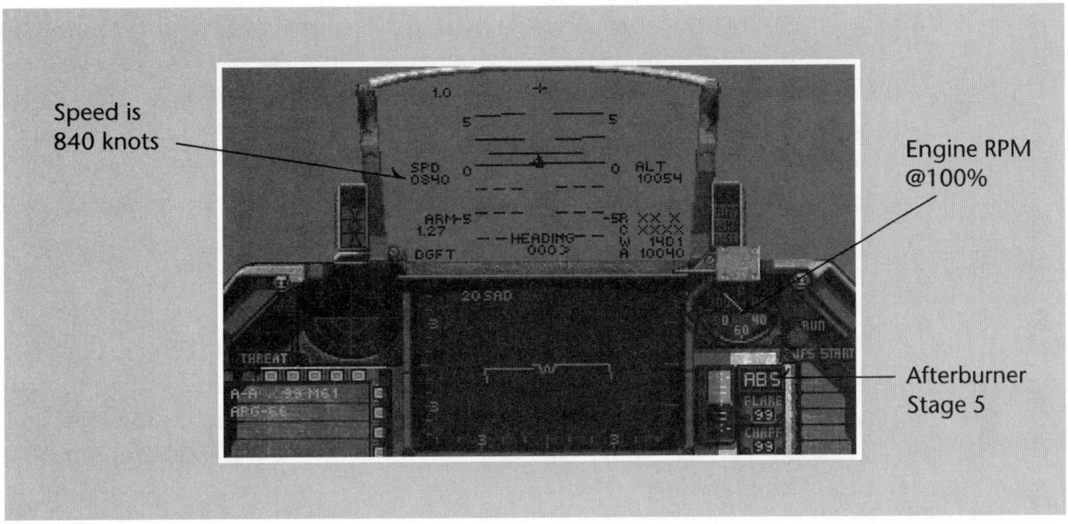

Figure 3-6 Fifth and Final Afterburner Stage

Once again, try climbing to 20,000 feet and diving back to 10,000 feet. You may notice that the control was a slight bit more sluggish due to the high airspeed. This feeling is much more intense at higher realism settings. Make sure you are level at 10,000 feet and turn off the afterburner by pressing [<] four times to return to AB1 and then pressing the [/] key to switch back to MIL (standard) power. It takes a few seconds for your airspeed to bleed off. Note that it is not mandatory to step down through the stages of afterburner before turning it off. You can press the [/] key to directly switch from AB5 to MIL.

- Before proceeding, reduce your speed by pressing [-] 3 or 4 times or until the engine RPM is at 80%. We are now ready for some banks and turns.

Banking the F-16 Enough of this straight and level stuff! Let's try banking the F-16. If you have not turned the aircraft, your heading (listed in the bottom center of the HUD) should indicate between 355 and 005 degrees. You are heading north.

- Push the stick to the left for a moment to bank the aircraft at a 45° angle. Use the horizon in front of you as your guide.

Observe the effects of this banking. The heading number should be decreasing, indicating you are turning in a counter-clockwise direction (as viewed from above). You may be losing or gaining a small amount of altitude depending on the initial position on the aircraft nose (pitch) when you initiated the turn. Your airspeed may also decrease slightly. These effects are not significant because of the BEGINNER difficulty level.

With a banking angle of 45°, try pulling back on the stick slightly.

You should experience two effects from this action. First, your altitude should increase due to the changing angle of the aircraft. You are pointing the nose of the aircraft up by pulling back on the stick. Second, your turn rate should also increase. Turn rate is how fast you are changing direction in the horizontal plane. This turn rate is evident by the heading number decreasing rapidly on the HUD.

If you want to change your heading without gaining or losing altitude, you must bank the F-16 at a 90° angle. Then pull back on the stick to rapidly change direction. This is a basic part of a dogfighting maneuver. Try the 90° bank angle and pull hard on the stick. Note the heading change is very rapid when doing this.

Figure 3-7 shows the effects of these maneuvers. You are rotating the aircraft on a different plane depending on the initial angle of the aircraft. The difficulty level prevents some of the forces from affecting the flight. For example, if you bank the Falcon at a 90° angle without adjusting any other controls, you lose altitude. The next lesson uses the INTERMEDIATE difficulty setting. You will learn how to offset the loss in altitude when banking.

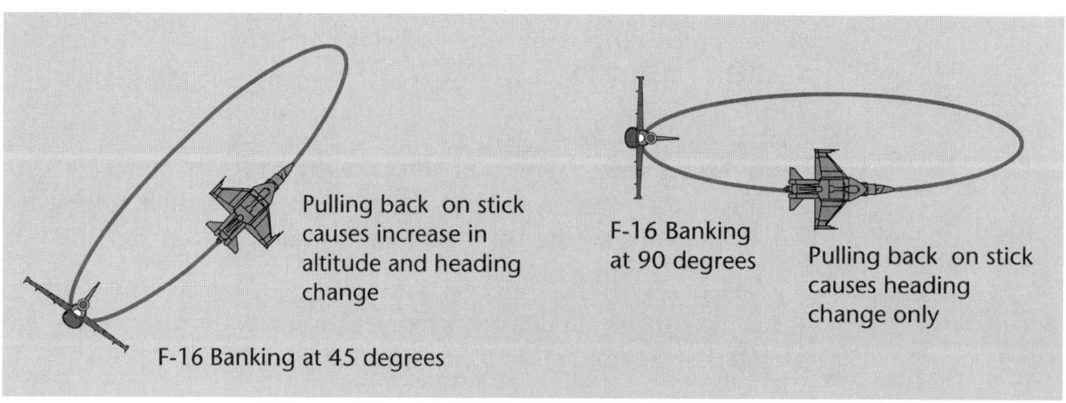

Figure 3-7 Combinations of Banking and Pulling Back on the Stick

Ending the Lesson To end the first training mission, bring up the menu bar by pressing (ESC). Select the FILE menu, then select END MISSION. This returns you to the Red Flag debriefing screen. This screen normally displays the results of the mission. If you destroy an enemy target or aircraft, or if the enemy destroys your aircraft, a message indicates the result. All of the missions in this chapter are passive. The skies are free and clear of enemy aircraft. Therefore, the debriefing screen only displays "THIS WAS THE PLANNED ROUTE." Clicking on the CONTINUE control causes the debriefing screen to display "THIS WAS THE ACTUAL ROUTE." The mission map displays a representation of your actual mission route.

Click on NEXT MISSION to return to Red Flag Control. At this point you are ready to load and fly the next mission. Let's take a look at what we have learned during our first flight.

Debriefing: The Takeoff The Takeoff lesson introduced the necessary tools to get the F-16 in the air. You've seen that it takes a certain amount of speed to create the necessary lift. This speed is around 150–160 knots for the Falcon. Also, you learned that the weight of the aircraft affects the takeoff procedure.

Once airborne, you learned how to climb and descend by pulling and pushing on the stick. You also found that speed affects our ability to climb and change direction. You will see more examples of this effect in upcoming lessons. You demonstrated the effects of banking the F-16. Banking enables you to change your heading. Pulling back on the stick in combination with banking increases the rate that the heading is changing. To change heading quickly and maintain a constant altitude, you must bank the F-16 to 90° and pull back on the stick.

You now have the ability to takeoff and maneuver the F-16. Reload and fly the Takeoff mission as many times as you want. We will change the difficulty settings for the next mission and start to feel the effects of gravity forces.

Flight Lesson #2: The G-Forces

This lesson introduces the undesirable effects of accelerative forces, or G-forces. While you are sitting, reading this book, you are experiencing one G (1G). This means that you are under a force equal to the force of gravity. Acceleration causes these forces on your body to increase. This causes the gravity forces to become greater than one G. The F-16 is capable of placing you in situations that require your body to withstand up to nine Gs. That is up to nine times the normal force of gravity! Normally, high Gs occurs in tight high-speed turns or climbs.

What happens to your body when it is subjected to such high G-forces? Your blood pushes down towards your feet and away from your brain. This results in a *blackout* in which your normal vision first becomes solid white. A few seconds later, you will blackout completely. Not a desirable situation when you are flying a supersonic aircraft!

You will also experience the opposite effect of the blackout, the *redout*. A redout occurs with exposure to *negative* G-forces. This causes the blood to run to your head, which in turn causes your vision to turn solid red. Negative Gs occur as a result of sharp dives at high speeds. Once again, this is not something to look forward to.

Although both positive and negative Gs are undesirable, positive Gs are more tolerable. Falcon 3.0 simulates these effects graphically by causing the display to fade to white when you *pull too many positive Gs* and fade to bright red when experiencing negative Gs. Prolonged exposure to either force results in the screen going completely blank.

In this lesson, you learn maneuvers that produce the high G-forces and ways to keep them to a minimum. You also learn some new maneuvers, including the loop.

> **NOTE:** The remaining missions in this chapter require the INTERMEDIATE difficulty setting. Set the difficulty before starting the G-forces lesson. For information on setting difficulty levels, refer to "Difficulty Levels" in Chapter 2, *Introduction to Falcon 3.*

Lesson Objectives In this lesson you:

- Examine the *A*-model HUD.
- Perform an afterburner takeoff.
- Execute Low-G turns.
- Execute High-G turns.
- Simulate blackout and redout conditions.
- Execute the loop.
- Execute an inverted dive.
- Recover from a stall condition.

Ground School We are using the INTERMEDIATE difficulty level which automatically selects the MODERATE flight model and the A-model HUD. The flight model change makes it more difficult to maneuver the aircraft. Banking the aircraft at 90° does not necessarily maintain your altitude. Other factors, such as your airspeed and aircraft weight, affect the response of banking. The A-model HUD displays more detailed information about the status of the aircraft. For example, scales replace the altitude, airspeed, and heading indicators in the A model.

Load the GFORCE lesson in Red Flag Control now. Pass through the F-16 Pilots and F-16 Armament screens to get to the runway. Do not touch the throttle yet. First, let's take a look at the differences the A-model HUD has to offer.

The A-Model Head-Up Display The A-model HUD represents the actual F-16 cockpit more accurately than the C model used in the first lesson. Figure 3-8 shows the new model HUD and calls out the differences. You should be sitting on the runway, ready to take off at this time.

The major differences in the A-model HUD are the scales used for speed, altitude, and heading. The scales scroll as their respective values change. For example, the altitude scale scrolls downward during takeoff. The G-force indicator was present on the C-model HUD. This feature did not have as much meaning due to the simplified flight model that disabled the effects of Gs. One addition to the A-model HUD is the Maximum G indicator. This displays the highest G-force that you have experienced during the current flight or mission.

The scales take a little getting used to, but they provide more visual feedback than the C-model digital readout. When you are diving, the

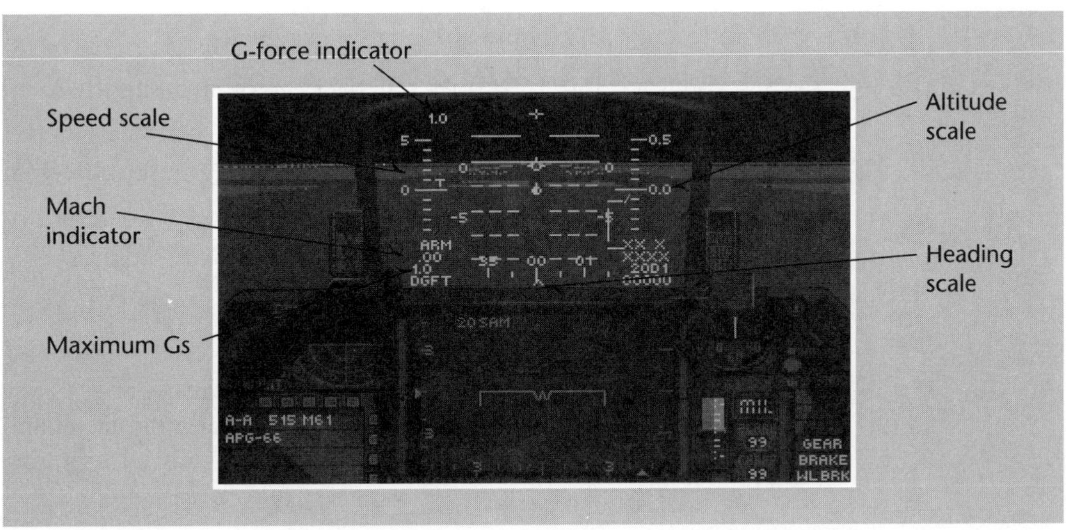

Figure 3-8 Features of the A-Model HUD

altitude scale scrolls to indicate the loss in altitude. Each notch on the scale represents 100 feet. The HUD also displays each 500 feet increment in digital form. For example, 0.5 indicates 500 feet. You can monitor the scales without taking your eyes off the center of the HUD.

The cockpit is basically the same as the C model. The radar has changed, but that does not affect the following lesson. We will discuss two of the three radars used in Falcon 3.0 in the following chapter.

Back to the Skies Takeoff again, but with a slightly different procedure. You are going to execute an afterburner takeoff. Engaging the afterburner during a takeoff is not a requirement in Falcon 3.0, even with a heavy load aboard. It can, however, create a more realistic takeoff and get you in the air and on your way faster.

- Engage the wheel brake first by pressing the W key.
- Start the JFS and engine by pressing + once.
- Release the wheel brake when the JFS run light turns green.
- As you start your roll down the runway, increase the throttle to 100% by pressing the + repeatedly. For realism, it is best to increase the throttle gradually. However, make sure you do not run out of runway!
- Once you have reached an RPM of 100%, kick in the afterburner with the / key. Note that the MIL/AB switch indicates AB1. You are in the first stage of afterburner.
- Step up to stage AB3 by pressing the > key twice.
- When you reach 150–160 knots, pull back on the stick slightly to lift off. Keep an eye on the altitude scale.
- As soon you have an indication that you are off the ground, raise your landing gear by pressing G.
- Pull back on the stick until you are climbing at 15–25° angle.
- Level off your F-16 when you reach an altitude of 15,000 feet (15 on the altitude scale).
- Switch off the afterburner. You can turn it off by pressing the / key again or you can press the − key to disengage the afterburner and decrease the throttle simultaneously. Press the − until the engine RPM reads 80%.

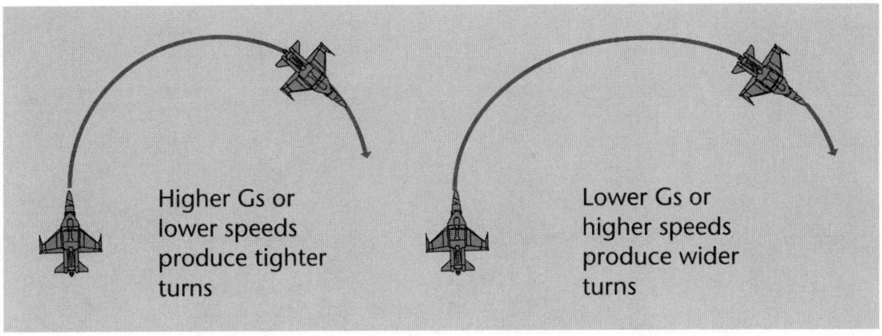

Figure 3-9 G-Force and Speed Effects on Turning Radius

- Once you are flying straight and level, adjust the throttle to set an airspeed to 300 knots. You can press the (−) key to decrease the RPM and watch the speed indicator. As soon as your speed drops to 305–310 knots, press the (+) key to stabilize this speed.

This may take a few tries. You may also have to pull on the stick slightly to maintain level flight at the lower airspeed. Remember that decreasing thrust decreases lift. You can always offset a loss in lift by pulling back on the stick unless you fall below stall speed.

The Low-G Turn Press the (P) key to pause the simulation while you read the following information. The ability to turn the F-16 *properly* becomes essential when you face the enemy in a dogfight for the first time in Chapter 5, *Using Weapons*. Properly, in this case, means whatever it takes to position yourself to shoot down an enemy aircraft. Basically, you control turning radius by two things: Gs and speed. Higher G-forces produce tighter turns. Higher speeds produce wider turns. Speed has a much more significant effect on turn radius. You must use tighter turns in a dogfight situation. Figure 3-9 illustrates the effects of Gs and speed on turning radius.

You can control the G-forces with the flight control stick. The harder you pull back on the stick, the higher the G-force. Higher speeds also produce higher Gs, but the gain in Gs does not affect the turning radius because the higher speed and higher Gs cancel out.

- Resume the simulation by pressing the (P) key. Try out a low G-turn.
- Bank left to approximately 90° then pull back on the stick hard. You should be turning at a fairly high rate. The heading scale should scroll from left to right.

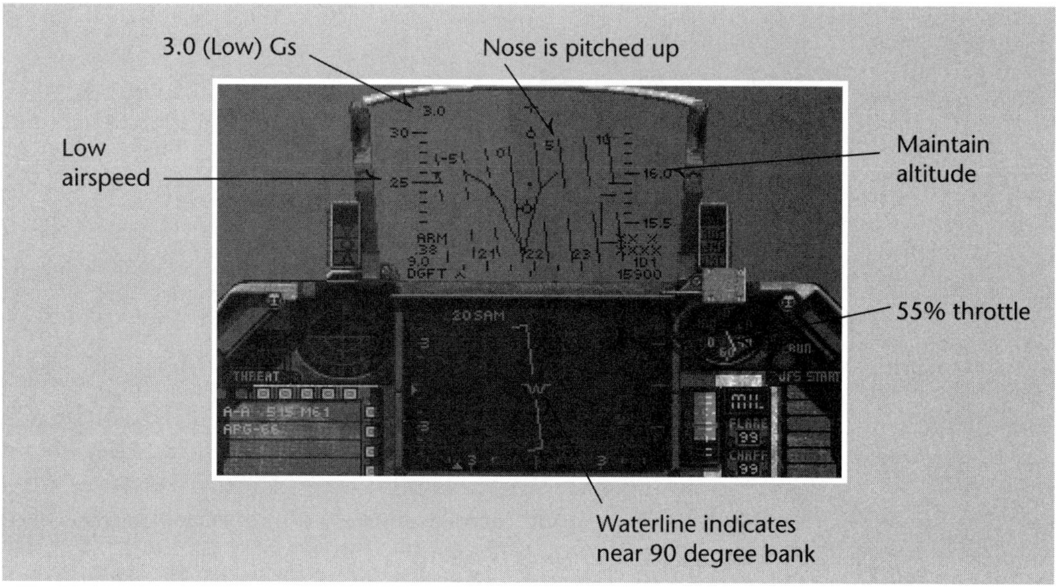

Figure 3-10 Cockpit View of a Low-G Turn

Figure 3-10 illustrates the low G-turn. It requires more effort to keep the F-16 from climbing or diving when executing this turn. This is due to the change in difficulty level. You may find that it is necessary to bank at an angle of slightly less than 90°. This keeps the nose of the aircraft up and helps stabilize the turn. Note the G-forces that you are being exposed to in this maneuver. The indicator should read about 2.5 to 3.5 Gs for this turn. If the reading is higher, level off and try again, making sure that your airspeed is approximately 300 knots before starting the turn.

After a few seconds of turning, level off the F-16 by pushing the stick to the right.

You are able to turn in the tight radius because of the combination of low speed and the ability to withstand 3 to 4 Gs. Of course it's very easy to take 4 Gs while sitting at your computer keyboard. Real-life pilots are not so fortunate. After an extended period of time, G-forces can take their toll on a pilot. What you can do with the press of a key, the pilot must do with his entire body. You will see some of the effects of Gs on the Falcon 3.0 pilot later in this lesson.

High-G Turns Make sure you are flying level and have enough altitude for another turn. You should get in the habit of checking this information repeatedly during flight. It is very easy to fly into the ground with an aircraft

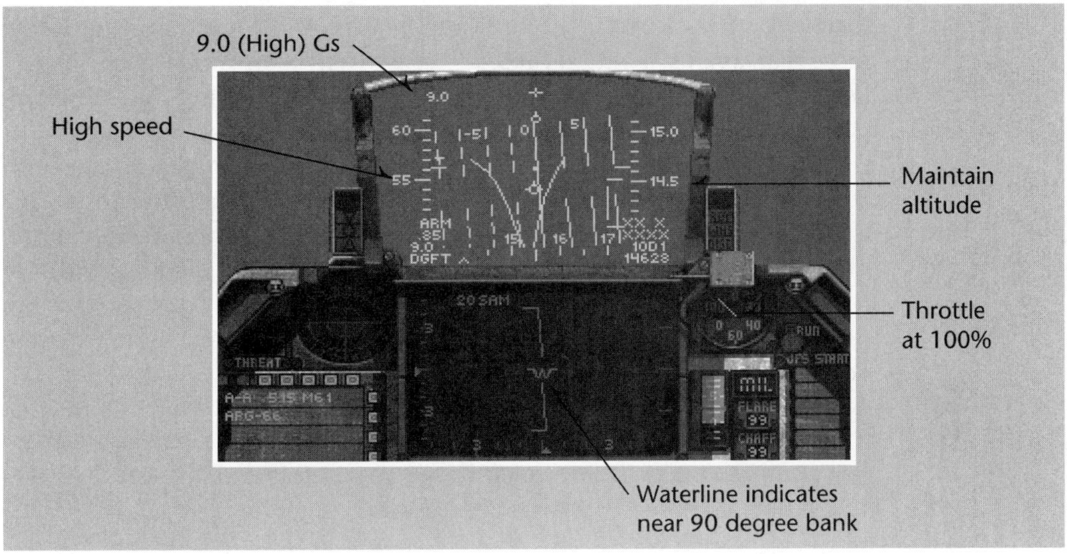

Figure 3-11 Cockpit View of a High-G Turn

that flies at supersonic speeds. Once you are at a comfortable altitude (over 10,000 feet), increase the throttle RPM to 100%. Get ready for a high-G turn.

Let's start the high-G maneuver. Wait until your speed stabilizes before starting the turn. Try turning the aircraft to the right this time.

- Bank the F-16 to the right at 90° by pushing the stick to the right. As soon as you reach the desired angle, pull back on the stick and hold it back for a second or two.

You may have to make small adjustments to the left and right with the stick to maintain a constant altitude. Figure 3-11 illustrates the high-G turn. Notice the G-force indicator in the upper left portion of the HUD. You should get an indication of 9 Gs.

Although it may not be apparent, you are not turning as sharply as the low-G turn. The high speed and sheer momentum keep you from making a tight turn. This becomes very important when engaging in a fight with an enemy aircraft. You have a good chance at winning the air-to-air battles when you can out-turn and out-maneuver the other.

- Pull out of the turn by pushing the stick to the left and level the F-16 out.
- Decrease the throttle to 80% by pressing the – key a few times.
- Pause the simulation by pressing the P key.

Redout / Blackout As mentioned before, if you experience high Gs for more than a few seconds, it causes a negative effect on your vision. You can take 3 or 4 positive Gs for a long period without blacking out. However, pulling close to +9 Gs for more than a few seconds causes a blackout.

A pilot cannot withstand –2 or –3 Gs for more than a few seconds without causing a blackout. Pushing hard on the stick pushes the nose of the F-16 down and causes the pilot's blood to rush to his brain. Falcon 3.0 simulates the redout/blackout conditions by altering the graphics on the screen.

Let's create a redout and a blackout condition. We start with the redout since it is easier to generate negative Gs.

- Unpause the simulation by pressing the P key again.
- Ensure you are flying level, above 10,000 feet and between 350–500 knots. Make adjustments if necessary.
- Push on the stick and hold it. The screen should start to turn red simulating your blurred, blood-red vision. Note the negative Gs on the HUD. Be ready to pull back on the stick soon!
- If you hold the stick forward for a few seconds the screen starts to turn black. This simulates a near loss of consciousness.
- Pull back on the stick to level out the aircraft and recover from the redout condition.

Now let's simulate the whiteout/blackout state. This requires a high speed to produce the high Gs required to generate the effect.

- Level out the F-16 at 10,000 feet.
- Turn on the afterburner by pressing the / key, then increase to stage AB3 by pressing the > key. Accelerate to 600+ knots.
- Bank the aircraft either direction at 60 to 90 degrees, then pull hard on the stick and hold. The G indicator should indicate +9Gs.
- After a few seconds the screen should start to fade to white. This simulates your eyesight turning white. Like negative Gs, positive Gs eventually cause you to completely blackout .
- Push on the stick to level out the aircraft and bank it back to level flight. Turn off the afterburner by pressing the / key.
- Pause the simulation by pressing the P key.

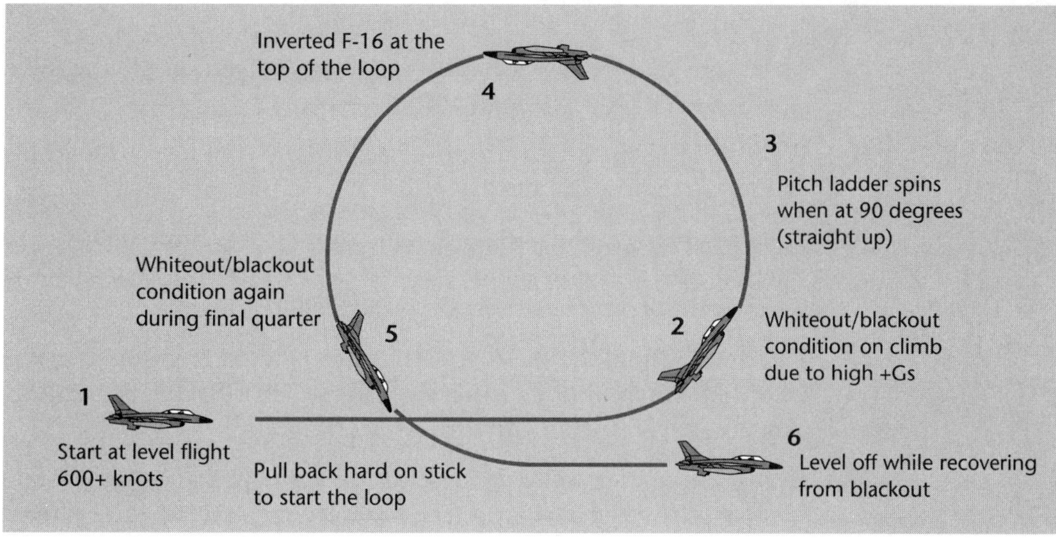

Figure 3-12 The Loop

You will experience these effects during air-to-air battles with the enemy. It is important to know how to recover from the conditions before an enemy takes advantage of your temporary loss of faculties. Pulling on the stick reduces the effects of negative Gs while pushing the stick offsets the effects of positive Gs. It also helps to know your altitude before making any sudden maneuver. You may fly into the ground while in a redout or blackout state.

The Loop If you have previous flight simulator experience, you probably have tried to execute the loop. Attempting a loop in a small aircraft like a Cessna is difficult. The aircraft design coupled with slow speed make the loop a very difficult maneuver. It requires a steep dive to gain the necessary speed to complete the loop without stalling.

The F-16 Falcon is definitely not a Cessna! The speed and raw power of the Falcon permit you to execute the loop with ease. You only need to achieve the proper speed before starting your initial climb.

You will experience a whiteout/blackout condition twice during the loop. You will generate high positive Gs when flying straight up and pulling hard on the stick. This also occurs as you pull out of the loop to level the aircraft. Figure 3-12 shows the F-16 loop and the blackout points.

You may want to read through the following steps before attempting your first loop. It is difficult to follow the steps and perform the maneuver simultaneously.

- Unpause the simulation by pressing the P key.
- Make sure you are above an altitude of 10,000 feet and flying level. Always start a loop at a high altitude.
- Press the + key until the throttle is at 100%. Make sure you have fully accelerated before the next step.
- Pull back hard on the stick and hold. You start to climb rapidly. At a pitch of 25–35° the screen quickly fades to white and then to black. This condition corrects itself as you near 90° (straight up).
- Continue to hold the stick back. The pitch ladder spins around as you pass +90°. You may not see this if you are still in a blackout condition. You are now in the second quarter of the loop.
- Keep holding that stick back! The inverted horizon comes into view as you pass the top of the loop. The pitch ladder starts to go negative.
- You're almost there! The pitch ladder spins around once again as you pass –90°. You may have to give a small amount of left/right stick to keep the F-16 level at this point in the loop.
- You start to black out once again due to the increase in speed. Note the pitch as you start to black out.
- You have to judge where 0° (level flight) is because of the blackout condition. Let go of the stick when you feel you are approaching level flight. After practicing the maneuver several times, you can start to sense the correct time to let off the stick. Experience is priceless!
- Level off and pause by pressing the P key.

That's it! The loop is a fairly easy maneuver in the F-16. It's not a common maneuver in combat, but every pilot has to show off now and then!

Execute the loop several more times before continuing the lesson. Try to achieve a perfect loop. For example, note your heading at the start of the loop and strive to end the loop with the same heading. It is very easy to stray from the desired heading, especially when you are in the final quarter of the loop. Remember to level out and pause the simulation before proceeding.

Inverted Dive We have seen how easy it is to cause a redout condition by pushing forward on the stick. This is very undesirable when in a combat situation. We need some way to dive without causing this problem. The *inverted dive* is the answer.

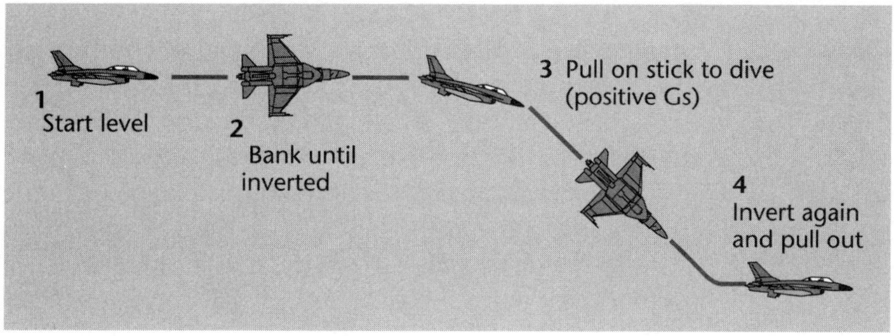

Figure 3-13 The Inverted Dive

The inverted dive consists of rotating the F-16 over to an inverted position, then *pulling* on the stick to dive. Instead of negative Gs, this maneuver causes positive Gs. Figure 3-13 illustrates the inverted dive. Let's try this essential maneuver.

- Make sure you are flying level and set the throttle for 80%. As with all training maneuvers, start with enough altitude (10,000+ feet). Wait for your speed to stabilize before proceeding.
- Bank your aircraft hard to the left until you are flying upside down. Use the horizon or the waterline to track your position. You may have to make a small stick adjustment to keep from gaining or losing altitude.
- Once you have stabilized the inverted position, pull hard on the stick to dive for a moment. *Keep an eye on your altitude!*
- As you are nearing the desired altitude (5,000 feet or so), bank the aircraft again to return to right side up, then pull back on the stick to level off.
- Pause the simulation by pressing the P key.

The inverted dive is very useful in combat situations. It lets you dive quickly to a lower altitude to engage an enemy. Diving by pushing on the stick is not recommended because of the effects of negative Gs. This trick eliminates the effect by employing a positive G move instead.

Practice the inverted dive until it becomes second nature. Try to combine the movements by pulling back on the stick as you are rolling the F-16 over. In combat, it is often necessary to perform several maneuvers simultaneously.

Recovering from a Stall Sooner or later you will find yourself in a *stall* situation. Recall that a stall is a loss of lift caused by an excessive angle of attack. The stall speed of the F-16 varies based on several factors such as pitch, airspeed, and altitude. As pitch increases, drag increases which in turn raises the stall speed. For example, you can fly the F-16 at 0° (level flight), an airspeed of 200 knots, and an altitude of 10,000 feet. If you pitch the aircraft up to 45° without increasing airspeed, you stall. The stall speed has increased.

The air density also affects the stall speed. As you gain altitude, the air becomes less dense. This raises the stall speed. Eventually you reach an altitude where the stall speed exceeds the maximum airspeed. This occurs between 50,000 and 60,000 feet for the F-16. We refer to this as the *ceiling rating* or altitude limit for the aircraft.

The best way to prepare yourself for the inevitable stall is to stall on purpose and recover from it. Surprisingly, both of these tasks are quite easy. Climbing at a steep pitch and a slow speed causes a stall. Recovering from the stall involves nothing more than diving to regain the airspeed, then pulling out of the dive. Figure 3-14 illustrates the stall and the stall recovery.

Try to create and recover from a stall now!

- Climb to 20,000 feet, level off, and adjust your airspeed to 300 knots.
- Pull back on the stick until the pitch ladder indicates 65–70°.
- Note that you are climbing; however, you are also losing airspeed.

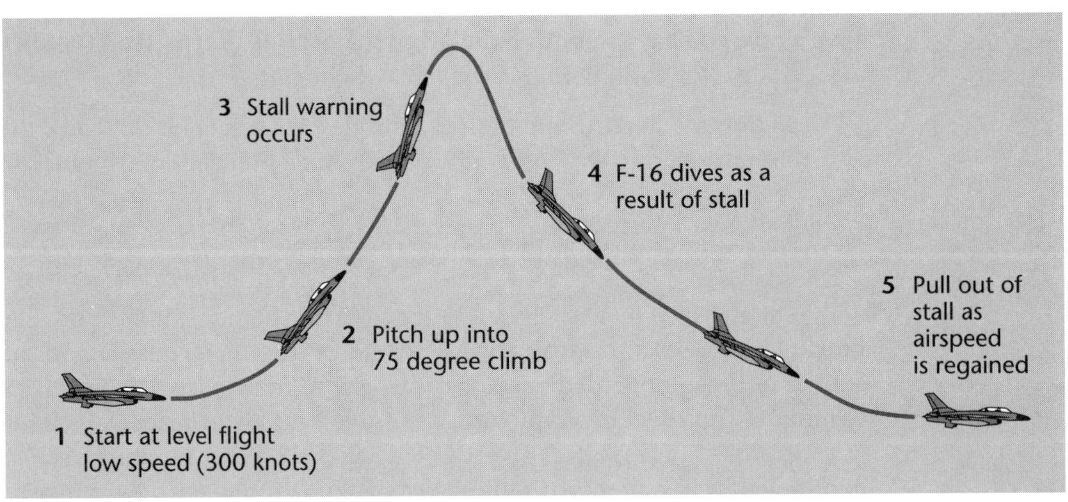

Figure 3-14 Stall and the Recovery

- When your airspeed drops below 200 knots, the stall light comes on in the cockpit. A horn also indicates the stall if you have sound enabled in your system setup.
- The nose of the aircraft starts to drop as a result of the stall. Be ready to correct any left or right movements with the stick.
- Let the aircraft dive on its own until it starts to regain the airspeed.
- As soon as the airspeed is over 225 to 250 knots, start to pull out of the dive by pulling back on the stick and level off.

It is very easy to recover from a stall. You just have to trade some altitude for speed. You will find out later that fighting an air-to-air battle often comes down to this simple equation; altitude for speed or speed for altitude.

It is important to note that stalling at very low altitudes usually proves fatal. You cannot recover your speed (apart from additional throttle) without giving up some altitude. If you are at 1,000 feet and stall, you may not have enough altitude to make the trade! You also may not have enough time to eject and save yourself!

This completes the G-forces lesson. Press the (ESC) key to bring up the menu bar, then select FILE-END MISSION. This sends you back to the Debriefing screen in Red Flag. Click on NEXT MISSION to return to Red Flag Control. You are ready to load the next lesson.

Debriefing: The G-Forces The G-forces lesson introduced the A-model HUD. The A-model HUD provides more detailed information about the status of the F-16. The INTERMEDIATE setting in the CONFIG screen automatically selects the A-model HUD. The remainder of the lessons in this chapter require this setting.

You also executed an afterburner takeoff. This helps you get into the air and to your desired altitude faster. The afterburner consumes a high amount of fuel. The afterburner directly injects jet fuel into the exhaust of the engine. It is not a requirement to engage the afterburner during takeoff.

Once you leveled the F-16 out at a safe training altitude (10,000–20,000 feet), we performed some low-G and high-G turns. You found that higher speeds cause the turning radius to increase. Lower speeds allow you to make tight turns. This becomes more of a factor when engaging in air-to-air combat where it is important to make tight turns. You also saw the conditions of whiteout, blackout, and redout. Excessive Gs can cause these conditions.

Just for fun, you executed the *loop*. The only necessary element to successfully carry out the loop in an F-16 is *speed*. You have to provide the speed to keep from stalling in the middle of the loop.

Pushing on the stick to dive causes negative Gs. The *inverted dive* lets you quickly obtain a lower altitude without the nasty side effects of negative Gs. By inverting your F-16 first, this lets *you* pull on the stick to dive. This creates positive Gs that are much more tolerable to the human body.

Finally, you forced the F-16 into a stall and recovered from it. You can easily overcome most stalls by diving to trade altitude and regain airspeed. Avoid stalling at low altitudes where there is no room for you to recover.

Flight Lesson #3: The Views

So far you have viewed your flight from the cockpit, looking straight out the F-16 canopy. You can access several other views in Falcon 3.0. Views are available from inside the aircraft as well as many views from an outside perspective. Some views let you access indicators like available fuel and backup speed indicators. Many views are not practical for combat, but prove useful in learning how to fly and observing how a new maneuver looks from outside the aircraft.

It is important to familiarize yourself with the various views before entering combat situations. We will cover the keys used to select the views as well as when and when not to use them.

It is not important where you fly in this mission. Just be sure to keep the aircraft at a safe altitude unless otherwise directed. You will fly close to the ground while checking out some of the views. If you crash, restart the lesson, takeoff, and skip to the view you were using when the crash occurred.

Lesson Objectives In this lesson you:

- Use the in-cockpit front, left, right, up, and rear views (low and high).
- Use the satellite and ground views.
- Use the track and chase views.
- Use the view zoom and rotation keys.
- Use the wingman view.
- Use the wingman commands.

In addition to using these views, you also will see when and why to use each of them. You also have a friend along on this mission . . . a *wingman*! Your wingman flies behind you and slightly to the right of your flight path. You will command the wingman to perform basic maneuvers while you continue to fly straight and level.

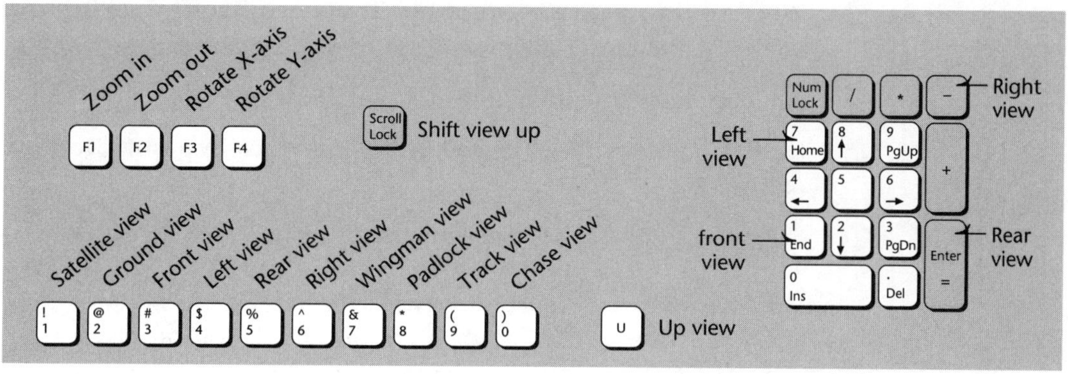

Figure 3-15 Keys Used in the VIEWS mission

There are two additional views, padlock and missile/enemy, that are not covered in this lesson. We discuss the padlock and the missile/enemy views in Chapter 4, *Radar and Enemy Identification*, and Chapter 5, *Using Weapons*, respectively.

Ground School Before you start to access the various views, let's verify the configuration and load the VIEWS lesson. As we mentioned earlier, set the difficulty level to INTERMEDIATE for the balance of the lessons in this chapter. If you are in the War Room, select a squadron and enter Red Flag. Load the VIEWS lesson using the Red Flag Control screen. Click on F-16 PILOTS (note the wingman F-16 on the left side of the screen), then LOAD ARMAMENT, and then TAKEOFF. You should be sitting on the runway.

Before you takeoff, take a brief look at Figure 3-15 which shows the keys you will use on this mission. You can select each of the views before taking off. We cover the views in detail while in flight. Note that you can access some of the inside views with more than one key. Return to the front view by pressing the 1 key on the numeric keypad or the 3 key on the upper row numeric keys.

The Takeoff It's time to check out the views while in flight. Feel free to pause the simulation during the lesson. Perform the following steps to take off and level your F-16 before looking at your first view.

- Set the wheel brake by pressing the W key.
- Start the JFS by pressing the + key once.
- Release the brake with the W key and start to smoothly accelerate down the runway by pressing the + until the throttle is at 100%.

- When your airspeed is between 150–160 knots, lift off by pulling back on the stick slightly. Raise your landing gear by pressing the G key.
- Pull back until the pitch indicator is at 25–30°.
- Climb to approximately 15,000 feet, then level off by pushing forward on the stick.
- Pause the simulation by pressing the P key.

> **NOTE:** The simulation must not be paused when switching views. To switch views during this lesson: Take the simulation off pause by pressing the P key, switch views, then pause the simulation again by pressing the P key.

The Front View You have been using the front view exclusively up until this lesson. Configuration options, such as difficulty level and the HUD switch setting, affect the front view only. Recall that you selected the A- or C-model HUD by the HUD switch position and/or overall difficulty setting in the Difficulty screen. The C-model HUD is easier to read, but provides less information, while the A-model HUD is more difficult to read, more realistic, and provides detailed information. Figure 3-16 shows the A-model HUD and the cockpit front view.

There are a few additional details called out in Figure 3-16. The RDY light indicates that the landing gear is intact and operational. The WHS light indicates that the stick has control of the nose wheel instead

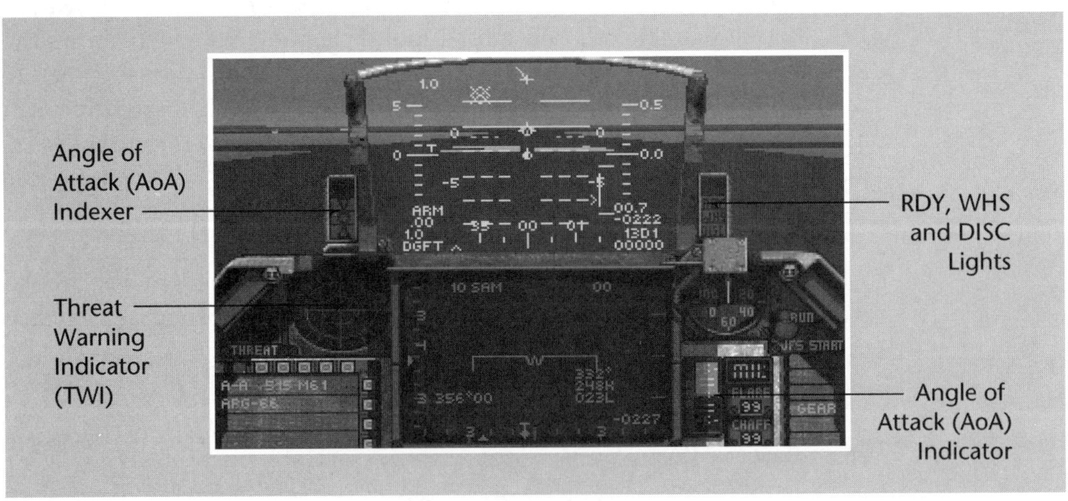

Figure 3-16 Cockpit—Front View

of the ailerons. When the WHS light is on, you are able to use the stick to steer the aircraft on the runway. The DISC light informs you that you are off the ground and the flight stick controls the ailerons. You will use the angle of attack (AoA) indexer and AoA indicator for landing procedures in subsequent lessons.

The Threat Warning Indicator (TWI) displays enemy radar activity and is useful in determining the type of enemy radar. We discuss enemy radar in Chapter 4. The Stores Control Panel displays the available weapons and is a part of the preflight check routine for proper weapon loading.

Press the SCROLL LOCK key to change the view angle of the cockpit—front view (remember to unpause, switch views, then pause again for each view). Notice that the cockpit controls are not visible, but more of the sky above the HUD appears. Use this view angle when you have visual contact with the enemy. Return to the normal cockpit view by pressing the SCROLL LOCK key again.

The Right View Select the right view by pressing the 9 key on the numeric keypad or the 6 key on the upper row numeric keys. Figure 3-17 shows the right view. This view depicts your right (the pilot's stick) hand. The right view also contains an analog clock. This clock indicates the current *mission time*. The Falcon 3.0 software selects a mission time randomly at the start of each mission. The mission start times are either early morning, high-noon, late afternoon, or night. You can always cycle to a desired mission time by pressing SHIFT-T. This will not, however, change the clock display.

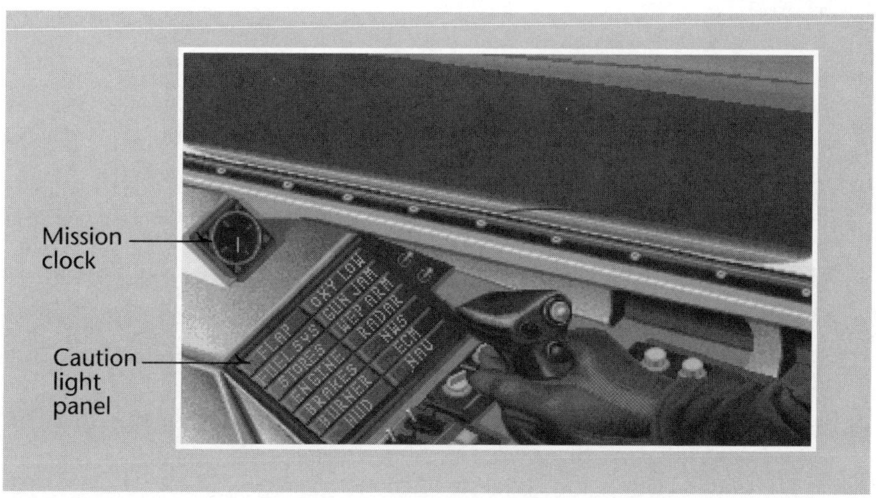

Figure 3-17 Cockpit—Right View

If the light displays...	this means that...	Take the following action:
FLAP	the flaps are damaged and are frozen in current position.	Continue mission at *high risk* or return to base.
FUEL SYS	fuel is leaking.	Monitor fuel and return to base.
STORES	you are unable to fire weapons.	Return to base.
ENGINE	the engine is destroyed.	Land immediately or eject if in slow spin.
BRAKES	the air brake is damaged and is frozen in current position.	Return to base if frozen on
BURNER	afterburner is destroyed.	Continue mission if you no longer need the afterburner.
HUD	HUD is destroyed, no info will be displayed.	Return to base if possible.
OXY LOW	cockpit is punctured	Return to base. Keep aircraft under 10,000 feet.
GUN JAM	20mm gun is jammed.	Return to base *only if* air-to-air weapons are used up.
WEP ARM	weapon arming mechanism is not functional.	Return to base.
RADAR	radar and electro-optical display destroyed.	Return to base or continue mission at very *high* risk.
NWS	nose wheel steering is damaged.	Complete mission and land as smoothly as possible.
ECM	ECM pod is destroyed (if loaded).	Return to base or continue mission at *high* risk.
NAV	map system is destroyed.	Return to base if possible.

Table 3-1 Caution Lights and Suggested Action

The most important items in the right view are the *caution lights*. All of the caution lights should be out at this time, unless you damaged the aircraft during the takeoff procedure. Anytime the aircraft suffers damage, a CAUTION light comes on in the cockpit—front view. The system will also speak to you if you have speech enabled and the appropriate hardware installed. Whenever this occurs, switch to the right view to assess the damage. Switching to the right view also stops the audible caution message. Use Table 3-1 to assess the damage and make a decision based on the damage.

If enemy missiles or guns hit your F-16, they often cause damage to the entire aircraft (all caution lights come on). For this condition, eject immediately by pressing CTRL-E three times in succession.

The right view is not a great view for dogfighting or flying in general. You should only access this view when you get the caution or warning message or you want to check the mission time.

Press the SCROLL LOCK key to change the viewing angle of the right view. You are now looking out the right side of your F-16. Use this view to look at friendly or enemy aircraft that are flying to your *starboard* (right) side. Do not stay in this view for more than a few seconds. You will not have a good indication of the direction and pitch of your aircraft when using this view.

The Left View Select the left view by pressing the 7 key on the numeric keypad or the 4 key on the upper row numeric keys. Figure 3-18 shows the left view. This view depicts your left (the pilot's throttle) hand. This view provides fuel status, a backup airspeed gauge, a compass, an IFF (Identification Friend or Foe) light, landing gear lights, and the AVTR (Airborne Video Tape Recorder) control panel.

The fuel status consists of a gauge with two *hands*. The long hand indicates the external fuel loaded and the short hand represents the main fuel storage. As the F-16 consumes fuel, the hands rotate counter-clockwise. The F-16 uses the external fuel tanks before the main tanks. When the external (long) hand reaches zero, the main tanks will take over automatically. The HUD (front view) displays the word FUEL when the main tanks are near empty. It is advisable to plan your fuel consumption before starting a mission.

Let's look at some examples of fuel consumption. If you fly an *empty F-16* (no weapons or other stores loaded) in level flight at 10,000 feet, at 80% throttle, and an airspeed of approximately 450 knots, the main tanks would allow for 600–630 nautical miles for the trip. If you loaded the F-16 with four Mk-84 2,000 pound bombs and a few air-to-air missiles, you would be able to fly only 400–430 miles before exhausting the main fuel supply. Or, if you

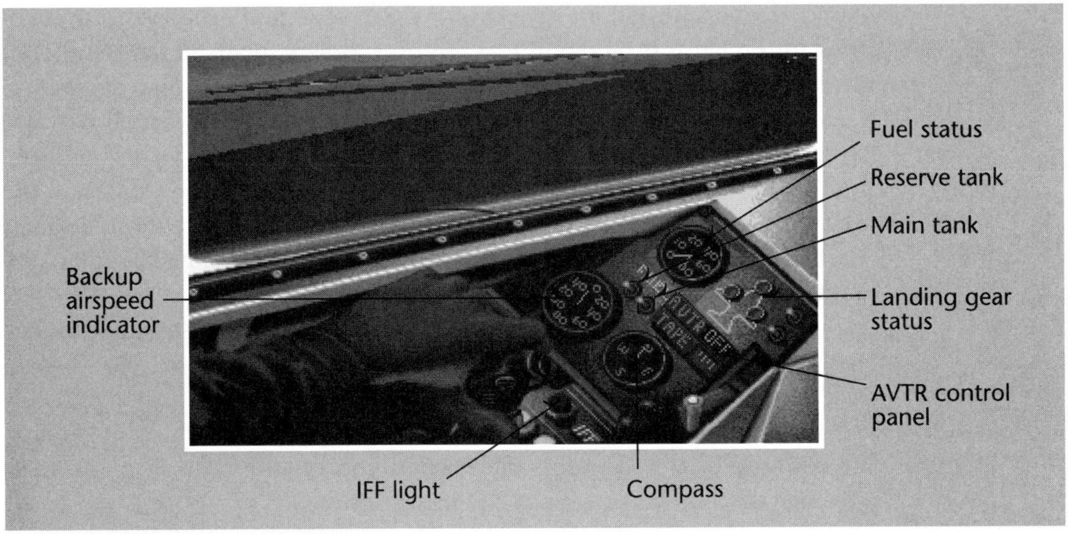

Figure 3-18 Cockpit—Left View

take the empty aircraft and engage the afterburner to the fifth stage (approximately 830 knots), the main tanks would be empty in less than 300 miles!

The main tanks hold close to 6,950 pounds of fuel. Two forms of external tanks are available to extend the range of your F-16. You have the choice of loading two wing-mounted tanks or a *centerline* tank (under the fuselage of the F-16). There is a drawback to the additional tanks, however. The placement of the wing mounted tanks restrict the loading of some weapons. The placement of the centerline tank prevents the installation of electronic-countermeasures gear which can be critical to avoiding enemy missiles.

You will find the backup airspeed gauge in the lower left portion of the left view control panel. The numerals on the dial indicate tens of knots. For example, if the backup airspeed gauge indicates between 40 and 60, this would represent an airspeed of 500 knots.

Located to the right of the backup airspeed gauge is the compass. You can use the compass to navigate if the HUD should become damaged. It is helpful to have a carefully planned route for all missions. The compass and knowledge of the route are the only forms of navigation outside of the HUD information.

Located below the compass is the Identification Friend or Foe (IFF) light. You use this light to check the status of unknown aircraft when you fly missions. You send an electronic code to the unknown aircraft by pressing the N key. If the aircraft is friendly, it responds with the correct code, a tone sounds (if sound is enabled in configuration), and the IFF light comes on.

The landing gear lights are to the right of the fuel gauge. There are three lights for each of the landing gear assemblies. These lights should be off during flight. If you damage the landing gear, the lights stay on, even if you attempt to raise the gear by pressing G. The NWS caution light (in right view) will also be on for this condition.

The Airborne Video Tape Recorder (AVTR) control panel lets you see the current status of the onboard mission tape recorder. The AVTR indicator glows green to indicate that you are taping the mission. The TAPE indicator lets you know how much room you have left to record mission data. The amount of tape you have left depends on the amount of expanded memory installed in your computer. You must have expanded memory to use the AVTR feature. The AVTR feature is discussed in detail in "ACMI" in Chapter 2, *Introduction to Falcon 3*.

Press the SCROLL LOCK key to change the viewing angle of the left view. You are now looking out the left side of your F-16. Use this view to look at friendly or enemy aircraft that are flying to your *port* (left) side. Do not stay in this view for more than a few seconds. As with the right view, you do not have a good indication of the direction and pitch of your aircraft when using this view.

The Rear View Select the rear view by pressing the 3 key on the numeric keypad or the 5 key on the upper row numeric keys. Figure 3-19 shows the rear view. You can use this view to observe aircraft that are directly behind you. You can also see chaff and flares as you drop them. Chaff and flares confuse and decoy incoming enemy missiles.

Figure 3-19 Cockpit—Rear View

Take a look at the effect of dropping chaff and flares now. Press the P key to take the simulation off pause. Switch to the rear view if you haven't already done so. Press the DEL and the INS keys one at a time. When you press the DEL key, you should see a small white cloud emerge from the rear of the aircraft; this is chaff. When you press the INS key, you should see a reddish colored cloud emerge from the F-16; this is a flare. We will discuss chaff and flares in detail in the next chapter.

Press the SCROLL LOCK key to change the viewing angle of the rear view. This provides another angle of the rear view. Do not stay in this view for more than a few seconds. As with the right and left view, you do not have a good indication of the direction and pitch of your aircraft when using this view.

The Up View Press the U key to switch to the up view. You should see nothing but blue sky and maybe a few clouds depending on the configuration and weather conditions. This view is not very useful for combat situations or controlling your aircraft. Occasionally, you may be able to locate an aircraft flying above you in this view. Press P again to pause before continuing.

The Outside View Control Keys The outside views have some features that are not available in the cockpit views. The outside views have controls to zoom and rotate the perspective of the viewer. With these controls, you can modify the view of: your F-16, your wingmen, other allied

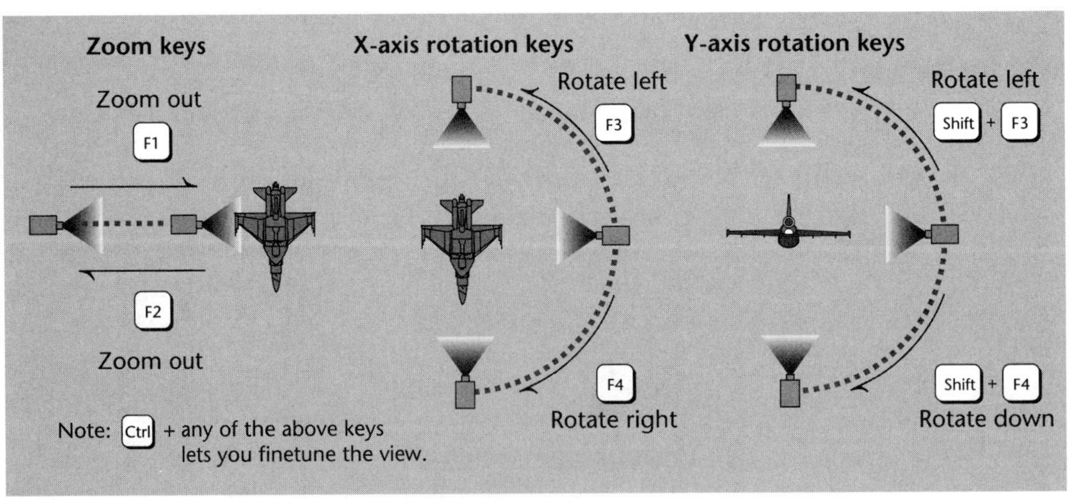

Figure 3-20 Outside View—Zoom and Rotation Keys

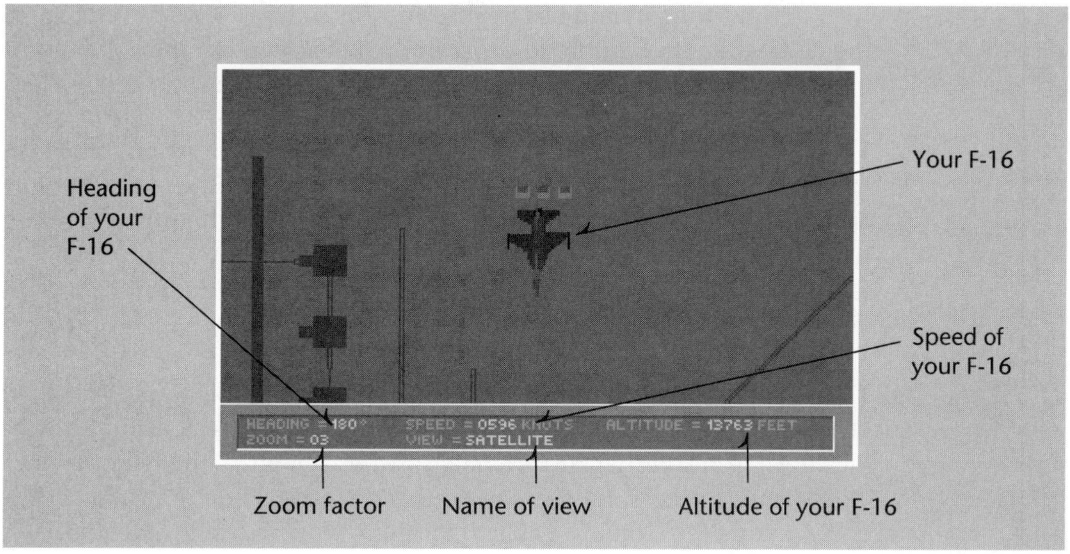

Figure 3-21 Outside—The Satellite View

aircraft, enemy aircraft, missiles, and ground targets. All outside views start with a default position or *point of reference*. You can modify this point of reference by using the controls listed in Figure 3-20.

It makes no sense to rotate some views. For example, if you are rotating the ground view on the Y-axis, you will not be able to see half (180°) of the view because it is under ground. Always make sure the flight of your F-16 is stable before using the outside views for any length of time. After some practice, you will be able to perform maneuvers while watching the results from an outside view. It is not advisable to use the outside views for combat.

Satellite View Press the 1 key on the upper row numeric keys to select the satellite view. This provides a viewpoint from above your F-16. Try out the zoom keys by pressing F1 and F2 to zoom in and out. Figure 3-21 shows the satellite view and the information panel at the bottom of the display. The information display is virtually the same for all outside views.

The HEADING, SPEED, and ALTITUDE values represent conditions for the displayed aircraft. Recall that you can display other aircraft, missiles, and even ground targets. The information given in the control panel is for the displayed item. The ZOOM value represents the amount of zoom. You can adjust this value from zero to 15. Zero represents full scale, while 15 represents minimum zoom. The VIEW entry displays the selected VIEW. This should indicate SATELLITE at this time.

Try zooming in and out by pressing F1 and F2. Note the change in the ZOOM number on the information panel as you use the controls. As mentioned before, the rotate keys are not very useful in the satellite view.

The Ground View Press the 2 key on the upper row numeric keys to select the ground view. This view is similar to the satellite view. The only difference is the point of reference. You will view the F-16 from a point on the ground looking up.

Once again, try using the zoom controls with the ground view. This view is not useful for combat or piloting the aircraft.

The Track View Press the 9 key on the upper row numeric keys to display the track view. The track view displays your F-16 as if you were viewing it from another aircraft. If you are flying with a wingman, the track view displays your F-16 at an angle that also tracks the wingman in the background. You should be able to locate your wingman in the track view now. You can track the aircraft as you perform maneuvers. If you are comfortable flying the Falcon, you can use this view for long periods of time during the flight. You should not use the track view for combat at any time.

You can use the track view to view your F-16 from any angle. Try using the zoom and rotation keys to position the view. Figure 3-22 shows the track view above and in front of the Falcon.

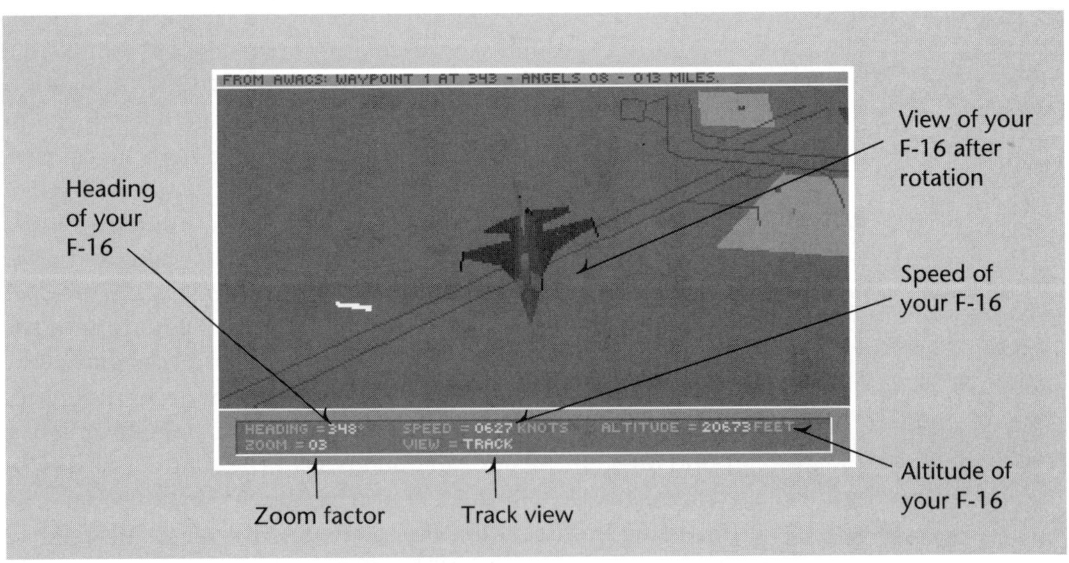

Figure 3-22 Outside—Track View (Rotated)

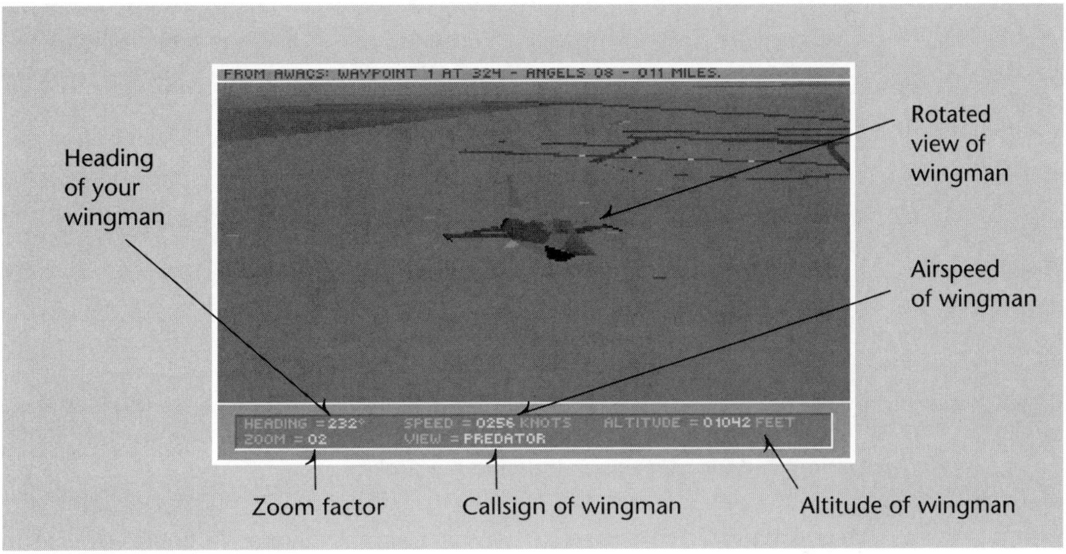

Figure 3-23 Outside—Wingman View

The Chase View Press the 0 key on the upper row numeric keys to select the chase view. This view is similar to the track view except it uses a fixed point of reference. It simulates a view from a chase plane. The view is from a point directly behind the F-16. Rotating in the chase view simulates looking around from this point. For example, use the X-axis rotation keys to rotate the view until you can see the wingman plane. The wingman should be behind and slightly to the starboard (right) side of your F-16.

The Wingman View Press the 7 key on the upper row numeric keypad to select the wingman view. You can use this view to observe the movements of your wingmen. This lesson only has one wingman assigned. If more than one wingman is assigned to a mission, pressing the 7 key repeatedly cycles through the wingmen. The view tracks the movements of the wingman and keeps the leader's aircraft (your F-16) in view. Figure 3-23 shows the wingman view.

This view has one major difference when compared to the other outside views. The HEADING, SPEED, and ALTITUDE values are no longer the values of your F-16. They are the values of the wingman aircraft. The VIEW entry displays the *callsign* of the wingman currently being viewed. The callsign is a nickname for the wingman. You can change the callsigns of the selected squadron pilots using the methods described in Chapter 2, *Introduction to Falcon 3*. Make sure the simulation is paused before proceeding.

Wingman Command	Wingman Action	Key
Break left	Bank left	SHIFT-A
Break right	Bank right	SHIFT-D
Break high	Climb	SHIFT-W
Break low	Dive	SHIFT-X
Level out	Return to level	SHIFT-S
Silence	No radio messages	SHIFT-R

Table 3-2 Wingman Commands and Keystrokes

Wingman Commands You can command your wingman to perform basic maneuvers during the mission. Normally, the wingmen follow the leader F-16 (your aircraft). The wingman commands let you direct the aircraft to break from normal flight. The wingmen will always return to the "follow the leader" mode a few moments after performing the command. Table 3-2 shows the basic wingman commands and their keystroke assignments. Additional wingman commands are covered in Chapter 6, *Introduction to Red Flag*, and Chapter 7, *Introduction to the Campaigns*.

Try out the wingman commands. Unpause the simulation. If you are not at the wingman view, access it by pressing 7 on the upper row. Be sure you are flying straight, level, and at a safe altitude before monitoring a wingman for an extended period of time.

Press SHIFT-A to command the wingman to break left. The wingman displays a message at the top of the screen indicating that he has received and is executing your command. Also notice that the wingman banks his F-16 to the left. If you have Radio Messages enabled in the Falcon 3.0 configuration, the wingman speaks the message "breaking left." After a few moments, the wingman banks back into formation with your F-16.

Try out the remaining wingman commands. Pressing SHIFT-R will silence the wingman messages. This becomes very useful when you are flying with several wingmen and allied aircraft. If the chatter becomes excessive, you can silence them with this command.

End the mission by pressing the ESC key to access the menu bar. Select FILE-END MISSION from the menu bar. Click on NEXT MISSION at the debriefing screen. This places you at Red Flag Control, ready for your next mission.

Debriefing: The Views This lesson emphasized the visual aspects of the simulation rather than maneuvers. We can break down the Falcon 3.0 views into two categories: inside cockpit and outside cockpit. Most of the views presented in this lesson are for entertainment purposes only; you should not use these views for combat.

The inside cockpit views consist of four selections: front, right, left, and rear. Use the front view the majority of the time because it displays the cockpit control panel and the HUD. You use the front view extensively in combat situations presented later in the book. Use the right view to check the caution light panel. This panel provides status on damage to your Falcon, as well as a clock. You can obtain a host of information (such as fuel, landing gear, AVTR, and heading status) from the left view. A backup airspeed gauge is also available. The rear view does not provide additional information. You can observe chaff and flares being dropped by using the rear view.

The outside views used in the lesson were: satellite, ground, track, chase, and wingman. The satellite and ground views provide perspectives from above and below the F-16. We can set the zoom factor by using the zoom keys (F1 and F2). You can use the track view to observe your F-16 from any viewing angle. You can control the viewing angle using the control keys for the track view as well as any outside view. Use the chase view to get a perspective of an aircraft chasing your F-16. You can observe the movements of your wingman by selecting the wingman view. This view provides heading, altitude, and speed information on the wingman. It also lists the callsign of the wingman.

As mentioned before, most of the views are for entertainment only. You usually use the front view in normal flight. The track and chase views provide an interesting viewpoint while flying; it is not advisable to use them for combat. Combat situations require the front view or the padlock view. We will discuss the padlock view in detail in Chapter 4, *Radar and Enemy Identification*.

Flight Lesson #4: Waypoints

You have been flying around in the F-16 without paying much attention to where you were heading. Navigation is a big part of being successful in a mission. Knowing the general direction or the description of a target is usually not enough information to go on. The easiest way to locate your target and return home is to use *waypoints*.

The F-16 is a complicated machine. As with most modern aircraft, the F-16 has onboard computers. You may have heard the Falcon referred to as a "fly-by-wire aircraft." This means that computers ultimately control the surfaces of the aircraft (ailerons, rudder, etc.). For example, when the pilot manipulates the flight stick, sensor information is sent to the computer. The computer, in turn, sends commands to the ailerons or rudder to carry out the action.

One advantage of onboard computers is their ability to *store* the upcoming mission in the form of waypoints. Waypoints represent points on the battlefield. You can use these waypoints to guide your way while carrying out the missions. You can also use waypoints to direct the F-16 when you enable the autopilot. You can use waypoints to determine the action to take at a particular location (bomb a target, intercept enemy aircraft, etc.). This lesson concentrates on using waypoints for navigational purposes.

Lesson Objectives In this lesson you:

- Fly a mission with eight waypoints.
- Use the HUD to determine waypoint distance and bearing.
- Use the autopilot to follow waypoints automatically.
- Use accelerated flight to speed up missions.
- Record a landing using the AVTR.
- View an autopilot landing.

Learning how to use waypoints helps follow mission routes. This proves to be invaluable in missions that involve finding a ground target to destroy or intercepting a group of enemy bombers on their way to destroy an allied site.

Like most training missions, this assignment is free from enemy activity. This allows you to concentrate on navigation without having to dogfight or avoid enemy missiles.

Ground School If you are in the War Room, access Red Flag Control by clicking on the Red Flag screen. Load the WAYPOINT mission by highlighting the mission name, clicking on LOAD MISSION, and pressing Y to confirm the mission selection. Click on F-16 Pilots, then LOAD ARMAMENT, then TAKEOFF. You should be sitting on the runway.

Before you takeoff, look at some new HUD information you will use during this lesson. Figure 3-24 shows how the HUD should appear when you are ready for takeoff.

You will use the *waypoint* caret to guide us during this lesson. Note that it is located on the left side of the HUD. This indicates that the next waypoint is to the left of our current path. After you takeoff, you will bank

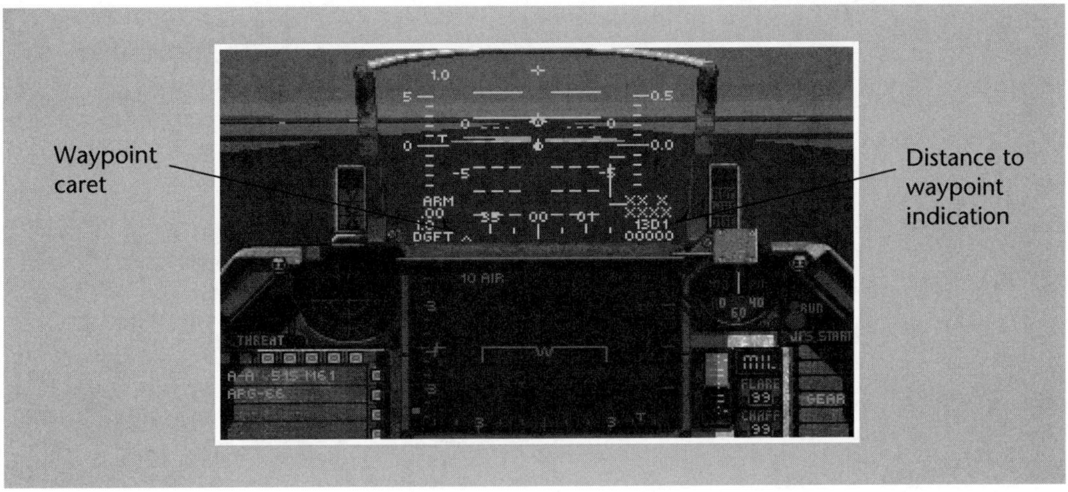

Figure 3-24 Cockpit View—Waypoint Information

left to start to head in the direction of the waypoint. As your flight path starts to line up with the waypoint, the caret moves towards the center of the HUD. You will be traveling directly toward the next waypoint when the waypoint caret is in the center of the HUD.

The distance to the next waypoint is above the altitude indicator. The onboard computer updates the reading as you fly towards the waypoint. For example, the waypoint distance should read 13D1 as you sit on the runway. This means you are 13 nautical miles from waypoint 1.

Figure 3-25 shows a map with the waypoints listed on it. Notice that the first waypoint is northwest of the starting point. This is why the waypoint caret is toward the left side of the HUD. Your F-16 is facing north or at a heading of 0°. The mission consists of eight waypoints. The eighth waypoint is where the aircraft lands. You fly to the fourth waypoint, then let the autopilot take over. The map also indicates that you fly over a chemical weapons plant.

The Takeoff Get in the air and follow the waypoints! Pause the simulation during the lesson to stop and read the steps. Perform the following steps to takeoff, line up with the first waypoint, and level your F-16.

- Set the wheel brake by pressing the W key.
- Start the JFS by pressing the + key once.
- Release the brake with the W key and start to smoothly accelerate down the runway by pressing the + until the throttle is at 100%.

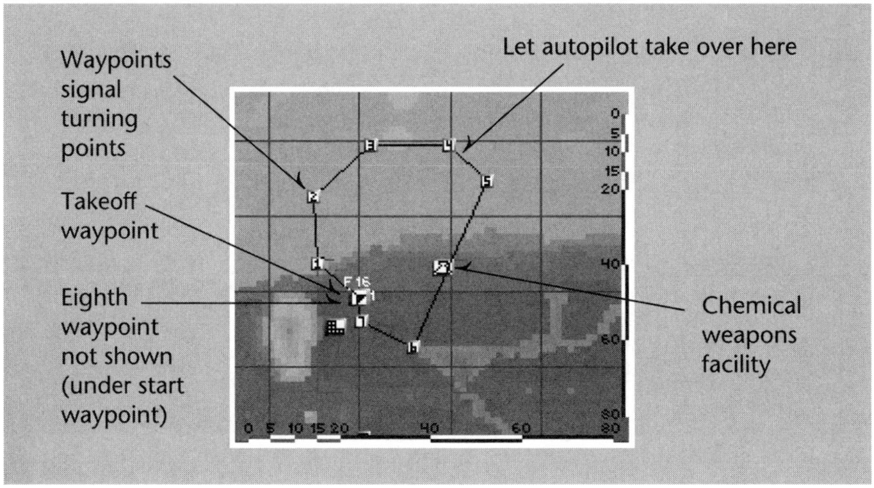

Figure 3-25 Waypoints

- When your airspeed is between 150–160 knots, lift off by pulling back on the stick slightly. Raise your landing gear by pressing the G key.
- Pull back until the pitch indicator is at 10–15°. Bank to the left at an angle of approximately 30°.
- Bring the throttle back to 80% by pressing the - key four times. Maintain an airspeed of 400 to 450 knots.
- Keep an eye on the waypoint caret. As you approach a heading of approximately 325°, the caret should move towards the center of the HUD.

NOTE: If you stray off the designated course, the AWACS system reports the condition at the top of the screen (and with digital speech if Radio Messages is enabled in configuration). For example, if waypoint 1 is at a heading of 325° and you are heading 300°, the bar at the top of the screen displays "FROM AWACS WAYPOINT 1 AT 325 - ANGELS 08 - 013 miles." This informs you of the location of the next waypoint if you are off course. Bank the F-16 to the reported heading to fly directly at the waypoint. ANGELS 08 indicates the altitude for the current waypoint. It is not imperative in the lessons to maintain the correct altitude. It is more important in Campaign mode.

- When you have centered the caret, bank your F-16 to level by pushing the stick to the right.
- When you reach an altitude of approximately 8,000 feet, level off by pushing forward on the stick. Make sure your altitude is 8,000 feet AGL, not ASL. Use the numeric altitude readout in the lower right corner of the HUD. You will be flying over a mountain range. The ASL indicator (the scale) should read around 12,000 to 12,500 feet.
- Pause the simulation by pressing the P key.

You should be heading directly towards waypoint 1 at this time. The distance to the waypoint should be decreasing. Continue on to the next waypoint.

- Unpause the simulation by pressing the P key.
- Proceed to waypoint 1. It may be necessary to bank left or right slightly to maintain the center position of the waypoint caret.
- As you see the distance-to-waypoint indicator reach 0D1, this indicates that you have reached waypoint 1.
- After a few seconds, the waypoint caret jumps to the right side of the HUD and the distance-to-waypoint indicator should read 16D2. This indicates that you need to bank to the right and you are 15 miles away from waypoint 2.
- Bank to the right until you have centered the waypoint caret again. This should occur at approximately 0°. You may receive messages from the Airborne Control and Warning System (AWACS) that you are off course. The messages stop when you center the caret.
- Proceed to waypoint 2. Maintain an altitude of 7,500 to 8,000 feet AGL. Keep the waypoint caret centered by banking gently in the direction of the caret.
- After a few minutes, you should reach waypoint 2. The caret should jump to the right side of the HUD indicating the direction of the next waypoint. The distance should read 19D3. Bank to the right until you have centered the waypoint caret, then level off.
- Continue on your way to waypoint 3 and waypoint 4. The distance between waypoint 3 and waypoint 4 should be approximately 14 miles.
- After you pass waypoint 4 and line up waypoint 5 with the caret, pause the lesson by pressing the P key.

This is the point in the lesson that you let the autopilot take over. The autopilot will follow and adjust the speed and altitude for each of the waypoints. You can learn a lot from watching the autopilot in action. The autopilot can teach you to land, locate the enemy aircraft, and even destroy the enemy aircraft! Let's take a look at autopilot.

- Take the simulation off pause by pressing the P key.
- Turn on the autopilot by pressing the A key.

The autopilot starts to make adjustments in the flight depending on your initial speed, heading, and altitude. The F-16 should start to descend and slow to approximately 350 knots. You may see the autopilot turn the speed brake on and off to maintain a steady speed.

Notice that the distance-to-waypoint indicator is counting down as you approach waypoint 5. The heading indicator should read 140°. You should be at an altitude of 5,000 to 6,000 feet. Keep an eye on the screen as the F-16 approaches the waypoint.

When the distance to waypoint indicator reads 0D5 the waypoint caret shifts to the right. The autopilot banks the aircraft to the right to line up the waypoint caret. You are heading for waypoint 6. The distance indicator should read 46 miles to waypoint 6.

Falcon 3.0 provides a way to accelerate past the boring parts of a mission. For example, we have 46 miles to the next waypoint. There is only one interesting site along the way. Let's accelerate the simulation.

- Press SHIFT-TAB to enable the mission accelerator. The words ACCELERATED MODE should appear on the HUD. Keep an eye on the distance-to-waypoint indicator.
- When the distance to waypoint 6 is 30 miles (30D6), turn off the accelerated mode by pressing the TAB key.
- The chemical weapons plant should be coming into view. If you received a random night mission, the lights from the plant should be visible.
- Check out some of the views you learned in the previous lesson. The track view provides an interesting perspective as the Falcon flies over the enemy plant. Figure 3-26 shows the F-16 flying over the weapons plant.
- Switch back to the cockpit view by pressing 1 on the numeric keypad. Accelerate the lesson by pressing SHIFT-TAB. Press the TAB key to turn off the acceleration as the F-16 reaches waypoint 6.

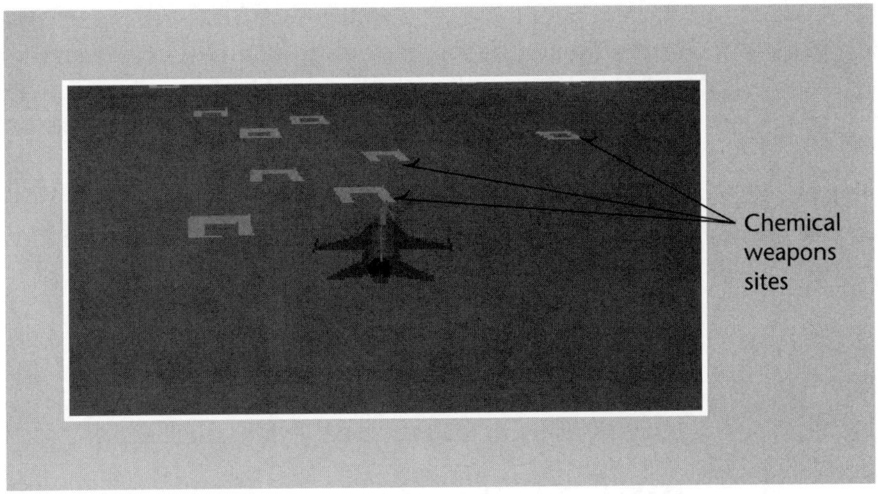

Figure 3-26 The Falcon Flies over a Chemical Weapons Facility

If you have expanded memory in your computer, you can record the landing sequence and view it using ACMI. Press CTRL-R to start the tape recorder. You can check the left view to see if the AVTR is on. If you do not have expanded memory, proceed without taping the mission.

Sit back and watch the rest of the mission as the autopilot brings the Falcon back to base. The aircraft should be heading for waypoint 7 at 290°. As the F-16 reaches the waypoint, the autopilot banks right, heading due north for the runway. You should see the aircraft start to decelerate to 300 knots and descend slowly.

The runway should be coming into view when the distance-to-waypoint indicator reads 4D8. As the Falcon reaches the runway, it should have an altitude of 500 feet. The autopilot starts the landing sequence. The Falcon 3.0 autopilot always performs a *military style* landing as opposed to a straight-in landing. Military landings involve lining up with the runway, flying over parallel to the runway, circling around 360°, then landing.

Watch the cockpit gauges and the HUD instrumentation closely as the autopilot performs the landing. As the aircraft reaches the runway, the autopilot banks hard to the right, initiating the 360° maneuver. The speed decreases slightly as the aircraft is in the turn. The autopilot has set the speed brakes. In the final stage of the turn, the autopilot sets the flaps. The flaps give the aircraft the additional lift it needs at lower speeds.

The autopilot should lower the landing gear as the runway comes into view again. The F-16 should touch down gently on the end of the runway as the autopilot lowers the throttle to 5–10%. When the speed drops below 70 knots, the autopilot steers the aircraft off the left side of the runway using the rudder. The autopilot sets the wheel brakes and the Falcon comes to a stop.

This concludes the lesson on waypoints. Access the menu bar by pressing the (ESC) key. Select FILE-END MISSION. If you recorded the mission, the AVTR control panel pops up. Click on the filename box, type WAYPOINT as the video tape filename, then click save to save the recording. You should end up in the Debriefing screen. Click on CONTINUE to review the flight path of your F-16. Note how you followed the path (the starting waypoint through waypoint 4) compared to the autopilot path (waypoint 4 to landing). The Debriefing screen takes a few seconds to display the route. Click on NEXT MISSION in the Debriefing screen. You should be at Red Flag control, ready to load the next lesson, the *landing*.

Debriefing: Waypoints This lesson discussed waypoints and their navigational value. You programmed the F-16 with the route before taking off. Then you simply followed the waypoint caret displayed on the HUD. If the caret was to the left of the center of the HUD, this indicated that you needed to bank in that direction to direct the nose of the aircraft toward the next waypoint.

Once you were heading for the next waypoint, you monitored the distance-to-waypoint indicator. For example, when the indicator read 13D2, this indicated that you were 13 miles from waypoint 2. As soon as you reached the waypoint, the onboard computer automatically switched to the next waypoint. You repeated the entire procedure for the subsequent waypoints.

About halfway into your mission, you let the autopilot take control of the F-16. You found out that each waypoint has an assignment for speed, altitude, and heading. This caused the autopilot to climb, dive, bank, and control the throttle to follow the waypoint instructions. You will be setting your own instructions in Chapter 6, *Introduction to Red Flag*. You can create your own missions from scratch and use waypoints to define actions as well as navigation points.

You took advantage of the autopilot to check out some out of cockpit views. The autopilot takes care of the details of keeping the F-16 in the air. This gives you time to check out the various views without worrying about crashing into the ground.

When the mission calls for long distances between waypoints, you can accelerate the simulation by pressing (SHIFT)-(TAB). Pressing (TAB) by itself returns to normal speed. There are dangers involved when using the accelerated mode. Switching to the accelerated mode without engaging the autopilot can be very hazardous. Very small stick movements may cause you to crash in this situation.

The training missions in this chapter do not contain enemy activity. Once you have begun to battle the enemy, you may think about switching to accelerated mode to get you home in a hurry. Doing so is very chancy. You never know when an enemy aircraft will sneak up on you. Accelerated mode only helps him sneak up on you faster!

If you recorded the flight, refer to "ACMI" in Chapter 2, *Introduction to Falcon 3*, for information on playing back the tape. Careful review of the tape may be helpful before attempting your own landings. You also can tape your own landings, then play them back to analyze your strong and weak points.

Flight Lesson #5: The Landing

Landing an aircraft can be one of the most difficult goals to achieve. Several things happen in a short period of time. If you concentrate too long on one thing, you may find yourself overlooking something else and crashing to the ground.

The purpose of this lesson is to guide you, step by step, into a perfect landing. This may take more than a few tries before you set the Falcon down in the right place, but after all, this is training! Keep trying and most of the movements and checks will become automatic.

You will use the ILS (Instrument Landing System) feature. This displays information on the HUD that aids in making a safe landing. You may have watched an autopilot landing in the previous lesson. It is highly recommended to watch an autopilot landing before trying it yourself.

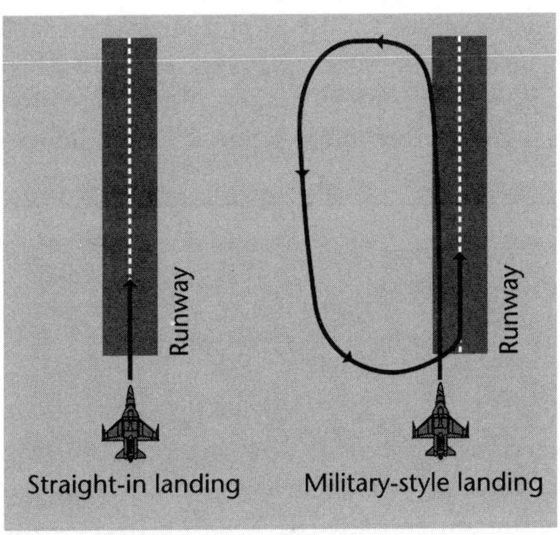

Figure 3-27 Straight-In and Military (360°) Style Landings

You will execute the straight-in landing first to get a feel for the procedure without worrying about banking. You will be in the air, a few miles out, and lined up with the runway when the mission starts. After you become comfortable with the straight-in landing, switch to the *military style* landing. This involves flying over the runway, circling, then landing your F-16. The second mission involves lining up with the runway before landing. Figure 3-27 shows a top-down view of straight-in vs. military style landings

Lesson Objectives In this lesson you:

- Learn the Instrument Landing System (ILS) of the F-16.
- Perform a straight-in landing.
- Learn how to line up for a runway approach.
- Perform a military style landing.

There are not as many objectives in this lesson as compared with previous lessons. Yet this will be one of the most difficult lessons to finish successfully. The best advice here is to not give up. Keep trying until you have the landing sequence down.

In campaign mode you takeoff, complete your mission, return to base, and *land*. The results of a campaign mission depend on your ability to perform the whole job.

Ground School If you are in the War Room, access Red Flag Control by clicking on the Red Flag screen. Load the LANDING1 mission by highlighting the mission name, clicking on LOAD MISSION, and pressing Y to confirm the mission selection. Click on F-16 PILOTS, then LOAD ARMAMENT, then TAKEOFF.

As soon as the cockpit view appears, press the \ key to select the Instrument Landing System (ILS) HUD mode. *Press P to pause the simulation and read the remaining ground school information before proceeding.*

The Instrument Landing System requires that the landing airfield be equipped with ILS gear. This consists of electronic equipment that is capable of sending signals to incoming aircraft. The ILS displays the results of these signals on the HUD so you can adjust for the proper glide slope when landing. This will prevent you from coming in too steep or too shallow for a proper landing.

> **NOTE:** Not all Falcon 3.0 airfields are equipped for ILS landings. Practicing landings with ILS turned off before entering the campaign mode is recommended. You may find it necessary to land at an alternate airfield that may or may not be set up for ILS landings.

Take a look at the ILS display. Figure 3-28 shows the ILS HUD display. The ILS mode is the current selection as shown by the indicator in the lower left corner of the HUD. The horizontal bar is the *Glide Slope Deviation* bar, or GSD. If the GSD bar is above the center of the HUD, your F-16 is coming in too low. If the GSD bar is below, your F-16 is coming in too high. The vertical bar is the *Localizer Deviation* bar, or LD. If the LD bar is to the left of

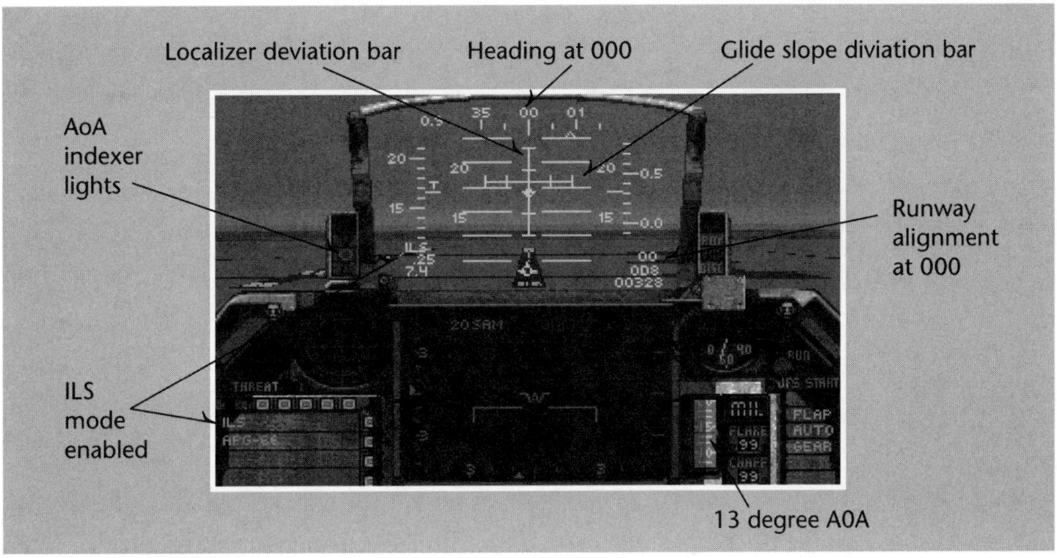

Figure 3-28 The Instrument Landing System (ILS) HUD

the center of the HUD, your Falcon is to the left of the runway. This means that you need to bank right to correct your course.

As of revision 3.0d, the ILS feature has some problems in Falcon 3.0. Its operation closely resembles that of an Automatic Direction Finder (ADF). For ground school only, we will describe the correct operation of an ILS system. For the actual flight, you will land the F-16 by visual flight rules (VFR). Enable the ILS on approach, but use the altimeter and your eyesight to guide you to the runway. Future versions of Falcon 3.0 may have an improved ILS feature.

Instrument Landing System Operation By reading the ILS, you can approach the runway lined up properly and at the correct *glide slope*. Glide slope is the angle at which your aircraft is descending. The Glide Slope Deviation (GSD) bar helps you approach at the optimum angle for a landing. Coming in too steep may cause you to crash onto the runway, while a too shallow slope may end up in a stall.

The ILS also tells you if you are off center of the runway by the Localizer Deviation (LD) bar. You normally make this adjustment several miles out to avoid last minute jockeying of the aircraft. The Falcon 3.0 ILS feature supports this. If you are off center of the ILS runway, the LD bar indicates this, allowing you to make the necessary corrections. Figure 3-29 illustrates correct ILS operation.

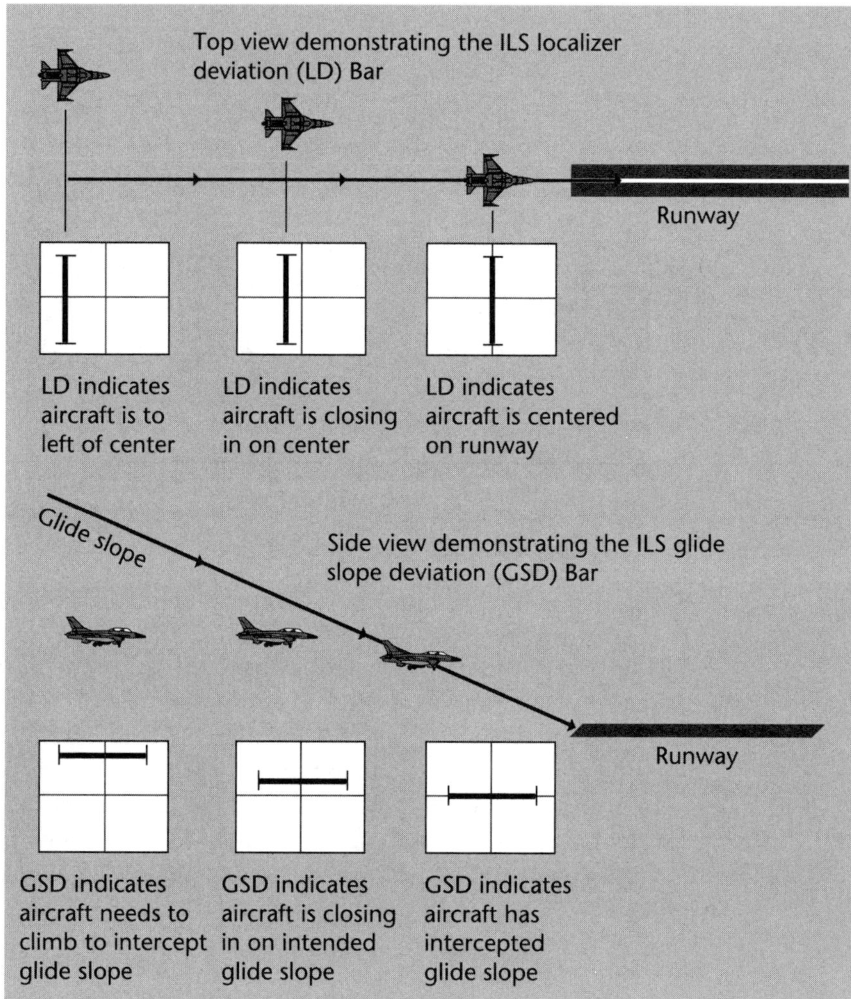

Figure 3-29 Using ILS to Land the F-16

Remember that the landing is one of the most difficult procedures in Falcon 3.0. You may have to try several times before touching down safely. The proper procedure is to set the Falcon down with an angle of attack greater than 8°. This will be very difficult without a lot of practice. Fortunately, the simulation is forgiving and will allow safe landings under the eight degree limit.

F3MAPS, a utility included on the Falcon 3.0 Flight Disk, can modify ILS operation. For additional information, refer to Appendix C, The Skunk Works Utilities.

The Rudder In addition to the ILS key, the landing lesson introduces two new keys: the rudder control keys ([and]). The rudder lets you make the fine adjustments necessary to make an accurate approach to the runway. Using the ailerons (banking) late in the landing approach can be hazardous. Always use the rudder to make the last minute alignment to the runway.

Don't give up on the landing procedure! At first it may seem tough, but it will get easier with each attempt. Let's try a straight-in landing now!

The Straight-In Landing We have designed this lesson to make your first landing as easy as possible. You should be paused at this time. The mission starts about seven to eight miles away from the base at an altitude of about 4,000 feet. Keep in mind that this would normally be too low an altitude for eight miles out. However, this gives you a little time to get adjusted before starting to descend. You may want to read all of the steps before trying the landing procedure. Remember to pause if you need to stop and read the instruments. However, the ultimate goal is to perform this procedure without pausing at all.

- Unpause the simulation by pressing the P key.
- Make sure you have displayed the ILS before starting the procedure. If it isn't, select it by pressing the \ key. The HUD should have the GSD bar and LD bar displayed.
- Immediately cut the throttle to 55–60% by pressing the - key. Try to get the speed down under 350 knots. Apply the speed brakes if necessary (the B key).
- As soon as you can see the runways, line up with the right runway by pressing the rudder keys. Press [for left rudder or] for right rudder. This redirects the nose of your F-16 without banking.
- If you are not descending, push the stick forward to point the nose down a little. DO NOT DIVE!
- When you are under 350 knots, set the flaps by pressing the F key. This will give the F-16 additional lift at a slower speed. You should see the speed decrease slightly.
- Cut the throttle two or three more notches with the - key.
- Continue to monitor your alignment with the runway. Use the rudder to maintain alignment.

- Approximately one mile from the runway, lower the landing gear by pressing the G key. The nose will drop slightly and you will lose more altitude. Pull back *slightly* on the stick to compensate for the drop. Do not pull up into a climb!
- Aim for the very start of the runway. Adjust the throttle so your airspeed is 150–170 knots when you reach the runway.
- As you reach the runway, pull back gently to make sure the nose is up. Do not fly into the runway nose down (negative AoA).
- As soon as you touch down, push forward on the stick to keep the F-16 from bouncing back up into the air. Cut the throttle to 5%.
- As the airspeed drops below 70 knots, the WHS light should light indicating the flight stick has control over the front wheel. Push the stick to the left to steer off the runway.
- Engage the wheel brake by pressing the W key and cut the throttle to 0% after you have come to a complete stop.

That's it! You have the makings of a top pilot if you were able to pull this off on the first try. If you crashed or missed the runway, try again! Landings will get easier with each attempt.

Keep in mind that the goal is to arrive at the start of the runway at an airspeed of 150–170 knots. If your speed drops off too fast, you will stall and crash. If your speed is too high, you may damage the landing gear.

If you are missing the runway left or right, use the rudder more. Do not press and hold the rudder keys; just touch them to make small adjustments. The biggest mistake you can make is overreacting to a condition when a small adjustment will suffice.

Bring up the menu bar by pressing ESC and select FILE-END MISSION. Click on NEXT MISSION to return to Red Flag Control. If you are uncomfortable with the straight-in landing, rerun the mission as needed. If you feel that there is not enough challenge in the straight-in landing, load the LANDING2 mission and press on!

Military Style Landing For this landing attempt we throw in a few new problems. You are not lined up with the runway in this lesson. Also, instead of a straight-in approach, you land *military style*. The military style landing consists of lining up with the runway, flying over the runway, turning 180°, flying out a couple of miles, turning 180° again as you make the approach, then landing. You will notice that this is similar to the procedure that the Falcon 3.0 autopilot uses.

This type of approach may take several attempts before your first success. Making consistent, smooth turns is an important part of this landing. You also have to adjust your speed and line up with the runway while coming out of the turns.

Getting Lined Up for the Approach Later in the book, you will be engrossed in tough campaign missions. Completing mission objectives is tough, whether you are attacking enemy aircraft or bombing a bridge. After you have accomplished the mission objective, however, you still have to find your home base and set your F-16 back on the ground safely.

You may find yourself approaching the runway at the wrong heading when you are getting ready to land. The runways in Falcon 3.0 have a north-south or east-west alignment. The lower right corner of the HUD displays the current runway heading when you have the ILS feature turned on. If you are heading for the runway at 140° and the runway is at 180°, you will have to correct your heading before you get to the runway. There are several ways to correct for this situation. Figure 3-30 illustrates the procedure you use in the LANDING2 mission to line up with the runway.

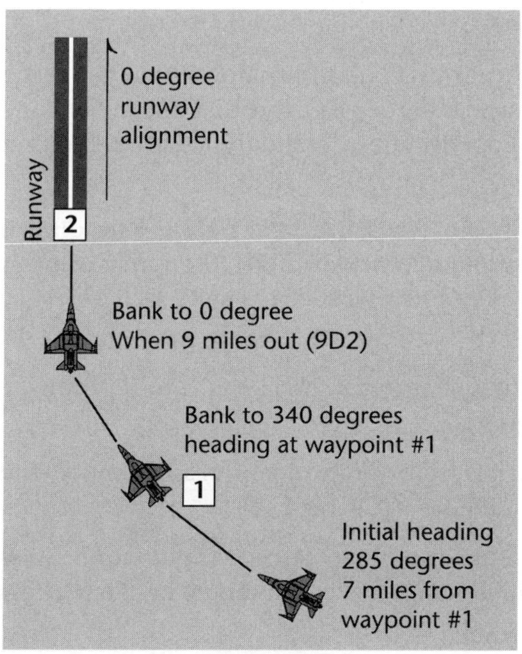

Figure 3-30 Lining Up with the Runway Using Waypoints

The waypoints in this lesson direct you to the runway regardless of the runway alignment. It is up to you to correct the alignment. You can use the waypoint to help you achieve this alignment. If the waypoint caret is to the left of the runway direction, adjust your heading even further to the left of the caret. This causes the caret to move towards the desired position (although it may be out of the HUD view). For this example, the waypoint caret has you aligned with 350° or so. If you fly to the left at approximately 340°, the caret moves towards 0°. You eventually *intercept* the proper line to approach the runway.

You do not have to line up with the runway from the distances used in this lesson. As you gain experience with landing, the alignment becomes easier. If you are still having problems with the landing procedures, try to line up with the runway as far out as possible. This way you will have one less thing to worry about during your landing.

There is one last important point to remember for this mission. If you feel that you have not lined up the Falcon with the runway properly or the approach angle is not right, pull up and try another pass. It is not a good idea to try to force a landing.

If you have loaded the LANDING2 mission, get in the air by clicking on F-16 PILOTS, LOAD ARMAMENT, and TAKEOFF. Pause the simulation immediately after the cockpit appears. Read through and become familiar with the following instructions before proceeding.

- Unpause the simulation by pressing the P key.
- Immediately cut the throttle to 70% by pressing the - key. You should be descending slightly.
- Your heading should be 285°, your altitude is 8,000 feet, and you should be six or seven miles from waypoint 1. Note that waypoint 1 is not the landing waypoint; waypoint 2 is the air base.
- Continue to descend. Level off when you reach 6,000 feet.
- Keep an eye on the distance-to-waypoint indicator. When you reach waypoint 1, bank right to a heading of 340°. Note that this will not line you up with waypoint 2 properly. The caret should actually be around 350° or so.
- When the distance-to-waypoint reads 9D2, bank right to a heading of 0° . The waypoint caret should coincide with 0°. You may want to pause by pressing the P key and refer back to Figure 3-30 to review what you have done.
- Switch to the ILS view by pressing the \ key. Note the runway indication of 0° (zero degrees).
- When you can see the runway, start to fine tune your alignment to the right runway with the rudder keys ([and]).
- Cut the throttle to 60% and continue to descend. Try to drop 1,000 feet in altitude for each mile. For example, you should be at 6,000 feet and 6D2, 5,000 feet at 5D2, and so on.
- As you approach the runway, level off at 500 feet and fly directly over the runway.

- As you pass the end of the runway, bank to the right and start a 180° turn. The bank angle of the turn is not that important. It should be greater that 45°, however. Being consistent is very important! Try to keep it as smooth as possible. Pull out of the bank at a heading of 180°.
- At this point, you may want to check out the right view. You should be passing the runway. If you want to concentrate on the landing, skip the view checks.
- Set the flaps by pressing the F key. Your airspeed should drop. If your airspeed is not down to 250–275 knots, cut the throttle some more or turn on the speed brakes.
- When you are two or three miles out from the end of the runway, start another 180° turn. Hint: Watch the distance-to-waypoint indicator or check the rear view. Try to make the turn as similar to the first as possible. This will result in correct runway alignment.
- As soon as you reach a heading of 340–350°, start to bank out of your final turn. Adjust your heading for 0°. Use the rudder to line up precisely with the runway.
- Lower your gear and cut the throttle again. Try to acquire an airspeed of 170–180 knots. Decrease to an airspeed of 150–170 knots by touchdown.
- As you reach the runway, pull back gently to make sure the nose is up. Do not fly into the runway nose down (negative AoA).
- As soon as you touch down, push forward on the stick to keep the F-16 from bouncing back up into the air. Cut the throttle to 5%.
- As the airspeed drops below 70 knots, the WHS light should indicate the flight stick has control over the front wheel. Push the stick to the left to steer off the runway.
- Engage the wheel brake by pressing the W key and cut the throttle to 0% after you have come to a complete stop.

Did you make another perfect landing? If not, don't get discouraged, just try again! That is precisely what the lesson missions are for. You can use them over and over again until you are comfortable landing your F-16. The goal is to avoid crashing or damaging the aircraft. In campaign mode you are assigned a limited number of aircraft. It is one thing if the enemy shoots you down, but don't help them by destroying your own F-16s.

Press (ESC) to bring up the menu bar and select FILE-END MISSION to return the debriefing screen. Click on NEXT MISSION to return to Red Flag Control.

Debriefing: The Landing The LANDING1 and LANDING2 missions introduced you to landing the Falcon. The ability to land is equally as important as dogfighting or bombing. It may not be as exciting, but there is nothing more discouraging than returning 100 miles from a successful bombing run, only to plow into the runway in a ball of flames.

The Instrument Landing System is a feature that allows you to align yourself with the runway using the HUD. The airfield transmits ILS signals that the electronic gear of the F-16 picks up. The F-16 computer converts these signals into two bars on the HUD-ILS display. A vertical bar, called the Localizer Deviation (LD) bar, indicates if you are off course to the left or right of the runway. A horizontal bar, called the Glide Slope Deviation (GSD) bar, indicates if you are approaching the runway at the correct angle.

You can use the ILS or combinations of instrument and visual procedures to land the F-16. Although it is not essential to align your F-16 with the runway early in the landing sequence, doing so makes that actual landing easier. By monitoring the waypoint caret (when the waypoint is a runway), you can adjust your alignment from several miles out. Runways in Falcon 3.0 have a north-south or east-west alignment. The HUD displays the runway alignment when you select the ILS feature.

The actual landing procedures are a matter of personal taste. There are several ways to land safely. Equally, there are several ways to fail to land properly. Your style of landing may be a slow descent over a great distance, or it could be a steep landing from a short distance. Of the two approaches, the latter is safer. Shallow landings allow more time for error and the possibility of stalling before you reach the end of the runway.

You can use the AVTR to record your mission and play it back at any ACMI location in Falcon 3.0. ACMI is available from debriefing screens as well as the War Room. Watching mission replays is highly recommended for failed landings. You may be able to pinpoint problems in your landing procedure by watching yourself land or crash. The external views in ACMI can provide a different and perhaps enlightening perspective on a failed landing.

When you fly campaign missions, you can always skip the landing by selecting the menu bar and ending the mission prematurely. If you choose to do this, the computer determines the result of the mission for you. It is better to have fate in your own hands. Learn to land!

Flight Lesson #6: Advanced Maneuvers

With the advent of modern-day supersonic fighters, the techniques and rules of air-to-air combat have changed. Maneuvers have to allow for the high speed and power of today's aircraft. Falcon 3.0 contains many different types of opponent aircraft, ranging from high-speed MiGs to hovering Gazelle helicopters. It is wise to put together your own "bag of tricks" to confront the many enemy types.

The F-16 is a "turning aircraft" when it comes to dogfighting. It is known for its superior turning ability in comparison to other aircraft. The cockpit design lets the pilot sustain high-G turns for longer periods of time. This means that the F-16 pilot usually tries to out turn the enemy in a one-on-one confrontation.

We cover the turning technique in the following chapter. This lesson introduces some additional maneuvers than can be performed with your F-16. This provides an excellent opportunity to continue to practice flying and controlling the Falcon. Who knows, you may even come up with a new maneuver that will rival heroes from the past!

This lesson consists of four maneuvers: the Immelmann, the Split-S, the Scissors, and the high-speed Yo-Yo. We preface each maneuver with a short ground school segment. You only need to load one Red Flag mission file for all four maneuvers. Just pause the simulation while surveying the ground school segments.

Lesson Objectives In this lesson you:

- Perform the Immelmann maneuver.
- Perform the Split-S maneuver.
- Perform the Scissors maneuver.
- Perform the high-speed Yo-Yo maneuver.

It is not essential that you complete the lesson maneuvers in the above order. However, we have listed them in order of difficulty. Try the lessons in order if this is your first time through the chapter.

Load the mission before proceeding with the ground school segments. If you are in the War Room, access Red Flag Control by clicking on the Red Flag screen. Load the MANEUVER mission by highlighting the mission name, clicking on LOAD MISSION, and pressing Y to confirm the mission selection. Click on F-16 PILOTS, then LOAD ARMAMENT, then TAKEOFF. You should be in the air at 12,000 feet (AGL) with 85% throttle. Your speed may be decreasing slightly. Press the (P) key to pause the simulation, then select the ground school for the maneuver of your choice.

Ground School—The Immelmann WWI ace Max Immelmann originated the first maneuver. You will perform a modification of the original maneuver more suited to a high speed aircraft like the F-16. The original Immelmann used a hard turn in the midst of a climb to reverse direction; the modern maneuver changes direction by rolling the aircraft as the aircraft is climbing. The primary purpose of the modern maneuver is to change direction.

Refer to Figure 3-31. You must meet one condition before initiating the maneuver: the airspeed must be high enough to sustain a half-loop. The maneuver starts with level flight. A hard pull on the stick causes a steep climb into a loop. When you are inverted, perform a half-roll back to level flight. Watching the pitch indicator and the actual horizon aid in successfully performing the maneuver.

The Immelmann provides a way to change direction quickly. You can change your heading by 180° in a matter of seconds as well as gain a significant amount of altitude. It does have some drawbacks, however. First,

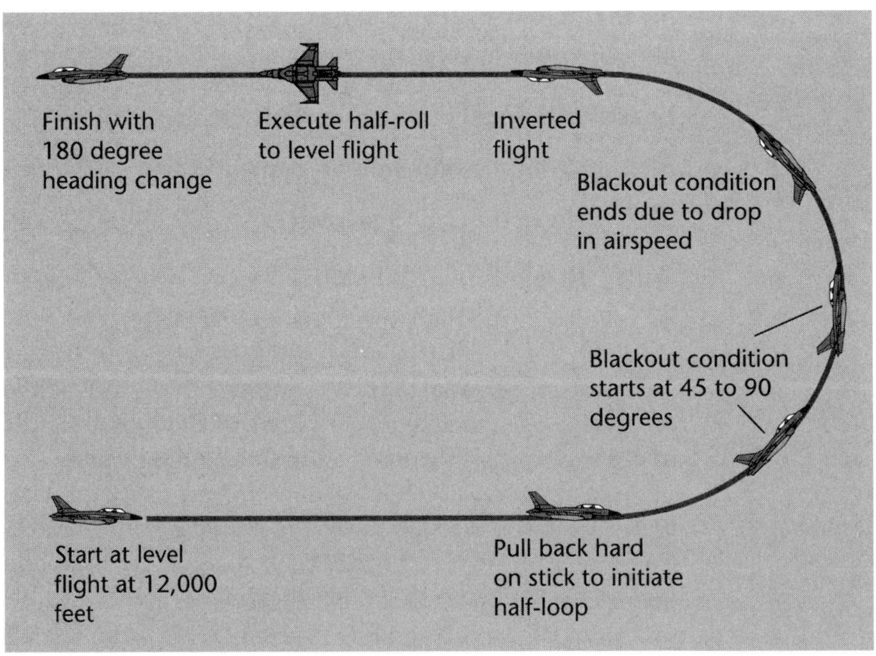

Figure 3-31 The Immelmann

you lose speed as you initiate the climb. It may be necessary to turn on the afterburner to complete the maneuver. Also, if you have an enemy on your tail, you may pull up into a position that will allow him to get a clean shot at you. It is important to note the position of the enemy and analyze the consequences before starting any maneuver.

As with many maneuvers, the Immelmann can subject your body to high Gs. Be prepared for a possible blackout during the maneuver. Because of the high speeds involved, the Immelmann also consumes a lot of fuel. If you are in an air-to-air battle with low fuel and you are quite a distance from home, do not attempt the Immelmann. Head for home instead.

Performing the Immelmann Try your first Immelmann. Before taking the simulation off pause, check that the throttle is at 100% and the altitude indicator reads approximately 12,000 feet. If this does not check out, adjust your F-16 to achieve this condition. Always try new maneuvers at a high altitude to allow time to recover from any possible mishap.

- Unpause the simulation by pressing the P key.
- Be sure you are flying level at an airspeed greater than 550 knots.
- Pull back on the stick to start the climb. You should see the pitch ladder start to roll. Do not move the stick left or right.
- Depending on airspeed, you may start to black out when you reach a pitch of 45 to 90°. *Do not let off the stick!* The blackout condition will self-correct due to a drop in airspeed and the attitude of the F-16 as it starts to become inverted.
- When you see the pitch ladder approach 0°, start to push forward on the stick to level out. The Falcon is completely inverted at this point.
- Push the stick hard to the left to roll the Falcon over to level flight. Be sure to let off the stick just before the aircraft levels out.
- Pause the simulation if you intend to complete the remaining maneuvers, or press ESC to access the menu bar and end the mission.

How did you do? This maneuver is fairly simple to execute. There are only a few things to cause a possible failure: initial airspeed too low, banking left or right during the climb, and letting off the stick if a blackout occurs. The worst that can happen is a temporary stall. You can recover from a stall as long as you are at a high enough altitude before attempting the maneuver. You can also come out of the maneuver at an undesired heading. This is usually the result of banking during the half-loop.

The goal of this maneuver is to achieve a new heading that is 180° from the start heading. For example, if you are at a heading of 260°, performing the Immelmann will result in a new heading of 80°. Practice this maneuver until you feel comfortable with the results. If you crash, simply reload the mission file at Red Flag Control and try again.

Ground School—The Split-S The Split-S is the complement of the Immelmann. The outcome is identical as far as the heading of the aircraft. The opposite effects are altitude and speed. In the Immelmann, you gained altitude while losing airspeed. The Split-S results in an increase in speed but a loss in altitude.

Refer to Figure 3-32. For the Split-S to be properly executed, initial altitude is more important than airspeed. You perform a half-roll first, then a hard pull on the stick results in a sharp dive. As with the Immelmann, the pitch indicator and the horizon to track the relative attitude of the aircraft during the maneuver. You level out the aircraft at 0°. Because of the initial inverted position, the result will be level flight after you have executed the half-loop.

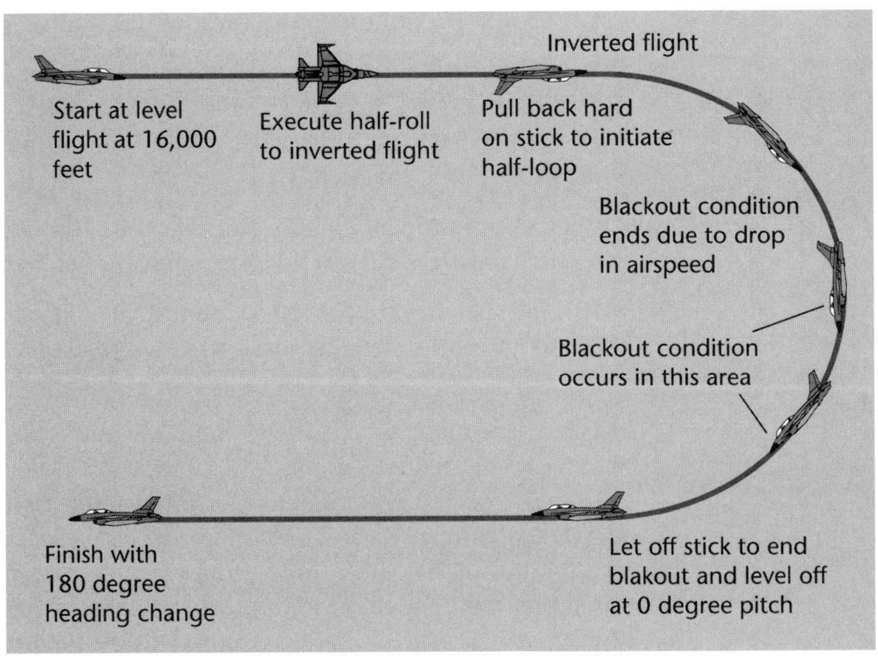

Figure 3-32 The Split-S

The purpose of the Split-S is to change directions quickly. There are also drawbacks to consider when executing the maneuver. You will always lose a significant amount of altitude. If the result of the maneuver leaves you beneath an enemy attacker, this may result in giving him an advantage. The air-to-air combat game is always a trade-off of altitude for speed and speed for altitude.

The Split-S is also a high-G maneuver. The high-G point in the maneuver differs from that of the Immelmann. You experience the blackout condition during the last part of the half-loop. This is due to the increase in airspeed at the bottom of the maneuver. You will have to judge when you arrive at 0° and let off the stick. If you continue to pull back on the stick, you will sustain the blackout until you are climbing straight up. This factor makes the Split-S maneuver execution slightly more difficult.

Performing the Split-S It's time to try the Split-S. Before attempting this maneuver, be sure you are at an appropriate altitude (above 15,000 feet). If you just performed the Immelmann from a starting altitude of 12,000 feet, you should be at an altitude of 15,000 to 16,500 feet. Recall that the Immelmann gains altitude. You will lose from 7,000 to 10,000 feet in altitude by executing the Split-S.

- Press the P key if the simulation is already paused or load the MANEUVER mission if you ended the mission after completing the previous segment.
- Make any adjustments necessary to ensure you are above 15,000 feet and flying level.
- Cut back on the throttle by pressing the − key. Set the throttle for 75–80% RPM and wait for your airspeed to stabilize. Keep an eye on your altitude; be sure you are not descending.
- Execute a half-roll by pushing hard on the stick to the left. Stop pushing the stick when you have nearly inverted the F-16.
- Pull hard on the stick to cause the F-16 to dive into a half-loop. Remember that you will start to blackout near the end of the half-loop. *Do not let the aircraft start to bank left or right.*
- Keep a close eye on the pitch ladder when you start to black out. Try to estimate a point when the pitch ladder will reach 0°. Let off the stick at this point. The blackout condition should end. Make sure you are at 0° or above when the blackout fades. If you are still diving, pull up to 0° and level off.

- Pause the simulation if you intend to complete the remaining maneuvers, or press (ESC) to access the menu bar and end the mission.

It is normal to experience more difficulty executing the Split-S. There are three major concerns with this maneuver. The first and most important concern is initial altitude. You *must* be above 11,000 to 12,000 feet in order to safely execute the Split-S. The second concern is the late blackout. You have to judge when it is time to release the stick and come out of half-loop. If you release the stick too soon, it will result in your F-16 continuing to dive. This may result in a crash before the blackout effect has subsided. The third concern is heading. The F-16 will have a tendency to bank left and right on its own during the half loop. Small left-right stick adjustments may be necessary.

As with the Immelmann, the goal of the Split-S is to quickly change direction by 180°. You will find that it requires more practice to master a perfect 180° Split-S. It is worth the practice, however. The Split-S may get you out of a tight situation with an enemy MiG hot on your tail! The following maneuver is also useful to shake (and attack) an enemy that is directly behind you.

Ground School—The Scissors There will be times when you notice an enemy directly behind you during air-to-air engagements. This is known as having the enemy on your "six o'clock" or your "six." This is perhaps the least undesirable position to be in. The enemy aircraft may be equipped with infrared (heat-seeking) missiles and here you are with your red hot exhaust staring him in the face! The Scissors cause a quick exchange in position, which will put you on the offensive.

Refer to Figure 3-33. The figure calls out the movement of both the enemy and your F-16. You will perform this exercise with no enemy present. It is better to practice new maneuvers with as little interference as possible. Enemies with missiles can cause quite a bit of interference!

The exercise assumes that an enemy is behind you. You initiate a turn to one side. This normally is towards the side the enemy is favoring. The enemy aircraft usually follows your movements. When the enemy starts in the direction of your turn you react by turning sharply in the other direction cutting your airspeed, opening the scissors. When the enemy reacts and turns back toward you, turn hard in the opposite direction, cut more airspeed, and cross paths with the enemy aircraft. You are in a position where the enemy overshoots your F-16. One more hard turn will line you up for a passing gun attack, closing the scissors.

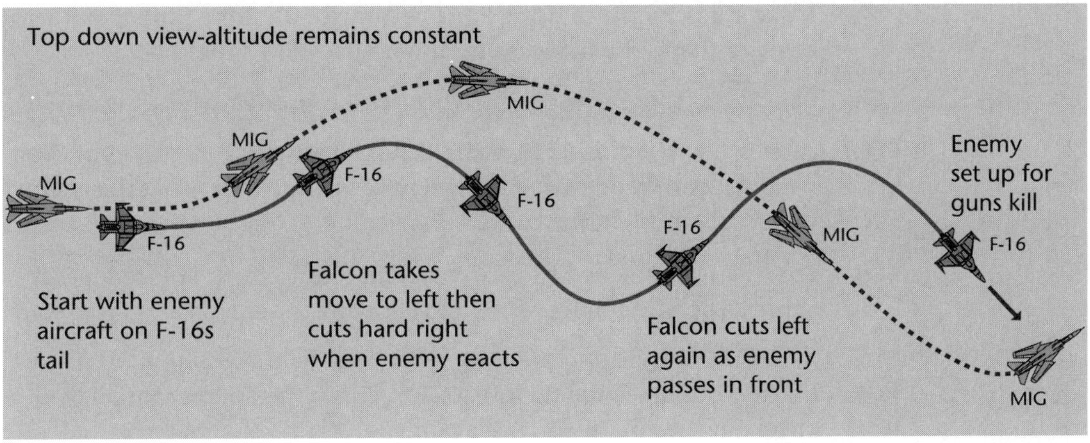

Figure 3-33 The Scissors

Use this lesson to become familiar with the moves. As mentioned before, there are no enemies involved in this exercise. Concentrate on getting the moves down while simultaneously dropping your airspeed. Also try to maintain a steady altitude throughout the move. One of the most common errors is to overreact to turns. You can see how this overreaction by the enemy can work to your favor.

The Scissors maneuver does not require sustaining high-Gs. You will be executing tight turns, but the time in each turn will be brief. The blackout effect should not come into play. This maneuver is very simple to practice without the enemy; it becomes very difficult when an enemy is present. The Enemy Logic Level setting in the Difficulty Levels screen will have a direct bearing on the reactions of enemy pilots. The lower the skill setting, the more apt the enemy will be to fall for the maneuver.

Performing the Scissors Let's execute the Scissors! For training purposes, it is important to start at a heading of 0°. We will call out specific headings in the following steps. Of course, in actual battle the heading will not be important; how the enemy reacts to your moves is very important! Because you maintain a steady altitude throughout the Scissors move, the initial altitude is not critical. Starting anywhere between 5,000 and 20,000 feet will do.

- Press the (P) key if the simulation is already paused or load the MANEUVER mission if you ended the mission after completing the previous segment.

- Make adjustments to bring your heading to 0°. Adjust the throttle to achieve airspeed of 450 knots (about 80% RPM should do).
- Bank 90° to the left and pull on the stick. Level out at a heading of 330°.
- After a few seconds, start a sharp turn (bank 90°) to the right. You would normally do this when you have visual contact that the enemy is reacting to your first move.
- Press the (-) key two times during the second turn. This reduces the throttle, opening the scissors, and allowing the enemy aircraft to start to overshoot.
- Pull out of the second turn at 30–40°. This is the point that you would check on the enemy aircraft again.
- After a few seconds at the 30–40° heading, bank 90° left again and pull hard on the stick. Reduce the throttle two more notches with the (-) key. Unless the enemy made a move to counter, he should be passing your F-16 at this point.
- As soon as you reach 345°, bank your aircraft back to 45° and hit the guns (press the (SPACEBAR)). If the enemy falls for your maneuver, you will nail him at this point. We will discuss the use of the guns in Chapter 5, *Using Weapons*.
- Check your altitude to see if there is any change from the start of the maneuver.
- Pause the simulation if you intend to complete the following maneuver, or press (ESC) to access the menu bar and end the mission.

This maneuver may seem very easy to complete in the absence of enemies. It will be a different story when in actual air-to-air combat. It is better to practice the maneuver alone first than be thrust into battle with no experience. Chapter 6, *Introduction to Red Flag*, will show you how to add enemy aircraft to a mission. You can even add enemy aircraft and take away their weapons. Hardly fair, but great for training!

There are a few important things to consider when executing the Scissors. The most important concern is maintaining a constant altitude. If you gain or lose altitude during the maneuver, you will not have the enemy lined up for the shot when the time comes. Another concern is reacting to the enemy. Don't start your next move until the enemy has reacted to your previous move. If you do, you may help the enemy line up a perfect shot at you!

Keep in mind that all enemy pilots are not *greenhorns* (beginners). You may run into some experienced pilots that will fall for the Scissors. However, most experienced enemy pilots will not fall for anything! That is when the ordinary task becomes the true challenge.

Ground School—The High Yo-Yo A pilot can change his aircraft's aspect angle or relative distance to another aircraft by maneuvering vertically. A maneuver of this type—called a Yo-Yo—is named after the pilot who invented it, rather than the stringed toy. Such association is not inappropriate, however, since an aircraft executing a Yo-Yo moves sharply up and down to change the combat situation.

There are numerous variations of the Yo-Yo. One version enables slower aircraft to close on faster ones and another helps slow circling planes to turn inside of their quicker turning counterparts. One particular variant is quite useful to Falcon pilots: the high Yo-Yo. This move enables a fast aircraft like yours to engage a slower plane without overrunning it. You might use the high Yo-Yo, for example, to attack a MiG-19 Farmer.

To execute the high Yo-Yo, climb rapidly above your slower opponent. The steep climb bleeds speed but keeps you on his "six." Once above and behind your adversary, descend upon your hapless prey. In order to keep sight of the MiG, you should roll your aircraft during the steep climb.

Refer to Figure 3-34. The Yo-Yo starts with your aircraft on the enemy's tail. Once again, practice the maneuver without an enemy present. The initial move is a sharp climb from the six o'clock position of the enemy.

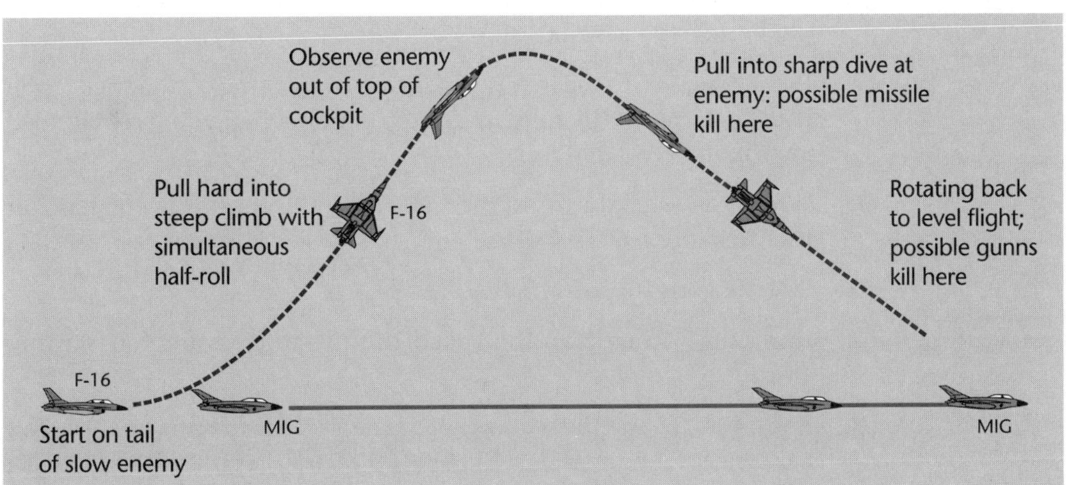

Figure 3-34 The High-Speed Yo-Yo

During the climb, you initiate a half-roll. You will be able to see the enemy out the top of the canopy. When you have separated from the enemy by approximately 4,000 to 6,000 feet, you initiate the dive sequence. At this point you can line up the enemy and fire a missile or wait until you get close for a guns kill. You will end up passing the enemy from high to low.

Since the MANEUVER mission file does not contain enemy aircraft, concentrate on the motions of the maneuver. The following steps give you checks along the way to ensure you are performing the procedure correctly.

Performing the High-Speed Yo-Yo It's time to try the Yo-Yo! This maneuver will require an initial heading of 0°. This allows you to track the exact position throughout the maneuver. In actual battle, the enemy would compel you to make adjustments throughout the maneuver. This is normal for air-to-air combat.

It is necessary to have a starting altitude over 15,000 feet. You can execute the Yo-Yo at much lower altitudes, but use high initial altitudes for training purposes.

- Press the P key if the simulation is already paused or load the MANEUVER mission if you ended the mission after completing the previous segment.
- Make adjustments to set your heading to 0°. Adjust the throttle to achieve an airspeed of 450 knots (about 80% RPM should do). Make a mental note of your starting altitude.
- When you are ready to start the Yo-Yo, pull up on the stick until the pitch indicates a 50–60° climb.
- Rotate the F-16 to the inverted position by pushing on the stick to the left. Try to reach the fully inverted position when you have climbed approximately 5,000 feet.
- When you reach the top of the 5,000 to 6,000 foot climb, pull hard on the stick into a 60–70° dive.
- Fire the guns by pressing the SPACEBAR.
- Invert the F-16 again and pull out of the dive after passing your starting altitude.
- If you want to end the training, press the ESC key to bring up the menu bar. Select FILE then END MISSION. You will return to the Red Flag Debriefing screen. Select NEXT MISSION to return to Red Flag Control. You can also level off, adjust your altitude, and try the mission again.

This maneuver is very difficult to perform in combat. Because the Falcon is such a superior turning aircraft, you may want to simply out turn your opponents in air-to-air conflicts. However, some enemy aircraft can turn as fast as you can. The Yo-Yo may be the move that will knock out the aircraft that you cannot out turn.

The main consideration for choosing the Yo-Yo is relative airspeed. After identifying an enemy aircraft, determine if it is a slower type aircraft. If the aircraft is slow, try the Yo-Yo (or hard turns). If the aircraft is faster, try the Scissors (discussed previously).

Debriefing: The Advanced Maneuvers You know the F-16 Falcon for its ability to produce tight, high-G turns, without causing the pilot discomfort. The aircraft design allows you to sustain high Gs for longer periods in comparison to other aircraft. Knowing this, you would think that this is the only type of maneuver necessary to win air-to-air confrontations. This is not the case. In Falcon 3.0, you can build your own personal "bag of tricks" when preparing for engagement with the real enemy. This was an introduction to the types of maneuvers that you can execute on the battlefield. We introduced four maneuvers.

You executed the Immelmann first (invented by famous ace Max Immelmann). You used this maneuver to change direction by 180°. It consists of a half-loop to an inverted position followed by a half-roll to level flight. The advantages are the quick change in direction and the gain in altitude. The drawbacks are significant loss of airspeed and possibly giving an enemy aircraft a good target!

Next you tried the Split-S. This is the complement move of the Immelmann. The goal remains the same: change the heading of the F-16 by 180°. The Split-S requires a half-roll to an inverted position be performed first, followed by a half-loop. The advantages of the Split-S are a large gain in airspeed and a quick change in direction. The primary disadvantage is the loss in altitude. You can use this maneuver to escape (at least temporarily) a pursuing attacker.

The next maneuver you explored was the Scissors. You used this strategy to fake an enemy fighter into overshooting the F-16 to set up for a guns kill. You performed the motions of the maneuver without an enemy present. The move consists of sharp turns from side to side. The goal is to get the enemy out of synch with your turns, eventually causing him to fly directly in front of you. In actual combat, the procedure requires constant monitoring of the enemy position. You will have a difficult time getting experienced enemy pilots to fall for the Scissors. Try this maneuver again when you learn how to track down the enemy in the next chapter.

The last maneuver was the High-Speed Yo-Yo. You can use this move against slower opponents. It starts with a steep climb in combination with a roll to an inverted position. After obtaining visual contact with the enemy (through the top of the cockpit), you pull hard on the stick and dive towards the enemy. If you can line the enemy up quickly, there may be time for a missile shot. Otherwise you attack with the guns.

The purpose of this lesson is to become familiar with the ways the F-16 responds when under certain circumstances. Everything should come together when you are in the presence of enemy aircraft. You also need additional training on using the padlock view and weapons (covered in Chapter 4, *Radar and Enemy Identification*, and Chapter 5, *Using Weapons*.). Knowing how to perform these basic maneuvers allows you to learn these new features without having to struggle with flying the Falcon.

Summary

We've covered several topics in this chapter. You have learned everything from theory of flight to performing advanced maneuvers. This material provides a solid foundation in the fundamentals of flight, especially as they pertain to the Falcon 3.0 version of the F-16.

You discovered that there are four fundamental elements that affect the flight of an aircraft: lift, gravity, thrust, and drag. Air flowing over the wing creates a pressure differential; this differential is lift. Gravity is a constant force that we are exposed to in our every day lives. Gravity and lift are opposing forces. When the lift generated exceeds the force of gravity, the aircraft can take off. Every aircraft has a power source that generates thrust. In the case of the F-16, it is a Pratt and Whitney F-100 Turbofan capable of producing over 20,000 pounds of thrust. You can describe drag as air friction. It affects airspeed and significantly affects fuel consumption. Loading heavy iron bombs increases drag because of the bombs large surface area. This surface area is the source of friction.

Six lessons made up the remainder of the chapter. These lessons covered flight from the basic through more advanced maneuvers. Here is a summary of the six lessons presented in Chapter 3:

- Lesson 1: The Takeoff—You saw the C-model head-up display and cockpit familiarization. Also, we covered the basics in taking off and achieving level flight. We also discussed banking the aircraft and using the afterburner.

- Lesson 2: The G-Forces—We covered the causes of G-forces and the effects they have on the body of the pilot. You flew a sample mission and executed both high- and low-G turns. You flew basic maneuvers that demonstrated the undesirable effects of G-forces. You intentionally caused blackout and redout conditions to view their effects on the simulation (and on you as a pilot). You also learned how to perform a loop, an inverted dive, and a recovery method for stalls. We also introduced the A-model HUD.
- Lesson 3: The Views—You used the several in-cockpit and out-of-cockpit views provided with Falcon 3.0. You learned about the caution lights, their meanings, and the proper recovery action to take. You also accessed other gauges that are not on the cockpit front view (fuel gauge, backup airspeed, AVTR control, etc.). You observed a wingman that was following our F-16 in formation.
- Lesson 4: Waypoints—You learned how to use waypoints to navigate around the three-dimensional world of Falcon 3.0. You set waypoints before the start of a mission and stored them in the onboard computers of the F-16. You flew an eight-waypoint mission that directed you over a chemical weapons plant. You also covered the accelerated mode and watched as the autopilot maneuvered the F-16 and landed safely.
- Lesson 5: The Landing—We discussed ways to make one of the most difficult maneuvers easier. You enabled the Instrument Landing System (ILS) to help align your Falcon with the runway before making the final approach. You executed two types of landings: straight-in and military style (360° approach).
- Lesson 6: Advanced Maneuvers—You performed four maneuvers that may have some value when we introduce air-to-air combat in subsequent chapters. The Immelmann and Split-S are evasive maneuvers that allow you to change headings by 180° quickly. The Scissors is a maneuver used to fake an aircraft into passing in front of the Falcon's guns. You will use the high-speed Yo-Yo when battling a lower speed aircraft.

If you have difficulty mastering the fundamentals of flight, you can use the mission files again for additional training. You can never get enough training, even after being involved in a campaign with several *sorties* (missions) under your belt. If you don't receive the proper training, the chances of mission successes are weak.

Exercises

1. Load and fly the NORTHWST mission. This mission starts you in the air and guides you through the northwest region of the Red Flag training area. Follow all of the waypoints and try to fly low to view the sights. Don't forget to use outside view keys!

2. Load and fly the CANYON mission. This mission guides you through the Grand Canyon area if you follow the waypoints. If you look close, you may even spot tourists and donkeys in the canyon! You may want to select autopilot to fly this mission.

3. Load and fly the LONGFLGT mission. If you follow the waypoints, this mission will take you all over the Red Flag area. There are other aircraft (friendly and enemy) assigned to this mission. You may run into some of them during the flight. The mission has unarmed enemies, so don't worry about an attack.

4

CHAPTER 4

Radar and Enemy Identification

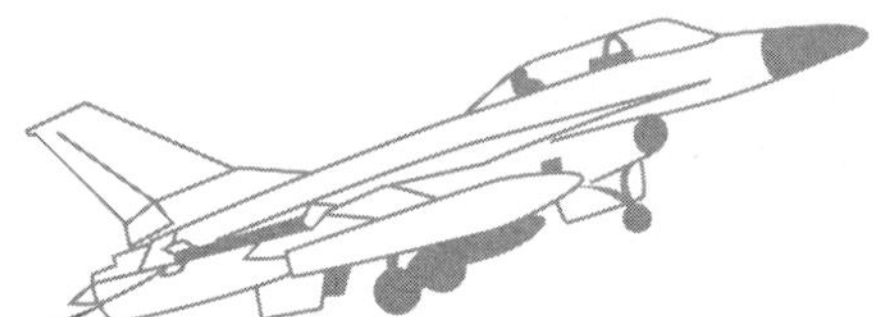

Technology plays a major role in modern combat. Sophisticated electronics gear has replaced or enhanced what used to be done by humans. The F-16 itself is a technological wonder, referred to as a "fly-by-wire" aircraft because of its computer controlled surfaces. Without the advanced, onboard computer systems, the pilot would not be able to fly the Falcon. The electronics are not used solely for flying the aircraft, however. The F-16 and Falcon 3.0 have many more electronic capabilities. This chapter explores them.

Most of this chapter discusses the subject of tracking and identifying aircraft. It is very important to have the ability to make split-second decisions in combat. If you encounter an aircraft, you must quickly determine its status. Is it friendly? Is it an enemy? Slow decision making can be fatal if the incoming aircraft is an enemy. Likewise, firing a missile at a target without determining its status can result in a quick court-martial if the unknown aircraft happened to be friendly. We also introduce a new view in this chapter to help you identify aircraft, the *padlock view*.

We will discuss the methods the enemy uses to track your aircraft as you enter enemy territory. You will encounter ground forces equipped with *anti-aircraft artillery* (AAA) and *surface-to-air missiles* (SAM). Some of these weapons use radar to guide them to your aircraft. You will learn techniques to escape and avoid these attacks.

First up is the definition of radar. We discuss some principles to help you understand how you can find the enemy (and how the enemy can find you) by using radar. You learn about the various types of radars and how they work. After we have built this foundation, we will discuss two of the three types of Falcon 3.0 radar. Then it will be time to climb back in the cockpit and fly more training missions.

Principles of Radar

In order to use radar effectively, it helps to understand how it works. Although we commonly refer to radar as a noun, it actually originated from an acronym: the letters in RADAR stand for RAdio Detection And Ranging. Radars are used in several different applications. There are short-range search radars used by airports to track the position of the aircraft in the local airspace. Powerful long-range radars have been used for decades to guard the shores and borders of countries. Primarily, the purpose of the radar is to detect airborne activity and give a representation of the range (distance) and the azimuth (direction) of the target.

How Does Radar Work?

Radar uses radio frequency energy, or RF, to generate a signal to transmit into space. When this signal meets an object, the RF is reflected and the *echo* is received by the radar receiver. All radars consist of a transmitter and a receiver. The transmitter must be capable of producing a high-powered RF signal. The receiver must be sensitive enough to receive even the weakest of signals.

Aircraft that are picked up by radar are called *targets*. In order to determine the target range, the radar uses the time between transmit and receive in a calculation. Figure 4-1 illustrates the key to radar range detection, the *radar mile*. A radar mile is 12.36 microseconds. Why? RF energy travels at the speed of light or approximately 300 million meters per second. This means that it takes the RF energy 6.28 millionths of a second (referred to as microseconds) to travel one mile. But radar depends on the

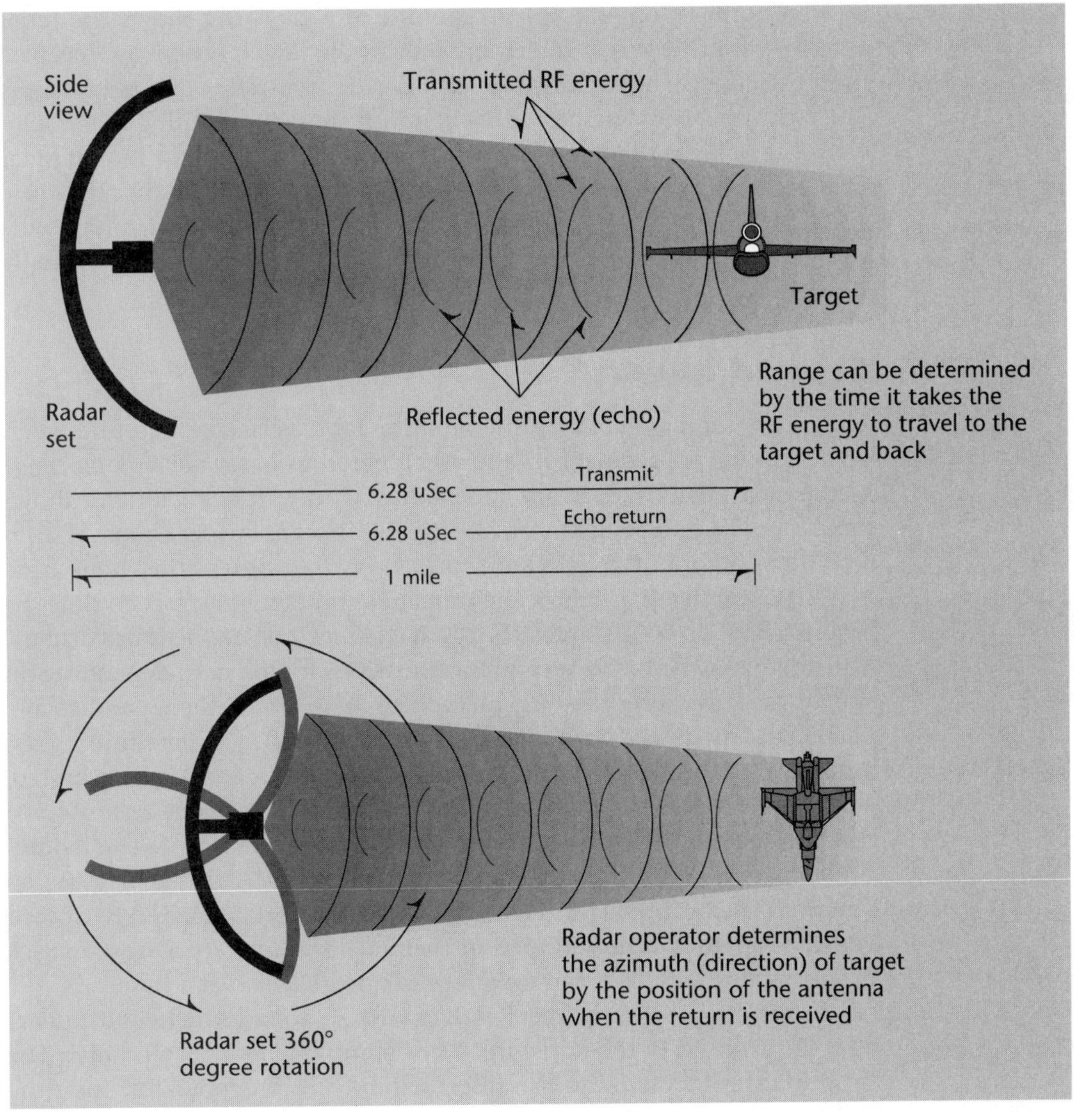

Figure 4-1 The Principles of Radar

energy being reflected back; therefore, it has to make the return trip (another 6.28 microseconds). The total is 12.36 microseconds, which is the radar mile.

The *azimuth* (direction) of the target is determined by the position of the radar when the echo was received. For example, the figure shows one possible form of obtaining the azimuth of a target. It shows the radar antenna rotating. When the antenna faces the target, echoes are received from the target. The rotating antenna is synchronized with a radar scope. The radar operator determines the azimuth simply by reading the scope.

The radar in the figure is a *search* radar. The beam of the search radar can capture every target from ground level up to 100,000 feet or more. The antenna is designed to shape the beam into a narrow horizontal, wide vertical form. This allows it to be selective on azimuth and accept virtually all altitudes.

Ground Radar

All of the examples of radar principles thus far have been for ground radar. There are many different types and uses for ground-based radar. Long-range search radars can cover a very large radius. If an unfriendly aircraft shows up on the scope, the operator will notify the appropriate personnel. Within seconds, a flight of fighters can be on its way to intercept the enemy.

The search radar rotates and transmits simultaneously. Each time the antenna lines up with a target, the result is *painted* on the operator's display. The target may be hit by several transmissions in one pass, depending on the range. This causes the target to appear as an arc on the radar display.

Older models of radar did not have the capability of determining the altitude of the aircraft. Without this ability, an additional radar is required, a *height-finder*. Height-finder radars can transmit in only one azimuth at a time. Instead of the antenna rotating, it nods up and down. The height-finder antenna is also shaped much differently than that of a search antenna. The beam of the height-finder is wide horizontal and narrow in vertical. Height is of importance and azimuth is secondary. One drawback of the height finder is it can only face in one direction at a time.

How does the radar operator know where to face the height finder? First the azimuth of the target must be determined by a search radar. The height-finder is rotated to the target azimuth by the operator, then the height is determined by the nodding antenna.

Modern radar has the capability of determining all three essential items about the target: range, azimuth, and height. All of this can be accomplished by one radar.

Finding information about the location of aircraft is not the only function of military radar. The enemy in Falcon 3.0 uses radar to guide the surface-to-air missiles at your F-16. You will learn methods of distracting this radar and ultimately distracting the guided missile.

Aircraft Radar

Most aircraft radar is forward seeking. The radar does not receive echoes from 360° around the aircraft. Since the aircraft is moving forward (usually at high airspeeds), there is a premium on what is in front of the aircraft. This does not mean you can ignore everything to the rear. You never know when an enemy will sneak up on your six and send you a detonating welcome message!

Aircraft radar is not as powerful as ground radar; therefore, the maximum range is normally much less. Ground radar has the valuable resource of a virtually unlimited power supply. Power is limited for the aircraft radar due to size and weight restrictions.

Not all aircraft are limited to forward seeking radar. The E-3C Sentry, nicknamed AWACS (Airborne Warning and Control System), is a large aircraft with full-search radar capabilities. The E-3C is built using the frame of a Boeing-707. A large radar dome is mounted to the top of the fuselage. The sole mission of the AWACS is to fly in a fixed pattern behind enemy lines, gathering information. This information can be transmitted to other friendly aircraft.

A ground based radar obtains data on range, azimuth, and altitude. The Falcon's radar and onboard computer can provide even more information about a target. By comparing echoes over a period of time, the heading and speed of the aircraft can be determined!

F-16 Radar—The APG-66 Pulse-Doppler Radar

The APG-66 is a *pulse-Doppler radar*. As the first half of the name implies, the APG-66 emits pulses of energy which are reflected by objects in front of the radar. By measuring the time between when the pulse is sent and when a reflected signal is received, the distance to the object can be calculated. The radar energy dissipates the longer it travels, so by ignoring reflected signals below a specified power level, or by ignoring reflected signals received after a set time limit, the APG-66 focuses on a fixed range and *filters out* targets beyond that range. The maximum range of the APG-66 is 80 nautical miles.

The second half of the term pulse-Doppler refers to the Doppler effect. A full discussion of the Doppler effect is beyond the scope of this book; however, in summary, the movement of objects emitting and reflecting radar energy cause shifts in the frequency of that energy. This shifting follows a constant set of rules and can, therefore, be reliably used to glean additional information from the reflected energy. By measuring the Doppler shift of the returned signal, the speed of the object can be calculated.

By comparing multiple signals reflected from a single object, information such as the object's direction of travel (heading) can be determined.

Primary Advantage of Doppler Radar Doppler radar can ignore returns with a given frequency shift. Normally, all objects on the ground, including the ground itself, reflect radar energy. These annoying reflections are called *ground clutter.* Since the ground is stationary, any Doppler shift of the reflected energy is caused by the speed of the transmitting aircraft. To avoid cluttering the radar display with reflections from dirt, Doppler radars measure the frequency shift and ignore any returns from objects that appear stationary. Moving ground objects, such as cars, also reflect radar energy. However, since these objects have a known, average speed (say 60 mph), the Doppler shift can be used to ignore returns from these objects, also.

Look-Down, Shoot-Down Capability Non-Doppler airborne radars cannot be pointed downwards; ground clutter will overwhelm the radar screen and render it useless. Since Doppler radars filter out ground clutter, they may be pointed down with no ill effects. This is called *look-down* capability.

Not all radar-guided missiles are capable of measuring Doppler shifts. Missiles that cannot measure Doppler shifts will be confused by ground clutter when fired downwards at a target. Newer missiles, such as the U.S. built AIM-120, can measure Doppler shifts and can, therefore, be launched downwards at a target. This is called *shoot-down* capability.

Using the APG-66 and AIM-120 missiles, the F-16 has full look-down, shoot-down capabilities. Many older aircraft, especially older Soviet aircraft, are not look-down, shoot-down capable. These aircraft cannot track or fire missiles at targets below them.

Drawbacks of Doppler Radar However, this results in the primary disadvantages of the Doppler radar. First, slow-moving airborne targets, such as a hovering helicopter, may be filtered out. Second, objects that have no motion relative to the transmitting aircraft appear stationary and are filtered out.

For example, suppose an F-16 using Doppler radar is flying due North (0 degrees) toward a MiG-29 flying due East (90 degrees). The MiG-29 is not moving either toward or away from the F-16. The only motion between the MiG and the F-16 is the F-16's movement toward the MiG. The Doppler shift of the reflected signal is (for the moment that the MiG is flying exactly perpendicular to the F-16) exactly the same as the Doppler shift from a stationary ground object. The radar, therefore, filters out the return, and the MiG momentarily appears invisible!

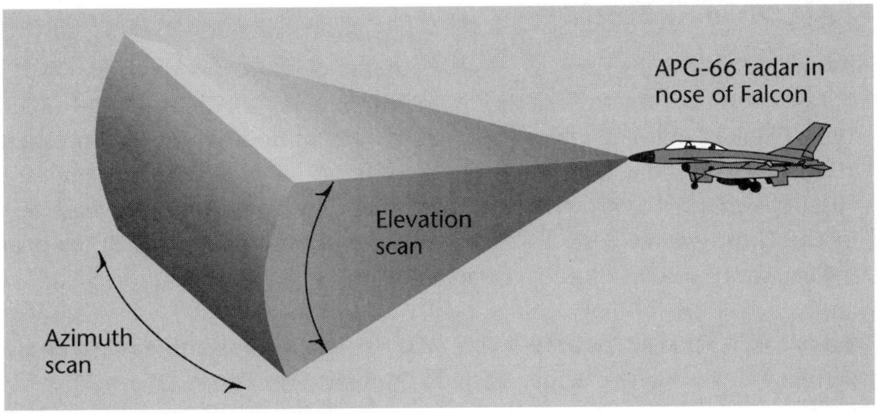

Figure 4-2 The F-16 APG-66 Radar

The Antenna

The APG-66 uses a relatively small, moving radar dish, or antenna, located in the nose of the aircraft. The antenna moves both horizontally and vertically emitting radar pulses, then waits for reflected signals. The horizontal and vertical movements of the antenna are controlled by the pilot. Horizontal, or *azimuth*, movement is measured by the number of degrees the radar scans on either side of the F-16. The vertical, or *elevation*, is measured in vertical movements called *bars*. The bar is a band of varying height dependent upon the radar's exact mode. Figure 4-2 illustrates.

For example, a bar may be defined as 10 degrees. A scan pattern may be defined as two bars and +/–30 degrees width. In this case, the antenna would scan a zone that extends 30 degrees both right and left of the center and from 0 to 10 degrees above the aircraft. Then, the antenna moves and a zone 0 to 10 degrees below and 30 degrees both right and left of the aircraft is scanned. Figure 4-3 illustrates this example.

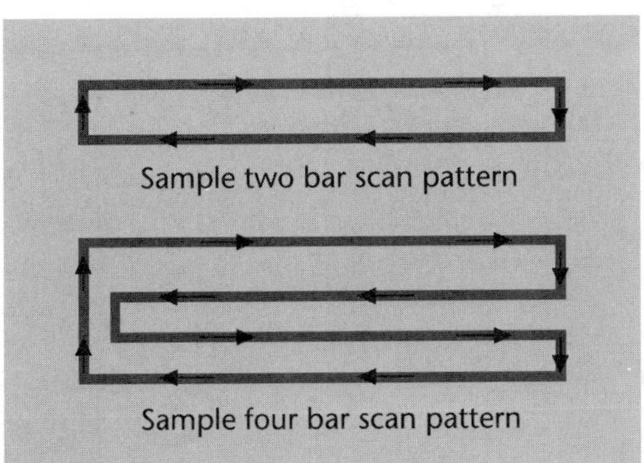

Figure 4-3 Scan Patterns

You must be very adept at flying and controlling the radar before battling the enemy. If you are fumbling with the radar controls, you may find yourself headed for the dirt, or on the wrong end of an enemy missile's path! Practicing reading and interpreting the radar is as important as practicing maneuvers.

Falcon 3.0 Radar

Falcon 3.0 provides three versions of radar: Situation Awareness Display (SAD), Situation Awareness Mode (SAM), and High-Fidelity Radar (HFR). We will take a detailed look at the first two radar modes in this chapter. The High Fidelity Radar is more complex; Chapter 8 is devoted to the High Fidelity Radar. You can select the radar mode in the Difficulty Levels screen in the Config area. Refer to Chapter 2, *Introduction to Falcon 3,* for more information on configuration options.

The SAD Radar Mode The SAD radar mode is the easiest to use. Figure 4-4 shows the Radar Electro-Optical display (REO) for the SAD mode. The location of your F-16 is represented in the center of the REO. The current maximum range is displayed in the upper left corner. This indicates the maximum range from top to bottom of the display. The range is selected automatically in the SAD mode. Since you are in the center of the display, the range from your Falcon is half of the maximum range. For example, if the REO displays 10 SAD, this indicates that the active range from top to bottom of the REO is ten miles. A target at the top of the display is five miles in front of you. All targets below the center of the REO are behind you. The maximum range is 80 nautical miles or a 40 mile range to the front and a 40 mile range to the rear. Tracking aircraft activity that is behind the F-16 is useful to new users; however, it is a very unrealistic representation of the APG-66.

The SAD mode displays targets with a color coding scheme. A white target indicates an aircraft that is within an altitude of 3,000 feet of your

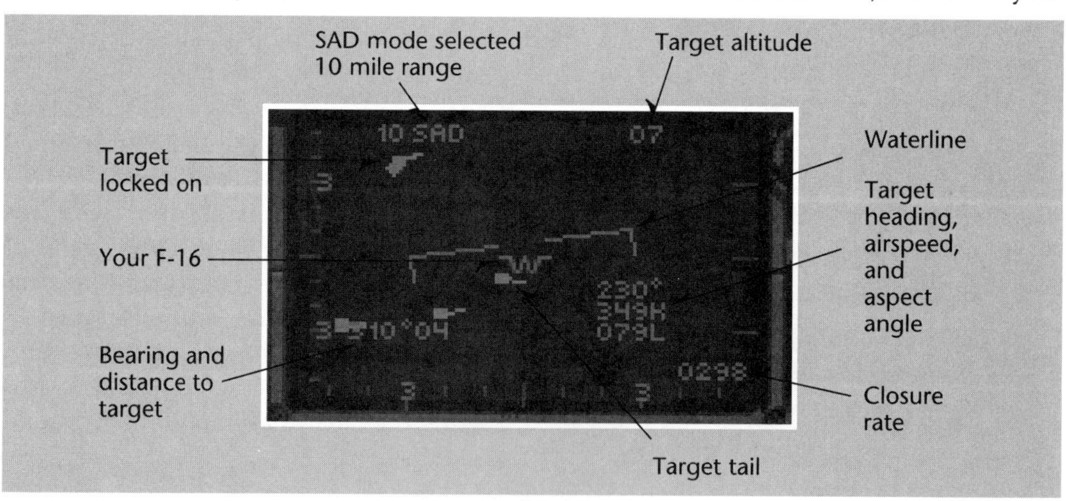

Figure 4-4 SAD Mode Radar Electro-Optical Display (REO)

F-16. A yellow target is more than 3,000 feet over your Falcon. A blue target is more than 3,000 feet below you. In addition, each target on the REO has a tail. This tail represents the exhaust of the aircraft. Each target is heading in the opposite direction of the tail on the REO.

The REO displays one target as a diamond instead of a square. This indicates your F-16 has *locked on* a target. In air-to-air combat, you normally lock on to an aircraft before you pursue it. Having a target locked makes it easier to track using the HUD. The computer automatically locks up the nearest target. Pressing the T key toggles through the targets (if more than one is within the range of the radar). You will see this demonstrated in the lessons in this chapter.

The waterline is an artificial horizon indicator. As you bank the F-16, the waterline moves to represent the horizon. Two lines extend from either end of the waterline to point in the direction of earth. These lines will point up when your F-16 is inverted.

The REO displays detailed information about the target lock-on. The target heading, airspeed, and aspect angle are on the right side of the REO. The distance to the target and target bearing are on the left side. The altitude (in thousands of feet) of the target is in the upper right corner. The *closure rate* is in the lower right corner. The closure rate indicates the rate (in miles per hour) at which you are gaining or losing on the target. A positive closure rate indicates you are gaining, while a negative rate indicates you are falling behind. You perform some exercises to become familiar with the SAD mode radar in Lesson #2.

The SAM Radar Mode The Situation Awareness Mode (SAM) provides a more realistic radar display. Notably the radar is forward facing. Figure 4-5 shows the REO for the SAM mode. The nose of your F-16 is at the bottom center of the display. Every target on the REO is in front of your aircraft. In order to see if there are any targets behind you, you must fly in that direction to face the APG-66. Of course you would only do this if all is clear in front of you. The last thing you want to do is turn your back on an enemy.

The range of the SAM radar mode is extended. Since you can no longer view targets to the rear, the front gains the additional distance. For example, if the computer sets the range to 80 miles, the SAD mode uses 40 miles for the front and 40 miles for the rear. The SAM mode uses the entire 80 mile range for the front.

Some of the information used in SAD is not available in SAM. The targets are no longer color coded to indicate relative altitude. You must lock a target and obtain its altitude on the REO, then compare it with your

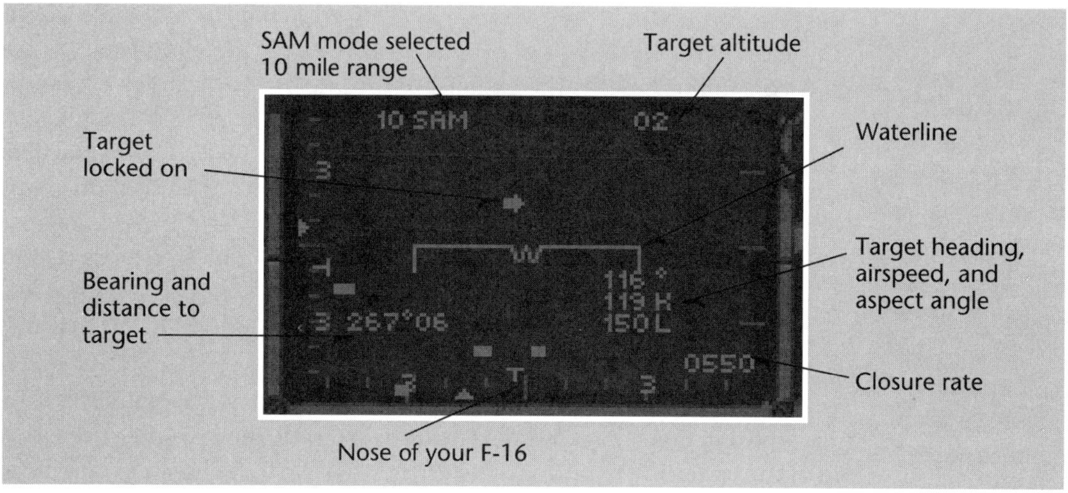

Figure 4-5 SAM Mode Radar Electro-Optical Display (REO)

altitude. The computer automatically locks up the nearest target. As with the SAD mode, pressing the T key toggles through the targets (if more than one target is within the range of the radar). There are no tails on the targets in the SAM mode. In order to determine the heading of the aircraft, you can lock up the target and read the heading on the REO.

The SAM mode requires more attention than the SAD mode. After becoming more familiar with reading the display, you will be able to gather information at a glance and return your attention to the HUD, where it belongs. You perform exercises in Lesson #3 to become familiar with using the SAD mode.

Radar Avoidance and Deception

You need to use your F-16 radar to your advantage in Falcon 3.0. However, the enemy is well equipped with radar also. Most of the enemy radar is in the form of missile guidance. There are various techniques when it comes to handling these types of radar. You can avoid the radar completely by flying around its transmitting range. Although some missions require you to fly near the radar sites to get to the primary target.

You can destroy the radar that is guiding the missiles. This requires that you carry the ordnance to do so. Since the Falcon can only carry so much, this may not be feasible. You can also use *countermeasures* to trick and confuse the enemy radar and missiles. Let's take a look at some methods of deception and avoidance.

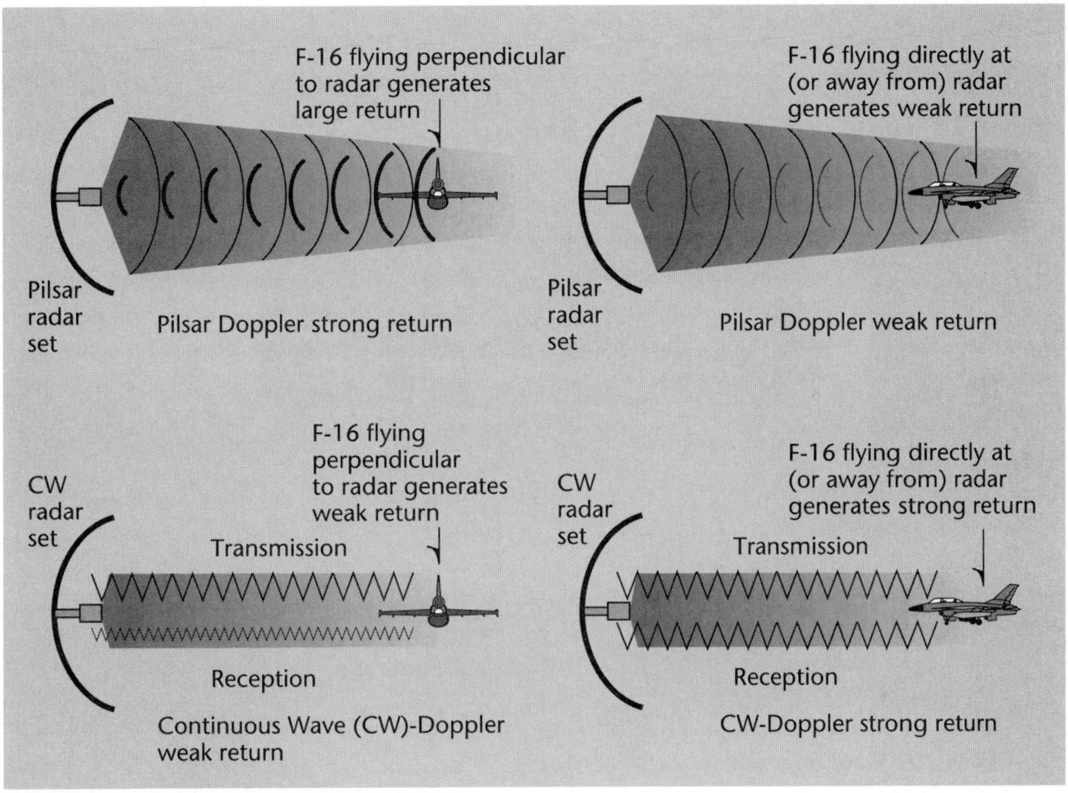

Figure 4-6 Avoiding CW and Pulse-Doppler Radar

Avoidance Tactics There are two types of ground radar used by the enemy in Falcon 3.0: CW-Doppler and pulse-Doppler. CW stands for continuous wave. The methods of avoiding the two types are quite different. Figure 4-6 illustrates the effects of flying perpendicular or directly at the transmitting radar.

As mentioned earlier, the Doppler radar detects *moving* targets and filters out stationary targets. The pulse-Doppler radar receives better quality returns (echoes) when a large area is hit by the RF energy. The CW-Doppler radar receives better returns when the target is moving toward or away from the radar set. It depends upon a *phase shift* in the signal to properly display a return.

To avoid detection by a pulse-Doppler radar you can fly directly towards or directly away from the transmitting radar. This presents the smallest target; therefore, the reflections will be faint. Flying perpendicular to the pulse-Doppler radar presents a large target, hence the returns are strong.

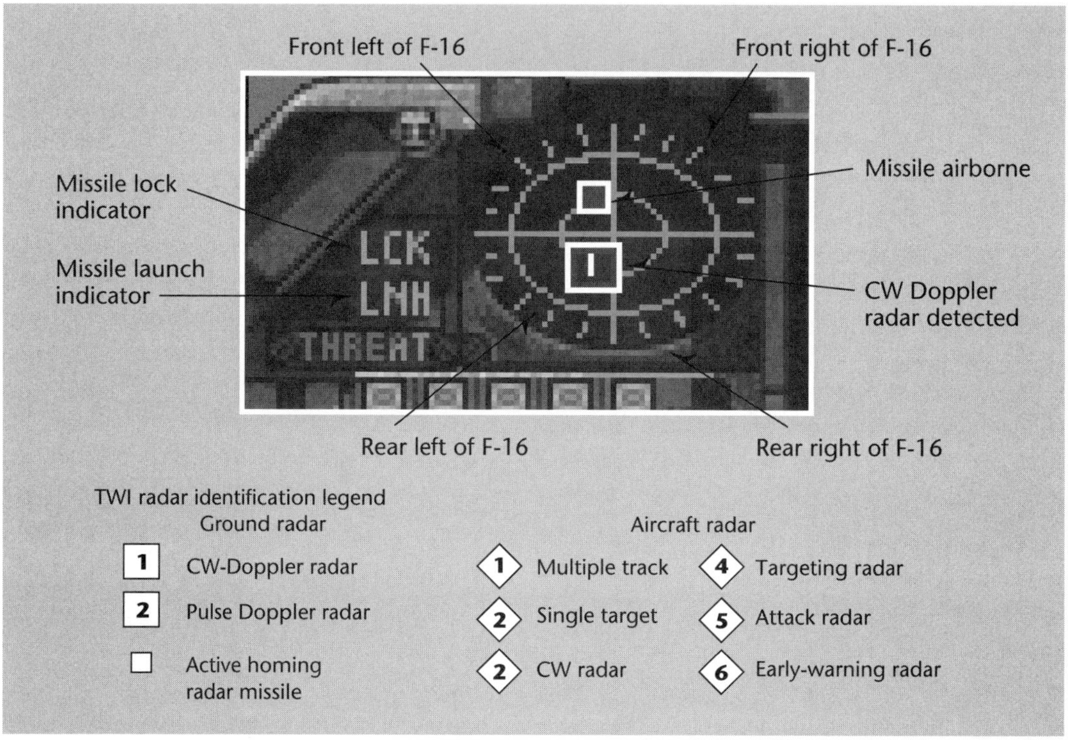

Figure 4-7 The Threat Warning Indicator (TWI)

Avoiding the CW-Doppler radar is virtually the opposite of the pulse-Doppler. Flying directly at or away from the CW causes the greatest phase shift which generates a strong return. Flying perpendicular to the CW simulates a stationary target (as far as range goes). This can reduce the returns to a level that the CW-Doppler radar cannot detect.

If you are flying very close to either type of radar, the return will probably be strong enough to detect you regardless of your relative heading. How do you know if the enemy radar is detecting you? What is the enemy radar type? How do you know the bearing of the enemy radar? The Threat Warning Indicator (TWI) has the answers to these questions and more.

The Threat Warning Indicator (TWI) The Threat Warning Indicator (TWI) is an integral part of your F-16. It is on the left side of the front cockpit view. Figure 4-7 shows the TWI and calls out several of the features. The heart of the TWI is a circular scope that represents a top-down view of the environment with your F-16 in the center. Everything that appears in the top half of the circle is in front of you. Everything in the lower half is behind you. For example, the figure shows the TWI detecting a missile radar behind and to the left of the Falcon. A missile is also on its way. The homing radar missile is currently to the front left of the Falcon.

The TWI also has the ability to determine if an enemy aircraft or ground unit has a lock on your F-16 or if a missile has been fired. The LCK indicator lights when a missile radar or aircraft radar has achieved a lock on your Falcon. An audible tone accompanies the indicator (if sound is enabled on your system). This condition requires constant monitoring and possible evasive action. However, no missile has been fired yet. The LNH indicator lights when an air-to-air missile or a surface-to-air missile has been launched. This usually requires immediate action. You will practice evasive maneuvers and deception techniques in Lesson #5.

Falcon 3.0—Radar and Avoidance

Let's put the textbook aside, climb back in the cockpit, and get back in the air. The first three lessons in this chapter are passive. Enemy aircraft are present but they are not loaded with any air-to-air weapons. The last two lessons require the enemy aircraft to be armed. You may get shot down a few times, but it will be a learning experience none the less. It is better to get shot down during a training lesson than during the mission that would have won the campaign for the allies.

The first lesson introduces the *padlock view* and *Identification Friend or Foe (IFF)*. The padlock view helps overcome the narrow perspective limitation of computer flight simulations. The IFF feature helps us determine whether an aircraft is friendly or not *before* it is in visual range. You take a look at the SAD and SAM radar modes in the second and third lessons, respectively. In the fourth lesson, you use the Threat Warning Indicator to spot some missile radar. Unfortunately, where there is missile radar, there is missile activity. Prepare to get shot down a few times in this one! The last lesson teaches you how to avoid the missile onslaught.

The Lesson Format

The lesson format is very similar to the format used in Chapter 3, *Learning to Fly*. You load a mission at the Red Flag control screen. Then you receive some last minute ground school instruction. Along with the ground school, you are given a list of lesson objectives listing the goals, information, and knowledge you will receive from the lesson. Then, using step-by-step instruction, you perform the lesson. At the end of the lesson you receive a review in the form of a debriefing. You can analyze your results and determine if you need another pass at the lesson. The Red Flag missions can be used over and over. The more comfortable you are with the radar and avoidance tactics, the more successful you will be in the campaigns.

If you need any help loading missions or getting to the runway, refer to Chapter 3 for detailed instructions. You bypass the F-16 Pilots and the F-16 Armament screens on your way to the start of each lesson. All lessons in this chapter start with your F-16 in mid-flight. It is not necessary to take off in this chapter.

Radar Lesson #1: The Padlock View and IFF

Falcon 3.0 has a unique feature that makes the simulation more realistic and, as a result, easier to play. This feature is the padlock view. Flight simulators designed to run on personal computers have always been plagued with a nagging problem; there is not enough sensory feedback. The computer-user "pilot" cannot feel the results of pulling hard on the flight stick or experience the sickening feeling of negative Gs. One sense that is severely limited in computer simulations is sight. The amount of visual feedback is confined to one narrow view. In the last chapter, you found that there are several views available in Falcon 3.0. The views are great, but you are saddled with the task of changing from one view to the next. This doesn't present a problem when you are flying around sightseeing. However, in a vicious dogfight you have enough to worry about without trying to switch views. The padlock view is born!

The padlock view simulates the actual view of a pilot during visual range combat. After a target is locked using the radar you can switch to the padlock view. Padlock view does not require radar lock; however, it's easiest to obtain radar lock before switching to padlock view. The view follows the target whether it is in front or behind your F-16. The only place the padlock view cannot track is directly below the aircraft. The padlock view also displays the aircraft type you are up against. This simulates a pilot *visually* identifying the aircraft. However, it is best to identify an aircraft *before* it is in visual range. The IFF feature helps you make this identification.

The F-16 is equipped with Identification Friend or Foe (IFF) gear. This equipment sends an encrypted message to an unidentified aircraft upon command. If the aircraft also has IFF equipment, it receives the code and sends a response back. In Falcon 3.0, this response is a short buzz. The IFF light in the left view also turns on for a few seconds. If the aircraft is not equipped with the IFF gear (enemy), it does not respond. You will know that the aircraft is not friendly. Let's see how all this works!

Lesson Objectives In this lesson you :

- Access the padlock view.
- Use the IFF feature to identify friendly aircraft.
- Use the IFF feature to identify enemy aircraft.

Ground School Go to the Red Flag Control screen and load the PADLOCK mission. You can fly this mission or use the autopilot to guide your F-16. If you choose to fly the mission yourself, be sure to keep your aircraft as level as possible and to follow the waypoints. Let's take a look at what you will be seeing before you start the mission.

We introduce a few new keys for this lesson. The padlock view can be accessed by pressing the 8 key on the upper row numeric keys or the * key on the numeric keypad. You can press the T key to select between multiple targets. The F-16 radar automatically selects the first target for you. Pressing the N key sends the IFF query to the selected target.

The Components of the Padlock View The padlock view is divided into four sections, or windows. Figure 4-8 shows the padlock view. The largest section of the screen is the main window. This is a view of what you are currently looking at. The upper left section of the padlock screen is the status window. This provides information on the status of your F-16. The top center portion of the display is the 360° window. This lets you see what portion of the 360° view is displayed in the main window. The upper right part of the screen is the target locator window. You can use this window to help find aircraft and monitor the position of your aircraft with respect to the ground.

The status window provides information about your F-16. The cockpit control panel and sometimes the entire HUD are invisible while tracking an aircraft. Therefore, it is important to have the ability to monitor this data during a dogfight. The TARGET entry will change depending on the status of the target being tracked. For example, in the figure we are tracking a target on radar (box in main window), but the target is not within visual range. If the target is not visible, TARGET indicates NONE. If the target is in visual range, but is not identifiable, TARGET indicates UNKNOWN. When the target is identified, TARGET indicates the type of aircraft (F-15, MiG-29, etc.)

The 360° window is used in combination with the main window. The center of this window represents the front of the F-16, the far left portion

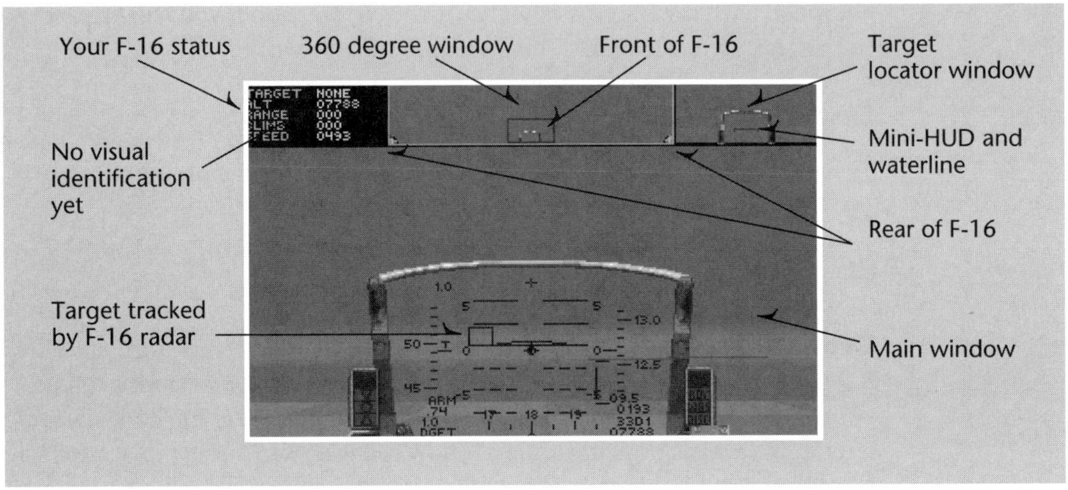

Figure 4-8 The Padlock View

represents the left rear of the F-16, and the far right indicates the right rear of the F-16. A tracking box follows the target around the aircraft. For example, if the tracked aircraft was directly to the left of the Falcon (9 o'clock), the tracking box would appear between the left and the center of the 360° window.

The target locator window has two purposes. It displays a line, extending from the top of the miniature HUD, that indicates the direction of the designated target. It also has a waterline (like the waterline on the REO) to help maintain the position of the Falcon with respect to the ground. For example, if the small lines that extend from the waterline are pointing up, this indicates that you are flying inverted.

The main window displays the portion of the 360° window that is marked by the tracking box. This view will move around in synchronization with the tracked target. This simulates your head turning around to keep your eye on the target.

Use the padlock view to observe some friendly and enemy aircraft. You will also use the Identification Friend or Foe to determine the status of aircraft that are beyond visual range.

Back to the Skies! Get in the air by passing through the F-16 Pilots and F-16 Armament screens. As soon as the cockpit screen appears, press the (P) key to pause the simulation. Note that there is a square on the left side of the HUD. This is an indication that the radar has detected a target. However, the target is not within visual range yet. You may want to read though the following steps before flying the mission. Remember to press pause any time you need to stop and read or look around the displays.

- Press the P key to unpause the simulation.
- Press the A key to engage the autopilot. This helps keep your F-16 on course while you check out the padlock view. If you choose to fly the aircraft, be sure to keep the altitude at around 8,000 feet, the airspeed at 450 knots, and follow the waypoints. You may not see some of the targets if you stray from this course.
- Press the * key on the numeric keypad to switch to the padlock view (you can also use the 8 key on the upper row numerics). Note that TARGET indicates NONE at this time. You cannot see the aircraft yet although the radar is tracking the target.
- Press the N key to send an IFF query to the target. You should hear a buzz (if sound is enabled). You can also switch to the left view by pressing the 7 key on the numeric keypad and viewing the IFF light. The sound method is preferred because it reduces the switching of views. You now know that the aircraft is friendly before he is in visual range!
- The square should cross from left to right on the HUD. Keep an eye on the TARGET indicator. It should switch to UNKNOWN for a few seconds. This means that we see the aircraft, we just don't know the aircraft type. A few seconds later the TARGET indicates that the incoming aircraft is an F-15 Eagle.
- Notice that the view in the main windows shifts to follow the F-15. This simulates your head turning as it follows the target.
- Press the T key a few times. Notice that the view shifts to two other F-15s. By pressing T, you are telling the radar to lock on a different target. When the radar lock changes, the padlock view follows.
- Press the T key to select the F-15 that you first locked on. It should pass your Falcon on the left-hand side. Watch the track box in the 360° windows as it follows the Eagle. Figure 4-9 shows this action.
- The F-15 should continue past you. When the target gets behind you, the word REAR appears in the target locator window. This is another indication that the target is behind you.
- Monitor the target RANGE in the status window. You slowly get farther away from the Eagle group. When the RANGE gets to three

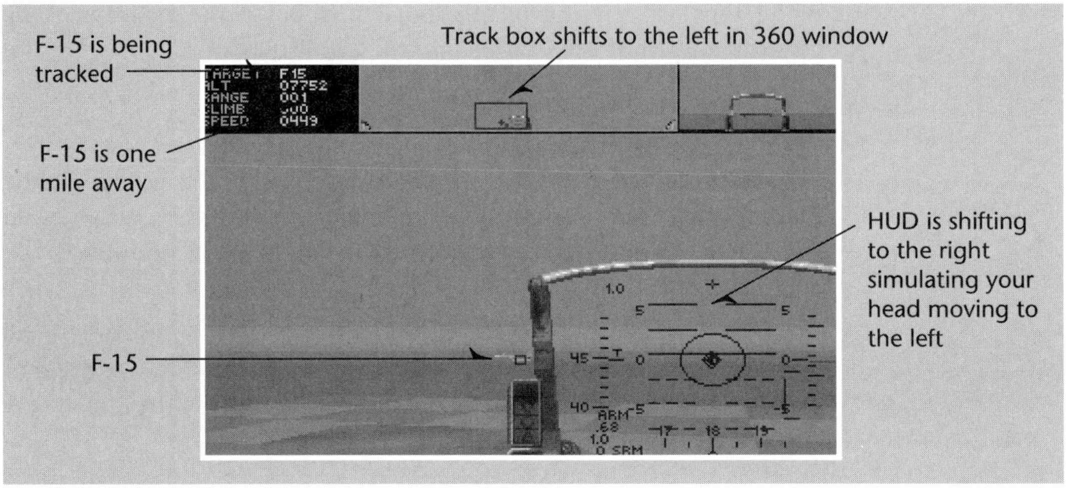

Figure 4-9 Observing a Passing F-15 in Padlock View

miles, TARGET indicates UNKNOWN again. A few seconds later TARGET changes back to NONE. You are out of visual range of the Eagles. The tracking box swings around to the front. This is the normal position for the tracking box when no targets are within visual range.

- Continue the flight. Monitor the distance to waypoint in the lower right portion of the HUD. You will pass the first waypoint. When the distance indicator reads 32D2, the radar locks on a new target.
- Press the N key to send an IFF query to the new target. No IFF sound or IFF light? This must be an enemy! Don't worry though. We've made sure that this enemy is not armed.
- Watch the TARGET indicator. It should change from UNKNOWN to MiG-23 very quickly. This is due to the high airspeeds of the MiG and your Falcon. By the time you see the MiG you can recognize him!
- Press the T key to see if there is another target. You should find a MiG-19 flying with the -23.
- The two MiGs get behind you (on your six!). Figure 4-10 shows this action. This is a position you want to stay away from in air-to-air combat!
- A few seconds later, the MiGs give up on you and turn away. Press ESC to bring up the menu bar. Select END MISSION from the FILE menu. Click on NEXT MISSION to return to Red Flag Control.

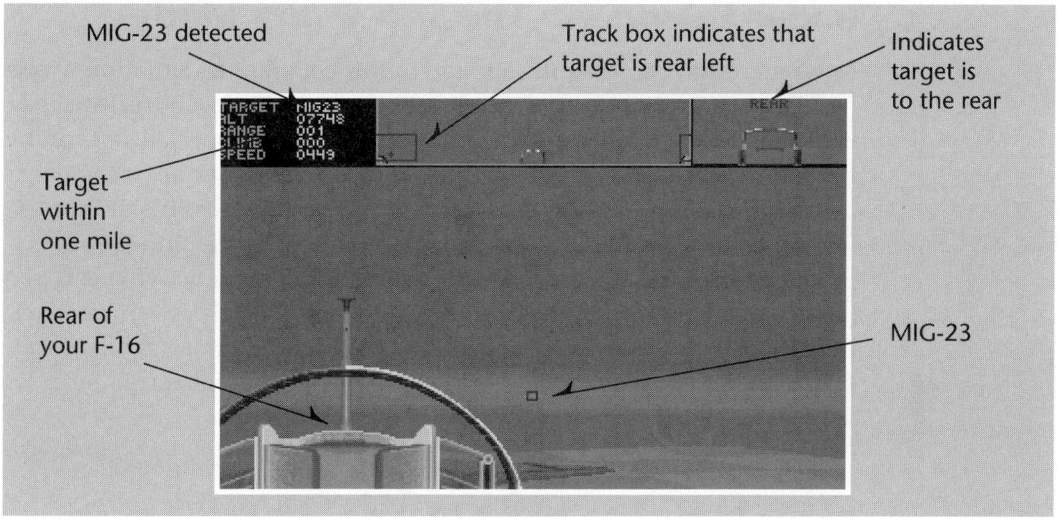

Figure 4-10 A MiG-23 On Your Tail!

Debriefing: The Padlock View and IFF This lesson gave you a look at the padlock view and the IFF. A real F-16 pilot can see virtually 360° around him. This is a big advantage in close-range dogfighting. It is very important to maintain sight when you are engaged with an enemy aircraft. Some fighter aircraft have a sunken-style cockpit; the pilot cannot see activity to the rear. The Falcon, with its big bubble canopy, lets the pilots see everything clearly. The Falcon 3.0 padlock view was designed to simulate this ability.

You will use the padlock view often in air-to-air combat. Getting used to the view can be tricky. After some time, it becomes as natural as the normal front cockpit view. The remaining lessons will call on the padlock view again. This provides the additional practice you may need.

The latest revision of Falcon 3.0 (revision D), as of this writing, has enhanced the ability of the padlock view. In addition to tracking aircraft, you can also track an incoming missile. This improves your ability to perform the avoidance and distraction tactics demonstrated in Lesson #5 of this chapter.

The Identification Friend or Foe (IFF) feature is very valuable. There are times when the sky is filled with air activity. Some aircraft are friendly, some are not. Participating in a friendly fire incident means immediate court martial in a Falcon 3.0 campaign. Pilots and aircraft are precious commodities in the campaigns. It is important to manage them wisely. Don't send a pilot home early by shooting down a friendly aircraft. Always use your IFF!

Radar Lesson #2: The SAD Radar Mode

As we mentioned in the introduction to this chapter, the Situation Awareness Display (SAD) mode is the easiest to use, but it is most unrealistic radar in Falcon 3.0. If you are new to flight simulators, and especially air combat simulators, you may want to use the SAD mode during your first campaign. I strongly suggest learning the SAM mode as soon as possible. It increases realism and, as a result, increases your enjoyment of the simulation.

You will take a short flight and observe the radar activity. It is very important to follow the prescribed waypoints at the airspeeds indicated in the lesson. You may want to rely on the old faithful autopilot once again! This will free your hands and allow you to focus your attention on the lesson objectives. Let's see if we can track down some aircraft.

> NOTE: This lesson requires the selection of the SAD radar mode in the Difficulty Settings screen. Set the RADAR switch to SAD or choose the BEGINNER setting to automatically choose SAD. For information on setting difficulty levels, refer to "Difficulty Levels" in Chapter 2, *Introduction to Falcon 3*.

Lesson Objectives In this lesson you will:

- Track targets on the REO.
- Find the status of a target (heading, speed, etc.).
- Identify a target as friendly or enemy.
- Use the wingman view to observe friendly aircraft.

Ground School Go to the Red Flag Control screen and load the SAD mission. You can fly this mission or use the autopilot to guide your F-16. If you choose to fly the mission yourself, be sure to keep your aircraft as level as possible and follow the waypoints. Take a look at what you will be seeing before starting the mission.

You use the padlock view (the * key on the numeric keypad) and the IFF query (the N key) in the lesson. If you are not familiar with these keys, perform Lesson #1 in this chapter first. You also use the wingman view in this mission (the 7 key on the upper row). Although there is no wingman present on this mission, the wingman view lets you look at friendly aircraft when they are in visual range. This view can be zoomed and rotated using the F1 through F4 keys.

Routine Patrol Procedures This lesson simulates a patrol mission. Normally, patrol missions require that you attack and destroy any enemy aircraft that crosses your designated path. You should never stray too far from the assigned waypoints while on patrol. However, the enemy is not armed in this mission so you will observe only.

The sequence of events that occur when you see that blip on the scope should become second nature. Try to make the following steps a habit.

- Observe the target on the REO.
- Lock it up on radar (the T key).
- Check IFF (the N key).
- If the target is an enemy, assess the situation and take *necessary* action.

The action you will take varies depending on your role in the mission. For example, you are assigned to escort a bomber to its target. On the way you lock up a target on radar 35 miles away. Upon checking the IFF, you get no response. Do you attack? The answer is no! To do so would leave your bomber unguarded. After taking care of the enemy and returning, you may find that another enemy has downed the bomber. It is important that you study the REO carefully before making a decision. Is the target closing in? Is the target running away? You don't always have a lot of time to make this decision. That is what this lesson is all about. Let's practice reading the F-16 radar, the SAD mode.

On with the Hunt! Now is your chance to look for air activity. Remember, the goal here is to find aircraft and quickly determine whether they are friendly or enemy. Also note the heading, airspeed, and altitude of the aircraft. SAD is the only radar mode that has the relative altitude color coded.

Click on F-16 PILOTS, F-16 ARMAMENT, and then TAKEOFF. Immediately turn on autopilot with the A key, then pause the simulation by pressing P. If you do not use autopilot, be sure to maintain an altitude of 8,000 feet and follow the waypoints.

- Press the P key to unpause the simulation. You should be at an approximate heading of 45°. 20 SAD appears in the upper left corner of the REO.
- Two blue targets appear at the top of the REO. Press the T key to lock up one of the two targets. The range may change to 40nm. One of the targets changes to a diamond shape and additional information

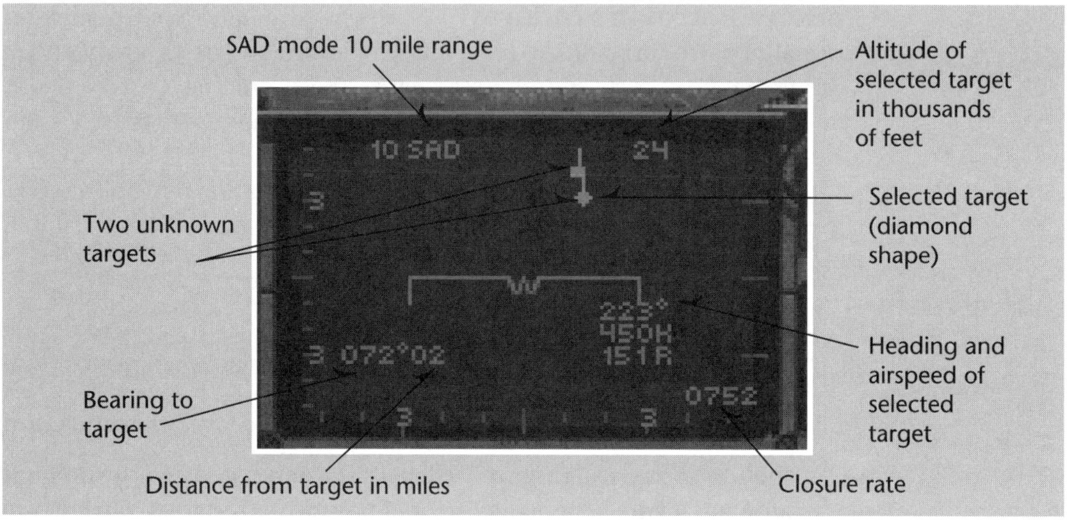

Figure 4-11 SAD Mode REO Tracking Two Unknown Targets

appears on the REO. Figure 4-11 shows this information and the targets as they close in on your F-16. Remember, blue targets are more than 3,000 feet above you. The REO shows that the locked target is at 24,000 feet.

- You may want to pause the simulation and study the figure and your REO.
- Press the N key to send an IFF query. Is the aircraft friendly? You should hear a buzz indicating this. If you do not have sound enabled, check the IFF light in the left view while pressing N.
- Let's take a look at padlock view (the * key on the numeric keypad) to find out the type of aircraft we are dealing with. Once the aircraft get in range you will see they are F4 Phantoms.
- Press the T key to toggle between the two aircraft. The padlock view moves to track the selected F4.
- Return to the front cockpit view by pressing 1 on the numeric keypad or 3 on the upper row numeric keys.

You should be getting close to waypoint 1 at this time. If you are not using autopilot, be sure to follow the waypoint caret. Check your altitude and stay in the 8,000 feet AGL range. The AGL altitude indicator is directly below the distance-to-waypoint indicator.

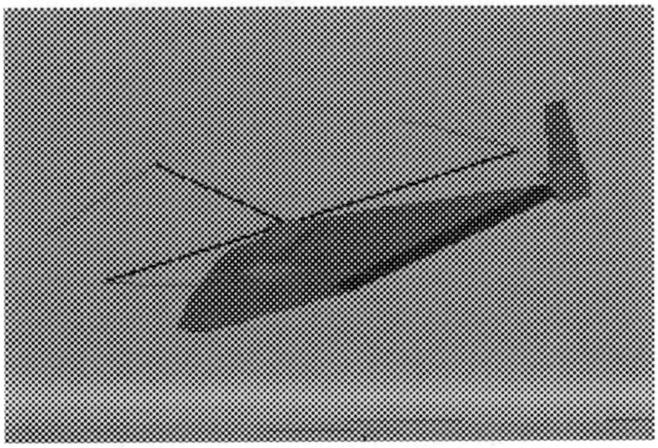

Figure 4-12 An Apache Helicopter Observed from Wingman View

- After making a bank to the left, your F-16 should be at a heading of approximately 315°.

- A few miles after making your turn, one or two targets will appear. Lock a target as soon as it appears on the REO. Press N to check IFF. Is the aircraft friendly? Once again, you should hear the buzz (or see the light).

- Switch to the padlock view when the target nears visual range (five to seven miles). Stay in padlock until you get a target ID.

- It's an AH-64 Apache Helicopter patrolling the area! Press the 7 key on the upper row to switch to wingman view. The wingman view provides a close up of the target lock-on when the target is in visual range. Figure 4-12 shows the Apache in action. You can use the zoom and rotate keys in this view (F1 through F4).

- As the AH-64 passes by, switch back to front cockpit view. Try pressing the T key to lock up the target when it is behind your F-16 (lower half of the REO). This will not work because you cannot lock up a target that is behind you.

- The Apache should drop off the bottom of the REO and out of site.

Now you should be reaching waypoint 2. The remainder of the mission is a zigzag pattern. You will fly northeast (45°), then northwest (315°), and so on until the mission is over. Back to the hunt!

- After you pass waypoint 2, three targets should appear. The targets may be white or blue. Lock one up with the T key as soon as they are visible.

- Press the N key to check IFF. There is no buzz? Looks like we are going to run into a few enemies after all!

- As the targets approach, switch to the padlock view and see what type of enemy aircraft you are dealing with. Use the T key to see if all the aircraft are the same type. This should be two MiG-27s and one SU-27. These aircraft may have more interest in your F-16 than the friendlies did. That's okay, they are free of weapons in this training lesson.

Figure 4-13 The F-117A Stealth Fighter Observed from Wingman View

- Proceed to waypoint 3. After making the turn at the waypoint, more activity should appear on the REO. Go through the routine. Lock it up, IFF check, and use padlock to identify aircraft type. You should find that the aircraft is enemy and the type is MiG-29. 29s can be tough opponents. Be glad they are not armed for now!

- Proceed to waypoint 4 and make the final turn. You should get the IFF signal for friendly aircraft. When you get close, use the wingman view (the 7 key upper numeric). You should see something similar to Figure 4-13.

- This is the end of the hunting using the SAD mode. Press ESC to access the menu bar. Select END MISSION from the FILE menu. Click on NEXT MISSION at the Debriefing screen. You are back at Red Flag Control.

Debriefing: The SAD Radar Mode You can see how easy it is to track targets using the Situation Awareness Display (SAD) radar mode. Being able to locate and quickly determine the details about air activity is very important in Falcon 3.0. The SAD mode gives you some additional assistance. The targets are color coded for relative altitude, and the heading of the aircraft can be determined by the tails on the targets. Keep in mind that the heading or relative altitude could be determined by locking up a target, then using the target data on the REO.

Every target you see on the REO during a mission should be checked out using the routine we discussed in the lesson. Observe the target, lock it up on radar, check the IFF, and take action if necessary. If the aircraft is friendly, no action is necessary. If the aircraft is an enemy, whether or not to attack depends on your assignment. We will learn how to make this crucial decision in Chapter 5, *Using Weapons*.

Which mode of radar (SAD, SAM, or HFR) you use is a matter of personal preference. When you start your first campaign, you may want to try easier difficulty settings, including using the SAD radar mode. If you want to obtain the most realism, the HFR mode is the best choice. Learning the SAM mode is the next logical step in getting ready for HFR.

Radar Lesson #3: The SAM Radar Mode

The Situation Awareness Mode (SAM) provides less information but increases the realism of Falcon 3.0. Since you are already familiar with the SAD mode, learning the SAM mode should be easy. Some of the principles are the same for this mode. For example, you use the same routine when a target becomes visible on the REO. The same keys are used as well. The T key locks up the target and the N checks IFF.

Take a short flight and observe the radar activity using the SAM mode. It is very important to follow the prescribed waypoints at the airspeeds indicated in the lesson. Using the autopilot is recommended. If you don't see some of the targets that are mentioned in the text, start the mission over and use autopilot. Let's try out the SAM radar mode!

> **NOTE:** This lesson requires the selection of the SAM radar mode in the Difficulty Settings screen. Set the RADAR switch to SAM or choose the INTERMEDIATE setting to automatically choose SAM. For information on setting difficulty levels, refer to " Difficulty Levels" in Chapter 2, *Introduction to Falcon 3.*

Lesson Objectives In this lesson you:

- Track targets on the REO.
- Find the status of a target (heading, speed, etc.).
- Identify a target as friendly or enemy.
- Use the wingman view to observe friendly aircraft.
- Check for targets to the rear of the F-16 using padlock.
- Check for targets to the rear of the F-16 by circling back.

Ground School Go to the Red Flag Control screen and load the SAM mission. You can fly this mission or use the autopilot to guide your F-16. If you choose to fly the mission yourself, be sure to keep your aircraft at an AGL altitude of 7,500 to 8,000 feet and follow the waypoints. Take a look at what you will see before starting the mission.

The most important thing to remember when learning the SAM mode is the location of your F-16 on the REO. Figure 4-14 illustrates this location. This indicates that you can no longer observe a target that is behind you. There are two ways around this. For visual range, you can use the padlock view. Padlock view always displays targets within visual range, even if an

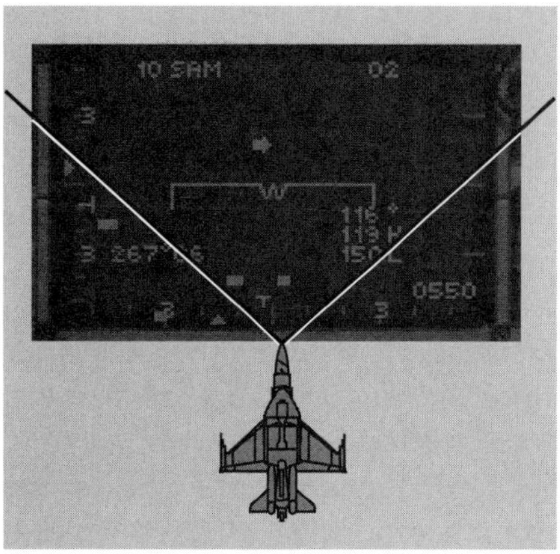

Figure 4-14 REO Display of the Situation Awareness Mode (SAM)

aircraft is behind your F-16. For *beyond visual range* (BVR), you must fly in a circle and check out the REO for air activity to the rear.

The SAM mode does not automatically lock on a target. You must press the T key to lock a target. After the target is locked, the REO displays information about the target. If you encounter a *flight* (group) of aircraft on radar, sending an IFF inquiry to only one of the targets is not sufficient. You should always toggle through all of the targets with the T key and press N for each one. You never know when a friendly might need help in a dogfight! The SAM mode automatically selects the range of the radar, based on target activity. Let's see what kind of activity is out there in the SAM mission!

The SAM Radar Mode Hunt Use your observe, lock, and IFF inquiry routine to check out all unknown aircraft in this mission. Enemies are out there, but they are unarmed once again. Get in the habit of checking out the heading, airspeed, and altitude of the target.

Click on F-16 PILOTS, F-16 ARMAMENT, and then TAKEOFF. Immediately turn on autopilot with the A key. If you do not use autopilot, be sure to maintain an altitude of 7,500 to 8,000 feet, an airspeed of 450 knots, and follow the waypoints. This is very important for this mission!

- You should be heading north (approximately 0°). Keep an eye on the REO for aircraft. When you see activity on the scope, pause the simulation by pressing the P key.

Wait a minute! Where did they come from? Three targets should have appeared at the bottom of the REO.

- Unpause the simulation by pressing P again. Lock up a target with the T key and press N. Hear the buzz? They are friendly.

- Quickly check out the padlock view to get a visual ID. You should find three F/A-18 Hornets. Switch back to cockpit view (1 key on the numeric keypad) and pause the simulation again with P.

It is a good thing the fighters were friendly because an enemy could have fired a missile up your tailpipe or nailed you with guns! There are ways to avoid this, however. You will see one of the ways later in this lesson.

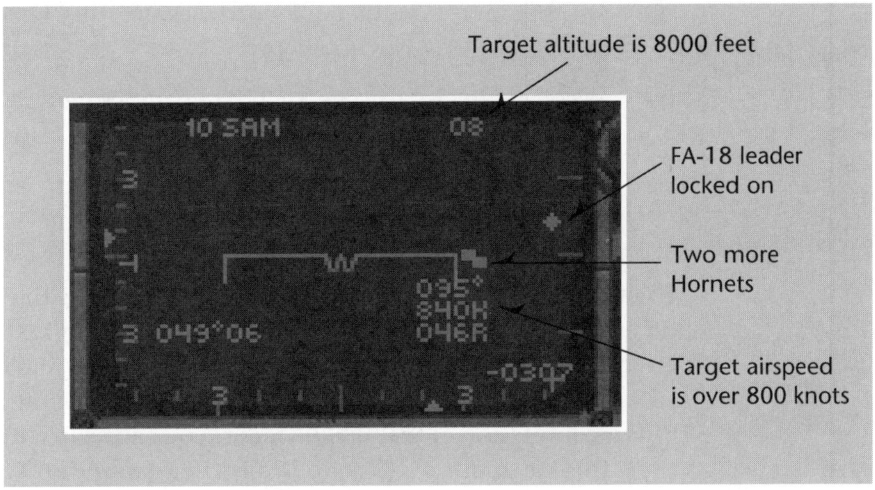

Figure 4-15 SAM REO with Lock on F/A-18 Hornet

Check out the REO. Did you notice the airspeed of the target when you locked on? Over 700 knots! No wonder the Hornets went buzzing past your F-16! Figure 4-15 shows the REO with a Hornet locked on. Back to the mission!

- The three Hornets should bank to the east and fly off the REO.
- Continue north towards waypoint 1. You may have noticed two targets at the top of the REO. They should reappear after you pass waypoint 1.
- Lock up one of the new targets with the T key and check IFF with N. Do the same for the other target. Are they both friendly?

Figure 4-16 Wingman View of A-10 Thunderbolt

- As you get within visual range, switch to padlock view and identify them. You will find two A-10 Thunderbolts (affectionately known as *Warthogs*). Switch to wingman view (the upper row 7 key) to get a better look. Figure 4-16 shows the wingman view of one of the A-10s.
- Continue to waypoint 2. The F-16 autopilot banks to the left, aligning the waypoint caret and heading for waypoint 3.

- Another target should come into view shortly. Lock it up and check IFF. No tone? This is an enemy.
- As you get in visual range, switch to padlock view. It's a MiG-29. Note the airspeed of the MiG. It looks like he's in a hurry!
- Proceed to waypoint 3. After making the turn and lining up the waypoint caret, pause the simulation.

Preventing Attack from the Rear You saw the F/A-18s sneak up on us at the beginning of this lesson. You need a method to prevent being attacked in that situation. Figure 4-17 illustrates one of the methods. If you continue to fly straight on course, you are vulnerable to attack from the rear. This is a limitation of the APG-66 radar. You can only see targets in front of the F-16. One solution is to periodically circle around 360°. This way you can scan the rear for targets.

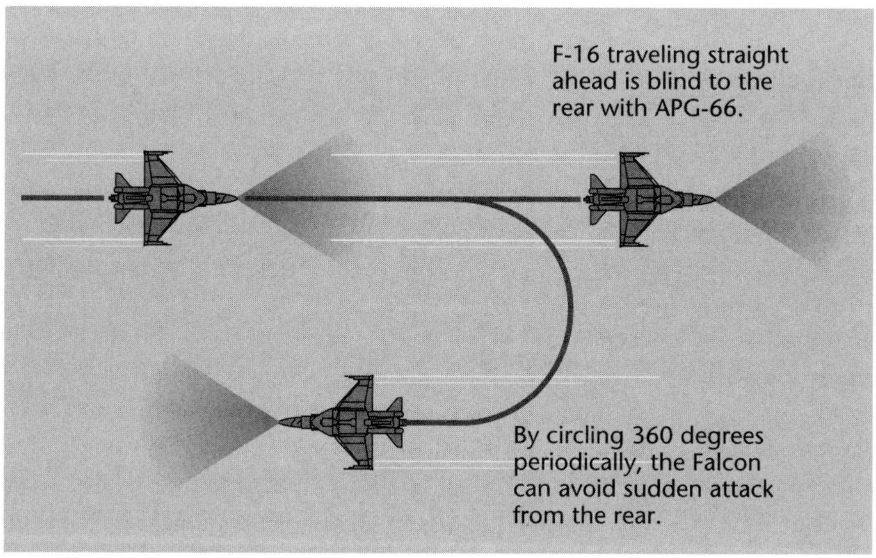

Figure 4-17 Circling to Prevent Attack from the Rear

How often to perform this maneuver depends heavily on the situation. Chances are if you are flying over friendly territory you do not need to do this. But if you are escorting B52s to a bombing site, it's your job to get them to the target intact. You should circle every few minutes to make sure nobody is sneaking up on your bombers.

Let's assume you have been over enemy territory for a while and it's time to check for a rear enemy attack.

- Unpause the simulation and turn off the autopilot.
- Start your circle by banking to the right. You may want to pull back on the stick a little at a time to accelerate the process, but this is not the time for a high-G turn.
- Keep an eye on the REO as you make your turn. At 50–80° (depending on how fast you are turning) some targets should appear.
- Lock up a target and check IFF. It's a good thing you checked the rear! Here comes the enemy! Note the high airspeed. In a real campaign mission, it would probably be time to run unless you had some wingmen along to even the battle or you are highly skilled in dogfighting.
- Switch to padlock view and fly towards the targets. Don't be concerned if you hear alarms go off. They indicate that the incoming aircraft are locking on you, but once again they are harmless. You should verify that the enemy is a flight of French-built Mirage F-1s.
- If these enemy aircraft seem more aggressive than usual, there is a reason for that. These enemies have been instructed to intercept any aircraft that violates their airspace, and you have done so. If their F-1s were loaded with weapons they would be using them on you!
- This is the end of the lesson on SAM mode. Press ESC to access the menu bar. Select END MISSION from the FILE menu. Click on NEXT MISSION at the Debriefing screen. You are back at Red Flag Control.

Debriefing: The SAM Radar Mode The Situation Awareness Mode (SAM) represents the APG-66 radar more accurately in that it only scans forward. No target information is available from the rear. The SAM mode does require you to manually lock up a target, but the range is automatically selected. Chapter 8, *Using High Fidelity Radar,* discusses the next level of radar, the High Fidelity Radar (HFR). The HFR is by far the most realistic form of the APG-66 radar in Falcon 3.0.

The SAM mode does not color code relative altitude or display a tail on the target to simulate target heading. You must manually lock up a target, then read the information of the REO. You can also get an indication of the heading by watching the target move over time.

Locking up a target and checking IFF are no different than in the SAD mode. It is essential to know the status (friendly or enemy) of all targets that appear on your REO. The locking and checking procedure should become second nature. This way you will be prepared to take what the enemy has to offer. Also, and perhaps more importantly, you will not shoot down a fellow airman.

The SAM mode took away your ability to see targets to the rear. However, the overall range of the SAM radar is double that of the SAD mode. You saw that you are prone to attack from the rear. The risk of such an attack can be cut significantly by circling periodically to check for an impending attack. Doing this is more necessary during escort missions and especially over enemy territory. You can also use the padlock view to see if anyone is lurking behind you (within visual range only).

You heard the alarms when the last group of Mirage F-1s locked onto your F-16. These alarms are part of the F-16 Threat Warning Indicator (TWI). This system can help prevent sneak attacks by detecting the incoming aircraft's radar. Our next lesson explores the TWI.

Radar Lesson #4:The Threat Warning Indicator (TWI)

The Threat Warning Indicator (TWI) is a *passive* (does not transmit) device that receives radar signals from other aircraft and ground units. These signals are displayed on the round scope on the left hand side of the cockpit control panel. Each ring on the scope indicates 10 miles, giving the TWI a range of 30 miles. The TWI is able to differentiate between types of radar (ground or aircraft, pulse-Doppler, CW-Doppler, etc.). The TWI is capable of receiving signals from all directions (omni-directional). The only time the TWI can display anything is when a radar is transmitting. An enemy aircraft can still sneak up behind you if his radar is off.

Figure 4-18 shows the TWI display and a list of possible warnings. In Falcon 3.0, ground radar is associated with ground-to-air weapons. Surface-to-air missiles (SAM) and some anti-aircraft artillery (AAA) units are guided by radar signals. The radar operator locks on your F-16 and fires the missile. The missile is guided by feedback from the lock. The TWI gives you advance warning of this occurrence. The SAM radar appears on the scope first. It's a square with a number one or two (depending on the type of radar) in the center of it. The LCK light follows indicating that the radar has locked on your aircraft. When a missile is launched, a small square appears on the TWI and the launch indicator (LNH). These conditions continue until you break the lock or you are hit by the missile.

The TWI shows aircraft radar as a diamond with a number one through six, depending on the type of radar. Knowing the radar type of an aircraft

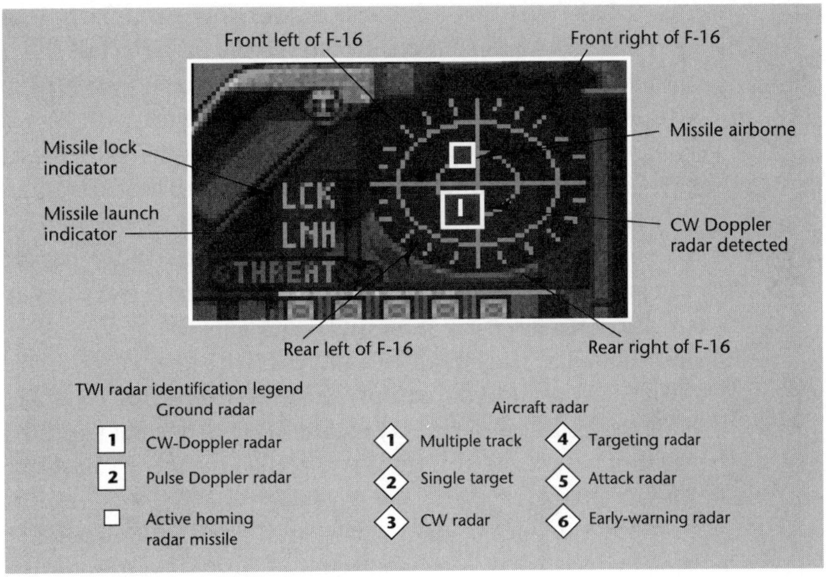

Figure 4-18 The TWI Display with Warning Indicators

can be of some value in Falcon 3.0. For example, if your mission is to intercept three MiG-29s and two MiG-27s, the aircraft would be represented on the TWI by three diamond's with a one inside and two diamonds with a two inside. However, there is one condition that must be met for all of this to work. *The MiG's radar must be transmitting*! The TWI relies on receiving radar transmissions to display activity. As a result, the TWI should not be used to identify aircraft; it can help to confirm the aircraft. Keep in mind, friendly aircraft also transmit radar signals that appear to be identical on the TWI. Don't attack everything that appears on the TWI. Use the REO and IFF to determine the status of all aircraft.

Lesson Objectives In this lesson you:

- Use the TWI to identify aircraft radar type.
- Observe an aircraft radar lock (LCK).
- Use the TWI to identify ground radar type.
- Observe a surface-to-air missile launch.

Ground School There are two separate mission files available in Red Flag Control. TWI1 demonstrates the effects of enemy aircraft radar on the TWI. TWI2 shows the effects of the SAM radar and a missile launch.

The TWI1 mission has several enemy aircraft in the air. You may have to run the mission a few times to see the full effect of the radar. The enemy aircraft have artificial intelligence; they have minds of their own. Sometimes they turn on their radar, sometimes they don't. If you run the mission two to three times, you should see all of the radar activity that is called for. The steps that follow tell you what signals to look for and when you should see them.

When designing the training missions, the enemy aircraft part is easy. The enemy transmits even when there are no weapons aboard. The TWI2 mission is a different story. In order to get the SAM or AAA operator to turn on the radar, they must be equipped with the weapons. You have a missile fired at you and you will probably be hit in this mission. You can always restart the mission and try again. The purpose of this lesson is to see what a launch looks like on the TWI. You learn how to avoid these missiles later in this chapter.

In Falcon 3.0, most aircraft and some ground forces have a radar type associated with it. Helicopters, tanks, and other units are not equipped with radar that is detectable by the TWI. Table 4-1 shows the aircraft and ground units, their radar type, and the number (signature) that appears on the TWI.

Enemy Radar Aircraft / Ground Force	Radar Type	Radar Signature
IL-76 Mainstay	EW Radar	6
SU-24 Fencer	Attack Radar	5
Mirage III	Targeting Radar	4
Mirage 5	Targeting Radar	4
Mirage F1	Targeting Radar	4
MiG-21 Fishbed	CW Radar	3
MiG-23 Flogger-B	Single Target	2
MiG-25 Foxbat	Single Target	2
MiG-27 Flogger-D	Single Target	2
SA-8 Gecko (SAM)	Single Target	2
MiG-29 Fulcrum	Multiple Target	1
SA-6 Gainful	Multiple Target	1
SU-27 Flanker	Multiple Target	1
ZSU-23-4 Shilka (AAA)	Multiple Target	1
ZSU-57-2 (AAA)	Multiple Target	1

Table 4-1 Aircraft and Ground Radars Displayed on TWI (*continued*)

(Continued from previous page)

Friendly Radar Aircraft / Ground Force	Radar Type	Radar Signature
E-3 Sentry	EW Radar	6
B-52 Stratofortress	Targeting Radar	4
KFIR-C7	Targeting Radar	4
F-16 Falcon	Single Target	2
F-4 Phantom	Single Target	2
F-111 Aardvark	Single Target	2
Roland (SAM)	Single Target	2
F-14 Tomcat	Multiple Target	1
F-15 Eagle	Multiple Target	1
F/A-18 Hornet	Multiple Target	1
Tornado	Multiple Target	1
M-163 Vulcan (AAA)	Multiple Target	1
Wildcat (AAA)	Multiple Target	1
Shahine (SAM)	Multiple Target	1
Patriot (SAM)	Multiple Target	1

Table 4-1 Aircraft and Ground Radars Displayed on TWI

Refer back to the table during the mission to confirm the radar types of the aircraft you encounter. For example, if a MiG-29 approaches you and turns on its radar, you will see a diamond with a 1 in the center of it. The IFF check will be negative (no tone) and the padlock view should show a MiG-29 when the target is in visual.

Let's get back in the air and check out the TWI. Remember that aircraft do not always turn on their radar.

Observing Enemy Aircraft Radar Go to Red Flag Control and load the TWI1 mission. Click on F-16 PILOTS, then F-16 ARMAMENT, and then TAKEOFF. You should fly level at an altitude of 7,000 to 8,000 feet. You can use the autopilot or fly the mission yourself. The waypoints for this mission take you directly south (180°). Identify all the aircraft and the radar types as you progress and compare your notes with the information at the end of the lesson.

- Soon after you start the mission, a target should appear on the REO. Lock it up and check IFF. The target is an enemy.
- Watch the TWI closely. If the incoming aircraft turns on its radar, you see an indication of the type of radar. Make a note of the type. If

nothing appears on the TWI, continue the mission. You can retry the mission after completing the first pass.

- When the first target is within visual range, switch to padlock to check the aircraft type. Make a note of the aircraft type.
- Switch back to the cockpit view.
- Proceed to the south. You should see another target on the REO almost immediately. Lock it up, check IFF, and watch the TWI. Note any TWI activity.
- Use padlock again to check the aircraft type. Note the aircraft type and switch back to cockpit view.
- Soon after the second aircraft passes, three targets appear at the top of the REO. Lock up each one individually and check IFF. Once again, note any TWI activity. Figure 4-19 shows how your cockpit view may look.

Figure 4-19 Three Targets Approach with TWI Radar Activity

- Use the padlock view to try to get an ID on each of the three aircraft. The LCK indicator may light on the TWI if any of the aircraft lock onto your F-16. If the enemy were armed, you could expect a missile any time! Figure 4-20 shows an aircraft with a single target type radar locking up directly on the tail of the F-16.
- This is the end of the aircraft radar ID portion of the TWI lesson. Press (ESC) to bring up the menu bar and select END MISSION from the FILE menu. Click on NEXT MISSION to return to Red Flag Control.

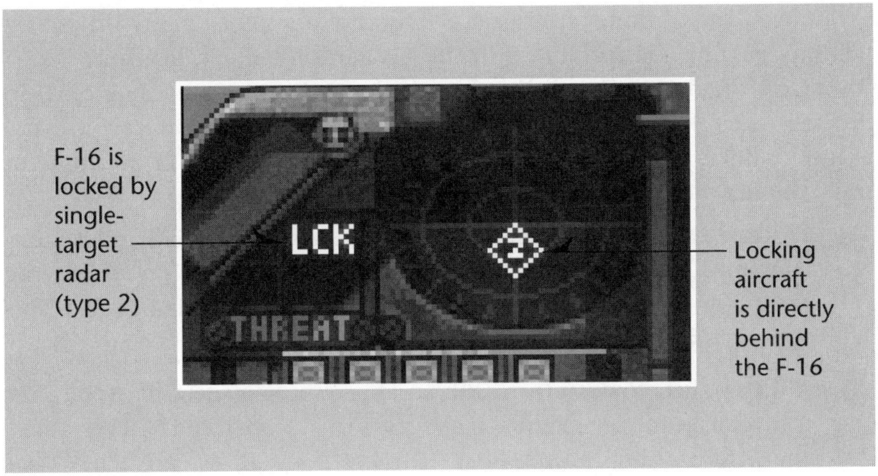

Figure 4-20 TWI Indicates F-16 is Locked Up by Single Target Radar

If you didn't get a radar ID for each of the aircraft encountered, you may want to fly the mission again. It may take several tries before you get every aircraft to turn on its radar. This is a summary of the aircraft you should have encountered and their radar IDs:

- First flight: One MiG-29, radar type 1
- Second flight: One Mirage III, radar type 4
- Third flight: One MiG-21, radar type 3; One MiG-23, radar type 2; One SU-27, radar type 1

Observing Enemy Ground Radar In the introduction to this chapter, you learned that enemy radar is primarily used to guide missiles in Falcon 3.0. When a square with a number in it appears on the TWI, it is time for action! If a ground missile radar detects you, you can be sure to see the LCK (lock on) indicator light followed by the LNH (launch) light. Your assignment dictates the action you take. For example, you may be assigned to a "wild weasel" mission. This means it is your job to make sure the enemy SAM units turn on their radar, thus allowing available aircraft to take the SAM out with anti-radiation missiles. Not a fun job!

The TWI2 mission has several enemy SAM units assigned to it. They are all bunched together about thirty miles south of your initial location. The heading of the Falcon will start at 180°, so you are heading right for them! It is very likely that you will be shot down by a missile. Don't worry about avoiding them for now. Just replay the mission as many times as it takes to become comfortable with the TWI and missile indication.

Go to Red Flag Control and load the TWI2 mission. Click on F-16 PILOTS, then F-16 ARMAMENT, and then TAKEOFF. You can use the autopilot or fly the mission yourself. Don't worry about your altitude for now, the missiles will find you as long as you fly south!

- Proceed to fly south. As you reach approximately 50 miles from waypoint 1, you should hear the lock alarm go off. The TWI shows the radar icon for CW-Doppler ground radar (a square with a 1 in it). This is most likely an SA-6 Gainful SAM unit.
- At this point, you can turn 180° and run. You may get out of the SAM unit's range in time. Figure 4-21 shows this. Note that the TWI shows the SAM unit behind the F-16.
- If you get away from the radar lock, turn back to a 180° heading. Fly south until you get another lock on. This time continue to fly south.
- The LNH indicator lights, indicating that a surface-to-air missile is on its way. The TWI displays a small square representing the incoming missile.

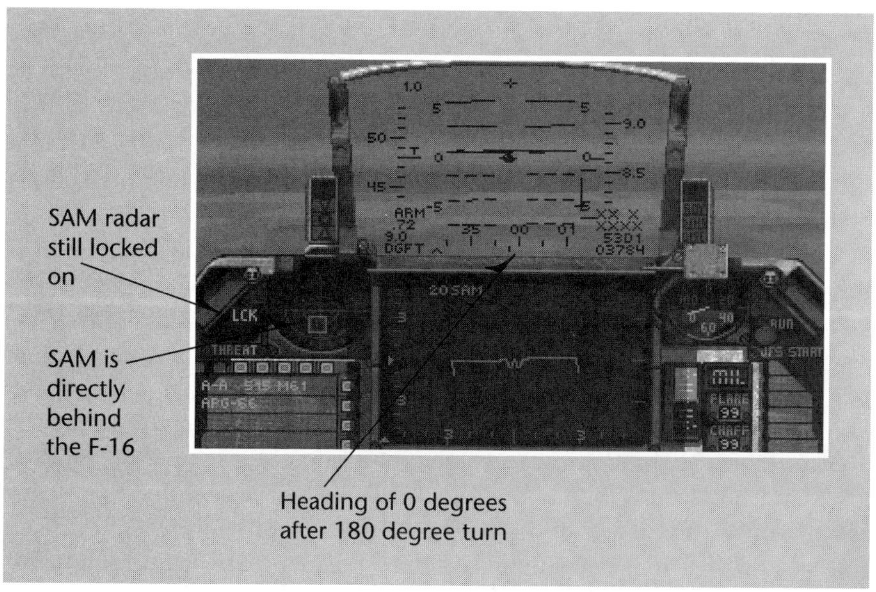

Figure 4-21 The Falcon Attempts an Escape from the SA-6 Gainful Radar Lock

- You can fly around to try to avoid it, but this type of missile is very smart and accurate. If you are hit you can try the mission over. You will return to the Debriefing screen automatically if your aircraft is destroyed.
- Press (ESC) to bring up the menu bar. Select END MISSION from the FILE menu. Click on NEXT MISSION to return to Red Flag Control.

Don't worry if you keep getting shot down. The next lesson introduces some techniques for avoiding and distracting the missiles.

Debriefing: The Threat Warning Indicator The Threat Warning Indicator gives the F-16 pilot the ability to monitor possible threats in a complete 360° circle. The system can pick up signals and determine the radar type and whether the radar is ground or aircraft. The TWI is a passive system. Enemy radar sets must transmit before the TWI can display anything.

The TWI shows aircraft radar as a diamond with a single digit in it. The digit indicates the type of radar. This can be used to narrow the list of possible aircraft that could be transmitting. It is not, however, a measurement of friend or foe. Enemy aircraft can still sneak up on your F-16 with their radar sets off. The TWI gives you no indication of this. If the aircraft fires a radar-guided missile at you, the TWI shows this by lighting the LNH indicator.

The TWI shows ground (missile) radar as a square with a single digit. The digit differentiates between CW and pulse radar. A TWI indication of ground radar is almost immediately followed by a LCK (lock on) condition. After the enemy establishes the lock, the LNH indicator lights and a small square appears on the TWI representing the missile. The surface-to-air missiles are very fast compared to the speed of the F-16. There is not much time to make decisions once the missile is on the way.

Inevitably you will face the issue of SAMs. There will be missions that require you to fly dangerously close to these sites. You must learn ways to avoid or distract the incoming missiles. The next lesson provides some of the avoidance and distraction techniques.

Radar Lesson #5: Avoidance Tactics

Except for the last mission, we have deliberately made the enemy weaponless. This is not reality of course, but it helps in the basic training of flight and navigation. When you enter a campaign things will be very different. Every mission (except for an occasional *milk run*) requires you to enter enemy territory or face the enemy on friendly soil. They are armed and they have one goal in mind: to shoot you and your wingmen down. You must be prepared to face threats from enemy aircraft as well as ground forces. The purpose of this lesson is to help you avoid and distract the enemy advances.

The enemy is equipped with a few air-to-air weapons that you must become familiar with. The AA-2 Atoll is a *rear-aspect, infrared-guided* missile. Rear-aspect means that the enemy pilot must gain a position close to your six o'clock before firing the missile. Firing the Atoll in any other position will most likely result in a miss. Infrared-guided means the missile will lock on a heat source (for instance, the tail of your F-16). The Matra R.550 Magic is an *all-aspect,* infrared-guided missile. Although the Magic locks onto a heat source, it no longer requires the pilot to be on the rear of the intended target. Hence the name all-aspect. The AA-7 Apex is a radar-guided missile that has a range of up to 25 miles. The techniques of distracting and avoiding these missiles differ slightly.

Your F-16 is equipped with two types of deception for incoming air-to-air missiles: *chaff* and *flares*. Chaff is a cartridge of metal strips that is fired out the rear of the Falcon. The cartridge bursts into a cloud. Radar-guided missiles depend on the reflections from the intended target. Dropping chaff causes the missile to chase the chaff instead of your aircraft. Flares are also dropped out the rear of the F-16. The flare burns and acts as a heat-decoy for incoming infrared missiles. Simply dropping chaff or flares any time you get a warning will not keep the missile from homing in on your aircraft. The timing of the chaff or flare drop is very important.

You will be faced with a few weapons from the ground also. Enemy forces in Falcon 3.0 have two types of surface-to-air missiles you must contend with. The SA-6 Gainful is a mobile SAM that fires CW radar-guided missiles at your F-16. The Gainful has a reported range of up to 30 miles and a ceiling (maximum altitude) of close to 50,000 feet. The SA-7 Grail is a very short range shoulder-mounted SAM that is not nearly as effective as the Gainful. The Grail uses infrared technology for homing in on the target. The SA-8 Gecko is a pulse-Doppler, radar-guided mobile SAM unit. The Gecko is a low-altitude, short-range SAM and does not pose as serious a threat as the Gainful. The last of the ground force threats is the ZSU-23-4 Shilka. The Shilka is an anti-aircraft artillery gun that is generally unguided. The Shilka operator fires shells into the sky to an altitude of 2,000 to 3,000 feet.

The primary device you use against these ground forces is the ALQ-131 ECM pod. ECM stands for electronic countermeasure. The ECM pod is mounted to the *centerline* (directly under the F-16 fuselage). When the pod is enabled, it generates signals that disrupt the reception of incoming radar missiles. The ALQ-131 is more effective against SAMs than incoming air-to-air weapons. You must resort to flares to avoid the shoulder-mounted infrared missiles; however, they will not be a significant threat in Falcon 3.0. The only way to avoid getting hit by AAA (triple-A) fire is to avoid flying low over the units. The chances of being downed by AAA is much less likely than SAMs, but they still pose a threat.

The techniques you learn in this lesson do not guarantee that you will never be downed by the enemy, but they will notably reduce the risk. Get ready to go head-to-head with some incoming missiles!

Lesson Objectives In this lesson you:

- Avoid an AA-2 Atoll missile attack with a flare drop.
- Avoid an AA-7 Apex missile attack with a chaff drop.
- Avoid a SA-6 Gainful SAM attack using the ALQ-131 ECM pod.

Ground School This lesson uses three Red Flag mission files: AVOID1, AVOID2, and AVOID3. AVOID1 puts a MiG-29 on your tail ready to fire an Atoll heat seeking missile. AVOID2 puts the same MiG on your tail, but this time he is armed with a radar-guided Apex. AVOID3 routes your Falcon directly to a busy SA-6 SAM site where the radar operator is itching to shoot you down. This mission does send you out with an ECM pod aboard, however.

Using Chaff and Flares The techniques for using chaff and flares are very similar. The main consideration is using the correct one for the job. For example, chaff does nothing at all to distract an infrared missile, nor does a flare distract a radar-guided missile. If the alarm is going off and you know the missile is near, there will not be a lot of time to read the label on the incoming missile! What do you do in this situation? Drop both chaff and a flare at the same time; it can't hurt.

You use two keys to drop chaff and flares. The INS key drops a flare and the DEL key drops a chaff cartridge.

Figure 4-22 shows one of the methods of using chaff to distract an incoming Apex. The top part of the figure shows what will happen if you ignore the TWI warning or try to get away by flying faster without changing direction. The lower portion of the figure shows the Falcon releasing chaff and turning 90° to avoid the incoming missile. The Apex (using radar as its guide) gets reflections off of the chaff. It follows these reflections instead of the F-16s. The F-16 makes a clean getaway

Does using chaff always result in the situation pictured in Figure 4-22? Definitely not! Using chaff properly involves timing and maneuvering. If

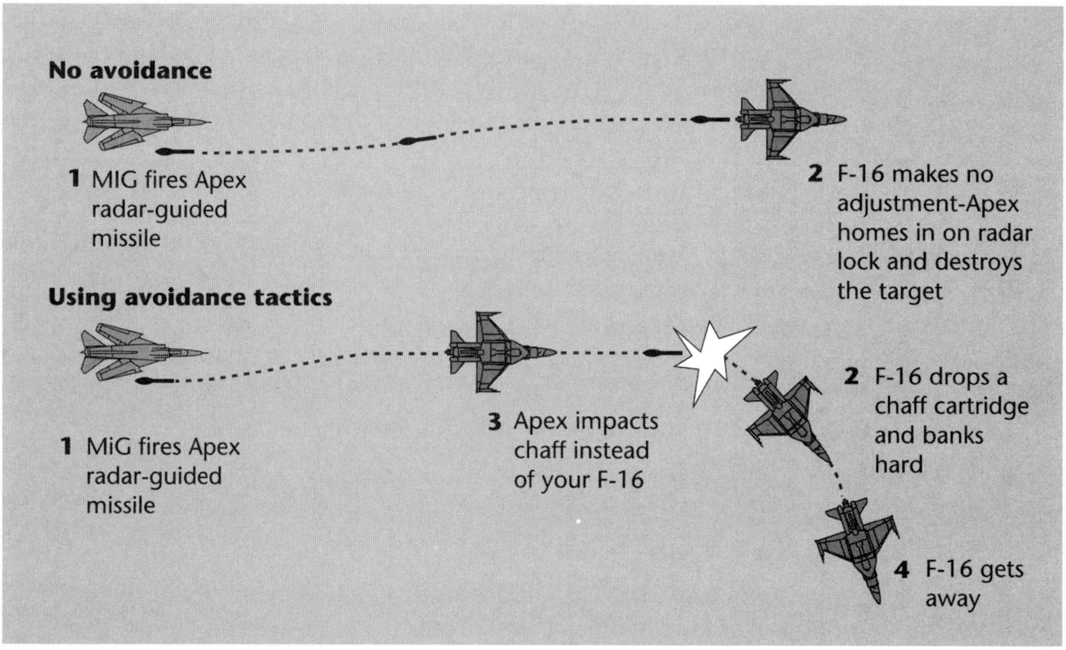

Figure 4-22 Using Chaff to Distract and Avoid an Incoming Apex Missile

you drop the chaff too early, the missile may be confused for a moment, only to re-acquire your F-16 as its target and blast into you anyway! You want to drop the chaff (the DEL key) as the missile approaches the Falcon, then bank sharply and accelerate. Learning where to make the drop requires practice. There are many ways to maneuver out of the way, but a 90° or greater turn is recommended. Do not continue to fly in the same direction. The Apex will be expecting you!

You can dispense flares (the INS key) using the same method as the chaff with a few exceptions. Do not engage the afterburner or climb steeply when an infrared missile is on its way. The last thing you want to do is expose a red-hot afterburner tail to a heat seeker. Dump the flare and bank hard. Try to make the missile see the flare and not your tail. Once again, practice is the key!

> **NOTE**: The Falcon 3.0D revision has the ability to display incoming missiles using the padlock view. As with displaying locked aircraft, the padlock view displays the range of the missile to your F-16. This is useful to gauge when to drop the chaff or flare. The padlock view also displays the missile type.

Using the ALQ-131 ECM Pod The ALQ-131 Electronic Countermeasure (ECM) pod is very easy to use. All you have to do is turn it on by pressing the E key. The ECM pod must be loaded on the F-16 before the mission begins. It is not automatically loaded like chaff and flares. In campaign mode, pods are a limited resource (as with all weapons). You have to choose which missions require ECM pods. The SAM avoidance training mission already has an ECM pod loaded for you.

However, there is more to consider when using ECM to avoid incoming SAMs than simply turning on the pod. You must move into a position where the SAM radar lock can be broken. This way you can turn the pod off again. There is one major drawback when using ECM. You call attention to yourself electronically. ECM generates strong signals that cause havoc with the guiding radar of the incoming SAM, but the same signals let enemy aircraft know where you are. Always turn off your ECM when there is no radar lock on your aircraft. Figure 4-23 shows one possible scenario of using the ECM pod.

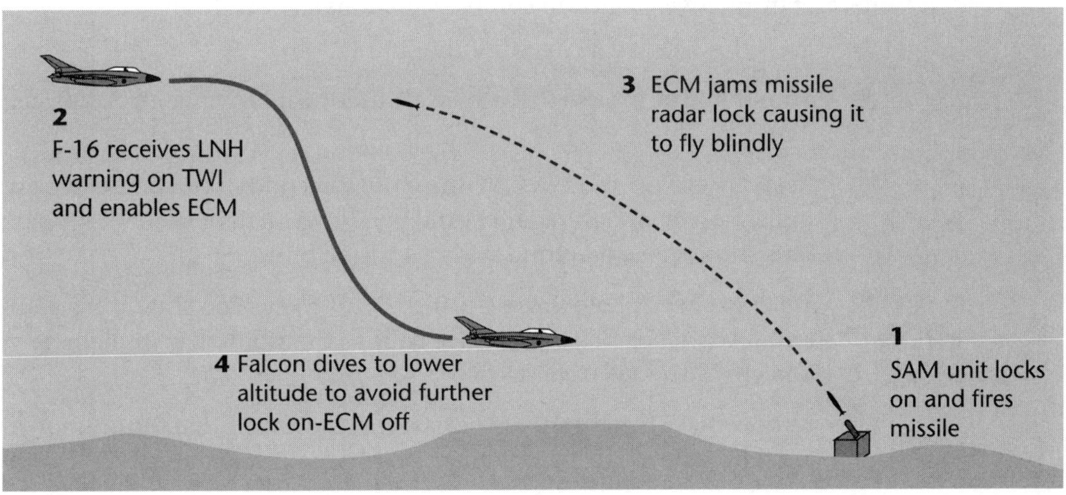

Figure 4-23 Using the ECM Pod to Avoid an Incoming SAM

What you do after breaking a SAM radar lock depends on the goal of your mission. You may simply fly out of the range of the SAM site and tend to your other duties, or you may have orders to destroy the SAM units using anti-radiation missiles. Whatever the goal, you do not want to loiter around SAM sites or keep your ECM pod running.

Your goal in this training mission is simple to state and difficult to achieve. You allow a SAM site to lock on to the F-16 and fire off a missile. You jam the missile (break the radar lock) with the ECM pod and escape from the area. If you feel your piloting skills are above average, you can fly at a very low altitude and sneak up close to get a look at the SAM site.

Taking On the AA-2 Atoll

In the first part of this lesson, you attempt to avoid an incoming infrared missile, the Atoll. Go to Red Flag Control and load the AVOID1 mission. Click on F-16 PILOTS, then F-16 ARMAMENT, and then TAKEOFF. Press the P key to pause the simulation as soon as the cockpit appears. You may want to read through the following steps before attempting this mission.

In addition to the normal flight and view keys, you will also be pressing the INS key to release flares. Use the index, middle, and ring fingers to control the movement of the F-16. Use your thumb to release the flares. You can also use your little finger to adjust your speed if necessary. Using this hand position minimizes hand movement. With practice, you will also be able to react instinctively when in combat situations such as this one.

- Press the P key to unpause the simulation.
- You should be in level flight at an altitude of approximately 8,000 feet AGL.
- Keep an eye on the TWI. Within a few seconds you should see an indication of aircraft radar behind you (lower half of the TWI scope). This should be a diamond with a 1 inside of it.
- Quickly check padlock view using the * key. You should have an unknown at six o'clock! Change back to the front view immediately and check the TWI again.
- By now the LCK light should be flashing, indicating that the unknown aircraft has you locked on radar. Do not make any moves yet! Don't panic.
- Shortly after the LCK light, the LNH will follow. The audible tone changes to reflect this. The missile is on its way.
- A few seconds after the launch, bank 90° to the left, pull hard on the stick, and drop some flares by pressing the INS key.
- Hold your turn at least until your heading passes 270° (at least a 90° turn). This should get the hot tail away from the incoming missile. If you have a properly timed flare drop, you should avoid the incoming Atoll.

- At this point, one of two things should have happened. The LCK and LNH lights went out signaling that you have successfully avoided the missile, or the caution light is on and you are hurtling towards the ground. You can press CTRL-E-E-E to eject if the missile strikes.

- Press ESC to bring up the menu bar. Select END MISSION from the FILE menu, then click on NEXT MISSION to return you to Red Flag Control.

It may take a few attempts to successfully shake the lock of the Atoll. If you can't seem to shake the missile, make sure you are dropping flares (not chaff) and try dropping your airspeed a little before starting your bank. Also, do not drop the flare too early and then wait. The missile may pass the flare and continue to lock on your F-16.

Flares are unlimited in the INTERMEDIATE skill level setting. You can limit the amount of flares to thirty per mission by increasing the skill level or turning on the LIMITED CHAFF/FLARES at the Difficulty Levels screen. Refer to Chapter 2, *Introduction to Falcon 3,* for setting difficulty levels.

Try this lesson until you feel comfortable that you can beat an incoming Atoll regularly. You won't be able to beat them all, but you should be able to beat most of them. Try avoiding the missile by other maneuvers. Remember that it is best to turn the tail of your F-16 away from the missile and the enemy aircraft to break the radar lock.

Avoiding the AA-7 Apex In the second part of this lesson, you attempt to avoid an incoming radar-guided missile, the Apex. Go to Red Flag Control and load the AVOID2 mission. Click on F-16 PILOTS, then F-16 ARMAMENT, and then TAKEOFF. Press the P key to pause the simulation as soon as the cockpit view appears. Once again, reading through the following information before attempting this mission increases your chances of success.

Since the Apex is a radar-guided missile, you want to drop chaff instead of flares. Chaff is released by pressing the DEL key (preferably on the numeric keypad). You use the same method of losing the missile as the previous mission. Wait for the missile launch, wait a moment longer, bank hard and pull, and drop chaff. The plane that is trying to take you down is a MiG-29.

- Press the P key to unpause the simulation.

- You should be in level flight at an altitude of approximately 8,000 feet AGL.

- Keep an eye on the TWI. Within a few seconds you should see an indication of aircraft radar behind you (lower half of the TWI scope). This should be a diamond with a 1 inside of it. This is the MiG-29.
- If the missile has not been fired yet, check padlock view. You should have an unknown on your six (of course we know it is that nasty MiG-29!) Change back to the front view immediately and check the TWI again.
- By now the LCK light should be flashing, indicating that the unknown aircraft has you locked on radar. The important thing is to stay calm and wait for the missile launch. Keep in mind that in actual combat, you would not set yourself up as target practice for a MiG!
- Shortly after the LCK light, the LNH follows. The audible tone changes to reflect this. The Apex is on its way. You may want to try the track view (the 9 key on the upper row).
- A few seconds after the launch, bank 90° to the left, pull hard on the stick, and drop a chaff cartage by pressing the DEL key.
- As with the flare drop, you want to turn the F-16 at least 90° before letting off the stick, then drop the chaff. Do not turn all the way around and face the enemy while the Apex is on its way! You may take it right in the cockpit!
- If you duped the Apex into going for the chaff instead of your F-16, the LNH light goes out. If you have broken the radar lock, the LCK light goes out.
- The MiG-29 may not give up so easily though. You may receive another enemy lock on. If this occurs, start the process again. After two tries with the Apex, the MiG should give up and go home.
- Press ESC to bring up the menu bar. Select END MISSION from the FILE menu, then click on NEXT MISSION to return to Red Flag Control.

Avoiding the Apex missile is slightly more difficult than avoiding the Atoll. The Apex can be fired at you from virtually any angle; the Atoll *required* the MiG to fire from the rear of your F-16. The key is to try to maintain an angle from the attack and drop the chaff as the missile nears. The track view may help visualize this action as it occurs. Do not continue to fly straight and level when the missile is inbound; this helps the Apex tremendously.

Chaff is unlimited in the INTERMEDIATE skill level setting. You can limit the amount of chaff drops to thirty per mission by increasing the skill level or turning on the LIMITED CHAFF/FLARES at the Difficulty Levels screen. Refer to Chapter 2, *Introduction to Falcon 3,* for setting difficulty levels.

Try the AVOID2 mission several times. Try to get your success rate above 50% before moving on to SAMs. Your practice will pay off when you are in a tough dogfight over Kuwait!

Confusing the SAMs One of your most deadly adversaries in Falcon 3.0 is the surface-to-air missile or SAM. SAMs are more difficult to avoid and require your immediate attention and time once you spot one on the TWI. Active SAM sites will show up as a square on the TWI with a number 1 or 2 in the center of it. The 1 indicates a SA-6 Gainful, while the 2 indicates the SA-8 Gecko. You're up against the tougher of the two in this mission, the Gainful.

Chaff is not nearly as effective against radar-guided SAMs as it was against the Apex. There are times when chaff and some violent maneuvering are your only hope! The top choice for evading and confusing the SAMs is the ALQ-131 ECM pod. The pod generates a strong signal that disrupts the guidance of an incoming SAM. It can also cause the SAM operator to lose the lock on your aircraft completely. There is a downside to the ECM pod. If you leave it on, enemy aircraft in the area will have no problem finding such a noisy target. You could end up with unwanted company in a hurry! The rule of thumb is turn off the pod when you have evaded the missiles or broken the SAM radar lock.

ECM pods must be loaded before a mission begins. The pod has already been loaded for this training flight.

Turning on the pod is very simple. Just press the E key. A light on the right side of the cockpit view indicates that the ECM pod is on. This lesson consists of a SAM site with no enemy aircraft. Get in the habit of turning the pod off when not in use, even though you do not have to worry about attracting enemy aircraft attention in this mission.

Go to Red Flag Control and load the AVOID3 mission. Click on F-16 PILOTS, then click F-16 ARMAMENT. Note that the ECM pod is mounted under your F-16 on the graphic display. Click on TAKEOFF and you are on your way. Read the following steps and pause the simulation when you need to during this mission.

- You start the mission flying south at an altitude of about 5,000 feet. Maintain the 180° heading.

- After a minute or so, you start to get a reading on the TWI. This is a square with a 1 inside it (CW radar SA-6).
- As you proceed south, the LCK light comes on when the SAM operator has locked on your F-16. An audible warning sounds. Don't make any moves yet.
- Shortly after the lock on the missile is launched. The alarm changes tone and the LNH light comes on. This time will vary from mission to mission. You may be able to catch a launch using the track view (the 9 key) and rotating the view with F3 or F4. Figure 4-24 shows SAMs being launched.

Figure 4-24 Surface-to-Air Missile Launch

- Turn on your ECM pod by pressing the E key, and start an evasive maneuver. For example, dive for a low altitude. You may want to attempt an inverted dive to prevent having to take on negative Gs.
- If the LNH light goes out, the missile has lost its lock. If the LCK light also goes out, the SAM operator has also lost track of you (temporarily). If the missile hits you, eject and restart the mission.
- If you have safely avoided the missile, turn off the ECM by pressing the E key again. Climb up to a higher altitude and let the SAM operator get another lock on your F-16.
- As soon as the LCK light comes on, turn on ECM and bank hard. You may be able to break the lock before a missile is launched. If they can't get a lock, they can't fire a SAM!
- Continue to make and break locks as many times as you can. If you cannot get a lock, you may have flown out of the range of the SAM. If this occurs, or you are shot down, start the mission over.

Press (ESC) to bring up the menu bar and select END MISSION from the file menu. Click on NEXT MISSION to return to Red Flag Control.

You can see how difficult it can be to avoid the SA-6. If you fly a mission without an ECM pod, getting close to any SAM site is very dangerous. You can try dropping chaff and flying in an erratic manner to lose the incoming missile, but this is easier said that done! When you are in campaign mode, you will be assigned missions that will take you over enemy SAM and AAA sites. You must either plan your mission carefully to avoid these enemy ground forces, carry an ECM pod, or both.

Fly the AVOID3 lesson several times to practice avoiding the missiles and breaking the lock of the enemy SAM units. If you fly low and dodge a few SAMs, you may even be able to fly up to the launch site!

Debriefing: Avoidance Tactics Facing enemy fire becomes commonplace during a Falcon 3.0 campaign. You must prepare yourself to take on enemies ranging from aircraft loaded with heat-seeking missiles to ground forces laden with accurate radar-guided SAMs. Knowing how to escape the incoming projectiles and turn the tables on the enemy is a requirement in winning any battle.

This lesson introduced three things you can use to avoid or confuse enemy missiles: flares, chaff, and the ECM pod. Flares are used against infrared or heat seeking missiles. They act as a heat decoy, diverting the missile's attention from the hot exhaust of your aircraft. The enemy has two types of infrared missiles. The Atoll is a rear-aspect missile that is only effective when fired directly at the rear of your F-16. The Magic is an all-aspect missile capable of scoring a hit from virtually any angle around the aircraft.

Chaff is used against radar-guided missiles. The chaff cartridge consists of a bundle of metal strips that burst into a small cloud when dropped. The incoming missile gets many reflections from the chaff cloud, luring the missile into the chaff instead of your aircraft. The enemy air-to-air radar guided weapon is the Apex. Generally, radar-guided missiles can be fired from a greater range and reach higher speeds. Both chaff and flare drops require timing and maneuvering to successfully shake the missile. Continuing to fly straight usually results in your destruction.

The electronic countermeasures (ECM) pod is used to break the radar lock of surface-to-air missiles (SAM). The pod transmits an electronic signal that interferes with the guidance system of the SAM. Like all missiles, the enemy must lock on to your aircraft first before firing the missile. If you can break the lock by jamming it with ECM, you can keep the missiles on the ground. If the SAM is launched, you still have time to use the pod to distract the missile. As when using chaff and flares, you usually need to maneuver the aircraft in addition to the ECM to shake the missile. The disadvantage to using the ECM pod is the attention you get from enemy aircraft in the area. Always turn off the pod if you are not locked by the SAM unit or an incoming missile.

Radar Lesson #6: Ground Map Radar

Up to this point you have been concerned with enemy aircraft and missiles. Many campaign missions in Falcon 3.0 require you to seek out targets on the ground and destroy them. You always receive a briefing before the mission with instructions on which targets to take out along with a map showing the *approximate* location of the target. The location is based on intelligence information that has been gathered by the allied forces.

How do you find the target once you are over enemy lines? Waypoints are set in the F-16 computer that guide you to the target. But the waypoint setting is entirely dependent on the intelligence data. Sometimes you need additional assistance to find your primary target. That is where ground map radar comes in.

Ground map radar mode displays ground targets on the REO for a range of twenty miles. It also lets you zoom in on a target while you are still several miles out. You often need to see ground targets from a distance to get in the proper alignment for a bombing run. For example, if your primary target is to take out a bridge, you will want to approach the target from end to end. This gives you more margin for error when you drop your load. If you drop a little early or a little late, you will still have a fair chance at accomplishing your mission. The primary target is marked by crosshairs on the ground map.

In addition to ground targets, the ground map radar also shows rivers and roads. This feature can be turned on and off. Rivers and roads are useful as landmarks when navigating. Studying maps before the mission helps in using these landmarks.

There is one drawback to using the GM mode. The REO can only be used for one thing at a time. Therefore, you cannot track enemy aircraft and look at the ground map at the same time. If you plan your missions right, you have additional flights of aircraft to take care of the enemy in the air, while you take care of business on the ground.

This mission does not have enemy aircraft. It is best to fly this mission on autopilot, at least for the first time through. Concentrate on using the ground map radar controls. Let's see what's in store for this mission.

Lesson Objectives In this lesson you:

- Learn the keys of the ground map radar.
- Track ground targets using the GM mode.
- Zoom in to verify particular ground targets (rail yard, nuclear plant, etc.).

Ground School The ground mode is fairly simple to use with no enemies to bother you. When no enemy is present, you have the time to casually switch between the different modes, switch views, zoom in, zoom out, and so on. However, when you are called on to switch to GM mode behind enemy lines, things can get a bit hectic. Use this lesson to get familiar with the keys that are new to the ground map radar.

You can access the ground map radar by pressing the F7 key while in the main cockpit view. The REO will change to a ground display similar to Figure 4-25. Rivers are represented by green lines and roads are shown as dim green lines. The rivers and roads display can be disabled by pressing the Y key. The *zoom box* defaults to the center of the REO when GM is first accessed. The zoom box represents the amount of the REO that will be displayed if you press the *zoom in* key. F1 zooms in and F2 zooms out. The zoom factor can be set to 1X, 2X, 4X, 8X, or 16X. This box can be shifted to any of nine positions by holding the SHIFT key and pressing any arrow key. For example, you could move the zoom to the upper left position by pressing SHIFT-↑, then SHIFT-←.

Targets are displayed on the REO as bright dots. You can position the zoom box over the target and zoom in to get a close up of the target. Each type of target (rail yard, factory, etc.) has a unique appearance on the REO. You will see examples of this as we fly the final mission of this chapter.

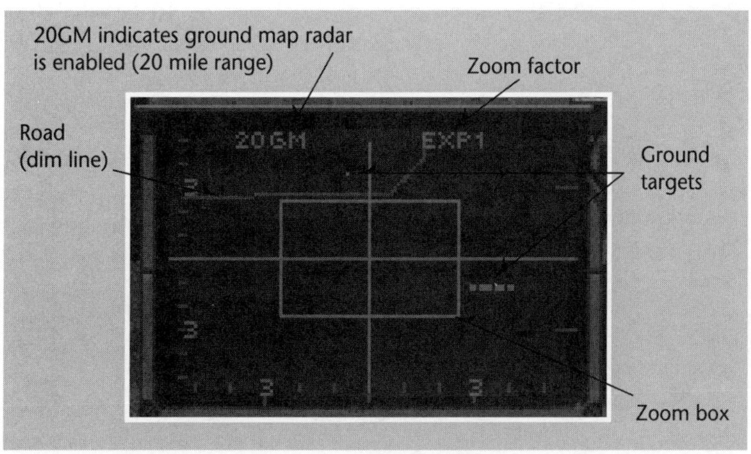

Figure 4-25 REO Display of Ground Map Radar

Zeroing in on Ground Targets The primary purpose of the ground mode radar is to zero in on ground targets. The waypoints for this mission have been set to guide you to four large ground targets. This frees your hands to learn the keys used with GM. The autopilot guides the F-16 low and slow. This gives you extra time to zoom in on targets and also to catch some out-of-cockpit views along the way.

Go to Red Flag Control and load the GMRADAR mission. Click on F-16 PILOTS, then F-16 ARMAMENT, and then TAKEOFF. Engage the autopilot as soon as the cockpit view appears by pressing the (A) key. You should be flying level at approximately 2,000 feet with an airspeed of 300 knots. You may want to pause between steps; some of the targets pass by quickly.

- Switch to ground mode by pressing the (F7) key. The REO should change to the GM mode. This is a top-down view. Your location on the map is at the bottom center.

- The first target is actually hidden by the vertical line on the REO. You are getting close to it, however. Check the distance to waypoint. It should read less that ten miles to waypoint 1.

- Hold down the (SHIFT) key and press the (↓) to move the zoom box to the lower center position. This moves the zoom region closer to the F-16 position.

- Press (F1) once. The zoom factor changes to EXP2. This indicates a magnification factor of two. Everything that was in the zoom box at EXP1 is blown up to the full size of the REO. The target should be visible as a tiny dot.

- Press (F1) three more times to zoom in to EXP16. The target is now shown as a small square. Figure 4-26 shows how the REO should look.

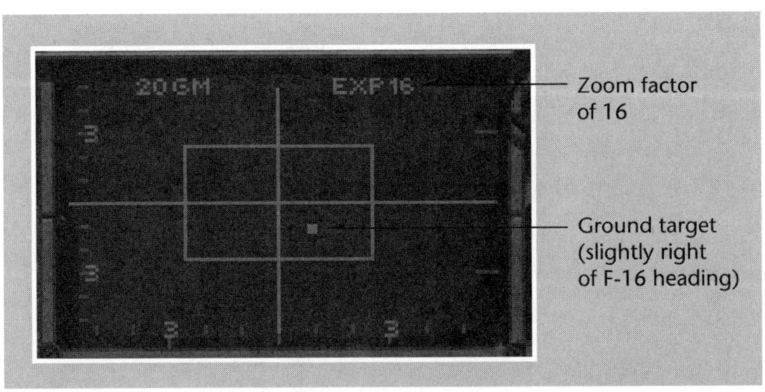

Figure 4-26 Ground Mode Zoomed to a Factor of 16 (EXP16)

- Note that the target is to the right of the vertical centerline of the REO. This indicates that the target is to the right of your current heading. Look out at the ground and try to spot the target. As you get closer (within 2 miles to waypoint 1), you should make out the target as a rail yard.

- Switch to track view (the 9 key) and watch as your F-16 passes over the first target. The autopilot banks to a heading of 305°, towards waypoint 2.

You have some time to experiment with the ground map keys on the way to the next target. Try moving the zoom box around to the nine possible positions and zoom in on any targets you may see along the way. Keep an eye on the distance-to-waypoint indicator. When it reaches 20D2, continue on with the lesson. Make sure the GM zoom factor is EXP1 before continuing.

- When you are 16 to 18 miles from waypoint 2, you should start to see some targets appear at the top of the screen. Let's investigate these targets from this long range.

- Press SHIFT-↑ to move the zoom box over the targets, then press F1 to zoom. Repeat this process until you are at a zoom factor of EXP8. These are generic targets.

- The targets should move from the top to the bottom of the REO as you get closer. Keep an eye on the waypoint.

- Switch to an out-of-cockpit view to check out the targets when you are within two or three miles of waypoint 2. Figure 4-27 shows the comparison of the zoomed GM display and the actual targets.

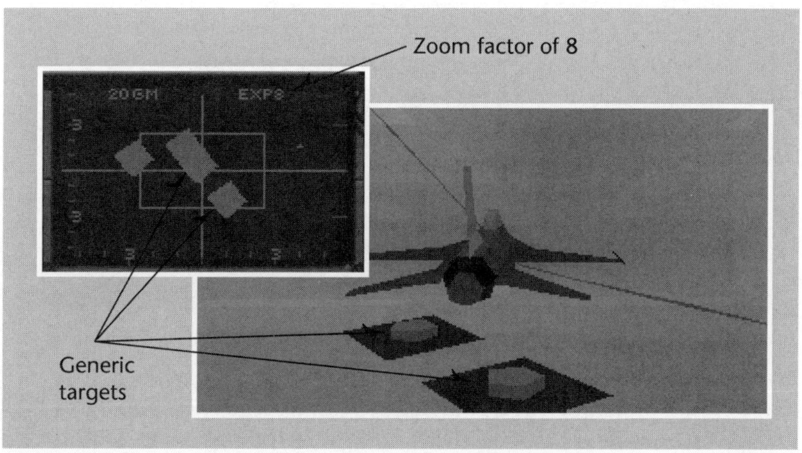

Figure 4-27 GM Display and Actual Generic Targets

- The autopilot banks the F-16 to a heading of 220°. You are on your way to waypoint 3 and our third target.

You can use the time between waypoints to check out more of the GM functions or you can advance to the next target by using accelerated mode ((SHIFT)-(TAB)). If you accelerate the mission, be sure to cancel the acceleration mode ((TAB)) *before* you are within twenty miles of waypoint 3.

- When you are 16 to 18 miles from waypoint 3, you start to see a new target appear at the top of the REO. It appears that a circle is drawn around the target. This is actually a road that surrounds the target which appears on the REO as a dim green line.
- Position the zoom box as you approach the target. Try various zoom settings on the target.
- Switch to track view when you are within visual range of the target. Two huge towers mark the location of a nuclear plant.
- The autopilot banks the F-16 to a heading of 315°. You are on your way to the final target. Accelerate to 20D4 if you want to speed up the mission.
- The last target appears at the top of the REO. Shift the zoom box up and zoom in to see the target. You should be able to make out three distinct targets. These are industrial targets (factories). Figure 4-28 shows another comparison of GM REO to actual target.
- Continue to fly towards the target. Switch to track view and watch the F-16 fly over the three factories.

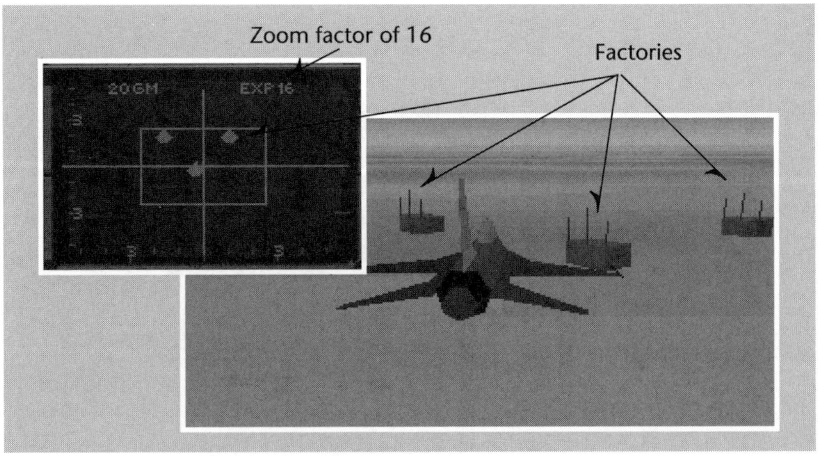

Figure 4-28 Factories on the REO and Rotated Track View

- This is the end of the flight. Bring up the menu bar by pressing ESC and select END MISSION from the FILE menu. Click on NEXT MISSION to return to Red Flag Control.

If you need further practice using the ground map radar, try flying the mission again without using the autopilot. This exercises your ability to control the plane and manage the radar at the same time.

Debriefing: Ground Map Radar The ground map radar lets you display ground targets on the REO at a maximum range of twenty miles. This information is useful in locating targets and lining them up for a bomb drop or air-to-ground missile strike. Waypoints can get you near the target, but the GM radar helps you zero in on a specific target. This is something that becomes necessary in campaign mode.

The GM radar introduced the use of some new keys in the lesson. It is important to be familiar enough with the operation to allow you to make quick changes during flight. Normally, the ground map mode is used behind enemy lines, where you may be attacked at any time. This is no place to fly around and play with the radar controls. Lingering around a potential target surely brings about unwanted company. Be sure you can operate the radar at an instinctive level. When on a ground attack, you will need to fly in, find your target, drop your ordnance, and get out!

Summary

Now that you have completed the lessons in this chapter, you should have the basic understanding of radar needed to survive longer and succeed in finding the enemy (and avoiding them when you need to). You learned that radar is a vital part of locating and tracking enemies in Falcon 3.0. Unfortunately, the enemy has radar capabilities also. You must be aware of this every time you climb into the cockpit to start a mission.

Radar is an acronym for radio detection and ranging. It works on the theory that radio-frequency energy travels at a constant rate (the speed of light). By transmitting a powerful pulse, then *listening* for a return (echo) with a receiver, the radar is able to time the echo which establishes the distance or range to a target. The longer the time between transmit and receive, the farther away the target is. Radar is used in many applications, from maintaining air traffic around an airport or an air base to missile guidance systems.

Although ground radar is important, the understanding of aircraft radar is essential in Falcon 3.0. The F-16 is equipped with the APG-66 pulse-Doppler radar. This is considered a medium capability radar with a relatively low cost. It has an 80 mile range and is forward facing. The pulse-Doppler radar has a slight drawback in that it sometimes loses targets that appear stationary. You will see this effect in particular on the HUD when we introduce the air-to-air weapons in Chapter 5, *Using Weapons.*

Falcon 3.0 supplies three versions of the APG-66. The Situation Awareness Display (SAD) is the easiest and least realistic form of radar. You can track altitude color-coded targets for 360° around your aircraft. In addition, the SAD mode displays targets with small *tails* that help determine the direction of the target. The only drawback to the SAD mode is that the maximum range is cut in half (40 miles). The Situation Awareness Mode (SAM) increases the realism factor, while increasing the range to eighty miles. You are responsible for locking an individual target and checking the altitude, heading, and airspeed figures to determine the intentions of an aircraft. The range of the radar is controlled automatically. The third mode, High-Fidelity Radar (HFR), is beyond the scope of this introduction to Falcon radar. Chapter 10, *The Campaigns: Tactics and Military Doctrine,* is dedicated to the subject of HFR operation.

You have the ability, independent of radar mode, to check aircraft for friendly/enemy status as long as a target is displayed on the radar and is in front of our F-16. You use the Identification Friend or Foe (IFF) feature to do this. By locking a target on radar, and pressing the N key, you can send an encoded message to an electronic box in the locked aircraft. If the response from the aircraft is correct, a tone sounds and the light on the left cockpit view comes on for a few seconds. Since only friendly aircraft have the capability of responding to the message correctly, you can determine the status of the aircraft. If there is no tone, it must be an enemy!

Once a target is in visible range, the padlock view can be used to maintain sight. You will find this view invaluable in a dogfight. The view is used to overcome shortcomings of the personal computer display, which is normally limited to a small viewing area. The padlock view simulates the pilots ability to turn his head virtually 360° to track a target.

The Threat Warning Indicator (TWI) is a passive device that displays radar activity happening around you. It is located on the left side of the cockpit control panel. The TWI consists of a round scope and two warning lights. The scope displays radar activity for a thirty mile radius. It is able to differentiate between types of radar. Aircraft radar is displayed as a diamond with a number in it. The number indicates the type of radar (CW, pulse-

Doppler, early warning, etc.) the aircraft is using. Ground radar is shown as a square with a number in it. There are only two ground radar types: CW and pulse-Doppler. The LCK (lock) light lets you know that an enemy aircraft radar has locked onto your F-16. The LNH (launch) light lets you know the missiles are on the way and to take evasive action.

After getting the basics down, you performed six lessons to exercise your radar usage and enemy radar avoidance technique. The following is a summary of those lessons:

- Lesson 1: The Padlock View and IFF—You used the padlock view to lock and track a target that was in visual range. You also learned to use the IFF feature to check the friendly status of an aircraft at long range.

- Lesson 2: The SAD Radar Mode—You were introduced to the Situation Awareness Display mode. You flew a short training mission and locked aircraft as they came into view on the REO. You tracked the aircraft and obtained information on altitude, heading, and airspeed.

- Lesson 3: The SAM Radar Mode—After changing the radar mode at the Falcon 3.0 Difficulty Settings screen, you journeyed out once again. You compared the SAM mode against the SAD mode. SAM mode required locking up targets individually to check their altitude, heading, and airspeed data.

- Lesson 4: The Threat Warning Indicator (TWI)—You were back in the air with hostile aircraft. The purpose of this lesson was to observe the enemy aircraft and ground radar on the TWI. You also looked at the LCK and LNH lights as the ground SAM units went into action.

- Lesson 5: Avoidance Tactics—This lesson provided an introduction to the avoidance and distraction techniques against enemy weapons. You learned about the use of chaff and flares to confuse enemy radar and infrared guided missiles. You also mounted an ALQ-131 ECM pod onto the F-16 and set out to confuse the enemy surface-to-air missiles.

- Lesson 6: Ground Map Radar—Your final lesson took a close look at the ground map radar. You flew a mission and used the zoom feature to identify ground targets from as much as fifteen to twenty miles away.

If you have problems with any radar related activity in the campaigns, refer back to these lessons to brush up on your skills. Proper use of the F-16 radar and the effective ability to avoid enemy attack are musts when it comes to success with Falcon 3.0. There are plenty of activities to attend to when flying a Falcon 3.0 mission, controlling the radar is yet another function you must master.

Exercises

1. Load and fly the TARGETS mission. This mission is filled with activity. No enemy aircraft are equipped with weapons. Follow the waypoints and query all incoming targets with IFF. Obtain as many visual IDs as possible during your journey.
2. Load and fly the AVOID4 mission. This is a very difficult mission that has you flying alone through enemy lines. You are equipped with chaff, flares, and an ECM pod. Try to get to waypoint 3 without getting shot down. This is a real tough one!
3. Load and fly the GMSEARCH mission. Just follow the waypoints and try to find as many ground targets as you can. You have permission from the squadron commander to venture away from the waypoint paths if you find a ground target off the mission route. Just turn back to following the waypoints after investigating the targets. This mission has six waypoints.

5

Using Weapons

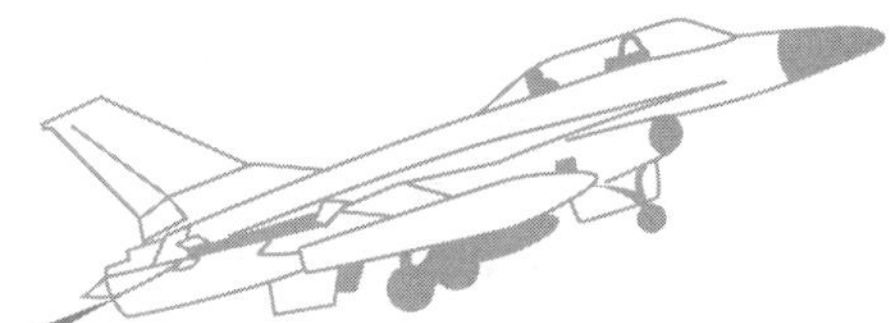

You have already had to face enemy aircraft with weapons and ground units with powerful missiles. Up to this point you have not retaliated for the enemy attacks. The time has come to strike back! This chapter covers the many weapons available to you in Falcon 3.0. We discuss every weapon and provide a lesson on each one to give you valuable practical experience delivering them.

The F-16 Falcon is a very versatile aircraft when it comes to weaponry. You can use the Falcon in a multitude of mission applications, all based on configuration of the armament. This aircraft has the capability and especially the maneuverability to engage in successful air-to-air engagements. Returning to base after an intercept mission, you could load the Falcon with iron bombs to take out a large factory or hardened aircraft shelter.

The theory in this chapter is presented in two segments: air-to-air and air-to-ground weaponry. The air-to-air segment introduces some basic fighting maneuvers (BFM) you use to locate and engage enemy aircraft. We lay the ground work for successful air combat in the lessons that follow. The air-to-ground segment shows the various methods used in delivering the many stores that can be loaded onto your Falcon. Since you can load the F-16 with such a wide variety of air-to-ground missiles and bombs, several different techniques are required.

It is essential to gain proficiency in using every weapon in Falcon 3.0. This chapter provides the theory, training, and the missions needed to help you achieve success. Let's take a look at the air-to-air ordnance of the Falcon.

Air-to-Air Weaponry

The air-to-air weapons of the F-16 consist of a gun and three different missile types. Which weapon you use depends on the individual situation. A limited number of missiles can be loaded on the F-16 at any one time. Also, missiles are limited in campaign mode to simulate real battlefield conditions where weapons are not an infinite resource.

M61A1 Cannon

The gun, an M61A1 20mm Gatling cannon, is used in close range dogfights. The range of the gun is approximately one mile. The HUD displays a *historical gunsight* when you select the cannon. This gunsight shows you where the 20mm shells would have hit if they had been fired one or two seconds before. This requires you to anticipate where the target will be in the future and act accordingly. The gun is the weapon of choice when you are in very close range to the enemy or you have exhausted your air-to-air missiles for the mission.

The AIM-9P Sidewinder

The missile you usually find to be the most plentiful in a campaign is the AIM-9P Sidewinder. This is the least expensive of the missiles in Falcon 3.0; therefore, you normally do not have a problem with availability. The AIM-9P is a *rear-aspect,* infrared missile capable of locking on the target at a range of one to five miles. The specifications list ten miles as the range of this Sidewinder; however, it is usually not possible to obtain a solid lock on at this range. As with the enemy AA-2 Atoll, you must provide a clear unobstructed path to the exhaust of the enemy aircraft. Figure 5-1 shows the successful *envelope* for the AIM-9P. The envelope is a description of all positions at which you can fire the weapon with a high rate of success. Firing outside of the envelope usually results in a wasted shot. The farther the F-16 is from the target, the more of a range difference there can be between the target and the F-16. All of this results in a weapons envelope that is shaped like a cone extending from the rear of the intended target, with the smallest portion of the cone at the rear of the target. The weapons system generates a tone (missile growl) to let you know that you are in the correct position (inside the envelope) to fire the missile. You will hear these tones in Lessons 1 through 3.

Simply firing the weapon from the correct position does not guarantee a hit. Enemy aircraft are equipped with chaff, flares, and ECM pods to help

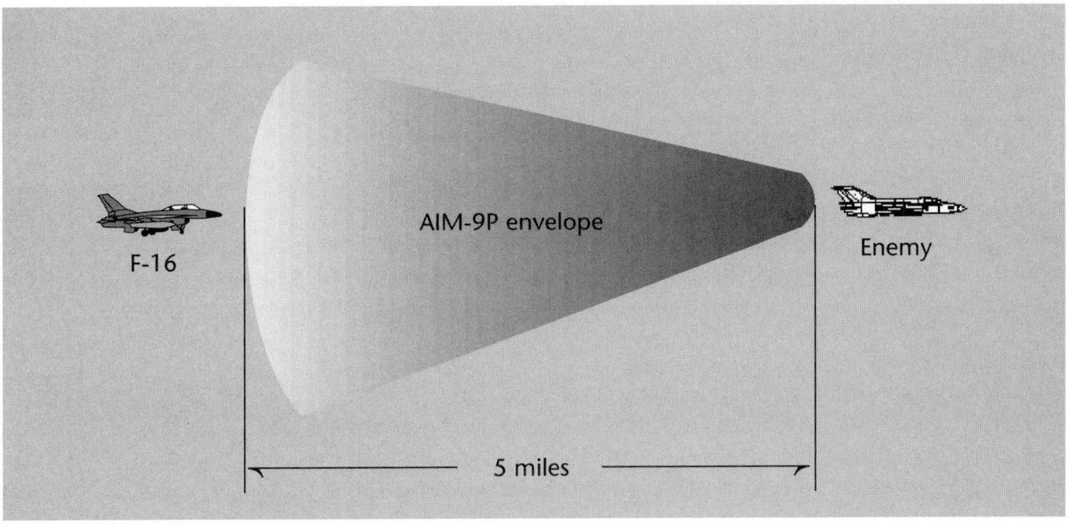

Figure 5-1 Weapons Envelope of the AIM-9P Sidewinder

fend off your attacks. Do not be surprised if the enemy drops a flare and performs evasive maneuvers causing your missile to run out of fuel and fall to the earth.

The AIM-9M Sidewinder

The AIM-9M Sidewinder is a step up in technology from the AIM-9P. This missile is more effective in that it is an *all-aspect* infrared missile. The sensors in the AIM-9M allow the missile to locate the heat source from any angle. It is comparable to the AA-8 Aphid. This allows you to fire the missile at an enemy target during a head-on pass, as well as other angles. Figure 5-2 shows the envelope of the all-aspect Sidewinder. The range of the AIM-9M is very similar to that of the AIM-9P (around five miles); however, you can fire the missile from virtually any angle around the enemy. The missile is not effective at very close range. The only drawback to the AIM-9M is that the supply may be limited during a campaign in comparison to the AIM-9P.

The countermeasure of choice for enemy aircraft is again the flare because the AIM-9M is an infrared missile. You may notice the enemy start to drop flares when you fire an infrared missile.

The AIM-120 AMRAAM

The AIM-120 AMRAAM (Advanced Medium Range Air-to-Air Missile) is a radar-guided, all-aspect missile. This type of missile lets you gain kills from

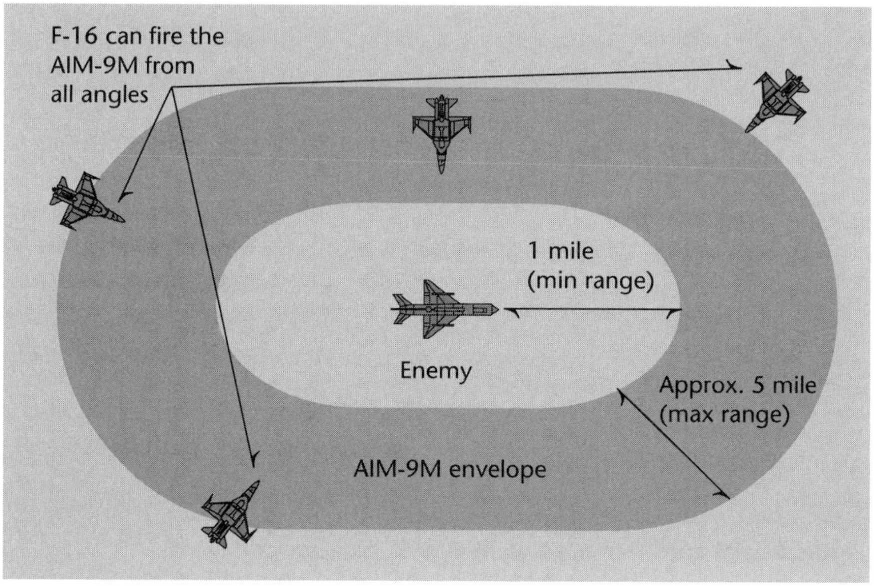

Figure 5-2 Weapons Envelope for the AIM-9M Sidewinder

beyond visual range (BVR). Specifications show the AIM-120 has a 25 mile range. However, you will find the lock-on range to be about 18–20 miles. This air-to-air missile is the hardest to come by in the campaign. This means you are responsible for managing the weapons supply. The weapons envelope for the AIM-120 is the same as the AIM-9M except for the longer range.

The enemy may counter the AMRAAM with chaff or an ECM pod because it is radar guided. AWACS reports ECM activity on the top of the Falcon 3.0 screen. This usually occurs when you lock on to the aircraft (before firing the missile).

Basic Fighting Maneuvers

You already learned some of the basic fighting maneuvers in Chapter 4, *Radar and Enemy Identification,* when you were required to avoid incoming enemy missiles. This is known as *defensive* maneuvering. Although knowing how to avoid the enemy advances is important, you also will be required to intercept and bring down hostile aircraft. Here are some of the fundamental moves to position your aircraft to fire and hit the enemy.

Aspect Angle One of the keys to gaining the proper position on the enemy is understanding the concept of *aspect angle.* The aspect angle is determined by drawing two lines. One line is drawn from the nose of your

F-16 forward, the other line is drawn from the tail of the enemy backwards. The intersection of these two line creates an angle; this is the aspect angle. Figure 5-3 shows two examples of the aspect angle. Note that the lower angles (less than 90°) mean that you are facing the rear of the enemy aircraft. Higher aspect angles (from 90° to 180°) mean you are facing the front of the enemy aircraft. An aspect angle of 0° indicates that you are directly on the enemy's tail while 180° indicates that you are flying head-on.

This is all great information, but how do you know what your aspect angle is in relation to a particular enemy? There is no time to get out the ruler and start drawing lines during a dogfight! You can get the aspect angle for any aircraft as long as you can lock him up on radar. The HUD and the REO do the rest of the calculation for you.

Using the HUD and REO to Find Aspect Angle What is the *desired* aspect angle? You will find out shortly that the answer to this question depends on whether or not you want to engage the enemy in the first place. Knowing the aspect angle of the aircraft and constantly monitoring the REO and HUD can prevent an unnecessary engagement. For example, if you are escorting bombers to a primary target, your mission is to protect the bombers along the way and shoot down any enemy that

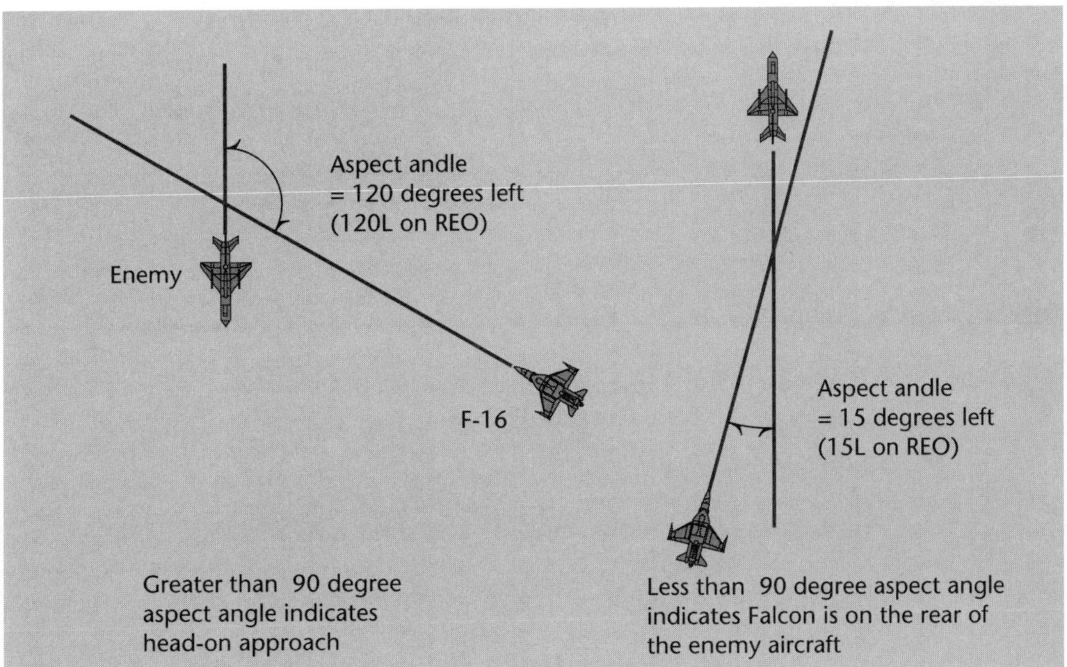

Figure 5-3 Aspect Angle

threatens the flight. The key word here is *threatens*. Just because a target appears at 40 miles out and IFF shows that it is the enemy doesn't mean you have to kick in the afterburner and go shoot him down. But, if you are monitoring the target and you notice that his airspeed is 600 knots with an aspect angle of 175°, there may be cause for alarm! The high aspect angle indicates that he is heading this way and with an airspeed of 600 knots, it won't be long before he gets here!

Let's take a look at what information the HUD and REO have to offer. Some of the information you have seen in earlier lessons. Now you will see just how valuable this information can be. For this example, we have selected a HUD view with the AIM-9P Sidewinder selected. Figure 5-4 shows the cockpit view. Information that is vital to air-to-air combat is called out.

There are many things to look at when in a dogfight situation. However, when you know where to look on the HUD or REO, it takes most of the confusion out of the process. Your attention and focus should always be on one thing in an air-to-air engagement, the enemy! Let's take a close look at Figure 5-4 and see what is taking place.

The lower left corner of the HUD displays the current mode. Currently the display indicates SRM (Short-Range Missile) mode. SRM appears for the AIM-9P and the AIM-9M. DGFT (Dogfight) appears when you select the Vulcan cannon, and MRM (Medium-Range Missile) appears when you choose the AIM-120.

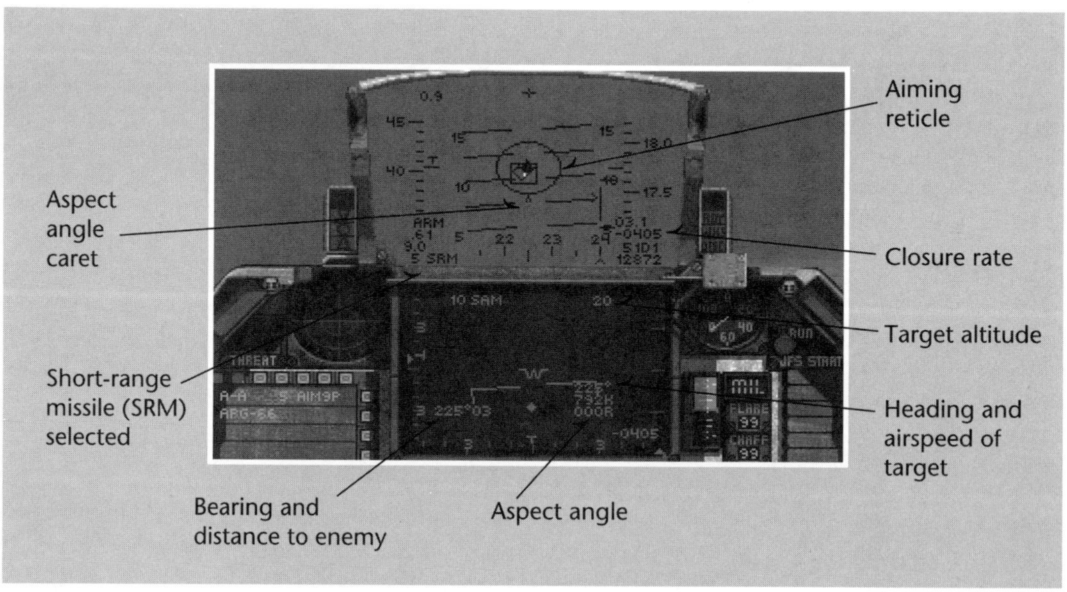

Figure 5-4 Cockpit View with AIM-9P Selected (Target Tracked)

This pilot has the enemy right where he wants him for an AIM-9P kill. The aspect angle can be found in two places in the cockpit. The REO displays the aspect angle in the lower right section, and the HUD displays the aspect angle graphically in the form of a caret. This caret points in at the edge of the *reticle* or aiming circle. If the target were heading directly for the F-16, the caret would be at the top of the reticle facing down. This target has an aspect angle of 0°. We are directly on the tail of the enemy; perfect conditions for a rear-aspect missile launch.

Another important indication on the HUD and the REO is closure rate. This is the enemy airspeed subtracted from the F-16 airspeed. Note that in the figure, the closure rate is negative (–0405). This indicates that the enemy is traveling away from the F-16 at a rate of 405 knots. The REO displays the enemy airspeed above the aspect angle. This example reads 792 knots for enemy airspeed. If the pilot does not fire the missile soon or accelerate, the enemy will be out of range and he will lose the lock. Figure 5-5 illustrates this scenario.

We will look into the HUD, REO, aspect angle, aiming reticle, and more when the lessons on air-to-air missiles begin. Let's look at the maneuvers that can gain desired positions on the enemy.

Head-On Approach There are at least three ways to attack on the head-on approach, depending on the loaded armament. Figure 5-6 shows three examples. The first is the beyond-visual-range kill. This can be accomplished only by the AIM-120 AMRAAM radar-guided missile. First the enemy aircraft is spotted and tracked on radar, then a radar lock is made on the target (about an 18 to 20 mile range for the AMRAAM). The F-16 pilot fires the long range missile as soon as the lock-on occurs. If the enemy aircraft does not have radar enabled, the incoming missile could be quite a surprise! The enemy aircraft may be able to spot the missile on the TWI and take evasive action (chaff or ECM).

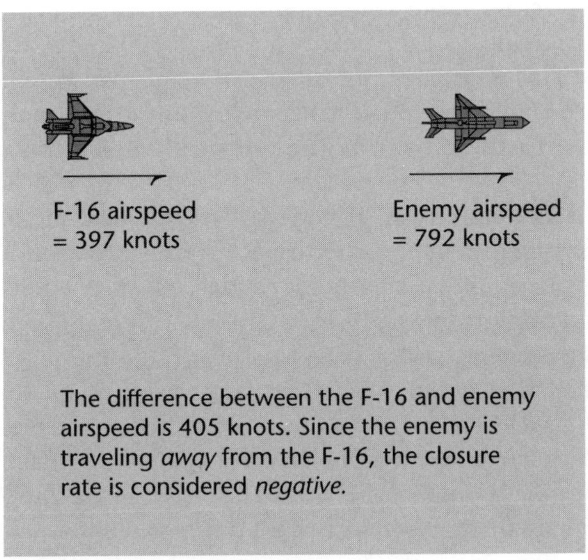

Figure 5-5 An Example of Closure Rate

The next scenario is one in which the AIM-9M can be deployed. As soon as the enemy is locked on (normally at five miles), the pilot fires the all-aspect missile. It is important to fire quickly

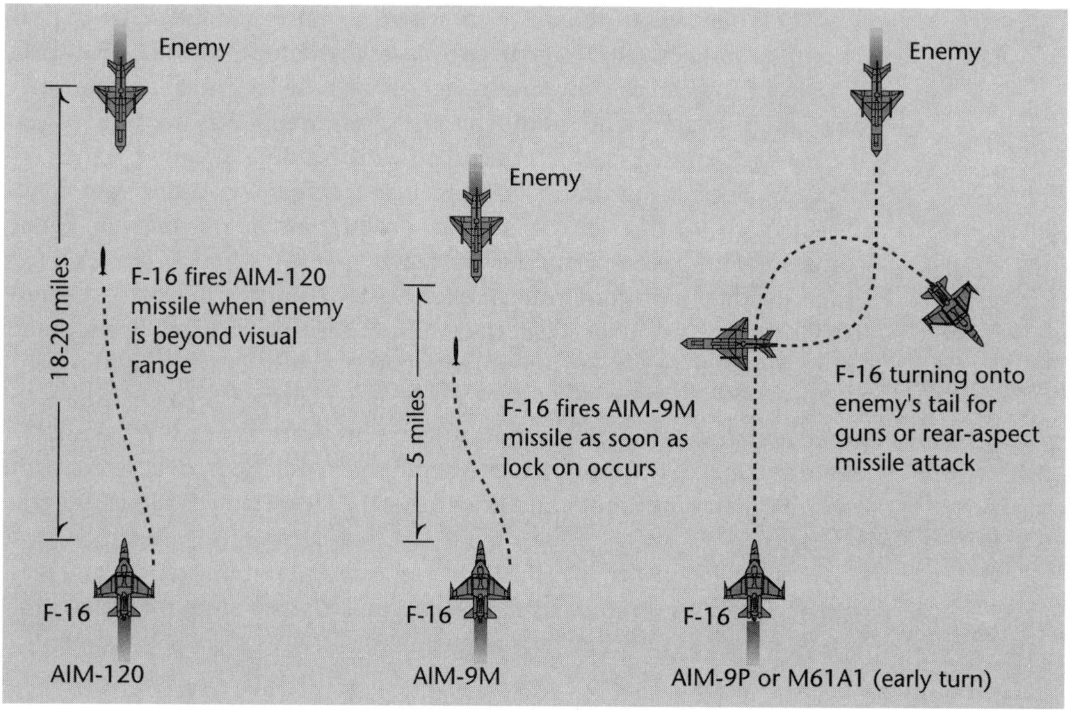

Figure 5-6 Three Head-On Engagement Scenarios

in a head-on engagement. Two supersonic aircraft flying directly at each other can create a very high closure rate. For example, if the airspeed of your F-16 is 475 knots and the airspeed of the enemy aircraft is 500 knots, the closure rate is 975 knots! This is faster than a quarter of a mile per second. If you do not fire the AIM-9M quickly, you soon may be inside the minimum effective range (too close to the target), resulting in the missile flying harmlessly into space.

The last scenario is the early turn. If you start a hard turn at the appropriate time, you will find the enemy turns to react to your move. What is the appropriate time? You can find that only by practice. If he is not quick on the draw you may find him in your sights for a guns kill or a rear-aspect missile. The skill level of the enemy pilot affects whether or not the enemy falls for this move. Recall that enemy skill level is determined by the configuration settings in the Difficulty Levels screen. The decision between guns and missile depends on range. Within one mile, try a guns kill. Outside of the one mile range, fire a Sidewinder (if you have one). If you are out of missiles, you better be talented with the guns or get out of the fight!

Getting the Enemy Off Your Tail (and Getting On His) You and your enemy have at least one thing in common during an air-to-air engagement: you both want the other to go down in flames! Since the best way to achieve that end is getting on the adversary's tail, it should not seem surprising that you will find the enemy on your tail from time to time. You need a method that turns the undesirable position into a desirable one. You have one great advantage over most of the enemy aircraft you face in Falcon 3.0: the F-16 Flying Falcon! The F-16 is known for its superior maneuverability. The aircraft design permits you to pull higher Gs for longer periods of time than other fighters. This means you can turn hard and tight, perhaps tighter than the craft you are up against.

Since your radar does not detect aircraft to the rear, it is best to use the padlock view to observe an enemy on your tail. It is a good idea to check the rear during a dogfight from time to time. For example, you decide to engage two enemy aircraft by yourself (not a good idea in the first place) and you have one target directly in front of the HUD ready for the kill. Where is the other enemy? He may be directly on your tail! Using the padlock view and pressing the target select key (the T key), you can check the location of the other enemy aircraft. It is sometimes better to concentrate on getting rid of an enemy on your tail even if you have his wingman lined up for the kill!

Figure 5-7 shows a maneuver you can use to get the enemy off your tail, and then turn the tables on the enemy pilot. This example is divided into

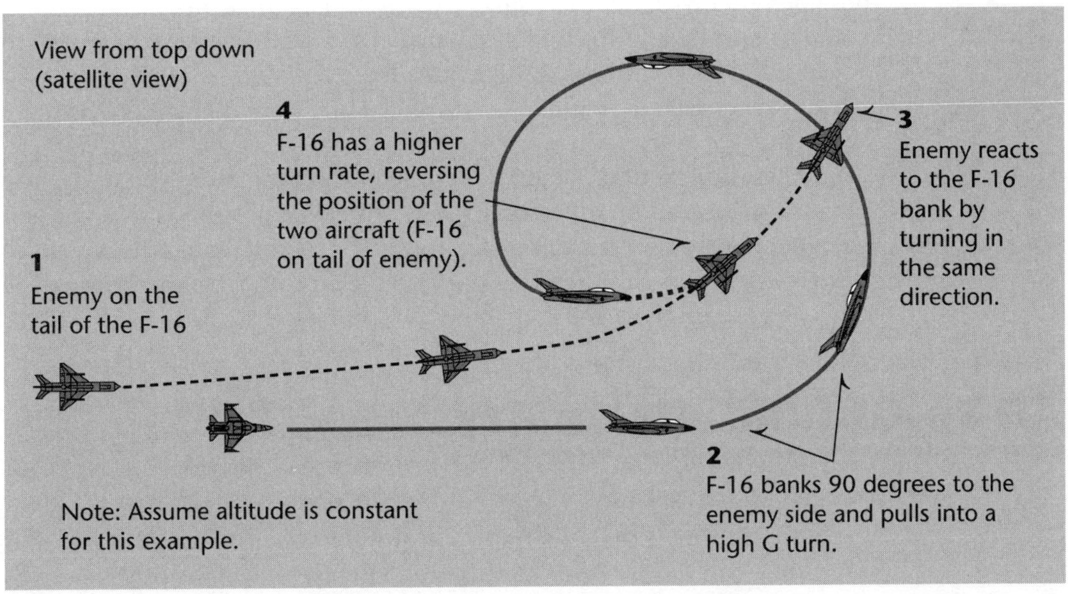

Figure 5-7 Maneuvering to Get a MiG Off Your Tail

four steps. In the first step, the enemy is on the tail of the F-16. You notice the enemy pilot over your left shoulder (you can use the padlock view in the lessons to observe the enemy). In the second step, you bank to the enemy (left) side and pull into a tight high-G turn. The enemy reacts by turning to follow the F-16 in the third step. The aircraft with the higher turn rate will ultimately win the battle of position. In the fourth step, the F-16 has turned farther and faster producing the desired result; you are now on the tail of the enemy.

There are other factors to consider when making this type of maneuver. You may come up against an enemy pilot with an aircraft that is capable of turning faster than your F-16. No matter how fast you turn, you just can't seem to shake the enemy off your tail. You can attempt to take the battle off the horizontal plane by diving or climbing or by varying your airspeed during the maneuver. In the lesson on G forces in Chapter 3, *Learning to Fly,* you learned that airspeed affects the turning radius of the aircraft. If your airspeed is 650 knots you will not be able to attain tight turns (although it will be easy to achieve high Gs).

There are many things to consider when you are in a dogfight. Your skill and abilities are major factors, as well as the skill and abilities of the enemy. The enemy skill level is set by selecting the Config screen in the War Room. The setting that affects the enemy skills is Enemy Logic Level. Four settings are available: Trainee, Cadet, Veteran, and Ace. The lowest level provides enemy pilots that cannot withstand high-G turns nor perform maneuvers outside of the horizontal plane; as a result they are the easiest to defeat. Each level introduces higher skilled enemy pilots capable of withstanding increasingly higher Gs and the ability to maneuver on virtually any plane.

There will be times when your mission orders require you to destroy a target on the ground. However, there is still a good possibility that you will encounter hostile aircraft along your route. It is for this reason that you *must* learn to engage enemy aircraft and win. More air combat maneuvers will be discussed in Lessons 1 through 3.

Air-to-Ground Weaponry

The are numerous air-to-ground weapons available for the F-16 and Falcon 3.0 pilot. Although these weapons are quite different in terms of size and what they can destroy, the method of delivery for groups of weapons is similar. For example, the cluster bomb (CBU-84) and the 2,000-pound iron bomb (Mk-84) are very different in size and purpose. The cluster bomb is used on *soft targets* (trucks, infantry units, etc.), while the Mk-84 is used against large targets (factories, aircraft shelters, etc.). However, both weapons have the same HUD display and are delivered in similar methods. They both use the *CCIP* (Continuously Computed Impact Point) HUD display for lining up and designating the target. This introductory section concentrates on the different HUD modes for air-to-ground weapons delivery. All weapons will be discussed individually in the lessons that follow.

Air-to-Ground HUD Modes

There are thirteen different types of Falcon 3.0 air-to-ground weapons. Each weapon type uses a specific HUD display that assists you in delivering the weapon. There are five air-to-ground HUD modes used in Falcon 3.0: A-R (Anti-Radiation), CCIP (Continuously Computed Impact Point), I-R (Infrared), E-O (Electro-Optical), and STRF (Strafe). The aircraft computer automatically selects the mode when you choose the weapon type in the cockpit. The lower left corner of the HUD displays the current weapons mode. This section shows the HUD view of each of the modes and describes several methods of delivering the weapons. You will put each of the methods into practice in the lessons that follow. Table 5-1 shows a summary of all of the weapons available to you and the HUD mode associated with each particular weapon.

Air-to-Ground Weapon	HUD Mode	Target
M61A1 Vulcan Cannon	STRF	Soft targets
LAU 5003A Rocket Launcher	CCIP	Soft targets
AGM-45A Shrike	A-R	CW radars
AGM-65B Maverick	E-O	Heavy armor
AGM-65D Maverick	I-R	Heavy armor
AGM-88A HARM	A-R	CW/pulse radars
CBU-84 Cluster Bomb	CCIP	Soft targets
BLU-107 Durandal	CCIP	Runways
GBU-15 Guided Bomb Unit	E-O	Bunkers, shelters
Mk-82HD Snakeye	CCIP	Tanks, small bldgs
Mk-82 Iron Bomb - 500 lb.	CCIP	Tanks, small bldgs
Mk-83 Iron Bomb - 1000 lb.	CCIP	Storage tanks, warehouses
Mk-84 Iron Bomb - 2000 lb.	CCIP	Factories, power plants

Table 5-1 Air-to-Ground Weapons with HUD Modes and Suggested Targets

Most of the F-16 arsenal uses the CCIP HUD mode, although the delivery of the weapons may vary. Note that the table lists some of the targets that these weapons may destroy. More information on targets is available in the weapons lessons. Let's take a look at the individual HUD modes and their similarities and differences.

STRF (Strafe) HUD Mode The only air-to-ground weapon that uses the STRF HUD mode is the M61A1 Vulcan cannon. This is the same cannon that is employed in the air-to-air combat mode. The HUD display is different when you select the air-to-ground mode and the M61A1. The air-to-air cannon displayed a historical gunsight while the air-to-ground cannon displays a small aiming *pipper* (aiming circle). As you point the nose of the F-16 towards ground targets, the pipper moves to indicate where cannon shells will strike when you fire. Figure 5-8 shows the STRF HUD mode.

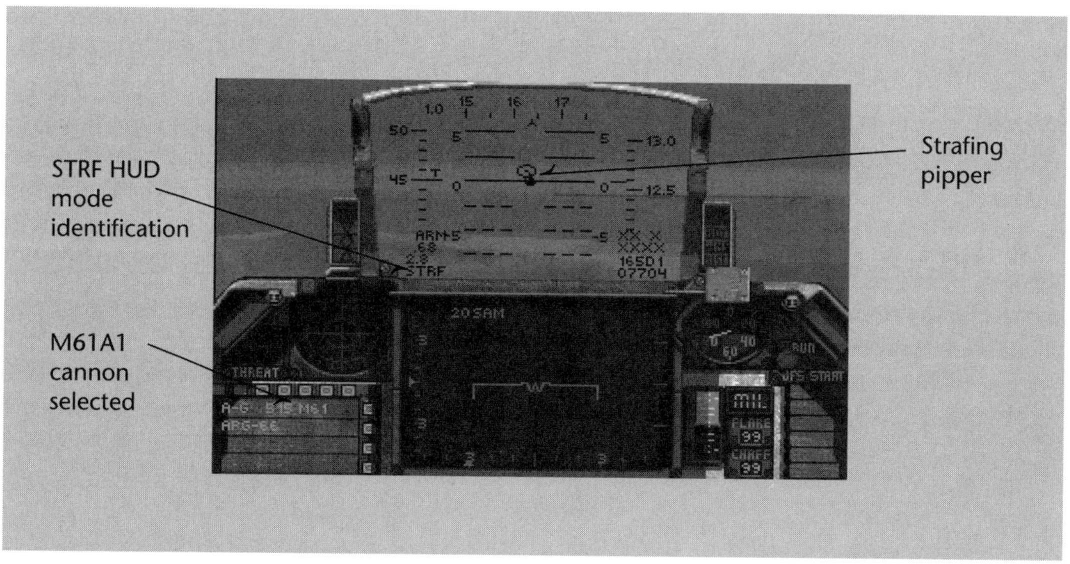

Figure 5-8 The STRF HUD Mode

Strafing ground targets with the F-16 is not a common activity. The only time it may be necessary is when you have exhausted the other air-to-ground weapons and there are soft ground targets left to destroy. If the soft targets are not part of the overall mission objective, it is best to leave the targets alone and head home. Many things can go wrong during strafing runs. You can crash into the ground or get hit by enemy fire. Flying at low altitudes over enemy territory for long periods is not advised.

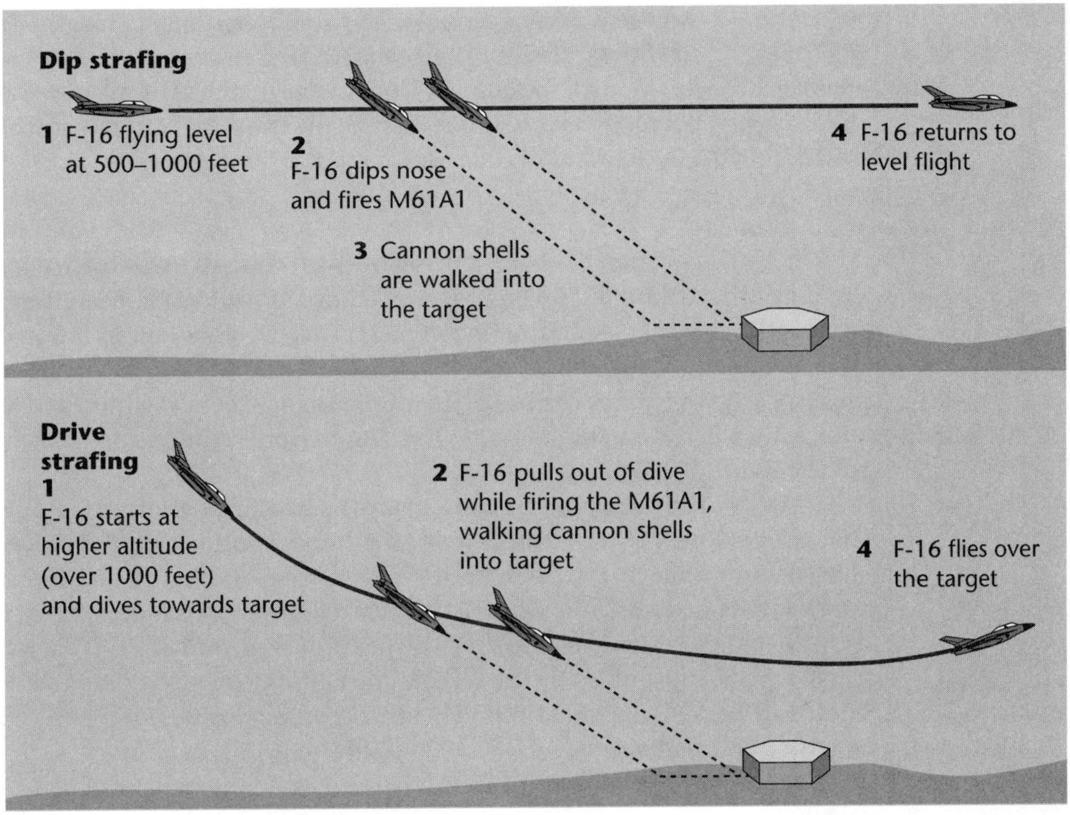

Figure 5-9 Strafing Methods

If you do wish to take the chance and take out some ground targets, Figure 5-9 shows a couple of strafing methods. Both methods have one thing in common. They start with the nose of the F-16 aiming at a point *before* the intended target and *walk* the gunfire into the target. Walking gunfire consists of firing shells into the ground at a point before the target, then flying to the target while continuing to fire.

A-R (Anti-Radiation)—I-R (Infrared)—E-O (Electro-Optical) HUD Modes The A-R, I-R, and E-O HUD modes are very similar in operation. Although the three modes control different types of weapons that destroy different types of targets, the delivery method is nearly the same for all three. This method combines the use of the HUD and the REO to help you find the correct target with the weapon. Let's take a closer look at the three individual modes and the weapons used in each mode.

The A-R (Anti-Radiation) mode is used to lock on to enemy radars and fire the Shrike or HARM missiles. The enemy radar must be transmitting to achieve the lock. Once the lock occurs, you fire the missile. The missile *rides* the radar signal directly to the source, destroying the radar. After firing the missile, no further action is needed on your part. This is referred to as a *fire-and-forget* missile. In Falcon 3.0, the A-R missiles are used to attack the SAM and AAA radars.

Only one weapon in Falcon 3.0 uses the I-R (Infrared) HUD mode. This weapon is the AGM-65D Maverick. However, two Mavericks (AGM-65B and AGM-65D) are available to the Falcon pilot. The "D" version uses infrared guidance technology, while the "B" version uses a television-imaging seeker. The I-R Maverick can be used at night, in inclement weather, and in situations where visibility is poor. The "B" Maverick cannot perform in these conditions.

The "B" Maverick and the GBU-15 are the two air-to-ground weapons that employ the E-O (Electro-Optical) HUD mode. Both weapons employ the television-imaging seeker. Both weapons are of the fire-and-forget variety. The major difference between the two E-O weapons is the way they are powered. The Maverick has a motor that propels the missile toward the target while being guided by the seeker. The GBU is a free-fall bomb that is guided by seeker-controlled fins. This is the primary difference between missiles and bombs.

The A-R, I-R, and E-O HUD modes all use a crosshair to mark the selected target on the HUD and some weapons display the target on the

Figure 5-10 The E-O HUD Mode for the GBU-15 Guided Bomb

Figure 5-11 Cockpit View of CCIP HUD Mode

REO. Figure 5-10 shows the E-O HUD mode for the GBU-15 laser-guided bomb. Note that the crosshairs on the HUD follow the target that is locked. The target is also displayed on the REO.

The figure shows the proper firing conditions for the GBU-15. Dropping the bomb at this point would probably result in a successful hit. However, everything does not always work perfectly on the battlefield. Each mission has a unique outcome in Falcon 3.0. Learning how to release the weapons at the appropriate time can significantly increase the chances of the target being hit.

CCIP (Continuously Computed Impact Point) HUD Mode Free-fall bombs employ the CCIP mode. As the name implies, the point of impact is continuously computed by the Falcon's onboard computer. The pilot first designates (selects) the target. From the time that you designate the target, the computer monitors the altitude and airspeed of the aircraft. The object of the CCIP is to release the bombs at the correct time. If all goes well, this results in the bombs landing on the target.

Before you make the designation, the bombsight is a vertical line that extends from the center of the HUD to a pipper (aiming circle) at the bottom of the HUD. You maneuver the F-16 into a position where the pipper is directly over the target. Designate the target by lining up a pipper over the target then marking the target position with the SPACEBAR. Figure 5-11 shows the cockpit view after the target has been designated. The vertical line has extended up to the top of the HUD and a short horizontal line is dropping from the top of the HUD. When the horizontal line drops to the center of the HUD, the bombs are automatically released. It is important to not make any sudden movements during the approach to the target.

Once a target is designated, you can cancel it by pressing the X key. This is useful when you designate a target and then notice an enemy missile has been fired in your direction. In this case, it is better to cancel the target designation and concentrate on avoiding the incoming missile.

Because of the powerless nature of free-fall bombs, you must drop them while the F-16 is relatively level. Missiles can be fired from almost any attitude; however, the release of free-fall bombs is restricted to certain positions. The HUD indicates when you cannot release bombs by displaying a short thick horizontal line above the pipper. You will see an example of this during the lessons using the CCIP HUD mode.

Methods of Free-Fall Bomb Delivery There are several methods that you can employ to drop free-fall bombs. The best way is to practice dropping each type of bomb and developing what works best for you. Figure 5-12 shows two examples of bomb delivery, dive bombing and level bombing. Both methods can be effective if executed properly. There is one important factor in any method of bombing. You must have sufficient altitude to keep from sustaining damage from your own bomb blast. The

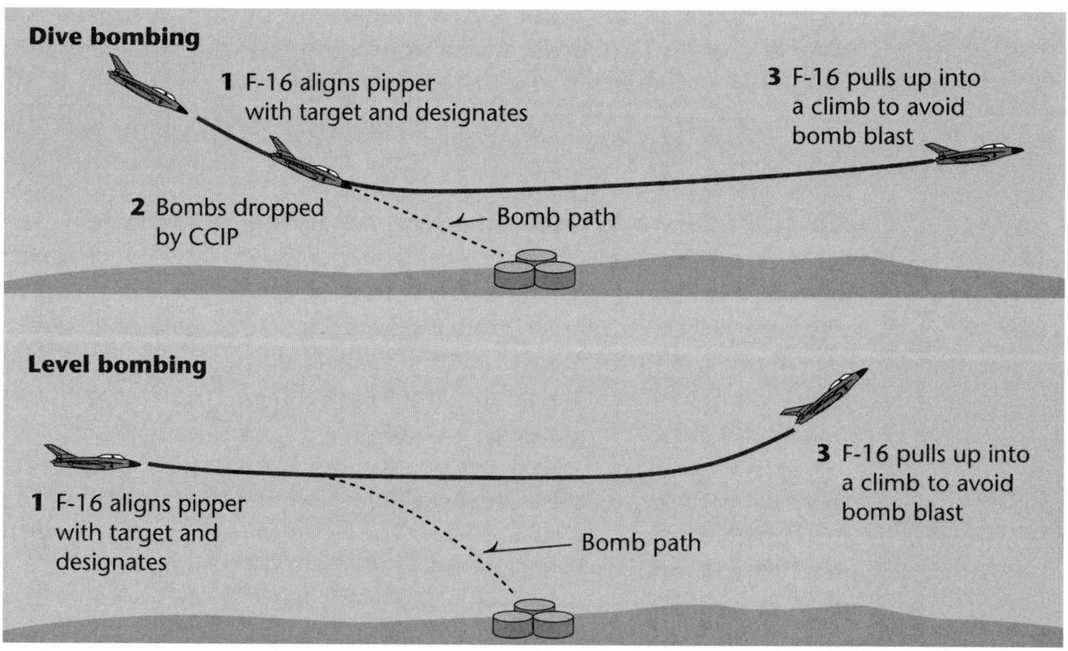

Figure 5-12 Free-Fall Bombing Methods

higher the bombs are dropped, the longer it will take for the bomb to reach the target and explode. You can turn away or start to climb once the bombs are dropped.

No altitudes are shown in the figure because this varies significantly between bomb types. Different bombs produce different amounts of blast. Although the dive bombing method is more realistic, you may find it easier to use the level bombing technique when you are learning.

Speed also plays a factor when using the CCIP mode. You will find that delivering free-fall bombs becomes increasingly difficult as airspeed increases. The margin for error is much smaller at higher airspeeds. The subsequent sections on individual weapons look closely at airspeed and technique.

CCIP for the LAU-5003A Rocket Launcher The CCIP HUD display is slightly different for the LAU-5003A Rocket Launcher. You still use the pipper, but it is located near the center of the HUD. The Rocket Launcher pipper resembles the HUD display of the M61A1 cannon when used in STRF mode (except this mode displays a horizontal line above the pipper when the target is in range). The LAU-5003A is the only CCIP weapon that is propelled, as opposed to the free-fall type.

Many Weapons for Many Purposes There are several weapons available to you as a Falcon 3.0 pilot. It is important to gain a high level of skill at each of them. The balance of this chapter is designed to help you do that. Ten lessons are presented to help you master each of the weapons, one at a time. All enemies that you encounter in the lessons are unarmed, except where it is absolutely necessary to arm them. For example, in order to use anti-radiation missiles, you must lock on to an enemy radar. SAM and AAA sites are the only enemies equipped to generate the radar signals. Let's get started with the lessons!

Falcon 3.0—Lessons in Weapons

Once again it is time to climb back into the Falcon and head for the skies. Only this time it is your turn to strike back. The lessons require that you have successfully completed the lessons presented in Chapter 3, *Learning to Fly*, and Chapter 4, *Radar and Enemy Identification*. You must know how to fly the F-16, use the views (including the padlock view), and use the APG-66 radar.

The first three lessons provide training for the air-to-air weapons in Falcon 3.0. The three air-to-air missiles are presented in the order of difficulty of use. The AIM-120 AMRAAM is usually fired from medium ranges and does not require sophisticated maneuvers to gain a position to fire the weapon. However, the AIM-9P rear-aspect missile requires a much higher level of maneuvering skill. Since the position needed to attack with the AIM-9P is also a good position for guns, the M61A1 cannon is introduced in the same lesson.

The remaining seven lessons are devoted to the thirteen air-to-ground weapons. Similar weapons are covered in the same lesson. For example, the delivery technique for the Mk82D, the Mk82, the Mk83, and the Mk84 are virtually the same. The major difference is the size and type of the targets that they are designed to destroy.

The Lesson Format

The lesson format is very similar to the format used in Chapters 3 and 4. You load a mission at the Red Flag control screen. Then you receive some last-minute ground school instruction. Along with the ground school, you are given lesson objectives listing the goals, information, and knowledge you will receive. Then, using step-by-step instruction, you will perform the lesson. At the end of the lesson, you will receive a review in the form of a debriefing. You will also use the debriefing feature built in to Falcon 3.0 to analyze your results and determine if you need another pass at the lesson. The Red Flag missions can be used over and over. The more skilled you are at delivering the many weapons of Falcon 3.0, the more successful you will be in the campaigns. Eventually, you will be called on to use each of the weapons in this chapter.

If you need any help loading missions or getting to the runway, refer to Chapter 3 for detailed instructions. You will bypass the F-16 Pilots and the F-16 Armament screens on your way to the start of each lesson. All lessons in this chapter start with your F-16 in mid-flight. It is not necessary to take off in this chapter.

> **NOTE:** All lessons in this chapter use the Intermediate setting in the Difficulty Levels screen. For information on setting the Difficulty Levels refer to "Difficulty Levels" in Chapter 2, *Introduction to Falcon 3*.

Weapon Lesson #1: BVR Kill

The weapon most capable of a BVR (beyond visual range) kill in Falcon 3.0 is the AIM-120 AMRAAM (Advanced Medium Range Air-to-Air Missile). The

AIM-120 is an all-aspect, radar-guided missile. Although the specifications list the AIM-120 as having a range of 25 miles, most target lock-ons occur around 18 to 20 miles from the target. Because of the long range, you must be absolutely sure the target is the enemy. If you fire the weapon and then find out the target is friendly, you had better hope the friendly can avoid it. Otherwise, you will most likely face a court-martial.

This lesson has two missions. In one lesson the enemy is approaching head-on (AIM120F). The other lesson shows the enemy flying away from the F-16 (AIM120R).

Lesson Objectives In this lesson you:

- Lock an incoming target at BVR and check IFF.
- Fire an AIM-120 for a BVR kill (high positive closure rate).
- Fire an AIM-120 for a BVR kill (negative closure rate).
- Use the threat/missile view.
- Use the Debriefing screen in Red Flag to observe results.

Ground School This lesson uses two new keys, the ENTER key and the Q key. The ENTER key has been used in several other screens before this mission, usually to accept a value. While you are in flight, the ENTER key cycles through the air-to-air weapons (including the M61A1 cannon). Since this mission only involves the AIM-120 missile, the ENTER key cycles between the cannon and the AIM-120. You will eventually have all three missile types loaded, in which case the ENTER key cycles through all three missiles and the cannon. The cannon is always loaded regardless of the mission. The Q key switches to the threat view (the enemy aircraft that is locked on by radar) or the missile view (after it is fired).

The MRM HUD Mode The MRM (Medium Range Missile) HUD mode is used exclusively with the AIM-120 missile. Selecting the MRM mode displays a few new items on the HUD. Figure 5-13 shows the MRM HUD mode. Some of the items have been present on the HUD during previous lessons. This is your first chance to use them.

This view of the MRM HUD mode is with no target in range. The REO is clear, indicating there is no activity to the front of the aircraft. The large circle in the center of the HUD is the *aiming reticle*. You try to get the enemy target in this circle before releasing the weapon. The small diamond in the center of the aiming reticle is the missile seeker head. This diamond moves and tracks a target when you have it locked on radar.

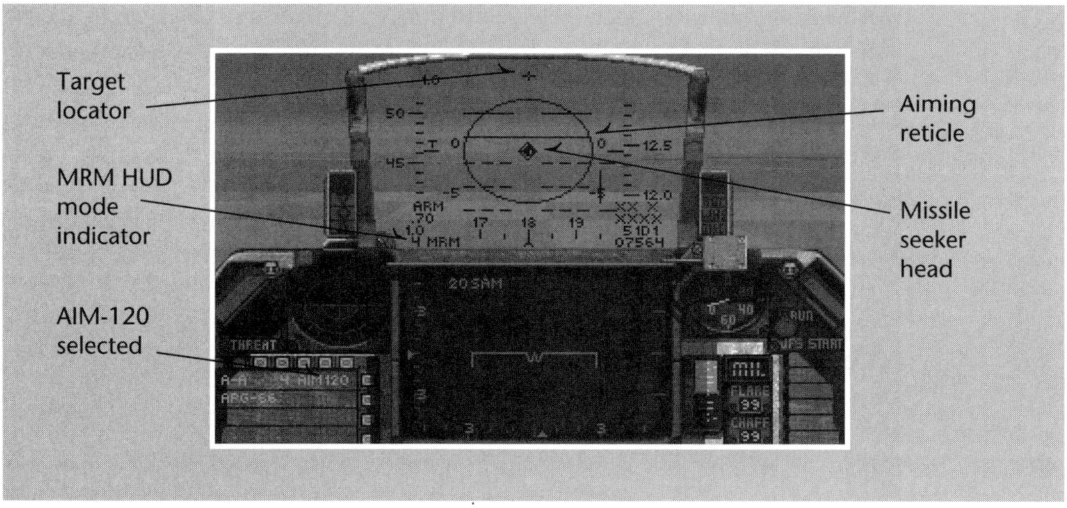

Figure 5-13 The MRM (Medium Range Missile) HUD Mode

The small cross at the top center of the HUD is the *target locator*. This feature is useful in locating targets that are being tracked by your radar, but out of the view of your HUD. When a target is in range and locked by radar, the target locator has a line extending from the cross indicating the relative direction of the target (compared to your F-16). For example, if the line extends up and to the right of the cross, this indicates that the target is above and to the right of the F-16. In this scenario, you could bring the target back to the center of the HUD by banking to the right and pulling on the stick to climb. Of course the enemy could continue to make evasive maneuvers.

The stores control panel (the lower left portion of the cockpit panel) indicates the selected weapon, in this case the AIM-120. The lower left corner of the HUD indicates that the MRM HUD mode is selected. The 4 indicates that four AIM-120 missiles are loaded. Up to eight AIM-120s can be loaded on the Falcon (depending on the other weapons loaded).

AIM-120 Tactics The AIM-120 is effective at longer ranges (from 5 to 20 miles) than the Sidewinder missiles. It is not nearly as effective at short range. If a target is approaching you at a high airspeed, the *closure rate* is very high. Closure rate is the rate (in miles per hour) that you are approaching the target. You can obtain the closure rate from the REO and the HUD. It is best to fire the missile as soon as you receive a lock in this situation. If you wait too long, you may find the enemy aircraft too close to fire the weapon.

The opposite of this situation is a *running* or *fleeing* enemy. The closure rate of an enemy on the run is usually negative. For example, if the enemy is traveling away from your aircraft at 550 knots and you are following at 450 knots, the closure rate is –100 knots. This means the enemy aircraft is separating from your F-16 at a rate of 100 knots. Whether or not to pursue the enemy in this situation depends on your mission assignment. If your mission orders are to guard a particular area, you should not break away from your patrol to chase an enemy aircraft. On the other hand, if you orders require you to intercept any enemy activity, then you should accelerate to catch and destroy the enemy aircraft.

The following lessons show both the positive and negative closure rate BVR attacks. Try both missions until you feel comfortable with the AIM-120. The enemy aircraft in this lesson is unarmed.

Head-On BVR Attack This mission sends a MiG-25 straight at you. Your goal is to lock it up on radar, check IFF to make sure it is the enemy, and fire an AIM-120 (or two) to destroy the enemy aircraft. You will take a look at the mission results at the Debriefing screen in Red Flag.

Go to Red Flag Control and load the AIM120F mission. Click on F-16 PILOTS, then F-16 ARMAMENT, and then TAKEOFF. Pause the simulation by pressing the (P) key. You start at an altitude (AGL) of 7,000 to 8,000 feet and an airspeed of approximately 450 knots. Are you ready to go after that MiG?

- Unpause the simulation by pressing the (P) key.
- Make any adjustments necessary to maintain a constant altitude, airspeed, and heading. Your heading should be 180°.
- The bottom left corner of the HUD indicates the DGFT mode is active. The stores panel indicates the M61A1 cannon is selected. Press the (ENTER) key to cycle to the AIM-120. The lower left corner of the HUD should change to 4 MRM.
- Monitor the REO. After flying a few miles, a target will appear on the top of the REO with the radar range set to 20nm (range is set automatically). The target may even appear briefly at the 40nm range (slightly above the center of the REO).
- Press the (T) key to lock up the target on radar. The target changes to a diamond on the REO. Press the (N) key to check the IFF. There is no tone because the incoming aircraft is the enemy.
- You hear an audible signal and the missile seeker head (diamond) will move to the target on the REO. Press the (P) key to pause the simulation as soon as you hear the tone. Figure 5-14 shows the AIM-120 locked on the enemy target.

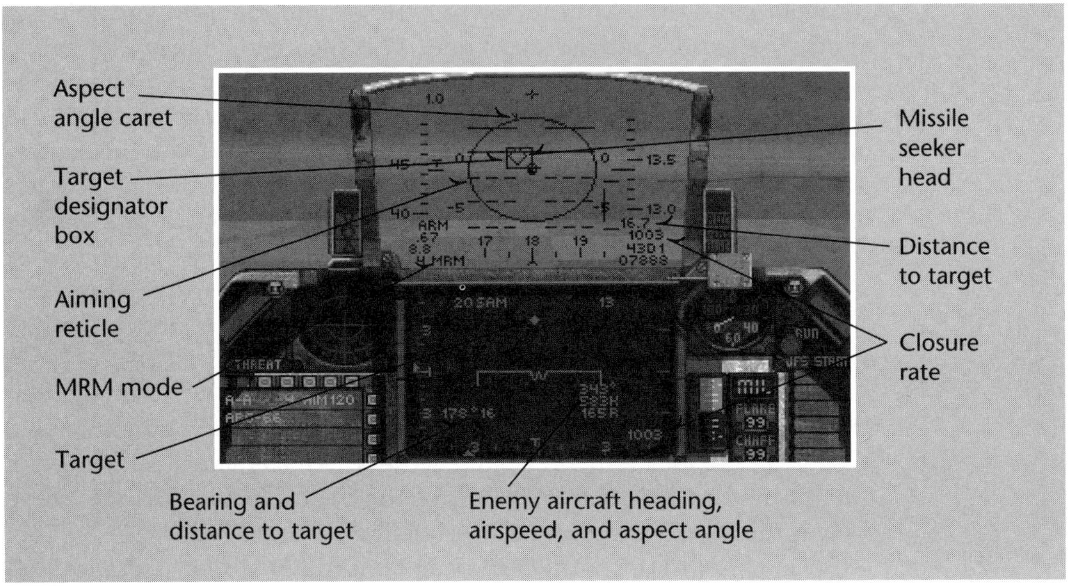

Figure 5-14 AIM-120 Locked On an Enemy Aircraft (positive closure rate)

There is a lot of valuable information on this screen. Take a look at the individual items while the simulation is paused. The more you practice using the HUD and REO indicators, the easier it will be in actual combat.

The target in the figure is 16.7 miles from the F-16. You can roughly determine the distance by using the REO. For example, the current range of the radar is 20 miles. Because the target is near the top of the REO, you can assume that the target is between 15 and 20 miles out. There is also an entry that will provide the distance to the target on the REO and the HUD. The entry on the HUD shows the enemy distance down to the tenth of a mile.

Another important item on the HUD is the aspect-angle caret. This caret provides a quick visual representation of the direction of the target. For example, in the figure, the caret is near the top, pointing down. This indicates the aircraft is flying nearly directly at you. The aspect angle is also available in numeric form on the REO. In the figure, the aspect angle is 165R. This means that the nose of the F-16 is 165° to the right of the tail of the target. Put simply, an aspect angle of 180° indicates the enemy is headed directly at the F-16, so the angle of 165R means the target is generally approaching head-on.

The next feature to observe is the closure rate. The closure rate can be found in the lower right corner of the HUD (under the distance to target indicator), or in the lower right corner of the REO. In this example, the closure rate is 1,003. This indicates that the F-16 and the enemy aircraft are closing in on each other at over 1,000 miles per hour! This is why it is necessary to be ready to fire in head-on situations like this.

The target designator box follows the incoming enemy aircraft, as well as the missile seeker head (diamond on the HUD). When you unpause the simulation, try to keep the box and missile seeker head inside the aiming reticle by making small adjustments with the stick. It is time to fire at the enemy.

- Unpause the simulation by pressing the (P) key.
- Check the missile seeker head to make sure it is following the target. If it is not, check to make sure the target is locked up by the radar. If you have lost radar lock, press the (T) to lock up the target again.
- Press the (Spacebar) to fire the AIM-120. You should hear the missile firing if you have sound enabled. The missile heads for the enemy aircraft.
- Press the (Q) key to toggle between the enemy aircraft and missile views. You may notice the enemy maneuvering wildly and dropping chaff to avoid the incoming missile. This is very similar to you noticing an incoming missile on the TWI, and making the moves to avoid it.
- If the enemy successfully avoids the AIM-120, the missile will eventually reach the ground. If the AIM-120 finds the MiG, you will see it go up in flames. You may even notice the pilot ejecting. Return to the cockpit view by pressing the (1) key on the numeric keypad.
- Press (ESC) to access the menu bar. Select END MISSION from the FILE menu to return to the Debriefing screen.
- Click on CONTINUE in the Debriefing screen. The simulated screen in the upper right corner displays "THIS WAS THE PLANNED ROUTE" followed by "THIS WAS THE ACTUAL ROUTE." Your route for the mission appears on the mission map as the small screen displays the summary of activity for the mission. For example, if you destroyed the MiG-25, the screen displays, "CAPTAIN HEPTIG DOWNED A MiG-25." (The actual pilot rank and name will vary on your system.)
- Click on NEXT MISSION to return to Red Flag control.

There are a few things to note before loading the next mission. In a campaign mission, it is not a good idea to use the threat/missile view for a long period of time. It is a good method to use to check to see if your weapon has been effective; but remember, the enemy is closing in while you are watching the missile. Keep this is mind in actual combat. If you feel there is a threat, stay in the cockpit or padlock view, do not watch missiles!

Another item is the debriefing screen. At the end of a campaign mission, the small screen displays more than a full page of information. You can use the scroll bars next to the screen to see the additional activity if it exists.

Rear BVR Attack This mission starts by placing your F-16 about 20 miles behind the MiG-25. The MiG's initial airspeed is higher than your aircraft's. This creates a *negative closure* rate. This means that the distance between you and the enemy aircraft is *increasing*. You need to close the gap by accelerating to get into range to fire the AIM-120.

Go to Red Flag Control and load the AIM120R mission. Click on F-16 PILOTS, then F-16 ARMAMENT, and then TAKEOFF. Pause the simulation by pressing the (P) key. Once again, you start at an altitude (AGL) of 7,000 to 8,000 feet and an airspeed of approximately 450 knots. Before you close in to fire the AIM-120 missile, take a look at the current situation.

Figure 5-15 shows the cockpit view for the start of the mission. Note that some of the information may be slightly different on the REO and HUD. One very important indicator in this figure is the *negative* closure rate (–106). This indicates that the enemy aircraft is running away from your F-16 (at least for now!).

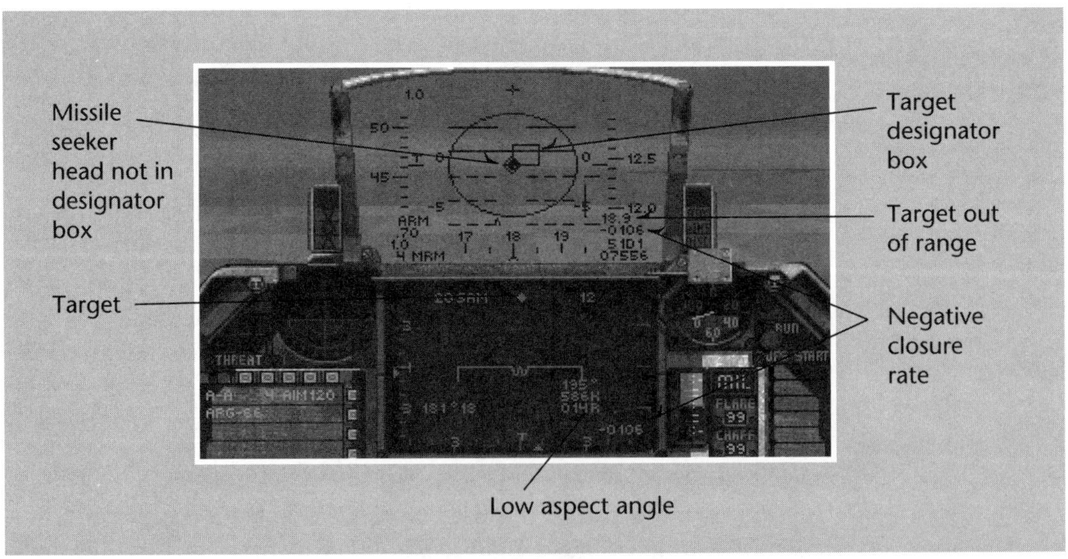

Figure 5-15 Enemy Target with Negative Closure and Low Aspect Angle

Also, the enemy is out of the range of the AIM-120. You have a radar lock on the target, but the missile is not locked on. The radar lock is signified by the diamond shaped target on the REO. The missile lock is normally indicated by the missile seeker head (small diamond) following the target designator box (and thus the target itself). In the figure, the missile seeker is resting in the center of the HUD. This is normal for the AIM-120 when there is no missile lock.

Note the low aspect angle (14R). This indicates that your F-16 is behind and to the right of the MiG by 14°. Zero degrees would indicate that you are directly behind the enemy.

You need to get your F-16 into the position needed to accurately fire the AIM-120 (into the *weapons envelope)*. The current RPM is around 80%. When you resume the simulation, be prepared to accelerate to catch the enemy.

- Unpause the simulation by pressing the P key.
- The bottom left corner of the HUD indicates the DGFT mode is active. The stores panel indicates the M61A1 cannon is selected. Press the ENTER key to cycle to the AIM-120. The lower left corner of the HUD should change to 4 MRM.
- Check the target for IFF by pressing the N key.
- Immediately go to full throttle (100% RPM) by pressing the + key repeatedly. Keep the target inside the HUD view by making stick adjustments.
- Keep an eye on closure rate. It should change from a negative to a positive number as you accelerate.
- Also watch the aspect angle. If the angle starts to increase above 90°, the enemy is turning towards you! He may have detected you on *his* TWI indicator.
- As soon as you get the missile tone and the missile seeker is inside the target designator box, fire the AIM-120 by pressing the SPACEBAR.
- Check to see if the missile hits the enemy by using the threat/missile view (the Q key). Fire another missile if necessary, you have four AIM-120s to launch! Return to the cockpit view by pressing the 1 key on the numeric keypad.
- Press ESC to access the menu bar. Select END MISSION from the FILE menu. Click on CONTINUE to see if you nailed the MiG. Click on NEXT MISSION to return to Red Flag Control.

Debriefing: BVR Kill The AIM-120 AMRAAM is the weapon of choice for BVR (beyond visual range) attacks in Falcon 3.0. It gives you the great ability to attack enemy targets early, perhaps before they are aware of your existence! Although specifications rate the AIM-120 with a range of 25 miles, you usually lock on to a target at a range of 18 to 20 miles. As always, never *assume that all targets are enemy!* Check all targets with IFF to make sure they are hostile before firing any weapon.

The AIM-120 is an all-aspect, radar-guided missile. You can fire it at any aspect angle as long as the seeker head is in the target designator box. The main drawback to the AIM-120 is the inability to strike targets at close range. In these cases, it is best to use the AIM-9M or AIM-9P.

You may wonder why you shouldn't load the AIM-120 on every mission. The answer is cost. The AMRAAM is a very expensive weapon. In training, you can use as many weapons as you want, of all types. There is no limit on supply. In campaign mode this will change. You will be required to ration the supplies over several missions. Save the AIM-120s for when you really need them. More information about weapons rationing is available in Chapter 7, *Introduction to the Campaigns.*

Weapon Lesson #2: All-Aspect Kill

The weapon to select for close range all-aspect attacks in Falcon 3.0 is the AIM-9M Sidewinder. The AIM-9M is an all-aspect, infrared missile. Although this Sidewinder uses heat to seek the target, it does not have to be fired at the rear of the enemy target. Successful hits can be made from virtually 360° around the target. Although the specifications for the AIM-9M list the range as ten miles, you usually lock the target up at a range of five to seven miles.

This lesson uses the AIM9M Red Flag mission. You will start with an F-16 loaded with four AIM-9Ms. If you follow the waypoints, you will run into three enemy aircraft.

> NOTE: Since the AIM-9M is an infrared (heat-seeking missile), it may occasionally lock on to the sun instead of the enemy. Try to avoid firing this missile when the enemy is between your F-16 and the sun. Continue to pursue the enemy until he changes direction.

Lesson Objectives In this lesson you:

- Lock and pursue an enemy target to Sidewinder range.
- Use the Target Locator and Diamond X to locate targets outside of the HUD.

- Fire the AIM-9M Sidewinder.
- Observe kill/miss using the threat/missile view.
- Use the Debriefing screen in Red Flag to observe results.

Ground School The same keys that were introduced in the previous mission are used in this mission. Use the ENTER key to cycle the air-to-air weapons and the Q key for threat/missile view. Use the standard radar keys (the T key to lock targets and the D key to check IFF).

The SRM HUD Mode The SRM (Short Range Missile) HUD mode is used with the AIM-9M and AIM-9P Sidewinder missiles. There are subtle differences between the HUD displays for the two weapons, however. Figure 5-16 shows the cockpit view with the AIM-9M missile selected. Note the changes from the MRM mode.

The aiming reticle is slightly smaller for the AIM-9M. This missile type requires you to be more precise in the delivery than the AIM-120. Also, the missile seeker head (small diamond) constantly scans the HUD looking for a target to lock on to. The diamond fills the target designator box as it did with the AIM-120. Note that the lower right corner of the HUD displays 4 SRM indicating four weapons loaded and the short range missile mode. The stores control panel displays 4 AIM9M, indicating the type of missile selected.

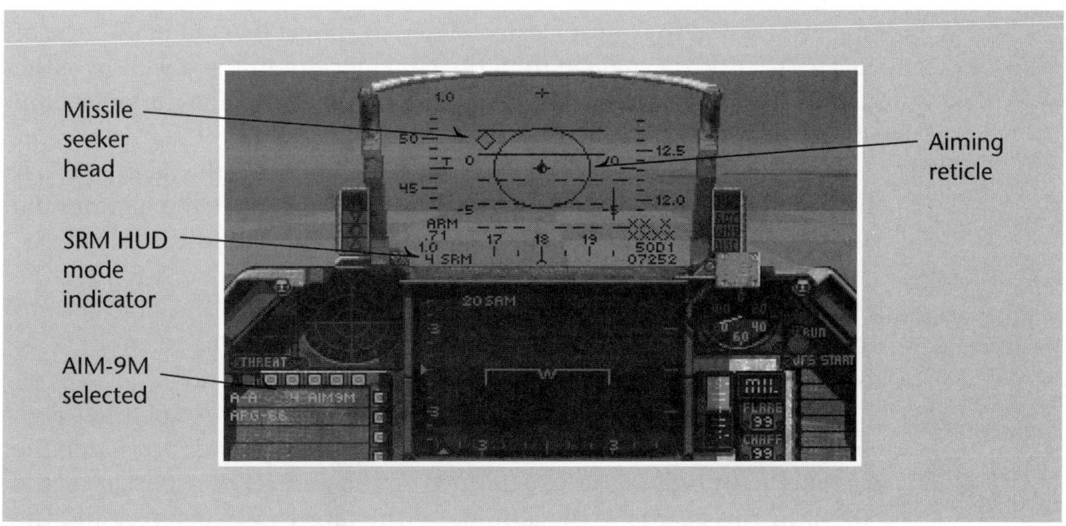

Figure 5-16 The SRM (Short Range Missile) HUD Mode

Up to six AIM-9Ms can be loaded on your F-16. The maximum amount depends on other air-to-air missiles loaded.

AIM-9M Tactics The AIM-9M is effective inside of five to seven miles. As mentioned earlier, it is an all-aspect missile. The direction of the enemy in relation to the F-16 is not as important as it will be in the next lesson (the AIM-9P rear-aspect missile). You want to concentrate on two things when preparing to fire an AIM-9M: getting the target in the aiming reticle (or at least the HUD view) and getting within range. Keeping an eye on the aspect caret, closure rate, airspeed, and heading of the enemy helps you close in on the enemy for a good missile shot. That is a lot of information to read and still fly the aircraft effectively. Once you close in on the enemy, it becomes more difficult to keep him in your sights. Since both aircraft are capable of supersonic speeds, reaction times must be virtually instantaneous. There are a few additional items on the HUD that help guide you to the proper position: the target locator and the diamond X.

The Target Locator and Diamond X You have already seen the target designator (small box) follow the target across the HUD to help you track the aircraft even if it is outside of visual range. This is a very helpful tool; but what happens if the designated aircraft flies outside of the view of the HUD? You need another tool to help maintain the track on the enemy. The target locator solves this dilemma.

Figure 5-17 shows the HUD with a target outside of view. In this example the target is being tracked by radar. How do you know where the target is? Look at the target locator. When the target flies out of the view of the HUD, a line is extended from the target locator in the direction of the target. This example shows the target locator indicating that the target is up and to the right of the F-16.

Another indication of the location of the target is the diamond *X*. If the target designator box moves outside of the HUD view (which means the target has done the same), the designator box becomes a pattern of four Xs. This pattern is referred to as the diamond X. The diamond X follows the relative position of the target. For example, in Figure 5-17 the target locator line indicates that the target is up and to the right. The diamond x is, therefore, located in the upper right corner of the HUD.

Another way to identify that the target is up and to the right is to compare the altitude of the target (located in the upper right corner of the REO) to the altitude of the F-16 (located on the scale on the right side of the HUD). In this example, the altitude of the target is 19,000 feet and the

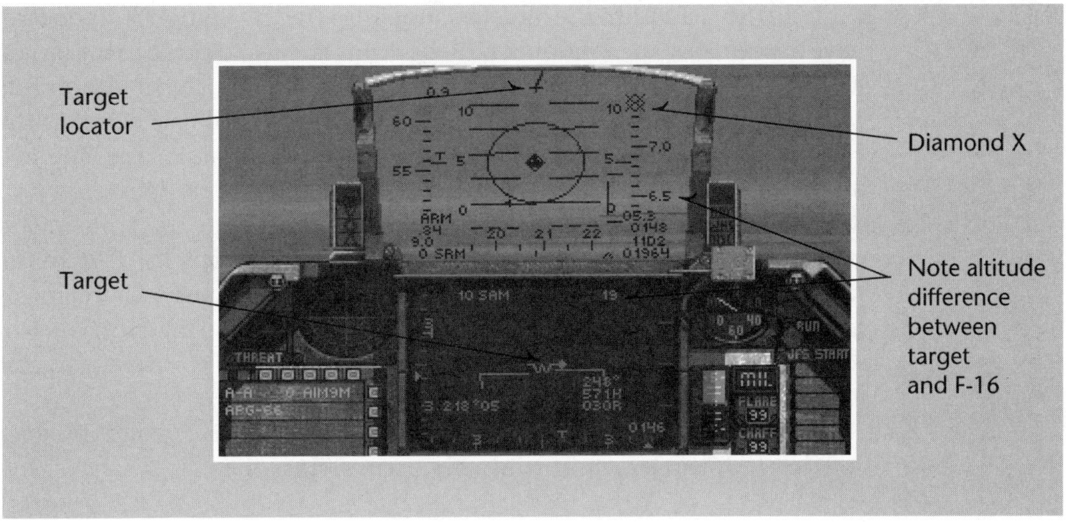

Figure 5-17 HUD View Using the Target Locator and Diamond X

altitude of the F-16 is between 6,500 and 7,000 feet. You can tell that the target is to the right by looking at the position of the target on the REO.

Now that you know where the target is, the next step is to maneuver the F-16 to place the enemy target back into the HUD view (and ultimately into the aiming reticle). Figure 5-18 shows one way to maneuver the Falcon to get the target back into view. This example uses the target locator. The initial position shows the target locator line extending up and to the right. This is much like the example of the HUD view in Figure 5-17. The F-16 pilot

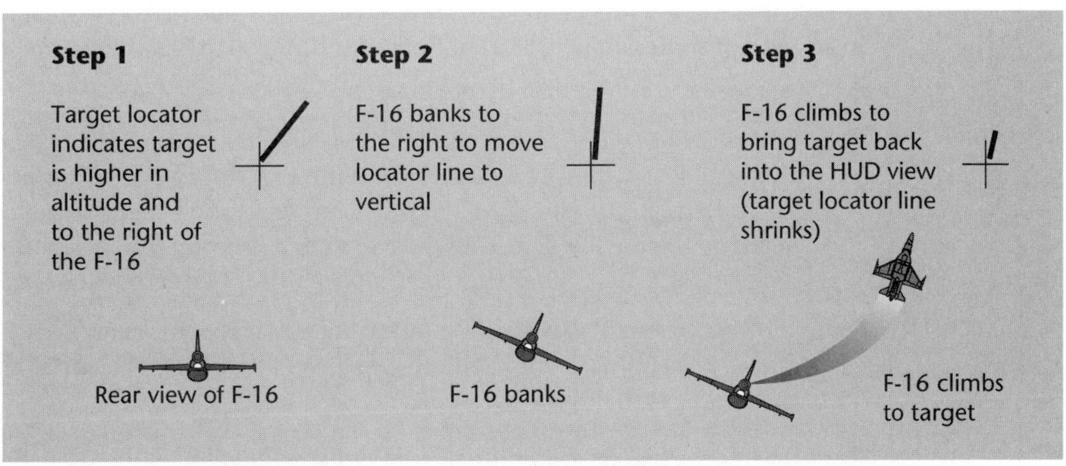

Figure 5-18 Using the Target Locator to Bring a Target Back Into the HUD View

banks to the right until the target locator line is nearly vertical (this doesn't have to be exact). Then the pilot pulls back on the stick to climb to the target. As the F-16 gets closer to pulling the target into view, the target locator line gets shorter. This is your indication that the target is getting closer to the HUD view. Once the target is back into view, the target locator line will disappear altogether and the target designator box will reappear.

As with most maneuvers in Falcon 3.0, there is more than one way to get the job done. You could start climbing first, then bank the F-16 to the right. Or you could perform the maneuvers simultaneously. It becomes a matter of personal preference. With experimentation and practice, you will soon have your own set of maneuvers to bring the target into view for a great missile shot!

The only time the target locator does not work is if you lose radar contact with the target. This usually occurs when the target flies behind your F-16.

Three Enemy Aircraft—Four AIM-9M Missiles This mission involves flying to three waypoints. Each waypoint is approximately 30 miles apart and has an enemy aircraft patrolling the area. You have four all-aspect Sidewinders loaded on your F-16. Don't waste all four on the first enemy! The goal is to take out all three enemy aircraft with the four missiles. The enemy aircraft have no weapons; however, they are equipped with flares. You may see the flares being dropped by the enemy pilot when you lock up the aircraft.

Go to Red Flag Control and load the AIM9M mission. Click on F-16 PILOTS, then F-16 ARMAMENT, and then TAKEOFF. Pause the simulation by pressing the P key. You start at an altitude (AGL) of 7,000 to 8,000 feet and an airspeed of approximately 450 knots. It is time for you to face the enemies!

- Unpause the simulation by pressing the P key.
- Press the ENTER key to select the AIM-9M. Note that the missile seeker head (small diamond) wanders around the HUD and a constant tone is heard. Recall that the AIM-120 only sounds a tone when a target is locked by the missile. The AIM-9M generates a constant low tone until a target is locked on. When the target is locked, the pitch of the tone rises.
- Continue towards waypoint 1, following the waypoint caret. Maintain a relatively constant altitude and airspeed. It is not essential to stay at an exact altitude, however.
- As you get closer to waypoint 1, a target should appear on the REO. The exact time the target appears varies from mission to mission depend-

ing on your airspeed and what the enemy aircraft does. Make sure you check IFF by pressing the N key. If there is no tone, it is okay to attack.

- The target designator box should be visible on the HUD once the target is locked up on radar. It may be necessary to press the T key to lock up the target. Also, if the target flies from left to right or right to left, maintaining a constant range from your F-16, you may lose radar lock temporarily. The target reappears after a few seconds if this occurs.
- Use your stick to keep the target designator box in the center of the HUD and the aiming reticle. Keep an eye on the aspect angle caret. This indicates the direction the aircraft is flying. Also, watch the distance-to-the-target indication on the HUD. You want to get within five or six miles to lock your Sidewinder on the target.
- If you see that the closure rate is negative, you may want to increase throttle slightly. Don't overdo it though. If your airspeed gets too high you may overshoot the target when you get close. You may not have time to fire the missile.
- Figure 5-19 shows an example of the desired position to fire the AIM-9M. You may want to pause the simulation (the P key) and review the figure before pursuing the target.

Note that the target designator is close to the aiming reticle and the missile seeker head is following it. The range is this example is 4.8 miles. This

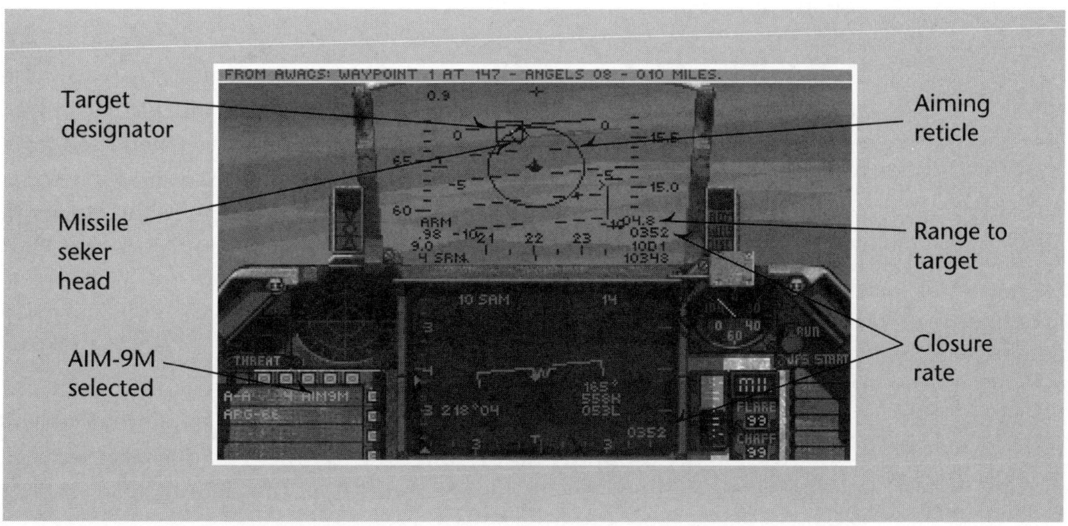

Figure 5-19 Proper Firing Conditions for the AIM-9M Sidewinder

is well within range for the AIM-9M Sidewinder. The closure rate is 352 miles per hour. This indicates that you better fire the weapon soon (using the SPACEBAR).

- Unpause the simulation with the P key and continue to pursue the enemy.
- When the target is in range (Sidewinder tone goes up in pitch and seeker head is in target designator box), fire an AIM-9M by pressing the SPACEBAR.
- Once a missile is fired, check the threat/missile view by pressing the Q key. Remember that pressing the key repeatedly switches back and forth between a threat (the enemy aircraft) and a track view of the missile.

At this point the mission takes on its own personality. It all depends on what you (and the enemy aircraft) do. All missions are different in Falcon 3.0. If you destroy the target, you may want to advance to the next waypoint (where the next enemy is) by pressing SHIFT-B (holding SHIFT and pressing B). You only have four weapons and there is an enemy waiting at each waypoint (three waypoints in total). Good luck!

When you have exhausted the four Sidewinders or downed all three aircraft, press ESC to bring up the menu bar. Select END MISSION from the FILE menu. Be sure to check out the summary of your actions at the Debriefing room by clicking on CONTINUE. Click on NEXT MISSION when you are done viewing the mission results.

Debriefing: All-Aspect Kill The AIM-9M Sidewinder is an accurate air-to-air, all-aspect infrared missile. It can be fired from virtually 360° around the enemy, although the AIM-9M is most effective when fired from the rear quarter. Normal lock-on range for the AIM-9M is around five to six miles. All you need to do is maneuver into a position to place the enemy in the HUD view (preferably in the aiming reticle), get in range for the AIM-9M to lock, and fire the missile. At that point the F-16 can fly to any position. There is no need to maintain the missile lock after the missile has been fired. The infrared seeker in the Sidewinder takes over and locks on to the heat of the target.

The enemy does have a defense to the AIM-9M: the flare. You will notice the enemy dropping flares from time to time. You may also see your expensive Sidewinder get distracted and follow the flare instead of your intended target. Not a pretty sight!

Once again, the AIM-9M is not the least expensive air-to-air missile available to the F-16. Therefore, the supply may be limited in a campaign. You usually have a fairly good supply of this all-aspect supply, but not as ample as the less expensive AIM-9P.

Weapon Lesson #3: Rear Aspect/Guns Kill

This lesson covers two weapons, the AIM-9P Sidewinder and the M61A1 cannon. They are the most difficult weapons to use, but they can be effective and are relatively inexpensive. It is not difficult to *fire* the cannon or AIM-9P at all. The difficult part lies in maneuvering to gain a position on the enemy that will *enable* you to use these weapons effectively.

The AIM-9P Sidewinder is a rear-aspect, infrared air-to-air missile. Rear-aspect indicates that it must be fired at the rear of the enemy aircraft in order to lock on to its hot exhaust. You can no longer fire at the enemy when you are passing head-on, face-to-face. You must maneuver into a position with the nose of your F-16 facing the rear of the enemy aircraft before achieving a lock. As with the AIM-9M, the missile can be fooled by the natural heat sources, so avoid firing when the target is between your F-16 and the sun.

The M61A1 cannon (referred to as *guns*) is not intended to be a great air-to-air weapon. However, it can come in handy during fierce, close-up dogfighting or for protection when all other air-to-air stores have been depleted. Although it is not necessary to get directly on the rear of an enemy aircraft to use the guns, it usually works out that way. Why? Because the range of the guns is short (around one mile). In order to keep an enemy target in your sights long enough to get a guns kill, you have to be on the rear of the aircraft. If you are passing head-to-head, you may be able to get off a shot, but the chances for success are slim. The enemy is only in your sights temporarily. You have to anticipate where the enemy is going instead of where he is now. If you shoot a stream of 20mm shells where the enemy *will* be, he will fly directly into the path of the stream of lead.

This lesson uses the AIM9M Red Flag mission. You start with an F-16 loaded with four AIM-9Ms. If you follow the waypoints, you will run into three enemy aircraft.

Lesson Objectives In this lesson you:

- Use the target locator and diamond X to locate targets outside of the HUD.
- Use the target aspect angle to plan an attack position on the enemy.

- Maneuver your F-16 to gain a rear-aspect attack position on enemy aircraft.
- Observe kill/miss using the threat/missile view.
- Use the Debriefing screen in Red Flag to observe results.

Ground School The same keys that were used in the previous mission are used in this mission. You use the (ENTER) key to cycle from guns to the AIM-9P Sidewinder. The (Q) key selects the threat/missile view. You also use the standard radar keys (the (T) key to lock targets and the (N) key to check IFF). The (SPACEBAR) fires the selected weapon.

Getting into Position to Fire the AIM-9P Because the AIM-9P is a rear-aspect missile, it becomes a bit more difficult to maneuver into a position to use it. You cannot simply fire when you are within the five to seven mile range. There probably will not be enough heat for the missile to lock on to if you fire at an aircraft that is headed towards you. When planning your attack from a distance (over ten to twelve miles), the most important reading in your cockpit is the aspect angle of the enemy. You use the aspect angle to determine the action necessary to place the nose of your F-16 on the tail of the enemy target.

Recall that the aspect angle is available in two forms. The REO displays the numeric value of the aspect angle. This value is between zero and 180 followed by an L or an R. The closer the number is to zero, the closer you are to being on the tail. Numbers between 90 and 180 indicate that the target is facing you (to some degree). The HUD displays a graphic representation of the aspect angle using the aspect caret. The caret is V-shaped with the point of the "V" touching the aiming reticle. Figure 5-20 shows the relationship between aspect angle and target position. One way to *read* the caret is to think of the point of the "v" as the front of the target aircraft. You may have noticed this caret when using the AIM-120 and AIM-9M. However, the position of this caret becomes more important with the AIM-9P.

Once you have determined the aspect angle, the next step is to try to get to the rear of the target aircraft. If your aspect angle for the enemy target is below 100°, you are already close to being on the tail. All you need to do is bank slightly in the opposite direction of the aspect-angle indication. For example, if the aspect angle is 90R, this indicates that you are off the right wing of the target. Banking slightly to the right starts your F-16 in the direction of the rear of the target aircraft. The enemy may make adjustments to counter this maneuver if he detects you, however. Once you see the

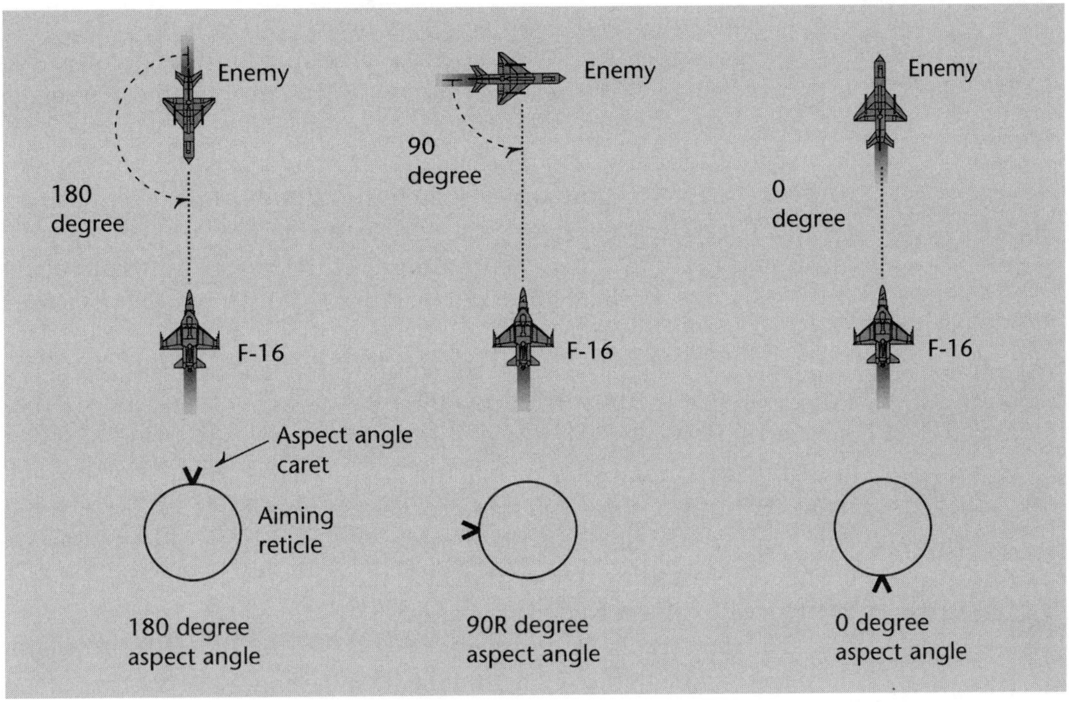

Figure 5-20 Relationship of the Aspect-Angle Caret to the Target Position

aspect angle get down below 45°, you can start to bank in the opposite direction to aim for the tail of the enemy (and hopefully a 0° aspect angle).

If the aspect angle is higher than 100°, you need to bank sharply in the opposite direction of the aspect angle first, then bank back hard as you pass the enemy and the aspect angle starts to drop. Figure 5-21 shows an example of moving from a high aspect-angle to the AIM-9P firing position. The

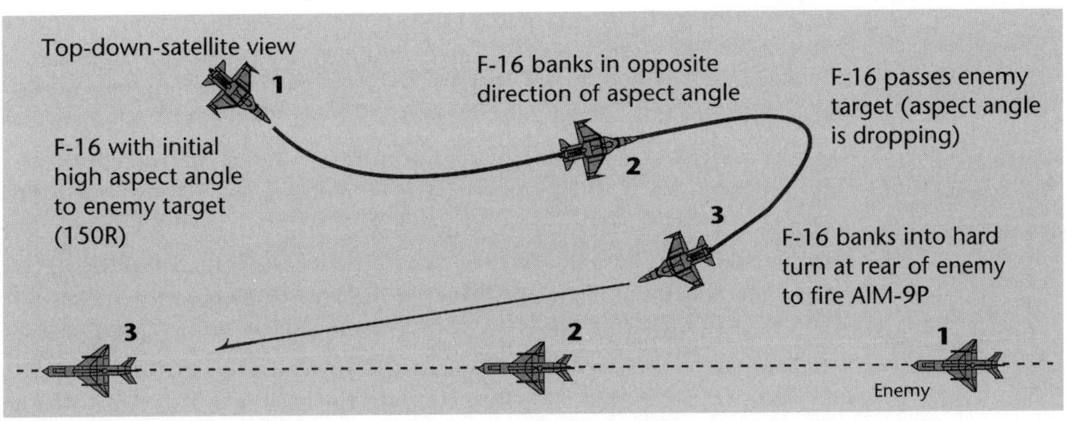

Figure 5-21 Using Aspect Angle to Gain the Proper Position to Fire the AIM-9P Sidewinder

enemy may make some counter movements (this is not shown in the figure). The higher the Enemy Logic Level setting in the Difficulty Levels screen, the harder it will be to perform these maneuvers without the enemy avoiding them.

The relative altitude and airspeed of the target is also important when using the AIM-9P. Always try to match the altitude of the enemy aircraft (+/–1,000 feet) before releasing the missile. If you spot an enemy target on radar, start to climb or dive to the altitude of the target immediately *before* you are in range of the target. Recall that the REO displays the target altitude in the upper right corner.

The desired relative airspeed (closure rate) depends on the situation. For example, if you are directly behind the enemy and slightly out of range for a missile shot, you want your closure rate to be positive. This means you are gaining on the target, which in this case is what you desire. On the other hand, if you are closing in on the tail of the enemy (within one or two miles), you may wish to decrease the throttle and keep from overshooting the enemy. The last thing you want to do is throw your F-16 out in front of the enemy so he can get a good shot at you.

The target range for releasing the AIM-9P is 1.5 to 6 miles. If you find the target in your sights, but within the 1.5 mile range, save your missile and switch to guns.

Using the M61A1 Cannon The M61A1 cannon is not a highly effective air-to-air combat weapon. It can be used in very close range situations or when the other air-to-air missiles have been fired. The key to using the guns is anticipation. You have to predict the next move of the enemy and instantly react to it. One method is to place a stream of 20mm shells out in front of the aircraft and let him fly into it. You also can go for the direct hit by flying up behind the enemy and firing directly at the tail. This is useful if you are in a position to fire an AIM-9P, but your high airspeed causes you to get too close to the target. If this happens, quickly switch to guns and fire!

The HUD also displays a few additional items that are useful in a dogfight. Figure 5-22 shows the five mile *radar ranging scale* and the *distance ranging scale*. The radar ranging scale is a vertical bar to the lower right of the aiming reticle. If a target is within five miles, a caret appears to the left side of the bar. A caret at the top of the bar indicates a target at five miles; the bottom of the bar indicates zero miles (the position of the F-16). Use the ranging bar or the digital readout in the lower right corner of the HUD (above the closure rate). The figure shows the caret towards the bottom of the scale (around one mile in range).

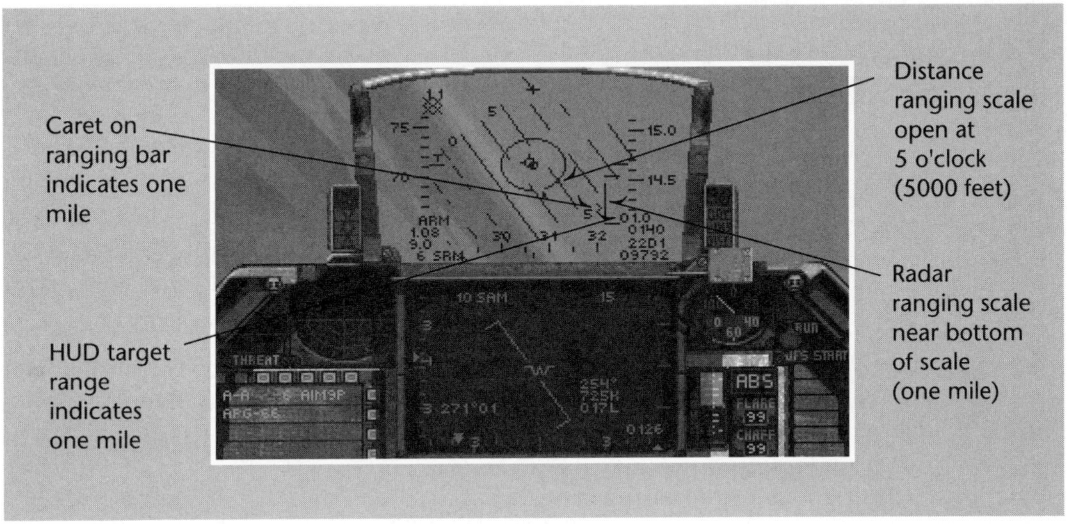

Figure 5-22 Radar Ranging Scale and Distance Ranging Scale

The distance ranging scale is a gap in the aiming reticle. If you are within 12,000 feet of the target, a gap opens up at the twelve o'clock position of the reticle. Eleven o'clock indicates 11,000 feet, 7 o'clock indicates 7,000 feet, etc. Figure 5-22 shows that gap open at about the five o'clock position. This indicates the target is at a range of 5,000 feet (about one mile). This coincides with the radar ranging scale and the digital range readout.

The example used in the figure calls for a switch to the M61A1 guns. This would not be a good time to fire the AIM-9P because of the close range.

Three Enemy Aircraft—Six AIM-9P Missiles As with the last mission, this lesson involves three enemy aircraft camped out at three waypoints. Waypoint 1 has a MiG-19 waiting for you. The MiG-19 is an older model aircraft that is not known for its maneuverability. This provides a good starting foe to learn to use the rear-aspect Sidewinder. Waypoint 2 has a MiG-25 patrolling the area. It presents a slightly more difficult challenge than the MiG-19. Waypoint 3 has the most difficult enemy in this mission, the MiG-29. All three enemy aircraft have the ability to use flares to try to avoid your Sidewinder assault. Remember that firing into the sun may also distract your missiles. Note that you have six missiles for this mission.

Go to Red Flag Control and load the AIM9P mission. Click on F-16 PILOTS, then F-16 ARMAMENT, and then TAKEOFF. Pause the simulation by pressing the P key. You start at an altitude (AGL) of 7,000 to 8,000 feet and an airspeed of approximately 450 knots. Once again, it is time for you to face the enemies!

- Unpause the simulation by pressing the P key.
- Press the ENTER key to select the AIM-9P missile. As with the AIM-9M, you hear a constant tone when the missile is selected. Note that the aiming reticle for the AIM-9P is the smallest of the three air-to-air missiles. This is because it is the most difficult missile to lock on to a target. Also note that the missile seeker head stays in the center of the HUD; it doesn't wander around like the AIM-9M seeker did.
- When you get within 10 to 20 miles of waypoint 1, you should pick up the first target on radar. The exact range depends on your airspeed and maneuvers on the way to the waypoint. Check the target IFF by pressing the N key.
- Try to keep the target designator box in the center of the HUD as you approach the target. Keep an eye on the aspect angle, closure rate, and distance from the target. Go on the attack, it's up to you now! If the target goes out of the range of the HUD, switch to padlock view by pressing the * key on the numeric keypad.
- Once you have flown to all three waypoints, press ESC to bring up the menu bar, then select END MISSION from the FILE menu. Click on CONTINUE in the debriefing room to see the summary of your actions during the mission. Click on NEXT MISSION to return to Red Flag Control.
- Continue to fly the AIM9P mission until you have destroyed all three enemy aircraft in one mission. You may want to read the rest of the lesson to help improve your skills and increase your mission success rate as a result.

Improving Your Falcon 3.0 Dogfighting Skills Because of the variable nature of Falcon 3.0, it is impossible to predict what is going to happen from this point on. The reactions of the enemy aircraft are based on artificial intelligence and, therefore, impossible to predict. However, here is some general advice to increase your AIM-9P and guns skills. Figure 5-23 shows a good position for an AIM-9P kill. The seeker head is tracking the designator box and the aspect angle is 013R (almost directly behind the target). The target is 1.7 miles away from the F-16. This is indicated in three areas: the digital readout (01.7), the radar ranging scale (the caret is close to the bottom of the five mile scale), and the aiming reticle (the opening at ten

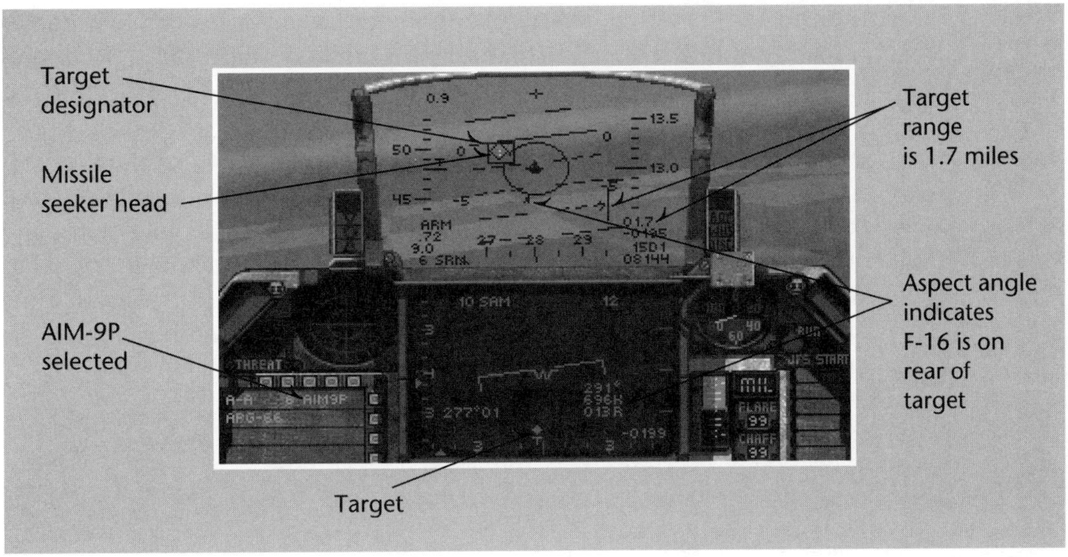

Figure 5-23 Firing Position for an AIM-9P Rear Aspect Sidewinder

o'clock shows that the target is 10,000 feet away, around 1.77 miles). If you keep the target in the center of the HUD, you should be able to gain this position.

One problem you will undoubtedly run into is overshooting the target. When this occurs, it is important to get out of this position immediately! If you don't, you will leave the enemy with a good shot at you. The objective is to get on the tail of the enemy, not the other way around. Besides overshooting the enemy, you will also encounter enemy pilots who are skilled enough to get on the tail of your F-16. You can use padlock view to help you get out of this situation.

Using Padlock View to Stay Out of Trouble It is a good idea to stay in padlock view as long as the target you are up against is in visual range. This enables you to maintain visual contact with the enemy aircraft even if it gets behind your Falcon. Using radar by itself is not that effective once you are in short-range missile or guns range. The target can get behind you and disappear from your APG-66 forward facing radar. If you stay in this position for too long you will end up going down in flames.

Figure 5-24 shows a time-lapsed example of using the padlock view to reverse the situation of an enemy aircraft on your tail. The main padlock window is not shown in the example. In the first phase, the pilot notices an enemy aircraft directly on the rear of his F-16. At this point, he decides which direction to bank the F-16. Normally, it is best to bank to the side that the enemy is favoring. In this example, the enemy is exactly behind the F-16; therefore, the direction of the bank is not important. The pilot chooses to bank to the right.

In the second phase, the padlock view shows the F-16 starting to pull around on the enemy. The target designator box is starting to move from the left side to the center of the 360° window. The waterline indicates that the F-16 is banking to the left (note the position of the small lines on the end of the waterline extending to the left). The target locator line extends showing where the target is located. This is the same as the target locator line on the HUD. At this point, the pilot sees the target locator line, adjusts the bank of the F-16, and starts to head for the target.

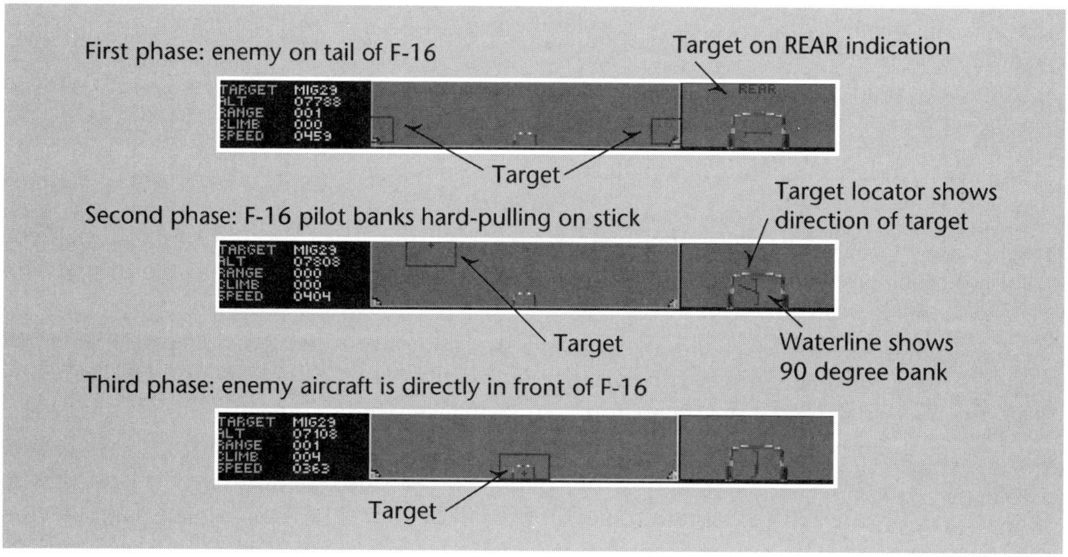

Figure 5-24 Time Lapsed Padlock View

The third phase shows the target in the center of the miniature HUD in the 360° window. At this point, the pilot can see the HUD and the target in the main padlock window. He can either pursue the enemy using the padlock view or switch back to cockpit front view. It is highly recommended to stay in padlock view and pursue the target. Doing so prevents you from losing sight of the enemy.

Debriefing: Rear Aspect/Guns Kill The AIM-9P Sidewinder is a rear-aspect infrared missile. Rear-aspect means that it must be fired at the rear of a target aircraft to gain a successful hit. The AIM-9P can be locked on in a range of five to six miles. The aiming reticle for this Sidewinder is the smallest of the F-16 air-to-air arsenal. As with all of the Falcon air-to-air missiles, the missile lock is required until the AIM-9P is fired. At that point, you can maneuver into another position.

The enemy pilot has flares to use as a countermeasure to the AIM-9P. The Sidewinder can be distracted by the flare, causing a wasted missile shot. The sun also distracts the AIM-9P because of the radiant heat. Always wait for a target to turn out of the line with the sun to avoid wasting a missile.

The AIM-9P is the least expensive air-to-air missile in Falcon 3.0. Therefore, there will be plenty available in campaigns. The only drawback to the AIM-9P is that the requirements to achieve a successful kill are greater. A skilled pilot should find that the AIM-9P is a formidable weapon. Practice using the AIM-9P until you establish a good success rate (30 to 50% is good). You will be glad you did when your squadron runs out of AIM-120s and AIM-9Ms in the middle of a campaign.

Weapon Lesson #4: The Mavericks

This lesson covers two weapons that are much alike, the AGM-65B and the AGM-65D Maverick missiles. Both weapons are used for air-to-ground attacks. The primary difference between the two Mavericks is the type of seeker head employed. The AGM-65B uses a television type seeker to guide the missile to the ground target, while the AGM-65D uses an infrared seeker. Because of its infrared nature, the AGM-65D is superior to its counterpart for night attacks.

Both Maverick types are of the fire-and-forget classification. This means that you can lock on to a different target or simply fly away once you have fired the missile. This is a great feature for this type of weapon; you may need a quick exit after an air-to-ground attack. In Falcon 3.0, you have to get within close range to the ground targets in order to lock on with a Maverick.

This lesson consists of two Red Flag missions, MAVRICK1 and MAVRICK2. The first lesson loads six AGM-65B Mavericks aboard the F-16. The second lesson loads six AGM-65D missiles. Both missions direct you to three waypoints where there is known to be ground activity. Most of the ground units you encounter are not equipped to attack your F-16. The last waypoint (waypoint 3), however, has infantry units that are equipped with shoulder-mounted SAMs. You won't see much action as long as you stay low, release your weapons, and fly away immediately. This adds a touch of realism as you get closer to participating in an actual campaign.

Lesson Objectives In this lesson you:

- Use waypoints (intelligence information) to locate regions where ground troops reside.
- Locate ground forces by patrolling or using rotated track view.
- Lock up a ground target with AGM-65B and AGM-65D (separate missions).
- Fire air-to-ground missiles and determine outcome with threat/missile view.
- Use the Debriefing screen in Red Flag to observe results.

Ground School In addition to the keys used to fly the F-16 Falcon, we introduce a few new keys for this mission. The BACKSPACE key cycles through the air-to-ground weapons that are loaded. Simultaneously, it selects an air-to-ground HUD mode that is associated with the type of weapon. For example, selecting the AGM-65B automatically selects the E-O (Electro-Optical) HUD mode, while the AGM-65D selects the I-R (Infrared) HUD mode.

The Maverick HUD Modes Although the delivery methods are virtually identical, the ways the AGM-65B and the AGM-65D lock on to a target are very different. The AGM-65B uses a television imaging seeker. The pilot uses the television signal to acquire and lock on to a target; therefore, the Electro-Optical (E-O) HUD mode is used for the missile. The AGM-65D requires heat to lock on to a target. This requires the use of the I-R HUD mode. Figure 5-25 shows the E-O HUD mode for the AGM-65B.

Selecting an air-to-ground weapon has significant effects on the cockpit view. The HUD displays the heading indicator at the top to allow better vision towards the bottom. This is useful for making visual identification of ground targets. The center of the HUD displays crosshairs that are used to aim at ground targets. Once a target is locked by the weapon, the crosshairs follow the target around the HUD (much like the way the missile seeker head did with air-to-air weapons). The REO displays the electro-optical image of the target if one is locked by the air-to-ground weapon. One drawback to using the REO for air-to-ground weapons is that the radar information is no longer displayed. This is no problem as long as you use the air-to-ground mode for short periods of time. Remember to switch back after using the weapons. You may spot an enemy target that would have gone unnoticed if you had not switched back to air-to-air mode.

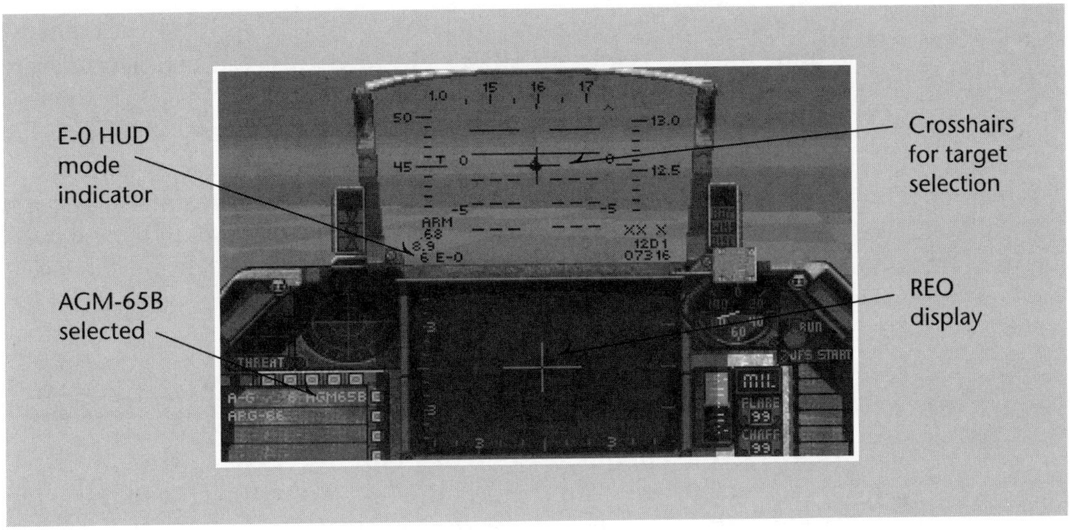

Figure 5-25 The Electro-Optical (E-O) HUD Mode for the AGM-65B

Finding Enemy Ground Targets In a Falcon 3.0 campaign, you receive intelligence information before setting out to destroy enemy ground units. This information has been gathered by reconnaissance aircraft and supplied to your squadron to plan the mission. From that information, you set waypoints that coincide with the location of the ground forces. Then it becomes a matter of following the waypoints. Will the enemy ground forces be exactly where the intelligence reports said they would be? Not exactly. You may have to search the area to find the ground targets once you arrive at the target waypoint. How close the intelligence reports are to the actual location is a function of the INTEL setting at the Difficulty Levels screen. The levels range from perfect (least realistic) to limited (most realistic).

Once you have arrived at, or as you approach, the target waypoint, you can find the targets using one of two methods. The first method, and the most realistic, involves searching the area using the cockpit view keys. The keys for the four cockpit views are the numeric keypad 1 (front), 7 (left), 9 (right), and 3 (rear). When you approach the target area, use the four view keys and watch the displays closely for small brown dots on the ground. Once you have identified the targets, maneuver the aircraft for a position of attack.

The second, less realistic, method of locating ground targets involves the track view and rotate keys. You can select the track view by pressing the 9 key on the upper row, and rotate the view around the F-16 by pressing F3 or F4. The ground units appear as small brown dots. When you locate the targets, note their location relative to your F-16 and start the maneuver to bring the targets into the HUD view. Once this is accomplished, switch back to cockpit view to start your attack.

You should be at a low altitude (1,000 to 3,000 feet) when searching for ground targets. There are times when AAA fire from enemy ground units may prohibit this. Make sure you do not attack friendly units. There is no IFF for ground units. You must make your decision based on visual identification.

> **NOTE:** Friendly ground units are dark green. Enemy ground units are brown. Always ensure the target is enemy before firing air-to-ground missiles or bombs. Failure to do so may result in a court-martial.

Locking the Target and Firing the Maverick Once the targets appear through the windscreen of the F-16, point the nose of the F-16 to place the HUD crosshairs over the target. When you are in range, the crosshairs will move to a target and the distance-to-target indicator becomes active (numbers displayed on HUD). The distance-to-target indicator displays Xs when the target is not locked. If a target is locked, the Maverick can be released by pressing the SPACEBAR. Figure 5-26 shows the proper firing conditions for the AGM-65B. The Maverick has been fired in this example.

Once the Maverick is on the way, you can switch to another target and fire again, or you can leave the area. The normal scenario for an air-to-

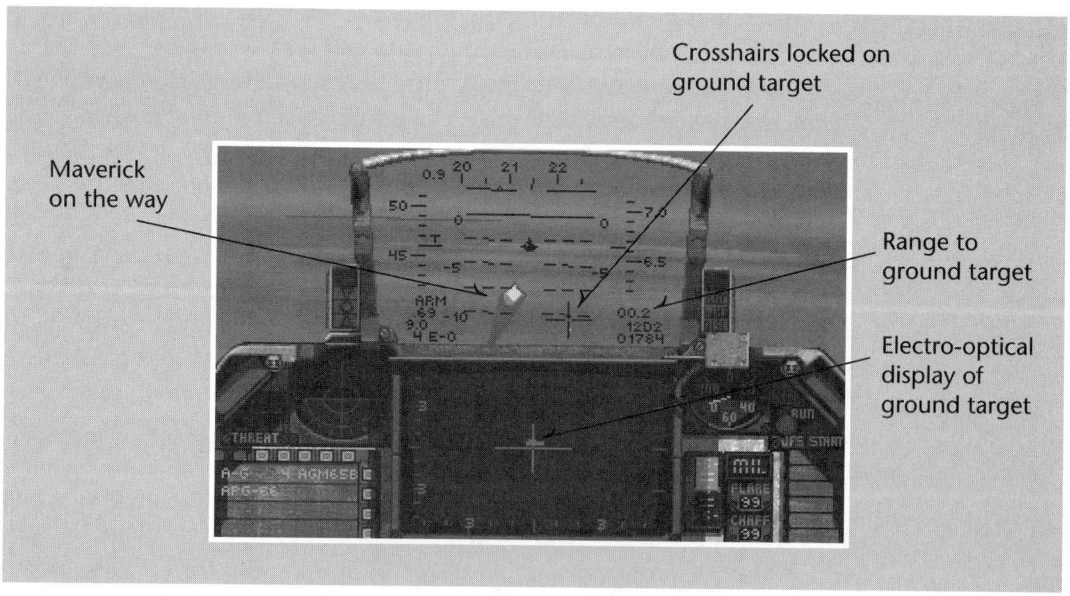

Figure 5-26 Proper Firing Conditions for an AGM-65B Maverick Missile

ground attack is to fly to the area, find the targets, unload the ordnance, and get out of the area as quickly as possible. In this mission, you will observe the missiles as they destroy the ground targets. You will not always have this time during actual combat missions.

Attacking the Ground Targets This lesson has two missions, one for the AGM-65B and one for the AGM-65D. The missions are identical except for the weapon type and the location of friendly forces. You fly over three waypoints. Intelligence has reported that ground forces are concentrated at each of the waypoints. Your goal is to destroy two targets at each waypoint. You have six Mavericks on your F-16, so don't waste a shot!

Go to Red Flag Control and load the MAVRICK1 mission. Click on F-16 PILOTS, then F-16 ARMAMENT, and then TAKEOFF. Pause the simulation by pressing the P key. You will start at an altitude (AGL) of 7,000 to 8,000 feet and an airspeed of approximately 450 knots. It is time to search out the enemy ground forces and destroy them.

> **NOTE:** Falcon 3.0 randomly selects a time of day for Red Flag Missions. If this mission starts at night, change to a daylight mission by pressing SHIFT-T. The AGM-65B is more effective in daylight missions.

- Unpause the simulation by pressing the P key. You should be heading towards the southwest. Maintain your alignment with the waypoint caret.
- Start a descent as you proceed to waypoint 1. Try to descend to between 2,500 and 3,000 feet before you are five miles from the waypoint (5D1). Decrease the throttle a few notches with the − key to set your airspeed to 350 knots.
- If you notice any ground targets along the way, make sure they are enemy targets (brown) before attacking. You should find enemy targets only within a one or two mile radius of a waypoint. Intelligence information should be fairly accurate for this mission.
- When you are within three miles of waypoint 1, start to scan by checking the left (numeric keypad 7), right (numeric keypad 9), and forward (numeric keypad 1) cockpit views. Keep an eye out for a group of small brown dots on the ground.
- Once you have spotted the group of ground targets, switch to air-to-ground mode by pressing the BACKSPACE key. The crosshairs for the Maverick appear on the HUD and the REO.

- Start banking to point the nose of the F-16 in the direction of the ground forces. For example, if you spot the ground forces out the left view, switch back to front view and bank the F-16 to the left.
- Once the forces are in sight through the HUD, nose down a bit to put the crosshairs on the forces. The crosshairs jump to one of the targets when the lock-on occurs. Keep an eye on your altitude; don't fly into the ground!
- When the lock occurs, press the SPACEBAR to fire a Maverick. Quickly press the T key to lock up a different target and press the SPACEBAR to fire another Maverick at the second target. Level out the F-16 and make sure you are not descending.
- Press the Q key to observe the missile view. Pressing the Q key again changes the view to a perspective of the target. Stay on this view as the missile slams into the target and destroys it. If the missile is not locked on to a ground unit, this view will be available.
- Pause the simulation by pressing the P key.

  Don't worry if you did not have time to switch to the target view. You still have two more waypoints to visit. Try the sequence again when you get there. Figure 5-27 shows the target view of a T-72 tank being destroyed.
- Unpause the simulation by pressing the P key.

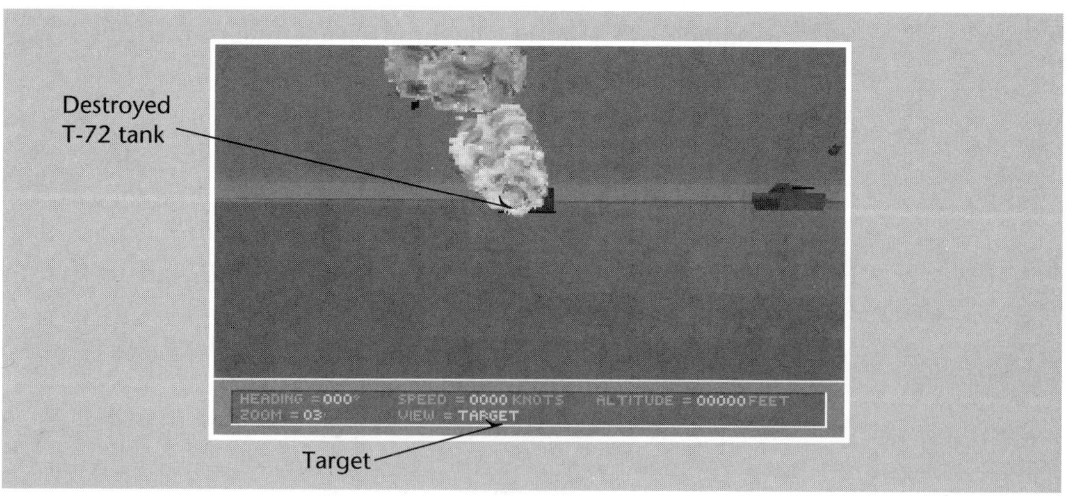

Figure 5-27 A T-72 Enemy Tank Is Destroyed by a Maverick Missile

- If the distance-to-waypoint indicator does not show waypoint 2 (*xx*D2), change it manually by pressing SHIFT-B (bypass waypoint).

- Climb back to 3,000 feet and switch back to air-to-air mode by pressing the ENTER key. Bank the F-16 to align the waypoint caret with the center of the HUD. Your heading should be in the southerly direction (approximately 180°).

- Repeat the same procedure as you approach waypoint 2. Use the views to locate the ground forces. Switch to air-to-ground mode by pressing BACKSPACE.

- Bank to line the Falcon up with the forces. Dip the nose to point the Maverick crosshairs at the targets. When the target is locked and the crosshairs move, fire the missile by pressing the SPACEBAR. Press T to lock up a second target and fire another missile with the SPACEBAR. Make sure that you lock a different target before firing or you will send a second missile at a target that you have already destroyed. This is a waste of a missile.

- Level off and press the Q key once to observe the missile view. Press the Q key again to switch to the ground target perspective.

- Return to cockpit front view by pressing the 1 on the numeric keypad. Bypass waypoint 2 (if necessary) and head for waypoint 3.

- When you reach waypoint 3, locate the ground forces and fire off your last two Mavericks. A word of warning, there is an infantry unit at waypoint 3. If you loiter around or get too close to the target, you may get a missile launch indication on your TWI. Refer to the TWI lesson in Chapter 4, *Radar and Enemy Identification*, for more information on missile avoidance.

- Press ESC to bring up the menu bar and select END MISSION from the FILE menu. Click on CONTINUE at the Debriefing screen to display a summary of your mission. Click on NEXT MISSION when you are done reviewing the summary.

Consider the mission a success if you destroy a ground target with each Maverick. Once you have successfully completed the MAVRICK1 mission, load the MAVRICK2 mission. The only difference is that the weapon, an AGM-65D, uses an infrared seeker. You can fly this mission at night; the AGM-65D is much more effective at night than the AGM-65B

Debriefing: The Mavericks The AGM-65B and AGM-65D Mavericks are air-to-ground missiles that are capable of destroying vehicles including armored personnel carriers and tanks. They can also destroy softer targets such as trucks and jeeps, although this is usually a waste of a Maverick. There are less expensive weapons that can destroy the softer targets. How do you know the type of target the Maverick locks on to? You will have to gain experience of making a determination by observing the REO image of the target. You won't have much time to make the decision in actual combat. While you are flying around trying to figure out if a target is a tank or a truck, an enemy is plotting to shoot you down!

In campaigns, you most likely use Mavericks when your assignment is to destroy a tank column or group of armored vehicles. You have to react quickly and get out of the area as soon as possible. Practice using the Mavericks with this lesson and you will be ready for action when called upon in a campaign.

Weapon Lesson #5: Anti-Radiation Missiles

This lesson covers the two anti-radiation missiles that are available in Falcon 3.0, the AGM-88A HARM and the AGM-45A Shrike. These missiles play an important role in destroying ground radar units that guide surface-to-air missiles, or SAMs. They are a must for missions that involve flying over SAM sites to get to the primary target. It may be necessary to send up a flight of F-16s to take out the SAMs so another flight can make its way to its destination unimpeded.

The AGM-88A HARM (High-speed Anti-Radiation Missile) is the more powerful of the two. It has a longer range of up to 30 miles, giving you more time to lock on to the SAM radar, fire the missile, and possibly avoid an incoming missile. In addition to the range advantage, the HARM is effective against both CW and pulse-Doppler radars. Most the SAM radar in Falcon 3.0 is CW; CW is represented by a 1 on the threat warning indicator. The only pulse-Doppler SAM in Falcon 3.0 is the SA-8 Gecko. This lesson uses SA-6 Gainful SAM units. The SA-6 employs a CW radar. Refer to the lesson on the TWI in Chapter 4, *Radar and Enemy Identification*, for more information on enemy radar.

The AGM-45A Shrike is only effective against CW SAM radars and has a shorter range (around 12 miles) than the HARM. Fortunately, most of the enemy forces employ CW radar. The short range presents a bit of a problem because you must get fairly close to the deadly SAM to lock on and fire a missile. The Shrike does have two major advantages over the HARM, cost and availability. The more powerful and versatile a weapon is, the higher the cost. When the cost is high, the availability in a campaign is seriously affected. Your arsenal in a Falcon 3.0 campaign will contain many more Shrikes than HARMS. It is important that you learn how to use both weapons effectively before committing to your first campaign.

Both of the missiles lock on to an enemy radar signal and ride the beam to its source. Once the missile is fired, the F-16 pilot can activate ECM, drop chaff, and take necessary evasive maneuvers to evade an incoming missile (if one exists). The HUD and REO displays for both weapons are virtually identical.

This lesson consists of a single Red Flag mission, ANTIRAD. This lesson has an additional risk factor built in. You have flown air-to-air combat against weaponless enemy aircraft and fired air-to-ground missiles against defenseless tanks and trucks. This mission pits you against SAM sites that are capable of destroying your F-16; they will fire back! This is necessary in Falcon 3.0 because SAM operators will not turn on their radar sets if they are not permitted to fire missiles. If they do not activate their radar, you will not be able to lock on to the target.

Your F-16 is loaded with two AGM-88As and two AGM-45As. An ECM pod is also loaded to help you avoid incoming SAMs. If you are not proficient at avoiding SAMs, we recommend you review "Lesson 5: Avoidance Tactics" in Chapter 4 before flying this mission.

Lesson Objectives In this lesson you:

- Cycle through multiple air-to-ground weapons.
- Allow a SAM unit to lock on to your F-16.
- Lock an AGM-88A and an AGM-45A on to the SAM radar signal.
- Destroy an SA-6 Gainful mobile SAM.
- Observe kill/miss using the target/missile view.
- Use the Debriefing screen in Red Flag to observe results.

Ground School No new keys are introduced in this lesson. You will use the (BACKSPACE) key to cycle through the air-to-ground weapons and HUD modes. You can fire the selected missile by pressing the (SPACEBAR). The (Q) key selects the missile/target views, and pressing (SHIFT)-(B) bypasses a waypoint. The HUD modes for the two anti-radiation missiles are both identical to that of the Maverick HUD mode. The missiles lock on at a much longer range than the Mavericks, however.

Using the Anti-Radiation Missiles You need steady nerves to use the anti-radiation missiles effectively. Figure 5-28 shows the process of destroying a SAM radar. In the first step, the Falcon flies into enemy territory. The enemy SAM radar locks up the target in step 2; an enemy missile could also be fired at this point. In step 3, the Falcon pilot observes the missile lock warning (LCK) on the TWI, maneuvers to lock up the target, and fires an anti-radiation missile. In step 4, the Falcon pilot starts evasive maneuvers and activates ECM to break the radar lock of the SAM unit (or avoid an incoming missile). The anti-radiation missile finds its target in step 5, destroying the SAM unit (no more lock on at this point). Step 6 shows the F-16, having suppressed the SAM unit, returning to level flight.

Of course not all attacks on SAM units go this smoothly. The anti-radiation missiles are by no means perfect; be prepared to escape the area even if your missile misses the mark. The training mission involves one SAM site at each of three waypoints. In actual campaign missions, SAM units are grouped together. It takes a team effort between you and your wingmen to get the job done. It is time for you to jump in the cockpit and destroy some SAMs!

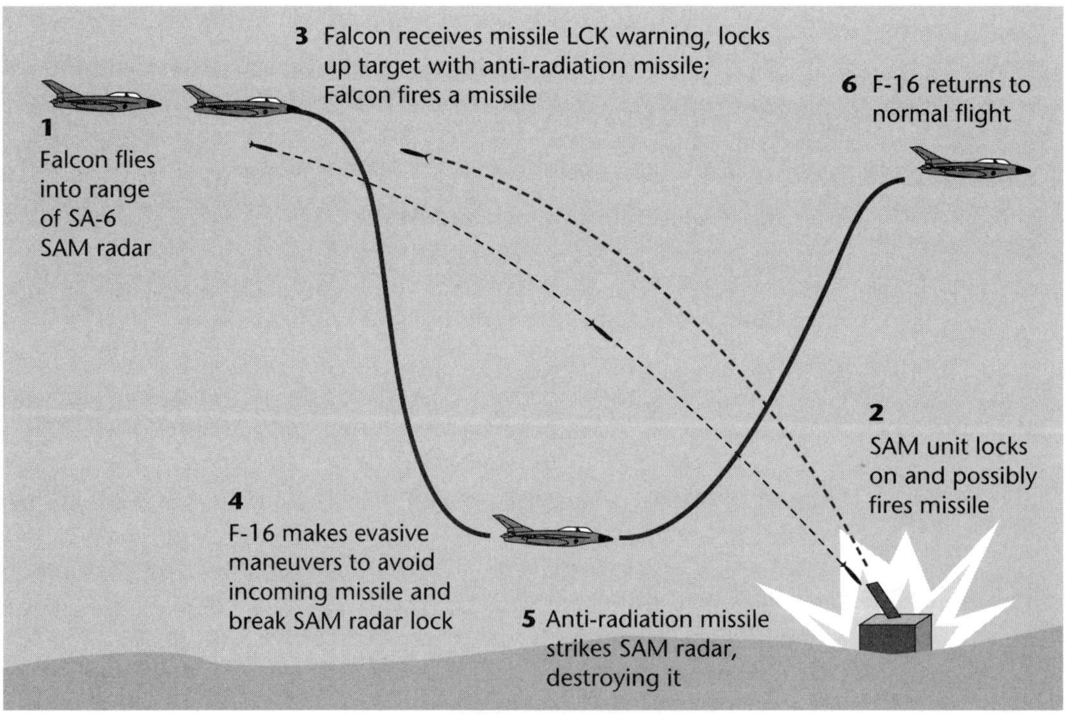

Figure 5-28 Destroying a SAM Radar with Anti-Radiation Missiles

SAM Hunting This lesson has only one mission, but it is a very difficult mission to master. The SAM radar operators are waiting for enemy aircraft to enter their area. Your job is to go out and destroy three SAM sites. Each SAM site is positioned near a waypoint. You will see the site's radar transmissions on your TWI long before you actually reach the site.

There is one final note before heading out. Falcon 3.0 missions are variable; a mission produces very different results each time it is flown. For example, in this mission, if you destroy the first two SAM sites, there is a chance that the third operator will get wise and refuse to turn on the radar. Consider this a success! You can't destroy a radar if the enemy doesn't turn it on. The enemy cannot fire a SAM with the radar set turned off either!

Go to Red Flag Control and load the ANTIRAD mission. Click on F-16 PILOTS, then F-16 ARMAMENT, and then TAKEOFF. Pause the simulation by pressing the P key. You start at an altitude (AGL) of 7,000 to 8,000 feet and an airspeed of approximately 450 knots. It is time to search out the enemy SAM units and destroy them.

- Unpause the simulation by pressing the P key. You should be 19 to 20 miles from waypoint 1.
- Continue towards waypoint 1. Maintain your current altitude and drop your airspeed to 375 knots (use the - key to cut the throttle).
- Press the BACKSPACE key until the stores control panel displays AGM-88. The BACKSPACE key will cycle through the three air-to-ground weapons (AGM-88, AGM-45, and M61A1 guns).
- When you are 10 to 15 miles from waypoint 1 (this may vary with each mission), you will receive a lock on warning on the TWI (LCK indicator). You may also receive a missile launch warning (LNH indicator). The TWI also indicates the relative position of the enemy radar on the circular display.
- Pause the simulation and refer to Figure 5-29. This is the position you are trying to achieve.

You must maneuver the F-16 to face the threat. For example, if the TWI shows the ground radar icon in the upper left quadrant, this indicates that the target is forward and to your left. Bank to the left to bring the target into view. If the target was in the lower half of the circular display, bank the F-16 hard to turn around and face the threat.

Once you are facing the threat and within range for the type of missile you have selected, the crosshairs move to the target indicating that the missile is locked on. If the target is slightly out of the view of the HUD, the

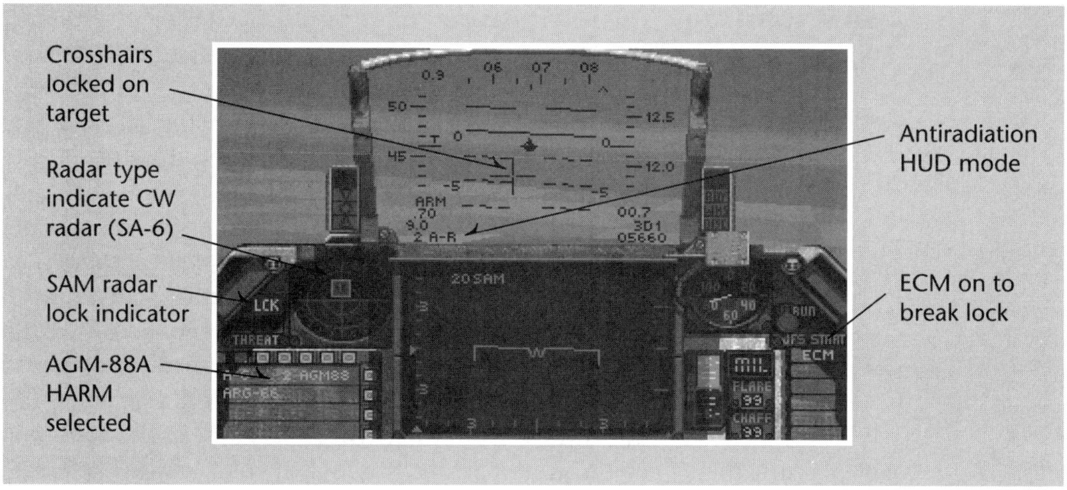

Figure 5-29 AGM-88 Locked on SAM radar

crosshairs will become dotted lines. When you get the lock-on position, fire the missile, turn on the ECM pod, and make your escape.

Now that you have the basics for attacking the SAM radar, head back to the cockpit to try it yourself!

- Unpause the simulation by pressing the P key.
- Bank the F-16 to face the threat. Use the TWI to guide you. You want the ground radar indicator (square with a 1 in it) to be in the middle and slightly toward the top of the TWI circle.

NOTE: If it takes you too long to set up for a missile shot and an enemy SAM is on the way (small square on TWI), activate the ECM pod by pressing the E key and start evasive maneuvers. Once you have successfully avoided the missile, turn off the pod and try the attack again.

- When you have the target in range and the crosshairs move to the target, press the SPACEBAR to fire the missile.
- Activate your ECM pod by pressing the E key and start evasive maneuvers. You can view the flight of the missile by pressing the Q key once, or you can view from the target perspective by pressing the Q key twice. *Be sure you are flying level with no impending threats when you switch views!*

- Once you are sure the missile has destroyed the SAM radar, switch back to cockpit view by pressing the 1 key on the numeric keypad. Turn off your ECM pod by pressing the E key again. If the SAM site was not destroyed, turn around and try again.
- Now that the threat at waypoint 1 is taken care of, press SHIFT-B to bypass waypoint 1 and head for waypoint 2. Remember to line up the waypoint caret.
- Repeat the same procedure when you get a lock from the SAM stationed near waypoints 2 and 3. Turn to face the threat, wait for the missile lock, and fire with the SPACEBAR. You will have to press the BACKSPACE key to cycle to the AGM-45 once you have fired the AGM-88s. Then take evasive maneuvers to get out of the way of any incoming missiles. The SAM operator at waypoint 3 may not turn on the radar if you have successfully taken out the units at waypoints 1 and 2.
- Once you have flown over all three waypoints, or you are out of anti-radiation missiles, press ESC to bring up the menu bar. Select END MISSION from the FILE menu. Click on CONTINUE at the Debriefing screen to get a summary of your actions. Click on NEXT MISSION to return to Red Flag Control.

Debriefing: Anti-Radiation Missiles Falcon 3.0 provides two anti-radiation missiles, the AGM-88A HARM and the AGM-45A Shrike. Both of the missiles have the same purpose, to destroy enemy SAM radar. The HARM is the more powerful and expensive of the two missiles. It can lock on targets up to a range of 30 miles. It also has the capability to lock on to CW and pulse-Doppler signals.

The Shrike is much less expensive and is usually available in quantity in a Falcon 3.0 campaign. The downside of the Shrike is that it is limited to CW radar and it has a shorter range (about 12 miles). It is very risky to get close enough to SAM radars to use the Shrike. It can be done, however, with practice and an ECM pod. An ECM pod is always recommended for a SAM hunting mission.

These anti-radiation missiles play a big part in the Falcon 3.0 campaigns. You will receive orders to attack targets that are far behind enemy lines. In many cases, the targets or the routes to the targets are heavily guarded with SAM and AAA units. You, as squadron commander, will decide how to handle the threat. You will assign a flight of F-16s to fly out ahead to clear a path for the remaining flights to use. You can even assign the mission to *your* flight if you feel you are an expert at killing SAMs. Whether you take the mission on yourself or assign it to another flight of Falcons, it is imperative that you understand what it takes to attack enemy SAM units.

Weapon Lesson #6: LAU and Strafing

This lesson introduces a new weapon, the LAU 5003A Rocket Launcher. You will also take another look at the M61A1 20mm cannon. This time you will use the cannon for air-to-ground attacks. Neither of these weapons is highly effective. They are designed for use against soft targets (jeeps, trucks, infantry). These two weapons can be extremely dangerous to use because you have to fly at a very low altitude to fire them effectively. You risk attack from a ground unit (AAA fire and SAMs) and you also risk flying into the ground.

The LAU 5003A Rocket Launcher is loaded under the wings in much the same way as air-to-ground missiles. Up to four launchers can be loaded depending on other loaded weapons. Each launcher is capable of firing 19 rockets, bringing the maximum number of rockets to 76. The individual rockets have no guidance system like the Mavericks, HARMs, and Shrikes. You aim a *pipper* at the target and fire. The HUD displays the pipper (a circle with a dot in the center of it) when the LAU is the selected weapon.

The M61A1 Vulcan cannon is the same one used in Weapon Lesson 3 for the guns kill. The only difference is that the HUD mode for the M61A1 air-to-ground is STRF (strafe) and the air-to-air HUD mode for the Vulcan was DGFT (dogfight). The DGFT HUD displays a historical gunsight. This funnel shows where the 20mm shells would have hit had they been fired a second ago. The air-to-ground STRF HUD mode uses a pipper (much like the LAU). The LAU pipper moves around depending on the motion of the aircraft. This calculation of plane movement and the position of the pipper is made by the Falcon's onboard computer. This is called the *Continuously Computed Impact Point*, or CCIP. We will discuss a slightly different version of CCIP in the next lesson on iron bombs.

Lesson Objectives In this lesson you:

- Locate soft ground targets on visual patrol with limited advanced intelligence.
- Attack soft ground targets using the LAU 5003A Rocket Launcher.
- Attack soft ground targets using the M61A1 Vulcan cannon.

- Use the Debriefing screen in Red Flag to observe your results.

Ground School No new keys are introduced in this mission. You select the air-to-ground weapons by pressing the (BACKSPACE) key. For this mission, the (BACKSPACE) key toggles between the LAU and the Vulcan (guns). The (SPACEBAR) fires the selected weapon. The threat/missile key does not function for either the LAU or the Vulcan. If you destroy a vehicle, you see it by looking directly out the cockpit windscreen.

Strafing Ground Targets Although the LAU is a very easy weapon to use (just point the pipper and shoot), the Vulcan cannon requires a little explanation before you head back for the skies. The technique used for air-to-ground cannon attacks is called strafing. Figure 5-30 shows two methods of strafing using the M61A1 cannon. The first method starts with the Falcon flying in level at a relatively low altitude (300–1,000 feet). As the F-16 nears the ground targets, the pilot pushes on the stick (dips), fires the Vulcan, and

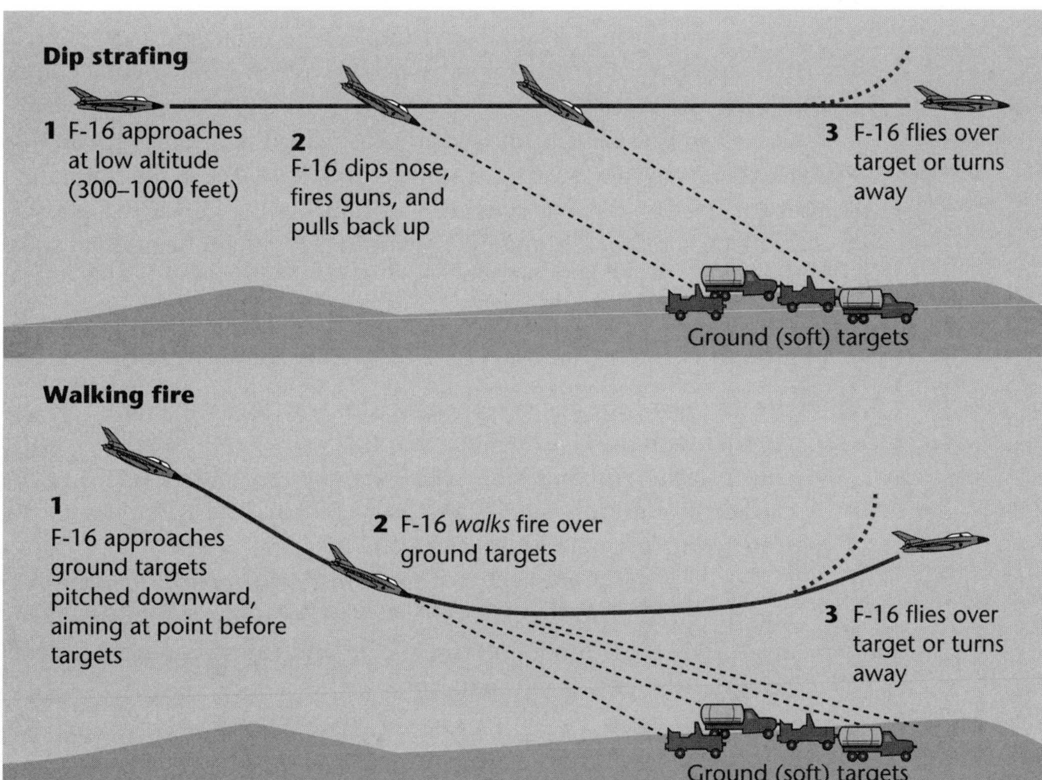

Figure 5-30 Two Strafing Methods Using the M61A1 Vulcan Cannon

then pulls up. If the F-16 has not flown over the targets, the pilot repeats the process.

The other method starts with the F-16 in a dive, with the nose pointed just before the ground targets. Just before the aircraft reaches ground level, the pilot pulls out and fires the cannon. This results in the cannon fire walking over the target. Both methods normally result in the F-16 flying over the targets or banking off to the side. It is not wise to hang around after strafing a ground unit. For this lesson, however, the enemy is unarmed, so you can make several passes to practice using the LAU and guns.

You are not limited to the above methods when using the Vulcan cannon. With some practice and experimentation you may find other ways to get the job done! In a campaign, you usually won't have a lot of time to hang around and play shoot 'em up.

Attacking with the LAU and Vulcan Cannon This lesson uses two waypoints. The ground targets are in a group somewhere in between the two waypoints. If you don't find the targets on the first time through, the waypoints cycle through again. For example, when you get to waypoint 2, the HUD automatically guides you back to waypoint 1. All you have to do is follow the waypoint caret.

Go to Red Flag Control and load the LAUSTRAF mission. Click on F-16 PILOTS, then F-16 ARMAMENT, and then TAKEOFF. Pause the simulation by pressing the P key. You start at an altitude (AGL) of 7,000 to 8,000 feet and an airspeed of approximately 450 knots. It is time to search out some soft ground targets to destroy.

- Unpause the simulation by pressing the P key. You should be around 12 miles from waypoint 1 traveling southeast (around 155°).

- Use the few minutes you have before reaching waypoint 1 to get familiar with the HUD. Notice that the M61A1 is selected (the stores control panel displays M61); however, the HUD mode is DGFT. The cannon is currently set for air-to-air combat. The A-A entry in the stores control panel also indicates this. Press the BACKSPACE key to select the air-to-ground mode. The stores control panel now displays A-G and the HUD mode switches to STRF (strafe). Press the BACKSPACE key again. The HUD mode indicates CCIP and the stores control panel indicates the LAU is selected.

- When you get to waypoint 1, the waypoint caret moves to indicate the direction of waypoint 2 (approximately 190°). Start a sharp descent. You want to search for ground targets, so descend to 1,000 to 1,500 feet.

- Start scanning the ground. Use the cockpit front (numeric 1 key), left (numeric 7 key), and right (numeric 9 key) views to search for the ground targets.

- When you spot the ground forces, maneuver the F-16 into a position where you will pass over the targets lengthwise. This gives you a better chance of hitting one of the ground targets. Figure 5-31 shows the F-16 cockpit view as the pilot approaches the ground targets. If you cannot locate the ground targets, fly to waypoint 2. The waypoint indicator switches back to waypoint 1. This directs you over the ground forces again. Be sure to fly low (1,000 to 1,500 feet).

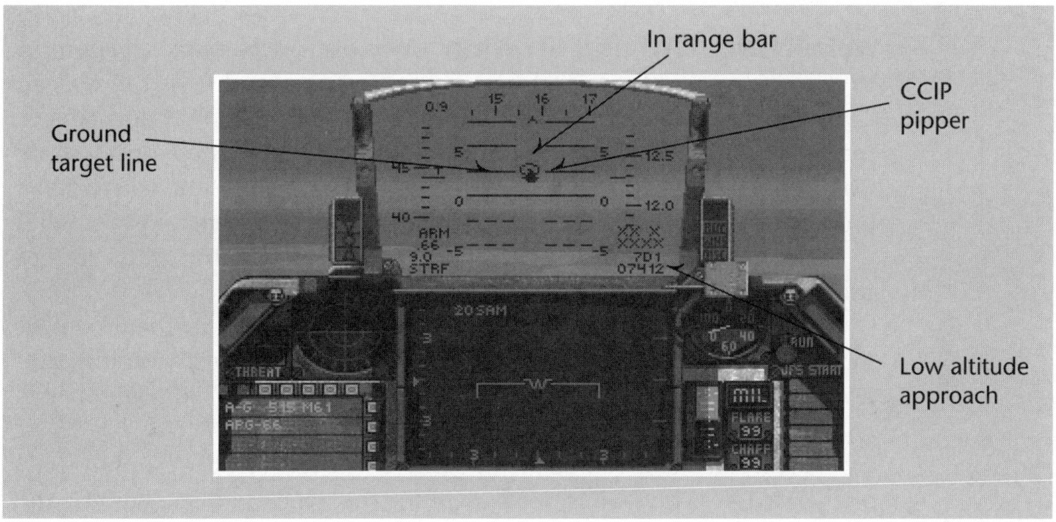

Figure 5-31 Flying Lengthwise Over Enemy Ground Forces

Figure 5-31 also shows some information about the LAU (CCIP) HUD mode. In addition to the pipper, the HUD displays an *in-range* bar when the target is in range of the LAU Rocket Launcher. The M61A1 cannon does not display the in-range bar.

- Make a pass over the targets, dip and aim the CCIP pipper at the targets, and press the SPACEBAR to fire the cannon. Each time you press the SPACEBAR, one rocket is fired. If you hold the SPACEBAR down, multiple rockets are fired. If you hit a target, it goes up in flames.

- Pull up and pass by the targets. Fly by two or three miles then turn 180° and return. Press BACKSPACE to switch back to the Vulcan and return to the targets. Each time you press the SPACEBAR, the Vulcan fires five

20mm shells. You can see the indication on the stores control panel. Each mission starts with 515 20mm shells.

- Continue to pass back and forth over the targets until you have exhausted the supply of weapons.
- Press (ESC) to bring up the menu bar and select END MISSION from the FILE menu. Click on CONTINUE at the Debriefing screen to display a summary of your mission. Click on NEXT MISSION when you finish reviewing the summary.

Try this mission several times. See how many ground forces you can destroy with the limited amount of weapons available.

Debriefing: LAU and Strafing Two of the lesser used weapons in Falcon 3.0 are the LAU 5003A Rocket Launcher and the M61A1 Vulcan cannon. Each weapon is designed for attacks against soft ground targets, such as jeeps and trucks. The Rocket Launcher uses the Continuously Computed Impact Point (CCIP) HUD mode. This enables the you to aim a pipper at the target and fire away. The F-16 must be flown at low altitudes to use the LAU with success. This increases the risk of being hit by ground fire or crashing into the ground.

The M61A1 cannon is the same gun employed in air-to-air combat mode (the DGFT HUD mode). The cannon is not very effective and should not be used unless all other weapons have been exhausted. The cannon uses an aiming pipper that reacts to the motion of the F-16.

Most Falcon 3.0 campaign missions will not require the use of the LAU or the M61A1. The F-16 is not known for this type of attack. Because the Vulcan is loaded on every mission, it may pay off to practice making the strafe attacks. You never know when it may come in handy.

Weapon Lesson #7: Iron Bombs

This lessons is devoted to the free-fall iron bombs. Falcon 3.0 offers four different types of iron bombs to load aboard your F-16. They are the Mk82, the Mk82D, the Mk83, and the Mk84. The main differences between these bombs are their sizes and the targets they are designed to destroy.

The Mk82 is a 500lb general purpose bomb. It can be used against small ground targets such as tanks, armored personnel carriers, and small structures. Up to 24 Mk82s can be loaded on the F-16. The Mk83 is a 1,000lb general purpose bomb. It is used against larger buildings like factories and warehouses. Up to eight Mk83s can be loaded on the F-16. The Mk84 is the largest iron bomb in the Falcon's arsenal, weighing in at 2,000 pounds. It is employed against the tougher, larger targets, such as bridges, hardened aircraft shelters, and, as you will see in this lesson, nuclear power plants. The Mk82D is virtually the same as the Mk82 (a 500lb bomb); however, the Mk82D employs a high-drag device that causes the bomb to decelerate quickly. This allows a lower altitude approach. Escaping the bomb blast is easier due to dropping the bomb in close proximity to the target. By the time the bombs explode, your F-16 is clear of the bomb blast. We will discuss more on this bomb in the Ground School section of the lesson.

Delivering the iron bombs requires practice; that is what this lesson is all about. You have to keep your Falcon steady on your approach to the target. Of course, you won't have the enemy tossing lead and fire at you from the ground in the lesson! This won't be the case when you are involved in a conflict in Kuwait, Israel, or Panama.

Lesson Objectives In this lesson you:

- Use the ground mode radar to locate the ground target.
- Select the CCIP HUD mode and designate a target.
- Cancel the target designation if required.
- Set the *ripple* number of bombs (multiple bomb drop).

Ground School Up to this point, you have used the SPACEBAR to fire weapons (both air-to-air and air-to-ground). For iron bombs, you use the SPACEBAR to first set the target designation. In other words you point at a target and press the SPACEBAR, which tells the onboard computer, "This is the target I want to bomb." At that point, the CCIP (Continuously Computed Impact Point) takes over. All you have to do is stay the course and the computer will release the bombs at the proper time, destroying the ground target. Sound easy? It can be with practice! Take a look at what you see when you select the CCIP HUD.

The CCIP HUD Mode The CCIP HUD mode is used for several weapons in Falcon 3.0, the four iron bombs in this lesson, plus the Durandal and cluster bombs yet to come. Master the CCIP in this lesson and the others will be easy. Figure 5-32 shows the cockpit view of the CCIP HUD mode; the Mk84 is selected. This CCIP mode is different from the one used with LAU Rocket Launcher. This mode has a bombsight. The bombsight is a vertical line that extends from the center of the HUD to the bottom. At the bottom of the line is a circle, the target locator. The dot in the center of the circle

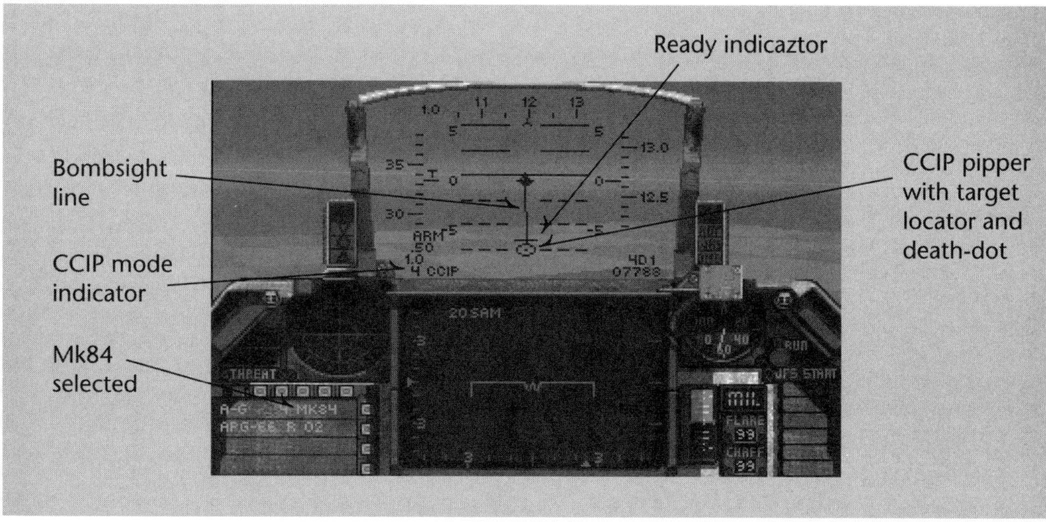

Figure 5-32 Cockpit View of the CCIP HUD Mode

is affectionately termed the *death-dot.* You aim at the ground targets by maneuvering your F-16 to cover the target with the locator and death-dot.

The Free-Fall Bombing Methods There is more than one way to deliver the iron bombs successfully. Although you will probably establish a method that you feel comfortable with, here are some of the fundamentals. Figure 5-33 shows different types of free-fall bomb delivery. Note that the steeper the angle, the higher the altitude at drop time. You are also closer to the target during the steeper releases.

Your airspeed is also a factor when dropping iron bombs. You do not want to approach the target with the afterburner glowing! Slower speeds give you a larger margin for error.

Dropping the Iron It is time for you to try out the CCIP HUD mode and iron bomb delivery. Four Red Flag lessons are available for iron bombs, MK82BOMB, MK82DBMB, MK83BOMB, and MK84BOMB. The MK82BOMB and MK82DBMB lessons use generic ground targets that are spread about the landscape in Red Flag. The lessons are identical except for the weapon type. The Mk82D will drop much closer to the target than the Mk82 because of a plume that opens, decelerating the bomb quickly. The MK83BOMB lesson guides you to a group of three factories. These heavier bombs are capable of destroying one of the factories.

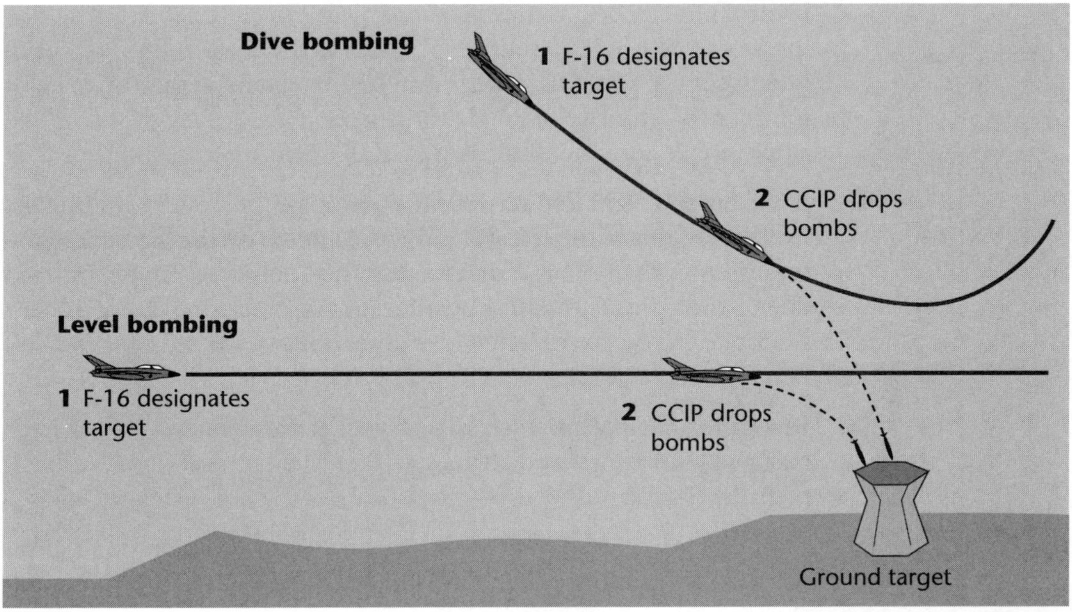

Figure 5-33 Delivery Methods of Free-Fall Iron Bombs

For now, let's step through the MK84BOMB mission. Your goal is to destroy a nuclear power plant.

Go to Red Flag Control and load the MK84BOMB mission. Click on F-16 PILOTS, then F-16 ARMAMENT, and then TAKEOFF. Pause the simulation by pressing the P key. You will start at an altitude (AGL) of 7,000 to 8,000 feet and an airspeed of approximately 450 knots. It is time to drop the heavy iron on the enemy's prized nuclear facility.

- Unpause the simulation by pressing the P key. You should be around 17 miles from waypoint 1 traveling southeast (around 120°). This gives you some time to check out the CCIP HUD mode.

- Press BACKSPACE to select the air-to-ground mode. This selects the CCIP mode and the Mk84. Press BACKSPACE a few more times. This toggles between the Mk84/CCIP HUD mode and the M61A1/STRF HUD mode. Make sure you leave the HUD mode in CCIP before proceeding.

- Decelerate to 350 knots by cutting the throttle a few notches (press the – key). Maintain level flight at 7,000 to 8,000 feet.

- Press the ; and ' keys to set the iron bomb *ripple*. Ripple indicates the number of bombs that will be dropped per designation. It is always in increments of two. The amount of ripple is indicated on the stores control panel (cockpit lower left) following the letter R. Pressing ' increases the ripple to four (R 04). This is the maximum number of bombs for the Mk84. The other iron bombs can be rippled up to eight for the MK83 and up to 24 for the Mk82s. The ; key decreases the ripple; make sure the ripple is two (R 02) before proceeding.

- Bank left and right and observe the action of the bombsight line. As the bombsight swings left and right, the line above the target designator becomes thick. This indicates that the bombs cannot be dropped due to the attitude (relative position to the ground) of the F-16. For example, if you fly inverted, the line would indicate that free-fall bombs cannot be released.

- Level off and line up with the waypoint caret once again. Check airspeed (350 knots) and altitude (7,000 to 8,000 feet). Make adjustments if necessary.

- Turn on ground mode (GM) radar by pressing F7. When you are five or six miles from waypoint 1, the targets (nuclear power plant towers) appear in the upper left quadrant of the radar.

- Bank left after reaching waypoint 1. Line up with the waypoint caret. Your heading should be approximately 90°. The targets on the GM radar should be near the vertical center of the REO.

- Check altitude and airspeed.

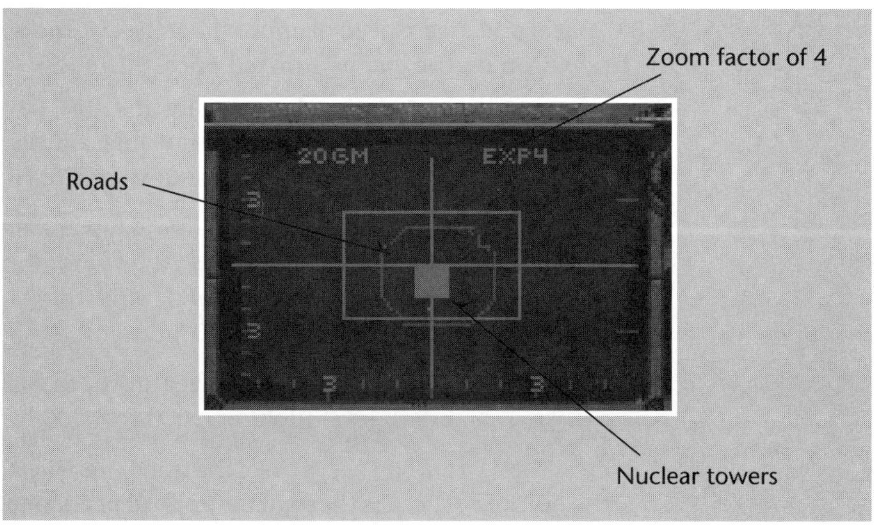

Figure 5-34 REO in GM Radar Mode — Zoomed Display of Nuclear Towers

- When the ground targets are in the center of the REO (about ten miles from waypoint 2), press F1 twice to zoom in on the towers. Your REO should resemble Figure 5-34.
- Decelerate slightly to around 325 knots (the - key).
- At the six mile point from waypoint 2 (6D2 on the HUD), the tower should come into view out your windscreen.
- Use the rudder (the [and] keys) to line up the bombsight with the tower. Don't worry about the designator yet, just align the vertical line and the tower. Nose down very slightly if necessary to check this alignment.
- At four miles out (4D2), nose down until the target designator is *below* the base of the tower. Hold this position, you're almost there!
- When the death-dot is on the *base* of the tower, press the SPACEBAR. This designates the target and activates the CCIP. Your HUD should resemble Figure 5-35. Pause the simulation by pressing the P key to check out the HUD. The bombsight line has extended to the top of the HUD and two horizontal lines appear. One line is in the center of the HUD, the other line is between the top and the center of the HUD and it is dropping. When this line reaches the line in the center of the HUD, the bombs will be released. This is the CCIP in action! Note the death-dot on the base of the target.

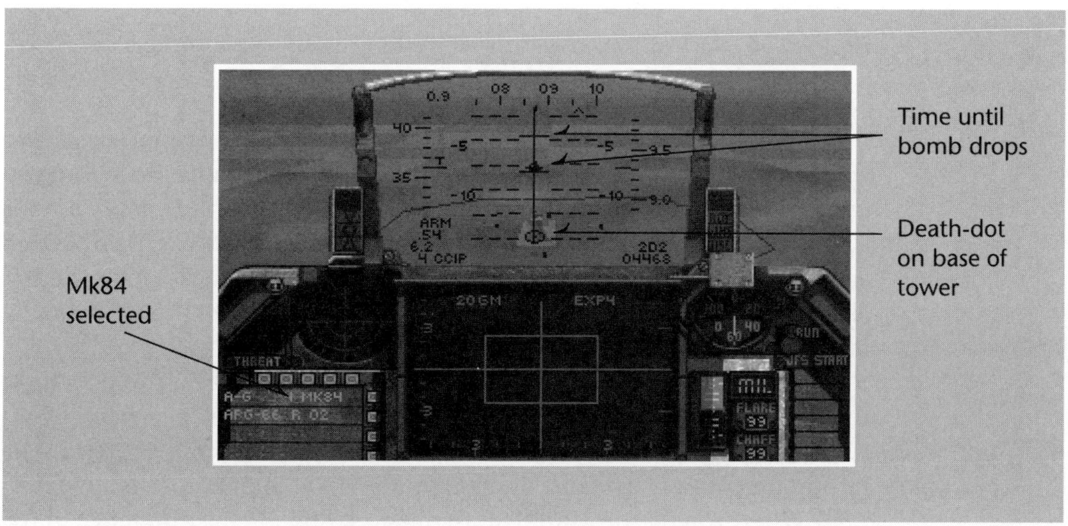

Figure 5-35 Nuclear Tower Is Designated—CCIP Activated

- Unpause the simulation by pressing the P key. Observe the horizontal line drop. When the line reaches the center, you will hear the bombs drop. Pull up to level off. Use the track view (the upper row 9 key) to check out an out-of-cockpit perspective of the bomb drop.
- After you have leveled off and passed the target, check the rear view (the 3 key on the numeric keypad) and pull up. You may catch a glimpse of the damage your iron bombs caused. Figure 5-36 shows the rear view after both towers have been destroyed.
- Climb back to 8,000 feet. After a few minutes of level flight, bank 180° and head back for the other tower (or the first one if you missed it).
- When you have exhausted your iron bombs, press ESC to bring up the menu bar. Select END MISSION from the FILE menu. Click on NEXT MISSION to return to Red Flag Control from the Debriefing screen.

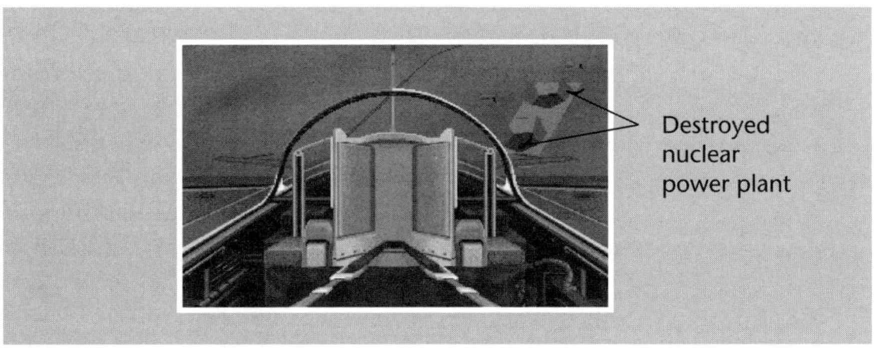

Figure 5-36 Nuclear Towers Destroyed by Iron Bombs—Rear Cockpit View

Try the other iron bomb missions. All of the missions have two waypoints; the target is located at waypoint 2. Use the same procedure you used to bomb the nuclear towers. The only difference in the missions is the total number of bombs available and the intended target. The MK82BOMB and MK82DBMB mission have 24 bombs available and the target is the Red Flag generic target. Your F-16 is loaded with eight bombs for the MK83BOMB mission; the primary targets are factories.

Because the other lessons have more bombs, you may want to increase the bomb ripple to increase the impact on the drop. The ' key increases the bomb drop count by two and the ; decrease the count by two. The minimum count is two and the maximum is the total bombs loaded.

When you fly the MK82DBMB mission, observe the difference in the bomb drop position when compared to the standard Mk82. You should notice that this type of bomb is released later and falls much more quickly. They are a better choice for low altitude, level bombing.

Debriefing: Iron Bombs The iron bombs play a big role in the Falcon 3.0 campaign. Taking out strategic targets with a single pass is a must. You can use the missions supplied with this lesson to improve your free-fall bombing skill. The CCIP HUD mode may seem difficult to grasp at first, however, the procedure becomes routine with practice.

Four free-fall iron bombs are available in Falcon 3.0. The major differences are size, maximum load, and the type of target the bomb is intended for. The MK84 is the largest bomb at over 2,000 pounds. It is designed to take out some of the "hard-to-destroy" targets like hardened aircraft shelters, bunkers, and, as you demonstrated in the lesson, nuclear power plants. Up to four Mk84s can be loaded per mission.

The Mk83 is a 1,000 pound bomb that is designed for use against large buildings, factories, and warehouses. Up to eight Mk83s can be loaded per mission. The Mk82 and Mk82D are both designed for small ground targets like tanks, armored personnel carriers, and other heavy armor. The primary difference between the Mk82 and the Mk82D is the way the bombs drop. The Mk82D releases a plume-like parachute that instantly decelerates the forward motion of the bomb. This is useful for low-altitude, level bombing.

Having a highly skilled, accurate heavy bomber in your squadron greatly increases your chances for success in a campaign. Practice and hone your skills here in the training missions; you won't have to rely on a computer pilot to get the job done for you!

Weapon Lesson #8: Guided Bomb Units

The Mk84 iron bomb does the job when it comes to destroying tough hardened targets. However, sometimes the iron bomb CCIP delivery can be imprecise. When you need absolute precision coupled with the power of the big iron bombs, the GBU-15 Guided Bomb Unit is the weapon of choice.

The GBU-15 has the same warhead as the Mk84 iron bomb, a 945-pound H-6, high-explosive warhead. The Mk84 bomb was a free-fall bomb that required correct timing and a precise approach to hit the target squarely. However, the GBU-15 employs a television-imaging seeker (sometimes an infrared seeker) to guide the bomb precisely to its target. The method of delivery is virtually identical to the Maverick's.

This lesson assumes that you have successfully delivered the Mavericks in Lesson 4. The Maverick lesson covers the E-O HUD mode, the same mode that the GBU uses.

Lesson Objectives In this lesson you:

- Use waypoint intelligence information to locate a missile site.
- Locate a missile site by visual identification.
- Lock up a ground target with the GBU-15.
- Fire an air-to-ground missile and determine the outcome with target/bomb view.

Ground School The ground school is fairly simple for this mission. No new keys are introduced in this lesson. The E-O HUD mode that the GBU-15 employs is identical to the Maverick (AGM-65B) HUD mode. All you will have to do once you are in the cockpit is find the target, select the GBU-15, and fire! You are one step closer to being fully trained!

Precision Bombing of a Missile Site Your mission goal in this lesson is to locate and destroy four missile sites. Your F-16 is loaded with four GBU-15s. Intelligence reports that the enemy missile site is near waypoint 2. Waypoint 1 is an intermediate waypoint; get ready for the GBU delivery on the way to waypoint 1.

Go to Red Flag Control and load the GUIDED missile. Click on F-16 PILOTS, then F-16 ARMAMENT, and then TAKEOFF. Pause the simulation by pressing the P key. You start at an altitude (AGL) of 7,000 to 8,000 feet and an airspeed of approximately 450 knots. It is time for you to take out that enemy missile site.

- Press the P key to unpause the simulation. You should be heading directly south (approximately 180°), about 6 or 7 miles from waypoint 1.
- Start to cut the throttle a couple of notches (the - key). Try to attain and maintain an airspeed of 375 knots or so. Follow the waypoint caret to waypoint 1.
- When you reach waypoint 1, the waypoint caret jumps to the right. Line up with waypoint 2.
- Start to descend by pushing the nose down a bit. Don't dive!
- Press the BACKSPACE key to select the air-to-ground HUD mode. The GBU-15 is selected (it is indicated by the stores control panel). The HUD mode indicates E-O (Electro-Optical).

- Try to arrive at an altitude of 3,000 feet (AGL) at the five mile mark (5D2).
- Pull the nose back to level (0° pitch) and bank to the left slightly. The targets should come into view. They appear as small green dots.
- Adjust the flight of your Falcon to point the crosshairs at the targets. When you are in range, the crosshairs move to cover a target. Figure 5-37 shows this action. The REO displays a representation of the target at closer ranges.

Figure 5-37 GBU-15 Locked On to Missile Site—E-O HUD Mode

- Press the SPACEBAR to fire a GBU-15. You should hear the sound of the bomb drop.
- Quickly press the T key to lock up a different missile site. Press the SPACEBAR to release another GBU. Repeat the procedure two more times to fire the remaining guided bombs.
- Check out the track view (the upper row 9 key) or the target/bomb view (the Q key. Make sure your altitude is steady before you check the views. Figure 5-38 shows the track view of a Falcon dropping a GBU-15. Although the lock and method of firing are similar, you may notice that the flight of the GBU-15 is quite different than that of a Maverick. This is primarily due to the fact that it is a *free-fall* guided *bomb* as opposed to a guided *missile*.
- Press ESC to bring up the menu bar. Select END MISSION from the

Figure 5-38 F-16 Dropping a Guided Bomb Unit (GBU-15)

- FILE menu. Click on NEXT MISSION to return to Red Flag Control from the Debriefing screen.

Debriefing:GuidedBombUnits

When you are called on to destroy a large or tough, hardened target, iron bombs come to mind. But when the word precision is added to the request, the GBU-15 is the answer. The GBU (Guided Bomb Unit) packs the wallop of an Mk84 2,000 pound iron-bomb, but has the accuracy of a Maverick missile. It is highly effective where a surgical strike is needed.

The GBU-15 uses the E-O (Electro-Optical) HUD mode. In a campaign mission, locating the target without getting shot down will be more difficult than firing and hitting a target with the Guided Bomb Unit.

Like most highly effective weapons, the availability of the GBU in campaign mode is less than that of the less expensive iron bombs.

Weapon Lesson #9: Durandals

The BLU-107B Durandal bomb is another variety of free-fall bomb. However, the Durandal was designed with one specific target in mind, the runway. When the Durandal hits a runway, it actually penetrates the surface of the runway, burying itself in the runway. After the bomb is under the pavement, the warhead explodes, severely damaging the runway, perhaps rendering it useless for the enemy.

The Durandal uses the CCIP HUD mode (as do most free-fall bombs). This lesson assumes you have completed Lesson 7 on the iron bombs. The delivery of the Durandal is virtually the same as the iron bombs. Make sure you are comfortable with the CCIP bomb delivery before attempting this lesson.

Lesson Objectives In this lesson you:

- Use waypoint intelligence information to locate an enemy runway.
- Align with the runway for an end-to-end approach using the GM radar.
- Drop the Durandal on or near the center of the enemy runway.

Ground School No new keys are introduced in this lesson. The BLU-107B Durandal is delivered using the same method as the Mk iron bombs, the CCIP HUD mode. Review the CCIP delivery method in Lesson 7 if necessary. Up to twelve Durandals can be loaded on the F-16. The maximum amount of Durandals are loaded for this mission.

Maximizing the Effect of the Durandal Attack You use waypoint information and the GM radar to locate the runway. However, finding the runway is just one phase of the Durandal attack. You must approach the runway at the correct angle to maximize the effect. Figure 5-39 illustrates this approach technique. The figure shows two separate F-16s making their approach to attack. The F-16 that is approaching from top to bottom has very little margin for error in timing. He could vary his bomb drop right or left and still hit the target, but dropping the bomb short (early bomb drop) or long (late bomb drop) will result in a sure miss. The only problem with this approach is that it is easier to be accurate left/right than it is long/short. The second F-16 (flying left to right across the figure) is flying over the length of the runway. This gives the largest margin of error for long/short bomb delivery. Note that the optimum location to drop the Durandal is the center of the runway. This effectively cuts the runway length in half, making it useless for the enemy. In the figure, two runways are cut in half by blasting their intersection.

Once you have bombed a runway, make sure you don't attempt a landing on it. Hitting the bomb crater will either seriously damage or

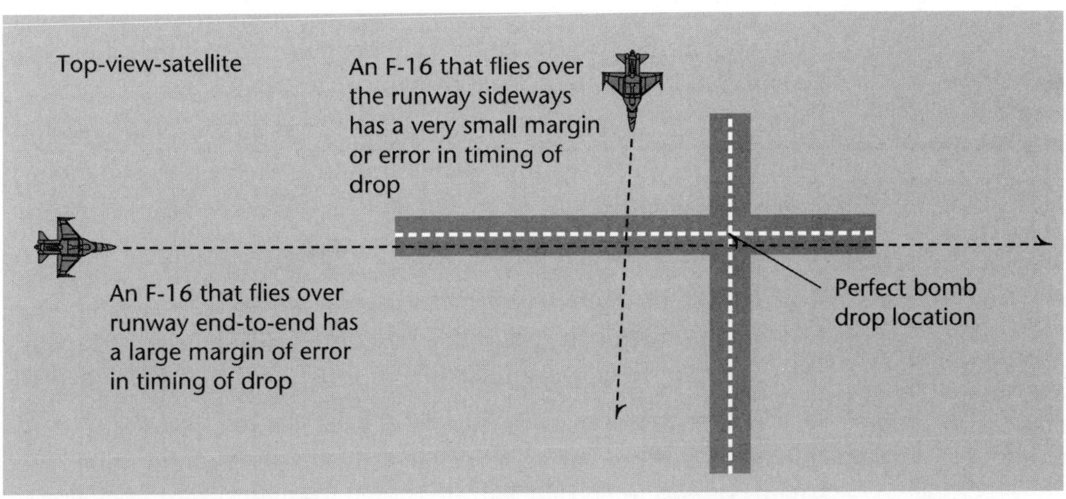

Figure 5-39 Durandal Runway Approach Technique

destroy your F-16. You never plan to land on an enemy runway, but you never know when you will sustain major damage and land in an emergency. It is probably better to eject than land at an enemy airstrip.

Taking Out the Runway This mission involves flying to an intermediate waypoint (waypoint 1), then heading for the bombing waypoint (waypoint 2). Intelligence reports that the enemy runway will be very close to waypoint 2. Your job is to shut down the airstrip by rippling twelve Durandals across the center of it; hopefully, you can hit the sweet spot that will disable both runways simultaneously.

Go to Red Flag Control and load the DURANDAL mission. Click on F-16 PILOTS, then F-16 ARMAMENT, and then TAKEOFF. Pause the simulation by pressing the P key. You start at an altitude (AGL) of 7,000 to 8,000 feet and an airspeed of approximately 450 knots. It is time to shut down a key enemy installation by taking out the main runways.

- Unpause the simulation by pressing the P key. You should be around 17 miles from waypoint 1 traveling southwest (around 205°).
- Cut your airspeed by pressing the − key. Try to attain and maintain 350 knots.
- Turn on GM (ground mode) radar by pressing F7. You should see the airstrip and enemy compound on the right side of the REO. They show up as small dots at this time.
- When you get to waypoint 1, bank the F-16 to the right to line up with the final waypoint. Your heading should be between 260 and 270°.
- Cut your airspeed to 300 knots for a slow accurate bombing approach. Maintain 7,000 to 8,000 feet for your altitude.
- Press the BACKSPACE key to select the A-G (air-to-ground weapons) mode. The stores control panel should indicate the Durandal is selected (12 DUR).
- Change the ripple from two (R 2) to all twelve Durandals (R 12) by pressing the ' key five times.
- At seven miles from waypoint 2 (7D2), nose down slightly into a gentle descent. Try to attain an altitude of 1,000 to 1,500 feet when the bombs are released. This may take some practice.
- Spot the runway out your cockpit windscreen. You are not aligned perfectly end-to-end yet. Bank to the left to angle toward an imaginary line extending out from the runway.

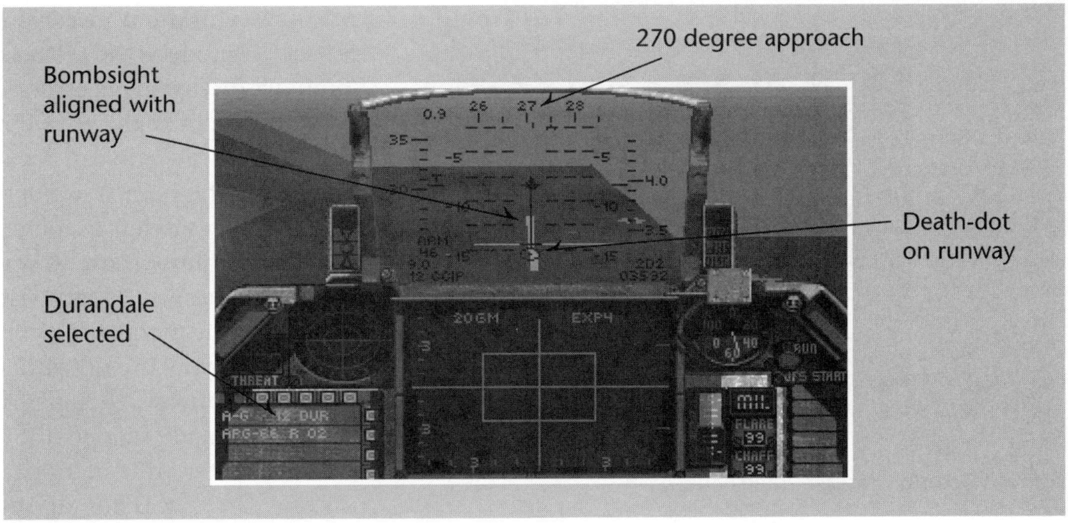

Figure 5-40 Lining Up with the Enemy Runway—Preparing to Drop the Durandals.

- Point the nose of your F-16 at the runway. Use the rudder (the [and] keys) to adjust your precise alignment with the runway. Line up the bombsight with the runway. Figure 5-40 shows this action.
- When the death-dot is in the center of the runway, press the SPACEBAR to designate the target. A short horizontal line should appear above the center of the HUD. The line will drop until it reaches the center, at which time the Durandals will be released by the CCIP system.
- Once the Durandals have been dropped, pull up into a gentle climb. Check the rear view (the 3 key on the numeric keypad) to assess the runway damage. Figure 5-41 shows the results of a perfect hit.
- Press ESC to bring up the menu bar. Select END MISSION from the FILE menu. Click on NEXT MISSION to return to Red Flag Control from the Debriefing screen.

Debriefing: Durandals The BLU-107B Durandal is a free-fall bomb with a single purpose. That purpose is to destroy enemy runways. The Durandal drives itself deep into the concrete runway before the warhead detonates. This causes serious damage as the runway buckles from the blast. Up to twelve Durandals can be loaded on the Falcon for each mission. As with the other free-fall bombs, the Durandal can be rippled in increments of two.

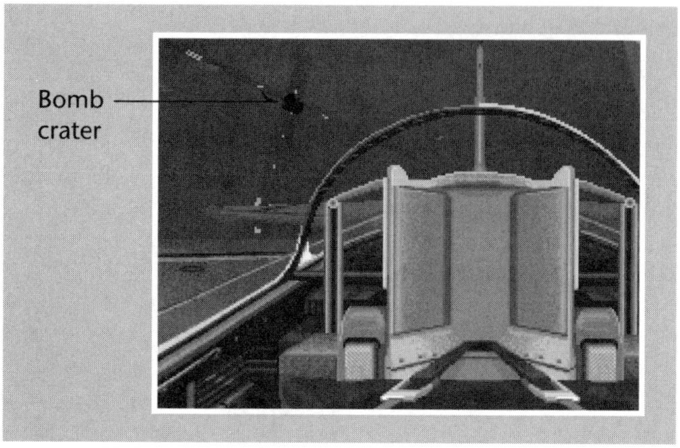

Figure 5-41 The F-16 Scores a Perfect Hit on the Enemy Runway (Bomb Crater in Intersection).

The Durandal uses the same HUD mode as the Mk iron bombs we discussed in Lesson 7. Using the bombsight to align with the runway, you can accurately drop the bombs, rendering the runway useless to enemy aircraft. It is important to approach the runway lengthwise to increase the margin of error. However, if you hit on either end of the runway, the enemy may still remain in operation with the shorter, still functional, runway. The key is to cut the runway in half.

Destroying enemy runways is a key element in winning a Falcon 3.0 campaign. It significantly affects the way the enemy engages in battle. If you destroy a runway on one mission, chances are you will not have to deal with as much hostile aircraft in that area on subsequent missions. Practice your Durandal delivery!

Weapon Lesson #10: Cluster Bombs

The CBU-84 Cluster Bomb Unit is more than a typical free-fall bomb. It is actually a couple hundred small bombs within a *dispenser*. The dispenser is a casing that resembles other free-fall bombs. When the CBU-84 is dropped, fins on the rear of the dispenser cause it to spin. As the bombs reach the target, the CBU throws the individual small bombs (bomblets) over a wide area. This bomb is designed for use against soft targets and light armor. You will not destroy too many tanks or armored personnel carriers with this weapon.

The CBU-84 uses the CCIP HUD mode. This lesson assumes you have completed Lesson 7 on the iron bombs. The delivery of the Cluster Bomb will be virtually the same as for the iron bombs. Ensure that you are comfortable with the CCIP bomb delivery before attempting this lesson.

Lesson Objectives In this lesson you:

- Locate soft ground targets visually (using limited advance intelligence).

- Select the CCIP HUD mode and designate a target.
- Set the ripple number of bombs.
- Use the Debriefing screen in Red Flag to observe the results.

Ground School No new keys or techniques will be used in this mission. The CCIP mode operates identically to the Mk iron bombs and the Durandals. Refer to Lesson 7 for more information on the CCIP HUD mode.

Dropping the Cluster Bombs This mission takes you over enemy territory; a portion of it contains hostile forces. You have limited intelligence information indicating that ground forces are located somewhere between waypoint 1 and waypoint 2. Reconnaissance information has not been obtained in days due to poor weather. Therefore, the exact location of the ground troops is unknown. Your goal is to seek out the targets and destroy as many as possible with CBUs.

Go to Red Flag Control and load the CLUSTER mission. Click on F-16 PILOTS, then F-16 ARMAMENT, and then TAKEOFF. Pause the simulation by pressing the P key. You start at an altitude (AGL) of 7,000 to 8,000 feet and an airspeed of approximately 450 knots.

> Warning: The preset weapons loadout for this mission exceed the limit for the Hi-Fidelity flight model. Do not use this mission with the Hi-Fi flight model unless you reduce the weapons loadout, otherwise your aircraft will crash due to excessive weight.

- Press the P key to unpause the simulation. You should be heading directly south (approximately 190°), about a few miles from waypoint 1.
- Start to cut the throttle a couple of notches (using the - key). Try to attain and maintain an airspeed of 350 knots or so. This should be a good patrolling speed. Follow the waypoint caret to waypoint 1.
- At waypoint 1, bank the F-16 to align with waypoint 2. The F-16 computer has loaded the waypoints to repeat. If you do not spot the enemy activity between waypoint 1 and waypoint 2, the waypoint indicator automatically switches back to waypoint 1. Continue the process until you locate the troops. They appear as small brown dots on the ground.

- When you locate the troops, press the BACKSPACE key to select the A-G (air-to-ground weapons) HUD mode. Verify that the stores control panel indicates the CBU-84.
- Press the ' key two times to increase the bomb ripple to six (R 6).
- Maneuver the Falcon so you will pass over the troops end-to-end. Falcon 3.0 ground troops are always aligned in a straight line. Figure 5-42 shows the end-to-end pass over the ground troops.

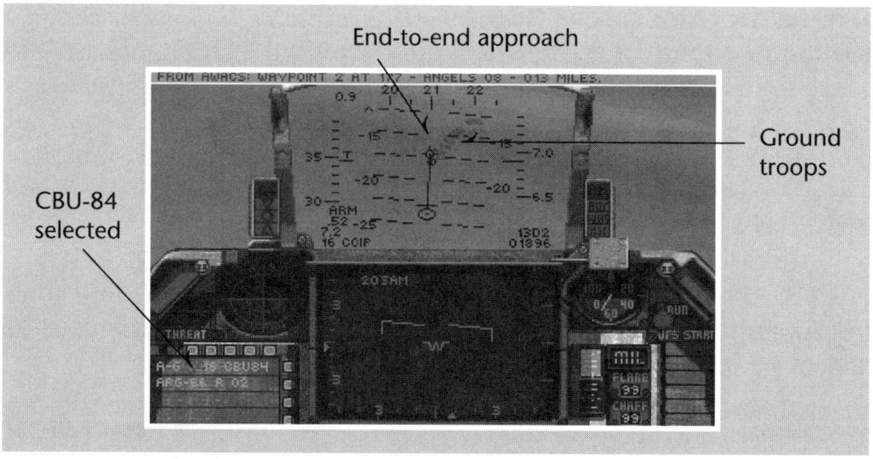

Figure 5-42 Passing Over Ground Troops—Setting Up to Drop the CBU-84 Cluster Bombs

- Line up the pipper on the center of the troops and press the SPACEBAR. Try to maintain an altitude between 500 and 2,500 feet as you pass over the target. The CCIP will release the bombs at the proper time as long as you do not make any sudden direction changes in altitude or heading.
- When the bombs release, pull up to a 15 to 20° climb.
- Switch to the rear view by pressing the 3 key on the numeric keypad. You should see the results of your bomb drop. Figure 5-43 shows the rear view after the Falcon CBU attack. Notice that the soft targets are destroyed, but the armored units remain intact.
- Press ESC to bring up the menu bar. Select END MISSION from the FILE menu. Click on NEXT MISSION to return to Red Flag Control from the Debriefing screen.

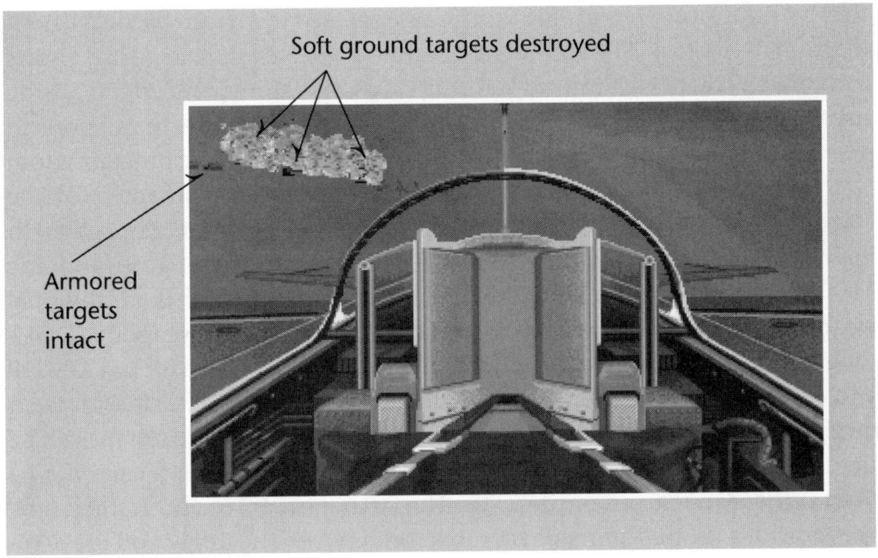

Figure 5-43 Results of the F-16 CBU-84 Cluster Bomb Attack

Debriefing: Cluster Bombs The CBU-84 Cluster Bomb is used to destroy groups of soft ground targets with one pass. The bomb actually consists of a dispenser that contains hundreds of small bomblets. Fins on the dispenser cause it to spin as it heads for the ground. The bomblets are spun out of the dispenser over a large area. The bomb is not effective against armored vehicles (tanks, personnel carriers, etc.).

The CBU-84 uses the CCIP HUD mode in the same way that all free-fall bombs in Falcon 3.0 do. Up to sixteen CBUs can be loaded per mission. The bombs can be rippled in increments of two up to the maximum load.

Use the CBU when you have to clear out large troop concentrations. The majority of these troops must be soft targets. You can use the CBU along with anti-armor weapons to cover all types of targets. However, loading the CBUs to the maximum prevents you from loading any other weapons (other than small air-to-air weapons) because of loading restrictions.

Summary

Now that you have completed the weapons lessons in this chapter, you are ready to go out and attack any enemy that Falcon 3.0 throws at you. The campaign mode requires a high level of skill in flying, using radar, avoiding enemy ground threats, and using weapons. You have covered all of this information. However, a pilot cannot be expected to go into battle without additional practice. The following chapter, *Introduction to Red Flag,* shows you how to create customized training missions against any enemy, using any weapon in Falcon 3.0. This way you will be able to create missions to practice any situation you can think of; the only limit is your imagination.

We started this chapter by showing you the fundamentals of the Falcon 3.0 weaponry. You learned about the air-to-air weaponry which included the three missiles (AIM-9P, AIM-9M, and AIM-120) and the M61A1 Vulcan cannon. Different HUD modes are used for the individual weapons. There are three possible modes for air-to-air weapons, DGFT (dogfight for the Vulcan cannon), SRM (Short-Range Missile for the AIM-9P and AIM-9M), and MRM (Medium-Range Missile for the AIM-120). Each missile has a "weapons envelope" which indicates where the missile can be fired from. For example, the AIM-9P is a rear-aspect missile; it can only be fired at the rear of an enemy aircraft. The farther the F-16 is from the target, the more of a range difference there can be between the target and the F-16. All of this results in a weapons envelope that is shaped like a cone extending from the rear of the intended target, with the smallest portion of the cone at the rear of the target.

You were introduced to the basic fighter maneuvers, or BFM. The key to understanding what the enemy target is doing is the aspect angle. The aspect angle is a representation of the intersection of two lines. One line is drawn from the rear of the target back, the other line is drawn from the nose of the F-16 forward. You don't have to worry about performing the geometry, though. The REO displays the numeric aspect angle of a target when you have a radar lock on it. In addition to the numeric display, the HUD displays an aspect-angle caret. The caret provides a graphical representation of the aspect angle. This lets you keep your eye on the target during an engagement.

You learned about the basics of air-to-ground weaponry next. There are several HUD modes available for air-to-ground weapons. HARMS and Shrikes use the A-R (Anti-Radiation) HUD mode. Use these weapons for attacking enemy radar. One of the Maverick missiles (AGM-65D) uses the I-R (Infrared) HUD mode, while the other Maverick (AGM-65B) uses the E-O (Electro-Optical) mode. Several free-fall bombs are available in Falcon 3.0. All free-fall bombs use the CCIP (Continuous Computed Impact Point). The M61A1 Vulcan cannon is also available in air-to-ground attacks and employs the STRF (Strafe) HUD mode. We discussed the basics of ground attacks including strafing, missile, and free-fall bombing techniques.

With the fundamentals of weapons delivery under you belt, you jumped into lessons on the individual weapons. The following is a summary of the lessons:

- Lesson #1: BVR Kill—You learned how to attack an enemy aircraft from beyond visual range (BVR) using the AIM-120 and the MRM HUD mode.
- Lesson #2: All-Aspect Kill—You learned how to attack the enemy at closer ranges from all aspects (directions). This lesson showed you how to use the AIM-9M infrared missile and the SRM HUD mode.
- Lesson #3: Rear Aspect/Guns Kill—In this lesson, you learned maneuvers to get on the tail of the enemy and fire the AIM-9P rear-aspect missiles of guns. You learned to use the SRM and DGFT HUD modes. You also used the padlock view to maneuver into a good position for firing a missile.
- Lesson #4: The Mavericks—You learned the E-O and I-R HUD modes for the two types of air-to-ground missiles (AGM-65B and AGM-65D). The lesson involved attacking a tank column.
- Lesson #5: Anti-Radiation Missiles—You learned how to approach a deadly SAM site and lock on to the SAM radar with the HARM and Shrike anti-radiation missiles. You also received additional training to avoid the SAM radar by using the ECM pod.
- Lesson #6: LAU and Strafing—This lesson covered the lesser-used weapons of Falcon 3.0. You were introduced to one version of the CCIP HUD mode for the LAU 5003A Rocket Launcher. You also strafed ground targets using the M61A1 Vulcan cannon.
- Lesson #7: Iron Bombs—The CCIP HUD mode was used in depth in this lesson. You flew a mission with the goal of destroying two enemy nuclear power plant towers. Other missions were used to demonstrate and practice the smaller free-fall bombs.
- Lesson #8: Durandals—This lesson covered the use of the runway-destroying, Durandal free-fall bomb. You attacked an enemy runway, dropping several Durandals. The CCIP HUD mode was employed.
- Lesson #9: Guided Bomb Units—The powerful and accurate GBU-15 was the root of this lesson. You attacked an enemy missile site with the precision and sheer power of the guided bomb. The E-O HUD mode was employed.

- Lesson #10: Cluster Bombs—This final lesson covered the deadly cluster bomb, the CBU-84. You attacked a troop concentration with a ripple of CBUs. The CCIP HUD mode was employed.

Exercises

1. Fly the WEAPON1 mission. This mission tests your skill in air-to-air weaponry. You must make it back to waypoint 4 and land. Don't waste a missile shot, you will need every one!
2. Fly the WEAPON2 mission. This mission involves taking out a tank column that is protected by a SAM site. The targets are at waypoint 3. Anti-radiation and Mavericks are loaded on your F-16 to help you get the job done. Land at waypoint 5.

6

Introduction to Red Flag

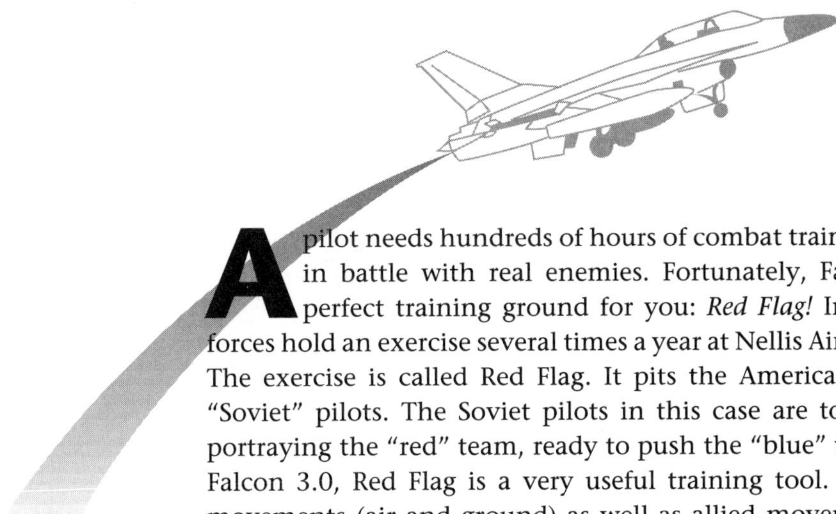

A pilot needs hundreds of hours of combat training before engaging in battle with real enemies. Fortunately, Falcon 3.0 offers the perfect training ground for you: *Red Flag!* In reality, the armed forces hold an exercise several times a year at Nellis Air Force Base, Nevada. The exercise is called Red Flag. It pits the American pilots against the "Soviet" pilots. The Soviet pilots in this case are top notch U.S. pilots portraying the "red" team, ready to push the "blue" team to the limit. In Falcon 3.0, Red Flag is a very useful training tool. You control enemy movements (air and ground) as well as allied movements. This lets you engage the enemy at a location that only you will know in advance. The enemy, however, will not have this advantage. This is precisely the advantage you need when learning the weapons and maneuvers of your F-16 Falcon.

You may already be familiar with Red Flag. The lessons included with Falcon 3.0 are Red Flag missions. In this chapter, you will create your own personalized missions using Red Flag. Save these missions using a descriptive name (BOMBING, MIGFIGHT, etc.). When you feel the need to practice using certain weapons or against certain aircraft, these missions can be used again and again. There is no substitute for experience. At Red Flag you not only gain experience, but you also increase the ratings of your squadron pilots. The ratings of your squadron pilots will become important when you are committed to a campaign. Training not only pays off for you, it pays off for your squadron as well.

The Tour: Red Flag

Before we get into the details of creating a mission, let's take a short tour and see what functions are available in Red Flag. After selecting your squadron, select the Red Flag monitor in the War Room. Figure 6-1 shows an overview of the screens you will encounter during the tour. Table 6-1 shows the purpose of each of the screens. This tour will present a lot of information in a short time. You do not have to squeeze all of this material into one mission. In fact, it is better to try new features one or two at a time. The instructional missions that follow will show you how to create missions from scratch.

Don't worry about remembering every detail and function of these screens. The purpose of the tour is to familiarize yourself with what is available and where to find it. Try some of the controls during the tour. We will clear any changes you make after the tour is over. The upper right corner of the screen will always display the name of the current screen. The following table is an overview of the Red Flag screens and their functions:

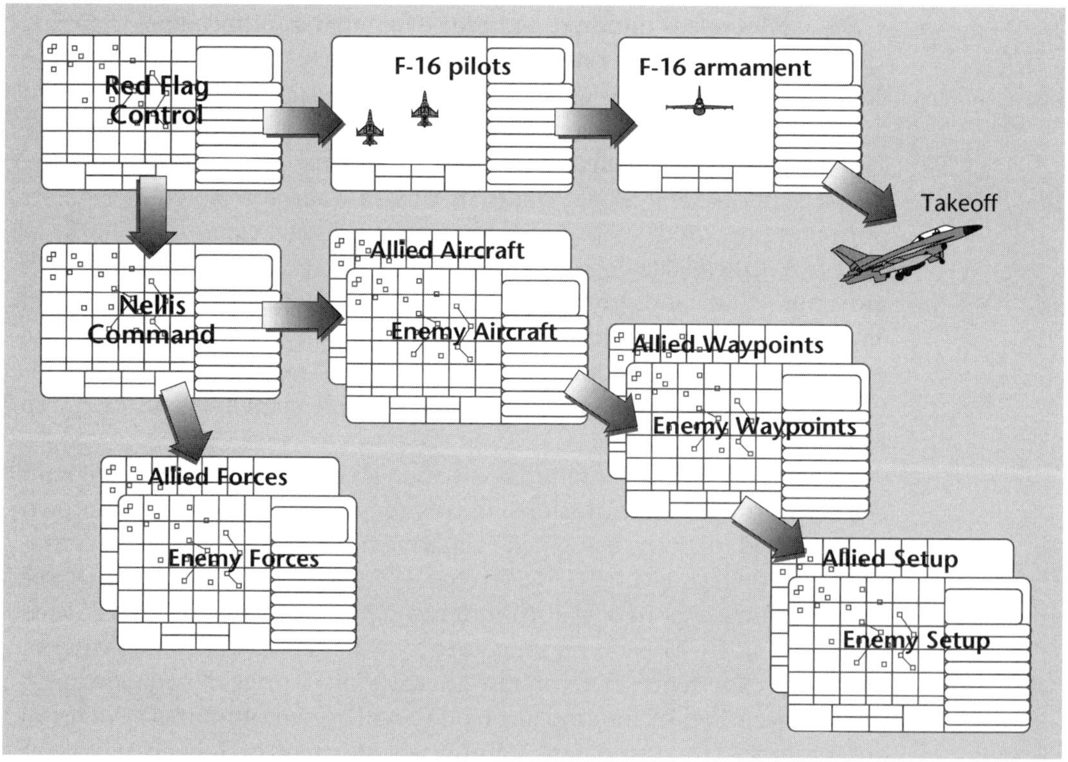

Figure 6-1 Red Flag Overview

Red Flag Screen	Function	Lets You:
RED FLAG CONTROL	Mission map view File management	View mission routes. Create, save, delete files.
NELLIS COMMAND	Access allied/enemy aircraft and forces	Access aircraft, forces, waypoints, and setup screens.
ALLIED/ENEMY AIRCRAFT	Define allied/enemy flights Adjust waypoints for direction & location	Set up flights. Locate waypoint icons.
ALLIED/ENEMY WAYPOINTS	Set waypoint action	Choose the action to be carried out at a waypoint.
ALLIED/ENEMY SETUP	Load weapons	Load air-air and air-ground (non-F-16 aircraft only) weapons to individual aircraft.
ALLIED/ENEMY FORCES	Define allied/enemy ground routes	Assign a path for ground forces to follow.
F-16 PILOTS	Assign F-16 pilots	Assign pilots from the squadron pilot roster.
F-16 ARMAMENT	Load weapons (F-16 only)	Load weapons, extra fuel, or ECM pods (for jamming radar missiles).

Table 6-1 Red Flag Screen Functions

Red Flag Control

The first screen, Red Flag Control, shows you the current mission and lets you perform mission file management. Figure 6-2 shows the Red Flag Control screen. The mission map on the left side of the screen represents Nellis Air Force Base and the surrounding area. The mission map shows several fixed targets (nuclear facilities, radar sets, bridges, etc.) that are ready to be attacked. Icons represent these targets on the map. For example, there is a nuclear facility in the northwest (upper left) corner of the map. Note that the top of the map indicates north or zero degrees. This map will be displayed on several of the Red Flag screens. For Red Flag Control, the map identifies the current mission selection. For instance, if you had designed a

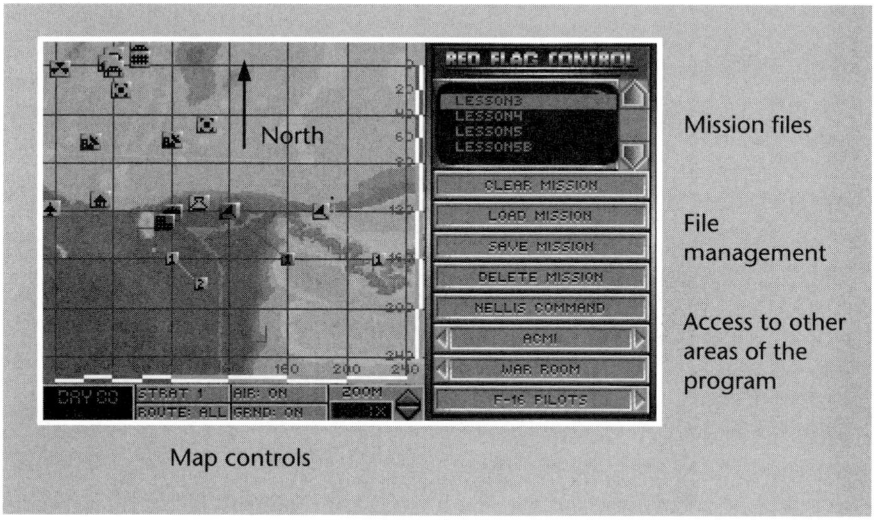

Figure 6-2 Red Flag Control

mission with allied aircraft flying from Nellis AFB to a radar installation, you would be able to identify the mission visually using this map. The mission map will always display the last mission loaded upon entering Red Flag Control. The map is currently displaying the default mission which consists of an allied (friendly) flight, an enemy flight, and an enemy ground route. The default mission is a good place to start when defining a new mission.

Mission Map Control The bottom of the screen has several controls for the mission map. You can display the map in various ways to gain a different perspective on a mission. The map is either displayed for tactical (TACT), which displays only the aircraft and ground route activity, or strategic (STRAT), which displays all activity plus fixed targets. Two different grid types are available, or you can disable the grid entirely. The grid indicates miles when you have STRAT 1 or TACT 1 selected. For example, each grid division is equal to 40 miles when Red Flag Control first displays the map. You can use the grid to reference alphanumeric coordinates when you select STRAT 2 or TACT 2. Settings of STRAT 3 or TACT 3 will result in no grid display. Clicking directly on the STRAT/TACT control lets you cycle through the six settings. The default setting is STRAT 1.

Using the ROUTE control lets you display all assigned flights in the mission or just a single one. This is useful for missions that have several flights; displaying all the routes sometime clutters the map with activity. You also can choose to display or hide the air or ground routes using AIR and GROUND. The zoom feature exposes more detail of the map and helps

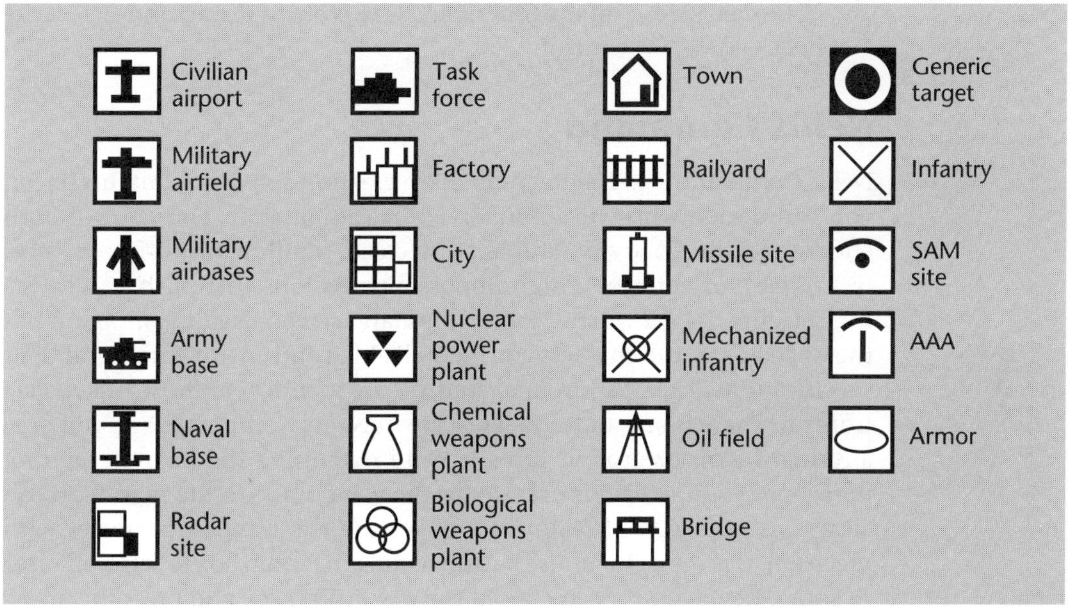

Figure 6-3 Mission Map Icons

ensure that you are sending aircraft and forces to the correct region. When entering Red Flag Control, the zoom will be set to full scale (1X). Objects that look close together at this scale may be actually 20 miles apart! The area displayed is over 240 miles wide and 240 miles tall. Over 60,000 square miles to fly, fight, and practice! You will use the mission map features in the tutorials that follow.

Mission Map Icons When you select the STRAT mode with the mission map controls, Red Flag displays all of the icons on the map. Figure 6-3 shows the mission map icons for Red Flag and the campaign mode. Not all icons appear in Red Flag.

Mission File Management The right side of the screen in Red Flag Control manages the files (missions) that you will create. The small screen in the upper right of Red Flag Control lists the available mission files. Use the up or down scroll arrows to display more files. You can create, save, load, clear, or delete mission files by using the controls located directly below the small screen. Controls are also available for accessing Nellis Command, Air Combat Maneuvering Instruction (ACMI), and F-16 pilots, or for returning to the War Room.

The next screen on the tour of Red Flag is Nellis Command. Select the NELLIS COMMAND control.

Nellis Command

Nellis Command is the center of mission creation activity. From this screen you can decide who will be involved in the mission. You control both enemy and allied activity. This lets you create training missions to try new techniques, or you can design impossible missions that push you to the limit! Figure 6-4 shows the Nellis Command screen. Nellis Command has the REPORT control that lets you view all allied and enemy forces and their specifications. The mission map controls are identical to those in Red Flag Control. There is one additional feature in Nellis Command. You can drag any flight icon or ground force icon to determine the mission starting positions. You can also move any of the waypoints on the map. You can always use the ZOOM feature to make sure the waypoints are set with precision. Use the right mouse button to drag the zoom box to select the area to zoom. Keyboard users can hold the right (SHIFT) key and press the arrow keys to move the box. You must move the cursor to the map area first using the (TAB) key.

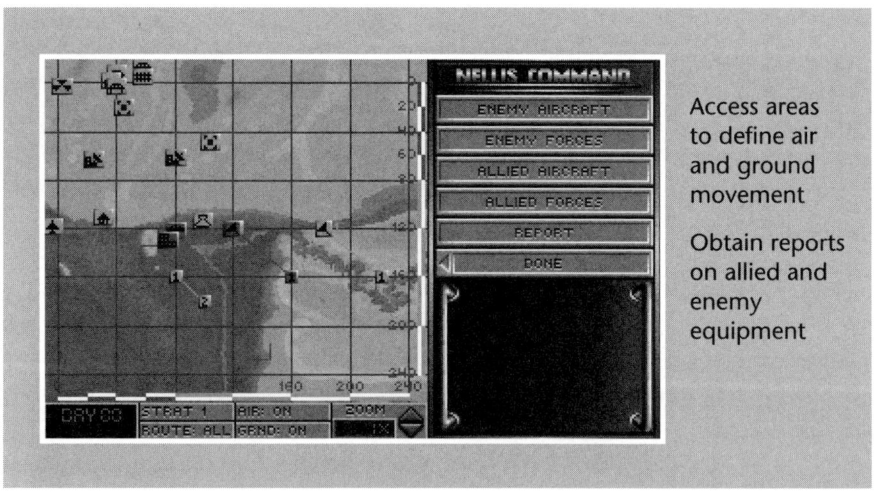

Figure 6-4 Nellis Command

Keyboard users can select waypoints with the left (SHIFT) key and drag them by pressing the left (SHIFT) key and using the arrow keys. This also requires you to position the cursor on the map first using the (TAB) key.

The controls on the right side of the screen allow you to access additional screens where you can control the movement of the aircraft and ground forces. Click the ALLIED AIRCRAFT control.

Allied Aircraft

This screen sets up groups of aircraft to participate in the mission. These groups of aircraft are called *flights*. Up to four allied (friendly) flights can be assigned to a mission and each flight can contain up to eight aircraft. You can assign a host of aircraft other than F-16s to the mission. For instance, you could create a flight made up of two B-52s and three F-16 escorts to carry out a bombing mission. You will always be assigned as the pilot for AIRCRAFT #1 in FLIGHT #1. The remaining F-16s will be flown by your squadron (computer) pilots. Figure 6-5 shows the Allied Aircraft screen.

The mission map buttons function as they do in Red Flag Control. However, if you set the route control to ROUTE: ONE, the map shows *only* the route of the selected flight. This feature is useful for missions with several flights and a high level of activity as it simplifies the map.

Flight# The small simulated screen in the upper right displays the allied aircraft available to help you carry out your mission. The up and down scroll arrows highlight the type of aircraft to assign to a flight. Located beneath the small screen is the FLIGHT # control. Selecting the FLIGHT # control cycles through the flights currently assigned to the mission. The mission map highlights the corresponding flight's route in yellow. For example if FLIGHT # 2 OF 3 is selected, flight #2 will be highlighted on the map. Each flight is identified on the map by its own flight icon, which also represents the mission starting point. The types of aircraft in the flight surround the icon. For example, if a flight with an F-16 and an F-111 was created, the map would display one icon with the characters F-16 and F-111 surrounding it. You can relocate the icons on the map; this will move both the F-16 and the F-111 along with it.

Add Flight—Delete Flight The next two controls let you assign additional flights or delete flights. Controls are disabled (grayed) if they have no use. For example, if there is only one flight assigned, the DELETE FLIGHT control will appear very dark. This is because at least one flight must be assigned to each mission. When ADD FLIGHT is selected, a new flight (one aircraft flying from northwest to southeast and back) is added to the mission map. This flight becomes the currently selected flight. This flight

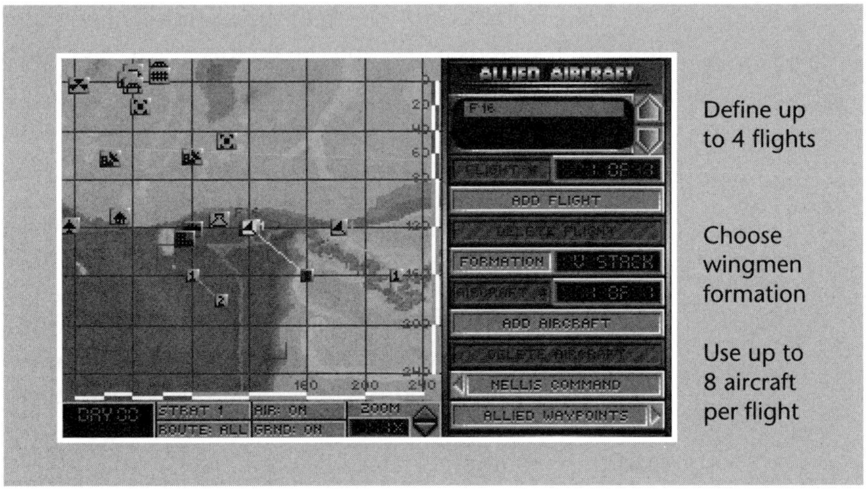

Figure 6-5 Allied Aircraft Assignment

can then be modified in several ways (adding aircraft, changing waypoints, etc.). When four flights are defined, the ADD control is grayed to indicate the maximum number of flights has been reached.

Formation Selecting the FORMATION control cycles through the available formations that can be assigned to the current flight. Each flight that has more than one aircraft assigned flies the mission in a formation. In multi-aircraft flights, one plane is assigned as the *leader* while the other planes are called *wingmen*. The arrangement of wingmen around the leader is the formation. Formations can be useful to fool the enemy. For example, a *C-stack* formation of eight F-16s (aircraft flying directly above each other) may appear as only one on enemy radar. Try various formations and chart your success.

Aircraft# The AIRCRAFT # control selects an aircraft within a flight. For example, if you want the aircraft #2 in a flight to be an F-117 Stealth Fighter, select AIRCRAFT # control until it displays 2 OF X (X is the number of aircraft assigned to the flight). Then use the scroll arrows in the top right corner of the screen to highlight F-117A. The label on the map then indicates that the F-117 is part of the flight.

Add Aircraft—Delete Aircraft The ADD AIRCRAFT and DELETE AIRCRAFT controls operate identically to the flight controls except they act on individual aircraft. Up to eight aircraft can be assigned to one flight. To add an aircraft, use the scroll arrows to select the desired aircraft type, then click on ADD AIRCRAFT. The name of the selected aircraft will be displayed on the map next to its assigned flight icon.

Selecting the NELLIS COMMAND control returns you to the command center to assign enemy aircraft or ground forces. After the allied flights are defined the next step is to define each flight's set of waypoints. Select the ALLIED WAYPOINTS control now.

Allied Waypoints

We introduced you to waypoints in Chapter 3, *Learning to Fly*. Until now, waypoints only designated turning points in a mission and kept your Falcon on course. But waypoints can also provide orders to flights at critical sections of the mission. The Allied Waypoints screen lets you set all friendly flight waypoints. The enemy waypoints screen is similar but affects enemy aircraft only. Figure 6-6 shows the Allied Waypoints screen.

Flight# The FLIGHT # control operates the same as in the Allied Aircraft screen. It lets you cycle through the flights assigned to the mission. Note that the selected flight is highlighted on the mission map. The selected route will be highlighted in yellow.

Waypoint# The WAYPOINT # control cycles through the waypoints assigned to the flight. Each flight waypoint has an altitude, speed, and action assigned to it. You can alter these values for each flight.

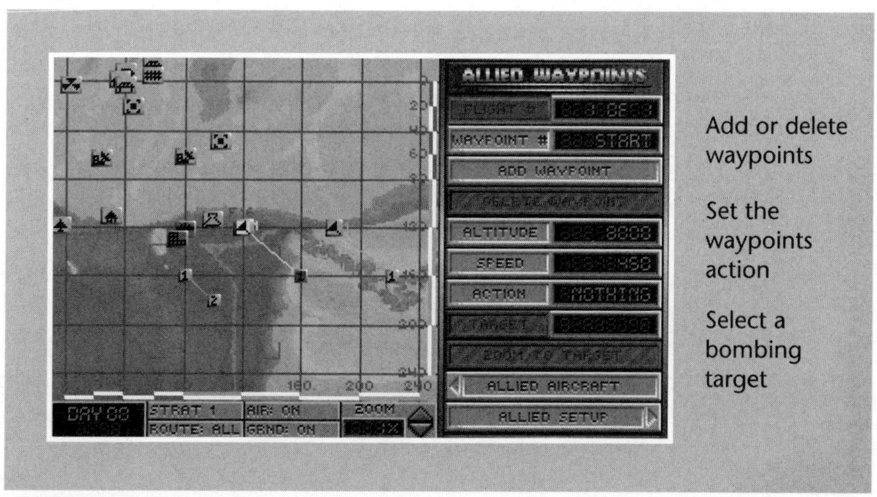

Figure 6-6 Setting Allied Waypoints

Add Waypoint—Delete Waypoint The default flight contains three waypoints (including the START waypoint). You can add additional waypoints using ADD WAYPOINT or delete waypoints using DELETE WAYPOINT. Waypoints will be inserted *after* the current (highlighted) waypoint. For example, if you want to add a waypoint after waypoint #2 of flight #1, you should select flight #1 with the FLIGHT # control, select waypoint #2 with the WAYPOINT # control (or by clicking directly on the waypoint icon 2 on the mission map), and then press ADD WAYPOINT. This adds waypoint #3.

Altitude and Speed The ALTITUDE and SPEED controls set unique values for each waypoint. The values will take affect until the next waypoint is encountered. For example, if waypoint #2 is set for 8,000 feet and 350 knots and waypoint #3 is set for 2,000 feet at 450 knots, the aircraft will begin diving from 8,000 to 2,000 feet *and* accelerate to 450 knots as it reaches waypoint #3. Of course, any enemy engagement during flight will cause the aircraft to temporarily (or perhaps permanently!) change from the intended flight path.

Action The ACTION control establishes what type of role the flight will be taking for the current waypoint. You could have the flight perform a search and destroy action for one segment of the mission and then switch to an intercept mode. Most actions are similar to the altitude and speed settings in that they take effect from waypoint to waypoint. Some actions, however, (such as BOMB) occur *on* the selected waypoint. Table 6-2 lists the actions and each action's meaning. Computer controlled aircraft will always defend themselves if attacked regardless of the action setting.

Target—Zoom to Target If the ACTION control is set to BOMB for a waypoint, two additional controls become available; TARGET and ZOOM TO TARGET. Selecting the TARGET control will cycle through the available targets in the vicinity of the waypoint. This also adjusts the waypoint to direct the aircraft to the exact location of the target. Once the target is designated, pressing the ZOOM TO TARGET control will display the target at a zoom factor of 999X (3D view). The view will rotate around the target until you press a key or mouse button. Knowing what the target looks like before starting the mission can be a great advantage! If you need to return to the previous screen, you can do so by selecting the ALLIED AIRCRAFT control. To continue with the tour, select the ALLIED SETUP control now.

Setting the ACTION to . . .	causes the flight to . . .
Nothing	take no action from waypoint to the following waypoint.
CAP (Combat Air Patrol)	protect the flight path by attacking enemy aircraft (will not stray from flight path).
CAS (Close Air Support)	actively pursue ground forces only. Set this waypoint at least seven miles from the previous waypoint to give the pilot time to select weapons.
S and D (Search and Destroy)	actively pursue all enemy aircraft and ground forces (may stray from flight path).
BOMB	bomb the target(s) specified by the TARGET setting.
INTERCEPT	actively pursues all enemy aircraft contacts. (may stray from flight path).
LOITER	return to previous CAP waypoint if fuel permits.
ESCORT	protect the escorted flight by attacking enemy aircraft which pose a threat.
LAND	land (set at last waypoint only).
TAKEOFF	affects only AIRCRAFT#1 of FLIGHT#1 (your F-16). Wingmen are in the air when the mission starts. Set at START waypoint and airfield location only.

Table 6-2 Waypoint Actions

Allied Setup

The Allied Setup screen lets you load weapons on all of the non-F-16 aircraft assigned to the mission. It is important to make sure that you equip every aircraft with the appropriate weapons before taking off. If you send out an aircraft empty, it probably will not return. Of course you have the same control over the enemy aircraft setup. Enemies without weapons can be useful when learning how to dogfight. Figure 6-7 shows the Allied Setup screen.

Loading Weapons (Non-F-16 Aircraft) To arm a plane, first select the appropriate flight # using the FLIGHT # control, then select the aircraft

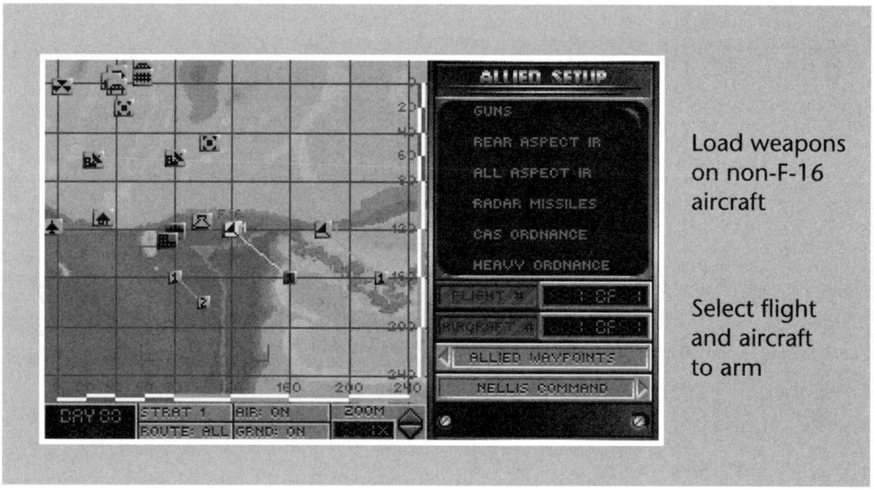

Figure 6-7 Allied Setup

using the AIRCRAFT # control. A list of armament appears in the small screen above the controls. The available weapons for the type of aircraft selected are identified by a hollow circle to the left of the weapon. Every weapon is not available to all aircraft. For example, you cannot equip a B-52 with air-to-air type weapons. To load the weapons, click on the hollow circle. The circle becomes solid, indicating that the weapon is loaded.

> **NOTE:** Enemy Aircraft, Enemy Waypoints, and Enemy Setup are the same as their allied counterparts. The only exception is the type of aircraft available. For example, you will find MiG-29s instead of F-16s.

At this point in mission design, you will have all the flights assigned, the waypoints set, and the weapons for non-F-16 aircraft loaded. Select the NELLIS COMMAND control to return to the control center.

At Red Flag you not only control aircraft (friendly and enemy), but you also control the ground forces. Select the ALLIED FORCES control.

Allied Forces

The Allied Forces screen places various formations of ground troops onto the battlefield. For instance, you can assign a column of tanks along with a squadron of SAMs (surface-to-air missiles) to move between specified points in the desert. These assignments are called *routes* in Falcon 3.0. You may notice the troop movement by flying over a ground force route at various times during a mission. Up to four routes (enemy and allied) can be assigned to a mission. Ground forces are given starting and end points for direction control. These points are labeled 1 (start) and 2 (end) on the mission map. Some of the terrain in the Red Flag training area is fairly mountainous, so don't expect rapid movement from the ground troops when they are assigned to cover this type of area. For training purposes, you will be defining more enemy forces. This will allow you to check your ability to fly through areas loaded with hostile ground activity, an event you will surely run into when engaging in a campaign. Figure 6-8 shows the Allied Forces screen.

Route#—Add/Delete Route The ROUTE # control lets you cycle through the routes that have been defined for this mission. Note that if both enemy and allied routes have been defined, only the *allied* routes will be accessible on this screen. For example, if ROUTE #2 of 4 and ROUTE #4 of 4 were defined as enemy force routes, the allied forces screen would display only ROUTE #1 of 4 and ROUTE #3 of 4. The ADD ROUTE and DELETE ROUTE controls let you add or delete an allied route.

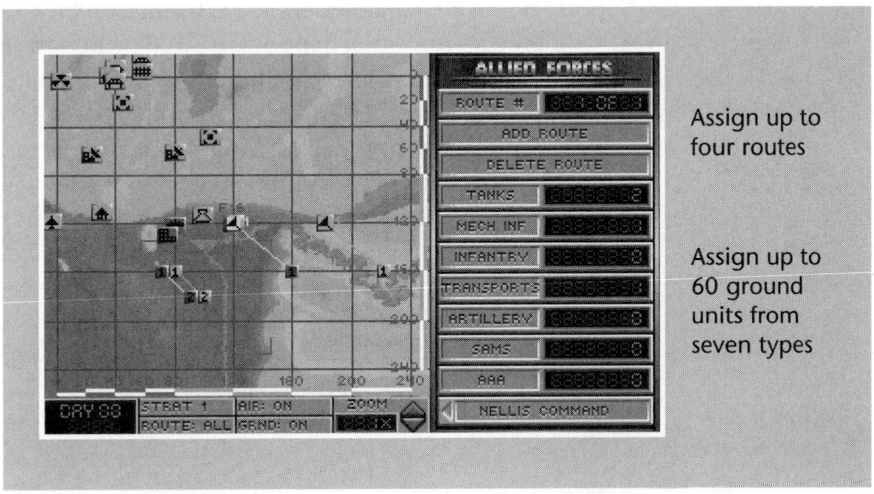

Figure 6-8 Allied Forces Assignment

Ground Forces Seven types of ground forces are available to assign to a route. They are: tanks, mechanized infantry, infantry, transports, artillery, SAMs, and AAA batteries. SAMs (surface-to-air missiles) and AAA (anti-aircraft artillery) are of particular interest to pilots. No more than seven of each type of ground force can be assigned to a route. Also, no more than 60 units total for all four routes can be assigned to a mission. If the total units assigned exceeds 60, all units will be scaled back proportionately. To set the number of units, click on the appropriate control with the left button to increase the number and the right mouse button to decrease the number. Alternately, keyboard users can use the arrow keys to position the cursor arrow, then press the INS and DEL keys to increment or decrement the forces. You cannot deplete all forces to zero. If you wish to get rid of all ground forces, delete the entire route instead.

> **NOTE:** The Enemy Forces screen is identical to the Allied Forces screen. The same types of ground units are available to the enemy forces. You will notice a difference when on the battlefield, however. Enemy ground forces are brown while allied forces are dark green.

The tour continues into the final stage: Selecting pilots and loading weapons for the F-16s assigned to the mission. Select NELLIS COMMAND to return to the command center. Click on REPORT.

Report

The Report screens lets you see detailed information on all allied and enemy aircraft and ground forces used in Falcon 3.0. The Report feature consists of two screens, the selection screen and the viewing screen. Figure 6-9 shows the Report selection screen. Report information is divided into four categories: Allied Aircraft, Enemy Aircraft, Allied Forces, and Enemy Forces.

You can select the type of information you want by clicking on the appropriate button. The Report screen displays the mission map, but it has

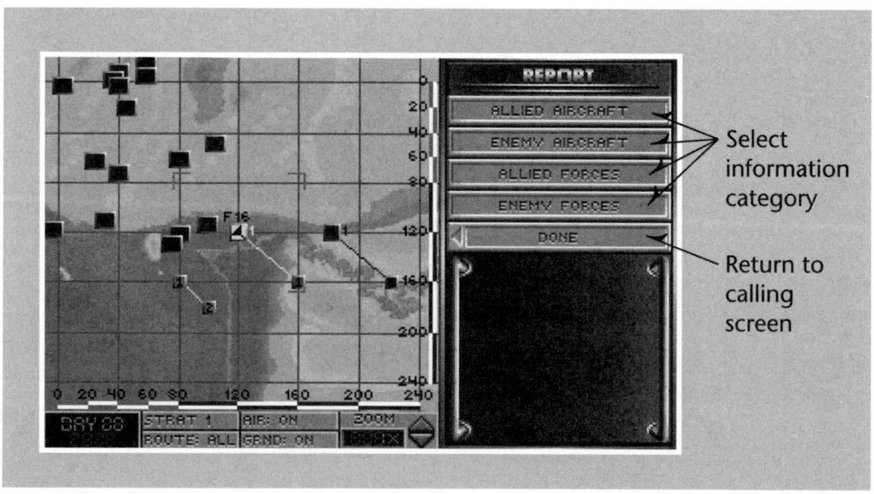

Figure 6-9 Report Selection Screen

Figure 6-10 Report Viewing Screen

no effect on the available information. The Report screen is available from several different screens in Falcon 3.0. For example, we selected the Report screen from Nellis Command. We can also access this screen from the F-16 Pilots and F-16 Armament screens. Click on Allied Aircraft. Figure 6-10 shows the Report viewing screen.

The Report viewing screen gives you statistical and visual information on all of the aircraft and forces included with Falcon 3.0. The screen is divided into four major areas: Information display, Digitized photo display, Falcon 3.0 Graphic display, and Controls. The screen in the upper left corner of the viewing screen is the information display. As you select different aircraft or ground forces, the information display shows statistics on the item in teletype fashion. The display shows information such as maximum speeds, ranges, radar types, and manufacturer names for each selection. The upper right section of the Report viewing screen shows a digitized photograph of what the actual selection item looks like. The lower half of the screen shows a graphic of how the selection will appear in a Falcon 3.0 mission. This is useful if you are having trouble locating or identifying certain enemy forces. The viewing screen has three controls. You can scroll the text on the Information screen by clicking and holding on the SCROLL

TEXT up and down arrows. You can choose the next aircraft or ground force by clicking on the VIEW left or right arrows. Clicking EXIT will return you to the calling screen, in this case, Nellis Command.

Try the VIEW and SCROLL TEXT arrows to view some of the other allied aircraft that are a part of Falcon 3.0. Click on EXIT when you are done viewing. Select DONE to return to Red Flag Control, then select F-16 PILOTS.

F-16 Pilots

A pilot must be assigned for every F-16 that is designated to participate in the mission. In Chapter 2, you created your own squadron. This squadron is made up of several pilots. Some are very skilled, some are greenhorns (beginners). Each pilot has ratings for specific areas such as bombing, dogfighting, etc. Falcon 3.0 will give different results based on these ratings. The ultimate question becomes "Which pilot do I assign to which mission?" Many factors make up the pilots' abilities. Some are great bombers, some are great dogfighters. All factors must be taken into consideration when making this decision. Fortunately, Red Flag is a training area. This is where the pilot has a chance to learn from his mistakes. You will find that the pilot skill levels will increase while attending Red Flag. For example, it is a good idea to assign a pilot that is weak in bombing skills to a bombing mission. He may fail, but he will gain experience and his ratings will increase as a result. Figure 6-11 shows the F-16 Pilots screen.

Flight# and Pilot Assignment The FLIGHT # control cycles through all flights that have at least one F-16 assigned. Flight #1 will have at least one F-16 assigned (your own!) When a flight is selected, up to eight F-16s will appear on the cloudy background on the left side of the screen. To select a pilot, highlight the pilots name on the small screen and then select the F-16 desired. The originally assigned pilot will return to the list of available pilots. If a pilot name is not visible on the screen, use the scroll arrows. The topmost F-16 will be designated as the *leader*.

> NOTE: In the case of FLIGHT #1, you will control the leader during the mission.

Pilot Information The PILOT INFORMATION control brings up detailed information on every pilot in your squadron. This screen also lets you change the name and callsigns of your pilots (abbreviated names like

Figure 6-11 F-16 Pilot Assignment

Bugout, Beowolf, etc.). Changing the names of pilots to names of your family members or friends can be helpful. It may help you associate the pilot name with performance and ability. Always pay attention to the callsigns of the assigned pilots. When the going gets rough on the battlefield, it may help to know which of your wingmen is sending you a message. All messages from wingmen are reported with callsigns. For example, if you receive the message: DEADEYE: I'M HIT!!! I'M HIT!!! and Deadeye is your bombing ace, it may be a good time to call off the bombing mission and head back to base. Without your bombing ace the chances for a successful mission are slim. The ultimate choice to complete or abort the mission is yours!

One final preparation before takeoff. We need to load the F-16 with weapons. Select the F-16 ARMAMENT control.

F-16 Armament

All F-16s must now be loaded with weapons and possibly extra fuel or anti-radar systems. Which weapons go on which F-16? To answer that question, it is important to remember the mission goal of that particular Falcon. Recall that the mission actions were defined when setting the waypoints. If the waypoints were set to INTERCEPT, the aircraft should be loaded with air-to-air weaponry. On the other hand if the mission is to take out a tank column (SEARCH AND DESTROY), air-to-ground missiles should be the priority. You will be responsible for loading all F-16s participating in the mission.

Chapter 5, *Using Weapons,* discussed the available weapons and their benefits in detail. Figure 6-12 shows the F-16 Armament screen.

Flight# The FLIGHT # control cycles through the F-16 flights assigned to the mission. The F-16 control cycles through the Falcons assigned to the current flight. If more that one F-16 is assigned to a flight, the first will be the *leader*. All other F-16s within that flight become wingman 1, wingman 2, and so on.

The F-16 Armament screen displays a front view of the currently selected F-16 on the left side of the screen. The weapons will appear on this screen as they are loaded.

Clear All Weapons The CLEAR ALL WEAPONS control will remove all weapons from the displayed aircraft, allowing you to start the loading procedure over.

Default Load The DEFAULT LOAD control will use computer intelligence to load weapons based on the waypoint actions assigned. It is important to note that this will not always result in the optimum weapon selection for the flight. You will gain the experience you need as you fly missions charting your success (and failure!)

Report The REPORT control works the same as in Nellis Command. It accesses reports on all allied and enemy aircraft and ground units.

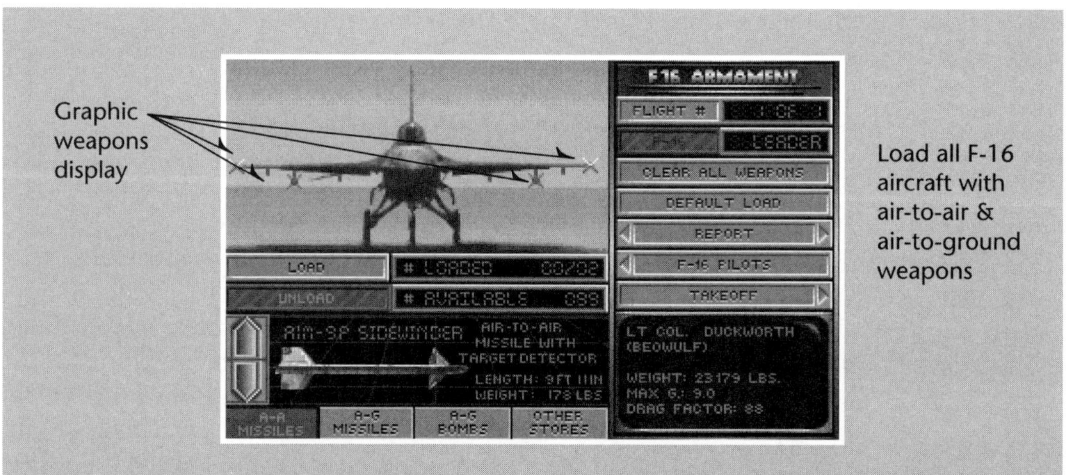

Figure 6-12 F-16 Armament

You can use several controls to select weapons manually. The type of weapons (or stores, as they are referred to) can be selected using four controls: A-A (air-air) MISSILES, A-G (air-ground) MISSILES, A-G BOMBS, and OTHER STORES. Once the basic type is selected, you can scroll through the available weapons using the scroll arrows to the left of the weapon's picture.

#Loaded The # LOADED status indicates how many of the current weapons are loaded out of the maximum load for that weapon. For example, the AIM 9-P Sidewinder indicates 00/06. This means that up to six Sidewinders can be loaded and that none are currently loaded.

#Available The # AVAILABLE status indicates how many of the current weapons are available for your squadron. This number is not important in Red Flag because it is reset after each mission. This status will become important in Campaign mode.

Load—Unload The LOAD and UNLOAD controls load and unload the displayed weapon. The LOAD control is disabled when the maximum load for the selected weapon type is reached.

The screen in the lower right corner displays the pilot and the callsign of the displayed F-16. It also displays the F-16's weight, maximum G, and drag factor. Maneuvering the F-16 becomes increasingly difficult as you load weapons, particularly heavy iron bombs.

F-16 Pilots The F-16 PILOTS control returns you to the pilot assignment screen. This is the normal selection when creating a mission for the first time. You will want to save the weapons information before flying the first mission.

Takeoff The TAKEOFF control takes you to the runway if the START waypoint action is TAKEOFF. You will start out in flight if the START waypoint has an altitude and speed assigned.

Tour Summary

This concludes the tour of the Red Flag facility. The purpose of Red Flag is to provide you with a training ground. It lets you create custom missions to test and measure your abilities. It's time to create our first mission using Red Flag: *Las Vegas Nightflight!* Before we get started, return to Red Flag Control by selecting F-16 PILOTS from the armament screen, then select RED FLAG CONTROL from the pilot assignment screen.

The Training: Mission Development

Now it's time for you to take control of Red Flag. This chapter provides three tutorials to help you discover how easy it can be to create missions that are fun, exciting, and educational. Each of the tutorials includes five sections: Overview, Mission Goals, Creating the Mission, Taking the Flight, and Experiments.

Overview is a description of the mission, Mission Goals describes what skills you will gain during the mission. Creating the Mission provides step-by-step procedures to create the tutorial mission. This section contains all the information needed to complete the mission. Taking the Flight gives you information on what to look for (and what to look out for!) during the actual flight. Experiments offer ways to modify the missions to make them more interesting and/or challenging.

Mission 1: Las Vegas Nightflight

Overview Have you ever wanted to gamble in Las Vegas? If you have, here is your chance to not only gamble, but to destroy ground targets as well. And you can do this while traveling at over 300 knots! Our first attempt at mission creation will be simple. You are going to start in the air at approximately 1,000 feet, south of Las Vegas, Nevada, heading for the city. After passing the first waypoint, you will bank towards the northeast and fly directly over the city lights. A few moments later you will arrive at waypoint 2 where you will make your final turn to the north, towards Nellis AFB. You will circle the base once, then land. Sound simple? Let's give it a try!

Mission Goals

- Using the external views during flight.
- Using autopilot.
- Observing the autopilot landing procedure.
- Designing a one-flight mission.

Creating the Mission You should be at Red Flag Control. If you are in the War Room, select a squadron and then the Red Flag screen. The last mission to be loaded or edited will appear on the mission map. Since we are creating a new mission, let's start out with a clean slate.

1. Select the CLEAR MISSION control and answer (Y) to the ARE YOU SURE? (Y/N) prompt. This will bring up the default mission. The default mission consists of one allied F-16 and one enemy MiG-29. Both aircraft are traveling southeast. An enemy ground route is traveling in the southeast direction. There must be at least one allied and one enemy flight defined for each mission. You cannot delete the MiG-29 flight. It is possible to delete the enemy ground route, although it is not necessary for this mission.

2. Now that we have a clear mission, select NELLIS COMMAND so we can adjust waypoints. You may recall from the tour that one purpose for waypoints is to provide information for navigation during flight. We can make some course and fine adjustments to the waypoints on the Nellis Command screen.

3. Select the F-16 flight icon and drag the icon to a point approximately 15 miles southwest of the Las Vegas icon. Notice that waypoint #2 was hidden under the F-16 icon. This is a course adjustment. Exact positioning will be done after all waypoints have be placed. Figure 6-13 shows the location of the Las Vegas icon.

4. Using the same method, move waypoint #1 to the Las Vegas icon. You may notice that the waypoint *snaps* or jumps to the Las Vegas icon when it is released.

5. Finally, move waypoint #2 to the Nellis AFB icon (the blue airplane icon). The same snap effect should occur.

All of the F-16 waypoints should now be in the immediate Las Vegas/ Nellis AFB area. With the waypoints concentrated in a small area, we can now use the ZOOM control to perform some fine adjustments.

6. The zoom box (red box with crosshairs) should have moved when you relocated the F-16 icon. If it did not move, or has moved since, adjust the box so it contains all waypoints. To move the box with the mouse, hold the right mouse button and drag. To move the box with the keyboard, move the cursor to the map with the (TAB) key, then move the box by holding down the right (SHIFT) key and using the arrow keys.

7. Adjust the zoom to 8X by clicking on the zoom arrows or by using the keyboard arrow keys. Adjust the map if you cannot see all waypoints at the 8X zoom factor. Each division on the grid will be 10 miles at the

8X setting. You may have to move the F-16 flight icon (starting waypoint) farther north to fit all of the waypoints in the 8X screen.

8. Select the ALLIED AIRCRAFT control. Since this will be a one-aircraft flight, there is no reason to add additional aircraft.

9. Select the ALLIED WAYPOINTS control. We will need to add a waypoint to direct the flight past a particular landmark. The waypoint should be added between the current waypoint #1 and waypoint #2.

10. Since waypoints are always inserted after the highlighted waypoint, select waypoint #1. This can be done by selecting it directly on the mission map or by using the WAYPOINT # control.

11. Once waypoint #1 is highlighted, select ADD WAYPOINT. The new waypoint is now called #2 and may appear directly over the waypoint on the Nellis icon. The former waypoint #2 now becomes waypoint #3.

12. Select our new waypoint #2 and move it approximately 2 to 3 miles south of Nellis AFB. Make sure the waypoint does not snap back to the Nellis icon. If it does, try moving it a little further from Nellis. Waypoint #2 is now in position.

Refer to Figure 6-13. Before proceeding, make sure the waypoints are in the following locations: Start (F-16 icon) is approximately 15 miles SW of Las Vegas, waypoint #1 is directly on Las Vegas, waypoint #2 is 2-3 miles south of Nellis, and waypoint #3 is directly on Nellis.

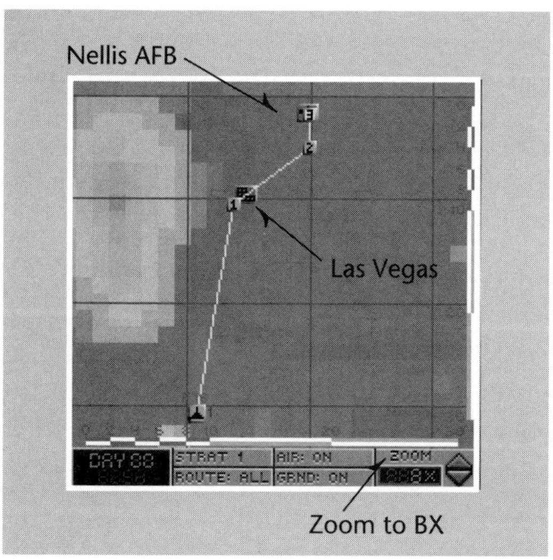

Figure 6-13 Las Vegas Nightflight—Mission Map

Now let's set the waypoint actions. Since this is a sightseeing flight, setting the waypoint actions will be relatively simple. Primarily, we will be concerned with altitude and speed settings.

13. Use the WAYPOINT # control to select START. The F-16 icon should be highlighted. The settings for START should read: ALTITUDE 8,000 feet, SPEED 450 knots and ACTION NOTHING. These are the default settings for waypoints before adjustments are made. We will start the mission already in the air to

save time. In this mission, you will fly very close to the ground. This is possible with the flat desert terrain.

14. Select ALTITUDE. This lets you type in a new altitude value. Type **2000** and press ENTER. The new mission starting altitude is 2,000 feet. For the START waypoint, we will leave the speed and the action at 450 and NOTHING.

15. Use the WAYPOINT # control to select waypoint #1. Adjust the altitude to 1,000 feet and the speed to 350 knots. As in the starting waypoint, leave the ACTION entry set to NOTHING. The lower altitude and speed will result in a relaxing cruise over Las Vegas.

16. Select waypoint #2. Adjust the altitude to 200 feet and the speed to 350 knots. The F-16 will skim the desert at this waypoint!

17. Finally, adjust waypoint #3 to an altitude of 700 feet and a speed of 350 knots. Use the ACTION control to cycle through the available actions. Select LAND as the action. If you cannot get LAND to come up as an option, make sure that waypoint #3 is on the Nellis AFB icon.

18. Select the ALLIED SETUP control. Because there are no non-F-16 aircraft assigned to this mission, the setup screen is not used. Select NELLIS COMMAND to return to the command center and select DONE to return to Red Flag Control.

Let's save our progress. Select the SAVE MISSION button in Red Flag Control. Press Y to confirm the save. A window appears to enter a filename. Type **SIGHTS** and press ENTER. (If your mission used weapons, you would first visit the F-16 ARMAMENT screen, then return to Red Flag Control to save your mission.)

Taking the Flight It is time to check out our first Red Flag Mission. We will let the autopilot do the work the first time through. Concentrate on using the view keys to enjoy this peaceful mission. They won't be peaceful for long!

Select F-16 PILOTS. Which pilot is selected is not important for this mission. You can change the name of the pilot to your own at this time if you want. Select F-16 ARMAMENT. No weapons will be carried on this mission.

The Takeoff The time has arrived! Select TAKEOFF and you will be instantly placed at 2,000 feet traveling at a rate of 450 knots. As soon as the cockpit comes into view, press the A key to enable autopilot.

Red Flag will randomly choose a time of day as early morning, high noon, late afternoon, or night. If the sky is not dark, try holding the right SHIFT key and pressing T until the sky goes dark. Remember, you can always pause the mission at any time by pressing P.

Try out several of the views while on the short tour over Las Vegas. The track view (press the 9 key) provides a nice perspective for most of the flight. The following is a list of things to look for on your flight between waypoints.

Start to Waypoint #1 Depending on where you initially placed your F-16 flight icon, you should be able to see Potosi Mountain to your left or behind you. You may have started your mission over part of the mountain. The concrete of Las Vegas should start to come into view shortly. Keep watching out the right side (the 9 key on the numeric keypad) for McCarran International Airport. From 1,000 to 2,000 feet, you should be able to see the control tower and runways. As you pass McCarran, switch back to normal cockpit view. You should be around 7 or 8 miles from waypoint #1 and Vegas itself. As you get close to Las Vegas the hotels and casinos start to come into view. As soon as you reach the heart of the city, the autopilot should bank your F-16 to the right. Figure 6-14 shows this action.

Figure 6-14 F-16 Track View over Las Vegas

Waypoint #1 to Waypoint #2 A quick check to the rear and you can catch a fading glimpse of the city. The autopilot should start a gentle descent to 200 feet. The freeway below you is Interstate-15. The lights from Nellis should be visible at the 10 o'clock position. You may even spot a marquis indicating that The King is still with us!

Waypoint #2 to Waypoint #3 Your Falcon should start to gain altitude to prepare for landing. Watching autopilot landings can help you improve your landing technique. After approaching the runway, you start a turn to the right. Continue for 360 degrees while the autopilot decreases the airspeed. Track view is a good choice when watching landings. After touchdown, the F-16 slows and turns off onto the infield and stops.

Press ESC and select END MISSION from the FILE menu to go to the Debriefing Screen. No activity with the enemy was involved in this mission, so select NEXT MISSION to return to Red Flag Control.

Experiments Here are some suggested modifications that may make your mission more enjoyable:

- Try taking the controls yourself and buzz Las Vegas! Remember that the altitude and speed settings for the waypoints affect only autopilot and other aircraft. Try adding weapons. If you get into trouble, you can always eject by pressing CTRL-E three times in succession.
- Try adding other aircraft on the ALLIED AIRCRAFT screen. Fly the mission with an F-117 Stealth Fighter. Use the ADD AIRCRAFT feature to make the added aircraft part of your flight.
- Revisit this mission and try bombing Las Vegas after learning how to use the weapons in the following chapter.
- Try adding new waypoints to extend the mission north of Nellis. Then land from the north. Notice any difference?

Mission 2: B52s in Action

Overview When you are flying in campaign mode, you will be asked to escort B-52s to their targets and also to assist them in returning. Normally, you would not be part of the B-52 flight. You would be part of a separate flight assigned to an escort mission. For our training mission, we will assign the F-16 to be a part of the B-52 flight. This is mainly for two reasons. It keeps the waypoint assignment simple and it permits you to see the big bombers in action! You will observe as these massive aircraft unload heavy armament on an enemy railroad yard. Let's get in the air!

Mission Goals

- Designing multiple aircraft flights.
- Setting flight waypoint action.
- Setting flight formation.
- Observing bombing waypoint action.
- Observing wingman formation.

Creating the Mission

You should be at Red Flag Control. If you are in the War Room, select a squadron and then the Red Flag screen. The last mission to be loaded or edited will appear on the mission map. Once again we are creating a new mission, so let's start out with a clean slate.

1. Select the CLEAR MISSION control and answer (Y) to the ARE YOU SURE? (Y/N) prompt. This default mission appears.

2. So far we have used the STRAT 1 setting on the mission map. This displays the strategic targets with a nautical miles grid. Select this control once to change to STRAT 2 to display strategic targets with a coordinate grid. This will help place the waypoints into proper position. The coordinates will be given with the vertical coordinate followed by the horizontal coordinate. For example, Las Vegas is at coordinate F-D.

3. Select the NELLIS COMMAND control.

4. Move the F-16 (START waypoint) to the center of coordinates 5-C. The F-16 icon may snap to the nearest strategic target. Don't worry about this for now. We can adjust it when we are zoomed in.

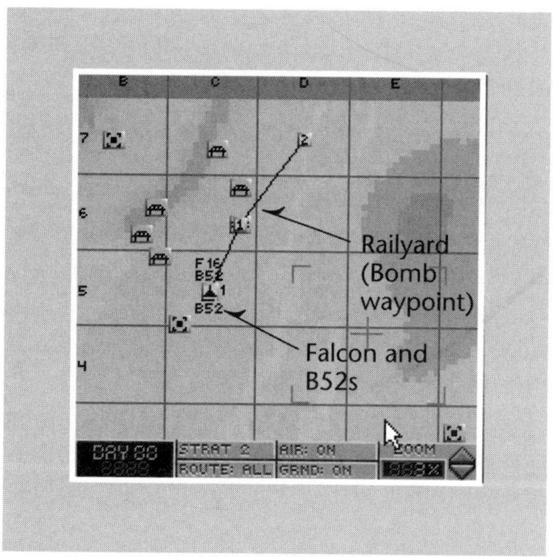

Figure 6-15 B52s In Action—Mission Map

5. Move the waypoint #1 icon to the rail yard icon (located at coordinates 6-C). Move waypoint #2 to the center of coordinate 7D.

6. Now that the waypoints are arranged, select ALLIED AIRCRAFT.

7. Select ADD AIRCRAFT and use the scroll arrows to highlight B-52, then select ADD AIRCRAFT again to add a second bomber. The mission map should indicate one F-16 and two B-52s. Figure 6-15 illustrates the B52 mission waypoints.

8. Use the FORMATION control to cycle to the WEDGE formation option. This will cause the bombers to fly to the right and slightly behind you until you give them permission to attack.

9. Select the ALLIED WAYPOINTS control.

10. Set the START waypoint for: ALTITUDE 3,000 feet, SPEED 300 knots, and ACTION NOTHING.
11. Set waypoint #1 for: ALTITUDE 2,000 feet, SPEED 250 knots, and ACTION BOMB. Two new controls were enabled when you selected BOMB, TARGET, and ZOOM TO TARGET. TARGET lets you cycle through the available bombing targets in the immediate area. For this mission, the target is 1 RAIL Y, which designates the rail yard for our primary target.
12. Select ZOOM TO TARGET. The map will automatically zoom to the 999X power and rotate around the target. This lets you see the target before starting the mission. Press any key to return to ALLIED WAYPOINTS.
13. Select ALLIED SETUP.
14. Now it is time to load the '52s. Select the AIRCRAFT # control to access 2 of 3 and 3 of 3. Notice that the only weapon available to load is heavy ordnance. The B-52's specialty is dropping bombs, the other weapons are of no use. Be sure to select heavy ordnance for both bombers before continuing.
15. Select NELLIS COMMAND to return to the command center and then DONE to return to Red Flag Control.
16. Select F-16 PILOTS and if you like, choose a different pilot.
17. Select F-16 ARMAMENT. Load your Falcon with 2 AIM-9Ms and 2 AMRAAMs for protection. This is not a necessity but it is good practice. It helps to have the air-to-air capability when escorting other flights.
18. Return to F-16 PILOTS and then to RED FLAG CONTROL.
19. Position the zoom box over the waypoints and zoom in to 3X. Verify that the START waypoint is in the center of 5C, waypoint #1 is on the rail yard icon, and waypoint #2 is in the center of 7D.
20. Select SAVE MISSION. Type **RAILBOMB** as the filename and press (ENTER). Press (Y) to confirm. Your mission is now complete.

Taking the Flight Let's watch as the B-52s tear up this strategic supply line! Let the autopilot do the work the first time through. Try to keep an eye on the bombers using the wingman view (the upper row (7) key) and other external views.

Select F-16 PILOTS and then F-16 ARMAMENT. You should see the loaded sidewinders and the AMRAAMs.

The Takeoff Select TAKEOFF and immediately select autopilot. You should be approximately 15–20 miles from waypoint #1. You can verify this using the distance-to-waypoint indicator located in the lower right corner of your HUD.

Exercise the different views while you are on your way to the target area. Try the padlock view (the * key on the numeric keypad). You should spot the two bombers flying off your right wing. Use the T key to toggle between the bombers in padlock view. Pressing the 7 (on the upper row numeric keys) will allow you to toggle between the views of your two large wingmen. You may find it necessary to adjust the zoom (F2) to see all of the B-52 in this view.

Periodically check your distance to waypoint #1. When you are two to five miles from the waypoint (target), one of the B-52 pilots will announce, "Request Permission to Attack." Hold the SHIFT key and press E to allow the aircraft to start their attack. The pilot will respond, "Attacking primary target." Figure 6-16 shows the big bombers and the destroyed rail yard.

The bombers will now prepare to fly over and drop their bombs on the rail yard. Try out several views to see the bombs' destruction as they hit (or perhaps miss) the target. Not all missions go exactly as planned. Try running this mission again. You will experience slightly different results each time.

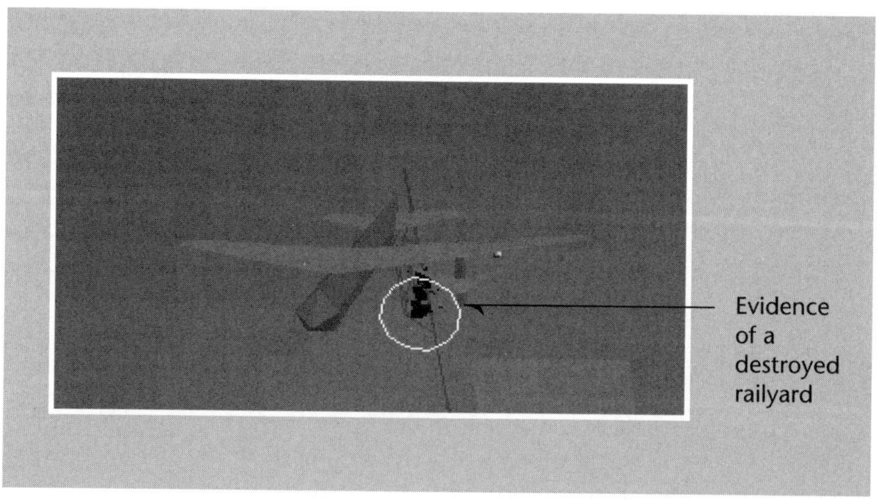

Figure 6-16 B-52 Takes Out the Rail Yard

When you are past the rail yard, press (ESC), select FILE and END MISSION. At the debriefing screen, select NEXT MISSION. You will return to Red Flag Control.

Experiments Here are some suggested modifications that may make the mission more enjoyable:

- Try taking the controls yourself during the mission. Keep in mind that you control the speed and altitude. If you fly too fast, the bombers will not be able to keep up with you. See how close you can fly to the target as the bombers unload. Be careful though! The bombers will not watch out for you!
- Try assigning aircraft other than the B-52s to carry out the bombing. Keep in mind that some types of aircraft cannot handle heavy armament.
- Load up with Mk84 iron bombs and try taking out the railway yourself!

Mission 3: MiG-29 Showdown

Overview So far the air has been clear and the enemy has been nowhere in sight. That is about to change. This mission brings three Falcons up against three of the best the opposition can offer, the MiG-29. We will send both the Falcons and the MiGs out looking for trouble by using the waypoint action INTERCEPT. The intercept action orders the aircraft to look for the enemy and engage. Both sides will find plenty of trouble in this training mission. Who will win this battle of the super-fighters? Let's find out!

Mission Goals

- Designing a multiple flight mission.
- Assigning a hostile ground route.
- Observing autopiloted dogfights.
- Observing air-to-air weapons delivery.
- Observing autopilot SAM avoidance tactics.

Creating the Mission You should be at Red Flag Control. If you are in the War Room, select a squadron and then the Red Flag screen. The last mission to be loaded or edited will appear on the mission map. Once again we are creating a new mission, so let's start out with a clean slate.

1. Select the CLEAR MISSION control and answer (Y) to the ARE YOU SURE? (Y/N) prompt. The default mission appears.
2. Set the map mode to STRAT 2. We will need the coordinate system to help place our flight and waypoint icons. We will also relocate the enemy ground route for this mission.
3. Select the NELLIS COMMAND control.
4. Let's relocate the allied flight first. Move the F-16 icon to the center of coordinate 3-0, move waypoint #1 to coordinate 3-1, and waypoint #2 to coordinate 5-3. The result is a route that starts facing due east, then banks northeast at waypoint #1.
5. Now relocate the enemy flight. Move the MiG-29 icon to coordinate 2-1, move waypoint #1 to coordinate 3-1, and waypoint #2 to coordinate 5-3. Notice that waypoints #1 and #2 coincide for the allied and enemy flights. A conflict indeed!
6. Finally move the enemy ground route. Move both points #1 and #2 to the lower center of coordinate 5-3. Even if the allied flight should make it past the MiGs, there is more trouble on the ground. Figure 6-17 shows the completed mission map.

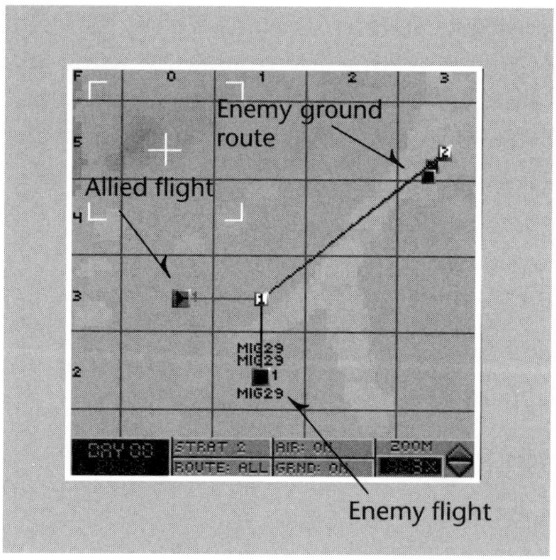

Figure 6-17 MiG 29 Battle—Mission Map

Now that the waypoints are in proper position, zoom to 3X and make adjustments if necessary. Select the ALLIED AIRCRAFT control.

7. Select the ADD AIRCRAFT control twice to add two additional F-16s to your flight. The icon on the mission map should note the additions. Select the FORMATION control to cycle to the WEDGE formation.
8. Select the ALLIED WAYPOINTS control. Adjust the START waypoint for the allied flight to ALTITUDE 12000, SPEED 450, ACTION INTERCEPT. Adjust waypoint #1 to ALTITUDE 8000, SPEED 450, ACTION INTERCEPT, and waypoint #2 to ALTITUDE 12000, SPEED 450, ACTION INTERCEPT.

9. Select the ALLIED SETUP control. Only F-16s are involved in this mission. Consequently no action is necessary at this screen. Select the NELLIS COMMAND control to return to the command center.

10. Now let's set up the enemy flights. Select the ENEMY AIRCRAFT control.

11. Select the ADD AIRCRAFT control twice to add two additional MiG-29s to the flight. The icon on the mission map should note the additions. Select the FORMATION control to cycle to the WEDGE formation.

12. Select the ENEMY WAYPOINTS control. Adjust the START waypoint for the enemy flight to ALTITUDE 12000, SPEED 450, ACTION INTERCEPT. Adjust waypoint #1 to ALTITUDE 8000, SPEED 450, ACTION INTERCEPT, and waypoint #2 to ALTITUDE 12000, SPEED 450, ACTION INTERCEPT. These are identical to the allied flight waypoints.

13. Select the ENEMY SETUP control. Use the AIRCRAFT # control to cycle through the three MiGs. Check the following weapons for each of the three MiGs: GUNS and REAR ASPECT IR. This equips the MiGs with the equivalent of the allied AIM-9P sidewinder. The sidewinder and other weapons will be discussed in detail in the following chapter. Make sure that all MiGs are loaded before proceeding.

14. Select the NELLIS COMMAND control. Once back at command, select the ENEMY FORCES control. One enemy route should be defined. This route should be located somewhere near waypoint #2. Let's add some additional ground forces to this route.

15. Click on the SAM control three times with the left mouse button to create three SAM units. Click on AAA with the left mouse button five times. The right mouse button will decrease the number. Keyboard users can move the cursor arrow to AAA or SAM, and then use the INS and DEL keys to increase or decrease the number of the forces. With three SAM and five AAA units, allied aircraft will find this area to be very hostile.

16. Select NELLIS COMMAND. Once you are back at command control, select DONE to return to Red Flag Control.

17. The final item for this mission is loading the appropriate weapons on the three F-16s. Select the F-16 PILOTS and change pilots if you want.

Select the F-16 ARMAMENT control. A-A MISSILES should already be selected (dark gray). If not, select it now. Use the scroll arrows to bring up the AIM-120 AMRAAM, select the LOAD control. The # LOADED window should indicate that two AIM-120s are loaded. You should also see the weapons appear on the wings of the F-16.

18. Notice that the F-16 indicator displays LEADER. This indicates that only the flight leader's aircraft is currently being displayed. Load the remaining two F-16s with two AIM-120s by selecting the F-16 control to cycle to the next aircraft and LOAD to load the 120.

19. Use the scroll arrows to bring up the AIM-9M sidewinder. Load four sidewinders (the LOAD control twice) on each F-16. Run through all three F-16s to ensure they are properly loaded before continuing.

20. We need to save the mission before takeoff. Select F-16 PILOTS then RED FLAG CONTROL to return.

21. Select SAVE MISSION. Type MIGFIGHT and press ENTER to save the mission, then confirm by pressing Y.

Taking the Flight Air-to-air battles can be hard to follow. You have to change views quickly to observe some of the techniques the computer pilots will use in a dogfight. It may be helpful to watch this mission several times. The outcome will vary from mission to mission.

Select F-16 PILOTS and then F-16 ARMAMENT. You should see the loaded sidewinders and the AMRAAMs. It is a good idea to check all of the F-16s for proper armament during this preflight check.

Select TAKEOFF and immediately select autopilot. You should be approximately 15–20 miles from waypoint #1. You can verify this using the distance-to-waypoint indicator located in the lower right corner of your HUD.

This will give you some time to use the views to observe your two wingmen. They should be located off your right wing (WEDGE formation). Try the padlock view (numeric keypad *), wingman view (upper row 7 key), and the track view (upper row 9 key).

You have several minutes to experiment with the controls. Try taking the aircraft off of autopilot (depressing the A key toggles autopilot status). Gently bank the aircraft to the left and observe the wingmen as they follow your lead. Change altitude by climbing or diving slightly. Each wingman constantly monitors speed, direction, and rate of climb. The reactions will not be instantaneous, however. The pilot needs to *see* your move, then react to it.

You should be getting closer to the confrontation with the enemy aircraft. Turn on autopilot before you are 11 miles from waypoint #1. Remember the distance-to-waypoint indicator is in the lower right corner of the HUD.

At approximately nine miles from waypoint #1 you should notice three targets appear in the upper right corner of your radar screen. You are flying east and they are flying north. One of your wingmen should request permission to engage. If this does not happen by the time your autopilot starts towards the MiGs, give them permission anyway. Hold SHIFT and press E to tell your wingmen to attack. You will hear one of two responses. *"Engaging!"* indicates that the wingman reads your command and is attacking one of the MiGs. *"Copy Fence Check!"* means the wingmen reads your command and will engage when necessary. The battle has begun!

The padlock view (* on numeric keypad) is a great view during dogfighting! You may even pick up a few pointers while watching. You will use this view often when engaging in air-to-air combat. The wingman view (upper row 7 key) can show some interesting angles. If you see a view of the front of your wingman, chances are that the enemy is on his tail! You may even see the MiG fire a rear-aspect IR missile. If your F-16 autopilot fires a missile, try pressing the Q key. This is the missile view key. It will toggle from the fired missile to the target lock-on. Figure 6-18 shows an F-16 attacking a MiG-29

Sometimes you win, sometimes you lose. Like all Falcon 3.0 missions, the results will differ each time the mission is flown. You may want to watch

Figure 6-18 F-16 Attacking MiG-29

your wingmen continue the mission if your F-16 was the first to be destroyed. You can press (ESC), select FILE then select END MISSION at any time to get to the debriefing screen.

Run this mission until the F-16s are successful against the MiGs. If you recall, our pilots have the ground forces near waypoint #2 to contend with.

You will hear the alarms go off, and the threat indicator (left-side cockpit) flashes as the enemy hurls surface-to-air missiles (SAM) and anti-aircraft artillery into the sky. Watch from the wingman or track views as the F-16s drop chaff and flares and try to evade the incoming threat. Chaff (an explosion of small metal strips) is dropped to confuse a radar missile while flares (a small hot missile) are dropped to confuse an infrared missile (heat-seeking). Sometimes the pilot does not have time to decide what type of missile is being fired at him, so he drops both!

Chances are the F-16 will not make it to waypoint #2. This provides an important lesson. Avoid enemy concentrations such as these or be more prepared for this type of situation.

When you are ready to end the mission, press (ESC), select FILE, and select END MISSION.

The debriefing screen can be used in this mission. Select CONTINUE on the debriefing screen. A tracer line is drawn on the mission map to represent your latest flight. At the same time, the small screen displays the actions that occurred during the flight. After the debriefing completes, you can use the scroll arrows to review all the mission events.

Experiments The following are some suggested modifications to make the mission more enjoyable:

- Add other weapons to the MiG-29s at the ENEMY SETUP screen. Try adding all-aspect IR missiles. This will make things much more difficult for the F-16s.
- Change the enemy flight to a large aircraft and two escorts, then attack the flight.
- Try the MIGBATTLE mission again with you at the stick instead of the autopilot!

Mission 4: SAMs and Strategy

Overview This Red Flag mission has the makings of a real campaign mission. When you receive a mission briefing in a campaign, you will have to make choices. You can send up to eight F-16s on a mission. How do you make efficient use of your F-16s to accomplish the mission objectives? You will not have to send all eight Falcons out on every mission. This mission gives some insight for this decision making process.

We can assign up to four flights in a single mission but, the optimum number of F-16s per flight is two. You can control what each of the flights will do during the mission, even if *you* are not part of that particular flight. This is done by setting the waypoint actions. For example, we could assign one flight with S AND D waypoint actions, which would cause that particular flight to search and destroy enemy ground and air units. We could assign a flight to escort our flight to a bombing target. There are endless possibilities, yet the selection process must be well thought out.

Most targets that campaign missions direct you to are well guarded. There may be an enemy airbase nearby. This causes a serious problem in getting to the intended target without being intercepted by enemy fighters. Often targets are guarded by SAM and AAA sites. We will design a mission that simulates this type of real campaign situation. We will also arrange two flights of F-16s to accomplish our mission goal: destroy a radar site. One flight will suppress the SAMs while the other carries out the primary mission.

Mission Goals

- Designing a campaign style mission.
- Assigning multiple F-16 flights with differing roles.
- Observing second flight destroying SAMs.
- Destroying a radar site with Maverick missiles.

Creating the Mission Go to Red Flag Control. If you are in the War Room, select a squadron and click on the Red Flag screen. The last mission that was loaded or edited appears on the mission map. We will start out with the default mission and modify it.

1. Select the CLEAR MISSION control and answer (Y) to the ARE YOU SURE? (Y/N) prompt. The default mission appears.
2. Set the map mode to STRAT 2. We will need the coordinate system to help place our flight and waypoint icons. We will also relocate the enemy ground route for this mission.
3. Select the NELLIS COMMAND control.
4. Let's move the default, allied flight waypoints. Drag the allied, flight-

START waypoint icon to the Nellis Air Force Base icon and release.

5. Move the #1 waypoint icon to a point 20 miles directly north of Nellis. Move the #2 waypoint approximately 20 miles directly north of the #1 waypoint. These are temporary positions for the waypoints.

6. Move the zoom box so the Nellis icon and the radar site icon (located directly north of Nellis) are both inside the box. Zoom in to 3X. Verify that the allied START waypoint icon is on the Nellis icon.

7. Move waypoint #1 to the bottom center of coordinate 2-E. Move waypoint #2 to the radar site.

8. Select ALLIED AIRCRAFT. Change the FORMATION to WEDGE, then click on ADD AIRCRAFT. The START waypoint icon should indicate two F-16s.

9. Select ALLIED WAYPOINTS. Select waypoint #2 by clicking on the WAYPOINT# control or clicking directly on the #2 waypoint icon. Click ADD WAYPOINT.

10. Move the new waypoint #3 to the bottom center of coordinate 2-D. Click ADD WAYPOINT again. Move waypoint #4 to the Nellis icon.

11. Use the WAYPOINT# control to select the START waypoint. The ALTITUDE entry should read 8,000. If it doesn't, set it now. Click on the SPEED control, type in 350, and press ENTER. Click on the ACTION control until it displays TAKEOFF.

12. Set the remaining waypoints by clicking on the WAYPOINT# control to cycle through them one at a time. Set these waypoints to the following:

    - Waypoint #1: ALTITUDE: 10000, SPEED: 350, ACTION: NOTHING
    - Waypoint #2: ALTITUDE: 2000, SPEED: 350, ACTION: S AND D
    - Waypoint #3: ALTITUDE: 8000, SPEED: 450, ACTION: NOTHING
    - Waypoint #4: ALTITUDE: 8000, SPEED: 350, ACTION: LAND

13. Click on ALLIED AIRCRAFT and return to a zoom factor of 1X.

14. Click on NELLIS COMMAND, then select ENEMY FORCES.

15. Move the #1 and #2 enemy force route icons to a location that is directly between Flight #1's waypoint #1 and #3.

16. Zoom in to 3X and verify that the ground route icons (1 and 2) are very close together and between the Flight #1 icons.

17. Set the number of SAM sites to 2 by clicking on SAMS twice with the left mouse button. Keyboard users can move the cursor arrow to the SAMS button, then press (INS) twice. These SAM sites will simulate the enemy protecting the radar site to the north.

18. Zoom back to 1X and then select NELLIS COMMAND.

19. Select ALLIED AIRCRAFT and click on ADD FLIGHT. This will add a default flight to the southeast of the activity we have defined so far. Click on ADD AIRCRAFT to add a second Falcon to the second flight. This flight will be used to clear a path for flight #1 through the SAMs.

20. Adjust the waypoints for the new flight. Move the START waypoint to the Nellis icon. Move waypoint #1 to a point between Nellis and the ground routes. Move waypoint #2 on top of the ground routes.

21. Zoom in to 3X and compare the map to Figure 6-19.

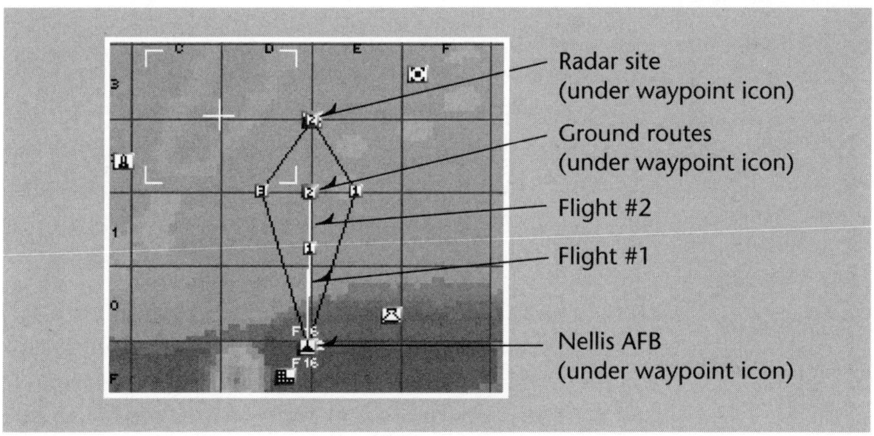

Figure 6-19 Mission Map—SAMs and Strategy

22. Select ALLIED WAYPOINTS, select waypoint #2 of flight #2, then click on ADD WAYPOINT.

23. Move the new waypoint #3 of flight #2 to the Nellis icon. Ensure that the correct waypoint moves.

24. Set the waypoints for flight #2 using the following information:

    - Start waypoint: ALTITUDE: 8000, SPEED: 450, ACTION: NOTHING
    - Waypoint #1: ALTITUDE: 8000, SPEED: 450, ACTION: NOTHING
    - Waypoint #2: ALTITUDE: 1500, SPEED: 350, ACTION: S AND D
    - Waypoint #3: ALTITUDE: 8000, SPEED: 450, ACTION: LAND

25. Now we have a flight that will fly out at a higher airspeed and attack the SAMs before flight #1 gets there. Click on ALLIED AIRCRAFT, then NELLIS COMMAND, and then DONE. You are back at Red Flag Control.

26. Before we save the mission, let's add the weapons for the two F-16 flights. Select F-16 PILOTS, then F-16 ARMAMENT.

27. The first aircraft to load will be the LEADER F-16 of FLIGHT #1 OF 2. Since flight one is responsible for taking out the radar building to the north, we will load Mavericks to do the job. The radar to the north is not transmitting; therefore, Shrikes or HARMs will not have a radar signal to lock on to, rendering them useless. Click on A-G MISSILES.

28. Use the scroll arrows to the left of the weapons display to select the AGM-65B Maverick. Click LOAD three times. This will load three sets of Mavericks, six in total. You should see the weapons on the graphic display. Figure 6-20 shows a loaded aircraft for flight #1 and #2.

29. Click on F-16 to display the 1ST WING. Click on LOAD three more times to load your wingman with six Mavericks.

30. Click on FLIGHT# to select FLIGHT# 2 OF 2. These aircraft are responsible for taking out the SAM units. Use the scroll arrows to select the AGM-45A Shrike. Click on LOAD twice to load four Shrikes. Since the SAMs operators will turn on their radar to attempt to shoot us down, the second flight aircraft can lock a Shrike onto them and destroy the offending SAM ground unit.

31. Click on OTHER STORES. The weapons display shows an ALQ-131 ECM pod. Because this flight is subject to incoming SAMs, let's load a pod. Click on LOAD once.

32. Click on F-16 to select the 1ST WING of FLIGHT# 2 OF 2. Use the A-G MISSILES and OTHER STORES to load up the Falcon with the same stores as the leader aircraft: four Shrikes and an ECM pod. Figure 4-20 shows a loaded aircraft from each flight.

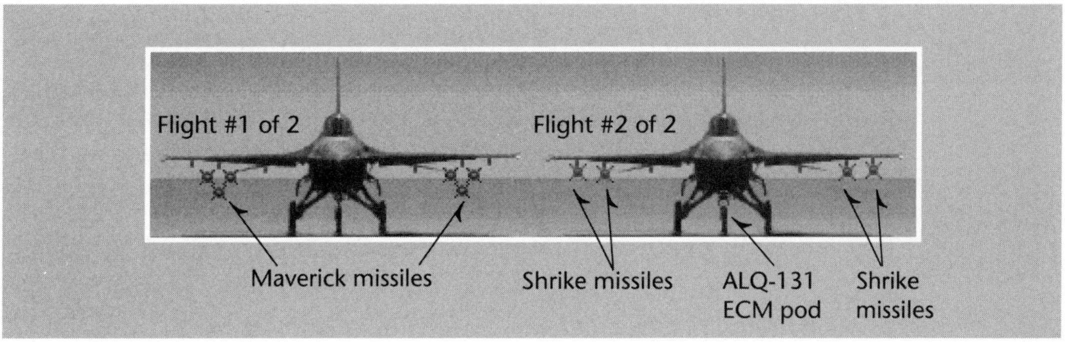

Figure 6-20 Loaded F-16s

33. Select F-16 PILOTS then RED FLAG CONTROL. Click on SAVE MISSION, type **SAMBUST**, press ENTER, and press Y to confirm the save. The mission is complete.

Taking the Flight In campaign mode, you will have control over the number of flights taking part in the mission, where the aircraft will fly, what the goal of the flight will be (waypoint actions), and what weapons the flights will carry. In effect, you are the squadron commander. Falcon 3.0 will generate a default mission or missions with waypoints and waypoint actions already set. However, these will rarely be adequate to successfully complete the mission.

In this mission, we intentionally routed flight #1 around the SAM site. This way, even if flight #2 does not destroy the SAMs, we still may be able to evade them. The campaign mode would have directed flight #1 in a "closest distance between two points" fashion. This would send flight #1 directly over the SAM sites. The Falcon 3.0 mission computer would probably not have the SAM destroying flight #2 that we added to this mission. You, as commander, are required to make these decisions.

Let's fly this mission and see how the four Falcons do. You can use the autopilot to guide you through the mission, but the following information will assume that you are controlling your F-16 (leader in flight #1).

Select F-16 PILOTS and then F-16 ARMAMENT. You should see the weapons that we loaded a few moments ago. It is a good idea to double-check all of the F-16s for proper armament during this preflight check.

Click on TAKEOFF. You are sitting on the runway facing north. Notice that the waypoint caret is off to the right slightly. Our first waypoint is to the northeast and around 40 miles away.

The Takeoff Use your normal takeoff procedure. After your gear is raised, pitch up into a 15° climb and bank to the right to line up with the waypoint caret. Your heading should be around 15° once you are lined up. Adjust your airspeed to 350 knots. This may require additional adjustment when you level off. Level off at 8,000 to 9,000 feet (ASL—the graduated scale on the right side of the HUD). Your AGL is going to fluctuate due to the area's mountainous terrain.

You should be able to see flight #2 on your REO. Notice their airspeed is 450 knots. Switch to wingman view by pressing the 7 key on the upper row. Pressing the wingman key repeatedly will cycle through three aircraft, your wingman and the two F-16s from flight #2. You can identify the flight #2 aircraft by the 000° heading and the 450 knot airspeed. It may help to jot down the callsigns of the two aircraft in flight #2. This will help when you receive radio messages.

Switch back to the front cockpit view (the 1 key on the numeric keypad) and verify you are still flying level and heading for the waypoint. Wait until you receive a radio message from one of flight #2 pilots. The message will be "closing on ground targets." Switch to the wingman view when your hear the message. Make sure you are flying level before switching. Maintain 350 knots as well.

The SAM Attack Watch the flight #2 aircraft as they approach the SAM sites. You may see a lot of banking going on with the addition of chaff drops. This indicates that the SAM site has locked on the Falcon and has fired a missile. One or both of the Falcons may get hit. This will vary from mission to mission. Eventually, one of the aircraft will fire a Shrike or two at the SAM sites. Recall that we placed two SAM sites when we created the mission, so it will only take two Shrike hits to take out the SAM units. You can also switch back to the cockpit view periodically and observe the TWI for SAM radar activity.

After (and if) flight #2 destroys the SAMs, they will fly over the enemy ground forces. After the enemy sites, the Falcons will bank towards home to a heading of 180°. This should be visible on the status panel in wingman view.

Switch back to cockpit view. Check the distance-to-waypoint indicator. You should be approaching waypoint #1. When you reach the waypoint (0D1), the caret will shift to the left, guiding you to waypoint #2 and the primary target. You are about 20 miles away. Bank your Falcon to the left and start a descent. Your heading should be approximately 335°. Try to maintain an airspeed of 350 knots while descending to 2,000 feet AGL (the numeric altitude readout).

Attacking the Primary Target Switch to Ground Map mode radar by pressing the F7 key. Observe the primary target. You can use SHIFT and the arrow keys to move the GM zoom box and F1 and F2 to zoom in and out. The target should appear near the center of the REO as long as you are lined up with the waypoint caret.

Switch to air-to-ground HUD mode by pressing the BACKSPACE key. Crosshairs appear on the HUD and the REO. The HUD displays six E-O in the lower left corner. The stores control panel indicates that AGM-65B are selected. If this is not the case, press BACKSPACE again. Maintain 2,000 feet AGL.

At approximately twelve miles from the primary target, your wingman will radio, "Closing on ground targets." Around eight miles out, he will radio, "Request permission to attack." Press SHIFT-E to give permission. The wingman responds, "Attacking ground targets."

At a range of four or five miles, the crosshairs on the HUD will move to a target. The REO will also display the target. This indicates that the target is locked. Press the SPACEBAR to fire a Maverick. Press the T key to attempt to lock up another target. If the crosshairs move, press the SPACEBAR again to fire another Maverick. Use the Q key to observe the Maverick as it slams into the target. Figure 6-21 shows the F-16 firing an AGM-65B Maverick.

Switch back to the front cockpit view. Fly over the site and observe the damage. Bank to the left when you reach waypoint #2 and head for waypoint #3. Your heading should be around 205°. Climb to 9,000 feet and level off.

Figure 6-21 The Falcon Fires a Maverick at a Radar Site

Heading Home Switch back to air-to-air HUD mode by pressing the ENTER key. The REO displays the normal radar output. Waypoint #3 was intentionally located to the west of the SAM sites, just in case flight #2 did not accomplish its mission. If we directed flight #1 to fly back at a heading of 180°, the SAMs may attack if they are still operational.

After passing waypoint #3, make the final bank towards Nellis. Your heading should be around 165°. Use your own landing procedure once you return to base. You can land straight-in, military style, or use the autopilot to land for you.

Press ESC to bring up the menu bar. Select END MISSION from the FILE menu. Click on CONTINUE at the debriefing screen. The mission map displays the path of your flight while the screen displays the events of the mission. You can use the scroll arrows next to the screen to review the mission. Click on NEXT MISSION to return to Red Flag Control.

Experiments The following are some suggested modifications to make this mission more challenging and enjoyable:

- Reverse the roles of Flight #1 and Flight #2. This will require changing the waypoint actions and locations. Because you will always be the leader of Flight #1, this changes your role to taking out the SAMs instead of the radar site. If you don't accomplish your mission, Flight #2 will be in danger.
- Try sending up the SAM killer flight without an ECM pod. This will demonstrate the importance of ECM pods when flying close to SAMs.
- Add some enemy air activity to the mission. Then add a third F-16 flight (two more F-16s) to fly intercept or combat air patrol.

Summary: Return to Red Flag

Falcon 3.0 provides the ultimate training facility for you to learn and excel with the simulation Red Flag. Modeled after the real Red Flag exercise, the missions help you build confidence when you succeed . . . and learn from your mistakes when you fail. You can create any type of mission from *sightseeing* to *impossible to survive!* You set the limits and the difficulty. Using Red Flag also increases the skill ratings for the pilots in your squadron. This will become an important factor when entering into campaign mode later in this book.

You can use the tutorial missions included in this chapter as a springboard to create challenging new assignments. You can also start with a clear mission map and create entirely new scenarios.

Even after becoming a *veteran* at campaigns, you should visit Red Flag often to sharpen your skills . . . and to find skills you didn't even know about!

Exercises: Challenges and Adventure

1. Create a mission to escort two bombers to the nuclear plant (coordinate 5-9) and back to a fixed waypoint. Assign some enemy flights that cross your flight path along the way. Let the autopilot fight the battles until you are familiar with the weapons.
2. Create a mission with a heavily guarded (five or six MiGs) transport plane moving from waypoint to waypoint. Try to take out the transport with a flight of three F-16s and escape the MiGs intact.
3. Set up dogfighting missions near the mountain ranges or near the Grand Canyon (coordinate E-6). If you can win a dogfight in the canyon without crashing, you may be ready for the real thing!

7

CHAPTER 7

Introduction to the campaigns

You are now one of thirty highly trained F-16 pilots assigned to a Falcon 3.0 squadron. You have learned how to fly your Falcon with great precision. Identifying and tracking targets on the REO is second nature to you now. You can deliver any of the F-16's weapons with repeatable accuracy. You participated in Red Flag missions that developed your skills to the highest level possible without actually engaging "real adversaries." Now it is time to find out if all of the training will pay off. You are about to enter into the ultimate challenge, the Falcon 3.0 campaign. You will fly, fight, and represent the United States in a grueling conflict in one of three regions: Israel, Panama, or Kuwait.

This chapter introduces you to the overall mechanics of a campaign. We discuss every detail, menu, and screen that makes up the Falcon 3.0 campaign mode. Although the chapter does cover some of the initial strategies that are necessary to complete a campaign, the emphasis for the chapter is on operation. Chapter 10, *Tactics and Military Doctrine,* provides additional information to increase your individual mission and overall campaign success rate.

What Is a Falcon 3.0 Campaign?

Campaign mode is the supreme challenge in Falcon 3.0. Not only are you responsible for your own actions in a single mission, you must now take on many additional responsibilities. In essence, you are the squadron commander. The United States is at war and the Allied High Command has assigned your squadron to the hostile region. You start the campaign with eighteen F-16s and thirty pilots.

Each day your squadron flies four missions each at different times of day: early morning, noon, late afternoon, and night. You, as squadron commander, are responsible for planning the individual missions, as well as participating as a pilot. Up to eight pilots and four *flights* can be assigned to each mission. A flight is a small group of aircraft with the same mission objective. Each flight has a leader and one or more wingmen.

When you receive your individual mission orders, Falcon 3.0 prepares a default mission as a starting point. One or more flights are defined, general waypoints are set, pilots are assigned to the F-16s, and the aircraft are loaded with weapons. It is your job to adjust and fine-tune the mission to produce the greatest chance for success. The default mission settings do not consider many important factors such as hostile areas, air support, weary pilots, and a limited weapons supply. You must analyze these factors and build your own mission around them.

Mission Planning

Planning each mission involves four basic steps. They are assigning flights, setting waypoints for each flight, choosing pilots for each F-16, and loading each Falcon with the proper weapons for the mission.

The flight assignment depends on where your mission takes you on the mission map. For example, if a mission requires that your squadron fly deep into enemy territory and bomb a target, you may want to assign an additional flight of two F-16s to escort and protect the bombing flight. On the other hand, if you are patrolling a border near friendly territory, a single flight of two or three aircraft may suffice. There can be up to four flights assigned to each mission. Each flight has its own mission goals.

Setting the waypoints is an important part of mission planning. Your squadron receives intelligence information that you can use to direct the F-16s to areas that will be the least hostile, but still perform the primary mission. Waypoints are set for an entire flight, not individual aircraft. The waypoints also determine what action each flight will take (bomb, combat air patrol, escort, etc.). For example, the default waypoints may guide a flight directly over a high concentration of SAM units. You may be able to move the waypoints into a configuration that will route the Falcons around the hostile area to the target. Of course, some targets are so well guarded that contact with the enemy is unavoidable.

Assigning pilots to each mission is another task that requires careful attention. At the start of the campaign, your squadron has thirty pilots of varying skill levels. You must match the pilot skill and the assignment. For example, if the mission orders state that there is to be an intercept of enemy flight, this would require a pilot with above average flying and dogfighting skills. The fatigue of the pilot also plays a role in the selection process. Sending your ace pilot on several missions in a row will result in high fatigue. He may end up making a mental mistake that will cost him the mission (and perhaps his life!)

The last step before takeoff is weapons selection. Each flight has a mission objective. It is essential that you supply the weapons for the flight to complete that objective. For example, you set up a two-flight mission. The first flight's objective is the primary mission, bombing a bridge. You would load the flight 1 aircraft with iron bombs capable of taking out the bridge (Mk84s, for example). The second flight's objective is to escort the first flight. Therefore, flight 2 would need the necessary air-to-air weapons to defend the bombing flight. Perhaps you would select a combination of Sidewinders and AAMRAMs.

At this point, the flights would be ready to take off and head out to achieve their mission objectives. Upon the flight's return (or demise), you receive a debriefing letting you know how your mission plan worked. This provides the information you need to learn from your mistakes and improve. You don't want to make too many mistakes or the campaign will end in allied defeat.

Day to Day

You continue the cycle of four missions a day until the campaign ends. Each mission flown has an impact on the outcome of the campaign. For example, a mission objective is to destroy a runway at an enemy airbase. If your squadron successfully takes the runway out of service, it affects the amount of enemy air activity in that area in subsequent missions. If the mission is a failure, the air activity will still be present, continuing to hamper allied air and ground forces.

The outcome of your daily missions are reflected on the mission map. If you are gaining ground and winning your individual missions, some of the strategic icons change color from red (enemy) to blue (allied). Of course, if you are losing the bulk of your missions, the opposite effect occurs.

Your squadron is not exclusively responsible for the outcome of the campaign. Other factors play a role as well. Ground forces and other fighter/bomber squadrons have an effect on the campaign result. However, if your squadron consistently accomplishes its mission objectives, the campaign will most likely end in success.

The daily mission activity varies depending on the campaign region. Let's take a look at three campaign regions of Falcon 3.0.

The Regions

Three areas of conflict, or campaign regions, are available in Falcon 3.0. (Spectrum Holobyte plans to release additional campaign disks in the near future.) Each of the three regions provides different scenarios, which in turn require different styles of mission planning strategy. The type and significance of enemy aircraft also varies from region to region.

You do not need to be concerned about planning for the entire region. Concentrate on the individual missions for your squadron. Central Command takes care of the details for the region and supplies orders to your squadron.

Israel—A Defensive Operation The Israel campaign simulation takes place after Desert Storm. Syria is the primary aggressor in this region. The goal in this campaign is to protect Israel by heading off the Syrian

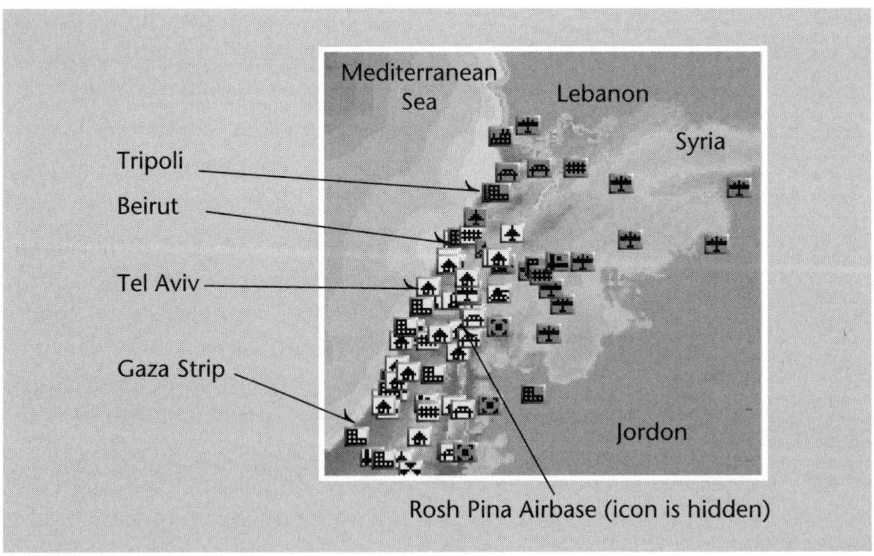

Figure 7-1 The Israel Theater.

advances. Your squadron is assigned to Rosh Pina Airbase. This provides a good position to fend off the enemy attacks. Figure 7-1 shows the Israel theater and some of the major cities of the region. Note that the darker icons are enemy controlled and the lighter icons are allied controlled. The map icons are red for enemy and blue for friendly.

The Israel region is fairly difficult to defend. You will be called on to fly several combat air patrol and intercept missions. Some missions will target routes that the Syrian troops are using to enter the area (bridges, rail yards). The region is very sensitive due to the heavy civilian population. Try to hold off the advancement until reinforcements arrive.

Kuwait—Desert Storm II This scenario is a simulation of the start of Operation Desert Storm. The Iraqi army has attacked Kuwait. The ground forces have dug in and are ready for any Coalition attack. Your squadron is assigned to King Khalid Military City. The majority of the icons at the start of the conflict are enemy. As you may recall, the Coalition was severely outnumbered at the start of the air war. Your goal is to drive the Iraqis out of Kuwait. Perhaps you can even take Baghdad! Figure 7-2 shows a map of the Kuwait region.

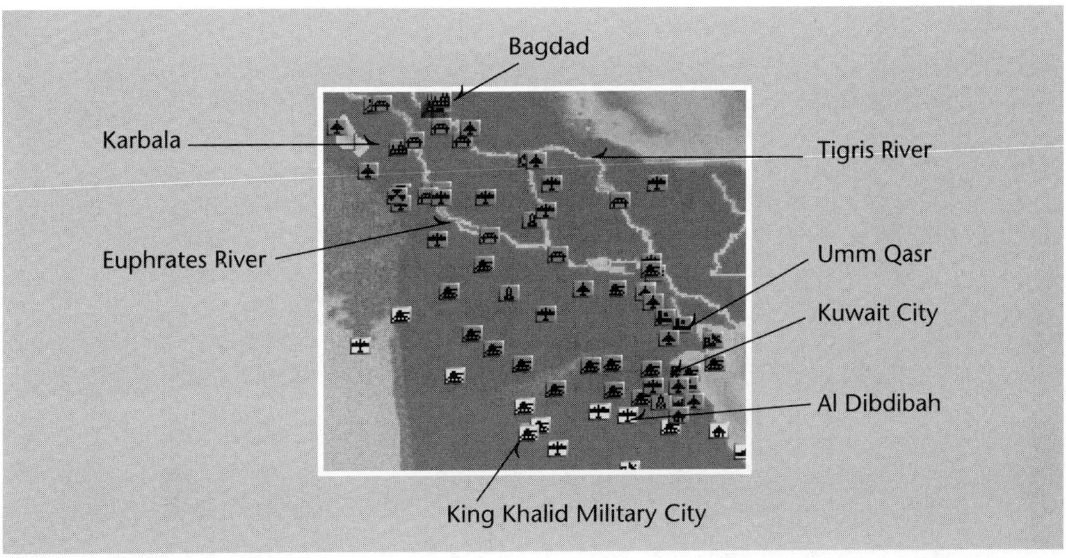

Figure 7-2 The Kuwait Theater

The Kuwait theater offers a variety of missions from intercept to strike missions. Your squadron will most likely be called on to bomb and attack enemy command and control centers as well as critical supply routes. Strike missions play an important role in cutting off supplies to the enemy troops dug in along the Kuwait-Saudi border. It is very important to have successful air-to-air battles. Achieving air superiority makes subsequent missions easier.

Panama—Restoring Order in Central America This campaign starts with Central America in turmoil; the risk of the government of Panama being overthrown is high. Your squadron of Falcons is assigned to Howard Air Force Base. The majority of the map is covered with allied icons at the start of this campaign. Your goal is to maintain order until reinforcements arrive. Because of the small size of the region, the missions usually are shorter than those in Kuwait or Israel. Figure 7-3 shows the Panama region and some of the major cities and airbases.

As with the Kuwait theater, Panama requires that your squadron participate in a wide variety of missions. Initially, your squadron heads for the Porta Belo area for the majority of missions. These missions do not require much time to fly and provide a good starting point for new campaigners.

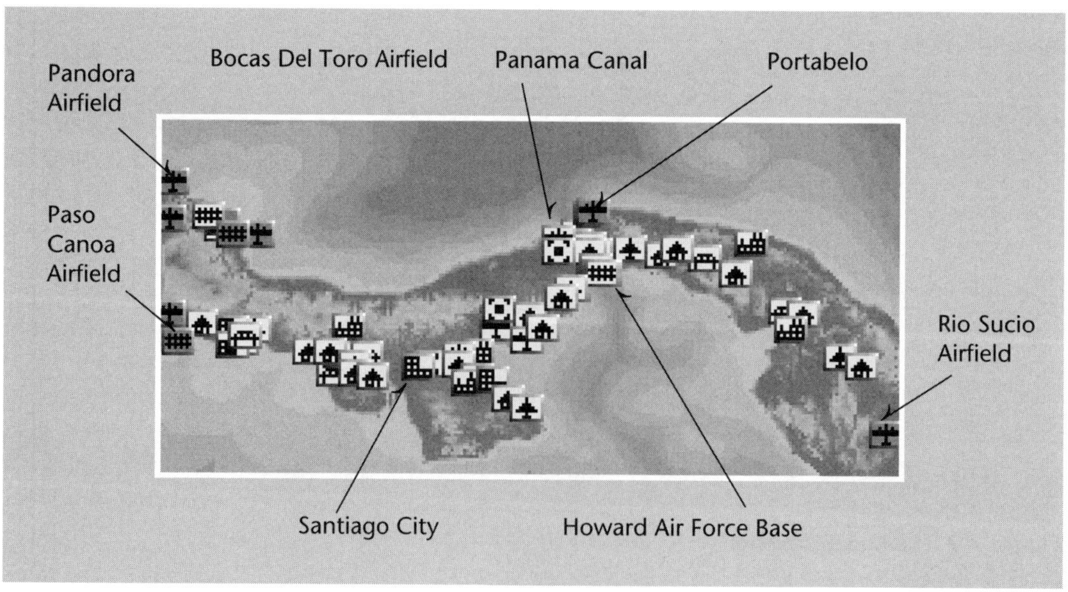

Figure 7-3 The Panama Theater

The Campaign Mode

Before the campaign begins, you must select a squadron and the region to participate in. Your squadron receives orders with a brief explanation of the causes of the conflict. The daily routine begins at this point. Your squadron flies four missions a day until the campaign ends. Figure 7-4 shows an overview of the entire campaign process.

If you leave the program at any time during the campaign, Falcon 3.0 automatically saves your progress. The only way to lose campaign information is to assign your squadron to another region or deactivate the squadron. The next section, "Committing to a Campaign," explains these options further.

Each of the steps in Figure 7-4 is part of overall mission planning. The following sections discuss each of the steps in detail, along with suggestions to improve your success rate.

Committing to a Campaign

You may want to follow through the rest of this chapter, using the material as a tutorial. Before the campaign begins, you must select a squadron that will participate and commit the squadron to a region. This activity takes place in the War Room. Figure 7-5 shows the War Room. The lower right portion of the screen is enlarged to show the detail of the area that pertains to squadron and campaign selection.

> NOTE: If you have already formed a squadron, click on the insignia screen until your squadron insignia appears. You can skip to the next section, "Theater Selection."

Forming a Squadron Before a squadron is selected, the FORM light is flashing. To form a squadron, click on the FORM button. The world map at the top of the screen displays, "Forming new squadron. Press arrows to select insignia. Press insignia to choose squadron." The arrows are located to the right of the squadron insignia. A green arrow indicates that more selections are available in that direction, a red arrow means that you are at the end of the list.

Once the insignia of the desired squadron appears in the insignia window, click directly on the insignia (or on the button below the insignia box) to activate the squadron. You can form more than one squadron; however, only one squadron can be *active* at any one time. The active

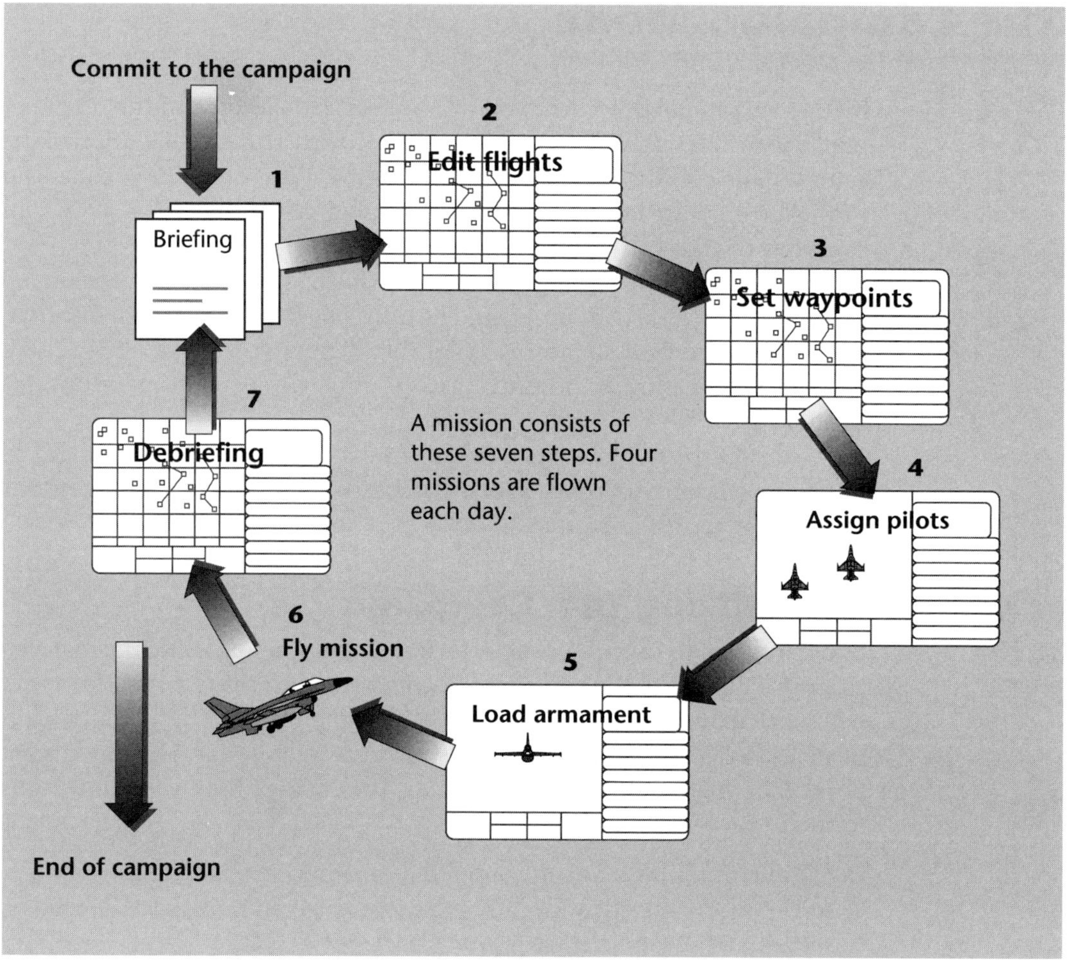

Figure 7-4 The Campaign Process

squadron name appears on the world map as the current squadron and the squadron insignia appears in the insignia window.

Once a squadron is selected, the FORM light and the light above the phone flash alternately with the DEACTIVATE and THEATER lights.

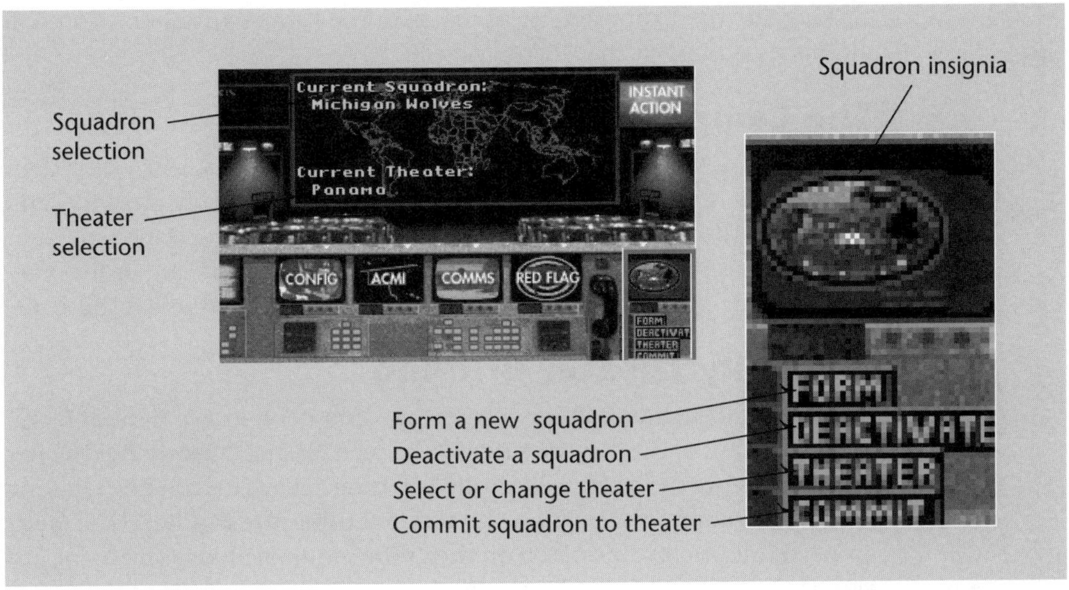

Figure 7-5 Squadron Selection and Committing to a Campaign in the War Room

Deactivating a Squadron If you choose to delete an entire squadron, click on the DEACTIVATE button. If you click on this button, the world map will display, "WARNING! If you continue you will lose ALL information in this squadron. Press 'Y' or 'N'." Pressing Y removes the squadron from the current campaign region (if any) and *deletes all squadron records*. Make sure this is your intention before pressing Y.

Theater Selection and Committing Now that you have selected a squadron, the next step is to select the campaign region. Click on the THEATER button. The world map displays the name of a region and highlights the region directly on the map with a green box. Repeatedly pressing the THEATER button cycles through the available regions.

> **NOTE:** If you have previously committed your squadron to a region, the world map will display, "WARNING! If you change theaters at this point you will lose this squadron's current campaign! Press 'Y' or 'N'." Pressing Y aborts the current campaign and resets all campaign statistics.

Once you have highlighted the desired region, click on the COMMIT button to send your squadron to the region. The campaign orders will scroll up the screen followed by the first mission status briefing. Pressing ESC or clicking the right mouse button will skip the campaign orders. You will ultimately end up at the Briefing screen.

The Campaign Orders

At the start of each campaign, you will receive your squadron's campaign orders from the Central Command. These orders briefly describe and summarize the events that led up to the conflict. The orders also spell out your squadron's role and broad goals for the campaign. The orders vary slightly from campaign to campaign, but the general message is the same.

The Daily Theater Briefing

At the end of each day (following the mission debriefing), Central Command displays a theater briefing. The screen flashes "Receiving Theater Briefing" before the briefing is scrolled up the screen. This briefing lets you, as squadron commander, know the status of the entire conflict. The results given in this briefing are based on the entire group of allied forces, not just your squadron (although your individual mission results have a bearing on the overall brief). The briefing breaks down the summary into Allied Gains and Enemy Gains. The effects of the gains/losses report can be seen on the mission map during the next day (the colors of the mission map icons change to reflect the new owner).

> **NOTE:** You will not receive this briefing at the beginning of day 1 of the campaign. You will go directly to the mission information briefing instead.

Mission Information

At the start of each mission, you will receive a mission information briefing that provides an overall look at the logistical state of your squadron and the campaign region. The screen will flash "Receiving Satellite Downlink" before the briefing is scrolled up the screen. The briefing supplies useful information for planning missions. The following is a breakdown of the individual items available in the mission briefing.

Mission Day/Time The briefing displays the day of the campaign followed by the mission time. The time is in military format. Four missions will be flown daily at 0600 (6 AM), 1200 (noon), 1800 (6 PM), and 2100 (9 PM).

Available Aircraft This entry shows the number of F-16s available for missions. You start the campaign with eighteen Falcons. This number goes down if an F-16 is destroyed and goes up as replacements arrive. Regardless of the number of available F-16s, the maximum that can participate in any one campaign mission is eight.

Available Pilots The entry shows the number of pilots who are able to participate in missions. You start the campaign with thirty pilots. This number goes down if a pilot is killed (KIA), missing (MIA), or injured. The number of available pilots increases as replacements arrive.

Current Weather—Tomorrow's Forecast The Current Weather entry shows the weather for today's mission. Tomorrow's Forecast shows the weather prediction for the following day's weather. As with most weather forecasts, it may or may not be correct. The cloud ceiling is also given for Tomorrow's Forecast.

Resupply Date This is an estimated date as to when you will receive supplies. The supplies consist of weapons, jet fuel, and other stores. Your squadron's morale is dependent on the supplies arriving safely at your airbase. You may be asked to escort the two C-130 transports that will deliver the goods.

Replacement Date This is the date that your squadron will receive replacements for pilots and aircraft. As with the resupply date, this is an estimate. Also, there is no guarantee that the replacements will be available. Do not make them part of your plan. No escort mission is necessary for the replacement.

Briefing Screen

The Briefing screen consists of the mission map and some controls. The small screen in the upper right corner displays the primary objective of the mission. There may be other elements that affect the planning of the mission (avoiding hostile ground troop concentrations, enemy airfields, etc.). Figure 7-6 shows the Briefing screen for an intercept mission.

Mission Map Controls The mission map controls function identically to those in Red Flag with the exception of TRACE and RECON. These controls replace the AIR and GROUND route controls from Red Flag. TRACE and RECON are discussed in the following Edit Flights section.

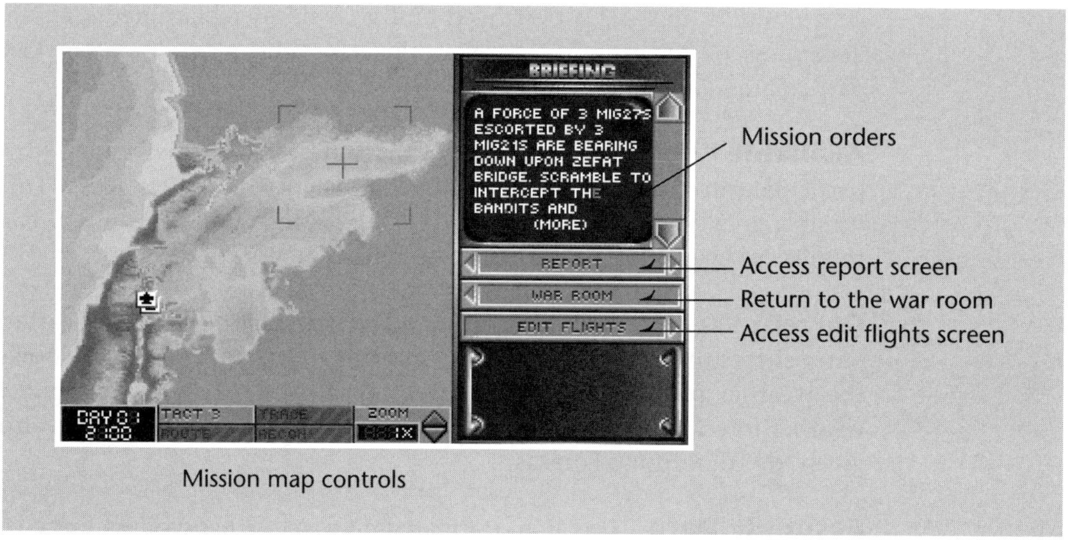

Figure 7-6 The Briefing Screen

Mission Orders Carefully read the mission orders. This is the primary goal of the mission. In order to gain a rating of successful at the end of the mission, your squadron must meet the goal set out in the briefing. If the orders are more than a full screen, use the scroll arrows to display the remainder of the text.

Report

One of the controls available in the Briefing screen is REPORT (you can also access this screen from the Edit Flights, Assign Pilots, and Load Armament screens). Click on the REPORT button to display the Report screen. Some of what the Report screen has to offer is the same as that in Red Flag. However, there are some additions to the screen for campaign mode: CAMPAIGN STATUS, SUPPLY STATUS, and OCCUPATION. Let's take a closer look at the additions. Click on the CAMPAIGN STATUS button to access the campaign statistics.

Campaign Status Figure 7-7 shows the Campaign Status screen. This provides an overall picture of the campaign as it relates to your squadron and the allies in general.

The following data is available on the Campaign Status screen:

- Campaign Zone Update—Shows the allied and enemy percentages of current occupation for the campaign region.

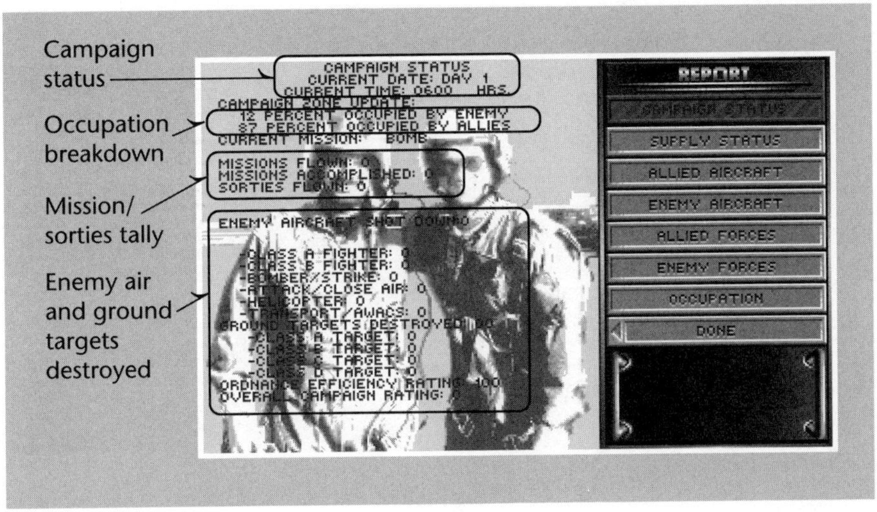

Figure 7-7 The Campaign Status Report Screen

- Current Mission—Lists the type of the next mission that your squadron will participate in (i.e. BOMB, INTERCEPT).
- Missions Flown—Lists the total number of missions flown. This equals the four a day mission total. For example, at the end of day 2, this entry will indicate that eight missions have been flown.
- Missions Accomplished—Lists the number of missions that your squadron met the criteria for a successful mission.
- Sorties Flown—Lists the mission total for all of your squadron's F-16s. For example, if three F-16s participate in a mission, this would total one mission and three sorties.
- Enemy Aircraft Shot Down—Lists the total number of enemy aircraft downed in combat. This is followed by a breakdown of aircraft type (Class A, Class B, etc.).
- Enemy Ground Targets Destroyed—Lists the total number of enemy ground targets destroyed by your squadron. As with the enemy aircraft totals, this is followed by a breakdown of the ground target types.
- Ordnance Efficiency Rating—This is a numeric value that reflects the percentage that your air-to-ground ordnance hits the intended target.
- Overall Campaign Rating—This a numeric value that reflects your squadron's overall performance in the campaign. You can use this number as a reference value from campaign to campaign.

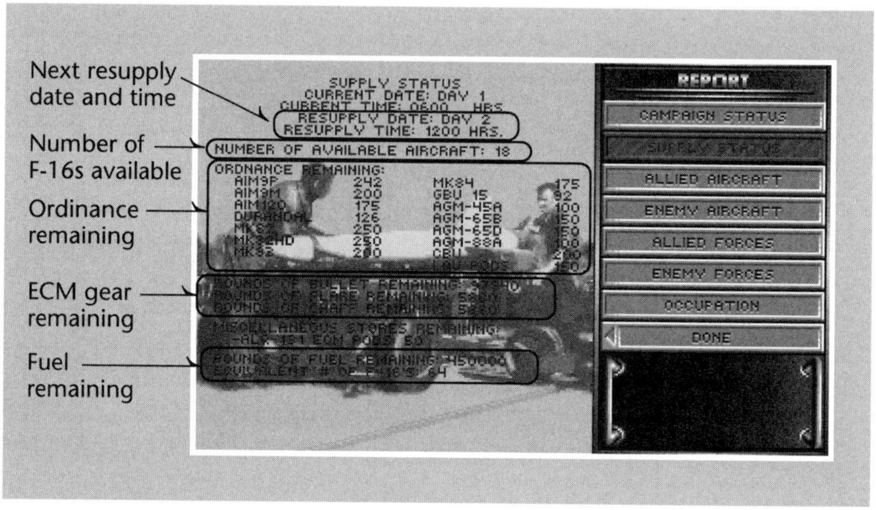

Figure 7-8 The Supply Status Report Screen

Supply Status Click on SUPPLY STATUS. Figure 7-8 shows the Supply Status screen. As squadron commander, you can use this screen to monitor the usage of weapons and other stores. Should you load up your Falcons with AIM-120s next mission or are they scarce? This screen provides the answers. If a resupply mission is successful, you will notice the effects of it on this screen.

Enemy/Allied Aircraft and Forces The Enemy/Allied Aircraft and Forces screens function identically to those in Red Flag. Refer to the Report section in Chapter 6, *Introduction to Red Flag,* for detailed information on these screens.

Occupation Click on OCCUPATION. Figure 7-9 shows the Occupation screen. The map of the campaign region is overlaid with two colored areas. The blue area represents the allied (friendly) occupation. The red area indicates enemy occupations. The area that is a mix of red and blue is in conflict. Your squadron's next mission may have an effect on the outcome of these territorial conflicts.

Click on DONE to return to the Briefing screen. Click on EDIT FLIGHTS to start your mission plan.

Edit Flights

The primary function of the Edit Flights screen is to set up the number of flights and the number of F-16s assigned to each of the flights. Falcon 3.0

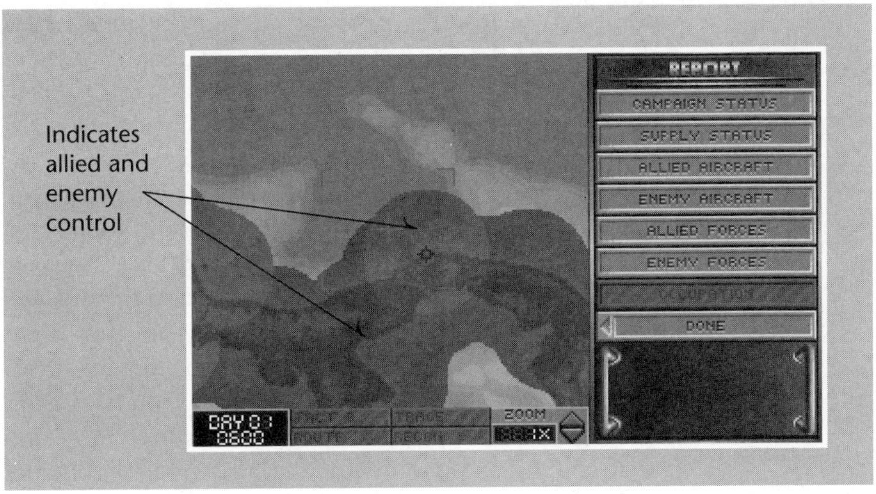

Figure 7-9 The Occupation Report Screen

assigns a default number of flights (and F-16s) to the mission. This is not always the optimum setting for a successful mission. You are responsible for setting up the flights to maximize your squadron's chances for a mission victory. Figure 7-10 shows the Edit Flights screen. Most of the functions

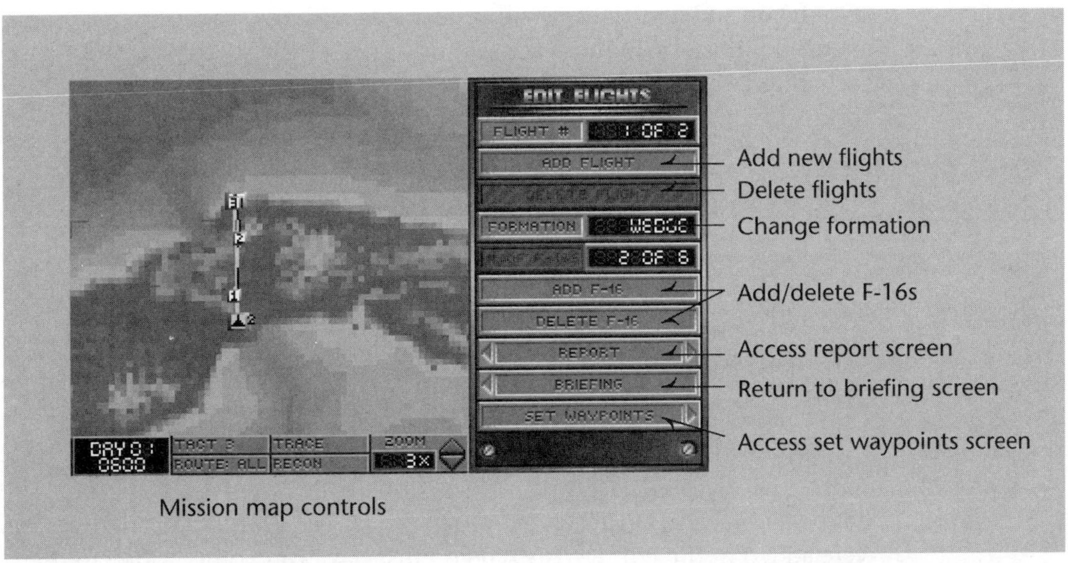

Figure 7-10 The Edit Flights Screen

(adding and deleting flights, F-16s, etc.) are the same as in Red Flag. If you are not sure how to use these controls, review Chapter 6, *Introduction to Red Flag*.

Choosing the Number of Flights You can assign up to four flights for each campaign mission. Should you always assign four? The answer is no. You should assign the number of flights that will accomplish the mission. There is no reason to subject additional aircraft to attack and possible destruction if it is not necessary. You should always assign the aircraft in groups of at least two. Do not send up an F-16 on its own. Also, you should have enough flights to guard the main flight from harm. For example, your squadron has received orders to bomb a runway. The default setting has two flights of F-16s (four Falcons total) heading to the target and bombing the runway. The runway is surrounded by SAMs (we will discuss how to check for SAMs and other hazards in the Set Waypoints section). You should assign a flight of two Falcons to reach the target area *before* the main flights to clear out the SAMs. You will load the new flight with anti-radiation missiles and an ECM pod at least. Another idea is to assign a flight of two Falcons to protect the bombing flight along the way. The possibilities are endless.

Some missions may not require additional flights at all. For example, if your squadron has received orders to intercept incoming enemy aircraft near the allied enemy airspace, a single flight of three Falcons should be able to get the job done.

If you add flights, they will appear with a START waypoint only at the assigned airbase. You must add, adjust, and set the waypoint actions for each flight in the Set Waypoints screen. Click on SET WAYPOINTS to continue with the mission plan.

Set Waypoints

Each flight of F-16s assigned to the mission must have a set of waypoint assignments to guide and direct them throughout the mission. Figure 7-11 shows the Set Waypoints screen. Most of the functions work identically to the Red Flag waypoints screen. Refer to Chapter 6, *Introduction to Red Flag,* for detailed information. The exceptions are in the mission map controls: TRACE and RECON have replaced AIR and GROUND.

The waypoints define the path that the flights will take. They also define the airspeed, altitude, and action to be taken (if any) for each waypoint. Each flight receives its own set of waypoints. Any flights that were added in the Edit Flights screen must have waypoints added to them using ADD WAYPOINT on this screen. You can then adjust the position of

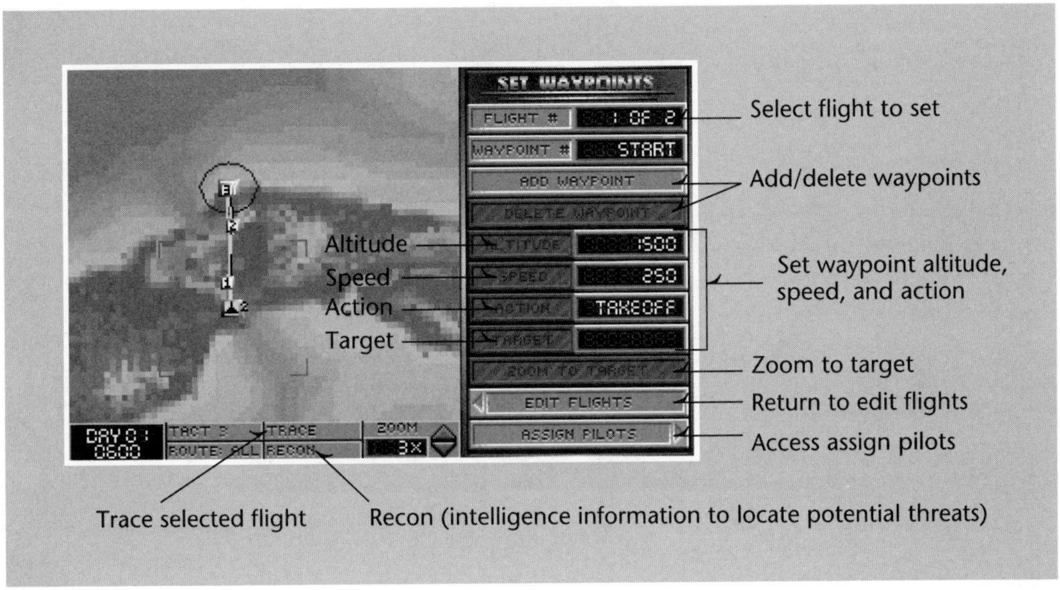

Figure 7-11 The Set Waypoints Screen

the waypoints by dragging them to the desired location on the mission map.

Strategically placing the waypoints is an important step in a successful mission. The default mission waypoints are usually not adequate to complete the mission. You must adjust the waypoints to minimize conflicts with the enemy along the way. How do you predict where the conflicts will arise? The trace and recon tools help you plan for this.

Using Trace Clicking on the TRACE button causes the mission map to trace the current waypoint path of the selected flight. The selected flight (highlighted in yellow) is set by clicking on the FLIGHT# control in the upper right corner of the Set Waypoints screen. Keep in mind that each flight has its own set of waypoints. You should use trace on each flight individually to check for conflict. Figure 7-12 shows an example of the Trace feature.

While the trace is following the proposed path of the F-16(s), the small screen displays the activity along with a number. This number also appears next to an icon on the mission map. The trace mode automatically adjusts the zoom factor while the trace is taking place. The numbers on the mission map correspond to the listing on the small screen.

Once the trace is completed, click on DONE to return to the Set Waypoints screen. You can rearrange the waypoints to attempt to direct the

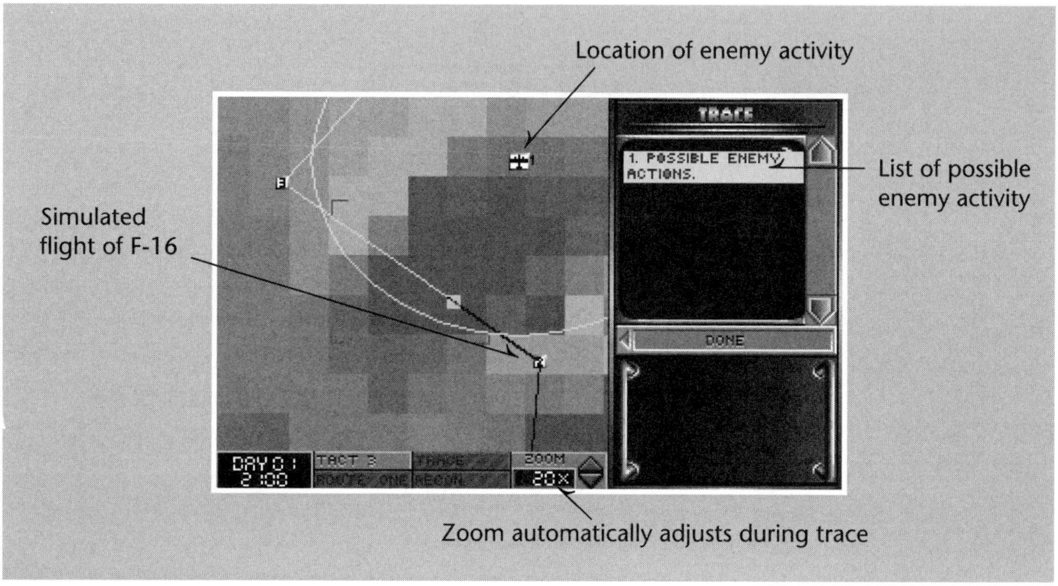

Figure 7-12 Tracing a Flight to Check for Enemy Activity

flight away or around the enemy activities. Some flights will have no choice but to fly close to enemy activity to accomplish a mission objective (such as a bombing). All of the trace information is based on intelligence information. This can be accurate or inaccurate depending on the INTELLIGENCE setting in the Difficulty Levels screen (refer to Chapter 2, *Introduction to Falcon 3,* for instructions on setting this value).

Using Recon Recon is another feature that can help you find out what your squadron flights will be up against in the mission. Recon is short for reconnaissance. Reconnaissance data on enemy activity is gathered by other forces in Falcon 3.0. You can view the results of the data gathering by selecting an area with the zoom box then clicking on the RECON control. The RECON view automatically zooms into the region selected by the zoom box. Figure 7-13 shows the RECON view of an enemy airfield and surrounding territory.

If enemy units are in the area of the zoom box crosshairs, Recon displays the units on the mission map along with a corresponding list on the small screen. The zoom automatically adjusts to a factor of 50X.

The Recon information can be used for two purposes. As with the trace screen, you can fine-tune the waypoints by using the Recon screen to avoid enemy conflict. The other use is landmark identification. For example, you

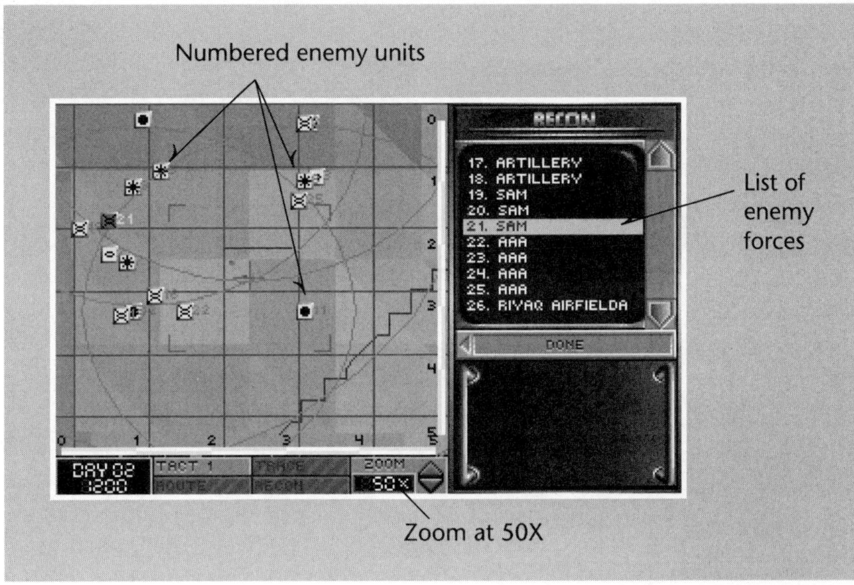

Figure 7-13 The Recon Display of an Enemy Airfield and Surrounding Area

may notice that a bombing target is near a characteristic bend in a river. When you are flying the mission, you can look for the river bend on GM radar to help locate the target. Remember, the accuracy of Recon information is affected by the INTELLIGENCE setting in the Difficulty Levels screen.

Clicking directly on the mission map icons or the small screen highlights one icon on the mission map. This is useful to find the names of airfields and key enemy installations.

Click on DONE at the Recon display to return to the Set Waypoints screen. If you have to add or subtract flights or F-16s, you can return to the Edit Flights screen by clicking on EDIT FLIGHTS. Once the waypoints for all of the flights are set, you are ready to assign pilots to the mission. Click on ASSIGN PILOTS to continue planning the mission.

Assign Pilots

Each F-16 in each flight must have an assigned pilot. You start a campaign with thirty pilots to choose from; each pilot has different levels of skill in bombing, flying, and dogfighting. All levels of skill can be adversely affected by a fatigue factor. Falcon 3.0 automatically assigns default pilots for each mission. *Do not use the default pilots!* Falcon 3.0 simply assigns pilots off the top of the list. You must consider the nature of the mission when assigning

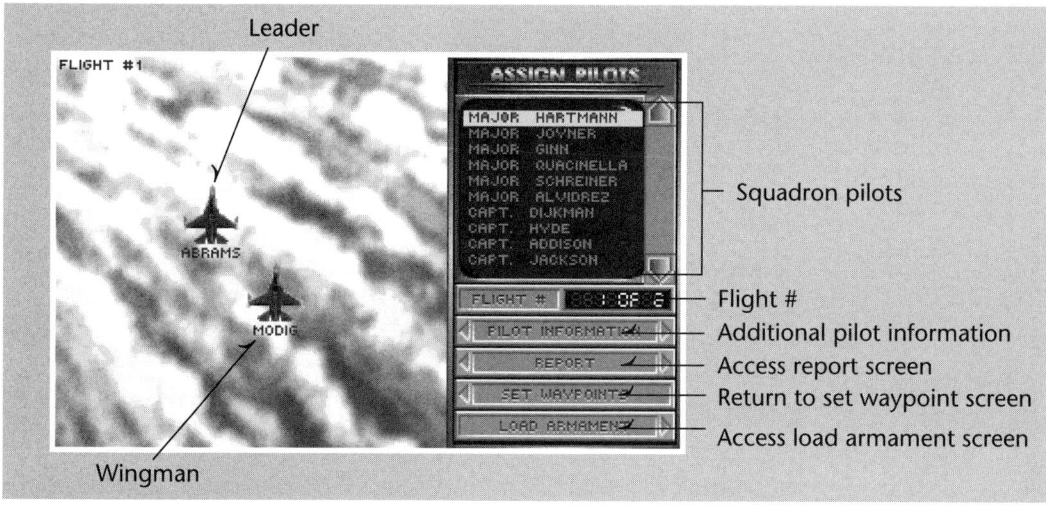

Figure 7-14 The Assign Pilots Screen

a pilot. Figure 7-14 shows the assign pilots screen. The majority of the Assign Pilots screen is identical to the F-16 Pilots screen in Red Flag. Refer to Chapter 6, *Introduction to Red Flag,* for detailed information on how to use the Assign Pilots screen.

> **NOTE:** Do not worry about the skill levels of the leader aircraft in Flight #1. You will be responsible for flying F-16 #1 of Flight #1. Pilot skill levels affect the computer controlled pilots only.

Basically, you select a pilot by clicking on the name on the small display on the upper right side of the screen (you can use the scroll arrows to view other pilot names). Once the name is highlighted, select the flight with the FLIGHT# control, then click on the F-16 graphic on the left side of the screen to assign the pilot.

Choosing the Right Pilot for the Mission/Flight Here is a short example of selecting a pilot for a particular mission. Assume your squadron has received orders to carry out an escort mission. In this case, you should look for pilots with high flying ability and dogfighting skills, since these skills are likely to get called on for the mission type. You can click on Pilot Information to get detailed information of the pilot skills. Once you have found the correct pilots, return to the Assign Pilots screen and assign them to the flight.

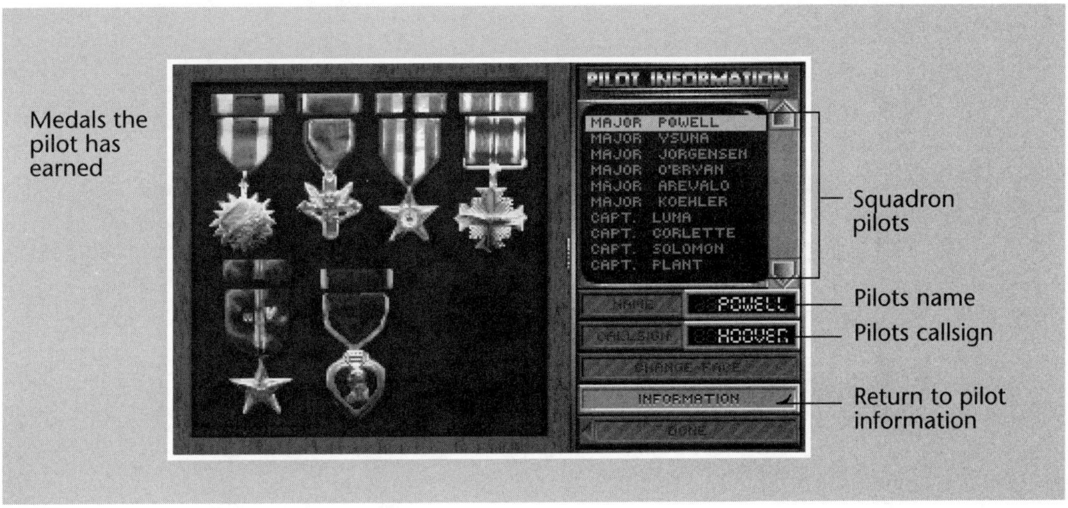

Figure 7-15 The Pilot Awards Screen

Pilot Awards While you are in the Pilot Information screen, you can click on AWARDS to view the awards that each of the pilots has earned. Click directly on any pilot's name on the right side of the screen; the awards display changes to reflect the awards of the selected pilots. Figure 7-15 shows the awards screen.

All pilots start with a clean slate (no medals). They earn the medals by flying campaign missions while under your control as squadron commander. Click on INFORMATION to return to the Pilot Information screen, then click on DONE to return to the Assign Pilots screen. You may wish to return to the Set Waypoints screen to make final adjustments. When you are satisfied with your pilot selection, click on LOAD ARMAMENT to continue with the final phase of planning the mission.

Load Armament

Loading up the Falcons is the last phase of the mission plan before taking off. Once again, Falcon 3.0 assigns a default weapons load for the mission based on the objectives for the F-16's flight (based on waypoint actions). The default load usually will not suffice for the mission. For example, Falcon 3.0 never loads an ALQ-131 ECM pod on the aircraft. If any of your Falcons will be subjected to SAM batteries along their mission route, it is essential that you the load the Falcons with ECM pods, thus overriding the default load. Figure 7-16 shows the Load Armament screen.

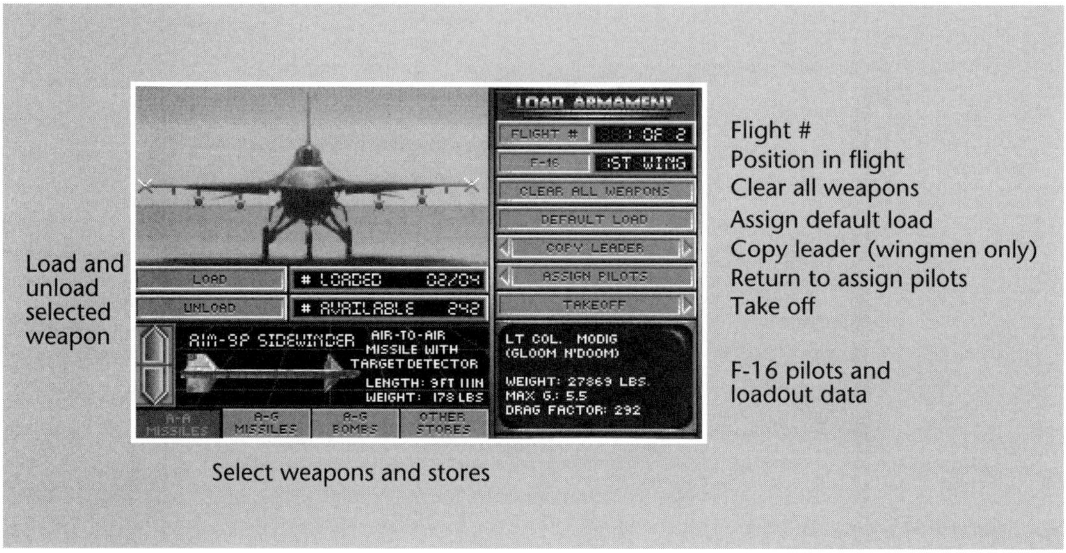

Figure 7-16 The Load Armament Screen

> **NOTE:** A common mistake is to forget to load flights other than Flight #1. Toggle through all flights (with the FLIGHT# button) and all F-16s (with the F-16 button) before clicking on TAKEOFF.

Copy Leader Flights of F-16s always have the same mission objective (determined by waypoint actions). Therefore, it is convenient to copy one aircraft's weapons configuration to another. The COPY LEADER control appears for all wingmen in the flight. Normally, this control is REPORT. To use the feature, load the Leader aircraft (designated next to the F-16 button) with the desired weapons. Then click on F-16 to select one of the wingmen (REPORT changes to COPY LEADER). Click on COPY LEADER. After a few moments, the wingman's F-16 is loaded to match the leader of the flight.

Choosing the Right Weapons for the Mission/Flight You must know the mission objective of each flight before assigning the weapons. The default weapons load usually provides a good starting point for loading weapons. You can modify the default load based on threats that you know the flight will face along the way (obtained from the Recon and Trace features). One factor that affects the weapons load is the supply of weapons. Recall that you can find out the quantity of weapons available by clicking REPORT and SUPPLY STATUS. The Report screen is only accessible in the Load Armament screen while the leader F-16 is selected.

Flying the Mission

This is where all of the training and hard work truly pay off. It will take some time to gain the experience necessary to win the majority of your squadron's missions and ultimately win the campaign. It is a good idea to make notes of each mission, describing the mission objectives, weapons configuration, pilots assigned, and so on. If you have trouble with a specific thing in a campaign, return to the lessons in Chapters 3, 4, and 5. For advanced strategy campaigns, refer to Chapter 10, *The Campaign: Tactics and Military Doctrine.*

Ending a Mission

You can end a mission at any time by pressing (ESC) to bring up the menu bar, then selecting END MISSION from the FILE menu. You will normally do this after you have flown to the mission objective area and returned to base. Falcon 3.0 campaigns do not require that you land the Falcon to gain a successful mission rating. If you end a mission prematurely, Falcon 3.0 will project the outcome of the mission. The mission is automatically ended if all friendly aircraft assigned to the mission are destroyed. In both cases, you end up at the Debriefing screen.

If Your F-16 Is Destroyed

If your Falcon is destroyed on a mission (or you eject), you will be able to view the rest of the mission using standard wingman view. If this occurs, pressing the upper row (7) key cycles through active aircraft. This way you can observe the remaining assigned pilots as they continue to carry out their mission orders.

Aborting a Mission

You can abort a mission at any time by pressing (ESC) to bring up the menu bar, then select ABORT MISSION from the FILE menu. Aborting a mission returns you to the War Room. When you reenter the campaign (by selecting COMMIT), your squadron faces the same mission that you chose to abort.

The Debriefing

When the mission has ended, you will be placed at the Debriefing screen. The debriefing consists of three parts: the route summary, medals, and mission summary. Figure 7-17 shows the Debriefing screen (a portion of the mission summary is shown).

Figure 7-17 The Mission Debriefing Screen

Route Summary The mission map displays the planned versus actual route. You can use this feature to see how far, if at all, you strayed from the planned mission route. The small screen on the right side of the display indicates the planned and actual routes. The Debriefing screen displays all of the encounters of the F-16s that participated in the flight. You can click CONTINUE to proceed with the debriefing or click NEXT MISSION to immediately go to the next mission.

Medals The Debriefing screen displays medals awarded (if any) for the mission and the pilot's name. If more than a screen of medals are awarded, you can use the scroll arrows to see the whole list. Click CONTINUE to proceed with the debriefing or click NEXT MISSION to immediately go to the next mission.

Mission Summary The mission summary shows the outcome of the mission (successful or failure) followed by the enemy and allied losses. The losses are separated into aircraft and ground unit losses. You can use the scroll arrows to view the remainder of the mission summary. The mission summary also lists the status of each pilot (Active, MIA, or KIA). Click CONTINUE to proceed with the last segment of debriefing or click NEXT MISSION to immediately go to the next mission.

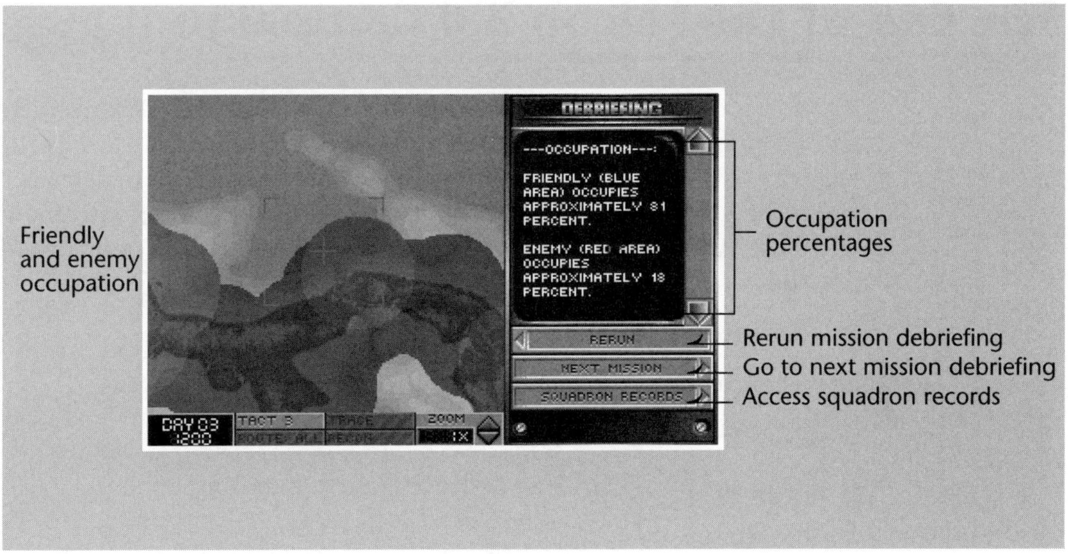

Figure 7-18 The Debriefing Occupation Screen

Occupation The last Debriefing screen shows the occupation breakdown of the campaign region updated through the end of the mission. Your mission outcome will not always directly affect the occupation breakdown for that particular mission. For example, your squadron destroys a key enemy bridge which counts as a successful mission. You may not see the effect of the bridge loss for a day or so. Figure 7-18 shows the Debriefing Occupation screen. The Debriefing screen displays the percentages of occupation on the small display.

You can rerun the entire debriefing by clicking RERUN. Click NEXT MISSION to go to the next mission briefing (starting with mission information). Click SQUADRON RECORDS for a breakdown of the squadron's mission totals. Squadron Records is discussed in detail in Chapter 2, *Introduction to Falcon 3.0.*

The End of the Falcon 3.0 Campaign

Winning a campaign is the ultimate goal in Falcon 3.0. Getting there requires intense practice and careful mission planning. You will eventually reach one of three results for the campaign: victory, stalemate, or defeat. Of course the goal is to achieve out and out victory. The final outcome is determined by your squadron's performance throughout the campaign. A campaign ends when:

- The allied forces have reached their campaign objectives.
- The enemy forces have reached their campaign objectives.
- A cease-fire is declared.
- Your squadron has been destroyed (aircraft and/or pilots).

Your success or failure is determined at the end of the campaign. An appropriate graphic appears as a testimonial to your campaign performance. You can start a new campaign in the War Room by selecting a region and committing your squadron to the region.

Aborting a Campaign

There are two ways to abort a campaign. The first is to select another theater in the War Room. All campaign statistics are lost; the squadron remains intact, however. The second method is to click on the DEACTIVATE button in the War Room. In this case, all data (campaign and squadron) is lost.

Summary

The heart of the Falcon 3.0 simulator is campaign mode. It is where all of the practice and training at Red Flag pays off. This chapter served as an introduction to campaign mode and provided information on mission planning. Falcon 3.0 always generates a default mission for every campaign mission flown. Your squadron's success rate can increase significantly by choosing the best route to the target.

After forming a squadron and committing to a campaign region, you and your squadron will fly four missions a day: morning, noon, late afternoon, and night. You will receive a mission briefing for each mission and a theater briefing each day. This continues until the end of the campaign.

You can choose from three campaign regions when initiating a campaign. A squadron can be assigned to only one campaign region at a time. Changing regions discards accumulated campaign data. Deactivating the squadron discards all squadron and campaign data. You can choose to battle in Israel, Panama, or Kuwait. Each theater provides a different type of campaign. For example, you will fight an aggressive war in the Kuwait region. However, you will be on the extreme defense while protecting Israel. The Falcon 3.0 software generates the missions for your squadron based on the region and previous campaign activity.

As mentioned earlier, Campaigns consist of four missions per day. Each campaign mission plan is broken down into four steps: Edit Flights, Set Waypoints, Assign Pilots, and Load Armament. This is where you get the chance to override the default selections.

At the Edit Flights screen, you determine the number of flights that will participate in the mission. You also set the number of F-16s per flight. You should always assign at least two Falcons to each flight.

After the number of flights has been determined, waypoints for each flight should be set. As in Red Flag, each waypoint has an altitude, airspeed, and an action in addition to the direction guidance. This lets you adjust the mission route that the flight(s) will take and possibly avoid enemy concentrations on the ground.

The pilots' assignment must consider the type of mission. Each pilot in your squadron has a unique set of combat skills. Some pilots are better dogfighters while others are better bombers. In addition to skills, fatigue plays an important role in pilot assignment. A pilot cannot fly four missions a day. You have to spread the mission assignments throughout your squadron to keep them well rested.

The last step before taking off is loading the Falcons with the necessary weapons to get the job done. The target is the primary issue when selecting the weapons. For example, if your squadron is assigned to intercept a flight of enemy fighters, you would select air-to-air weapons and leave the air-to-ground weapons on the ground. You also have to consider the supply on hand when making the decision. If you load up your Falcons with expensive AIM-120 radar-guided missiles for each mission, you will undoubtedly run out.

With the mission defined and the Falcons ready, you take off and follow the waypoints and the mission objective. The mission ends when you arrive safely back at the base (or all friendly aircraft are destroyed). You receive a full debriefing informing you of enemy and allied losses, medals, and updated occupation maps.

The campaign continues until all campaign objectives are met for the allies or the enemy. Losing all of your squadron F-16s or pilots also ends a campaign. You have to plan well and fly well on every mission to expect to finish victoriously.

8

Using High Fideltiy Radar (HFR)

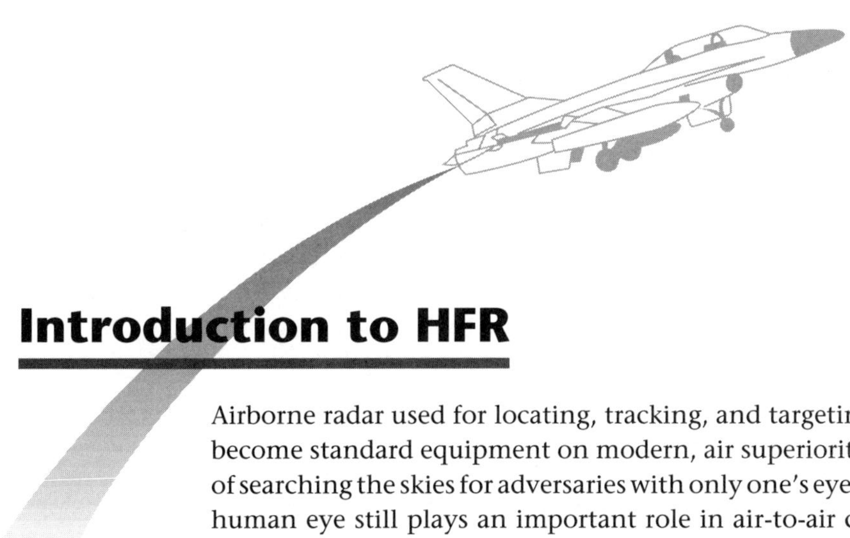

Introduction to HFR

Airborne radar used for locating, tracking, and targeting other aircraft has become standard equipment on modern, air superiority fighters. The days of searching the skies for adversaries with only one's eyes are over. While the human eye still plays an important role in air-to-air combat, the human visual range is limited to a few miles at best. Using air-to-air radar, fighter aircraft can locate and engage enemies *Beyond Visual Range* (BVR), sometimes at ranges greater than 100 nautical miles.

The F-16 employs a medium-capability radar unit designated the APG-66. While the APG-66 isn't as complex as and doesn't have the range of the radars used by the F-15 or the F-14, it is still a formidable radar package. In Falcon 3.0, the HFR mode most accurately simulates real-world operation of the APG-66.

NOTE: You must select HFR as the radar type from the configuration menu before proceeding with this chapter.

Falcon 3.0 has three radar operation modes: *Situational Awareness Display* (SAD), *Situational Awareness Mode* (SAM), and *High Fidelity Radar* (HFR). SAD and SAM modes are training modes that greatly simplify the operation of the APG-66. SAD mode allows an unrealistic 360 degree view of the world with simplified lock-on procedures and color-coded displays. SAM mode offers slightly more realism, but severely limits performance of the APG-66. SAM limits scans to a +/–60 degree cone in front of the F-16, and has an oversimplified lock-on procedure. Their complete operation is discussed in Chapter 4, *Radar and Aircraft Identification*. HFR mode, however, models the actual operation of the APG-66. The Falcon 3.0 pilot using HFR radar has precise control over the radar's range, azimuth, and elevation, as well as realistically modeled lock-on procedures.

Why Use HFR?

HFR, while being much more complex than SAD or SAM, allows the Falcon 3.0 pilot to control range, azimuth, and elevation scans, as well as precise control over target selection. HFR is the most realistic simulation of airborne radar available on the PC. Those who strive for maximum realism from a flight simulator will want to use the HFR mode exclusively. However, in unskilled hands, the HFR mode can be overwhelming. This chapter teaches you the in-depth details of HFR usage. With a little practice, you'll be an expert user of HFR. This chapter discusses the following topics:

- HFR components and modes: the components that make up the HFR and what they tell you.
- Operating the HFR: the keys used to control the HFR.
- Practical use of the HFR: detailed description of the practical use of HFR. Includes a custom Red Flag training mission.

HFR Components and Modes

HFR uses the same components as the other radar types: the *Heads-Up Display* (HUD) and the *Radar/Electro-Optical* (REO) display. However, HFR uses these devices differently. HFR has different modes of operation and displays different types of data depending upon the current mode.

The talk of types and modes may initially be confusing. However, it's actually very simple. Falcon 3.0 has three radar types: SAD (Situational

Awareness Display), SAM (Situational Awareness Mode), and HFR (High-Fidelity Radar). HFR radar has four modes of operation (described later). Each HFR mode will be discussed in detail. Throughout this chapter, the term *mode* refers to the individual HFR operating modes, not the Falcon 3.0 radar types. To add to the confusion, enemy air defense missiles, or *surface-to-air missiles*, are called SAMs. Do not confuse surface-to-air missiles with radar modes.

HFR Operating Modes

HFR has four operating modes:

- Normal Air Mode (NAM): This mode is used to search for new contacts. Selected by pressing F5, NAM mode allows you to scan different range, azimuth, and elevation values. Airborne contacts are displayed as green squares. Other than displaying relative position to the F-16, NAM mode gives little information about the target.
- Situational Awareness Mode (SAM): This is a little confusing. The acronym SAM is used to denote both a Falcon 3.0 radar and an HFR mode. Throughout this chapter, unless otherwise stated, SAM refers strictly to the HFR operating mode.
- When a desired target is locked on to from NAM mode, SAM mode is automatically selected. SAM continues to display the green blips for all radar contacts, but also provides heading, range, altitude, airspeed, and closure rate of the selected target.
- Air Combat Mode (ACM): This mode changes the azimuth and elevation scans to a tighter pattern that, during typical combat, is likely to keep radar contact with the target. ACM mode always acquires and locks the *closest* target it detects, regardless of whether it's a friendly or enemy aircraft. Select ACM by pressing F6.
- Single Target Track (STT): This mode is the radar equivalent of tunnel vision. The radar locks on to a single target and ignores all other contacts completely. This mode is usually only used during close range dogfights. This mode may be selected after acquiring a target in either SAM or ACM modes by pressing the T key. STT mode will be selected automatically when a target is locked on to at ranges under 10 miles.

The Radar/Electro-Optical Display

The REO, or Radar/Electro-Optical display, is the primary component of the HFR radar. Although some data is presented on the HUD as a convenience to the pilot, the full gamut of information is available only on the REO. Each HFR mode uses the REO slightly differently, but uses the same set of codes and indicators. Because it is such an integral part of HFR, we'll review the basics of the REO.

The Top Row

The first functional section of the REO is the top row. As shown in Figure 8-1, along the top are the *range indicator, mode indicator, and altitude data*. These three positions may appear slightly different in various modes, but data displayed at these locations always refers to range, mode, and altitude.

The Artificial Horizon

Centered in the REO is the horizon, or *waterline*. The "W" in the center of the waterline represents the nose of your F-16, aptly named the *nose indicator*. This is an artificial display of the horizon in relation to the nose

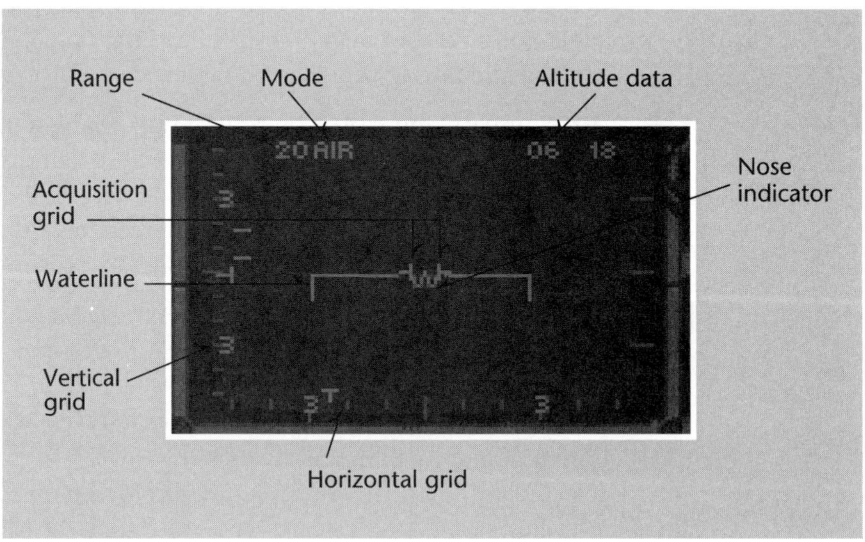

Figure 8-1 Basic Components of the REO

of your F-16. If you're flying straight and level, the waterline will be a horizontal line centered in the REO. If you're banking, the waterline will appear as a diagonal line parallel to the horizon. If you're climbing, the waterline will move toward the bottom of the REO, so that the nose indicator is above it. If you're diving, the waterline will move toward the top of the REO, so the nose indicator will be below it. The waterline is always parallel to the horizon and the nose indicator indicates the position of the F-16's nose with respect to the horizon.

Acquisition Corrals

Two vertical bars normally centered around the nose indicator are called the acquisition corrals, or the *captain's bars*. These bars move to surround the currently selected target. When no target is selected, the bars normally will be centered around the nose indicator. The horizontal scan, no matter what width is selected, *always uses the acquisition corrals as center*. If a +/–20 degree scan is selected, the radar will scan 20 degrees right and 20 degrees left of the corrals.

Ranging Grids

The grids on the REO display are actually quite complex. The horizontal scale along the bottom and the vertical scale along the left edge display data on range, altitude, and antenna scans simultaneously. Tick marks on the grids have multiple meanings depending on how you read them.

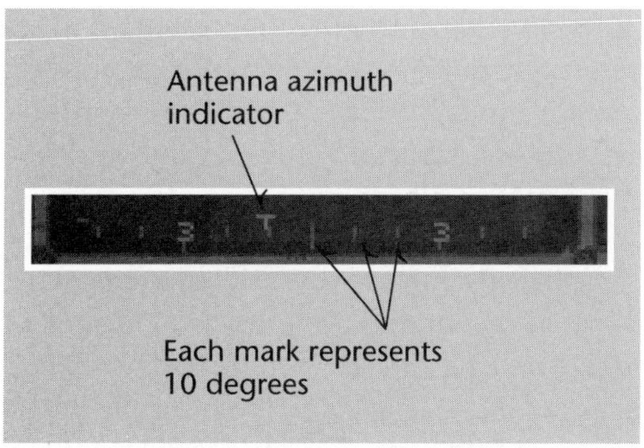

Figure 8-2 Horizontal Ranging Grid

Horizontal Ranging Scale Refer to Figure 8-2. Each mark along the bottom edge of the REO represents 10 degrees offset from the center of the aircraft, covering a range from 60 degrees left to 60 degrees right. Two "3" symbols indicate the +/–30 degree points for quick reference. A small *antenna azimuth indicator* symbol (similar to a "T") moves along this grid as the radar antenna pans back and forth. By observing this symbol, you can determine how wide the radar is scanning, as well as the direction the antenna is facing at any given time.

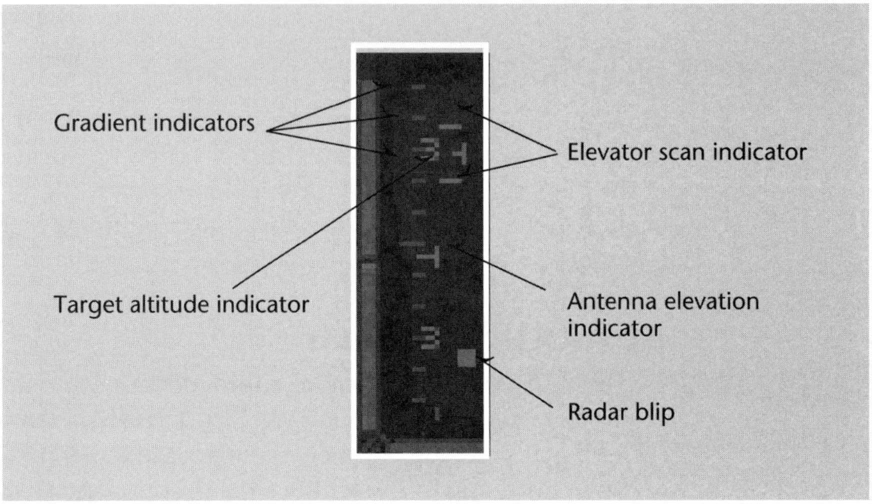

Figure 8-3 Vertical Ranging Grid

Vertical Ranging Grid Figure 8-3 illustrates the vertical ranging grid. The vertical grid along the left edge of the REO is much more complex than the horizontal grid. It displays three types of information: target range, target altitude, and antenna elevation, simultaneously!

Target Range First, imagine the REO to be laid flat on a table before you, with the bottom edge closest to you, facing up. The edge farthest from you (the top of the REO) indicates the currently selected range. For example, if the current range is 40, the nearest edge of the REO represents 0 miles away, and the farthest edge represents 40 miles away. Radar blips, according to their distances, are displayed accordingly. A target 20 miles away would be displayed in the center of the REO. A target 10 miles away would be displayed one-quarter from the bottom, or closer, edge.

Target Altitude Second, the vertical center of this grid also represents 0 feet altitude. Each tick mark above center represents 10,000 feet of altitude. When a target has been selected, its altitude is indicated by a small mark (shown in Figure 8-3), the *target altitude indicator*. For example, if the selected target is at 20,000 feet, the horizontal mark is placed near the second grid indicator above center. The upper "3" represents 30,000 feet. The lower "3" has no meaning with respect to the target's altitude. In Figure 8-3, the target's altitude is approximately 30,000 feet.

Antenna Elevation The vertical grid reports two things regarding the antenna: the vertical scan height range and the current position of the antenna. Two horizontal bars called the *elevation scan indicators* (illustrated in Figure 8-3) show the upper and lower altitudes the radar is scanning. For this purpose, the grid marks still represent units of 10,000 feet.

The *antenna elevation indicator* displays the current vertical pitch of the antenna. For this purpose, each grid mark represents units of 10 degrees above and below the aircraft. The two "3" symbols represent 30 degrees above and 30 degrees below the aircraft's horizontal axis.

The elevation scan indicator and the antenna elevation indicator are independent measurements. The elevation scan indicator reports (in feet) the altitudes being scanned; the antenna elevation indicator reports the pitch of the antenna. In Figure 8-3, altitudes from 20,000 feet to approximately 40,000 feet are being scanned while the antenna is currently pitched downwards approximately 5 degrees.

> NOTE: The vertical ranging grid simultaneously displays different data in units of miles, feet, and degrees. Depending upon the data being read, each tick mark may represent miles from the F-16, altitude, or degrees above and below the F-16.

Monitoring the Antenna Scan By watching the azimuth and elevation antenna indicators, you can monitor the location of the radar antenna at all times. Depending upon the number of bars and the width selected, you will see the elevation antenna indicator move, then remain steady as the azimuth antenna indicator moves. Then the azimuth indicator will stop, and the elevation indicator will move to a new position and the process repeats. This will be demonstrated later.

Historical Track

Referring to Figure 8-4, next comes the actual radar contacts, usually referred to as *blips*. As the radar scans back and forth, contacts are displayed as bright green squares. When the radar makes the next scan, all blips displayed on the last scan are changed to a darker shade of green, and blips from the current scan are displayed in bright green. This process repeats until four colors of green varying in intensity are displayed. This is known as a *historical track*. By carefully analyzing the historical tracks you can determine the relative movements of the contacts.

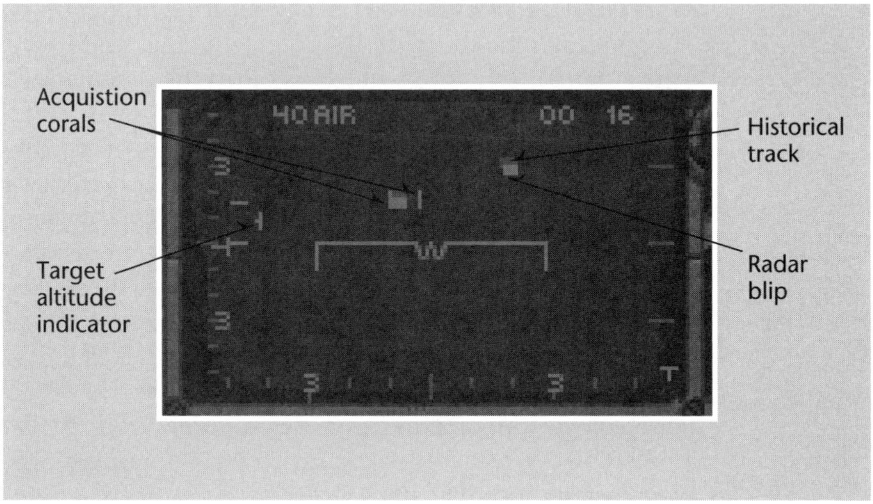

Figure 8-4 Historical Track

NOTE: Radar contacts displayed on the REO have no relation to the waterline. If a blip is displayed above the waterline, that does not mean that contact is above your aircraft.

Radar blips are called various names depending upon the situation. Contacts that have been identified as allied forces are called *friendlies*, contacts that have been identified as enemies are called *bandits*. When it is not known if the contact is friendly or hostile, the contact is called a *bogey*.

Bearing and Range

The lower left corner of Figure 8-5 contains the *bearing and range indicator*. The bearing and range indicator has two numbers separated by a circular symbol. The first number is the heading (in Figure 8-5 it's 341) you must fly to point your nose directly at the target. The second number is the distance in nautical miles to the target.

Target Data Block

Referring to Figure 8-5, next comes the *target data block*. This position displays the heading, airspeed, and intercept angle of a selected target. The top number is the target's current heading; the middle number is the target's current speed (the letter "K" indicates the speed is measured in knots). The bottom number is the *aspect angle*. As you will recall this is the angle between the bearing to the target and the heading of the target. This number will be

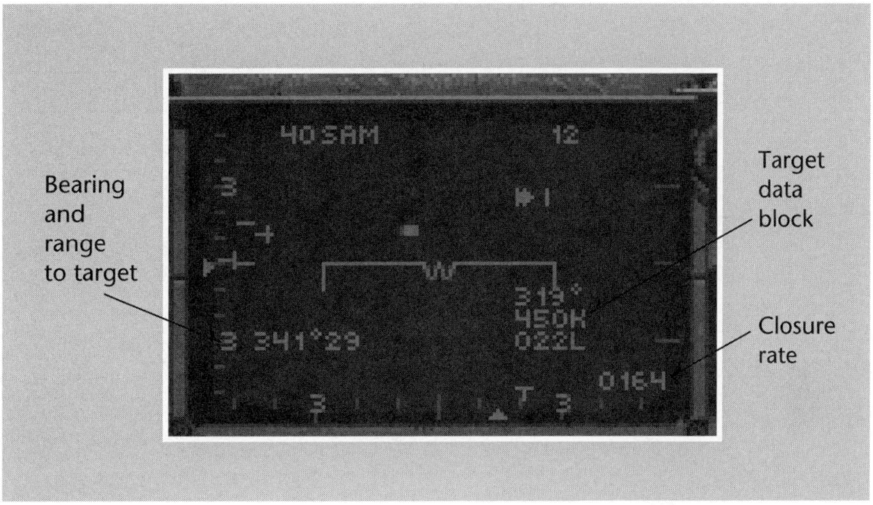

Figure 8-5 Target Data

zero when you are directly behind the target. The letters "L" and "R" following the number indicate which side of the target you are on.

For example, if the you are traveling 0 degrees and pointing directly at a target heading 90 degrees, the aspect angle would be 90R. The difference between the direction to the target and the direction the target is traveling is 90. If the targeted pilot looked over his right shoulder at that instant he would see your F-16. In Figure 8-5, the target is flying at a heading of 319 degrees. The direct heading to the target is 341 degrees. If you were flying at a heading of 341 degrees, the difference between your flight path and his would be 22 degrees and you would be on his left side. Figure 8-6 illustrates the concept of an aspect angle.

Aspect angle plays an important role in determining when to fire a missile at the target. A low aspect angle means the target is basically heading the same direction as the firing aircraft; therefore, the missile has to make few turns to track the target. A high aspect angle means the target is turning away from the launching aircraft. The missile will have to turn sharply to continue tracking the target. Some older heat-seeking missiles, such as the AIM-9P, can only track a target if it is directly behind the target at a low aspect angle. The infrared seeker in the missile is unable to detect the heat of the target's exhaust unless the exhaust is pointed directly at the missile.

> **NOTE:** The lower the aspect angle, the greater the chance that a missile will hit the target.

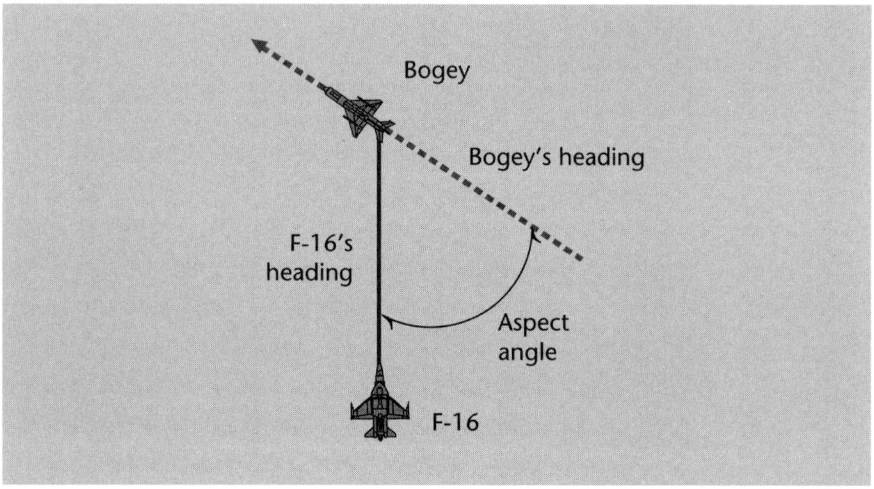

Figure 8-6 Aspect Angle

Closure Rate

Lastly, Figure 8-5 shows the *closure rate* between you and the target. Closure rate is the relative speed between you and the target. When the range between you and the target is decreasing, closure rate is positive. When the range between you and the target is increasing, the closure rate is negative. The value of the closure rate shows what your speed would be if the target were stationary.

For example, two aircraft both flying at 500 knots traveling directly toward each other would have a closure rate of 1,000. This would be equivalent to an aircraft traveling at 1,000 knots toward a stationary object. If an F-16 is headed 90 degrees at 400 knots following a MiG-29 also headed at 90 degrees but traveling at 500 knots, the closure rate would be –100 because the MiG is traveling away from the F-16. A closure rate of –100 would be the equivalent of an aircraft traveling at 100 knots away from a stationary object. Closure rate also takes into account the pitch angles of the two aircraft.

NOTE: Closure rate translates the rate at which the distance between you and your target is changing and displays that as what your speed would be if the target were stationary.

The Heads-Up Display

Modern HUDs are designed to provide pilots with all the mandatory data required during combat. HUDs display summaries of flight attitude data (altitude, pitch angle, speed, etc.), weapons information (weapon type selected, aspect indicators, gun sights, etc.), and navigation information (range to waypoint, heading to waypoint, etc.). Repeats of critical data gathered by the APG-66 are also displayed.

Figure 8-7 shows a typical HUD. Please note that of the two HUD types available from the CONFIG menu (the "A" version and the "C" version), the "A" version is the appropriate model for the particular model of F-16 simulated in Falcon 3.0. While some users may prefer the aesthetics of the "C" version, this chapter will use the "A" version exclusively.

Target Designator Box

Refer to Figure 8-7. First is the *target designator box*. In SAM and ACM modes, the APG-66 determines the exact location of the selected target, then passes that data to the HUD computer. The computer controlling the HUD then calculates (based on the target's position and the pilot's viewing angle) where the target would be viewed in the display. The HUD computer then

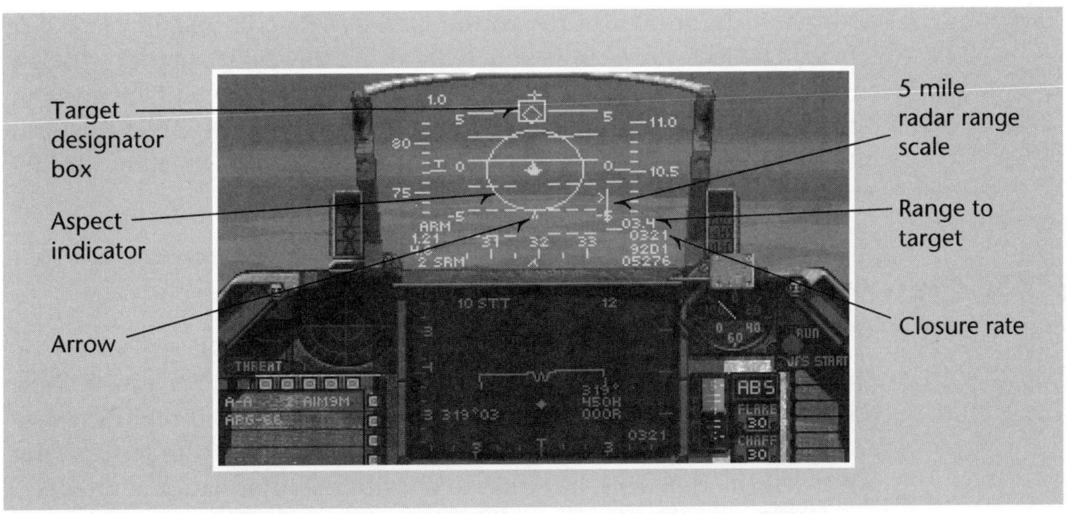

Figure 8-7 Radar Information on the HUD

highlights this spot by superimposing a small square around it. This way, even when the target is far beyond visual range, the pilot knows its exact location: inside the target designator box.

Range and Closure Rate

Also visible in Figure 8-7 are repeats of the range to the target and the closure rate. These values are used so often during combat that they're presented on both the HUD and REO. During a dogfight, the pilot never has to look far to find these critical pieces of data.

5-Mile Radar-Ranging Scale

The "A" version of the HUD also includes a *5-mile radar-ranging scale,* also visible in Figure 8-7. This line appears when the selected target is within 5 miles of your F-16. The top of the line represent a distance of 5 miles, while the bottom of the line represent 0 miles. The arrow on the left side of the line marks the distance the target is from your F-16.

Aspect Indicator

When an air-to-air missile is selected, the target's aspect angle is repeated on the HUD in graphic format. The circle represents 360 degrees. The arrow points the direction the target is heading *with respect to your aircraft.* For example, if the arrow is at the bottom of the circle pointing up, the target is heading directly away from you. If the arrow, however, is at the top of the circle pointing down, the target is flying directly toward you. This gives an estimate of the aspect angle to help you determine if the target is within missile launch parameters or not. In Figure 8-7, the target is heading directly away from the F-16.

HFR Operating Modes

Now that you know what components make up the HFR, it's time to learn how to operate it. To effectively use the HFR, Falcon 3.0 pilots need to develop a philosophy, or *system,* of usage. The pilot needs to understand not only what the HFR does, but what to do with the information it provides.

Do not think of the four HFR modes (NAM, SAM, ACM, and STT) as independent entities or unrelated views. Instead, visualize an automobile with three rear view mirrors: one mounted on the driver's door, one in the center of the windshield, and one mounted on the passenger's door.

Depending upon which of three mirrors the driver looks at, a different view of the road behind the car is seen. Individually, each of three views are important; however, to get a complete understanding of the area behind the car, the driver must use all three views in conjunction. The driver must know what information each mirror presents, as well as when to look at it. Likewise, HFR modes present separate views of the same airspace depending on how the pilot chooses to look.

Returning to the automobile analogy, knowing when to look is as important as knowing how to look. The driver will choose different mirrors to view at different times, depending upon the traffic, driving conditions, etc. Likewise, the Falcon 3.0 pilot will select different HFR modes depending upon the "view" the pilot requires.

NOTE: To summarize: each of the four HFR modes of operation (NAM, SAM, ACM, and STT) present the pilot with different views of the same airspace. Depending upon the pilot's current situation, different modes are selected.

Executing an Attack: The Three Steps

A combat pilot should never charge an enemy blindly. Instead, you should take the time to use all the available views and gather as much information as possible about the enemy. Normally, this process follows these three steps:

- Search for targets.
- Track and identify a target.
- Pursue and destroy a hostile target, repeat as necessary.

Each HFR mode has been designed to execute one of these tasks. We'll study what each mode does and how it relates to one of the above three steps. The following two Red Flag training missions, CHAP8EX1 and CHAP8EX2, are designed to teach you how to control HFR modes, as well as how to use them effectively in combat. At this time, you should enter Falcon 3.0, select your favorite squadron, enter Red Flag, and load CHAP8EX1. Next, assign a pilot and takeoff.

NAM Mode Operation

Normal Air Mode, or NAM, is designed for the first step in executing an attack: search for targets. The pilot configures NAM mode radar for specified range, azimuth, and elevation to scan. NAM mode displays the current position and historical tracks for all radar contacts within those scans on the REO, but does not give detailed information on any single contact.

NOTE: Use NAM mode to search for new contacts at long ranges.

NAM Keyboard Summary NAM mode employs a total of six keys:

- F5 selects NAM mode.
- F8 adusts the range scan.
- F9 controls the azimuth scan.
- F10 changes the elevation scan.
- T designates target.
- X clears target designations and resets the REO.

Selecting NAM Mode Before selecting a radar mode, make sure your APG-66 radar is activated by checking the stores panel in the lower left corner of the cockpit. If the stores panel does not display "APG-66," then the radar is turned off. Use the R key to toggle the radar on and off. Once the radar is active, select NAM by pressing F5.

NOTE: The mode indicator in Figure 8-8 reads "AIR" to indicate that NAM radar is selected. This is somewhat confusing. You will have to remember that the word "AIR" actually indicates NAM mode.

Adjusting the Range Scan When you first select NAM, the range is automatically set to 20 miles, the azimuth scan is set to +/–60°, and the elevation scan is set to 4 bars. This will rarely be suitable for air-to-air searches. You have four possible range values: 10, 20, 40, or 80 nautical miles. Press F8 to adjust this value. Each time F8 is pressed, the next lower range value is selected until the minimum of 10 nautical miles is selected. Pressing F8 again resets the range to the maximum of 80 nautical miles. Pressing SHIFT-F8 reverses the selection order. Begin your air-to-air search with an 80 nautical mile range. Press F8 until the range indicator displays 80, as shown in Figure 8-8.

Adjusting the Azimuth Scan There are three possible azimuth scans: +/–60°, +/–30°, or +/–10°, selected by pressing F9. Each time F9 is pressed the next wider scan is selected until the maximum of +/–60° is achieved. Pressing F9 again resets to the minimum width of +/–10°. Pressing SHIFT-F9 will reverse the selection order. Usually, you should initiate air-to-air searches with a +/–60° scan. Press F9 while watching the azimuth indicator (shown in Figure 8-8). Continue to press F9 until the azimuth indicator moves completely across the bottom of the REO.

There is no display other than the antenna azimuth indicator that identifies the current azimuth selection. To determine what width is currently being scanned, you have to observe the movements of the antenna azimuth indicator against the horizontal ranging scale. In Figure 8-8, the antenna azimuth indicator is currently only two degrees to the left of center.

Adjusting the Elevation Scan There are three choices of elevation scan (1 bar, 2 bars, or 4 bars) selected by pressing F10. As with range and elevation, the elevation scan will continually cycle through the three possible values each time F10 is pressed. Also like the range and azimuth, pressing SHIFT-F10 reverses the selection order. You should begin an air-to-air search with the maximum elevation scan.

There is no actual indicator to show how many bars are currently selected. Instead, watch the numeric maximum and minimum altitude scan indicators change as you press F10. The greater the difference between these two numbers (the greater the vertical scan), the greater the number of bars. Typically, you will be more concerned with the values of the minimum and maximum altitude scan indicators than with the actual number of scan bars. If the antenna is scanning the desired altitudes, the number of bars being used is irrelevant. In Figure 8-8, the antenna is scanning between 0 and 32,000 feet.

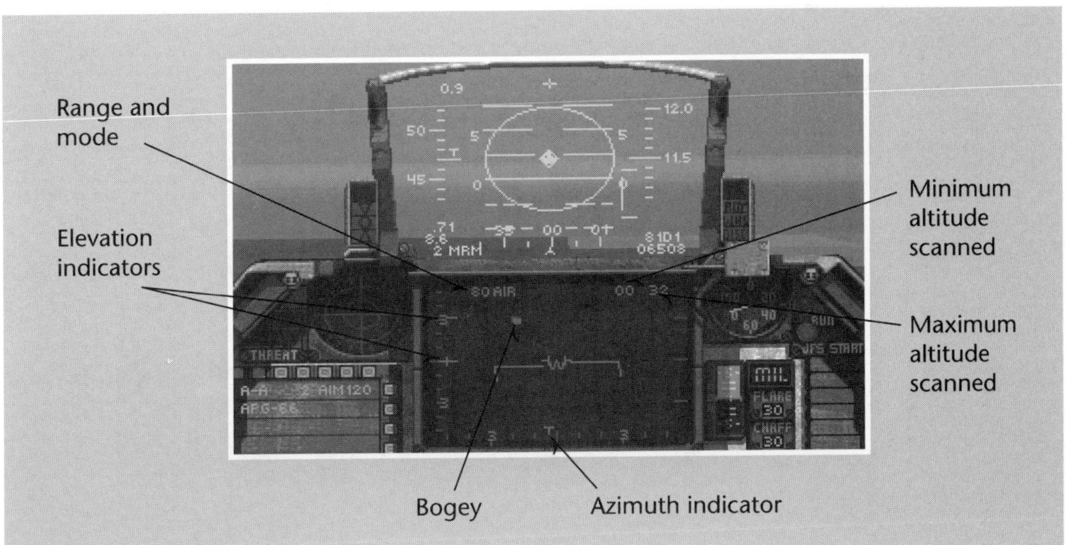

Figure 8-8 NAM Display

Your NAM radar is now configured for a maximum coverage scan. A green blip, as shown in Figure 8-8, should soon appear on your REO. This is your first radar contact, or bogey.

> **NOTE:** Radar contacts within the specified range but outside of the azimuth and/or elevation scans will not be displayed on the REO. For Example, in Figure 8-8 a radar contact 15 miles away at 40,000 feet would not be displayed because the radar is only searching to 32,000 feet.

Target Designation NAM mode is designed for long-range, wide-area scans while monitoring multiple air contacts, not for tracking a single target. The second HFR mode, SAM, is used for tracking and identifying a specific target. However, before a target can be tracked in SAM mode, a contact must be designated via the T key in NAM mode.

Pressing the T key moves the acquisition corrals from the center of the REO to one of the radar contacts. This contact is called the *designated contact*, meaning it has been designated for further scrutiny. Repeated pressing of the T key designates each contact in sequence until all contacts have been designated once. Pressing T again re-designates the original target and the cycle starts over again. Press the T key now to designate this bogey.

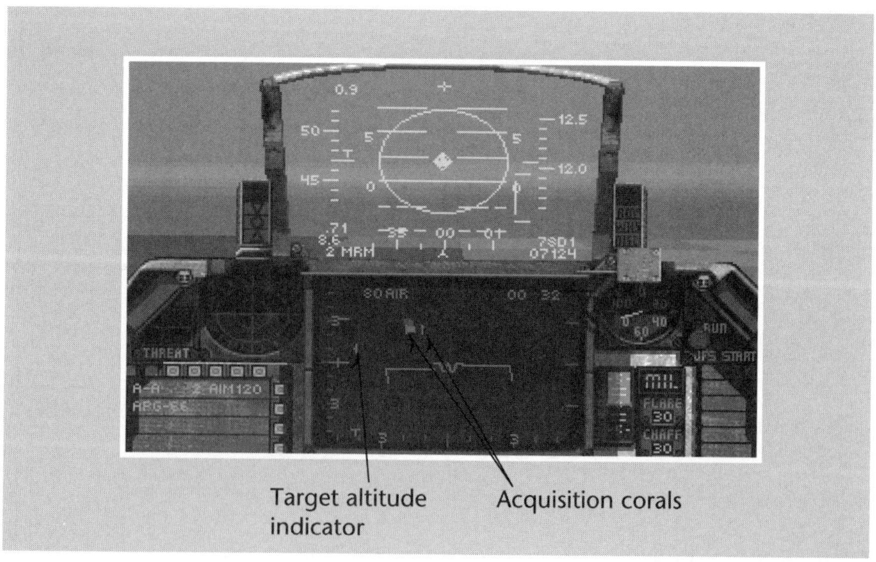

Figure 8-9 A Designated Target

Figure 8-9 shows what you should now see. The target altitude indicator will appear along the right side of the vertical ranging grid once a radar contact has been designated. For the purpose of reading the target's altitude, each mark on the grid represents 10,000 feet. In Figure 8-9, the designated target is slightly below 10,000 feet.

Range to Target The range to the target is determined by the distance the contact is from the bottom of the REO. In Figure 8-9, the contact is approximately three-quarters above the bottom of the REO. The displayed range is 80 nautical miles, so the range to the target is three-quarters of that, or about 60 nautical miles away.

Clearing Designation The X key breaks any radar lock or target designation. Pressing the X key clears the REO of all radar contacts until the next scan is completed. Press the X key now and observe the results. All contacts on the REO are erased, and the target altitude indicator is no longer displayed. As of Falcon 3.0D, pressing X will leave the acquisition corrals "stuck" in their last position on the REO. This can cause problems with subsequent air-to-air searches. See the "NAM Mode Pitfalls and Caveats" section for more details.

Clearing a designation does not stop the radar from scanning. As you fly, watch the azimuth indicator continue to move. Once it has panned across the bottom of the REO, the contact will again be displayed on the REO. Press the T key to designate the target again. Pause the simulation by pressing P and proceed to the following section.

NAM Mode Pitfalls and Caveats

There are several obstacles you must be aware of when using NAM mode: blind spots, range changing, azimuth centering, and radar beaming.

Radar Blind Spots The radar scans a cone extending from the radar antenna. The elevation and azimuth scans determine how large the base of the cone will be at the selected range. Targets within the range selection but outside of the cone will not be displayed on the REO. Bandits can hide in these radar blind spots and surprise you. You should occasionally adjust your altitude and heading and look at these blind spots. Figure 8-10 illustrates.

Changing the Range Value As of Falcon 3.0D, changing the range value resets the elevation scan to a default two bar scan. The smaller scan will result in a smaller radar cone. A contact 18 miles away that was within

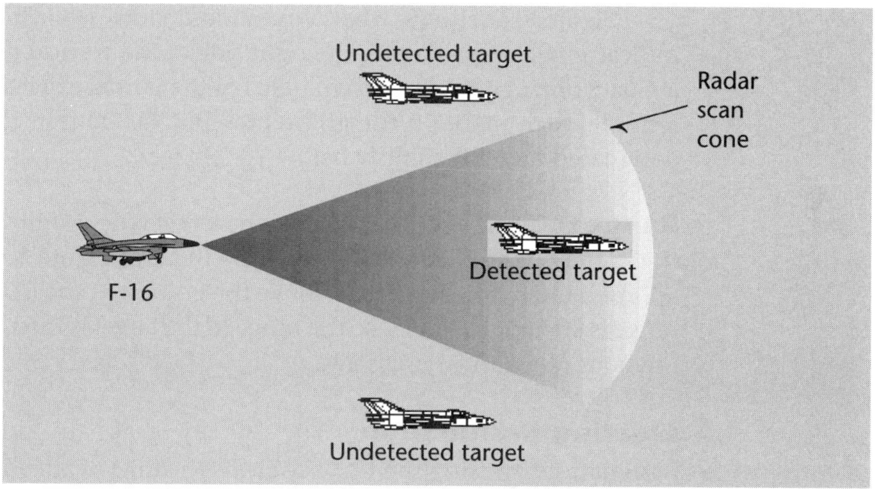

Figure 8-10 The Radar Scans a Cone Forward of the Aircraft

the cone at a 40-mile, maximum elevation scan may be suddenly placed outside a 20-mile, default elevation scan. If you press F8 to reduce the range and the contact disappears, readjust the elevation scan with F10.

Azimuth Scan Centering The azimuth scan always centers around the acquisition corrals. If the corrals are not in the center of the REO, the scan will be skewed to one side of the aircraft. Contacts on the opposite side of the aircraft may, therefore, fall outside the azimuth scan.

> WARNING: By designating a contact, you adjust the azimuth scan, thereby possibly placing the other contacts in your radar blind spots. You must remember to constantly check your blind spots lest a bandit sneak behind you and ruin your day.

Centering the Azimuth Scan As explained, when you press X to clear the target designation in Falcon 3.0D, the acquisition corrals remain in their previous position instead of returning to the center of the REO. It is possible that future versions of Falcon 3.0 will correct this problem, but in the meantime there is a fix.

Centering the azimuth scan is tricky. It requires the proper timing of a two-key keystroke sequence. You must first press the X key to clear the REO of all targets. Then you must *quickly* press the T key. The contacts will be redisplayed on the REO when the next scan is made. If you press the T key too late, you will simply re-designate one of the radar contacts. You must press the T key *while no contacts are displayed on the REO*. This returns the acquisition corrals to the center of the REO and resets the azimuth scan. The timing is tough and it will probably take you a few tries to get it down. After a little practice, it will become second nature to you.

Doppler's Weak Spot As explained earlier, Doppler radars filter out contacts with a 90 degree aspect angle because the Doppler shift from these contacts falsely represents them as stationary. The Doppler radar is fooled into believing these contacts are merely reflections from the ground. This is known as *beaming* your radar. If you lock a target that is flying at a 90 degree aspect angle, your radar lock-on will probably break quickly. There's only one thing you can do in this case: alter your heading so that the aspect angle is no longer 90 degrees.

SAM Mode

Situational Awareness Mode, or SAM, radar is designed for the second step in executing an attack: tracking and identifying a specified target. Like NAM mode, you have complete control over the range, azimuth, and elevation scans in SAM mode. However, SAM mode also provides detailed information about the designated target in addition to the data provided by NAM.

NOTE: SAM mode can be selected only after a target has been designated in NAM mode.

SAM Keyboard Summary SAM mode uses three keys:

- Z radar locks the designated contact.
- X unlocks the designated contact.
- N identifies the locked target as friendly or hostile.

Selecting SAM Mode SAM is designed for the second phase of air-to-air attacks: tracking and identifying targets. There's only one way to select SAM mode radar. You must first select NAM mode radar, locate a contact, and designate it with the T key. After the acquisition corrals are centered around the desired target, press the Z key to obtain a radar lock. The radar blip will change from a square to a diamond, indicating the lock and the radar mode will change to SAM. SAM will continue to scan like NAM mode while reporting detailed information on the locked contact.

Unpause the simulation. You should still have a contact displayed and designated from the previous exercise. Press the Z key to lock on. Your screen should now look like Figure 8-11.

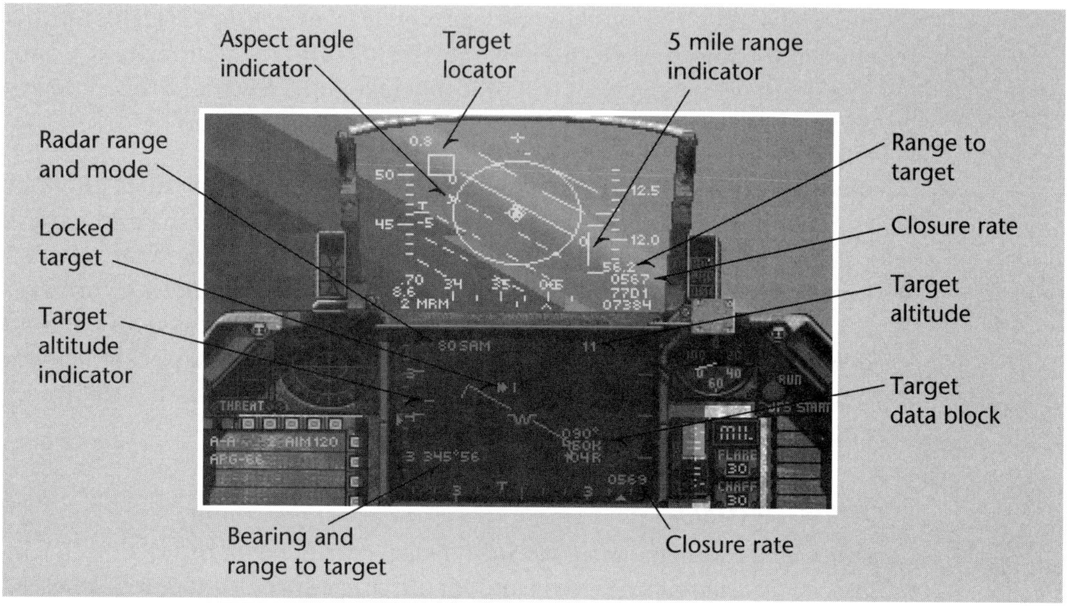

Figure 8-11 Radar Lock-On in SAM

Referring to Figure 8-11, you can determine that the target is 56 miles away, at a bearing of 345°, traveling at a heading of 90°, moving at 450 knots, flying at 11,000 feet, with an aspect angle of 104°. Closure rate is positive 569 knots, indicating you are gaining on the target. The blip for the locked target has changed from a square to a diamond to indicate the lock.

Breaking Radar Lock The X breaks radar lock-ons, clears target designations, and reselects NAM. Press X now. Your radar lock is now broken, the additional displays on the HUD are gone, and the REO has been cleared. The acquisition corrals remain unmoved; you must use the procedure described earlier to center the corrals in the REO.

Since you're again in NAM, the radar continues to scan after the lock has been broken. If it hasn't done so already, the contact will soon reappear on the REO. Designate the target again with the T key and reacquire lock-on by pressing Z. Pause the simulation by pressing P.

Advantages of SAM Despite the radar lock, SAM mode continues to scan the selected azimuth and elevation settings. If a wide azimuth and/or a tall elevation has been selected, the radar will scan the target less often than with a narrow search pattern. This works to your advantage due to the operation of enemy radar detectors.

Almost all combat aircraft carry a device called a *Threat Warning Indicator* (TWI). The TWI is a radar detector, similar to those used in automobiles, but more complex. TWIs monitor how often they are scanned by hostile radar beams. When the number of times the aircraft is scanned in a certain period of time exceeds some predetermined number, the TWI alerts the pilot that his aircraft has been locked on to by activating the "RADAR LOCK" warning light. However, SAM mode continues to make broad searches, possibly only scanning the target once every few seconds. In this case, the enemy's TWI will not detect the lock; you're deceiving him.

Identify, Friend or Foe As missile technology and ranges improve, aerial battles occur at greater distances between the combatants. The pilot with the longest-ranged weapon has a distinct advantage: attack the enemy at a distance from which the enemy can't return fire. However, even at close ranges, it's often difficult to determine the identity of another aircraft. Is your target an enemy MiG waiting to pounce on you or is it a friendly F-15 that has strayed off course? At missile ranges of 15 or more miles, it's impossible to visually identify the target.

So, most modern combat aircraft carry equipment called *Identification Friend or Foe* gear, or IFF for short. When you verify the identity of the target (called "checking IFF"), your F-16 transmits encrypted signals to the target. If the target has a friendly IFF transponder unit, it will transmit special encrypted signals back to you. Your IFF gear verifies the validity of the returned signal and informs you whether the target is a good or bad guy. If the target is a good guy, the green IFF light on the left side of the cockpit will illuminate. To check this light, you have to press the 4 key and observe the left cockpit view. Besides seeing the IFF light illuminate, you should also hear a loud buzz indicating the target is a friendly.

> **NOTE:** You must radar lock a target before you can check its IFF signature.

Press P to unpause the simulation. Check the IFF of the locked target by pressing the N key. If the target is a hostile aircraft nothing will happen. If the target is a friend, you should hear the loud buzz and see the IFF light illuminate. This target is a friendly aircraft; you should now hear the IFF buzz.

Automatic Ranging SAM mode also has a feature called *automatic ranging*. When a locked radar contact moves close enough to the F-16 that it becomes visible on the next closer range scale, SAM mode automatically changes to the next scale. For example, suppose you set the SAM mode range to 40 nautical miles, lock a target that is 30 nautical miles away, and fly toward it. When the distance between you and the target closes to less than 20 nautical miles, SAM mode will automatically change the range to 20. At first this may seem disruptive; however, this is an actual feature of the real APG-66 radar. Falcon 3.0 is correctly modeling the operation of the F-16 radar.

Approaching the Target Increase speed to 500 knots and fly directly toward the target. The aspect angle (refer to Figure 8-11) of 107° is near enough to the 90°-aspect blind spot of Doppler radars that the radar lock may suddenly break. When the lock breaks, the REO will revert back to NAM. Simply repeat the designation and lock-on procedures described above. You may have to repeat this procedure several times until the aspect angle changes sufficiently. Continue flying toward the target until the range is less than 40 nautical miles. Notice, when the range drops to 40 nautical miles, the REO automatically switches to a 40 nautical mile range. Pause the simulation by pressing P.

If you close to within 10 nautical miles of the locked target, the radar mode is automatically changed from SAM to a dedicated tracking mode called *Single Target Track* (STT). Briefly, STT mode is designed to maintain a radar lock on a maneuvering target at ranges less than 10 miles. Complete details of STT mode are discussed later in this chapter.

SAM Mode Pitfalls and Caveats

In addition to the problems with NAM mode, SAM mode has an additional obstacle. As described above, when the range is changed in NAM mode, the elevation scan is reset to a default bar scan. As of Falcon 3.0D, SAM mode's automatic ranging feature also readjusts the elevation scan. When the target crosses the threshold and the range is automatically changed, the elevation scan will also be changed. *In many cases, this bug causes the target to be outside the new elevation scan, thus breaking the radar lock.* This is one of the most dangerous bugs remaining in Falcon 3.0.

Automatic Ranging Hazards If you have a target locked on the 40 nautical mile scale and it automatically switches to the 20 nautical mile scale and breaks the lock, you can be 99.9% certain that the elevation scan is too shallow. Once the lock is broken, however, the radar resorts back to NAM mode and the contact will not be visible on the REO.

However, due to the prior lock, you should know the target's altitude. Quickly readjust the elevation scan to once again encompass the target's altitude and the target should reappear on the REO. Designate the target again with the T key and radar lock it again with the Z. You should be back in business.

Automatic STT Mode Selection As stated above, when the automatic ranging function selects a 10 nautical mile range, the radar mode is also switched from SAM to the dedicated tracking mode, STT. Complete details on STT will be discussed below in a separate section. However, you should be warned at this point that STT will only display information regarding the locked target on the REO. *Other, un-locked targets will no longer be displayed on the REO.*

ACM Mode

Air Combat Mode, or ACM, does not fall cleanly under a single attack execution task. Instead, it combines activities from the first two tasks (locate a target, track and identify a target) at short ranges. Often referred to as "boresight" mode, ACM uses tight, non-adjustable azimuth and elevation scans and a fixed, 10 nautical mile range. ACM scans a narrow azimuth (+/–5 degrees) but a tall elevation (+/–20 degrees). Target selection is automatic: the closest target to the aircraft is automatically designated and locked, then ACM automatically switches to the dedicated tracking mode, Single Target Track (STT).

Typically, ACM mode is selected when engaged in a dogfight at ranges under 10 miles, especially against multiple bandits. ACM mode automatically locks the closest target it detects. The pilot now has "hands free" radar operation and can focus on firing weapons. *This training mission does not fully utilize ACM.* The following mission, CHAP8EX2, will explore the capabilities of ACM in combat.

ACM Keyboard Summary ACM mode uses only one key:

- F6 selects ACM mode.

All other ACM functions are controlled automatically.

Selecting ACM Mode ACM mode is designed for "hands-free" radar operation during combat. This allows the pilot to focus attention on the target and firing weapons. Unpause the simulation by pressing P, and select ACM mode by pressing F6. ACM mode is much simpler than either NAM or SAM; ACM has a fixed range of 10 nautical miles, narrow azimuth scan, and a tall elevation scan. Since the target is still over 10 nautical miles away, contact will be broken and the REO will be blank.

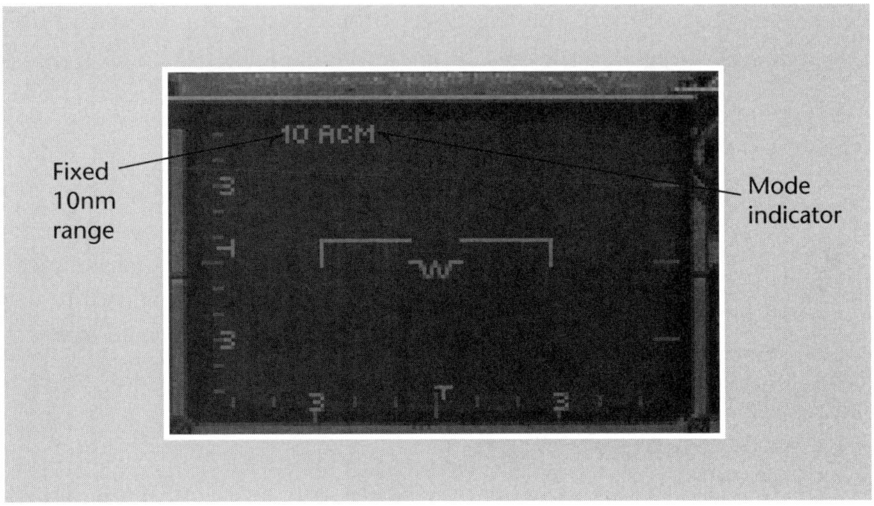

Figure 8-12 ACM Mode REO Display

ACM Displays Figure 8-12 shows the only REO display that ACM supplies. The range indicator is always set to 10 nautical miles. You may watch the azimuth and elevation scan indicators move, but you are unable to alter them. ACM mode is purely used for short range, hands-free scanning. As soon as contacts are detected, the closest one is locked and the mode automatically switches to STT.

Before proceeding to the next section, reselect NAM by pressing F5. Again designate the target by pressing T, then radar lock it by pressing Z. Pause the simulation and proceed to the next section.

STT Mode

Single Target Track (STT) is the final HFR mode. It is designed for the terminal phase of the attack: pursue and destroy the target. STT displays the same detailed information given by SAM mode about the locked target, but displays only the locked target. STT completely controls the elevation and azimuth scans; the antenna is kept centered on the target.

STT Keyboard Summary STT mode is also very simple and uses only three keys:

- Z selects STT mode after a target has been locked in SAM mode.
- X breaks the radar lock.

- N interrogates the target's IFF.

Selecting STT Mode There are two ways to select STT mode:

- From SAM mode: Pressing the Z key again will switch from SAM mode to STT mode, focusing the REO on the locked target. If you later press X to break the lock, the REO will revert to NAM mode.
- From ACM mode: No keystrokes are required. ACM mode automatically locks the closest contact it detects and switches to STT mode. If you later press X to break the lock, the REO will revert to ACM mode.

Unpause the simulation and press the Z key. Figure 8-13 shows how your REO should now appear. Pause the simulation.

STT Displays STT display modes are a subset of SAM mode's displays. The same HUD display is used in both STT and SAM. Identical REO displays are also used, with one exception. Whereas SAM mode displays both detailed data about the locked target and historical tracks for other contacts, STT mode displays only data regarding the locked target. Otherwise, the two

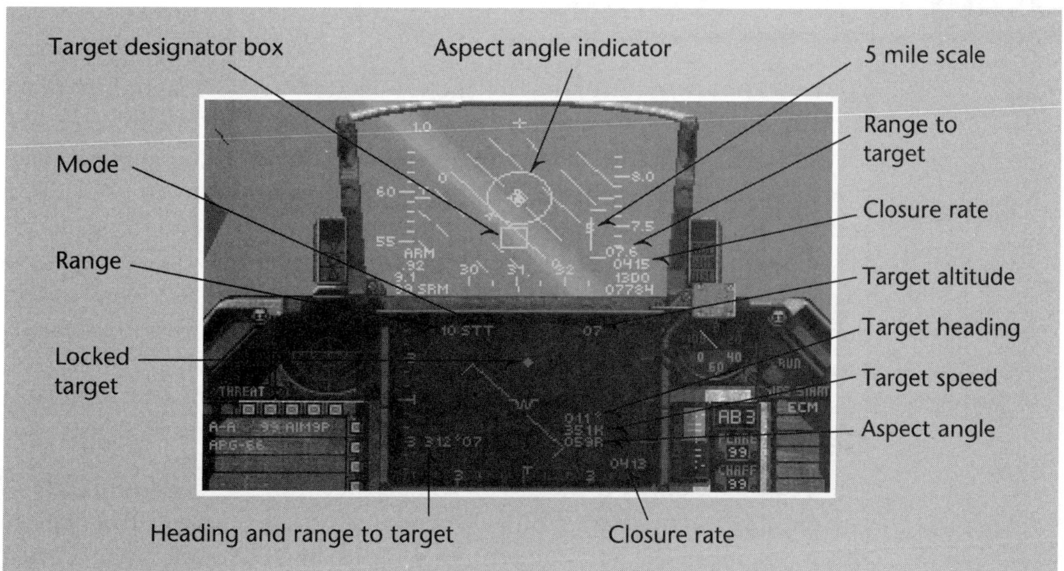

Figure 8-13 STT Mode Full Cockpit View

modes use identical displays. Figure 8-13 shows both a typical HUD and a typical REO when in STT mode.

Identifying the Target Interrogation of IFF transponders operates exactly the same in STT as in any other radar mode. Unpause the game and press the N key. Since this is a friendly aircraft, you should now hear the IFF buzz.

Breaking Lock-On Sometimes you may need to break the radar lock-on. Maybe the target is a friendly aircraft, or maybe the target is out of range for your weapons. You may break the radar lock at any time by pressing X. The lock will be broken and the radar mode will revert to the previous mode. For example, if you had previously been using SAM mode, the mode will revert back to SAM when the lock is broken. Likewise, if the previous mode was ACM, the mode will revert back to ACM when the lock is broken.

Experiment with the X key now. Break the radar lock, then repeat the designation and lock-on procedure. The lesson is over, you've learned the basics of HFR operation. The next section will teach you to use HFR during combat. Press ESC and end the mission when you are through experimenting.

Using HFR in Combat

You now know what all of the HFR modes are, how to select them, what keys control them, what displays they use, and what the symbols mean. However, knowledge with no practical application will not help you when there's a bandit on your six. This section teaches you how to use HFR in combat. For this training mission only, you may find it useful to set Enemy Logic Level to TRAINEE. Flying against simple targets allows you more time to operate the radar in your first combat mission using HFR. If you haven't done so already, enter Falcon 3.0, adjust the logic level from the config screen, select your favorite squadron, enter Red Flag, and load CHAP8EX2.

Getting Started

The Red Flag training mission you will be executing contains a mixture of friendly and enemy forces. Therefore, you need to exercise caution before firing weapons. This mission will fully utilize all HFR modes in a combat environment.

From the Red Flag Control menu, press the F-16 PILOTS button. Pilot selection for this mission is not important; use any pilot you wish. Next select the F-16 ARMAMENTS button. The default weapons load (two AIM-120 and two AIM-9M missiles) should be sufficient for this mission. Press the TAKEOFF button. You'll begin the lesson in the air traveling at 450 knots at an altitude of 14,000 feet.

Maximum Scan Configuration

As stated earlier, each attack consists of three steps, finding a target, identifying it, and attacking it if it is hostile. You'll begin the lesson by searching for targets. NAM mode is designed for this role, so select it by pressing F5. You should now see something similar to Figure 8-14.

Notice that the range is set by default to 20 nautical miles. Watch the antenna azimuth indicator move back and forth across the bottom of the REO. By default, it moves the maximum width of the REO, +/–60 degrees. Notice the default elevation range of 0 to 12,000 feet. Upon selecting NAM mode, the range will always be set to 20 and the azimuth scan to +/–60 degrees. The elevation scan will always initially be set to 4 bars; however, the actual altitudes scanned will vary based on your present altitude.

Trade-Offs Every good thing has a catch. HFR radar is no exception. Although you can scan a 60 degree cone extending 80 nautical miles in front of your F-16 for enemy aircraft, there's a cost penalty: time. The farther the

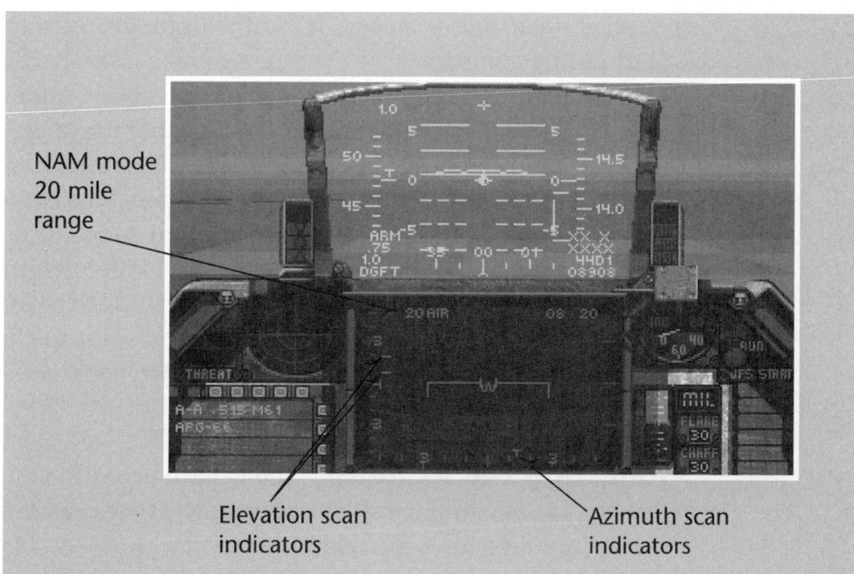

Figure 8-14 Initial NAM Display

antenna moves, the greater the area you scan. However, moving the antenna takes time. In some extreme cases, after the radar scans (or *paints*) the target, several seconds may elapse before the antenna returns to paint the target again. A target traveling at 600 knots travels 1 mile every 5.45 seconds. A high-speed adversary can make good use of 1.5 to 2 seconds between radar scans. The enemy could use this time to make radical altitude or heading changes. The next time your radar paints the target, it could be a considerable distance from its previous position.

> NOTE: Generally, it is a good idea to begin with a maximum scan and get a complete view of the area ahead. Then, as you locate targets, narrow the scan pattern to focus on the ones that pose a threat.

Selecting a Range When configuring the HFR scan, always set the range first. As of Falcon 3.0D, every time the range is changed, the elevation scan reverts back to the default values. If you set the elevation first, you'll just have to do it again when you set the range.

Personal preferences may vary, but normally you should begin with a range of 80 nautical miles. You should always search a wide area, identify targets and threats, then focus on a particular contact or set of contacts. *Tunnel vision*, or focusing concentration on a narrow area, is one of the most common errors made by novice pilots. A pilot must at all times be aware of the total environment. Keeping tabs on multiple contacts in all directions is called *situational awareness*. It is difficult to surprise a situationally aware pilot during combat.

As Figure 8-14 shows, the range value is always initially 20 when NAM mode is selected. Press F8 once and notice that the range decrements to 10 nautical miles. Press F8 again and observe the result. The range should have changed to 80 nautical miles. Pressing F8 again reduces the range to 40, and a second press returns the range to the initial 20 nautical mile range. Now, hold the SHIFT key down while pressing F8. Notice that the range increases each time instead of decrementing. Remembering to press the SHIFT key can save you several precious seconds when you want to change to the next higher range value. Using either F8 or SHIFT-F8, set your range to 80 nautical miles.

Adjusting the Azimuth The default azimuth scan is always +/–60 degrees, the maximum available. Keeping with the doctrine of using a wide search initially, this is the azimuth scan that you want. However, take a few moments to experiment.

Watch the antenna azimuth indicator as it moves completely from side to side across the bottom of the REO. Press F9 and observe the results. The antenna indicator now only moves as far as the first gradient mark on either side of center. This is the minimum scan of +/–20 degrees. Pressing F9 again causes the indicator to move three marks (30 degrees) left and right of center (+/–30 degree scan). Finally, pressing F9 again reselects the full +/–60 degree scan. As with the range, holding SHIFT while pressing F9 reverses the order. Using either F9 or SHIFT-F9 sets your azimuth scan to +/–60 degrees.

Elevation Scan Considerations As previously stated, as of Falcon 3.0D, every time NAM mode is selected and every time the range is changed, the elevation scan is also changed. The exact altitudes being scanned with this setting will depend upon the altitude of your F-16 and the current range setting, but will generally be insufficient for long range searches.

For example, increase throttle to 100%. Pitch the nose up about 20 degrees. As you climb, watch closely the maximum and minimum altitude scan indicators. You will see that as your altitude increases, so does the maximum altitude being scanned. However, so does the lower altitude. Eventually, you will reach an altitude where the radar no longer scans completely to ground level (0 feet).

> **NOTE:** Maximum and minimum altitudes being scanned are directly related to your current altitude. The higher your F-16 is, the higher the maximum scanned altitude. However, the lower scan limit also increases. Low-flying bandits may pass undetected beneath your radar.

Adjusting the Elevation Scan Elevation scan has three options, one, two, and four bars. Use the F10 key to select between these options. Continually press F10 to cycle through the three options and start over again. As with the range and azimuth controls, holding SHIFT while pressing F10 reverses the selection order.

Level your F-16 at 15,000 feet. Press F10 until your radar scans from 0 to about 34,000 feet. Typically, you want to make sure that your radar is scanning completely down to 0 feet. Enemy aircraft more frequently fly at low altitudes (attempting to fly under the scans of ground based radar) than at high altitudes.

> **NOTE:** Normally, an altitude of 8,000 feet will ensure radar coverage down to 0 feet. If, at your current altitude, you cannot set the elevation to scan to 0 feet, lower the altitude of your F-16.

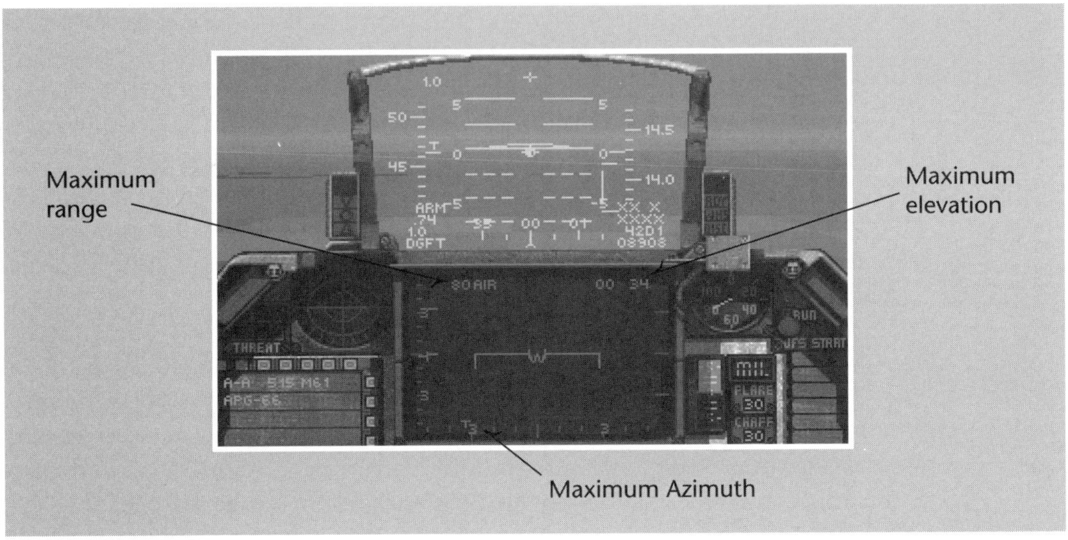

Figure 8-15 A Properly Configured REO for an Initial Search

Summary If you've followed the steps presented, your REO should now appear as in Figure 8-15. In the future, use the following guidelines when beginning an air-to-air search:

- Begin with the maximum scan available. Get a good picture of your environment, then focus your attention on contacts with the highest value or that pose the greatest threat.
- Set the range first and set it to 80 nautical miles.
- Set the azimuth scan to the maximum width of +/–60 degrees.
- Set your elevation scan last and select the tallest scan available.
- Adjust the altitude of your F-16 as necessary to ensure that the elevation scan extends to 0 feet. Depending upon terrain, this altitude will be between 8,000 and 9,000 feet.

Locating a Target

Now that your radar scan is properly configured, head for waypoint 2. Press SHIFT-B to bypass waypoint 1 and head for the new coordinates supplied by the AWACS. Shortly, green squares, or blips, should appear on your REO, as in Figure 8-16. These are your first radar contacts. They are near the top edge of the REO, indicating they are nearly 80 nautical miles away.

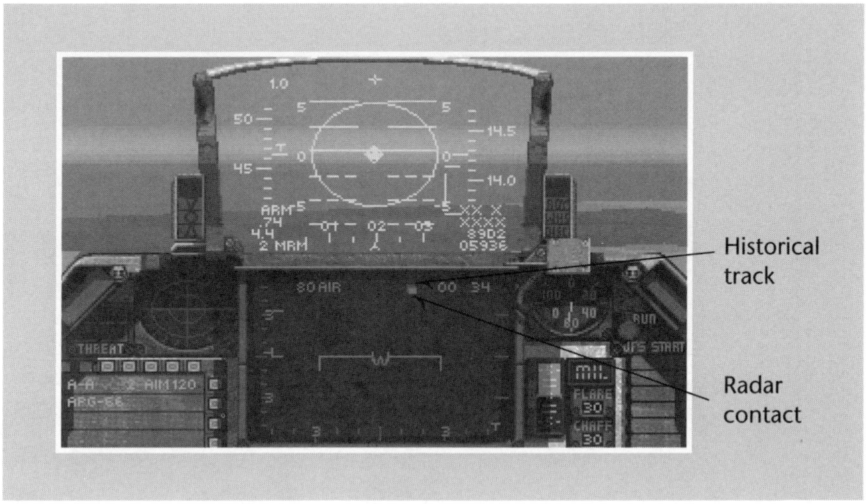

Figure 8-16 First Contact

Reading the Historical Track Fly toward the targets at a speed of 450 to 500 knots. As you fly, watch how the radar blips and their historical tracks move around the REO. Each time the REO is updated, the contacts are closer to you. This could mean that the contacts are headed toward you. It could also mean that the contacts are headed away from you, but moving slower than you and you're gaining on them.

Designate a Target Move the acquisition corrals to a target by pressing T. The corrals will surround one of the radar contacts as illustrated in Figure 8-17. Notice that the altitude indicator is now displayed along the left edge of the REO, just under the 10,000 feet mark. From this we can estimate that the target is flying around 9,000 feet.

Lock-On: Switching to SAM

You still don't know much about the target, though. It is now time to select SAM mode and check this guy out. Remember, there's only one way to select it: you must radar lock the designated contact in NAM mode. Radar lock the selected target by pressing Z. The square radar blip will now change to a diamond to indicate the successful lock. Figure 8-18 illustrates what you should now see.

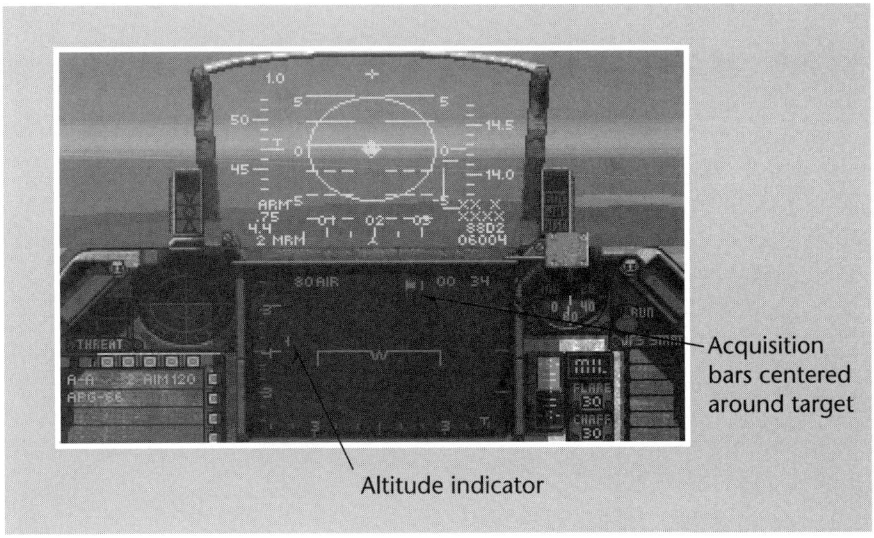

Figure 8-17 Designating a Target

Priority One: Identify the Target In this mission, you have an advantage because you know that all aircraft are friendly. In actual campaign missions, you won't have that luxury. Immediately after radar locking a target, you should always check its IFF signature. First, switch to the left cockpit view by pressing 4 and notice the gray color of the IFF light. Press N to interrogate the target's IFF transponder. If the target is friendly, you should hear a loud buzzing sound, and the IFF light will illuminate with a green glow. The buzzing will stop when you release the N key; however, the IFF light will remain illuminated as long as the friendly aircraft is radar locked. If the target had been a hostile aircraft, the IFF would not have illuminated and you would not have heard the buzz.

You were instructed to switch views for educational purposes only. Under normal circumstances, it is not necessary to verify the IFF light if you hear the confirmation buzz. Return to the normal cockpit view by pressing 3.

Target Data Block and Closure Rate Now check the target's data block. In Figure 8-18, you can see that the target is headed at 25 degrees (roughly the same heading as the F-16 in the figure) at a speed of 303 knots. This contact is flying an elliptical pattern. Depending upon how quickly

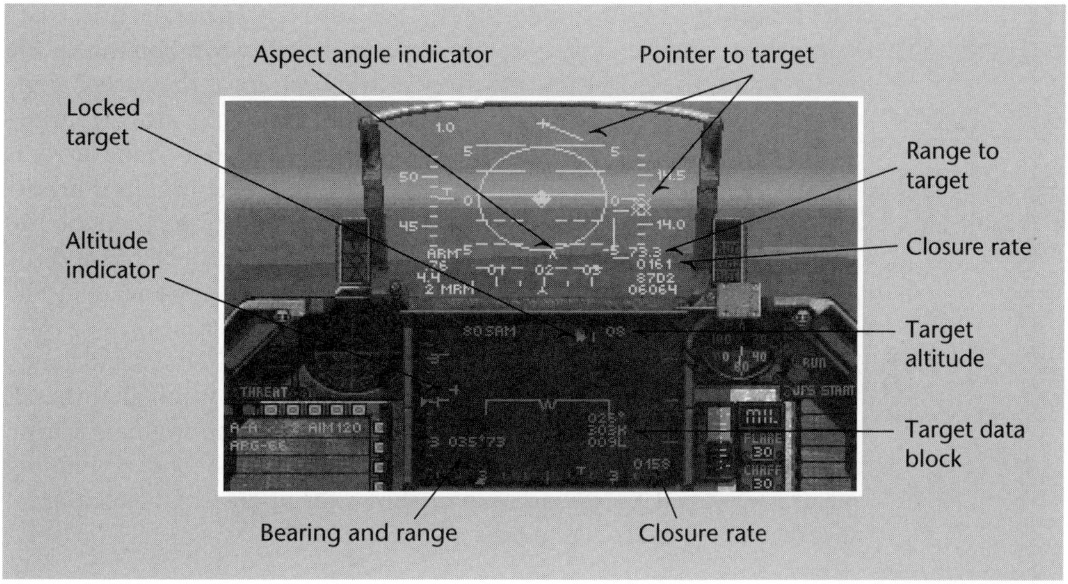

Figure 8-18 SAM Mode Lock-On

you locate and lock the target and how much you deviated from the assigned course, the values you see may vary. If you took a long time to lock the target, it may have reversed course and be headed toward you now. This text assumes you acquired the target within a reasonable amount of time and have a view similar to Figure 8-18.

In this example, the target is indeed headed away from you, but due to your superior speed, you are overtaking it. As the closure rate in the bottom right corner indicates, your speed is 158 nautical miles per hour greater than the target's. Next, the aspect-angle indicator reads 09 L, indicating you are almost directly behind the target. Remember from Figure 8-6, the lower the aspect angle, the closer you are to being centered behind the target.

Bearing, Range, and Altitude The bottom left corner of the REO indicates the bearing and range to the target. The number preceding the circular symbol is the heading you must fly in order to point directly at the target (in this case, 35 degrees). The number following the circular symbol indicates that the range to the target is 73 nautical miles. The numeric altitude indicator in the upper right corner of the REO shows the actual altitude of the target to be 8,000 feet.

HUD Display In SAM mode, the HUD will display repeats of critical data (aspect angle, range to target, and closure rate) as well as symbols indicating exactly where the target is. The arrow at the bottom of the aspect angle indicator shows that the target is heading almost directly away from the F-16, as previously indicated by the REO display. The range to the target is displayed as 73.3, slightly more precise than the range displayed on the REO. The closure rate is displayed as 163. This is slightly faster than the 158 displayed on the REO. Due to the rate at which data on the HUD and the REO are updated, sometimes there are negligible discrepancies in the displayed values.

When the target is within the borders of the HUD, a small target designator box is superimposed over it to highlight its position. In this case, the target is not visible in the HUD. Instead of a box, a line originating from the top center of the HUD points toward the target. The symbol resembling several overlapped Xs, or hash marks, shows the approximate position of the target along the HUD's border.

Focusing the Attack: Switching to STT

Suppose for a moment that this is a hostile contact and you want to devote your entire attention to it. You may encounter a situation where the REO is filled with friendly radar contacts that you want to ignore while you concentrate on the bandit. This is the role of STT: tracking a single target. Press the Z key again to switch to STT mode. Your screen should now appear as in Figure 8-19.

The HUD in this mode is identical to the HUD used by SAM mode. The REO is identical to the REO used by SAM mode—with two exceptions. First, no historic tracks are displayed, only the diamond radar blip is shown. Second, no other contacts are displayed. There may be over 100 aircraft flying in front of you, but only the locked target will be shown on the REO. STT mode must be used cautiously. Focusing too long on a single target allows other enemies to sneak up behind and kill you.

Breaking Lock

Because you've identified this contact as a friendly, you may want to ignore it and resume your long range search. You can break a radar lock in SAM or STT modes at any time by pressing X. This breaks the lock and the radar reverts to its previous mode. In the case of this lesson, breaking the STT lock will revert the radar back to NAM mode. Press X now and break the radar lock.

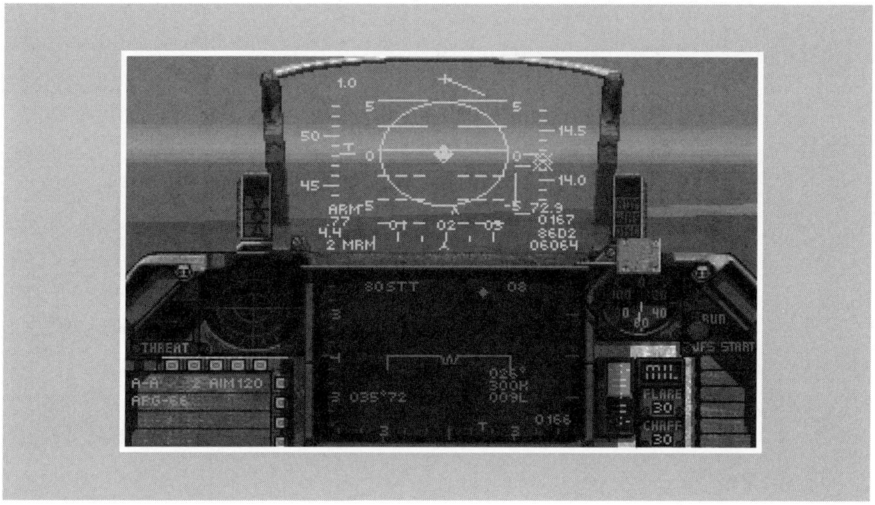

Figure 8-19 STT Mode Lock-On

Notice that the REO is cleared, but the acquisition corrals still remain over the last known position of the contact. As described in the section entitled "SAM Mode Pitfalls and Caveats," the azimuth scan will remain centered on these "stuck" corrals. You should now recenter the corrals by pressing X to clear the REO followed by T to move the corrals before any radar contacts are redisplayed. The timing is critical, and will probably take several attempts before you are successful. Sometimes, it may be useful to change the radar range to a lesser value so that no contacts will be displayed. Press T to center the corrals, then reset the range and elevation scans.

Heading for Waypoint 2

Press SHIFT-B to bypass waypoint 2 and head for waypoint 3. Unless you've grossly deviated from the assigned course, waypoint 3 should be almost due north of your position. Reconfigure your radar for a maximum scan. Reset the range to 80 by pressing F8, select a +/–60 degree azimuth scan by using the F9 key, and select the maximum elevation scan by pressing F10. Make sure that the elevation is scanning completely down to 0 feet. You may have to adjust your altitude to accomplish this. Shortly, your screen should appear similar to Figure 8-20.

In this example, the F-16 is flying at a heading of 5 degrees, at a speed of 550 knots, and an altitude of 19,600 feet. The NAM mode radar has a selected range of 80 nautical miles, and is scanning all altitudes from 0 to

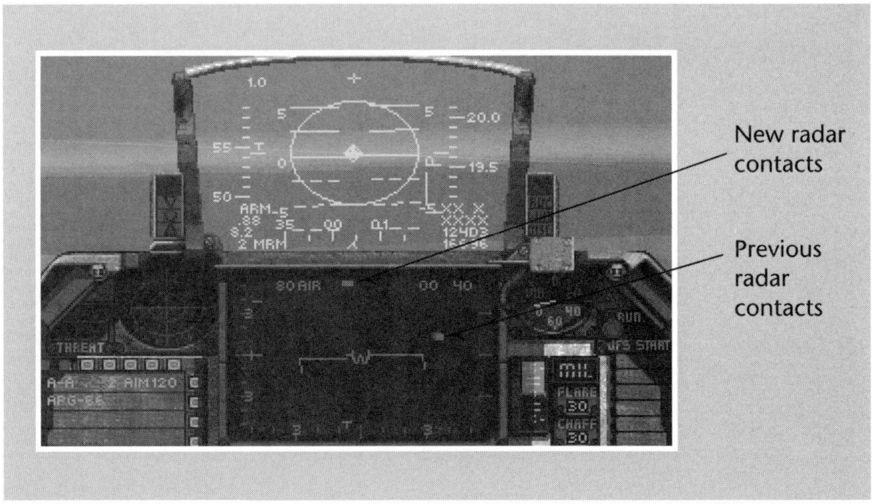

Figure 8-20 New Radar Contacts

40,000 feet. Because of the heading of the previous contacts, they are still visible on the right edge of the REO. They are slightly above the vertical center of the REO, indicating their range is approximately 50 nautical miles. New contacts just within the upper edge of the REO are almost 80 nautical miles away.

Focus on New Contacts

You've already determined thatthe original contacts are no threat and you have no further interest in them. As you'll notice in Figure 8-20, the old contacts are positioned just to the right of the 30 degree azimuth indicator. This tells you that if you select an azimuth scan of +/–30 degrees or less, the old contacts will no longer be displayed. Press SHIFT-F9 to select the +/–30 degree scan. The old contacts will disappear, and your attention is focused on the new contacts.

Lock and Identify New Contacts

Turn your F-16 so that the new contact is centered in the REO. This points your nose directly at this contact. Use T to designate a contact and Z to radar lock it to select the new contact and switch to SAM mode. You may have to press the T key several times before the desired contact is designated. When you have the new contact locked, press N to interro-

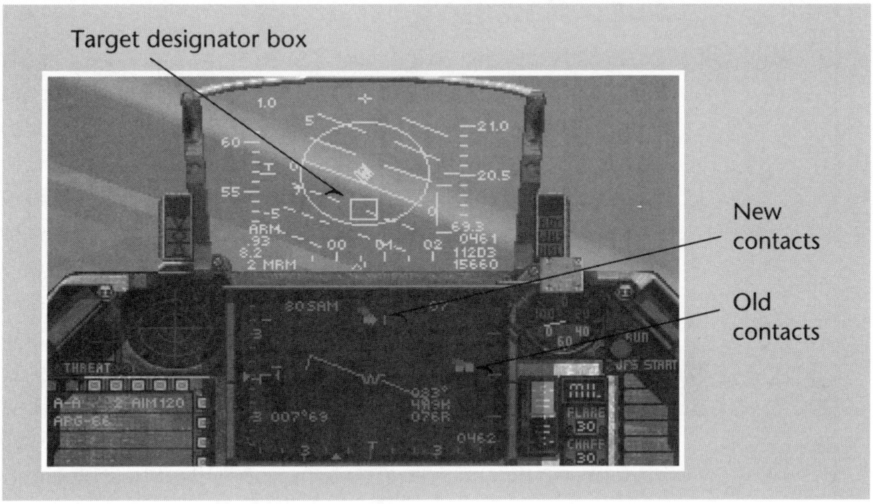

Figure 8-21 Radar Lock on New Contacts

gate its IFF signature. You should not hear the buzz; this contact is a bandit! Your screen should now resemble Figure 8-21.

These aircraft are flying an east/west race track pattern. Depending upon how quickly you encounter these aircraft, what you see on your screen may vary slightly from Figure 8-21. In Figure 8-21, a second square blip can be seen alongside the locked blip, indicating there are at least two aircraft in this group. They are heading 83 degrees, at a speed of 449 knots, and an altitude of 7,000 feet. Because of the huge offset between the F-16's heading and theirs, the aspect angle is high, 76R. Closure rate is 462 knots.

Doppler's Weakness: High Aspect Angles

This is a dangerous angle from which to approach the targets. As you continue to fly directly ahead, the aspect angle will begin to approach 90°. Not only is it difficult for missiles to track a target at a high aspect angle, but as you now know, Doppler radar sees little or no frequency shift in the radar reflections from targets at or near a 90° aspect angle. The radar, therefore, believes the target to be stationary and nothing more than a reflection from the ground. As you fly toward these aircraft, suddenly and without warning your SAM mode radar lock will break and the radar will revert to NAM mode. This is called *beaming*. Enemy fighters frequently try to break radar locks by beaming. There's only one tactic that is effective against this problem: alter your heading so that the aspect angle is no longer 90°.

Auto Ranging

Fly directly towards waypoint 3. Maintain radar lock on the targets north of you. Keep a close watch on the targets. If they beam your radar and break your lock, press T to designate a contact and Z to radar lock it. As you close on the targets, they will move lower on the REO. As the range approaches 40 nautical miles, the blips will move closer to the vertical center of the REO. When the range decreases to 42 nautical miles, watch the REO closely. When the range drops below 40 nautical miles, the radar range will automatically change to 40. Your screen should now appear similar to Figure 8-22.

The problem here is that the antenna elevation scan has been automatically adjusted too. As of Falcon 3.0D, any time the range is changed, whether manually or automatically, the elevation scan is also changed. In this case, the lower scan indicator no longer is set to zero. Sometimes the auto-ranging function will adjust the elevation scan enough that the target is no longer within the scan pattern and the lock is broken. If this happens, you must quickly use the F10 key and reset the elevation scan to regain the contact.

Close Range: Using Radar in a Dogfight

Turn your F-16 and head directly for the target. Watch the range closely. When you get within 12 miles of the target, select the close range, hands-free radar mode ACM by pressing F6. You will lose contact with the target,

Figure 8-22 40-Nautical-Mile Range Automatically Selected

Figure 8-23 Selecting ACM Mode

but only temporarily, so don't worry. Figure 8-23 illustrates how your screen should look.

Hands-Free Scanning: Using ACM ACM mode uses fixed values for the range, azimuth scan, and elevation scan. You have no control over where the antenna points. ACM will automatically designate and lock the closest contact it detects. You have no control over target designation. ACM mode is designed to provide close range searches and radar locks without pilot intervention. This allows the pilot to concentrate on maneuvering and using weapons. The only thing the pilot has to do is press the N key to interrogate the target's IFF signature. Select ACM mode when you're about to engage in a close range dogfight.

Automatic Target Selection When you close to within 10 miles of the targets, ACM mode will automatically radar lock the closest one and switch to STT mode. Your screen should resemble Figure 8-24. Refer to the previous sections on STT mode for details on HUD and REO displays.

Breaking Lock You may break radar lock at any time by pressing X. The radar will revert back to ACM mode. However, ACM mode will immediately reacquire the closest target and re-select STT mode. If you want to break the radar lock completely, you will need to switch to NAM mode by pressing F5.

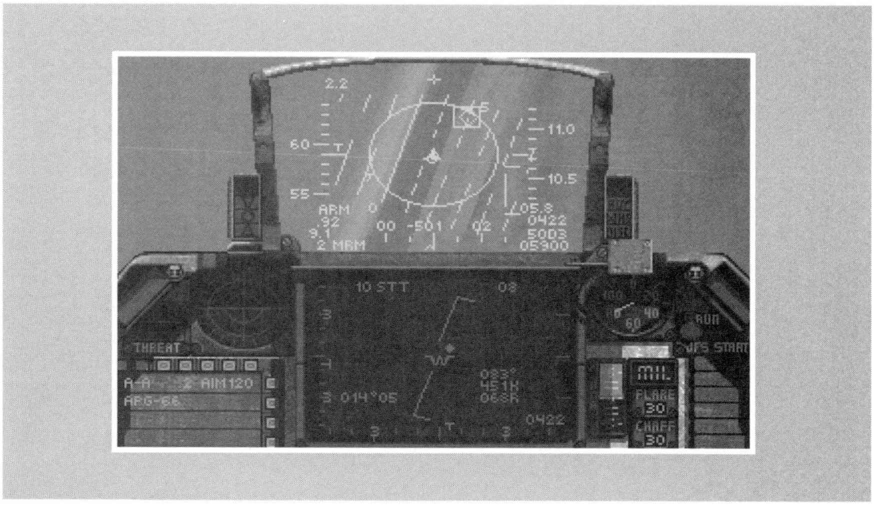

Figure 8-24 Automatic Selection of STT Mode

Combat End Game

You've nearly completed the training mission. The successful result of an air-to-air search is the destruction of an enemy aircraft. If you've followed the mission steps closely, you should now be about four miles from the bandit. Press ENTER repeatedly until the AIM-120 is the selected air-to-air weapon. The missile should immediately track and lock the bandit. Fire the missile and down the bandit to successfully end this exercise.

ECM and HFR

Falcon 3.0 versions prior to Falcon 3.0D had numerous problems with the usage of *electronic counter measures* (ECM) equipment, also known as *radar jammers*. Jamming equipment works in conjunction with the TWI. When the TWI detects that an enemy radar has locked on to your aircraft, the information is passed to the ECM gear which subsequently broadcasts high powered bursts of radar energy at the offending radar site. The bursts generated by the ECM gear become confused with the actual radar energy being reflected by your aircraft and the radar operator loses contact with you.

ECM Operation

In versions Falcon 3.0 through Falcon 3.0C, ECM acted like a magic shield. Once the pilot activated ECM, no radar could ever lock on to him. That was hardly realistic and has been changed in Falcon 3.0D.

Jamming One Radar at a Time In both the real world and Falcon 3.0D, ECM can jam only a single radar at a time. If multiple radar sites are locked on to a single aircraft, the ECM pod focuses on one radar source, ignoring all others. When the TWI indicates this radar is no longer locked on to the aircraft, the ECM pod then focuses on the next radar source, ignoring the previously jammed radar and all other radar sources. This procedure is repeated until all radars have been jammed.

Previously Jammed Radars Are Still a Threat For example, say an F-16 is flying an attack mission and is locked on to by three ground radar sites. The ECM gear focuses on a single radar and attempts to jam it. When the ECM gear switches its attention to a new radar source, the currently jammed radar is no longer affected. This radar is once again capable of locking on to the aircraft. While the ECM gear is busy with the second and third radars, the first radar may reacquire the F-16.

Many radar guided surface-to-air missiles receive constant guidance instructions from the ground radar. If the ground radar is jammed, the missile will be unable to track the target aircraft. However, if the jamming equipment switches to jam another radar and the first radar reacquires the F-16, new instructions are sent to the missile and it will again pursue the target aircraft.

> **WARNING:** ECM is not a magic shield. It will usually jam a single radar successfully, but it can only jam a single radar at a time. If a previously jammed radar reacquires radar lock on your F-16, new guidance instructions are sent to airborne missiles about the location of your aircraft. If multiple radar sites lock on to your aircraft, you must use a combination of ECM, chaff, and evasive maneuvers to evade incoming missiles.

ECM Against Air-to-Air Radars

Prior to Falcon 3.0D, ECM had no effect on airborne radars. Falcon 3.0D has changed that. ECM now has the capability to jam airborne radars as well as ground radars. ECM has two effects against an airborne radar:

- Breaks a radar lock-on—If an enemy aircraft has a radar lock on you, ECM may be able to break that lock. Due to the nature of enemy radar guided air-to-air missiles (see Chapter 9, *Red Flag: Advanced Flight School*, and Chapter 11, *Secrets and Tactics of the Enemy*, for details), enemy aircraft must maintain a radar lock on your aircraft until their missile impacts it. If the radar lock is broken, the missile will go awry.
- Creates *ghosts*—ECM can cause false images to appear on the radar operator's screen. These false images, called ghosts, quickly appear and disappear making it difficult for the operator to select a true target. Even if the operator gets lucky and happens to lock on to the real radar image, ECM will probably quickly break that lock, making the real target appear as another ghost.

Computer-Controlled Pilots and ECM

As of Falcon 3.0D, all computer-controlled pilots, both friendly and enemy, have the ability to use ECM. Before a friendly pilot can use ECM, you must load an ALQ-131 ECM pod onto his aircraft. Enemy pilots, however, are randomly assigned ECM gear; some aircraft will have it, some won't during each mission. Effective use of ECM is dependent upon the pilot's ability levels, whether he's a friendly or an enemy pilot. Pilots with lower ability scores are less likely to engage ECM than those with higher ability scores.

Enemy ECM Use

Whenever enemy aircraft use ECM, the jamming transmission will be detected by friendly AWACS aircraft. They will contact you over the radio and warn you of the enemy's use of ECM equipment. During aerial combat, you have to contend with the same effects of jamming that the enemy does: broken radar locks and ghost images.

You already know that an enemy pilot can break a radar lock by beaming your radar. That technique, however, only works at 90° aspect angles. If a radar lock is broken at some other aspect, you can be reasonably sure the enemy is using ECM. Be prepared; when the enemy uses ECM, many ghost images will rapidly appear and disappear on your REO.

> NOTE: By watching the ghost images, you can monitor the approximate direction to the enemy aircraft. However, you will be unable to lock on to this aircraft, determine its exact location, or its distance from your aircraft.

Countering ECM Usage

Radar energy dissipates as it travels. The farther away the target is, the weaker the reflected radar energy will be when it returns. At long ranges, the high-powered bursts from ECM equipment can completely hide low-power reflected signals. However, this changes as the distance from the radar to the target decreases.

As the range to the target decreases, the strength of the reflected energy is less affected. At some point, the strength of the reflected signals will be as strong as, if not stronger, than the strength of the jamming signals. This point is unique to every radar type and depends upon a multitude of atmospheric conditions.

Once the target is within this range, however, jamming has little or no effect. The strong reflected signals now mask the jamming signals and the radar operator clearly sees the true radar image instead of ghosts. This condition, where the reflected energy is stronger than the jamming signals, is called *burn through*. Once a radar is able to burn through jamming signals, ECM equipment is useless.

WARNING: The closer you get to a SAM launcher, AAA cannon, or enemy aircraft, the less effective your ALQ-131 ECM pod is against its radar. Eventually, your ECM effectiveness will dwindle completely. At close ranges, ECM has no effect against enemy radars. This works in both directions; the closer you get to an enemy aircraft, the less effective his ECM equipment will be against your radar.

Therefore, always keep the following in mind:

- Engage enemy ground sites at maximum range. This increases the effectiveness of your ECM equipment.
- When you encounter enemy aircraft using ECM, either disengage and flee, or fly directly toward them. Eventually, you will get close enough that their jamming gear has no effect against your radar.
- Enemy ECM, like yours, is coupled to their TWIs. If you stay in NAM or SAM mode and his TWI from activating (don't get a "hard lock" on the target) you can prevent his ECM from working against you. Avoid locking up an ECM-capable target until absolutely necessary.

ECM is a powerful tool, and you should be well versed in its operation. Use ECM gear liberally; it can save your pilots' lives.

Conclusion

You now know the ins and outs of HFR. A lot of data has been presented in this chapter, but true expertise in HFR can not be learned in a single lesson. It will take many missions and lots of practice to fully master HFR. At a very minimum you should remember the following key items:

- How to switch radar modes.
- How to adjust range, azimuth, and elevation scans.
- How to designate and lock a target.
- How to interrogate a target's IFF signature.

Questions: Using HFR

1. Name the four HFR operating modes.
2. What is the primary advantage of Doppler radar?
3. What does "beaming the radar" mean?
4. True or False: if the REO has been set to a 40 mile range and a blip is displayed just above the waterline, this means that the contact is at a higher altitude than your F-16.
5. What radar mode is used for short range, hands-free search and target acquisition?

Answers

1. NAM, SAM, ACM, and STT.
2. Radars can use the Doppler effect to filter out spurious returns from objects on the ground.
3. Flying perpendicular to the radar source, thus presenting no Doppler shift in the returned signal and breaking the radar lock.
4. False. The waterline has no relationship to the radar blips.
5. ACM.

9

CHAPTER

Red Flag: Advanced Flight School

"USAF Credits Realistic Training for Success of Desert Storm Operations."

"[Col. Gary] Voellger said [pilots] flying operation combat missions closely followed procedures they practiced in Red Flag [exercises]...."

> -*Aviation Week & Space Technology,* "USAF Credits Realistic Training For Success of Desert Storm Operations," p.25, March 4, 1991, McGraw Hill Publishing.

ZNR CCCCC
I 01 0830Z JAN 92

FM RED FLAG HQ DIV//GEN WAITE//
TO 386TH FSFORUM SQU CMDR//COL BASHAM//

BT
C L A S S I F I E D
REF: RED FLAG ADVANCED FLIGHT SCHOOL (C)
(C) THE 386TH FSFORUM "BASHERS" AND 387TH FSFORUM "CRUNCHERS" ARE ORDERED TO REPORT TO NELLIS AFB IMMEDIATELY TO ATTEND ADVANCED FLIGHT SCHOOL.
ET

There's a new training program available at Nellis AFB. You've been ordered to report back to Nellis to attend Advanced Flight school. The last time you were at Nellis you breezed through Basic Flight school and graduated with honors. Soon after graduation, conflict broke out in

Kuwait, Israel, and Panama. Because of the shortage of experienced squadron leaders and your exemplary record, you were assigned a squadron command and were quickly shipped overseas. Your squadron fought hard and costly battles in the following months. Many fine young pilots were lost to enemy weapons. Finally, a welcome, but costly, peace was achieved.

However, regional stability is questionable, to say the least. Around the globe, tense cease-fire treaties are cautiously being observed by the U.S. and its adversaries. Political negotiations are once again on the verge of breakdown and military forces around the world are poised on the brink of war.

Fortunately, this lull in combat provides you and your unit a chance to resupply and hone your war-making skills. To this end, you're returning to Nellis to undergo the most intensive training of your career. Good luck, you're going to need it.

Introduction

Before proceeding, you must first install the custom Red Flag training missions included on the accompanying floppy disk. If you have not already done so, refer to the instructions in Appendix A, *The Falcon 3 Flight Disk,* for installing the Red Flag mission files.

The Air Combat School Red Flag missions included in the Falcon 3.0 package teach you the basics of cockpit operations and weapons delivery in terms of a single aircraft operating alone in a hostile environment. However, actual Falcon 3.0 campaigns rarely (if ever) involve a single aircraft operating alone. Instead, success in campaign missions depends upon the coordination of multiple sections of F-16s from your squadron to maximize your offensive potential.

Additionally, there usually are unexpected friendly aircraft, known as *strangers,* operating in close proximity to your squadron. More important than delivering your weapons on target is avoiding so-called *friendly fire casualties,* a glorified phrase meaning that an individual or unit mistakenly attacked and injured another individual or unit from the same army or from the army of an ally.

Friendly fire usually results from a condition known as *the fog of war.* During poor visibility conditions (such as night, heavy rain, or cloud cover), locating a target becomes difficult. When the battlefield becomes heavily congested with friendly and enemy forces, it becomes even more difficult to determine if that target is friendly or hostile. Sometimes communication links break down, coordinated units lose track of one another and mistakenly attack each other. All of these situations describe war fog. Indiscriminate use of weapons under these circumstances is downright dangerous. Falcon 3.0 allows you to fire on an unidentified target. However, destroy a friendly unit and you'll promptly receive a court-martial and your flight status will be revoked.

The Red Flag missions in this chapter are designed to teach you to coordinate multiple flights of aircraft (in a congested and sometimes confused environment), so that you'll be able to overcome enemy defenses and achieve the primary objective. Each individual mission focuses on a single task, such as *Close Air Support* (CAS), *Strike missions,* and *Escort missions.* Additionally, each mission is part of an overall storyline from a typical campaign. Each mission advances the story as it trains you.

Each mission consists of:

- A tactical communication from Red Flag HQ to your squadron.
- A dialogue that advances the overall storyline.
- A briefing from your Red Flag instructor.
- A preflight mission analysis on objectives, waypoints, recon information, etc.
- A detailed walk-through of each mission complete with screen photos.
- A mission debriefing with the Red Flag instructor.

Configuration Requirements

Although you may configure Falcon 3.0 anyway you desire, the training missions assume that your system is configured with SKILL LEVEL configured to ADVANCED. All training missions use the High Fidelity Radar (HFR) mode, and either the COMPLEX or the HI FIDELITY flight model. Using other configurations will produce results that vary from the ones in this book. If you are unclear about how to set your configuration, refer to the "Configuration" section in Chapter 2.

If you have not done so, please read Chapter 3, *Learning to Fly,* Chapter 5, *Using Weapons,* Chapter 6, *Introduction to Red Flag,* and Chapter 8, *Using High Fidelity Radar.* To maximize training in flight school, you should be familiar with terms and jargon introduced in earlier chapters. Advanced Flight School missions discuss only the use of the HFR mode of radar.

The following missions are designed to teach advanced combat principles and doctrine. They are not designed to teach the beginning pilot how to operate weapons. Each mission introduces new material while building upon lessons learned from previous missions. To achieve full training benefit, *you should execute the following missions in order!* Each mission becomes progressively more difficult; the enemies will fire at you, and there will be friendly aircraft you must avoid shooting. Welcome to the major league, let the training begin!

ZNR CCCCC
I 10 0830Z JAN 92

FM RED FLAG HQ DIV//GEN WAITE//
TO ALL UNITS RED FLAG THEATER OF OPERATION

BT
T O P S E C R E T
REF: OFFENSIVE ACTION (T)
(T) TREATY NEGOTIATIONS HAVE STALLED. ENEMY FORCES ARE REDEPLOYING ALONG FRIENDLY BORDERS. INTEL ESTIMATES ENEMY FORCES WILL BE COMBAT READY IN 3 DAYS AND WILL PROBABLY ATTACK SHORTLY THEREAFTER.

THE PRESIDENT HAS AUTHORIZED PREEMPTIVE, OFFENSIVE MILITARY ACTIONS TO ENSURE THE SOVEREIGNTY OF THE UNITED STATES. THESE ACTIONS ARE UNDER THE DIRECT CONTROL OF GEN. WAITE, RED FLAG HQ.

INITIALLY, ENEMY AIR DEFENSES WILL BE ATTACKED TO OPEN A SAFE CORRIDOR INTO ENEMY TERRITORY. TACTICAL BOMBERS WILL INGRESS THROUGH THIS CORRIDOR AND ATTACK HIGH VALUE, STRATEGIC TARGETS.

ALL UNITS ARE HEREBY PLACED ON FULL ALERT. STANDBY FOR FURTHER ORDERS....

ET

Mission 1: Operation Lights Out

A Coordinated Attack on Enemy Nuclear Facilities

ZNR CCCCC
I 11 2345Z JAN 92
FM RED FLAG HQ DIV//GEN WAITE//
TO 386TH FSFORUM SQU CMDR//COL BASHAM//

BT
S E C R E T
REF: DAILY ATO, OP:LIGHTS OUT (S)
(S) TODAY'S TARGET IS THE NUCLEAR FACILITY NEAR THE BORDER OF QUADRANGLES MN AND NN. RECON ESTIMATES AIR DEFENSES TO BE HEAVY TO THE SOUTH AND EAST OF THE FACILITY, AND LIGHT TO THE NORTH AND WEST. ENEMY FIGHTER ACTIVITY IS EXPECTED TO BE LOW.

AIR ASSETS FROM THE 37TH TFW/ 415TH SQU HAVE BEEN ASSIGNED TO ATTACK THE FACILITY AT 1830 HOURS LOCAL TIME, APPROACHING FROM THE NORTH. YOUR SQUADRON WILL PROVIDE SAM SUPPRESSION AND TARCAP. ELIMINATE SURF TO AIR THREATS AND PROVIDE SAFE ROUTE OF EGRESS FOR ATTACK AIRCRAFT SOUTH OF THE TARGET. HAVE YOUR AC ON STATION BY 1830 HRS.
ET

Nellis AFB, NV—1600 HRS

You've just donned your flight suit, picked up your notepad, and are headed for your squadron's briefing room. Despite the serenity of the late afternoon sun, the entire air base seems ready to snap from the tension. For the last two weeks you've been performing drills, practicing bombing, and flying CAP sorties. You've been part of a routine defensive screen assigned to monitor enemy forces while high-level government officials negotiate treaties in Washington.

Rumors circulated that the talks were breaking down. The rumors were substantiated when the president announced that foreign government officials refused to negotiate and have walked away from the meetings. The president, having exhausted all other options, set a deadline for the opposing forces to comply with U.S. demands by 12 noon yesterday, Washington D.C. time.

The deadline came and went. Enemy forces, rather than standing down, went to full alert and began redeploying to counter U.S. forces assigned to the region. Your squadron waited nervously to see how the president would respond. Then, the communiqué arrived. The president authorized a preemptive strike against enemy forces to begin tonight.

You've been assigned to fly in the first wave of attacks against the enemy. Shortly, you'll be briefed on your mission objectives and be airborne over hostile forces. You breathe a sigh of relief knowing that this is all just a training mission... or is it?

You enter the briefing room, find a seat. The Red Flag instructor enters the room, steps to the podium, and begins to speak . . .

The Mission Briefing

"Alright, pay attention. We are now in a state of war. The president has ordered preemptive, first-strikes against the enemy forces before they can mobilize and attack us. "

The Mission: Support Stealth Fighters

"Red Flag HQ," the instructor continues, "has targeted an enemy nuclear facility that is being used both for power generation and weapons research. Destruction of this site will not only disrupt enemy command, control, and communications abilities, but will also halt their nuclear weapons program. The site is heavily defended to the south and east with AAA and SAMs, although the north and west are apparently unguarded. Enemy air activity is expected to be low.

"F-117A Stealth Fighters are scheduled to attack the facility at 1830 hours. The F-117s will ingress from the north to avoid enemy defenses, attack the primary target, and egress to the south. That's where this squadron comes in. We will fly four sorties in support of the Stealths. This mission will launch at 1800 hours. Aircraft are to be on station, or begin executing your attack, by 1830 hours. Two 2-plane sections will fly to the target area and arrive shortly before 1830 hours local time."

Flight 1: Your—Job Defense Suppression

The instructor continues, "The first section will locate and attack enemy surface-to-air defenses stationed south of the target. You are responsible for ensuring that the Stealths have a clear route of egress. This section will fly a high visibility profile, allow enemy radars to lock them up (thereby revealing their positions), and attack them with anti-radiation missiles. Each aircraft in section 1 will carry two AGM-88A HARM and two AGM-45A SHRIKE anti-radiation missiles, two AIM-9M air-to-air missiles, and an ALQ-131 Electronic Counter Measures (ECM) pod. "

Anti-Radiation Missile Basic Rules "Enemy surface-to-air radars employ two types of radar: continuous wave and pulse-Doppler. Continuous wave radars will be displayed on your Threat Warning Indicator (TWI) by a green box with the numeral '1' inside. Pulse-Doppler radars will be indicated on the TWI by a green square with the numeral '2' inside. AGM-88s are effective against both radar types and have a range of 30 nautical miles. The AGM-45s, however, are effective against continuous wave radars only, and have a range of only 12 nautical miles.

"Overall, the AGM-88 is a much more effective weapon, but it is much more expensive. At short ranges against continuous wave radars, you should fire AGM-45s and save the AGM-88s for standoff attacks. Remember, the F-16's TWI has a 30 nautical mile range. Therefore, any ground radar displayed on the TWI is fair game for the AGM-88."

Jamming Enemy Radars "The ALQ-131 ECM pod is highly effective against both continuous wave and pulse-Doppler radars. However, most radar sites will cease transmitting when they realize they're being jammed, and, thereby, greatly reduce the effectiveness (if not render useless) your HARMS and SHRIKES. Also, each time the enemy launches a radar-guided SAM (which will be designated by a small green square on the TWI) and the radar source shuts down, the missile will go awry and be lost.

"Therefore, the ALQ should not be activated while attacking a radar site. If the ALQ must be activated, the pilot should wait until at least one missile has been launched, resulting in at least the loss of missiles to the enemy. This is not as costly as the loss of the SAM launcher, but is better than nothing.

"A single ALQ unit can only jam a single radar source at a time. The ALQ transmits a burst of radar energy of the same frequency back at the radar transmitter. The flood of signals from the ECM drown out the radar's real returns, thus breaking the lock. If multiple sites are locked on to your aircraft, the ALQ will jam one, then the next, and the next until each lock has been broken. When the ALQ proceeds to the next radar source, the previous radar may reacquire a lock on your aircraft. The ALQ will continue to cycle through all radar threats, and will eventually focus on radars that were previously jammed, but have reacquired your F-16."

SAMs and AAA: The Enemy's Claws "The enemy is primarily equipped with Soviet-built hardware and fields three mobile, radar guided surface-to-air defense systems: the SA-6 Gainful SAM launcher, the SA-8 Gecko SAM launcher, and the ZSU-23-4 Shilka AAA cannon. Additionally, enemy infantry may be carrying SA-7 Grail, shoulder-launched, heat-seeking SAMs."

AAA: The 23mm Nightmare "The ZSU-23-4 cannons employ a continuous wave radar. Therefore, AAA sites will appear as a box with a '1' on the TWI. Both the AGM-45A and the AGM-88A are effective against this radar type. The ZSU-23-4 is a close-range weapon, having only a one mile range and a ceiling of 2,000 feet. Don't be fooled by its short range, though; its 23mm shells can ravage an F-16.

"The ALQ-131 will jam the ZSU's guidance radar; however, the cannon can still be fired 'blindly' at you. ZSU-23-4s usually are deployed in groups and can throw a lot of lead in the air. They don't have to hit you if they can make a wall that you can't fly through! Worse yet, a 23mm shell could hit your ALQ-131 and destroy it, leaving you naked against other radars. Stay at least 2,000 feet above ground level and AAA fire should be no problem."

Radar-Guided SAMs: The SA-6 and SA-8 "The SA-6 SAM launcher employs a continuous wave radar and will, therefore, be displayed as a box with a '1' on the TWI. Either the AGM-45 or the AGM-88 will be effective against the SA-6. The SA-6 has a 30 nautical mile range and an effective ceiling of 47,000 feet. This weapon, however, is useless if its guidance radar is jammed. Activating your ALQ-131 renders the SA-6 a non-threat.

"The SA-8 SAM launcher employs pulse-Doppler radar. Therefore, it will appear as a box with a '2' on the TWI. Only the AGM-88 is effective against this type of radar. The SA-8 has a 10 nautical mile range and a ceiling of 20,000 feet. Like the SA-6, though, when the guidance radar is jammed, the entire weapon system becomes useless. The ALQ-131 is highly effective against this weapon system."

SAMs May Reacquire Radar Lock "Don't forget, as long as a radar site has a lock, constant guidance instructions are sent to the SAM. If the

SAM is evaded and flies past the aircraft, but the ground operator still has a lock, the SAM will be redirected back at the targeted aircraft. Additionally, if the ECM gear successfully jams the radar, but the radar later reacquires the F-16, the missile will be directed back at the targeted aircraft. The ALQ-131 is effective, but it's not a magic shield. You will still have to rely on chaff and maneuvering to survive attacking SAMs."

Heat Seeking Threats: The SA-7 "Enemy infantry will probably be equipped with the SA-7 Grail infrared homing, shoulder launched SAM. This missile sports a one mile range and has an effective altitude of 12,000 feet. Because IR homing transmits no signals, it will not appear on your TWI. Other onboard sensors may detect the missile exhaust, however, and the MISSILE warning light will illuminate.

"The ALQ-131 has no effect against these missiles; you'll be totally dependent on flares and maneuvering to defeat them. Remember, IR missiles home on the heat from your exhaust. While it may seem advantageous to slam the throttle to afterburner and extend out of the missile's range, you'll probably only make yourself a brighter, more visible target. "

Evading SAMs "Instead, it is usually more effective to reduce throttle (thereby reducing heat), fire a series of flares, and make a sharp, out of plane maneuver, such as performing a split S, or breaking high. If you have visual contact with the missile, allow the missile to close, then break hard TOWARD the missile to cross inside the missile's turn radius. For example, if the missile is behind your right wing, break to the right. This procedure is also valid for avoiding radar guided SAMs (should your ALQ-131 be damaged), except you should fire chaff instead of flares and you should not decrease throttle."

Tactic Summary "Basically, the F-16s in section 1 should follow these tactics:

- Engage radar sites at maximum range. This allows the F-16 the option to extend beyond range of the radar source and escape.
- Fly a high visibility profile, allow radar sites to lock on.
- Use AGM-88s against all pulse-Doppler threats ('2' on TWI) at any range, and against continuous wave threats ('1' on TWI) at ranges of greater than 12 miles.
- Use AGM-45s against continuous wave threats ('1' on TWI) at ranges under 12 miles.

- Do not engage ECM unless a SAM is inbound.
- Extend away from AAA sites. ECM will jam AAA targeting radars, but AAA can still be fired 'blindly' in your direction.
- Do not attempt to use the ALQ to jam heat-seeking missiles.

"Above all else," the instructor concludes, "remain calm. Do not panic. The ALQ is highly effective against radar-guided SAMs. If you get in a jam, activate the ECM and get clear of the area. Once clear, reassess the situation and initiate a new attack."

Flight 2: Combat Air Patrol—Your Body Guards

The instructor shuffles his notes and continues, "The second section will provide CAP over the target. Section 2 is responsible for keeping all enemy fighters away and will stay on station until all friendly aircraft have left the area. Therefore, this section will carry an external fuel drop tank on the centerline station. Each aircraft in section 2 will have four AIM-120 AMRAAM and four AIM-9P air-to-air missiles.

"Both sections will fly in formation to a point about 50 miles south of the target. Section 1 will proceed north, then search for and destroy enemy surface-to-air defenses. Section 2 will then take up station around the primary target and intercept all inbound enemy aircraft. Neither section should stray far from the target zone.

"Okay, that pretty much covers it. Any questions? No? Alright, check out the maps and recon photos. Get real familiar with the area. I want all four aircraft to return to Nellis under their own power tonight, and that's an order. Dismissed."

Mission Analysis

This mission emphasizes four elements:

- Operating in an environment with multiple friendly and enemy aircraft. Pilots will have to take extra time to identify air targets before attacking.
- Attacking a well-defended target. Coordinated strikes will be required to neutralize enemy defenses and destroy the primary target. Each aircraft will depend on all other friendly aircraft to complete its assigned tasks.

- Operation and use of the AGM-88 HARM and AGM-45 SHRIKE missiles.
- The need to arrive at assigned waypoints promptly, execute the assigned task, and to depart on time.

Executing the Wild Weasel Mission

Each individual aircraft executing a mission is called a *sortie*. Groups of aircraft are interchangeably called *sections* or *flights*. You always fly the lead aircraft in flight 1. The mission of you and your wingman is to search for and destroy enemy surface-to-air threats. This is a dangerous job. You are basically a decoy, assigned to catch the attention of enemy radar operators while the main strike force, the F-117s, attack the primary target. While these activities, termed *wild weasel* or *defense suppression* operations, are not the primary role of the F-16, an F-16 equipped with anti-radiation missiles and ECM gear creates a formidable anti-SAM platform.

Most campaign missions require a flight of aircraft dedicated to defense suppression sorties. While you may not personally execute these sorties, you will assign the aircraft and pilots that do. You must understand the capabilities of the enemy in order to maximize effectiveness of the aircraft you assign to defense suppression.

Timing Is Everything

The F-117s are depending on you to clear a way home for them (they're hard to detect, but not completely invisible to radar), and they expect you to be on time. Once they attack the primary target, they expect you to have cleared the way home for them. If you're off doing some macho air-to-air jockeying instead of executing your mission orders, the F-117s are going to be exposed to unnecessary threats.

Other F-16s will be there to deal with air threats. Like the F-117s, they expect you to be on time. When they run low on fuel they're going to leave. If you're still cruising around in enemy territory, you're going to be left all alone. You must not only attack your target on time to protect the F-117s, you must also leave the combat zone in time to ensure that the other F-16s protect you. You are now ready to proceed to the mission walk-through.

Mission Walk-Through: Preflight

Upon entering Falcon 3.0, select a squadron. You may select any squadron you desire. Throughout this chapter, "386th FSFORUM" will be used to refer to your squadron. Enter Red Flag Control, and load the mission LITEOUT. Select Nellis Command, followed by Allied Aircraft, then Allied Waypoints. To remove clutter, set the map mode to TACT 1, set ROUTE to ONE, AIR to ON, and GRND to OFF.

The discussion of waypoint information will be brief and limited only to friendly aircraft. During an actual campaign you will never have information on enemy flight plans, so you shouldn't get used to using it now. Despite the brevity of this section, you should spend some time familiarizing yourself with each flight's plan and waypoint actions. It may even be useful to occasionally take a few notes on waypoint information for use during flight. You should attempt to keep track of all friendly aircraft at all times and avoid surprises.

NOTE: The Falconr utility on the enclosed Falcon 3.0 Flight Disk loads the two special squadrons, the 386th "Bashers" and 387 "Crunchers," mentioned throughout this chapter. You may wish to install those squadrons before continuing. Refer to *Appendix A, The Falcon 3.0 Flight Disk* for instructions on installing Falconr and the associated squadrons.

Analyzing Your Waypoints

You will always fly the lead aircraft in section 1. Figure 9-1 details (at 3X magnification) your flight plan. To save time, it is assumed that you are capable of taking off and flying to a specified waypoint. Therefore, this mission begins not at Nellis, but approximately 60 miles south of the nuclear facility.

Use the WAYPOINT button to review the assigned altitude, speed, and action at each of your waypoints. You begin at 8,000 feet at a speed of 450 knots. At waypoint 1, you execute CAS actions. It's here that you will search for and destroy enemy radar installations. Finally, waypoint 2 takes you back home to Nellis.

Flight 2: Combat Air Patrol

Now, select flight 2 of 4 via the FLIGHT # button. This force is your protection from enemy fighters. These guys hold your life in their hands. If you end up firing an air-to-air missile for some reason, be sure that it's not at one of these guys! This section of two F-16s starts ahead of you, and faster than you. They start at 500 knots and have their waypoint action set to ESCORT. They move into the combat zone ahead of you and draw enemy fighters away.

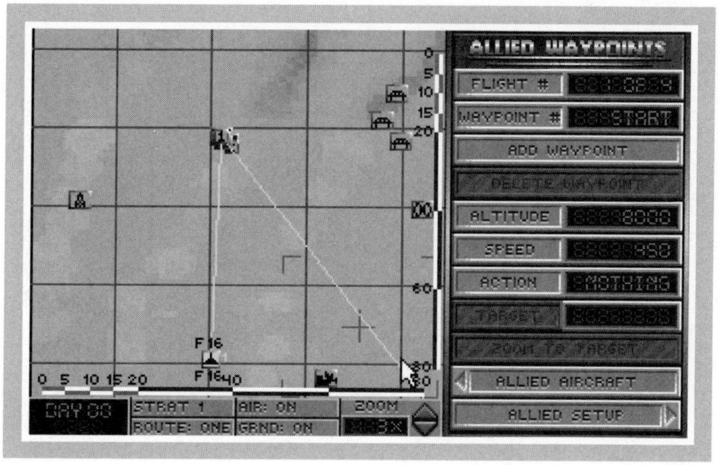

Figure 9-1 Your Flight Plan

Section 2 will proceed to circle the primary target for waypoints 1 through 4 at a speed of 450 knots and an action of ESCORT. Under these conditions, aircraft in section 2 will not stray far from their designated course, but they will intercept any enemy aircraft that enter the vicinity of their path.

With this speed and this course, section 2 won't hang around all that long. After they pass waypoint 4, they're headed for their fifth waypoint, Nellis. They should be on station long enough to allow section 1 to make two attack passes, and then they're going home. They expect section 1 to leave the area by then.

Flights 3 and 4: The Main Attack Force

Both of these sections consist of a single F-117A. Although each section follows a slightly different ground track, both sections have the same number of waypoints and the same actions defined at corresponding waypoints. For this reason, discussion will be limited to section 3; however, all comments apply directly to section 4 as well.

The F-117s begin the mission north of the target. They begin at a speed of 350 knots and a low altitude of 2,000 ft. Although the F-117s design is tailored to reduce the size of reflected radar energy, this alone is not sufficient to always defeat enemy radars. The F-117 must also use flight tactics to appear invisible to the enemy. Thus, the F-117s begin the mission flying very low, under the coverage of enemy search radars.

Waypoints 1 and 2 cause the F-117s to delay their attacks, allowing you and flight 2 to clear the area surrounding the nuclear facility. At waypoint 3, the F-117s *pop-up* or increase their altitude to 7,000 feet and begin their attack approach. They drop their ordnance at waypoint 4 and head for Nellis, waypoint 5.

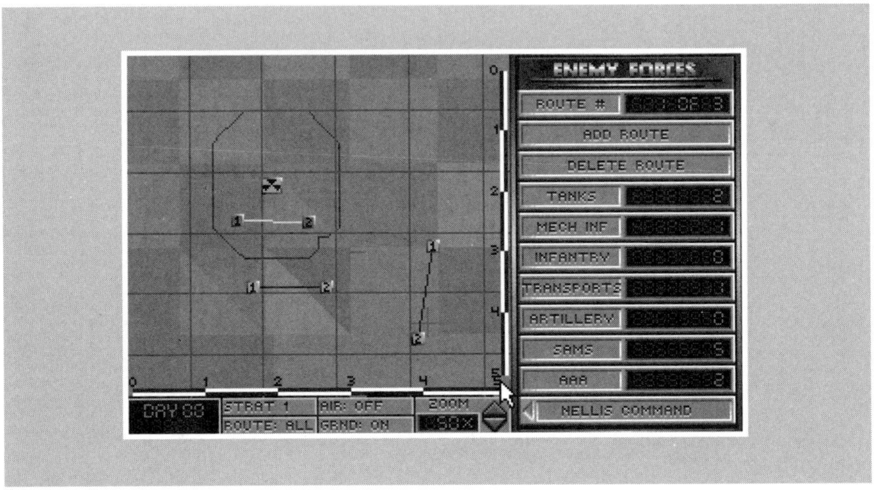

Figure 9-2 50x Magnification of Ground Forces

Tactical Recon

Normally, some amount of reconnaissance information about enemy ground forces is available. Collected from a variety of sources, including specialized aircraft, satellites, and other spacecraft, and ground forces, recon information is rarely complete, and often has inaccuracies. However, information is as powerful as any weapon, and you should take ample time to study all recon information supplied by Falcon 3.0.

Return to the Nellis Command menu and select ENEMY FORCES. On the map, be sure to set AIR to OFF and GRND to ON. Increase the zoom factor until your screen appears similar to Figure 9-2.

You now see the situation of ground forces with respect to the nuclear facility. Three individual units are positioned along the south and east sides of the facility, traveling along the displayed ground tracks. You now know the exact whereabouts of the enemy, a luxury you will never have in a campaign mission.

Mission Walk-Through: The Flight Line

When you've finished studying the enemy positions, return to Nellis Command and select DONE. This returns you to Red Flag control. Select ASSIGN PILOTS from this menu and assign your desired pilots to the F-16s. (Remember: Falcon 3.0 automatically assigns pilots to all non-F-16 aircraft.)

You should assign pilots with high bombing abilities to flight 1 and pilots with high dogfighting abilities to flight 2.

When finished, select F-16 ARMAMENT to view the weapons load out. Only F-16s are visible from this menu, so only flights 1 and 2 can be reviewed. These four F-16s will be configured as described by the Red Flag instructor during the mission briefing. You're now ready for the flight. Select the TAKEOFF button and away you go!

This mission is designed to be an afternoon mission; however, Red Flag randomly assigns a time to each mission. Once in the cockpit, press SHIFT-T, which will cycle between the four possible times (0600 hrs, 1200 hrs, 1800 hrs and 2100 hrs), until you reach 1800 hrs.

> **NOTE:** To find 1800 hrs, key off of late evening, or 2100 hrs. 2100 hrs is the only time with a dark sky and a glow on the instrument panel from the red cockpit lights. From 2100 hrs, press SHIFT-T SHIFT-T SHIFT-T to select 1800 hours.

Check your HUD. You are about 12,500 feet above sea level, but only 7,672 feet above ground level as you skim over the mountains to the south of the primary target. Your waypoint is directly ahead of you and your speed is about 470 knots. Adjust the throttle accordingly to maintain a speed of 450 knots.

Prepare for Battle

Your primary mission is air-to-ground in this lesson, so let's start by readying an air-to-ground weapon. The best weapon you're carrying for SAM busting is the AGM-88. It has a 30 nautical mile (nm) range and better homing logic than the AGM-45, so have it ready for use. Select air-to-ground weapons mode by pressing BACKSPACE. Your HUD will now change to an air-to-ground mode. Continue to press the BACKSPACE key until the Stores Panel (left of the REO) displays "2 AGM-88" as the selected weapon.

Next, review the friendly aircraft operating in the area. In the real world, Airborne Warning and Control (AWACS) aircraft would advise you of friendly aircraft near your position. Falcon 3.0 AWACS do not provide this service directly. However, you may use the 7 key to gain a fictitious view of all friendly aircraft nearby. Press the 7 key once. You will now have an external view of *your* wingman. Notice the information bar across the bottom of the screen as shown in Figure 9-3.

The top row of this bar shows the heading, speed, and altitude of the viewed aircraft. The bottom row shows the zoom factor (adjustable with F1

Figure 9-3 Wingman View Information Bar.

and F2 keys) and the callsign of the pilot flying the mission. By continuing to press the 7 key, you will step through views of all F-16s and any other nearby friendly aircraft. You have now "simulated" AWACS giving you an update on a particular aircraft.

Now, see if you have any hostile airborne company. Press 3 to return to the cockpit view. Select the NAM radar mode by pressing F5. Press F8 until the 80 mile range is selected, press F9 until the maximum azimuth scan (+/– 60 degrees) is selected, and press F10 until the maximum elevation scan is achieved, probably from 0 feet to 30,000 feet depending upon your exact altitude.

Bring On the Bad Guys

Continue to fly straight and level until bright green squares appear on the REO. They are *bogeys*. Due to their position on the REO, we can determine that the bogeys are between 10 and 20nm ahead. Depending on the actual ground track you have followed and the speed you have maintained, you may not see the bogeys yet. Turn your nose to about 345 or 350 degrees, and slow down to 400 knots if you haven't seen the bogeys yet. They'll show up.

> NOTE: Unidentified aircraft are bogeys, hostile aircraft are bandits, unexpected friendly aircraft are strangers.

When you finally do see all the bogeys, proceed to lock them up and interrogate them with IFF. Press the T key to move the two vertical "acquisition corrals" to the desired target, then press Z to lock him up. Since the closest bogey is probably the highest threat, use the T key to move the corrals until they're on the closest blip to you. Lock up with the Z key and you should see something like Figure 9-4 on your REO.

Typical of the automatic ranging function of the high fidelity radar, the range has switched to 20. In this example, the REO reports that the bandit is at 6,000 feet by the number in the upper right corner. The lower left tells us that the bearing to the bogey is 330 degrees at a range of 15nm. The lower right corner tells us he is heading 336 degrees (away from us) at a speed of 550 knots. If we wanted to intercept this bandit, we would turn right to 57 degrees. Our

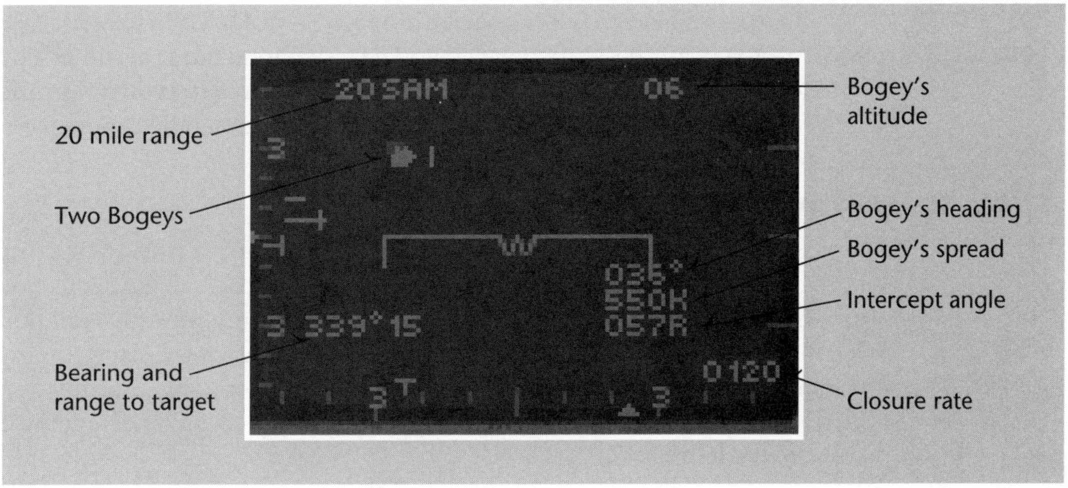

Figure 9-4 SAM Mode Air-to-Air Radar

closure rate is 120 knots, which means we're gaining on him.

Interrogate, or check the IFF signature of the bogey we just locked up by pressing the N key. Do you hear a loud buzz? If so, he's friendly and you shouldn't start shooting. In this example, the close bogey should always be a friendly; these are the CAP guys sent to protect you!

Break the lock by pressing X. Reset the radar to the 40-mile range by using the F8 key, and reset the antenna elevation to maximum by using the F10 key. Note that the antenna elevation is a function of your altitude. If you vary your altitude, you may be unable to set the antenna elevation exactly as it is described in the figures.

Continue flying toward your waypoint until, as Figure 9-5 illustrates, additional bogeys appear on the REO.

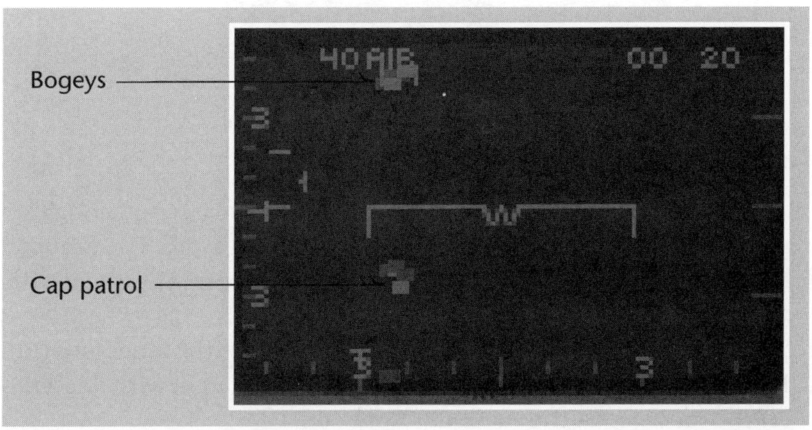

Figure 9-5
New Bogeys at 40 Nautical Miles

Use the (T) key to select one of the new bogeys, lock him up with (Z), and interrogate his IFF with (N). Did you hear that loud buzz this time? You shouldn't have; these are bad guys. You should endeavor to avoid them and proceed with your mission. The CAP guys are there to handle these jokers.

Moving In for the Kill

This is where it gets tricky. You're now in hostile territory on a SAM busting mission. The basic idea here is to fly around and let the bad guys lock you up and launch missiles at you. You retaliate by firing an anti-radiation missile in their face, activating your ECM gear, pulling a few Gs and hoping the inbound missile goes wild. This is one of the most dangerous mission assignments because you're going out of your way to give the enemy a chance to shoot at you.

Head back towards the first waypoint and get some altitude. Select the GM (ground map) mode radar by pressing (F7). In a little while things will start to happen. When the first LCK warning starts and you see a bright square on the TWI, pause the game. You'll probably see something like Figure 9-6.

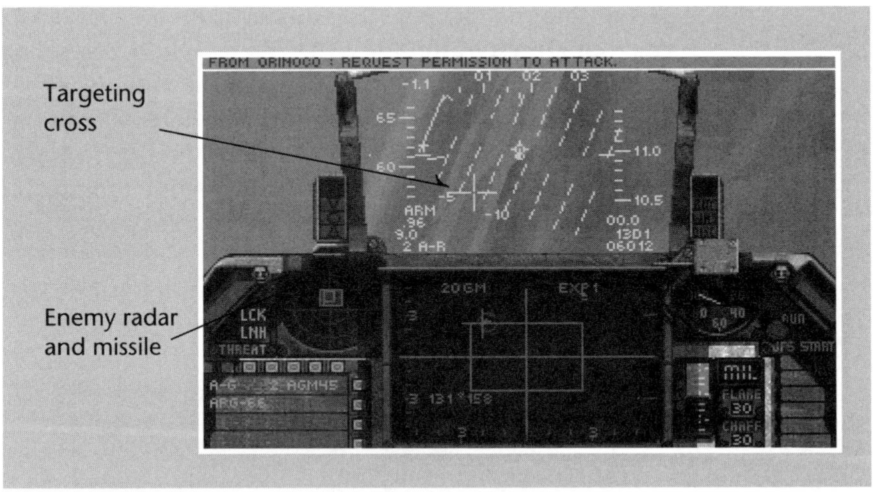

Figure 9-6 Lock-On by an Enemy SAM Site

First, look at the TWI on the left of the cockpit. The large green square denotes a ground-based radar dead ahead, about 10nm away. The numeral "1" in the box designates this as a continuous wave radar. This means the radar site is either a ZSU-24 AAA or an SA-6 SAM. Since the ZSU-24 only has an effective range of 1nm, this is probably a SA-6. Because the range is within the AGM-45's effective range, it is wisest to attack this target with an AGM-45. Select this missile via the (BACKSPACE) key.

Second, look at the REO. The ground map REO mode shows fixed ground targets within a 20nm range as bright dots on the REO. When the mission includes a primary target that one (or more) flights are to bomb, a cross hair is overlaid on the target. The bright box is a "zoom" box which may be moved by combinations of SHIFT plus the arrow keys. You may use F1 and F2 to zoom this box in and out. The magnification (1x, 2x, 4x, and 8x) is displayed after the EXP designation in the upper right corner.

In this example, the nuclear plant is near the upper edge of the zoom box, and the horizontal portion of the crosshairs is overlaid by the horizontal portion of the zoom box. For this particular mission, the GM radar mode has limited use. Its primary function here is to keep you informed of your position relative to the primary target. This keeps us from going off on a wild goose chase after SAMs that are no threat to our accompanying aircraft.

Third, look at the HUD. Notice the solid cross in the left of the HUD? That's the AGM-45 lock indicator. When you select an anti-radiation missile, a solid cross will appear in the center of the HUD. When an active radar is encountered, the targeting cross will move toward the site, thus acquiring the target. As soon as the targeting cross moves to the target, you may fire the missile. Both the AGM-45 and AGM-88 operate this way.

If you maneuver so that the radar site is no longer visible through the HUD, but is still ahead of the plane, both the AGM-45 and AGM-88 will maintain the lock. The targeting cross will drift to the edge of the HUD closest to the radar site and will turn from solid lines to dashed lines. The missile still has a fix on the radar site; however, to maximize your chances for a kill, you should place the radar site in the forward section of your HUD. Unpause the game.

Getting Mean

Once a SAM locks you up, you only have a few seconds to respond. First, despite your strongest impulses, *do not engage ECM*, at least, not yet. Quickly point your nose at the radar site and get your AGM-45 or AGM-88 locked up, *quick!* As soon as the targeting cross acquires a target, fire your missile by pressing SPACEBAR.

Now, play it cool. If there is no inbound missile, do not engage your ECM. Break away from the SAM site and prepare to make another pass. Never fly over the SAM site if you can avoid it. Even if their guidance radars are jammed, they may still have AAA guns which can be fired blindly into the air. A lucky piece of flak is just as deadly as an expertly guided SAM.

If there is an inbound missile, activate ECM with the (E) key. This should break the lock and send the inbound missile off chasing phantoms. Try to keep your heading perpendicular to that of the missile. If the ECM doesn't break the lock, keep the missile at 90 degrees deflection, pump chaff using the (DEL) key, and break hard into the missile. Generally speaking, however, ECM effectively spoofs enemy radar guided SAMs.

In some cases, the SAM operator may shut down his radar once he realizes he's being jammed. This will have an effect on your anti-radiation missiles. If the missile has already been launched and the radar site shuts down, the missile will continue towards the location where the radar was last active. If the missile has not been launched, the dashed targeting cross will return to the center of the HUD and await a new radar source.

Finally, Figure 9-7 shows a close-up view of SA-6 missile launchers over the shoulder of the lead pilot in section 1. You can clearly see a row of SAM launchers (one of which is smoking). If your attack is successful, you should see something similar.

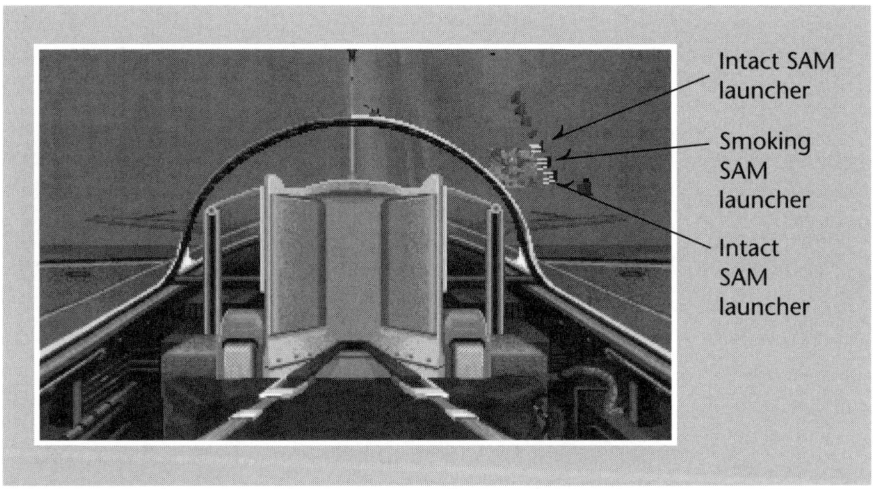

Figure 9-7 Intact Missile Launchers Adjacent to a Demolished SAM Launcher

End the mission now by pressing (ESC), selecting the FILE menu and selecting End Mission. You will be placed back to Red Flag in the de-briefing menu. Take a few minutes to review the mission briefing, analysis, and walk-through, then repeat the mission on your own.

Mission Debriefing

Did you survive Operation Lights Out? If not, you should consider the mission a failure and repeat it. If you survived, the mission still may not be a success. You may consider the mission a success if:

- You destroyed at least 5 SAM/AAA sites, and
- The F-117s successfully destroyed the nuclear facility, and
- Not more than one friendly aircraft was shot down.

Was your mission a success? If so, congratulations, you're ready for the next sortie. If not, what went wrong?

- Did you fail to destroy enough SAM/AAA sites? If so, repeat the mission. Targeting and attacking ground targets is difficult work and takes a lot of practice. Don't worry, though, you'll soon get the hang of it.
- Were too many friendly aircraft shot down? If so, and they were hit by SAM/AAA, then you failed to execute your task properly and you should re-execute the mission. If the friendlies were shot down by other aircraft, however, chalk it up to bad luck. Even the best pilots will eventually make a mistake and be shot down. There's little you can do about that, except be prepared in the future. When assigning sorties, *always be sure to have enough CAP aircraft assigned to be effective.*
- Were you shot down? If you were hit by a SAM or AAA, consider this a hard lesson learned. Be thankful that this was only a Red Flag mission that you can walk away from. Review the briefing, analysis and walk-through. Particularly, review the SAM evasion tactics, then re-execute the mission.

Mission 2: Operation Iron Breaker

An Attack on an Enemy Rail Yard

ZNR CCCCC
I 12 0600Z JAN 92
FM RED FLAG HQ DIV//GEN WAITE//
TO 386TH FSFORUM SQU CMDR//COL BASHAM//

BT
S E C R E T
REF: DAILY ATO: OP: IRON BREAKER (S)
(S) INTEL HAS LOCATED STOCKPILES OF MOBILE SS-21 SPIDER TACTICAL MISSILE SYSTEMS AT ENEMY RAIL YARD. FRIENDLY GROUND FORCES ARE ADVANCING ON THE YARD BUT WILL BE UNABLE TO STOP TRANSPORT OF MISSILES. THE 386TH FSFORUM "BASHERS" ARE ORDERED TO ATTACK RAIL YARD.

BE ADVISED ALLIED CASUALTIES HAVE BEEN INITIALLY LIGHT DUE TO HOSTILE FORCES' LACK OF READINESS. ENEMY FORCES ARE REGROUPING AND RESISTANCE SHOULD STIFFEN DURING THE NEXT 24 HOURS. ARMY AVIATION REPORTS THAT ONE UH-60 BLACK HAWK WENT DOWN WITH THE LOSS OF ALL CREW MEMBERS. AIR FORCE REPORTS AN F-111 IS OVER DUE, BOTH CREW MEMBERS ARE LISTED MIA.
ET

Nellis AFB, NV—0930 HRS

The first night of the war is over. Despite the fact that the enemy seemed unprepared for the attack, you heard that a UH-60 Black Hawk helicopter transporting a group of soldiers went down. Two crew members and six soldiers were killed. The pilot of another helicopter witnessed the crash and reported that the downed helicopter was hit by an SA-7 shoulder-launched SAM.

You turned on the morning news and watched a replay of the speech the president gave last night. He emphasized the commitment of the entire country to support what he termed, "a justifiable and necessary use of military force." The president promised that sufficient resources to ensure military victory would be supplied. "Nothing less than total and unconditional surrender by the enemy will be accepted," said the president.

Next, you watched the Pentagon's morning press conference. The Pentagon spokesperson reported the enemy was totally unprepared and allied ground forces made impressive gains. Additionally, a large number of strategic targets deep in enemy territory were attacked. Assessment of damage has only begun, but initial results are encouraging. Finally, the spokesperson stated that due to the surprise factor, few of the enemy's fighter aircraft were airborne during the night.

However, that's all changed now. The enemy is fully aware of the situation and is scrambling to field a defense. Enemy ground forces are reported to be fortifying their present positions and holding fast rather than moving to halt allied advances. It appears they plan to concede the territory between their current locations and the advancing allied troops in exchange for time to formulate a defense. Allied gains thus far have been hollow victories as no significant engagements have occurred. Enemy fighter activity is high and the battle for the skies has just begun....

The Mission Briefing

"Today," the Red Flag Instructor begins, "the 386th has been assigned to attack an enemy rail yard. Intel has located a shipment of Soviet-made SS-21 Spider missile systems. Initially, it was believed the enemy had already received and deployed these tactical missiles. It now appears that the shipment was delayed and the enemy is scrambling to deploy them. This mobile missile system can deliver a 900 pound warhead up to 75 miles. Available warheads include high explosives, chemical weapons, anti-personnel cluster bombs, and 100kT nuclear devices. These missiles are much more accurate than a run-of-the-mill missile like the Scud. Needless to say, these weapons pose a serious threat to front-line forces and field commands. We now have an opportunity to destroy them while they're still packed in their crates.

"Now then, there's good news and there's bad news. The good news is that this morning's satellite photos show few SAM launchers defending the rail yard. There's still a good amount of AAA visible; but with the proper tactics, we can defeat that. The bad news is the enemy has successfully fielded their fighters. Large numbers of MiG-21s have been on station since around 0500 hours, and MiG-29s have been spotted patrolling the primary ingress/egress routes from last night's sorties."

The Mission: Destroy Enemy Missile Stockpiles After a short shuffle of his notes, the instructor continues, "This mission consists of four sorties by two sections of aircraft. The first flight will consist of two aircraft and will attack the factories. The remaining two aircraft will compose the second section and will escort the first section to and from the target. Navy F-14s will patrol the area for enemy aircraft."

Your Job: Attack the Rail Yard "Each aircraft in section 1," the instructor states, "will carry two GBU-15 television-guided bombs and four AIM-9Ms. Additionally, this section will carry the ALQ-131 ECM pod. Initially, these F-16s will be very heavy and air-to-air engagements should be avoided. After the GBUs are delivered, however, the F-16s become agile, air-to-air platforms once again.

"Figure 9-8 shows the latest recon photo of the area. Notice the three concentrations of enemy forces situated close to the plant. These forces surround the plant and protect it from all directions of approach. These three concentrations are primarily armed with SA-7 Grail shoulder-launched SAMs and ZSU-23-4 AAA canons, which have only a one mile range and effective altitudes of 12,000 and 2,000 feet, respectively. Therefore, a high-altitude, steep-descent attack approach will provide the greatest safety. There are still a few SA-6 and SA-8 SAMs, but the ALQ-131, in conjunction with chaff, should provide effective defense against these weapons."

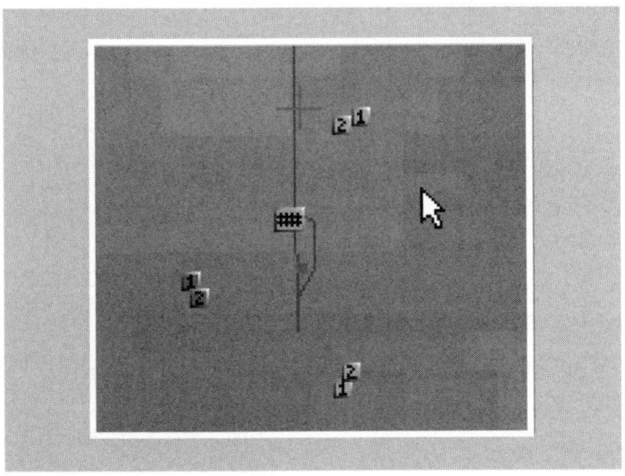

Figure 9-8 Reconnaissance Photograph of the Primary Target

Approaching the Target "Your attack profile will begin about 60nm due east of the primary target. You will climb to an altitude of 30,000 feet and a speed of 450 knots. Identification of ground targets at this altitude will be difficult, so you'll be dependent on your Ground Map (GM) mode radar for locating the target.

"Your first waypoint will be the primary target. Fly directly toward the primary target, using the GM radar image on the REO and the waypoint direction indicator to guide you. The GBU television-guided bombs only have a five mile range, so you won't begin the actual attack until you've closed to that range.

"When you reach the five mile distance, select the GBU as your active weapon. The map on the REO will be replaced with the image generated by the GBU's seeker. Push the nose of your aircraft down until the GBU locks on to a ground target and its image is displayed on REO. You'll probably have to nose down 60 or 70 degrees before the view is visible, so push the nose slowly to avoid pulling excessive negative Gs; you don't want to red out and temporarily lose vision during your attack. Cut the throttle to 60%.

"Once the image of the warehouse is displayed on the REO, no special procedures are required to drop a GBU-15; it's a glide bomb, and will use control fins to control its glide to the target it has designated. To avoid enemy defenses, under no circumstances should you dive below 12,000 feet.

"After release, pull the nose back to level while increasing to 100% throttle. Continue due west until clear of the rail yard, then return to base. This should be a one-pass clean delivery. Do not make multiple passes over the target."

The instructor now shifts discussion topics. He locates the pilots for section 2, and begins addressing their mission. "Section 2 will fly escort," he states, "for section 1. Each aircraft in section 2 will carry four AIM-120 AMRAAM and four AIM-9M Sidewinder missiles. This section will fly alongside section 1 and will protect it from threatening aircraft from all sides. However, section 2 will not stray far from section 1. Navy F-14s are flying CAP duties in the area, and will handle long range interceptions. Section 2 will only attack enemy aircraft directly threatening either themselves or section 1."

The instructor continues for some time discussing air-to-air concerns and escort tactics; however, your attention wanes. You focus your concentration on the maps and photos before you. Eventually, he finishes his lecture and dismisses you.

Mission Analysis

This mission emphasizes three elements:

- Operating in an environment heavily congested with friendly and hostile air traffic.
- Delivery of the GBU-15 television-guided bomb.
- Avoiding enemy defense with high-altitude, steep-dive attack profiles.

Survival: Every Pilot's Responsibility

Despite the terminology used during mission briefings, the *primary* responsibility of a combat pilot is to return home with both himself and his aircraft intact. A pilot's most dangerous mission is his first, the time when he's least experienced. However, pilots who survive that first deadly mission gain irreplaceable, first-hand lessons on combat. It's at this point that a pilot begins to "earn his keep" or maximize his effectiveness.

Weapons are expensive, there's no doubt about it, but few weapons approach the cost of a $20 to $30 million dollar aircraft. Likewise, training costs for pilots tally to huge sums, and few aircraft approach the cost of training a single pilot. Couple the high cost of training a pilot with the fact that his first mission will probably be his least efficient, one can quickly determine that a war of attrition, exchanging one pilot + one aircraft + one weapon for every enemy target, is far from cost effective, and rarely feasible. You can win a battle, but if your forces are decimated, you'll lose the war.

High Altitude, Steep Descent Attacks

Although all types of surface-to-air defenses are defending the target in this mission, the greatest threat to your airframe is presented by the smallest weapon system: the SA-7 Grail shoulder-launched, infrared homing missile. True, the SA-6 and SA-8 SAMs pack a much bigger punch than the SA-7; however, the ALQ-131 ECM pod is extremely effective against these threats, rendering them virtually useless. The 23mm artillery shells of the ZSU-23-4 cannon can disintegrate an F-16; however, it has an effective ceiling of only 2,000 feet. Flying above this level renders AAA harmless.

The SA-7, though, still poses a threat. Even though sensors may detect the incoming missile, since it uses *passive* (doesn't transmit any signals) infrared homing, the missile will not appear on your TWI. Your MISSILE light will illuminate, but you'll have no clues as to where or how close the missile is. Because the missile uses infrared homing, electronic jamming by the ALQ-131 has absolutely no effect. The missile has a short range of only 1nm, but an effective ceiling of 12,000 feet. With careful consideration and proper use of the F-16's capabilities, this threat can also be rendered harmless.

Six Basic Steps High altitude, steep descent attacks execute six basic steps:

1. Ingress at high altitude (greater than 25,000 feet).
2. Use ECM to defeat radar-guided SAMs capable of reaching that altitude (no infrared homing SAMs in Falcon 3.0 have that capability).
3. Close to within weapons range.

4. Dive steeply at the target.
5. Release ordnance while in a 65° (or steeper) descent.
6. Level the aircraft and egress before descending below 12,000 feet.

Using these tactics, attacking from a high altitude gives you sufficient time to acquire the target. At the same time, you never fly within the operational envelope of surface-to-air weapons that you can't jam.

Mission Walk-Through: Preflight

As described in mission 1, enter Falcon 3.0 and select the squadron you want to fly the mission. Enter Red Flag Control and load the mission "IRONBRKR." Proceed to NELLIS COMMAND, followed by ALLIED AIRCRAFT, and then to ALLIED WAYPOINTS.

Flight 1: Your Flight

Set the map mode to TACT 1, ROUTE to ONE and GRND to OFF. Again, in this mission you begin enroute to the target to save time. Your starting point is approximately 60nm due east of the rail yard. You begin at an altitude of 30,000 feet and 450 knots — the appropriate height and speed to execute this attack.

Tactical Recon: Zoom to Target Waypoint 1 lies directly over the enemy rail yard, your primary target. You'll notice that the ACTION for this waypoint specifies BOMB and the TARGET is set to 1 RAIL YARD. As explained in Chapter 6, *Introduction to Red Flag,* when a waypoint activity in a Red Flag mission is set to BOMB you have the ZOOM TO TARGET option available. Zooming to the target gives you a three-dimensional, rotating view of the target. While this option is unavailable in campaign missions or when the waypoint action is anything other than BOMB, this is a valuable source of information. Select the ZOOM TO TARGET button now. You should see something similar to Figure 9-9.

Consider this view a composite generated from the latest photos taken by an SR-71, RF-4, U-2, or another reconnaissance aircraft. Let the view rotate the rail yard several times until you are familiar with the target from all directions. Keep in mind, however, that this view only shows fixed targets. *It will not show enemy infantry, armor, SAMs, or AAA locations!*

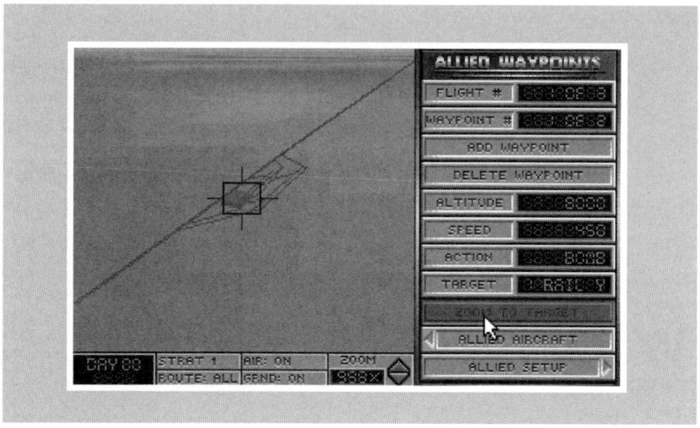

Figure 9-9 Reconnaissance View of the Enemy Rail Yard

Waypoint 2: Back to Nellis Finally, you return to Nellis after completing your mission. We typically do not discuss the waypoints of enemy forces (since you would never know this information during a campaign); however, you may notice that enemy aircraft will be patrolling the area between the rail yard and Nellis AFB. As you may have gathered, returning home won't be easy in this mission.

Flight 2: Your Escorts

This group of two F-16s is assigned one task and one task only: protect you. They begin their flight south of your position, then follow a path alongside yours. They've been assigned the ESCORT activity at their waypoints. They won't stray far from their assigned path, but they will attack any aircraft threatening the area either side of that path.

They won't follow you, either. As long as you stay on course they'll be nearby to protect you. If you wander off course, they're going to continue along their assigned route, and you'll be left hanging. As with mission 1, if you don't follow your orders, you'll be left alone in the cold.

Flight 3: Other Friendly Aircraft

There's a group of Navy F-14s on a CAP mission in your vicinity. Campaign missions almost always include other non-F-16 aircraft, but unfortunately, their waypoint information is never made available to you. You'll never know where or what type of aircraft they'll be nor how many. Therefore, it's a bad idea to get used to having that information in Red Flag missions. To prevent you from developing bad habits, we'll avoid discussing this flight.

Tactical Recon

By now you've learned the two primary sources of tactical information in Red Flag missions: the "zoom to target" feature on the Allied Waypoints screen and the manual zoom feature of the Enemy Forces screen. Since we've already discussed the data provided by the "zoom to target" function in the waypoints discussion, we'll now focus on the information available on the Enemy Forces screen. Select the ALLIED AIRCRAFT button, then the NELLIS COMMAND button to return to the Nellis Command menu. Select ENEMY FORCES, then set the map mode to STRAT 1, AIR to OFF, and GRND to ON.

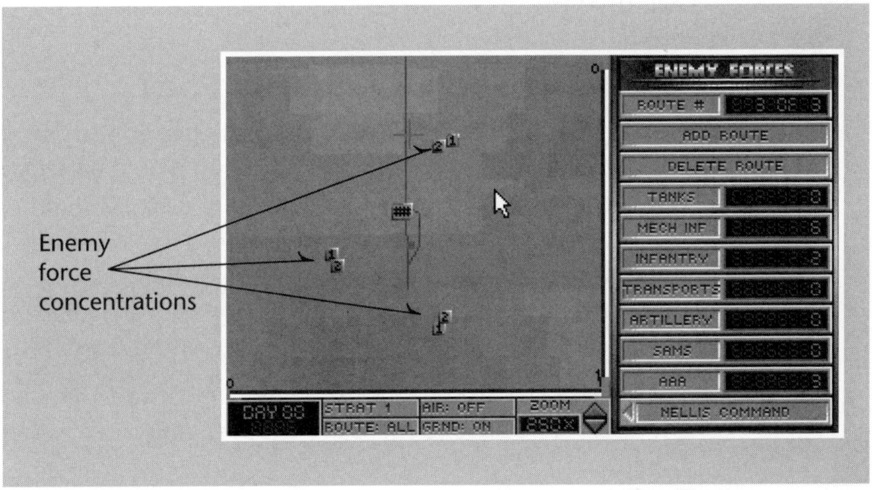

Figure 9-10 Enemy Forces at 250x Magnification

Increase the zoom level to 250x and your screen should appear similar to Figure 9-10. As the figure illustrates, three camps of enemy forces have taken positions around the rail yard. These forces are the main threat to your flight of aircraft. The tactics presented in this mission are designed to protect you from them.

As with the previous mission, there are few landmarks to help you locate and identify your target. You will be totally dependent upon waypoint guidance and the GM radar mode to locate the rail yard.

Head for the Tarmac Return to Red Flag Control. Select F-16 PILOTS and assign your pilots. Be sure to assign pilots with good air-to-ground skills in flight 1 and pilots with good air-to-air skills in flight 2. Press the F-16 ARMAMENT button and review your weapons load out. Press the TAKE OFF and enter the cockpit.

Mission Walk-Through: The Flight Line

You begin the mission cruising around 30,000 feet, headed due west toward the target zone. You're 60nm miles from the target, well beyond the 20nm range of the GM radar mode. As you fly toward waypoint 1, look for airborne. Select the NAM radar mode with the F5 key. Press F8 three times to select a 40 mile range. Press F10 until the upper right corner of the REO displays "27 40" meaning the radar is scanning altitudes between 27,000 and 40,000 feet. Press F9 until the horizontal pan mark scans the entire width of the REO. Your electronic eyes and ears are activated.

First Contact: Friend or Foe?

Fly directly toward waypoint 1 until a bogey appears on your REO. Who is this guy? An enemy interceptor, perhaps? You'd better check this guy out. Press the T key. The vertical acquisition bars should center around the bogey. Press the Z key to lock the bogey up. When the lock is successful, your screen should appear as in Figure 9-11.

You now know a lot about this guy. He's at 33,000 feet, moving at 770 knots directly toward you. Your closure rate is displayed as 1,094 knots.

> **NOTE:** Closure rate is positive when the distance between you and the target is decreasing, negative when the distance is increasing.

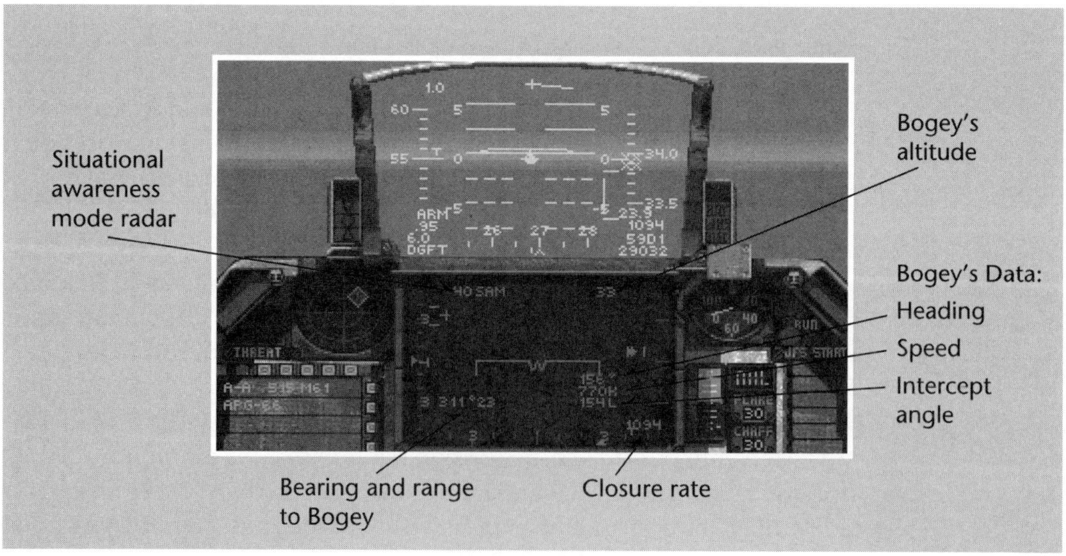

Figure 9-11 Lock the Bogey Up

The bottom line is: this guy is closing on you fast. You'd better identify him quickly. Press the N key to interrogate his IFF. Do you hear a loud buzz? You should have; this should be an F-14. You can also verify IFF by pressing 4 to view the left side of the cockpit. The green IFF light should be illuminated. If there's any doubt about his identity, contact your "simulated" AWACS controller by pressing Q. This gives you an external view of the target. You don't have this miracle view in the real world, but you normally have AWACS controllers you can contact who can identify the target for you.

Using Ground Map Radar

Leave the F-14s to their business. Continue directly toward waypoint 1 until you are approximately 20nm from it. Select GM radar mode by pressing F7. Figure 9-12 illustrates how your screen should now appear.

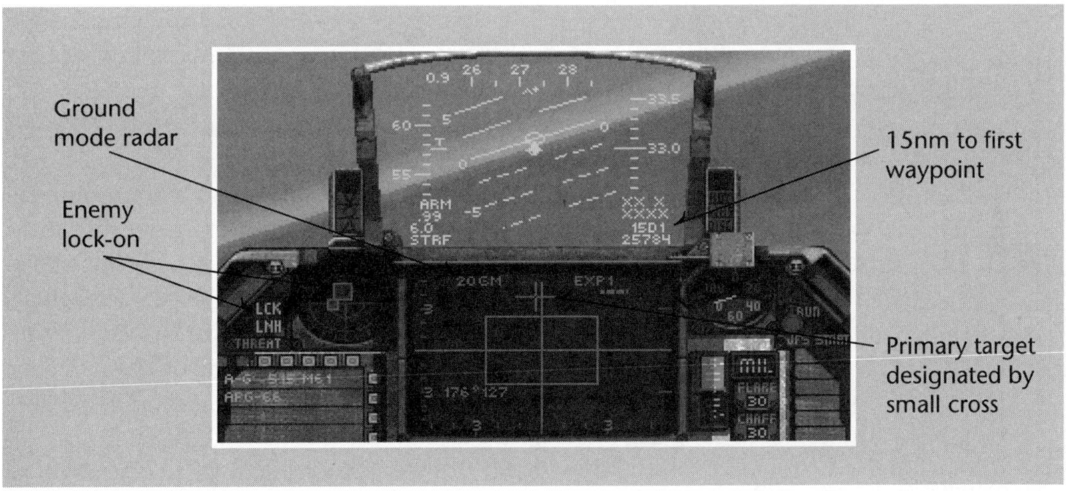

Figure 9-12 Ground Mode Radar

The GM displays ground targets less than 20 miles ahead of your aircraft as green lines and dots on the REO. Roads and rivers are displayed as dim green lines, while buildings are displayed as bright green boxes and or dots. The nose of your aircraft is "located" at the center of the bottom edge of the REO. An object midway between the top and bottom of the REO would be 10 miles in front of your aircraft.

When an object that has been defined as a target for a BOMB waypoint appears on the REO, it is designated by a bright green targeting cross, as shown in Figure 9-12. This cross has no operational affect on any weapons systems; it is simply an indicator of the target's location relative to the nose of your aircraft. It can be used for navigation along with the waypoint indicators. In Figure 9-12, the cross is one quarter from the top of the screen, indicating a range of 15 miles. Correspondingly, the HUD waypoint indicator shows that waypoint 1 (the primary target) is 15 miles away.

The Battle Begins

By this time, enemy SAMs probably have begun to lock on to you. Activate your ALQ-131 jamming pod by pressing E. The word ECM should appear on the display panel located along the right side of the forward cockpit view. Your ECM gear renders radar-guided SAMs ineffective, and your present altitude renders AAA and shoulder-launched SAMs harmless.

Delivering the GBU-15

You now want to fly directly toward the primary target until you get within the five-mile range of your GBU-15s. Align the GM targeting cross in the center of the REO and fly directly toward the target until the HUD waypoint distance indicator reads 5 miles. You are now ready to execute the attack. Press BACKSPACE to select air-to-ground weapons mode, then press BACKSPACE until the GBU-15 is the selected weapon.

First, the REO display is changed, quite literally, to a "bomb's eye" view. When the GBU acquires a target, an image of that target is displayed on the REO. Second, an aim-point cross appears in the center of the HUD. To acquire a target, move the aim-point over the desired target. The GBU's television guidance system uses image recognition systems to "watch" the target, thereby achieving a lock. An image of the target will be displayed on the REO and the aim-point cross in the HUD will remain superimposed over the target as long as you keep the target visible in the HUD.

Slowly, push the nose down. Pushing the nose fast will cause you to pull a high amount of *negative G-forces* which can cause you to *red out* or temporarily lose vision. Reduce throttle by repeatedly pushing the - key until the throttle reaches 60%. The lower your speed, the longer you can dive. The longer you dive, the more time you have to aim and deliver your weapons. You may also elect to engage the speed brake by pressing B. This will help control your speed, but you must remember to retract the speed brakes when you climb away from the target.

Continue to push the nose down until you can see the rail yard in the HUD. Depending on how quickly you push the nose down, your dive angle will be anywhere from 50 to 75 degrees. Even with the throttle reduced to 60%, if you do not engage the speed brake, your airspeed may climb as high as 600 knots. Turn your aircraft so that the aim point moves to cover the rail yard.

The GBU automatically locks on to the first structure its television system detects. This might be the rail yard, or it might be one of the many armored vehicles surrounding it. If the acquired target is not the rail yard, select a new target by pressing T. Figure 9-13 shows how your screen should appear when you have the rail yard acquired. Be very careful not to dive below 12,000 feet as displayed by the AGL indicator in the bottom right of the HUD. Remember, if you're at 20,000 feet above sea level, but only 6,000 feet above ground level, you are well within the 12,000 feet range of the SA-7!

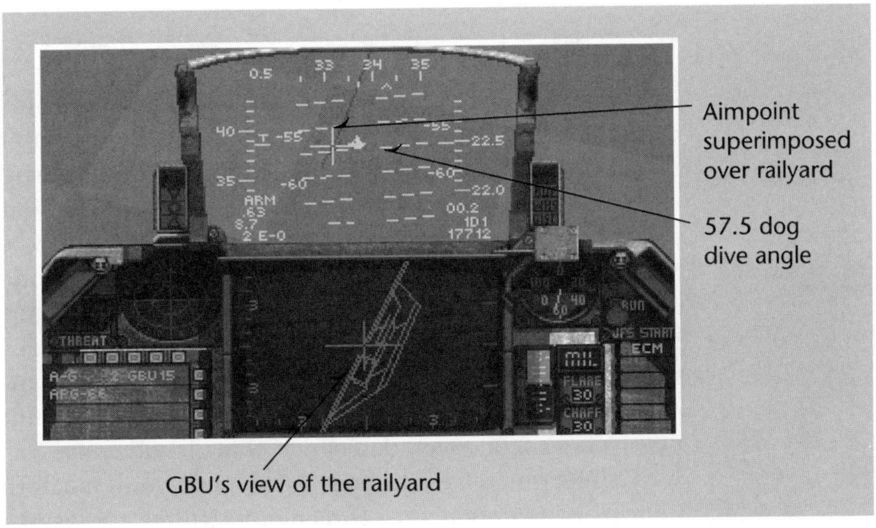

Figure 9-13 Delivering the GBU-15

When you have the rail yard acquired, drop the GBU on it by pressing SPACEBAR or the first joystick button. Once the first bomb is away, the second GBU will repeat the automatic acquisition procedure. Drop the second bomb by again pressing SPACEBAR or the joystick button. Don't sightsee. Quickly pull the nose level and apply 100% throttle by pressing the + key. Continue due west for a couple of miles, until you are clear of the rail yard.

The Trip Home

Congratulations, you've finished your assigned task. Now it's time to head for home. If the waypoint indicator in the HUD is not directing you to waypoint 2 (back to base), press ALT-B to bypass waypoint 1 and select waypoint 2. Although the actual attack run was certainly a harrowing experience, it's no time to get complacent. You're not out of the woods, yet.

You're still deep within enemy territory, streaking across a sky patrolled by enemy fighters. As you turn your aircraft toward waypoint 2, you must now reconfigure your electronic eyes and prepare yourself for further combat. First, if your ECM is still active, turn it off by pressing E. While its powerful electronic transmissions may cloud enemy radar screens and hide your exact location, the same transmissions still betray your presence to the enemy. It's better to deactivate the ALQ-131 when you don't need it, but stay alert, you may yet fly over enemy SAM sites. Be prepared to reactivate it on a moment's notice by pressing E.

Your Electronic Eyes

Next, reconfigure your air-to-air radar. Based on your current altitude, the configuration you can achieve varies. As a rule of thumb, your air-to-air radar is most effective when you're flying at an altitude between 7,500 feet and 9,000 feet. At this altitude, you can usually adjust the antenna elevation to scan all altitudes between 0 feet (ground level) and 15,000 or 16,000 feet. Most enemy fighters operate within this altitude band. If you're flying above 9,000 feet, your radar will be unable to scan completely to ground level, thus failing to detect low-flying bandits. On the downside, you'll be flying within the performance envelope of the SA-7, but on your current path back to base, you should encounter few enemy ground forces. If you're flying above 8,000 feet, descend to that altitude now.

Unfortunately, like your ECM pod, your radar transmissions announce your presence to the enemy. Unlike the ECM gear, your radar broadcasts your *exact* location! Your best bet for a safe trip home is to configure your radar as described, fly for not more than four minutes, then if you have no contacts, deactivate your radar by pressing R. Change your altitude and modify your course slightly. Fly along for another three or four minutes, then reactivate radar by pressing R and repeat the process. If you want an uneventful, safe trip home, this is the tactic for you. Your escorts can then deal with any enemy fighters.

Radar Contact

Depending on how long you loitered over the target and how much you've deviated from the assigned course, your encounters enroute to base may differ slightly from those described below. However, if you encounter the unexpected, don't despair; it's another lesson in handling the fog of war. Based on the variables listed, you should be heading 150 to 170 degrees toward Nellis AFB. At this time, Nellis should be approximately 110 miles away.

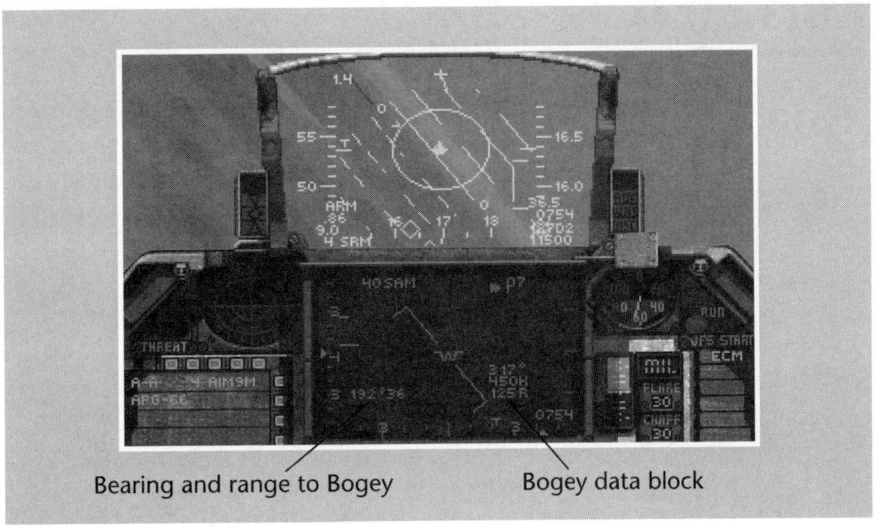

Figure 9-14 Radar Contact.

After a few minutes on this course, you should detect a radar contact on the right side of the REO. Lock the bogey up with the familiar key sequence of T and Z. Your screen should appear similar to Figure 9-14.

> **NOTE:** Use the key sequence of T and Z to lock bogeys, use N to interrogate IFF.

In Figure 9-14, the bogey is 36 miles away at a heading of 192 degrees (southwest) from your position. The bogey is traveling on a heading of 317 degrees at a speed of 450 knots and an altitude of 7,000 feet. Interrogate his IFF by pressing N. Do you hear the buzz indicating a friendly? Press 4 to view the left side of the cockpit. Is the green IFF light illuminated?

The answer to both questions should be negative. These are bad guys. You now have to make a decision: do you engage these guys or avoid them. Nellis is still 100 or more miles away. An engagement will expend precious fuel and weapons. If you *go winchester*, or run out of weapons, and encounter additional bandits on the way home, you'll be in serious trouble. So far, these bandits are not a threat. Your best bet is to avoid trouble and continue toward base. Keep a watchful eye open, however. If the bandits close on you, be ready to defend yourself. Remember that your escorts are still watching your back. If the enemy decides to attack, let the escorts take care of them.

Mission Debriefing

How did you do? If you correctly executed the tactics detailed in the walk-through, you should've had no problem executing the attack and returning to base safely. Assuming you survived, you may consider the mission a success if:

- You destroyed the rail yard, and
- You downed two MiGs, and
- No F-16s were lost to friendly fire.

Did you succeed? If so, proceed to mission 3. Otherwise, take a moment to analyze the results. What went wrong?

- Were you shot down attacking the rail yard? If so, you failed to properly execute the attack. Using the tactics described in conjunction with ECM gear, no enemy surface-to-air threat should be able to harm you. There are only two ways the enemy could've hit you: you forgot to turn your ECM on and a radar-guided SAM hit you, or you flew too low and were hit by an SA-7 or AAA fire. Repeat the mission taking care to avoid these hazards.
- Did your bombs miss the rail yard? If so, don't feel bad. Precision bombing, even with so-called smart weapons, is difficult. Practice is the only thing you lack. Repeat the mission.
- Were you surprised and shot down on the way home by enemy SAMs? If so, you probably fell victim not to the incoming missile, but to the pilot's greatest enemy: complacency. Long flights often tend to be boring, and the pilot's mind begins to wander. Suddenly, the pilot finds himself struggling for his life against an unexpected enemy. As often as not, the pilot loses this battle. If you successfully destroyed the rail yard, but were shot down under these circumstances, proceed to mission 3, but be more alert!
- Were you shot down by enemy fighters that slipped by the escort patrol? This, unfortunately, is one of the cruel realities of combat. The escorts assigned to you are not invincible and they sometimes make mistakes. There's little you can do but file this under the heading of bad luck. As stated in mission 1's debriefing, when assigning aircraft to a CAP or ESCORT mission, be sure to assign sufficient numbers of aircraft to be effective. If you successfully destroyed the rail yard proceed to mission 3. Otherwise, repeat this mission.

- Were you shot down in air-to-air combat? If this is the case, practice the basic fighter maneuvers presented in Chapter 6, *Introduction to Red Flag,* and Chapter 11, *Secrets and Tactics of the Enemy*. As with precision bombing, there's no substitute for practice. Brush up on your air-to-air tactics. Then, if you successfully destroyed the rail yard, proceed to mission 3.

Mission 3: Operation Ground Shaker

Escort B-52s Through Enemy Airspace

ZNR CCCCC
I 12 0600Z JAN 92
FM RED FLAG HQ DIV//GEN WAITE//
TO 386TH FSFORUM SQU CMDR//COL BASHAM//

BT
S E C R E T
REF: DAILY ATO: OP: IRON BREAKER (S)
(S) AS SUSPECTED, ENEMY GROUND FORCES HAVE DUG INTO BUNKERS AND ARE HOLDING POSITION AWAITING ATTACK. HQ ESTIMATES ALLIED GROUND FORCES NEED AT LEAST A 3 TO 1 ADVANTAGE TO PENETRATE THE ENEMY DEFENSIVE LINE. ALLIED GROUND FORCES ARE LOITERING ALLOWING USAF TIME TO INCREASE OUR ODDS. THE 386TH IS ASSIGNED TO ESCORT B-52S ON CARPET BOMBING SORTIES.

TERRITORIAL GAINS THUS FAR ARE NEGLIGIBLE. ONLY LIGHT GROUND ENGAGEMENTS REPORTED. ENEMY AIRCRAFT OPERATING IN AN ORGANIZED MANNER IN BOTH AIR-TO-AIR AND AIR-TO-GROUND ATTACKS.

AN F-16 FROM THE 387TH FSFORUM "CRUNCHERS" PILOTED BY COL M BARRS WAS SHOT DOWN DURING AIR COMBAT. WITNESSES REPORT COL BARRS SUCCESSFULLY EJECTED. CURRENT STATUS UNKNOWN.
ET

Nellis AFB—1030 HRS

You were just told the news: Colonel Barrs, the 387th squadron leader was shot down yesterday. His wingman reported they were jumped by a group of Su-27 interceptors, and Barrs' aircraft was hit by an air-to-air missile. The pilot of an A-10 they were escorting reported seeing Barrs eject and his parachute deploy. The A-10 pilot attempted to maintain visual contact, but had to withdraw when additional enemy fighters were spotted nearby. A search-and-rescue helicopter was unable to locate the Colonel before nightfall. Enemy air activity this morning has prohibited a follow-up search.

You halfheartedly head for the TV lounge down the hall from your room to watch the daily press conference. You learn that the total number of allied aircraft downed has risen to six, while 17 enemy aircraft have been destroyed. The ground offensive, for all practical purposes, hasn't started yet. The gains posted by the military spokesman were conceded by the enemy in exchange for time to regroup. Only minor skirmishes have occurred on the ground, usually nothing more than artillery duels. There have been a couple of injuries, but nothing major. A Marine armored recon patrol stumbled across an enemy T-72 platoon. The Marine M-60s surprised the T-72 force (which was apparently lost) and captured it.

The war is not yet 48 hours old. It's still too early to tell exactly how well things are going. What you do know, however, is that you have another mission to fly today. It's back to the briefing room...

The Mission Briefing

"Today," begins the Red Flag instructor, "the 386th will provide escort duties for a series of B-52s on carpet bombing missions. Enemy ground forces have dug into positions approximately 140 miles southwest of Nellis. SAC is sending B-52s from the 93d Bomb Wing to carpet bomb the area. We will fly four sorties to support the bombers. Section 1, consisting of two aircraft, will provide detached escort enroute to the target. Section 2, also composed of two aircraft, will take up a CAP station around the enemy position and provide reception escort."

Section 1: Escort B-52s

"Section 1 will initially fly due east from Nellis and rendezvous with the B-52s about 50 miles from the air base. The B-52s will fly southwesterly.

Once contact is made, maintain a tight escort and don't forget to constantly check all directions for enemies. They may show up where you least expect it.

"Section 1 will carry four AIM-9M Sidewinder heat-seeking missiles. They are all-aspect missiles, that means they will acquire a target from any angle, not just from the rear quarter. If the bandit is coming head-to-head with you, show your teeth and launch the Sidewinder in his face. Each aircraft will carry two AIM-120 AMRAAM radar-guided missiles. Both types are fire-and-forget missiles; that is, both the AIM-9M and the AIM-120 have their own internal targeting systems. Once either missile has acquired a target, no more guidance information is required from the launching aircraft."

Air-to-Air Missile Tips

"The AIM-120 requires the launching aircraft to first obtain a radar lock on the target. Once the missile is launched, however, the aircraft can break the lock, lock on to another target, or even shut down the radar completely. Regardless, the missile continues toward its target. The AIM-120 has a theoretical range of 30nm but rarely acquires a target farther than 15 miles away.

"The AIM-9M, while having a much shorter effective range of about 6nm, tracks the heat emissions of the target without transmitting any signals of its own. Although some sensors are capable of detecting the missile in flight, it will not announce itself like the AIM-120. Additionally, the AIM-9M has two methods of acquiring a target. First, like the AIM-120, it can acquire a target that is radar locked by the launching aircraft. Second, the missile can acquire the heat emissions of a nearby aircraft, even if the launching aircraft has radar shut off.

"As you approach the target zone, section 1 will hold back and the B-52s will proceed under the protection of section 2 and drop their ordnance. Section 1 should loiter at that position and avoid section 2's zone. We don't want the two sections to get confused and fire on each other. When the B-52s leave the target, section 1 will continue to escort them back to Nellis."

Section 2: Patrolling the Target

The instructor pauses briefly, then begins to address the pilots of the second section. "The second section," he says, "will leave Nellis before section 1. Section 2 will proceed to the target zone, then fly a racetrack CAP pattern around the area, providing a reception escort. Section 1 will ensure that the bombers arrive at the target area, section 2 will ensure that they aren't attacked when they get there.

"Section 2 should not stray far from the assigned path, and should not attempt to attack targets not threatening the B-52s. Each aircraft in this section will carry six AIM-9M sidewinders."

Know Thine Enemy

"Enemy aircraft known to be operating in the vicinity of your flight paths include MiG-21s, MiG-29s, and Su-27s. All are dangerous adversaries carrying a mixture of three types of missiles:

- The AA-2 Atoll—This is a heat-seeking missile, similar to AIM-9P because it requires an unobstructed view of the exhaust nozzles from the rear of the aircraft. It has a maximum range of five miles.
- The AA-8 Aphid—This is an improved heat-seeking missile, similar to the AIM-9M. While still having only a five-mile range, it has an all-aspect seeker like the AIM-9M. It can be fired at a target aircraft from any angle.
- The AA-7 Apex—This is the standard radar-guided missile of the Soviet arsenal. It has an effective range of 25 miles. Unlike our AIM-120, it has no active seeker and requires that the launching aircraft maintain a radar lock on the target aircraft during missile flight. A sharp maneuver that breaks the radar lock renders the missile useless.

"Finally," the instructor concludes, "both sections of aircraft must stay alert. Don't let an itchy trigger finger get the best of you. Try not to shoot each other down when you rendezvous at the target zone. Dismissed."

Mission Analysis

This mission emphasizes three elements:

- Coordination of multiple flights of aircraft.
- Escort duties.
- Air-to-air combat in an area congested with both friendly and hostile aircraft.

While escort missions are one of the most frequent fighter aircraft tasks, they are probably the least liked and most difficult to execute. Strictly speaking, fighter aircraft are offensive weapons designed to roam the skies freely in search of prey. Typically, the fighter's primary advantage is *initiative*, or the ability to sustain an offensive edge over the adversary. Even when providing a zone defense, fighters are free to maneuver against the enemy to maintain the offensive potential. When all else fails, the fighter's chief defense is to accelerate and escape. The fighter, in an offensive role, can appear from any direction at any time, concentrate its attack on the most vulnerable target, and then accelerate away before the enemy can retaliate.

The Disadvantage

Classic escort missions, in which a section of aircraft accompanies a massed formation of strike/bomber aircraft, tie the predatorial F-16 to slowly moving, highly visible targets. The fighter is still charged with attacking its prey, but it no longer has the advantage of freely roaming the sky and customizing attacks to meet the situation. It must maintain a position near the escorted aircraft and yield the surprise factor to the enemy. The fighter can no longer concentrate its attack on the most vulnerable target; it must now prevent any aircraft from penetrating the defensive zone around the escorted aircraft. When things get rough, the fighter cannot simply withdraw, or in fighter pilot lingo, *bug out*. The fighter must continue to defend the escorted aircraft.

The First Rule of Combat

Always keep the first rule of combat in mind: *never fight the enemy on his terms*. If the enemy is most effective at high altitudes, fight low. If the enemy can out turn you, use vertical maneuvers to counter. If the enemy has all-aspect weapons, don't go head-to-head. If the enemy has the initiative, devise tactics that seize it from him.

> **NOTE:** Never fight the enemy on his terms.

Escort tactics have been refined in accordance with this principle into a much more executable system. However, there's a trade-off. In the case of escort missions, the system is perfected by dividing the mission into separate tasks at the cost of additional aircraft. Unfortunately, there may not always be a sufficient number of aircraft available to properly staff the mission.

Types of Escort Missions

To regain the advantage, escorting fighters must return to the role of aerial hunter-killers, free to maneuver, attack, and escape. However, this role does not lend itself well to creating an impenetrable barrier between the enemies and the defenders. Despite the best efforts of friendly pilots, a few intent enemy fighters will always manage to pass through the defensive screen and harass the strike/bomber aircraft.

Therefore, a *layered defense* concept has been applied. Rings of aircraft assigned with slightly different tasks provide multiple layers of defense for the main body. Enemy fighters must penetrate multiple groups of escort aircraft (hopefully sustaining substantial losses from each group) before reaching the primary force of strike/bomber aircraft. Using the concept of a layered defense, four types of escort missions have been defined: *forward escort, wide escort, close escort,* and *reception escort.* We'll briefly analyze each type.

Forward Escort Forward escort aircraft form the first layer of defense. This section of two to four aircraft conduct hit-and-run sweeps well ahead of the main body. These aircraft attack all enemy aircraft they encounter and transmit warnings to the other friendly aircraft. Typically, forward escorts may be positioned as much as 150 miles ahead of the main body.

Wide Escort Next, the wide escorts provide the second layer. These aircraft are positioned around the main body at a range exceeding the maximum attack range of the enemy. This allows the wide escorts to attack enemy aircraft before the enemy aircraft can fire on the main body. These aircraft intercept enemies that manage to slip past the forward escorts.

Close Escort Third, we have the close escort, the final layer of defense. These aircraft are stationed close to the main body, around, above, and in-between. They have two responsibilities: assist the wide escorts and intercept bandits that slip past the wide escorts.

Reception Escort Finally, reception escort aircraft provide reinforcements. Reception escort aircraft are stationed at fixed points along the path of the main body, usually on the return route, allowing the main body to pass while intercepting trailing bandits.

In each of these roles, individual pilots have to rely on their personal judgment. Because you have a strict defensive role, attacking every bandit you detect is not feasible. You must save your limited amount of fuel and weapons to attack only those bandits that are a distinct threat to the bomber group. Attacking a Mig-29 patrol 100 miles from the bombers may be more fun and may increase your kill count, but it leaves the main body defenseless. You may return to the bomber group out of missiles and low on fuel, only to find that four MiG-19s have decimated the group and are waiting for you. No amount of air-to-air kills will generate a mission success if the main body is destroyed.

Conclusion

Fully implementing a layered escort, however, requires a large number of aircraft. If only two aircraft are assigned to each of the four tasks, that's eight aircraft unavailable for other missions. If other sorties, such as SAM suppression, are required, the total rises. The total aircraft required to completely protect the main strike body is usually prohibitively high. Falcon 3.0 campaigns allow a maximum of eight aircraft (usually less) from your squadron to participate in a given mission. Therefore, based on analysis of the probable threat, sacrifices are made.

Each individual you encounter must be evaluated. If the bandits pose little or no threat to the main body you are escorting, you must resist the urge to engage them. Keep a watchful eye on the bandits, but remember your main mission: protect the convoy. This may be the most difficult mission you must execute, but it also one of the most important.

Mission Walk-Through: Preflight

It's time to get down to business. Enter Falcon 3.0, select the desired squadron, enter Red Flag, and load the mission GRNDSHKR. As usual, we'll begin by analyzing the waypoints of friendly aircraft, so select NELLIS COMMAND, then ALLIED AIRCRAFT, followed by ALLIED WAYPOINTS. Set the Map mode to TACT 1, AIR to ON, GRND to OFF, and ROUTE to ONE.

Flight 1: Wide Escort

Your flight is charged with wide escort duties. As described above, you and your wingmen should follow a flight path similar to that of the B-52s you are escorting. Normally, you'd position yourself at a distance from the B-52s so that you could engage bandits before they could fire on the bombers. However, in this mission, you do not have the full complement of escort aircraft, you only have yourself and the reception escort patrolling the target area. Because of this, you'll have to do double duties between wide and close escort.

Your Waypoint Information You begin this mission almost directly above Nellis AFB headed east. You begin at an altitude of 8,000 feet and a speed of 450 knots. When you enter the cockpit, your first priority will be to locate the B-52s. No matter how many bandits you may encounter, no matter how many of your wingmen get shot down, you must at all times be aware of the B-52s' position. Lose track of the bombers and, while you're searching for them, bandits will surprise attack you every time.

Your first waypoint intersects the path of the B-52s. By the time you arrive at this waypoint you should have made radar contact with the bombers and verified their identity by their IFF signatures. The bombers, or big friends, will probably move south of this point before you arrive there. In such a case, you'll want to bypass waypoint 1 and stick with the big friends.

Your waypoint action is set to ESCORT. Although speed and altitude data are also set, to effectively perform the escort mission, you'll have to ignore them. As you'll soon see, the B-52s are flying at a high altitude of 30,000 feet. At short range (20nm or less), your radar will not be able to scan from ground level (0 altitude) to 30,000 feet, nor will you be able to guard all directions at this speed.

Rather, you'll have to use your own judgment and make altitude, course, and speed changes at regular intervals to guard all possible directions of attack. Enemy fighters may come in low and attack from below, or they may come in high and attack from above. You'll have to keep a constant vigil. We'll discuss how to do this shortly.

Hand Off Waypoint 2, also defined with the ESCORT action, falls short of the target area. Section 2, the reception escort, is circling the target area. Your second waypoint stops just short of their zone. You shouldn't enter their area of operations. There are already two F-16s on patrol and four B-52s on attack runs. You and your wingmen would just congest the air space and make target acquisition and identification difficult.

Consequently, you should pull short at waypoint 2 and not interfere with section 2's patrol. You should loiter around waypoint 2 and watch for incoming bandits. For a short time the reception escort essentially will switch roles to become close escort, and you'll temporarily have wide escort responsibilities. After a few minutes the B-52s will turn north and head back for Nellis AFB. When they leave the protective umbrella of section 2, you should rendezvous and escort them back to base.

Flight 2: The Reception Escort

While reception escorts normally provide a defensive screen around the home base for tired aircraft making their way home, reception escorts can be positioned anywhere along the flight path of the guarded aircraft. Sometimes, it may be to your advantage to post a reception escort at other points if the likelihood of attack is high in that area. This mission does exactly that. Section 2 provides reception escort at the primary target.

At the start of the mission, section 2 is already on station, well in advance of the upcoming strike. Like you, they are performing a combination of two escort types: remote and reception. By being on station already, you can assume that they've swept the target area of bandits, the task of remote escorts. Now, they patrol the area around the target to keep it devoid of enemies, the task of the reception escort.

Their action for the starting waypoint through waypoint 2 is CAP. Waypoint 3, however, is set to LOITER. When the F-16s in flight 2 reach waypoint 3, they will evaluate their fuel status. If they have enough fuel, they will make another pass through the circuit. However, if doing so would leave them with too little fuel to return to base, they will instead abandon their patrol and return to base. Thus, the F-16s will continue to provide cover around the primary target until their fuel status become prohibitive.

Flight 3: The Big Friends

Here come the behemoths of the skies: the B-52s. Four B-52s compose section 3. With their approximate payload of 100,000 pounds each, nearly 400,000 pounds of ordnance will soon fall on enemy positions! The B-52s begin their flight northeast of Nellis. Typically, B-52s are stationed far from their end targets and often fly thousands of miles (accomplished through inflight refueling) before dropping their ordnance. These B-52s are no exception; they originated their flight at Griffiss AFB, NY several hours ago.

The B-52s are high altitude, slow moving strategic bombers. As you can see from the ALTITUDE and SPEED displays, they'll begin this mission at 30,000 feet and 375 knots. Their slow speed makes them very vulnerable to nimble enemy fighters.

This is the reason for the mission: the delivery of weapons. Press the WAYPOINT button to view the data for this waypoint. Still at an altitude of 30,000 feet, their action has been set to BOMB. Note, however, that the TARGET display is blank. Although concentrations of enemy vehicles cannot be selected as the target for a BOMB waypoint, according to the Falcon 3.0 manual, Chapter 6: *Introduction to Red Flag,* aircraft with a BOMB action and no target will still drop their ordnance at that point. With that much ordnance falling, the chances of a hit are still high.

For variety's sake, these B-52s are not going to make the several hour trip back to their home base. Instead, they're headed with you back to Nellis. Your job ends only after the four B-52s land there safely.

Tactical Recon

This mission only involves air operations for your aircraft; you have little need of information on ground forces. The only ground forces you will encounter are those targeted by the B-52s. These troops have dug in and aren't going anywhere. Simply being aware of where they are located (knowing where flight 3's second waypoint is) is about all the useful recon information you can get. So, proceed directly to the tarmac.

Proceed to the Assign Pilots menu by pressing ALLIED AIRCRAFT, followed by NELLIS COMMAND, then DONE. You should now be back to the Red Flag Control menu. Select F-16 PILOTS. Choose your favorite pilots, preferably those with high air-to-air combat skills and high fatigue (well-rested) values. Proceed to load armaments by pressing the ARMAMENTS button. As with all Advanced Flight School missions, your aircraft will already have the necessary ordnance loaded. Finally, select TAKEOFF to get underway.

Mission Walk-Through: The Flight Line

Your first task is to locate the B-52s. You know from the waypoint analysis that they're east of your position, roughly 65 to 70 miles. You know they are headed southwesterly and flying at 30,000 feet. To locate them, you need to configure your HFR radar in the NAM mode to scan accordingly. Select the NAM radar mode (press F5), set your range to 80nm (using F8), set your azimuth scan to maximum width (using F9), and adjust the antenna elevation to scan between 0 and 30,000 feet (using F10). You may have to increase your altitude to 9,000 feet to achieve the proper altitude scan. Fly directly to waypoint 1 until you detect radar contacts.

This contact is probably the B-52s. Use the HFR lock up procedure described in the previous missions to lock them up and verify their identity. As before, press T to move the vertical acquisition bars over a radar blip, then press Z to lock. Your screen should appear similar to Figure 9-15. Please note that due to the dynamics of Falcon 3.0, the B-52s' actual path, speed, and altitude may vary slightly each time the mission is executed.

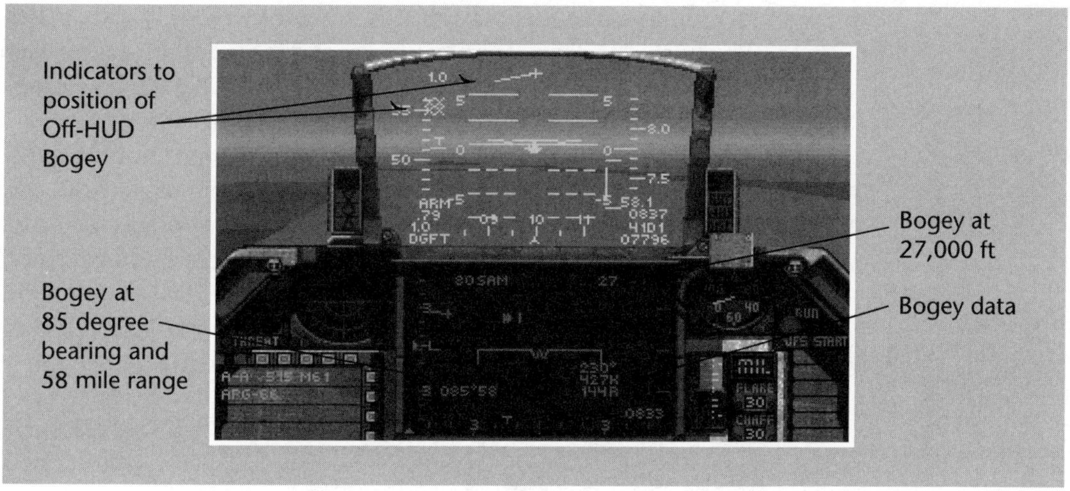

Figure 9-15 Radar Lock-On

In Figure 9-15, the bogeys are headed 230 degrees (southwest) and are at an altitude of 27,000 feet. This fits the profile of the B-52s. To determine if they are really your big friends, interrogate their IFF by pressing N. You should now hear the familiar IFF buzz indicating that they are friendly aircraft, the B-52s. For further verification, contact your simulated AWACS controller by pressing the Q key. This gives you a nice (albeit unrealistic) view of your target. In the real world, your AWACS controller could verify that the aircraft were indeed your B-52s. In Falcon 3.0, you have to devise your own AWACS controller.

Rendezvous with the bombers. If necessary, increase speed and bypass waypoint 1. Head directly toward the bombers. If they have already moved south of your first waypoint, press ALT-B to bypass waypoint 1. Close to about 30 miles from the bombers. You are now executing the role of a detached escort.

Looking for Bandits

Your electronic eyes (radar) and ears (TWI) are scanning the sky for enemies. To maximize your electronic eyes and ears you must turn your aircraft, just as you must turn your head to fully scan your surroundings with your real eyes and ears. Once you have linked with the B-52s, execute a tight turn to your left. Continue the turn until either a radar contact appears or you've turned a full 360 degrees and are once again headed toward your second waypoint. Remember, bandits may appear from anywhere. They're just as likely to try to bushwhack you from behind as they are to ambush you from the front. You should now press (ENTER) until the AIM-120 is selected. Shortly, you should see new contacts on the left side of the REO.

When you've turned to a heading of 70 degrees, you should see the B-52s headed south, to your right. In the upper left corner of the REO, just barely within the 80 mile range of your radar, are new contacts. Are they bandits? Are they strangers? Use the (T) key to select the closest bogey, press (Z) to lock him up, then press (N) to interrogate his IFF. Did you hear the IFF buzz? You shouldn't have. These bogeys are bandits. Once you've locked the closest bandit, your screen should look similar to Figure 9-16.

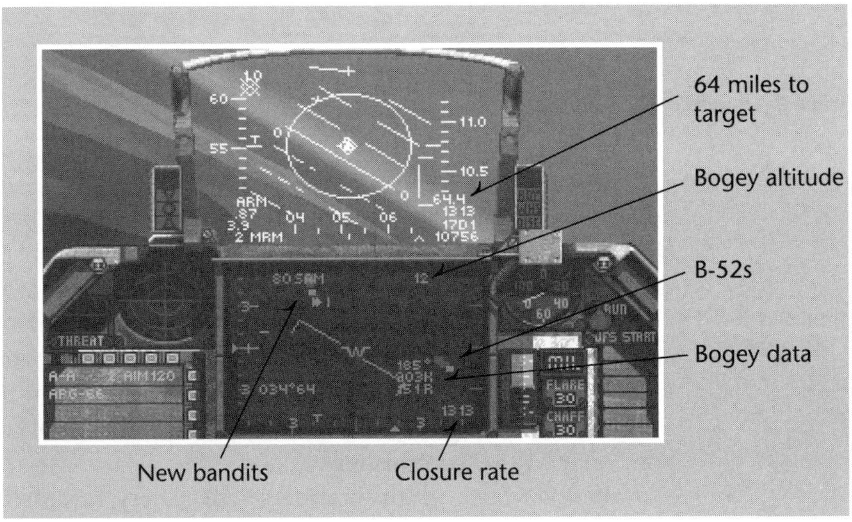

Figure 9-16 Lock Up the Bogey

Continue to turn north towards the bandits. They are headed 185 degrees at an altitude of 12,000 feet. They're 64 miles away at a heading of 34 degrees from your position. These bandits are headed straight for the bombers. It's your job to stop them. Make sure you have the lead bandit locked because he's the greatest threat. He's probably the most experienced, that's why he's leading the flight. Because he's closest to you, he'll be the first one that can shoot at you.

Air Combat Tactics

Pause the game by pressing (P). You are now about to enter a two-on-three dogfight. Multiple aircraft engagements such as this are known as *furballs*.

It will be difficult to coach you during this encounter because Falcon 3.0 bandits will execute different maneuvers each time the mission is performed. Your starting speed, heading, and altitude also will play a major role in the outcome. However, here are a few tips:

- Speed is life. Keep your speed high. Set your throttle to 100%. Keep your speed above 300 knots.
- Remember to conserve *potential* energy (altitude) and *kinetic* energy (speed). If you have to slow down (lose kinetic energy), try to do so by climbing (increase potential energy).
- Your missiles are fire-and-forget. Once you launch them you can break radar lock and attack another bandit if you want.
- Don't follow one bandit too long. While you're chasing him, his wingman will be moving into attack position behind you.
- Try to attack the bandits from their blind spot at 6 o'clock low (below and behind). However, if bandits are moving at a high speed, they may outrun you. If the bandits are coming in fast, stay between them and the bombers.
- Use the padlock view. It can save your life.
- Lead the target. If the bandit is turning to either the left or right, fire the missile slightly ahead of the target.

Unpause the game by pressing P. Your wingman is probably calling out radar contacts, and saying, "Request permission to engage." You definitely want him working with you in this mess, so press SHIFT-E to order him to engage. He should respond with, "Engaging." If, however, he responds with, "Copy fence check," he hasn't located a target yet. He'll quickly find and engage a bandit.

The bandits are coming in fast. You must get between them and the B-52s. Don't be afraid to get in there and mix it up with them. Increase throttle to 100% and head for the bandits. When you close to 15 miles, your AIM-120 should lock on a bandit. The missile circle will begin to flash and you'll hear a high pitched tone. Check the bogey's direction, then turn the nose of your aircraft to point slightly ahead of his path. Fire the AIM-120 by pressing SPACEBAR or the number 1 joystick button. Press P to pause. From here, things may proceed in a number of ways. Your missile may miss the leader. The enemy wingmen may execute different maneuvers. Be prepared for anything. When you get within visual range (five miles or less) of the bandits, select the padlock view by pressing 8.

Fighting with Padlock

Remember that padlock view will lock on friendly aircraft as well as enemy aircraft. Remember also that padlocking a bandit does not radar lock the bandit. You must still operate the radar normally. When in padlock view, the (T) key selects the target to padlock, not radar lock.

For best results, maneuver until the rectangle in the upper middle window overlays the HUD symbol. The bottom window should display the HUD at that point. The bandit will also be displayed in the bottom window inside a red box. You should then press (F6) to select ACM mode radar. The closest target within the 10 mile scan range will automatically be locked on to. The red box around the padlocked bandit will be replaced with the familiar green radar lock designation box. You will then be able to target your missiles.

> **NOTE:** Padlocking a bandit does not radar lock the bandit.

Before you unpause, be sure you're prepared. Be prepared for your missile to miss. Falcon 3.0 severely limits the effectiveness of the AIM-120. To ensure a kill, you may want to point your aircraft further ahead of the lead bandit and fire another missile. You may rather save your remaining AMRAAM and choose to close within six miles (AIM-9M Sidewinder range) before firing another missile.

The bogey will probably continue on a southerly heading, passing from left to right across your screen. You may choose to turn and follow him to ensure his destruction. If you do so, finish him quickly. When you turn to follow him, you'll place yourself between his aircraft and his wingmen, thereby becoming the victim of a classic maneuver known as *The Sandwich*. Figure 9-17 shows the dangers of this situation; as long as you remain in this

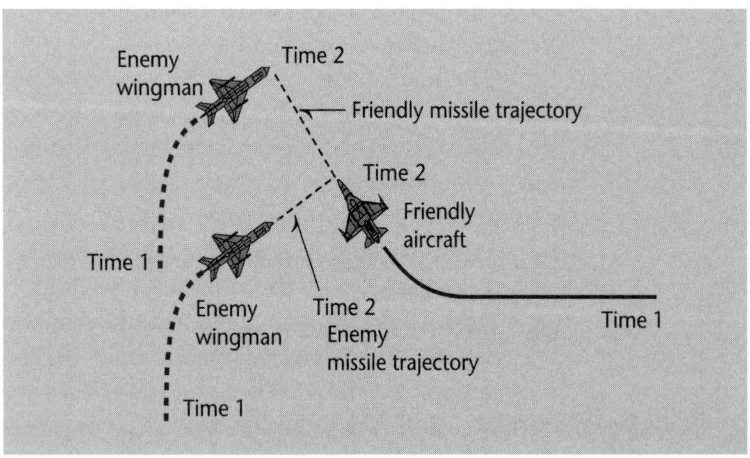

Figure 9-17 The Sandwich Maneuver

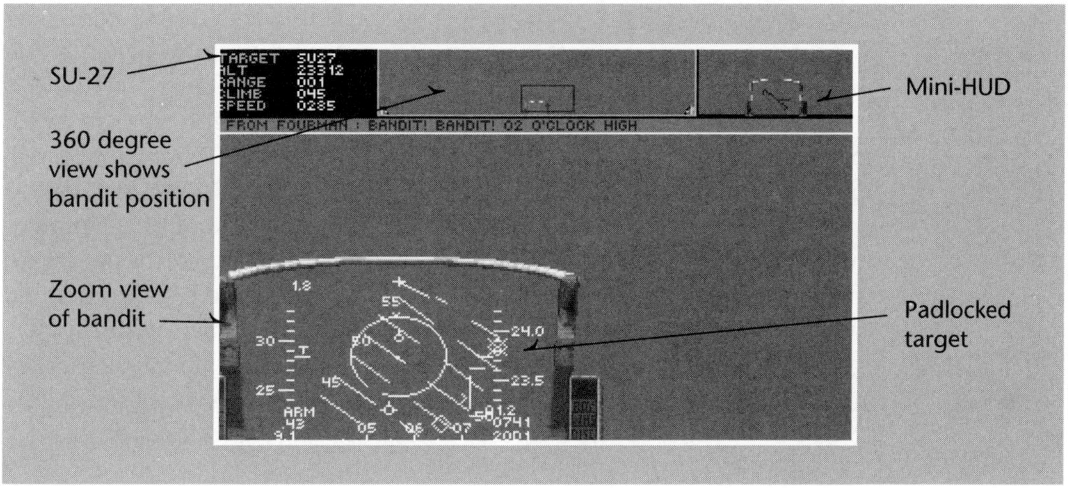

Figure 9-18 Padlock View of Su-27.

position you are a target for the enemy wingman. Alternatively, to avoid being the victim of a Sandwich, you may wish to change targets, thereby going head-to-head with one of the wingmen.

Figure 9-18 shows a typical padlock view of a dogfight. In this example, the bandit, an Su-27, is directly in front of the F-16. The rectangle in the upper middle window overlays the HUD symbol. The bottom window shows a close up view of the rectangle. The HUD is visible, as is the red box surrounding the padlocked Su-27.

Now it's time for you to execute your attack. Decide your tactic, be prepared for it to fail, and be ready to improvise. When you press P to unpause, your missile will continue on its course toward the bandit leader. Complete the dogfight, then press P to pause.

How did you do? Between you and your wingman, the three Su-27s should be reduced to smoking wreckage scattered across the desert sands. If, however, the Su-27s left you hanging from a parachute, don't despair. There's only one way to build expertise in air-to-air combat: practice. If you were shot down, proceed to the mission 3 debriefing. Otherwise, read on.

Not Out of the Woods Yet

If you survived the encounter, congratulations! While it's a great accomplishment, your job isn't over yet. How long did the encounter take? Where are the B-52s now? You may have earned a break, but you're not about to get one. If your waypoint indicator still points toward waypoint 1, press SHIFT-B to bypass and select waypoint 2. Check your necessary heading with AWACS by pressing SHIFT-N. A message from the AWACS controller should appear across the top of your screen indicating the heading and distance to waypoint 2.

As you turn toward the second waypoint, reconfigure your radar for maximum coverage. Make sure you have the 80 mile range selected, maximum azimuth scan, and a vertical scan from 0 to 30,000 feet. Unless you really went awry during the dogfight, waypoint 2 should be approximately 130nm away at a heading of 220 to 240 degrees. Continue toward this waypoint and you should catch the B-52s. After a short time, you should see new radar contacts. Lock and interrogate these contacts with the T, Z, and N sequence. You should hear the IFF buzz, indicating a friendly aircraft; these contacts are the B-52s. It's time to regroup with them. Close to within 10 miles of the bombers, increasing speed as necessary.

Fuel: The Life Blood of the F-16

So far, all of the missions you've executed have been short duration, short range missions where fuel consumption has not been a factor. This mission pushes the range of the F-16's internal fuel to the limits. Although you have an external tank also, long sprints at 100% throttle and/or afterburner use fuel at an alarming rate.

First, examine your current fuel status. Press 4 to view the left side of the cockpit. The fuel gauge has two needles. The longer needle reports the status of external fuel tanks, the shorter needle reports the current amount of internal fuel. The numbers on the gauge mark fuel amounts in hundred units. For example, "80" would mean "80 times 100" or 8,000 pounds of fuel. Based on your flying habits, the amount of fuel you have remaining may vary greatly. Simply keep the following in mind:

- You will need at least 3,000 pounds of fuel to travel from waypoint 2 back to base and land.
- Full throttle while cruising consumes large amounts of fuel. For efficient fuel consumption while maintaining a speed of 450 to 550 knots, set the throttle to 65%.

If you're low on fuel, you may have to abort the mission and return to base. You should have plenty of fuel remaining, however. If not, you need to modify your flying habits and ease up on the throttle in future missions.

A New Threat

As you close to within 100nm of waypoint 2, you should detect two new contacts on the edge of REO. Lock these guys up and interrogate their IFF.

Did you hear the buzz? You shouldn't have because they are bandits. Fortunately, the bandits are still almost 80nm away. You have plenty of time to devise your tactics.

Increase your speed and get between the bombers and the bandits. The bandits are probably around 8,000 to 11,000 feet high, so you should adjust your altitude likewise. Although, maintaining a height advantage over your adversary gives you additional potential energy during the conflict, you want to be sure that your target is kept well within the scan of your radar. For example, if your radar is scanning only down to 8,000 feet and the bandit is at 9,000 feet, a quick downward break of 1,500 feet by the bandit will take him below your lower scan boundary. Try to keep the bandit positioned so that it will be difficult for him to break your radar lock.

Press (ENTER) to select the longest range air-to-air weapon you have remaining. If you still have an AIM-120, select it, otherwise, select an AIM-9M. If you're completely out of missiles, select the 20mm cannon.

Threat Analysis

As you continue toward the bandits, what do they do? Do they point their noses toward you and charge, or do they continue away from you? Figure 9-19 shows what you probably see: these bandits are headed away from you.

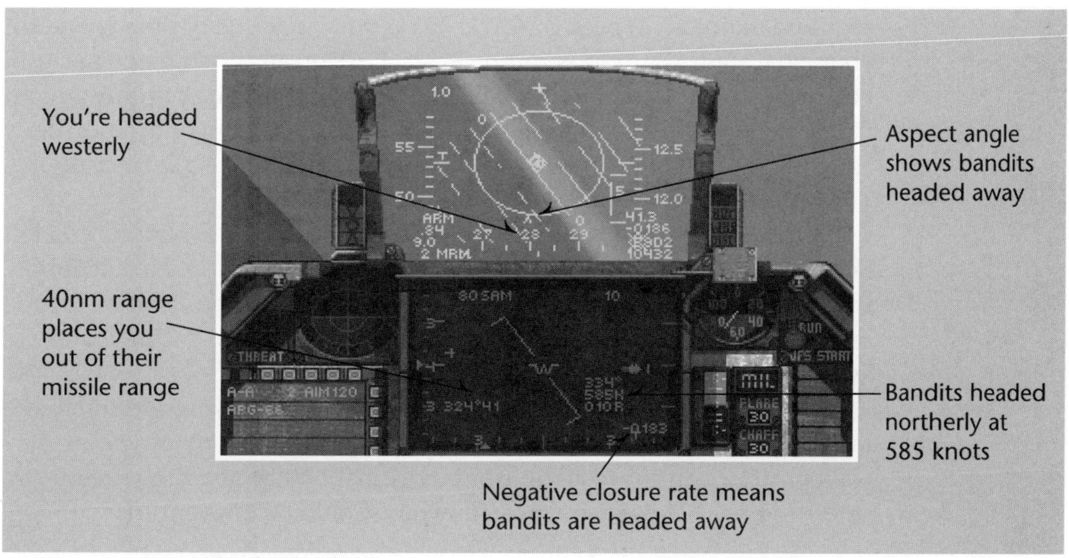

Figure 9-19 Bandits Headed Away

As stated earlier, when charged with an escort mission, you can't go gallivanting around the sky attacking every bandit you come across, and then run home when the weapons run out. In an escort mission, you must reserve your limited fuel and weapons for the protection of the escorted aircraft. If the new bandits close on you, attack and destroy them. If they continue away, leave them alone, but continue to monitor their location. As you continue onward, make an occasional circle to check behind you. If those guys try to sneak up behind you, you'll be prepared.

Approaching Waypoint 2

Rendezvous with the bombers and continue toward waypoint 2. Make sure you've configured your radar for maximum scanning and an 80nm range. As you close to within 60 to 80 miles of waypoint 2, you should detect two new bogeys. When you lock and interrogate them, you'll probably breathe a sigh of relief. They aren't bandits, they're the reception escort!

Now comes the hand-off. The B-52s will continue south to their target and the reception escort will provide cover for them. You are to loiter at waypoint 2 and wait for the bombers to finish. Once they've dropped their payloads, they'll turn north and head for Nellis. From the time they leave the protection of the reception escort until they land at Nellis, they will again be your responsibility.

You should set your altitude so that your radar scans between 0 and 30,000 feet at an 80 mile range. You should then set your throttle at about 65% and maintain a speed of 400 knots as you circle. Every time you point your radar southwards look for the B-52s. Lock up any aircraft you see until you locate them. They shouldn't be hard to find, they'll be the only aircraft flying at 27,000 to 30,000 feet. When their heading changes to a northerly course, you'll know they've finished their attack and are on their way home. They're once again your responsibility.

While you circle, keep an eye to the north for those bandits you left behind earlier. Don't let them sneak up behind you. In all likelihood, they're low on fuel and are returning to base; however, you can never be too careful. If the bandits begin toward you, destroy them. If they continue away, let them run.

When the B-52s head north, position yourself alongside them at a range of about 15 to 20 miles. As during the trip from waypoint 1 to waypoint 2, continue to circle around the main body, guarding their front, sides, and rear. The return trip, however, should be uneventful.

Mission Debriefing

You may consider this mission a success only if both of the following conditions are met:

- At least three of the B-52s land safely at Nellis, and
- You land safely at Nellis.
- Anything else results in a mission failure. If you failed, examine the results of your mission.
- Did your wingman get shot down but the mission still succeed? If so, chalk this up to bad luck and proceed to the next mission.
- Were you shot down? Brush up on your air-to-air skills. Review padlock view use, basic fighter maneuvers, and air-to-air weapons delivery in Chapter 5, *Using Weapons,* and the HFR radar use in Chapter 8, *Using High Fidelity Radar*. Then, repeat this mission. Preview advanced fighter maneuvers in Chapter 11, *Secrets and Tactics of the Enemy.*
- Were too many B-52s shot down? Escort missions are difficult, and it takes considerable practice and a little good luck to succeed. Review the briefing and analysis, then repeat the mission.

Mission 4: Operation Sand Blaster

A Close Air Support Mission

ZNR CCCCC
I 14 0800Z JAN 92
FM RED FLAG HQ DIV//GEN WAITE//
TO 386TH FSFORUM SQU CMDR//COL BASHAM//

BT
S E C R E T
REF: DAILY ATO: OP: SAND BLASTER (S)
(S) ENEMY FORCES HAVE SUCCESSFULLY REGROUPED AND HAVE BEGUN EXECUTING COUNTER ATTACKS. A LARGE CONVOY OF ENEMY GROUND VEHICLES HAS BEEN SPOTTED APPROXIMATELY 100 MILES NORTHWEST OF NELLIS AFB. THE CONVOY, COMPOSED OF ARMOR, INFANTRY, AND ARTILLERY, CONTAINS OVER 25 VEHICLES AND IS MOVING SOUTH. A NUMERICALLY SMALLER FORCE CONSIST-

ING OF ELEMENTS FROM THE 155TH ARMORED AND 32ND ARTILLERY BRIGADES IS MOVING NORTH TO ENGAGE. THE 386TH IS ORDERED TO EXECUTE CLOSE AIR SUPPORT SORTIES AGAINST THE ENEMY CONVOY BEFORE FRIENDLY FORCES ENGAGE.

FRIENDLY FORCES HAVE SUCCESSFULLY PENETRATED ENEMY LINES IN THREE KEY POSITIONS, RESULTING IN SIGNIFICANT TERRITORIAL GAINS. ENEMY FORCES HAVE FAILED TO SEIZE ANY SIGNIFICANT TERRITORIAL GAINS.

ENEMY STATE TELEVISION REPORTS OF CAPTURE OF COL M BARRS ARE UNCONFIRMED.
ET

Nellis AFB—0900 HRS

Ever since enemy press officials made the announcement, the news media has been swamped with rumors that Colonel Barrs is being held as a Prisoner of War (POW). It has been three days since the Colonel was downed behind enemy lines, and multiple search-and-rescue patrols were unable to locate him. Pentagon officials refuse to confirm or deny statements made in an enemy press conference. The enemy spokesman stated the Colonel was captured two nights ago and is being held at an unnamed enemy communications facility. The safety of the Colonel was assured—provided that allied forces do not attack said facility.

The fact that the enemy knows Colonel Barrs' name is a bad sign, indicating that they may indeed hold him prisoner. However, the possibility still remains that they observed his name on the wreckage of his F-16 or on some discarded piece of clothing, such as his helmet. You hope that he remains free.

Meanwhile, the war is definitely progressing well. Enemy casualties appear to be extremely heavy, while Allied casualties have been extremely light. Enemy forces have regrouped and begun coordinated counter attacks; however, it appears unlikely that they will be able to alter the tide. One enemy convoy has been spotted moving toward Nellis, near where Colonel Barrs was downed. The 386th is preparing to attack this convoy while it moves across the desert. With thoughts of Colonel Barrs, you head for the briefing room. Although you remain strictly professional at all times, deep down inside you have a personal score to settle on this next mission.

The Mission Briefing

"Enemy ground forces are on the move," begins the Red Flag instructor, "and the 386th will be there to greet them. Allied forces are making substantial gains against them, and they are desperately trying to mount a counter attack. One particular convoy was spotted four hours ago by an RF-4 approximately 100 miles northwest of Nellis. This convoy consisted of over 25 vehicles and is headed southerly, possibly planning to attack this airbase. There is a much smaller column of friendly vehicles moving northward to engage them. Our job is to even the odds by locating and destroying many of the enemy vehicles before our boys get there. This type of mission is called *Close Air Support,* or CAS."

Close Air Support: Two Versus Many

"Only a single flight of two F-16s will attack the convoy. That makes the odds about 30 to two. Each aircraft will carry six AGM-65D Maverick missiles and eight CBU-84 cluster bombs. With the proper tactics, the two F-16s should be able to reduce the convoy to less than ten operational units. There is no enemy air activity in this area, so there will be no need to carry air-to-air weaponry.

"In typical enemy fashion, the convoy was observed moving in a single file column across the desert. You should fly low (under 2,000 feet) and fast (over 500 knots) as you search for them. Once you've spotted the convoy, make multiple attacks from different directions. The Maverick missiles will be most effective when approaching the convoy from the sides. The cluster bombs will be most effective when flying the length of the convoy, allowing you to *ripple* the individual bombs along it.

"Finally," the instructor concludes, "no SAM or AAA units were observed in this convoy, although you can be certain that infantry units will be carrying SA-7 Grail, shoulder-launched, heat-seeking missiles. So, watch your backs. Dismissed."

Mission Analysis

This mission emphasizes three elements:

- Principles of CAS missions.
- Delivery of AGM-65 Maverick missiles.
- Delivery of CBU-84 cluster bombs.

When someone mentions the words "Air Force," the image of aerial combat usually enters the listeners' imaginations. Yet, the air-to-air combat role actually developed as a secondary mission. The first manned aircraft, simple balloons, made their combat debut as reconnaissance platforms during the American Civil War. Powered aircraft continued this role during the opening years of World War I. In response to being fired upon by ground troops, early pilots began dropping simple bombs on the forces they were monitoring. This spawned the use of aircraft to deny other enemy aircraft the opportunity to attack.

By the time World War II started, the armies of the world realized the destructive potential of aircraft in the ground attack role, due in part to the persistent advocate of air power, General Billy Mitchell. Although the public remains fascinated with the three-dimensional maneuvering of aerial combat, this alone is purely defensive. A fighter's true offensive potential lies in its ground attack capabilities.

CAS missions have become loved by modern ground forces. The ability to call for an aerial bombardment against one's enemy while remaining safely out of the battle has endeared airpower to most foot soldiers. As seen in the 1991 Gulf War, weeks of sustained bombardment by air power greatly reduced Iraqi military effectiveness, allowing Coalition forces a quick, devastating, 100 hour mop up.

Falcon 3.0 is no exception. Ground forces in campaign mode will often call upon your squadron for help. Sometimes, the friendlies are preparing an attack and want you to whittle the enemy down to size; at other times friendly forces are trapped by hostile troops and require your assistance to escape. The CAS mission is an extremely important task and should be approached seriously.

CAS Principles

While the need for CAS sorties is recognized by all, the requirements to perform such missions often fuel heated debates. Some advocate the use of low speed, heavily armored aircraft, such as the A-10. Others prefer attack helicopters, such as the AH-64. A third group recommends the use of high speed, lightly armored aircraft, such as the F-16.

Everyone agrees that the slower the aircraft flies, the more likely it is to be hit. Proponents of the F-16 believe that modern SAMs can penetrate the armor of slow moving aircraft. They instead rely on high speed, believing that the aircraft can escape the danger zone before the enemy returns fire. F-4s performing the CAS role in the Vietnam War also relied on this theory.

However, the faster the CAS aircraft approaches the target, the less time it has to target and deliver its weapons. If you are using guided weapons, such as the AGM-65, this may not present a problem. However the targeting of free-fall bombs requires a significant amount of time to ensure accuracy. The F-4s performing the CAS role in Vietnam had substantial difficulties delivering free-fall weapons on small targets while traveling at high speeds.

Speed Is Life

You do not have the luxury of choosing your approach tactic. Your F-16 is extremely vulnerable to enemy fire. You only have one engine; if it takes damage, you lose all power. You must approach your target at high speed, preferably above 450 knots. Fly slow, and you will be shot down.

Multiple Attack Passes—Altitude Kills

Normally, when attacking a ground target, you make a single attack run, flying high enough to avoid AAA fire and shoulder-launched SAMs. However, this rarely works for a CAS mission. Normally, a two plane group will carry sufficient ordnance for 14 to 16 kills against a group of 30 or more targets. A Maverick missile has a range of 14 miles. At 450 knots, your F-16 will cover 14 miles in about 1.6 minutes. That doesn't give you enough time to deliver all your weapons.

Therefore, you will have to make multiple passes over the target, and will need a tactic to minimize the additional risks. Your best bet is to fly very low, under 1,000 feet above ground level (AGL), making fast hit-and-run attacks from multiple directions. By flying low, the surrounding terrain will hide you from the enemy's radars and eyes. Each pass should be from a different direction, constantly surprising the enemy.

Use the Right Weapon for the Right Job

Low-level attacks, however, require some forethought. Dropping a 2,000 pound Mk84 bomb in the center of the convoy may ensure numerous kills, but even at high speeds, an F-16 flying under 1,000 feet will be damaged by the explosion. The following weapons are well suited for low-level delivery; all other ordnance requires additional altitude before firing.

- AGM-65 Maverick—This high speed missile flies much faster than the F-16, and has a relatively small 125 pound warhead. This missile does considerable damage to its target, without much *collateral damage* to the surrounding environment. Best used to destroy a specific target, like an individual tank.

- CBU-84 Cluster Bomb Unit—This device drops 202 small, free-fall bombs on and around the specified drop point. Excellent for attacking massed formations, these *submunitions* thoroughly cover the targeted area using ½ pound warheads. The small warheads are highly effective against light armor and infantry while posing little threat to the deploying aircraft.
- LAU 5003A Rocket Launcher—This weapon fires unguided rockets ahead of the aircraft. Rockets detonate ahead of the aircraft, posing little threat of self-injury. Very effective against light armor, trucks, and infantry.
- Mk82HD Snakeye—This free-fall bomb carries the same 275 pound warhead of the Mk82; however, it uses *drag-fins* which operate like a parachute to slow the decent of the bomb, thereby allowing the deploying aircraft sufficient time to escape. Effective against heavy armor and small buildings, the Snakeye requires precise CCIP bombing techniques to ensure a hit.

Different AGM-65 Versions

As discussed in Chapter 5, *Using Weapons*, there are two versions of the Maverick missile: the AGM-65B television guided, and the AGM-65D infrared guided versions. Both missiles are fire-and-forget missiles; once the missile has been released, the launching aircraft is free to select a new target or maneuver. The infrared sensor of the D version makes it much more effective at night than the B version. Not only can the D version target objects hotter than the background (such as a hot engine in a tank), but it can also target objects colder than the background (such as the cold chassis of a tank in a pre-dawn desert morning). You will carry six AGM-65D missiles during this mission.

AGM-65 Usage

Both versions of the AGM-65 operate the same. To acquire a target, simply point the F-16 at the desired target so that the target is visible in the center of the HUD. The AGM-65 targeting crosshairs will automatically move and superimpose the target signifying a lock. An image of the target as the missile sees it will be displayed on the REO. In case of multiple targets, press the T key to step through all available targets. If you want to break the lock completely, press the X key. As long as the target remains visible in the HUD, however, the AGM-65 will automatically reacquire it.

CBU-84 Usage

The CBU-84 uses standard Continuously Computed Impact Point (CCIP) bombing techniques. Also known as *iron bombing,* CCIP bombing depends upon the timing of weapons release to ensure that unguided munitions land on target. When a CBU-84 is selected, a small circle appears at the bottom of the HUD. The pilot steers the F-16 until this circle superimposes the target. The pilot selects that target by pressing SPACEBAR. No weapons are released, but the F-16's flight computer begins computing when to release the weapons to ensure a hit based on current altitude and speed. The computer automatically releases the bombs at the correct time.

The pilot can increase the chances of a hit by dropping more bombs at one time. The number of bombs dropped, called the *ripple value,* can be set anywhere from a minimum of 2, to a maximum of all bombs remaining. The ripple can be increased by the ' key and decreased by the ; key.

In this mission, your primary weapon will be the AGM-65 Maverick missile. Therefore, you only need an elementary knowledge of CCIP bombing techniques at this time. For complete details on CCIP bombing, refer to Chapter 5, *Using Weapons*. For further training on CCIP bombing, refer to Mission 6: Operation Falling Sky, later in this chapter.

Approach Techniques

How you approach the target is as important as what weapon you fire. As stated before, each pilot has a primary responsibility to return to base with both himself and the aircraft intact. The enemy will rarely be sitting still. Usually, the specified CAS waypoint will be in the general vicinity of the target, not an exact indicator. Flying fast and low usually complicates locating the enemy and delivering weapons. The following tactics will help these situations.

The Pop-Up Search Figure 9-20 illustrates the pop-up search. The attacking aircraft approaches the target area at low altitude and high speed. When near the target, the aircraft *pops up,* or quickly climbs several thousand feet, and rolls inverted, allowing the pilot a clear view of the

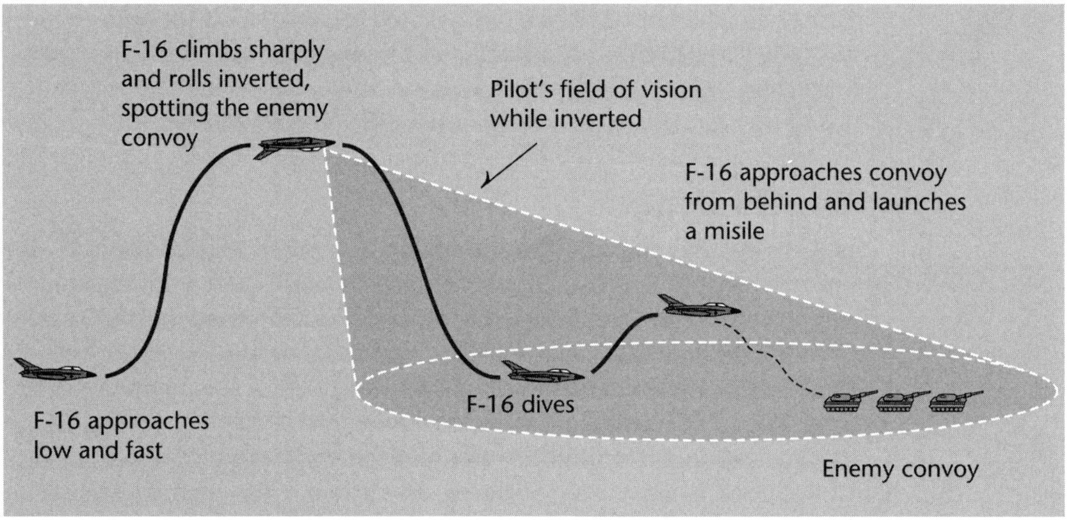

Figure 9-20 The Pop-Up Search

surrounding terrain through the top of the canopy. The pilot then quickly dives and rolls right side up again. The pilot repeats this procedure until the enemy has been spotted.

The Pop-Up Attack Very similar to the pop-up search, Figure 9-21 illustrates the pop-up attack. This maneuver is normally used when the location of the target is known and the attacking aircraft has ordnance that

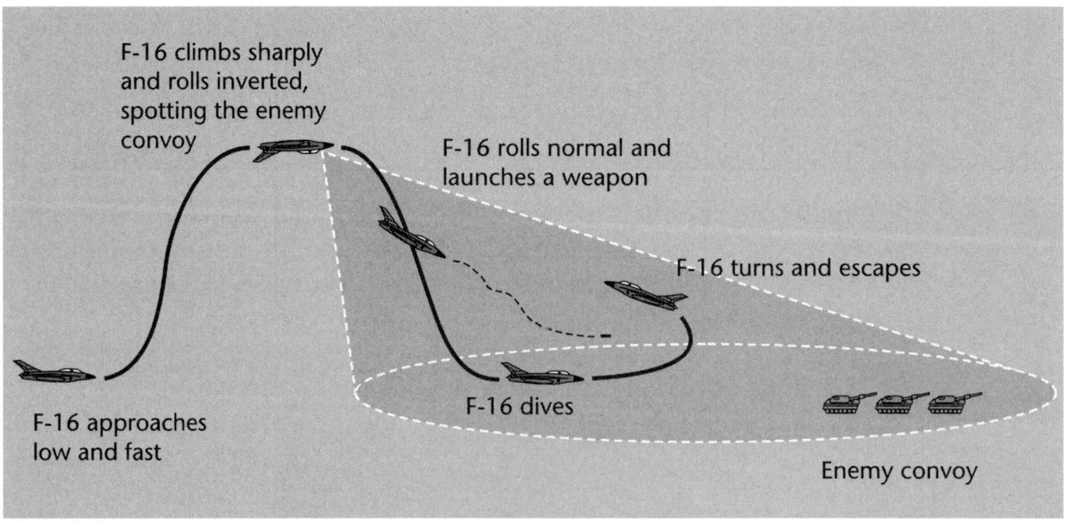

Figure 9-21 The Pop-Up Attack

requires additional altitude prior to release, or the pilot reacquires a new approach angle to surprise the target.

The pilot begins by approaching the target at low altitude and high speed. The pilot closes on the target until he is within weapons range, then climbs steeply and rolls inverted, gaining visual contact with the target. This time, however, the pilot fires a weapon at the target prior to diving.

> **WARNING:** During pop-up maneuvers, be careful not to remain at the high altitude very long. Remember: if you can see the enemy, the enemy can see you.

The Wingover The wingover maneuver helps you maintain visual contact with the target while providing additional altitude for weapons delivery; however, it also increases the length of time you are vulnerable to ground fire. Figure 9-22 illustrates.

The wingover begins while flying at low altitude searching for the targeted convoy. Upon locating the target, the aircraft flies over the target at low altitude and deploys any available low-altitude weapons. Then, after passing the target, the pilot applies full afterburner and pitches the aircraft's nose up to a 90° climb, then continues pulling the nose until the plane is inverted and the nose begins to fall. During this time, the pilot should be able to maintain visual contact with the target through the top of the

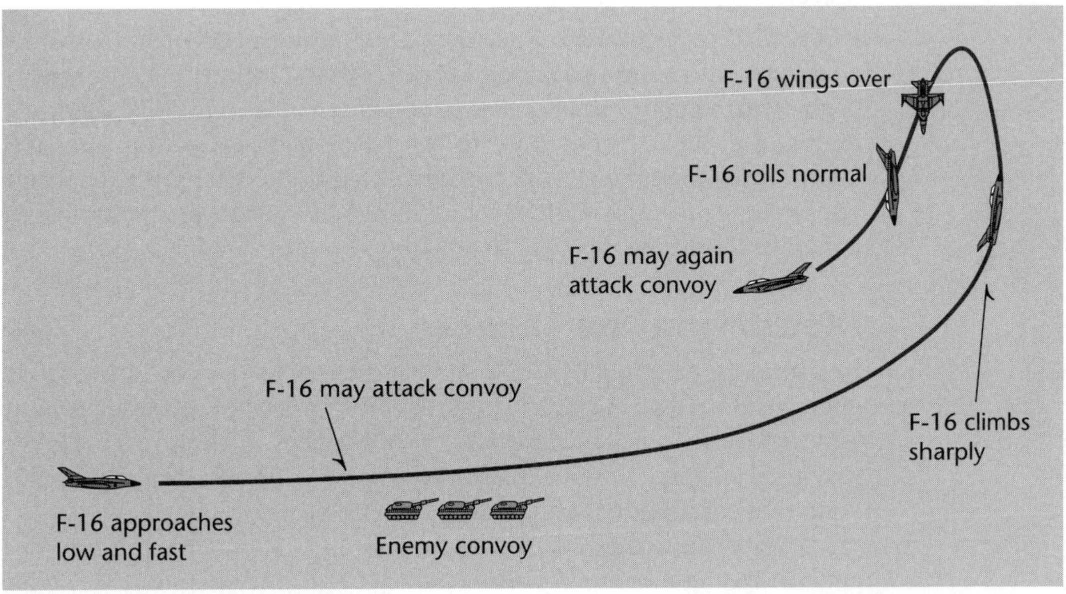

Figure 9-22 The Wingover Attack

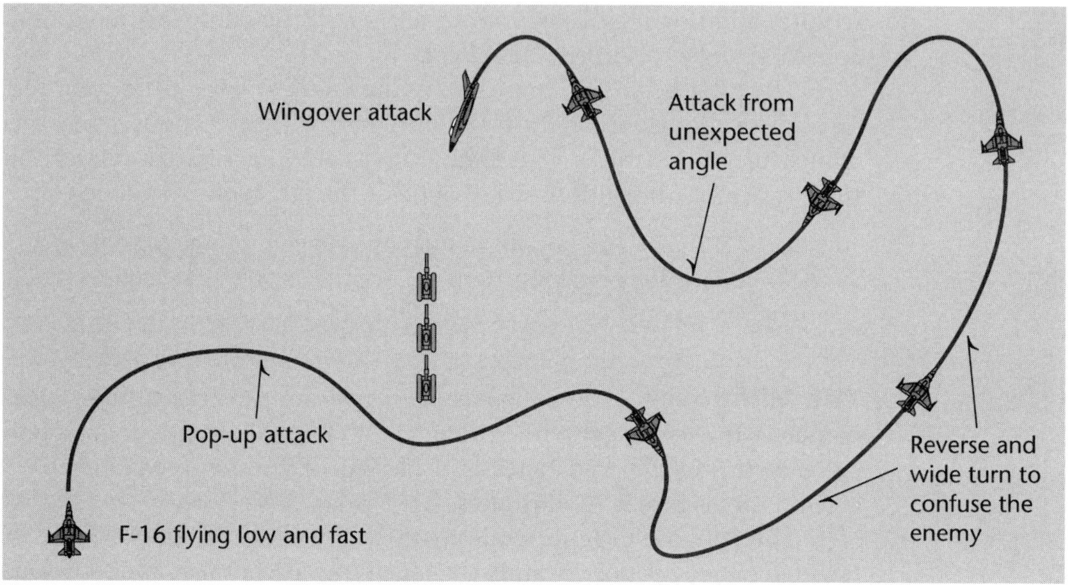

Figure 9-23 Overhead View of Multiple Approaches During a Typical CAS Mission

canopy. The pilot then rolls the aircraft to a conventional position and should see the target directly before him.

Combining Tactics

Rarely will you use a single approach tactic during a CAS mission. Instead, you will combine various maneuvers as shown in Figure 9-23. The mission begins with a pop-up attack as the pilot makes a wide right turn. Then, after diving, the pilot reverses hard to the left and makes a long turn, later approaching the convoy from an unexpected angle. After firing the second weapon, the pilot turns right, extends, executes a wingover, and attacks the convoy a third time.

Identifying the Target

Determining whether a ground vehicle directly before you is friendly or enemy is the single most difficult task of the CAS mission. Often, friendly and enemy forces will be positioned extremely near one another. It is very easy to accidentally attack a friendly target by mistake, thereby earning yourself a court-martial and ending your flying days.

There's only one way to tell the friendly and enemy ground forces apart in Falcon 3.0: observe the color of the ground vehicles. *All* friendly ground vehicles will be either green or gray. *All* enemy ground vehicles will be black or brown. Even at ranges where the vehicles appear as a single dot on your screen, all vehicles will adhere to this color scheme.

> **TIP:** Always remember the following rule: Use the first letter of the color of the target to identify it. If the color of the troops starts with the letter "g" (*g*reen or *g*ray), then the troops are good guys. If the color of the troops starts with "b" (*b*rown), the troops are bad guys. All ground forces in Falcon 3.0 are colored green, gray, or brown.

Other Search Methods

Besides visual searches, there are three other methods of locating ground forces: using the targeting systems of smart weapons, playing "professional target," and modifying the visual zoom factor. The first two are legitimate combat methods, the third is a cheat.

> **NOTE:** Mobile ground units, such as tanks and artillery, are not detected by GM radar. GM radar only detects fixed structures, such as roads and buildings. You cannot use GM radar to search for enemy convoys.

Smart Weapons Targeting Systems When a target is detected, smart weapons, like the AGM-65 and GBU-15, automatically acquire the closest target and display its image on the REO. When searching for enemy forces, you should select one of these types of weapons, even if you are unable to launch it due to your current altitude constraints. Execute a pop-up search. When you dive (thereby pointing the weapon at the ground), if there's a target within range, the weapon will lock on. The GBU-15 has only a 5 mile range; however, both versions of the AGM-65 have a 14 mile range.

Professional Target This is as dangerous as the name implies. When you just can't find the enemy, try climbing to 8,000 or so feet, and circle. If the enemy is nearby, you can bet they'll begin firing SAMs at you. You have made yourself a target.

You must keep alert while executing this maneuver. Once the SAM is airborne, you must not only execute evasive actions, but you must also mark where the missile originated relative to your current position. As you make wild maneuvers to evade the SAM, you must keep track of your heading and remember where the missile came from. Once you evade the SAM, you can focus your search around the origination area.

WARNING: Being a professional target is a dangerous tactic and should be executed only when you are fully capable of evading SAMs.

Cheating: Changing How You Look at the World Of course, you can always press the ESC key, select the Options menu, and adjust the view magnification to a higher value. In the real world, the pilot must always rely on the normal, 1x view. In Falcon 3.0, you can increase the magnification up to 8x. This does not affect unit positions or weapons ranges, it only makes objects appear larger. This visual distortion may lead you to believe you are closer to a target than you actually are. Using any magnification other than 1x is not recommended.

Mission Walk-Through: Preflight

Unfortunately, there's very little that can be done to prepare for a CAS sortie. Studying waypoints provides limited value because ground forces are usually moving. Rarely will your CAS waypoint precisely mark the location of the targeted convoy.

Furthermore, ground units are not affected by terrain in Falcon 3.0. Tactical chokepoints, such as mountain passes and bridges, have no effect in a Falcon 3.0 campaign. This isn't the deviation from reality it sounds like. Modern armies using mobile bridge laying equipment can ford most rivers with relative ease, and the terrain in the Falcon 3.0 theaters of operation may sometimes be difficult, but rarely impassable.

NOTE: You cannot use CAS waypoints as exact indicators of enemy positions because such units are usually in motion. Neither can you attempt to catch enemy forces as they move through tactical bottlenecks due to Falcon 3.0's disregard for the effects of terrain on ground forces.

As usual, you should study the waypoints of your flight and other allied aircraft to avoid war fog conditions during the mission. You should ensure that pilots with high bombing and flying skills are assigned to the CAS flight, and you should endeavor to arm the CAS aircraft with the best selection of ordnance, following the guidelines listed above. Otherwise, it is time to head for the cockpit.

Falcon 3.0 does not allow you to save the magnification. Every time you enter the simulation, it will reset to 2x. The F3maps utility on the enclosed Falcon 3.0 Flight Disk allows you to reset the default magnification to 1x, 2x, 4x, or 8x. This way, every time you enter Falcon 3.0, your preferences will already be configured. Refer to Appendix A, *The Falcon 3 Flight Disk* for details.

Mission Walk-Through: The Flight Line

Radar will be of little value during this mission. During Falcon 3.0 campaigns, the possibility of encountering the enemy always exists; however, for this training flight, there are no other aircraft, friendly or hostile, besides you and your wingmen. This mission focuses strictly on the CAS duties, and avoids cluttering the lesson with additional factors. Additionally, mobile ground units are not displayed on GM radar. While it may sometimes be useful to use GM radar to locate tactical landmarks such as roads, bridges, etc., this radar mode has no value during the actual attack. Since using active radar announces your presence to anyone equipped to detect it, it is strongly suggested that you do not activate the APG-66 until you have reason to do so. Shut the APG-66 radar off by pressing R.

Preparing for the Hunt

This mission again begins enroute to the target to save time; however, you still begin a considerable distance from the target area to allow time to appropriately configure your systems. Fly to waypoint 1, then turn and fly directly toward waypoint 2.

As stated in the mission briefing, you can augment your visual search for targets by keeping a guided weapon, such as the AGM-65 Maverick, selected as the current weapon. If you should happen to point the weapon at a target purely by chance, it will still acquire and lock that target automatically. For this flight, you are carrying six AGM-65s. Select the AGM-65 as the current weapon by pressing BACKSPACE repeatedly until your screen appears as in Figure 9-24.

Notice the altitude of the aircraft in Figure 9-24; it is 5,700 feet ASL, but only 836 feet AGL. During a CAS mission, you always want to remain low, hidden by the surrounding terrain. Always remain below 1,000 feet AGL unless executing a specific maneuver in order to evade a SAM or deploy a weapon.

HINT: Always monitor your AGL value instead of your ASL value when flying low. In Figure 9-24, the aircraft is 5,700 feet above sea level, but only 836 feet above the ground.

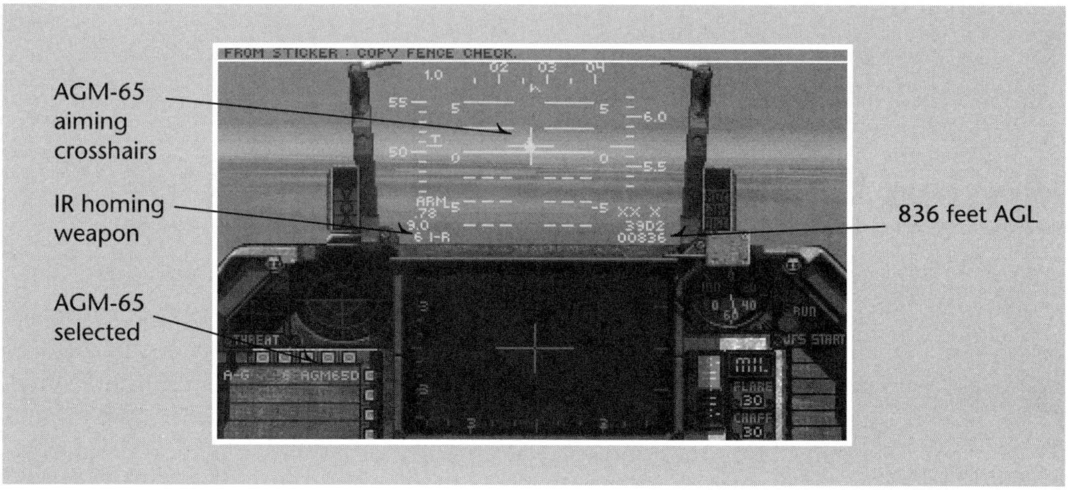

Figure 9-24 Initial Weapons Selection

The F-16 in Figure 9-24 is also traveling at slightly over 500 knots. Always remember, speed is life. When in a combat zone, circling, slowly moving, high-flying aircraft are excellent targets for enemy ground-to-air defenses. Your only hope is to constantly surprise the enemy, appearing and disappearing like a ghost. This requires you to maintain a very high speed while flying at extremely low altitudes.

> WARNING: High speed and low altitude form a deadly combination. You must remain alert and aware of your altitude at all times. One small mistake and you'll plow into the ground!

First Contact

Continue directly toward waypoint 2, flying at 450 to 500 knots and under 1,000 feet AGL. When you are approximately 33 miles from the waypoint, a single row of dots should appear on your screen, as shown in Figure 9-25. These dots are ground units; trucks, tanks, artillery, infantry, etc. What color are these dots? They are either green or gray, indicating they are good guys.

Even though you don't want to attack these guys, there's nothing wrong with getting a little extra targeting practice. Feel free to point the Maverick targeting crosshairs on the HUD at one of the friendly vehicles. When the missile locks on to the friendly vehicle, an image of the vehicle will be displayed on the REO. Do not fire a missile at any vehicle in this convoy!

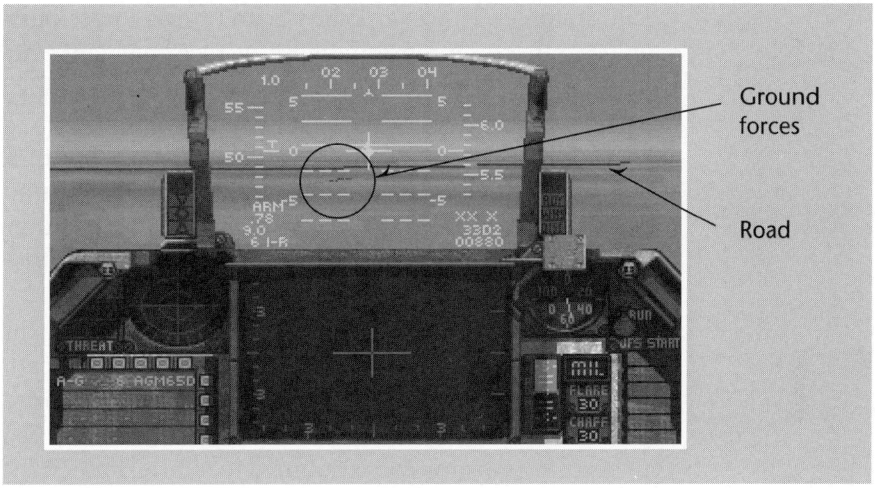

Figure 9-25 First Contact with Ground Forces

Waypoint 2: The Search Is On

Continue toward waypoint 2. Depending upon how much you deviated from the assigned course and how fast you fly, the enemy convoy will have had some time to move. By the time you reach waypoint 2, they may be located directly beneath you, or up to five miles from the waypoint! Your first order of business upon reaching waypoint 2 is to locate the convoy.

Use a Pop-Up Search The pop-up search is usually a good maneuver with which to begin. Execute a series of pop-up searches, each facing a different direction, forming a circle around waypoint 2. For each pop up, vary the maximum altitude and the length of time at that altitude, but never remain at altitude for more than ten seconds. Every second you remain at a fixed altitude increases the risk of drawing SAM and AAA fire by at least 10%. Stay high for over ten seconds and you're sure to have someone shoot at you.

There Are No Short Cuts There is no secret key that reveals the position of the enemy. There is no secret maneuver that always tells you where the bad guys are. There is no short cut that immediately positions you directly above the enemy.

During the 1991 Gulf War, several F-15E strike aircraft (among others) were assigned to locate and destroy Iraqi mobile Scud missile launchers. Due to the political ramifications of having these missiles fired at Israel, the destruction of Iraqi Scuds was crucial to maintaining the cohesiveness of the

Coalition forces. However, many Scud hunting missions ended unsuccessfully. Despite the intense network of reconnaissance aircraft and intelligence satellites, Coalition pilots frequently were unable to locate the mobile launchers and had to return to base empty handed.

Likewise, this may occasionally happen to you in Falcon 3.0. Sometimes, no matter how hard you try, you simply will not find the ground forces you were ordered to attack. Under such circumstances, you will have to return to base, your weapons still hanging unfired beneath your wings.

Cutting Losses If this happens to you, do not be disillusioned. True, the mission will be rated a failure, bestowing the ramifications of said failure upon all friendly forces theater-wide. However, it is unrealistic for you to expect to successfully complete all of your missions. Sometimes, despite your best efforts, a mission is doomed to failure. In such instances, it's better to cut your losses and take your aircraft safely back to base, instead of pushing your luck.

He who retreats lives to fight another day!

Listen to Your Wingman However, by executing the tactics described in the mission briefing, you should have little trouble locating the enemy forces. Your wingman is also searching for the enemy, and he may find them before you do. If your wingman states, "Closing on ground targets," followed by, "Request permission to engage," do not hesitate to give permission by pressing SHIFT-E. Once your wingman begins his attack, you can switch to padlock view and follow him to the target.

After the Convoy Is Located

Searching for the convoy is the difficult part. Attacking them is the dangerous part. Convoys usually travel in single file rows. Depending upon the angle from which you approach, different attack methods are required. Figure 9-26 illustrates.

Approach Zones: Aspect to the Target Figure 9-26 shows the four possible approach zones based upon the aspect between the approaching aircraft and the target. If the angle between the heading of the target and the heading of the aircraft is low, the aircraft will fly length wise over the convoy, maximizing the amount of time available to deliver weapons. If the angle between the heading of the target and the heading of the aircraft is high, the aircraft will quickly cross the line of vehicles, minimizing the amount of time available for weapons delivery.

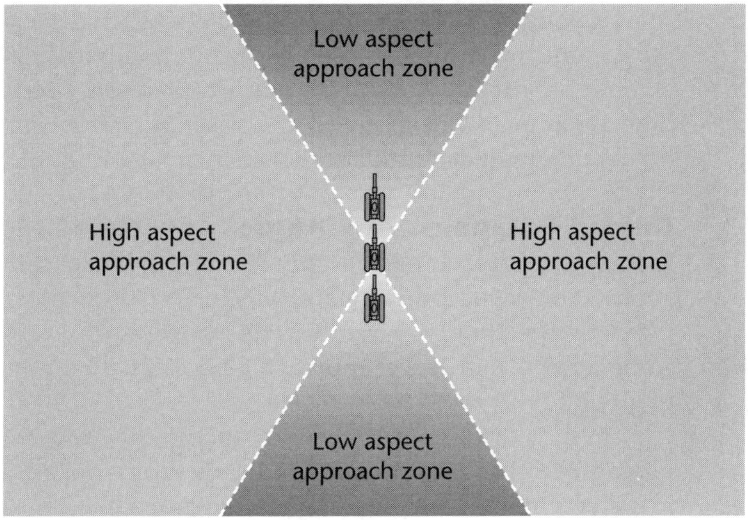

Figure 9-26 Approach Aspect Zones

Unguided Ordnance: Low-Aspect Attacks Only When approaching from a low-aspect zone, you will fly over the entire convoy from front to back (or vice versa). Low-aspect approaches provide the maximum time available for weapons delivery. Unguided ordnance, such as the CBU-84, are usually delivered in groups to increase the *probability of a kill* (PK). The size of the group is called the *ripple*. Ripple values may be set to 2, 4, 6, or 8 by using the ; to decrease and ' to increase. A ripple value of 4 means that 4 units of the selected weapon will be released at once. The ripple value is displayed on the stores panel, refer to Figure 9-28.

Because of the increased delivery time, and the ability to ripple release a series of weapons along a single line, unguided ordnance should be dropped only when approaching from a low-aspect zone. When a series of bombs is dropped along a straight line, the explosion of the bombs will only damage enemy targets at the point(s) where the line of bombs and the line of targets intersect.

For example, if a convoy is heading 0° and you drop a series of CBU-84 cluster bombs while traveling at 90°, the explosion from the cluster bombs will damage enemy vehicles only at the point where the two lines cross. However, if you drop the bombs while traveling at either 0° or 180° directly over the convoy, your bombs will damage multiple vehicles along the line.

TIP: When using unguided ordnance on CAS missions, set ripple values high and approach the target from a low-aspect zone.

If you must use unguided ordnance when attacking from a high-aspect zone, set the ripple value to the minimum of 2. This will reduce the amount of ordnance dropped on unoccupied soil. Because of the reduced time to set up a CCIP approach and lower PK, it is recommended that you do not use unguided ordnance when attacking from high-aspect zones.

Guided Weapons: Any Angle, Any Time No matter how you look at it, approaching the target from a low-aspect zone increases PK because you have more targets directly in front of your F-16. However, it also increases the time you are directly above enemy air defense systems. Sometimes, a high-aspect approach is necessary to minimize time exposed to ground fire.

In such cases, guided weapons, such as the AGM-65 Maverick, are the appropriate choice. Although guided weapons work equally well during low-aspect attacks, they are much more suited to high-aspect attacks than unguided ordnance. Guided weapons have a much higher likelihood of hitting their target, therefore, requiring fewer weapons fired per target than unguided ordnance.

Make the Decision, Choose the Weapon Continue touring the area surrounding waypoint 2 until you locate the enemy convoy. Remember to verify color; bad guys will always be either black or brown. Once you spot the enemy, you must do the following:

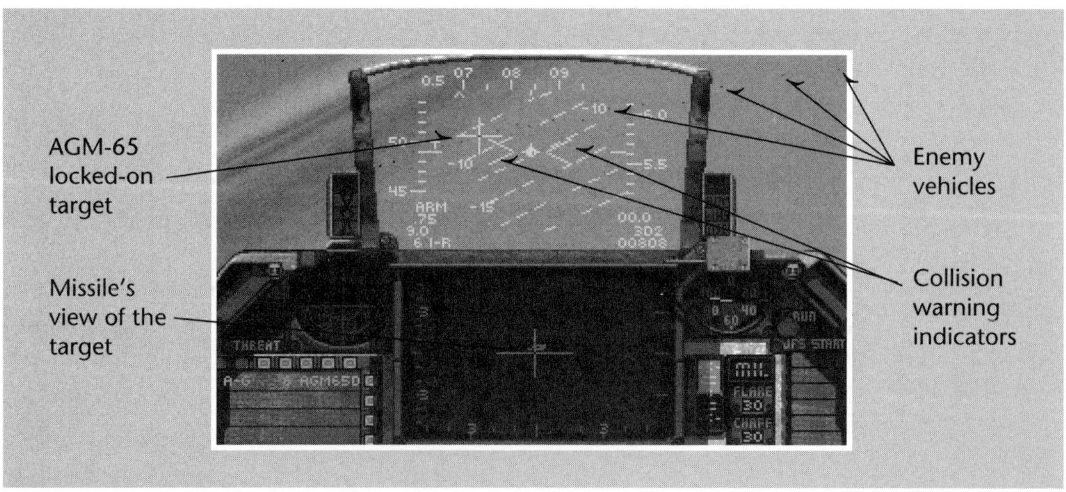

Figure 9-27 A Typical High-Aspect Approach

1. Determine if you are approaching from a high or low aspect angle, then choose either a guided or unguided weapon, respectively.
2. When selecting unguided weapons, remember to increase the ripple value by pressing ['] key. A ripple value of 4 generally works well, allowing at least two attack passes. For extremely low-aspect attacks, where the time over targets is long, higher values of 6 or 8 may be appropriate.
3. Deliver weapons and escape.
4. Check fuel and weapons status. If low on either, go to step 6; otherwise, proceed to step 5.
5. Execute maneuvers to prepare for next attack pass. Go to step 1.
6. Disengage and return to base.

Figure 9-27 shows a typical high-aspect approach using an AGM-65D. The F-16 is approaching the line of vehicles at nearly a 90° degree aspect angle. Due to the high aspect, an AGM-65D Maverick missile has been selected. The targeting crosshairs on the HUD are superimposed over one of the vehicles, indicating a lock. The target, as the missile sees it, is displayed on the HUD.

Figure 9-28 shows a typical, low-aspect approach using a CBU-84. The F-16 is turning left such that it can fly lengthwise over the column of vehicles. The ripple value has been set to 4, with 8 CBU-84 units remaining. Since each CBU-84 dispenses 202 submunitions releasing four CBU-84s will release 808 submunitions on the enemy!

Figure 9-28 A Typical Low-Aspect Approach

Mission Debriefing

You may consider this mission a success if all of the following conditions are met:

- You survived the mission, and
- You personally destroyed at least six enemy ground vehicles, and
- No friendly ground units were destroyed.

If you successfully completed this mission, proceed to the next. If not, what went wrong?

- Were you unable to locate the enemy forces? If so, chalk this one up to bad luck, but repeat the mission until you successfully complete it.
- Were you shot down? It cannot be emphasized enough: *your primary responsibility is to return your aircraft to base!* A war of attrition composed of suicide attacks can not be won. Repeat the mission, but take extra steps to ensure the safety of yourself and your aircraft.
- Did you fail to destroy the required number of targets? If so, keep practicing your ground attack skills. Repeat the mission.
- Were friendly ground forces attacked? In a campaign, attacking friendly units would get you court-martialed and end your flying days. American military leaders severely dealt with soldiers responsible for friendly fire incidents during the 1991 Gulf War. Repeat the mission and release your weapons on target this time.

Mission 5: Operation Fence Post

Intercept Inbound Bombers

ZNR CCCCC
I 15 1200Z JAN 92
FM RED FLAG HQ DIV//GEN WAITE//
TO 386TH FSFORUM SQU CMDR//COL BASHAM

BT
S E C R E T
REF: DAILY ATO: OP: FENCE POST (S)
(S) ENEMY FORCES HAVE FORMED AN AGREEMENT WITH MEXICO
REGARDING USE OF MILITARY FACILITIES. INTEL BELIEVES ENEMY

LEADERS HAVE PAID CASH AMOUNTS EXCEEDING $250 MILLION U.S. DOLLARS IN EXCHANGE FOR USE OF MEXICAN RUNWAYS.

TR-3 RECON AIRCRAFT HAVE SPOTTED TU-22S AND MIG-29S REDEPLOYED TO THESE SITES. INTEL BELIEVES THESE AIRCRAFT WILL ATTEMPT TO ATTACK NELLIS AFB BY SURPRISE. KEEP F-16S ON FULL ALERT AND BE PREPARED TO INTERCEPT INBOUND BOMBERS.

OVERNIGHT, ALLIED FORCES LAUNCHED A SECOND GROUND OFFENSIVE AND HAVE PENETRATED ENEMY LINES IN FOUR KEY POSITIONS. ACCORDING TO RUMOR, THE ENEMY PRESIDENT IS PREPARING TO FLEE AND IS REQUESTING SANCTUARY FROM OTHER NATIONS.

COL M BARRS HAS BEEN RESCUED. AFTER A COMPLETE MEDICAL EXAM AND DEBRIEFING, THE COLONEL IS SCHEDULED TO ATTEND A PRESS CONFERENCE.
ET

Nellis AFB, NV—0600 HRS

The good news spread through the camp like a runaway missile! Colonel Barrs was rescued late last night. Apparently, after ejecting he was captured by a small enemy patrol, but subsequently escaped. Using escape and evasion techniques learned during pilot training, the colonel was able to survive in the wilderness while being pursued by enemy patrols. While the details of his rescue have been strictly classified, rumor has it that the colonel was extracted by a U.S. special forces team.

In other news, Allied ground forces launched a massive second attack. According to the daily Pentagon news briefing, Allied forces have penetrated deep within enemy territory. Enemy ground forces are again in disarray, desperately attempting to regroup. Reports have surfaced that the enemy has struck a deal with nearby Mexico, trading huge cash sums for use of Mexican airbases. While attacks on targets in Mexico have not been authorized, American — Mexican relations are seriously strained. The president has stated that all aircraft in Mexican airspace will be closely monitored, and those attempting to cross the Rio Grande river will be considered hostile. Theater Command hopes to crush the enemy forces quickly and end the war before Mexican forces become involved.

Looking at your watch, you realize it's time for your mission briefing. You make your way to the briefing room. The instructor enters and begins the briefing....

The Mission Briefing

"Good morning, gentlemen," the instructor begins, "today we are assigned guard duty. We have been ordered to keep a flight of F-16s on *ready five alert* all day. If hostile inbound aircraft are detected, we must have intercepting F-16s on station within five minutes of the launch order."

The Mission: Intercept Inbound Bombers

"Enemy Tu-22 bombers and MiG-29 fighters have been redeployed to Mexican airbases, apparently attempting to open a new, southern front. Intel suspects that these bombers, escorted by the MiG-29s, will attempt to attack Nellis. Our job will be to intercept and destroy incoming enemy bombers before they reach Nellis.

"Due to logistic considerations, we are unable to launch more than two F-16s from this squadron at any given time. Until those two land, this squadron cannot launch any more aircraft. Therefore, this mission will be executed by a single flight of two aircraft. Pilots will remain on alert and in their aircraft, but will not launch unless inbound bombers are detected."

Flight 1: Your Job–Intercept Bad Guys

The instructor continues, "The two F-16s will be armed to the teeth with air-to-air weapons. Each F-16 will be carrying a full complement of eight air-to-air weapons, a full load of 20mm ammo for the internal cannon, and an ECM pod. Each F-16 will have four AIM-120 AMRAAMs, two AIM-9M all-aspect Sidewinders, and two AIM-9P rear-aspect-only Sidewinders. Quantities of the AIM-9M, or *Mikes,* are low, so only two are available for each aircraft. The AIM-9Ps, or *Papas,* supplement the Mikes. "

Air-to-Air Missile Strategies "Don't waste or misuse missiles. There may be a large group of incoming aircraft and every pound of ordnance loaded on the F-16s must be rationed accordingly. Keep the following rules in mind at all times:

- AIM-120 — Use this missile for long range shots only. It has the longest range of any missile you carry, and will be under-utilized if launched at close range.
- AIM-9M — While this missile has all-aspect capability, avoid using this missile for easy rear-aspect shots. The AIM-9M is perfectly capable of, and highly effective at rear-quarter launches, but is under-utilized in this role.

- AIM-9P — This is the least effective missile in your arsenal. It has the most restrictive targeting envelope and is only effective in rear-quarter shots. It should be used for the simple, close range, rear-aspect shots; thereby saving the more effective missiles for the more difficult targets."

Enemy Missile Performance "Using these rules," the instructor states, "will increase your effectiveness and your Probability of a Kill (PK). Keep in mind, however, the performance of enemy air-to-air missiles compared with your own. Review your notes from Operation Ground Shaker for details. In summary, enemy radar-guided missiles out-distance the AIM-120, but enemy heat-seeking missiles are out-distanced by either version of the AIM-9."

Electronic Counter Measures: The ALQ-131 "Each F-16 will carry an ALQ-131 ECM pod. As you recall from your training (Chapter 8, *Using High Fidelity Radar*), the ALQ-131 is effective against airborne, as well as ground based, radar units. Since all enemy radar-guided, air-to-air missiles are semi-active, radar homing (SARH), and require a constant radar lock on your aircraft, the enemy missile will go awry if the ALQ-131 breaks the radar lock, even for a second.

"Don't get complacent, however. The ALQ-131 is not always 100% effective, and may take a few seconds to break the radar lock. At long ranges of 20 miles or more, the ALQ will have plenty of time to spoof the enemy missile. However, if the enemy closes and fires a AA-7 at close range (under 5 miles) the ALQ may not have sufficient time to break the lock. Always keep your finger on the chaff dispenser button and be prepared to make evasive maneuvers. Of course, the ALQ-131 will have no effect against heat-seeking missiles."

Electronic Counter Measures: The Enemy "Some enemy aircraft also carry ECM equipment. Apparently, jamming equipment is in short supply, so only a few selected aircraft carry it. Little is known about its origin or capabilities, but it is suspected to be of French manufacture, possibly the Barax system. The Barax was designed for use with the Mirage series of aircraft, but enemy technicians may have modified it for use with MiG aircraft.

"Aircraft carrying these ECM devices can break your radar locks on them, and transmit ghost images on your REO. It may become difficult to determine exactly where the enemy is. If you suddenly and mysteriously lose radar lock on a target, it's highly probable the target is using ECM.

There are three ways for the enemy to break your radar lock:

1. Maneuver out of the area being scanned by your radar.
2. Beam your radar (see Chapter 8, *Using High Fidelity Radar*).
3. Use ECM.

Anytime the enemy uses ECM, the AWACS will notify you."

In-Your-Face Combat

"Intercept missions are straightforward. If you have the opportunity, sneak up on the enemy. Time is critical in an intercept mission, however, so you normally charge at full speed into the enemy's face and mix it up with him. Remember, the goal is to destroy aircraft capable of attacking Nellis. If you *splash,* or shoot down, all escorting MiGs but the bombers destroy Nellis, you lose and they win. All right, get out there and down some bad guys. Dismissed."

Mission Analysis

This mission emphasizes two elements:

- Air-to-air combat in an arena using both radar and ECM devices.
- Intercepting inbound aircraft.

The Intercept Mission

Intercept missions almost always place the participants in a race against time. Enemy pilots try to penetrate and attack targets before defensive actions can be taken; friendly forces frantically try to marshal defensive systems before the enemy delivers his weapons. Also called a *scramble,* pilots are often shaken out of bed at all hours and sent into the skies with only a few minutes notice.

The Difficulties of Intercepts

Although intercepts usually place fewer restrictions on pilots than escort missions, intercepts have their own unique set of problems. Like escorts, intercept pilots are charged with defending friendly forces. Unlike escorts, intercept pilots usually have been alerted where the hostile forces are coming from, and the approximate size of the inbound group.

However, enemy raiding parties often are composed of multiple aircraft types, usually bombers with fighter escorts. You must identify each aircraft in the inbound group and determine which ones are the highest threat. Remember, a single Tu-22 bomber dropping tons of ordnance on your airbase does more damage to the war effort than a fleet of escorting MiGs engaging a patrol of F-16s.

Role Reversal: Intercept Versus Escort

You have a distinct advantage, though, in this mission type. As you recall from Operation Ground Shaker, escorting fighters are severely bound by the aircraft they are charged to protect. They have little or no information on you, but must be always ready to fight you. Escorts usually use the layered defense concept discussed in Operation Ground Shaker. Aircraft intent on penetrating, not engaging, the escort have the advantage.

Of course, one cannot simply ignore enemy fighter escorts. You must take appropriate steps to defend yourself. However, always remember, the attacking bombers, not the escorting aircraft are the targets. If you destroy the bombers and the escorts flee, you've done your job quite well.

> **NOTE:** Remember the difficulties of the escort role and exploit them against the enemy.

Mission Walk-Through: Preflight

Start Falcon 3.0, select your squadron, enter Red Flag, and load the mission, FNCEPOST. Ground units play no role in this mission, so set the GRND option to OFF. Because you are protecting Nellis and, therefore, need to know your position relative to it at all times, set the map to STRAT mode. Make sure AIR is set to ON. When your mission begins, you will be off the ground, speeding toward inbound enemy aircraft!

Analyzing Your Waypoints

Waypoint analysis is very straightforward for this mission. You have only three, corresponding to three actions: start, intercept, and land.

1. Starting Waypoint—You start out flying low and slow over Nellis AFB, as though you had just lifted off. You are pointed toward waypoint 1 and are ready to roll.

2. Waypoint 1—You are assigned the INTERCEPT action at this waypoint. Waypoint 1 has been planted specifically in the path of the inbound aircraft. Flying to this point should guarantee radar contact with the enemy.
3. Waypoint 2—Return to base after completing the mission and land.

Reconnaissance Information

No reconnaissance information will assist you in this mission. You are not attacking ground targets, nor are they attacking you. You have one mission, fly to waypoint 1 and destroy all enemy aircraft found there. So don your flight gear, assign your pilots, and head for the tarmac.

Mission Walk-Through: The Flight Line

You begin the mission low over Nellis AFB; in reality, you would've been sitting in your cockpit, possibly for hours, with your aircraft parked on the tarmac, waiting for the order to launch. You've been saved this inconvenience; your mission begins just after takeoff.

Battle Preparations

This is strictly an air-to-air mission. Time is of the essence; you should accelerate to 500 knots and climb to 8,000 feet. Configure your HFR for 80nm range, +/– 60° azimuth scan, and maximum elevation scan using the procedures given in prior missions. Flying at 8,000 feet, your elevation scan should be from zero to 28,000 feet. Select the AIM-120 as the current weapon. You now have your radar and weapons systems configured for maximum range; he who shoots first usually wins. Fly directly to waypoint 1.

As you fly toward waypoint 1, you will eventually obtain radar contact with the incoming aircraft. Results will vary depending upon speed and course deviations, but you should achieve radar contact by the time you are 40nm from waypoint 1. As soon as a blip appears on your REO, use the lock-up sequence of T and Z to lock on to this target.

Bandits, Bandits Incoming!

You should now see something similar to Figure 9-29. The target is flying at 7,000 feet, heading 38°, and 499 knots. The aspect angle is 177, indicating

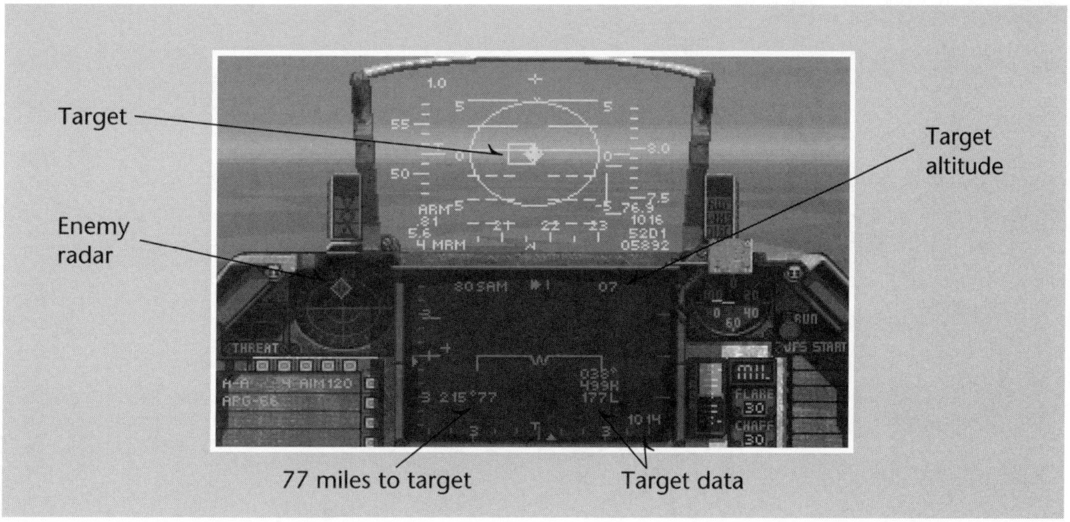

Figure 9-29 First SAM Radar Lock

the bogey is flying almost directly at you. In the figure, the F-16 is 52 miles from the waypoint and 77 miles from the bogey. Interrogate the bogey's IFF by pressing N. There should be no IFF buzz, this is a bandit.

Point your nose at the bandit and increase throttle to 100% power. While you don't specifically know it, this contact is probably a fighter escort, not one of the main bombers. It would serve little purpose to place the attacking aircraft ahead of the escorting fighters. Of course, you can always use the Q key to view the locked target.

Working with Your Wingman

Your AMRAAMs won't lock at ranges greater than 17 nautical miles. Fly toward the bandits and prepare to fire. Based on your air combat skills, you may want to try some of the advanced, multi-plane tactics available to you: the *bracket* and the *drag*.

The Bracket This maneuver requires coordination between you and your wingman. Figure 9-30 illustrates the maneuver. The wingleader and wingman break in opposite directions as they approach head on to the bandits. Then, both the wingleader and wingman break back towards the bandits. Whichever direction the bandits turn, they will engage one of the two F-16s head on, while the other F-16 drops in behind them.

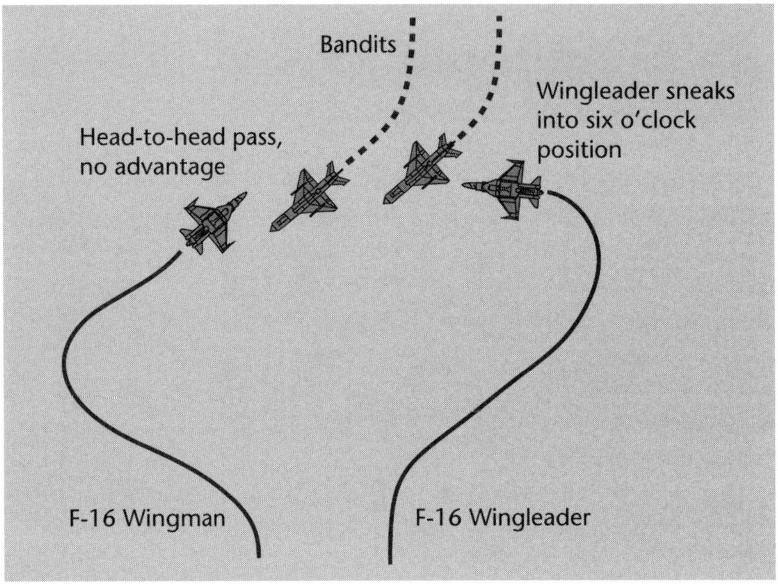

Figure 9-30 The Bracket

> WARNING: This maneuver requires coordination of both aircraft. The unengaged fighter must immediately assist the engaged fighter.

You may order your wingman to initiate the bracket in either direction. Press SHIFT-C to order the wingman to initially break right, press SHIFT-Z to order the wingman to initially break left. No matter which direction you order the wingman, you should break the opposite direction.

The range to the bandits must be greater than 15 nautical miles, or your wingman will reply, "Unable." Executing this maneuver at closer ranges increases the risk that the bandit will fire a missile at you before the maneuver is completed. Also, the bracket should be executed when the aspect angle to the target is between 160° and 200° at a range of 20 nautical miles. At aspect angles outside of this range, the bandits' direction of travel will make it difficult for both F-16s to circle behind them.

Countering the Bracket The enemy pilots, however, also know this tactic. While trainee pilots will rarely execute such complex stratagems, VETERAN and ACE level pilots are capable of both executing this maneuver and defending against it. You should likewise be versed in counter tactics; not only to defend against the bracket, but to be prepared for enemy defensive maneuvers. Figure 9-31 illustrates.

In Figure 9-31, the bandits execute a simple defense against the bracket. The bandits allow the F-16s to break apart, then approach from

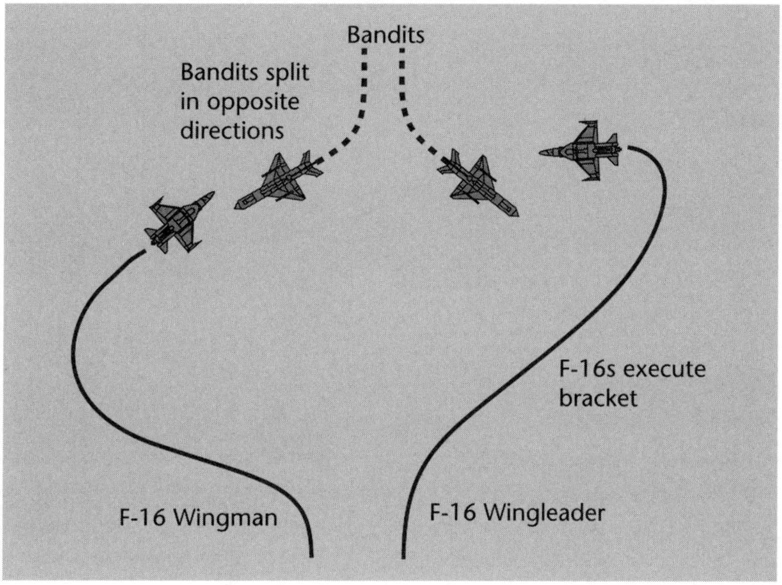

Figure 9-31 Countering the Bracket

opposite sides. As the F-16s approach within missile range, the bandits separate, each turning toward an attacker. Each bandit is now approaching head-to-head with an F-16, with neither F-16 gaining a superior position over the bandits.

If the enemy appears to be executing a bracket against you, use this counter tactic. Monitor their positions using the REO, TWI, and padlock view. When both bandits are outside of your formation, break towards one of the bandits, while ordering your wingman to break in the opposite direction by pressing SHIFT-A or SHIFT-C.

The Vertical Bracket Another option available only when flying in two-player or multi-player mode is the *vertical bracket*, also known as the defensive split. Instead of each F-16 breaking in opposite directions, one F-16 climbs sharply, executes a half-roll, then dives back against the bandits. Meanwhile, the other F-16 executes a half-roll initially, then dives sharply. Typically, one bandit will chase the low F-16 while the other climbs, as shown in Figure 9-32.

Next, the F-16s exchange bandits, as shown in Figure 9-33. F-16 #1 dives and attacks bandit #2, thus clearing the tail of F-16 #2. Meanwhile, F-16 #2 climbs and engages bandit #1, thus clearing the tail of F-16 #1, resulting in an all-around neutral position. However, sometimes the bandits may err, and both bandits will follow a single F-16. The *engaged* F-16 acts

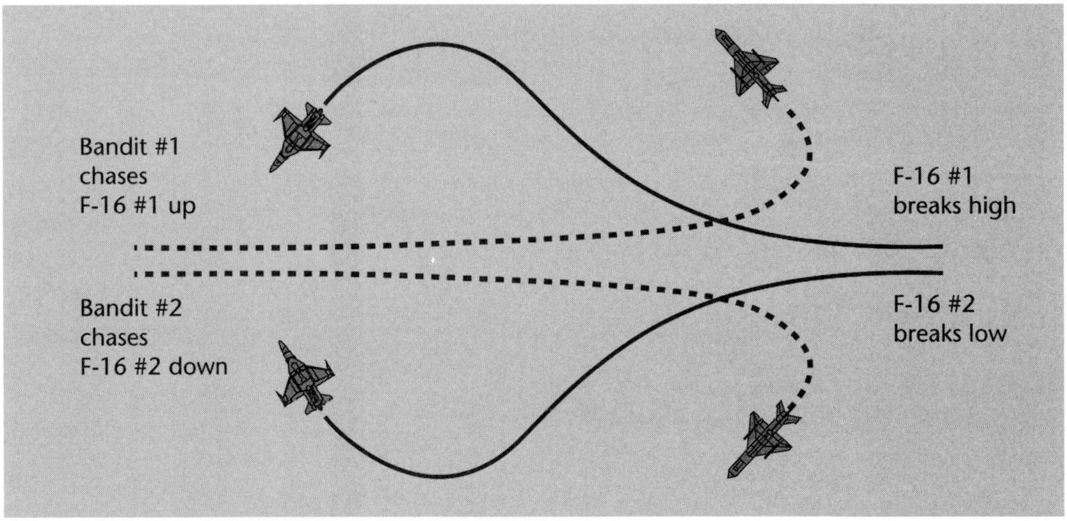

Figure 9-32 The Vertical Bracket — Phase One

as a decoy for both bandits while the *free* F-16 reverses and attacks both bandits from behind.

NOTE: There is no way to order a computer controlled wingman to execute a vertical bracket. This maneuver can only be executed during two-player and multi-player flights where the individual pilots may communicate with one another.

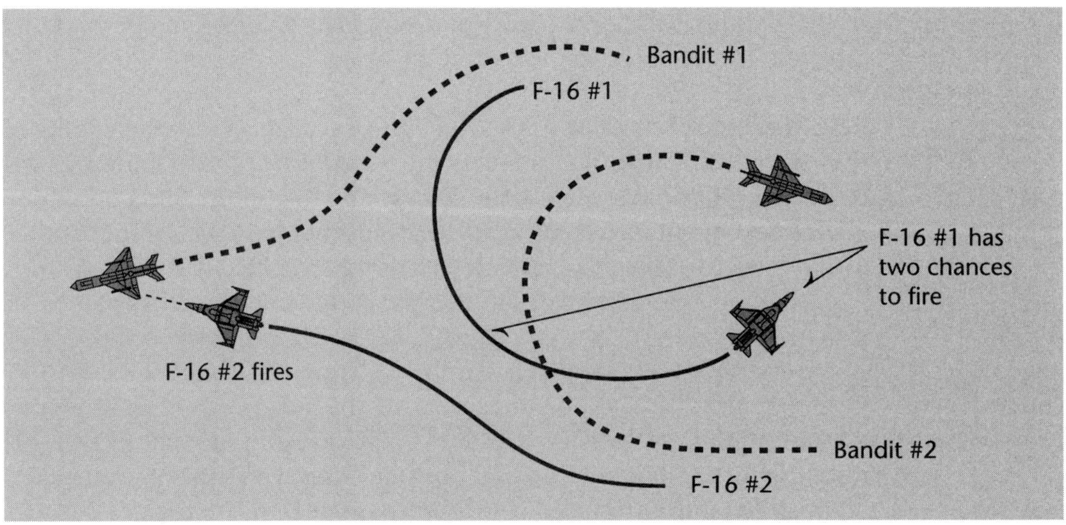

Figure 9-33 The Vertical Bracket — Phase Two

This maneuver is very difficult to coordinate. If the F-16s do not perfectly time their maneuvers, they will wind up out of position and unable to protect each other. Each F-16 will find a bandit planted squarely at its respective six o'clock position.

The Drag Figure 9-34 illustrates this maneuver. Like the bracket, both F-16s begin by breaking in opposite directions. However, the wingman continues to turn away from the incoming bandits, instead of toward them. The wingleader then reverses back toward the bandits. The bandits, seeing a six o'clock view of a lone fighter, will usually follow the wingman. The wingleader must quickly turn behind the bandits and engage them.

> **WARNING:** The drag command is extremely confusing. The drag-left command does not order your wingman to break left. Instead, the wingman will break such that the pursuing bandit will always remain on the wingman's left side.

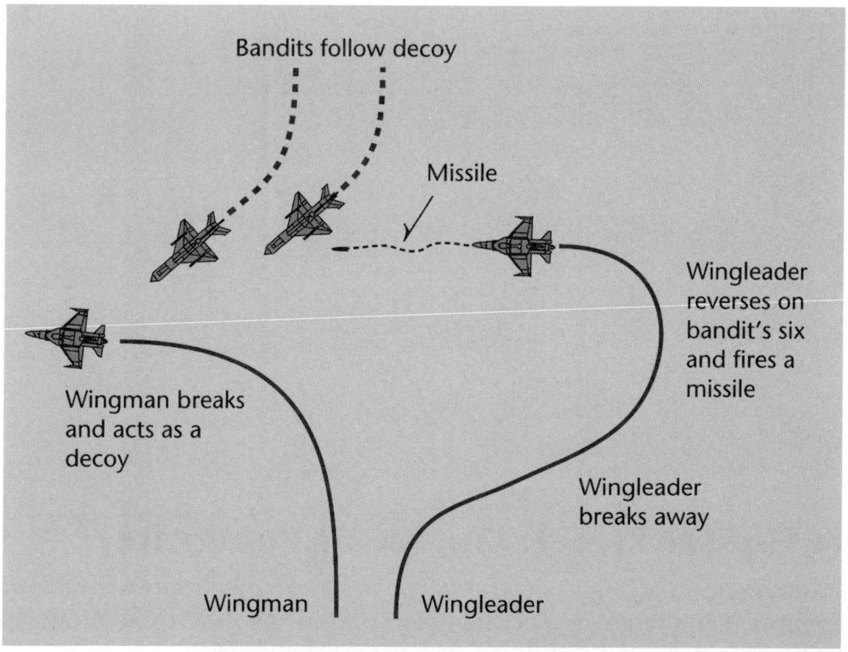

Figure 9-34
The Drag

> **WARNING:** This maneuver is very dangerous and requires precise timing by you. If you fail to reverse and engage the bandits quickly enough, they will down your wingman and then return for you. You must quickly move into the bandits' six o'clock position and attack.

This maneuver must be initiated when the range to target is greater than 10 nautical miles. Your wingman will respond, "Unable," if you try to initiate this maneuver at closer ranges. At ranges under 10 nautical miles, the enemy can close within range and fire a missile before the wingleader can reverse and engage him.

Countering the Drag Figure 9-35 illustrates how to counter the drag maneuver. As with countering the bracket, each bandit breaks in opposite directions. In this case, bandit #1 falls in behind the decoy F-16 for an easy rear-quarter shot. This F-16 is at a definite disadvantage. Meanwhile, bandit #2 turns toward the lead F-16 and engages it head-to-head. The lead F-16 is unable to assist the decoy.

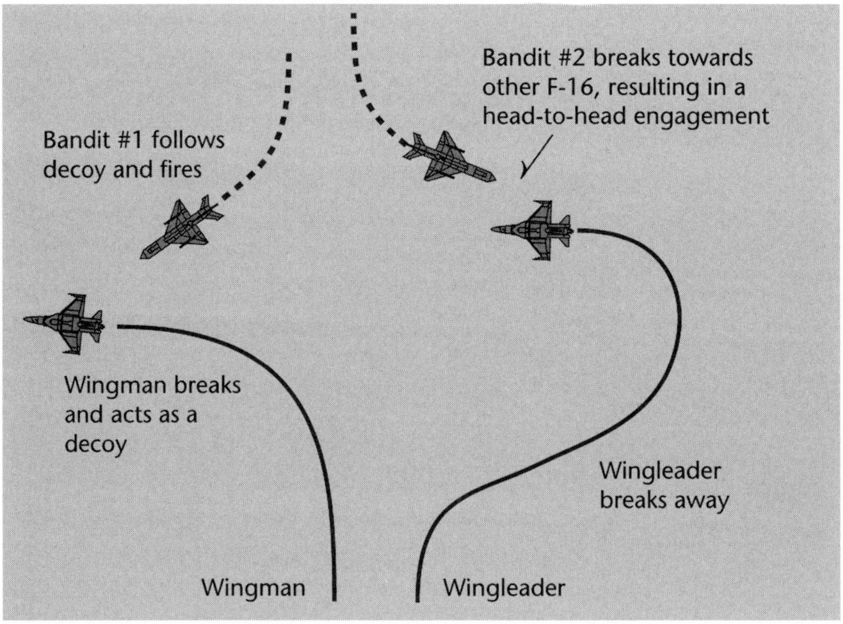

Figure 9-35 Countering the Drag

The Fighter Escort: Engage or Penetrate?

The bandits are rapidly closing on you; you must now determine what tactic to employ. If the target aspect angle falls within the 160° to 200° range, consider initiating a bracket. If the aspect angle falls outside of that range, consider executing a drag. If you feel capable of supporting your wingman in a drag, issue the engage command with SHIFT-E, ordering your wingman to engage under his own initiative. As you begin your attack, keep one vital point in mind: *this is not your primary target!* Don't waste time with these guys.

Quick Penetration Rather than mixing it up with the enemy fighters, you may opt to divide your force and go for a quick penetration. Depending upon the skill of your wingman, you may want to order the wingman to engage, but you increase to full afterburner and blast pass the enemy without a second glance. This frees you to search for the bomber group, but leaves your wingman in the precarious two-on-one situation. With TRAINEE and CADET enemy pilots or when the bombers are near the airbase, this a valid approach. However, with VETERAN and ACE opponents, your wingman is probably doomed. Use this tactic as a last resort, only.

Fighting It Out The other option is to stay and fight it out. Before attacking, take a quick survey of your systems. Select the AIM-120 AMRAAM as the active weapon, if you haven't already done so. Increase throttle to full military power. Activate your ALQ-131 ECM pod by pressing E. You're ready for combat!

Use the Padlock View Remember to use the padlock view when the battle gets close. Padlock view can save your life; not only does it give greater visual coverage of the target aircraft, it will also padlock inbound missiles. Padlock view greatly increases your awareness and understanding of the combat environment. Figure 9-36 shows a sample padlock view of the F-16 wingman engaging a MiG-29 with guns. Press 8 to select the padlock view.

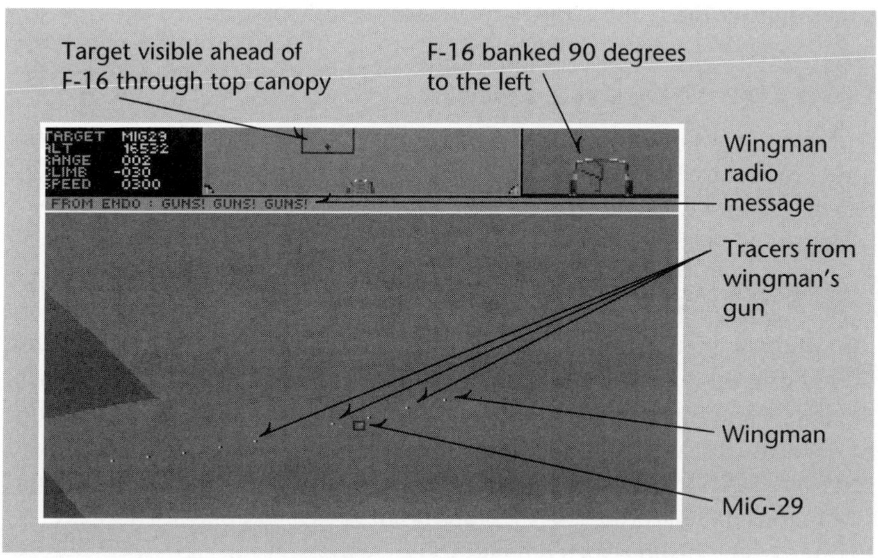

Figure 9-36 Padlock View of the Wingman Engaging a MiG-29

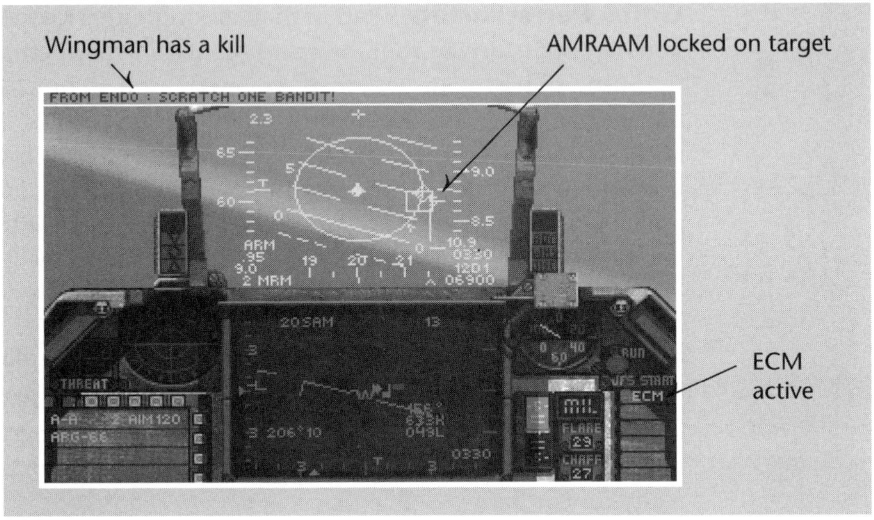

Figure 9-37 A Typical Air-to-Air Combat Scene

Figure 9-37 shows a typical air-to-air combat scene. In this particular example, the two F-16s split, each engaging a different bandit. The wingman, as indicated on the message bar in Figure 9-37, quickly maneuvered behind his bandit and downed it. The second bandit attempted to reverse and assist the first, but succeeded only in allowing the lead F-16 to *saddle up,* or achieve a rear-quarter firing position. The second bandit soon joined the first.

Find the Inbound Forces

Once you've dealt with the escort you must quickly locate the main bomber force. Normally, the lumbering bombers are slow, easily downed targets. However, always keep alert, there could be additional escorting fighters.

TIP: Always remain on the lookout. There may be more fighters flying close escort with the bombers. Be prepared for this.

Return to your specified course and fly toward waypoint 1. Depending upon how long you spent with the escorting fighters and how far you deviated from the assigned course, waypoint 1 should be between 5 and 10 miles away. Reconfigure the HFR for maximum coverage and fly directly to waypoint 1. Shortly, you detect new contacts. Use the sequence of T and Z to lock one of these bogeys. They should be the bombers, but press N to interrogate the bogey's IFF. You should hear no IFF buzz; these bogeys are the enemy bombers. Your screen should resemble Figure 9-38.

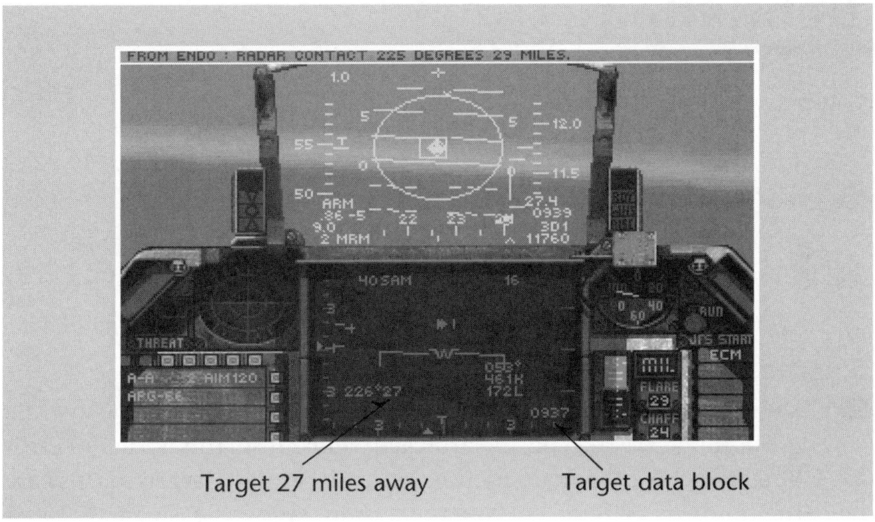

Figure 9-38 Radar Contact with Enemy Bombers

In this particular case, the two MiG-29s already encountered compose the entire fighter escort. Assuming that you downed both MiG-29s, there are no fighters left in this mission. The remaining group consists of four unarmed Tu-22 bombers; easy pickings for your F-16! Circle behind and pull up close behind the bombers. Issue the (SHIFT)-(E) command for your wingman and open fire! Figure 9-39 shows the rear view of a Tu-22 taken at 8X magnification. The bomber, having detected the radar lock of the lead F-16, has executed a break turn to the right. In typical, precautionary fashion, the bomber is dispensing both chaff and flares in anticipation of an incoming missile. The small dot indicating a burst of chaff can be seen in Figure 9-39, just behind the Tu-22. Finish the bombers off and return to base.

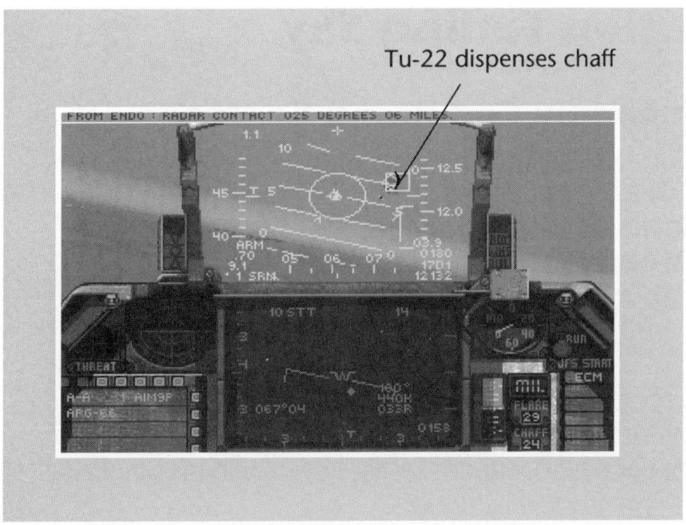

Figure 9-39 8X Magnification View of a Tu-22 Bomber

Mission Debriefing

You may consider this mission a success if:

- You survive the mission, and
- All four incoming bombers were destroyed.

If you were successful, proceed to mission 6. If not, analyze your results. What went wrong?

- Were you shot down by the MiG-29 fighter escort? If so, practice air-to-air combat and repeat the mission.
- Did you spend too much time focusing on the MiG-29s, meanwhile, the bombers passed you and attacked Nellis? If so, this is a major error. You must always remain focused on your primary target, in this case, the bombers. Killing MiGs may be more enjoyable, but a shattered runway at your home base can ruin your day. Repeat the mission and keep your mind on your primary task: intercepting inbound bombers.
- Did you fire all of your ordnance at the MiG-29s and had no weapons to fire at the bombers? This is also a major error. The MiGs are not a serious threat to the airbase; the bombers are. You must conserve your limited weapons for use against the primary threat. Repeat the mission and keep your mind on your primary task: intercepting inbound bombers.

Mission 6: Operation Falling Sky

Destroy an Enemy Command Center

ZNR CCCCC
I 16 1030Z JAN 92
FM RED FLAG HQ DIV//GEN WAITE//
TO 386TH FSFORUM SQU CMDR//COL BASHAM

BT
S E C R E T
REF: DAILY ATO: OP: FALLING SKY (S)
(S) INTEL HAS DETERMINED THE ENEMY'S AIRBASE IS BEING USED AS CENTRAL COMMAND HQ. THE ENEMY PRESIDENT AND HIS FAMILY ARE

BELIEVED TO BE IN THIS FACILITY WHILE PREPARING TO FLEE THE COUNTRY. DESTRUCTION OF THIS COMMAND FACILITY WILL SEVERELY DISRUPT ENEMY COMMUNICATION NETWORKS.

ENEMY FORCES ARE IN FULL RETREAT AT THREE OF FOUR KEY POSITIONS. COLLAPSE OF ENEMY FORCES IMMINENT. INTEL BELIEVES ENEMY PRESIDENT WILL ATTEMPT TO ENTER MEXICO AND PERSUADE MEXICAN FORCES TO JOIN THE HOSTILITIES AGAINST THE U.S. IN EXCHANGE FOR CASH PAYMENTS. INTEL ALSO BELIEVES THE ENEMY PRESIDENT WILL SURRENDER TO ALLIED FORCES IF UNABLE TO ESCAPE THE COUNTRY.

EFFECTIVE IMMEDIATELY, THE WHITE HOUSE HAS ORDERED THE U.S. - MEXICO BORDER CLOSED. ONLY U.S. CITIZENS WITH PROOF OF CITIZENSHIP WILL BE ALLOWED TO CROSS FROM MEXICO TO THE U.S. NO ONE IS PERMITTED TO CROSS FROM THE U.S. TO MEXICO, REGARDLESS OF NATIONALITY. TAKE ANY STEPS NECESSARY TO PREVENT PERSONNEL FROM ENTERING MEXICO. MEXICAN OFFICIALS HAVE PROTESTED THIS MOVE TO THE UNITED NATIONS.
ET

Nellis AFB, NV—0800 HRS

Enemy forces are on the run, apparently with little opportunity to halt the tide of advancing Allied forces. The enemy's only hope is to draw a new combatant into the game. The enemy president appears to be offering the Mexican government large cash payments to entice them into attacking the U.S. In a preemptive move, the U.S. president closed the U.S.–Mexico border and stationed additional troops there. Mexican officials protested, and retaliated by expelling five U.S. diplomats. The State Department has filed a complaint with the United Nations and has sternly warned Mexico to stay out of the war.

It is believed that the enemy president will surrender if unable to flee to another country. If he escapes, it is believed that he will be able to continue directing the war from exile, as well as recruit other radical and terrorist organizations to join the hostilities. Allied forces have been ordered to search for and capture the enemy president. The enemy is almost defeated, but if the enemy president escapes and persuades other parties to join the hostilities, the war could drag on for some time.

Colonel Barrs is listed as being exhausted, but in otherwise excellent condition. He is expected to return to flight status within three days. You are scheduled to attend dinner in his honor later today, after you return from today's mission. That is, if you return.... You gather your gear and head for the briefing room.

Mission Briefing

"Today we are targeting enemy *C3I,* or Command, Control, Communications, and Intelligence facilities," begins the instructor. "The communication center at the enemy airbase west of Nellis is believed to be the central node in the enemy's communication network. Destroying it should disrupt enemy comms abilities theater-wide. Rumors have it that the enemy president is residing in this structure; we are not, repeat, not attempting to assassinate him. If any members of the press question you on this matter, you are ordered to categorically deny it."

The Mission: Iron Bomb the Headquarters

"This mission consists of four sorties. The first section of two F-16s will *iron bomb,* or deliver free-fall ordnance on the communications building. The second section, also consisting of two F-16s, will provide defense suppression around the airbase. Enemy air activity is estimated as extremely light, despite being in the vicinity of an airbase."

Flight 1: Your Job—Iron Bomb Enemy HQ

"Each aircraft in flight 1 will carry four Mk83 iron bombs, two AIM-9M Sidewinders, two AIM-120 AMRAAMs, and an ALQ-131 ECM pod. Despite the lack of enemy activity, aircraft in the first flight will carry the air-to-air missiles as a precaution. This flight will ingress, deliver all eight Mk83s on the comms HQ building, then return to base."

Dropping Iron Bombs—CCIP Procedures "You pilots are well versed in the deployment of air-to-air missiles and ECM usage, so we'll proceed directly to discussion of the Mk83s. As you know, unguided, free-falling ordnance is usually referred to as an iron bomb. Iron bombs have no guidance or control systems at all. Their guidance to target is based wholly on the timing of their release, based upon such factors as the F-16s altitude and speed at the time of the release. In the old days, pilots had to *eyeball* their targets and guess when to release iron bombs. Today, the F-16s flight computer aids the pilot in this task through *Continuously Computed Impact Point* (CCIP) calculations.

"When you select a free-fall bomb as the active weapon, a circle will appear at the bottom of the HUD. This circle is known as the *pipper,* or *death-dot.* You steer the F-16 so that the death-dot is superimposed over the target, then you designate, or *pickle,* that target by pressing weapons release button. The weapon is not released, but the F-16 flight computer calculates when to release the iron bomb in order to strike the pickled spot. It is very important that you maintain a constant speed, heading, and attitude once you've pickled a target. Any deviations will skew the CCIP calculations and cause the bomb to miss.

"To increase the chances of hitting the target, more than one bomb can be released at a time. The number of bombs dropped is called the *ripple* value. The ripple value can be set to drop a maximum of all bombs at once to a minimum of only two bombs per release."

CCIP Approach Methods "The hardest part about CCIP bombing," states the instructor, "is the approach. With a perfect approach you can be relatively assured of a hit; with a less-than-perfect approach, you can be assured a miss. There are three possible target approaches: low altitude, level delivery; medium altitude, shallow dive delivery; and high altitude, steep dive delivery.

"Like the name implies, low altitude, level delivery approaches begin by flying very low, nape-of-the-earth (NOE) to the target, then flying level at 1,500 to 2,000 feet altitude over the target while dropping ordnance. However, the explosive concussion from large bombs can often damage the escaping F-16. The larger the bomb, the higher the F-16 must fly. Due to the strength of the Mk83, you will be unable to fly this approach during this mission.

"Medium altitude, shallow dive and high altitude, steep dive deliveries are closely related. As you recall from Operation Iron Breaker, you ingressed at very high altitude and released weapons while in a very steep dive. This is a typical high altitude, steep dive approach. Medium altitude approaches use the same techniques, except the dive is begun slightly sooner and is much shallower, thus preventing the F-16 from diving into the ground. For this mission, you should use a medium altitude, shallow dive approach."

Flight 2: Defense Suppression

Switching topics, the instructor begins to discuss your escorts, "The second flight will arrive slightly ahead of the target. Each aircraft in the second flight will be armed with GBU-15 television-guided bombs and AGM-88

HARM anti-radiation missiles. This flight will be responsible for destroying the massive SAM launchers positioned around the airbase before the main strike (the first flight) arrives. For self defense, the second flight will also carry AIM-9M Sidewinder missiles.

"Finally, after delivering weapons, both flights will return to Nellis," the Instructor concludes. "Don't forget that there will be a dinner in honor of Colonel Barrs at 1900 hours tonight. All members of the 386th are invited. Try to be on time. Dismissed."

Mission Analysis

This mission emphasizes a single element: CCIP bombing techniques. War-making technology is constantly advancing, making smarter, more accurate weapons. Guided munitions, under most circumstances, are nearly fool-proof. Point the crosshairs where you want the missile to go, and you are almost guaranteed a hit.

However, as the intelligence of weapons increases, so does the cost to build those weapons. Modern guided weapons cost so much to produce that the military cannot afford to build as many as it requires. Therefore, there will always be a place in military arsenals for cheap, unguided, free-fall munitions. Iron bombs, by comparison, are cheap and easy to produce, thus making them a perfect supplement to high-tech weapons. In most Falcon 3.0 campaigns, you can expect to have an insufficient number of Mavericks and GBU-15s to complete your assigned missions; you'll have to rely on iron bombs to round out your attacks.

Approach Tactics

As stated in the mission briefing, the key to iron bombing success depends solely upon your approach to the target. Although the computer calculates the best time to release the weapon, if your approach is erratic or skewed, the bombs are guaranteed to miss their targets. If your approach is perfect, however, you should have no problem hitting the assigned target. As mentioned in the briefing, there are three possible approach techniques. Each of these is now discussed.

NOTE: The biggest problem faced by computer pilots is the need to visually locate targets. In the real world, the pilot has a much wider angle of view, as well as the ability to see buildings and structures from ten or more miles away. In Falcon 3.0, most objects are visible at ranges under seven miles. Computer pilots dependent upon visual contact with their targets are at a distinct disadvantage.

To date, no computer-based flight simulation can represent the world in the same intricate detail that the human eye can perceive the real world in. Therefore, PC pilots must wean themselves of the need for visual verification and learn to trust their instruments. Using navigational instruments on the HUD and REO will greatly improve the pilot's ability to properly approach targets.

Low Altitude, Level Delivery

This is the preferred approach method for pilots who desire visual contact with their targets. Despite the fact that instruments will accurately direct the way to the target, many PC pilots feel the need to fly low so they can "see the target better." The majority of Falcon 3.0 pilots who have problems executing CCIP bombing runs are using this technique, and simply need to modify their approaches.

Visual Myths The belief that all targets are more easily located at low altitudes is nothing more than a myth. Although some small targets, such as tanks and trucks, cannot be seen from high altitudes, large structures, such as buildings and runways, can be seen when flying at 30,000 feet and seven miles away. However, at this range/altitude combination, the target is located below the nose of the aircraft, and the pilot must dive, often steeply, in order to see it.

During low altitude approaches, pilots fly toward targets at altitudes under 6,000 feet, sometimes as low as 2,000 feet. The pilots then fly nearly level over the target and attempt to release their weapons, often experiencing four problems: the ordnance misses the target, the ordnance won't release at all, the attacking aircraft takes damage from the explosion of the bombs, or the attacking aircraft is hit by ground fire. Usually, these problems are resolved simply by using a different approach.

Valid Low Altitude, Level Delivery Applications There are times to use this tactic, of course. CAS missions usually require the aircraft to fly extremely low to identify hostile vehicles and to use surrounding terrain as cover. However, always use the right weapon for the job. If you must drop iron bombs at low level, be sure to use less powerful weapons, such as the CBU-84, or use Mk-82 Snakeyes. The Snakeye version is a standard Mk-82 bomb equipped with drag fins that act as a parachute, slowing the descent of the bomb. The slower falling bombs allow the releasing aircraft sufficient time to escape the explosion.

Also, if no ECM gear is available, the attacking aircraft may choose to ingress at extremely low altitude in an attempt to evade enemy radar contact. While AAA and SA-7 Grail SAMs can be fired at low altitude targets, radar-guided SAMs (the SA-6 and SA-8) usually cannot. This approach is still dangerous, but may be less so than the alternatives.

Medium Altitude, Shallow Dive Delivery

This is the most common method of iron bombing. The attacking aircraft ingress at altitudes from 15,000 to 17,000 feet until they are about seven miles from the target. The aircraft then nose down into a 10° to 20° dive, whatever is necessary to bring the target into the HUD. The pilots pickle the target and pull out after weapons release, never diving below 10,000 feet.

Advantages This type of approach has many advantages. First, attacking aircraft remain at the upper altitude limit of AAA cannons and SA-7 missiles. If these units open fire, the aircraft can quickly climb and evade them. Of course, at these altitudes, SA-6 and SA-8 SAMs are serious threats. The pilots should be well versed in missile evasion tactics.

Additionally, the higher altitude translates into increased approach time. Given two aircraft both one mile away from the target, an aircraft at 20,000 feet simply has longer to setup its attack than an aircraft at 1,000 feet., Longer approach times generate more opportunities for course corrections. Since the accuracy of free-fall ordnance depends solely upon the accuracy of your approach, you always want to maximize the available approach time.

High Altitude, Steep Dive Delivery

As you recall from Mission 2: Operation Iron Breaker, high altitude, steep dive approaches go one step further. Attacking aircraft execute the same procedure used for medium altitude approaches, but from altitudes of 25,000 to 35,000 feet. This approach time provides additional immunity against AAA and SA-7s, as well as allows more time during the attack dive. However, high altitude approaches increase the likelihood of detection by the enemy. SA-6 and SA-8 SAMs are also a considerable threat.

> NOTE: Each of the three approaches has advantages and disadvantages. The greater the threat from enemy aircraft, the lower the attacking aircraft should ingress. The greater the threat from enemy ground units, the higher the attacking aircraft should ingress.

Conclusion

Always analyze each individual situation, considering the various threats and the weapons available, then determine which of the three approaches fit the mission. In this particular mission, a medium altitude approach is the most appropriate. There is little threat from either air or ground units, and the range to the target is short. A climb to high altitude would be very inefficient given the short distance to the target.

Mission Walk-Through: Preflight

Enter Falcon 3.0, select your favorite squadron, enter Red Flag, and load mission FALNGSKY. This mission involves multiple flights of aircraft, as well as fixed ground targets. Prior to flying the mission, you should familiarize yourself with the waypoints of the other flight as well as the target area. Select Nellis Command, then Allied Aircraft, followed by Allied Waypoints.

Flight 1: Main Strike Force

As always, you will be flying the lead aircraft in the first flight. Step through the three waypoints (starting point plus two regular waypoints) by pressing the WAYPOINT button. You begin the mission just west of Nellis, waypoint 1 marks the location of your primary target, and waypoint 2 brings you back to Nellis at the end of the mission.

Focus your attention on waypoint 1, the primary target. Notice that your target is a specific building, 5 Command, out of several buildings at the airbase. You'll have to know which building is your specific target before attacking it. Move the map crosshairs directly over the enemy airbase and increase the zoom factor to 120. Figure 9-40 shows how your screen should now look.

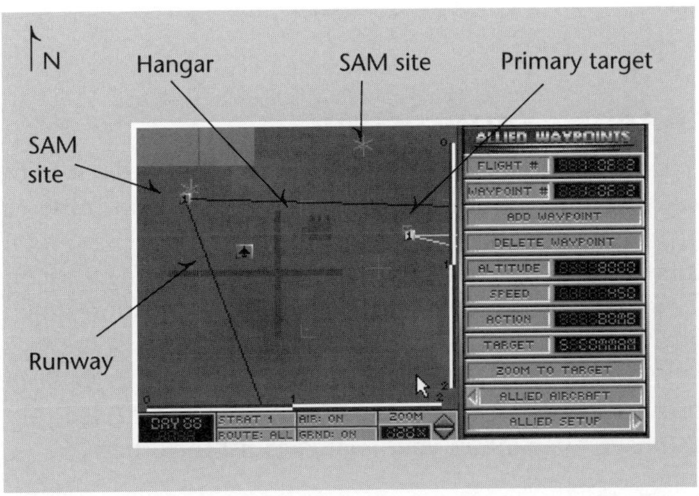

Figure 9-40 120X Magnification of the Target

This map follows standard conventions, up is always north. You now see your primary target, superimposed by the waypoint symbol slightly above and to the right of the runways. You know now that you are approaching from the east and that the target lies slightly northeast of the runways. You also can see two fixed SAM sites, one of which is superimposed by a waypoint icon from the other flight.

Press the ZOOM TO TARGET button. Figure 9-41 illustrates what you should now see. As you recall from Mission 2: Operation Iron Breaker, the ZOOM TO TARGET button increases the map magnification to 999, and displays a rotating, three-dimensional view of the selected target. From Figure 9-41, you can determine exactly what the target, as well as the immediate vicinity, looks like.

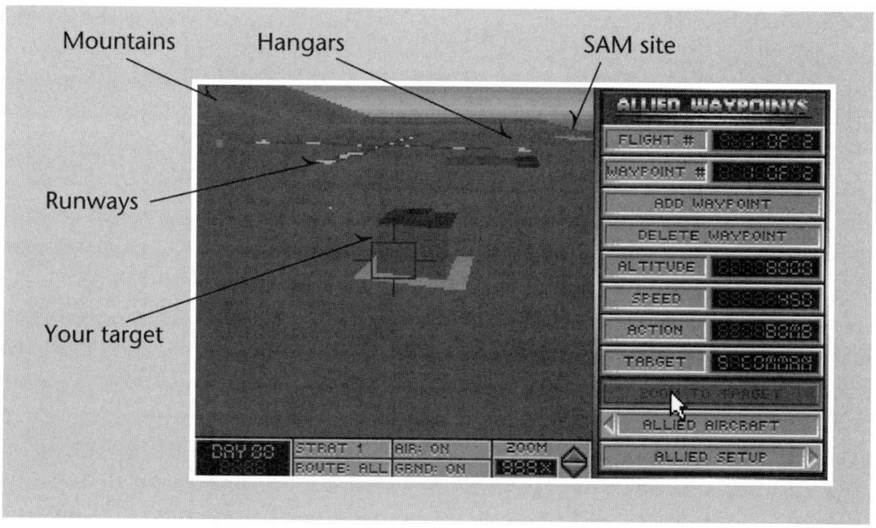

Figure 9-41 Your Specific Target

Flight 2: Defense Suppression

Press any key to disengage the ZOOM TO TARGET function and return to the normal Allied Waypoints screen. Press the FLIGHT # button and observe the second flight's waypoints. Like your group, the second flight has a total of three waypoints counting the start and land waypoints. Cycling through the waypoints, we see that the second group begins the mission much farther south and west than you do. They proceed to waypoint 1 where they bomb one of the two SAM sites, then waypoint 2 returns them to Nellis to land. Please note that this section is targeting only one of the two fixed SAM sites. You will still have to maintain your guard against the other.

Mission Walk-Through: The Flight Line

Study the views available from the Allied Waypoints screen until you are completely familiar with the enemy airbase and flight 2's course. Once finished, return to Red Flag Control, then proceed to the F-16 Pilots screen. Since all four aircraft are executing ground attack sorties, you should assign pilots with high ground attack scores to all four F-16s. Next, proceed to the F-16 Armament screen and verify the weapons loadouts: two AIM-9Ms, two AIM-120s, one ALQ-131, and four Mk83 bombs for each aircraft in flight 1; four AIM-9Ms, two AGM-88s, one ALQ-131, and two GBU-15s for each aircraft in flight 2. Select the TAKEOFF button and begin the mission.

Check for Airborne Company

As usual, configuring the HFR for maximum scan coverage is the first order of business; you must always know who you are sharing the skies with. Select NAM mode via F5, and using F8-F9, and F10 configure range, azimuth, and elevation scans for maximum coverage. Because there is little likelihood of an air-to-air encounter, go ahead and select air-to-ground mode by pressing BACKSPACE. Continue to press BACKSPACE until the Mk83 is the selected weapon. When the Mk83 is selected, the aiming pipper, or death-dot as it is usually called, will appear along the bottom edge of the HUD. Your screen should now appear similar to Figure 9-42.

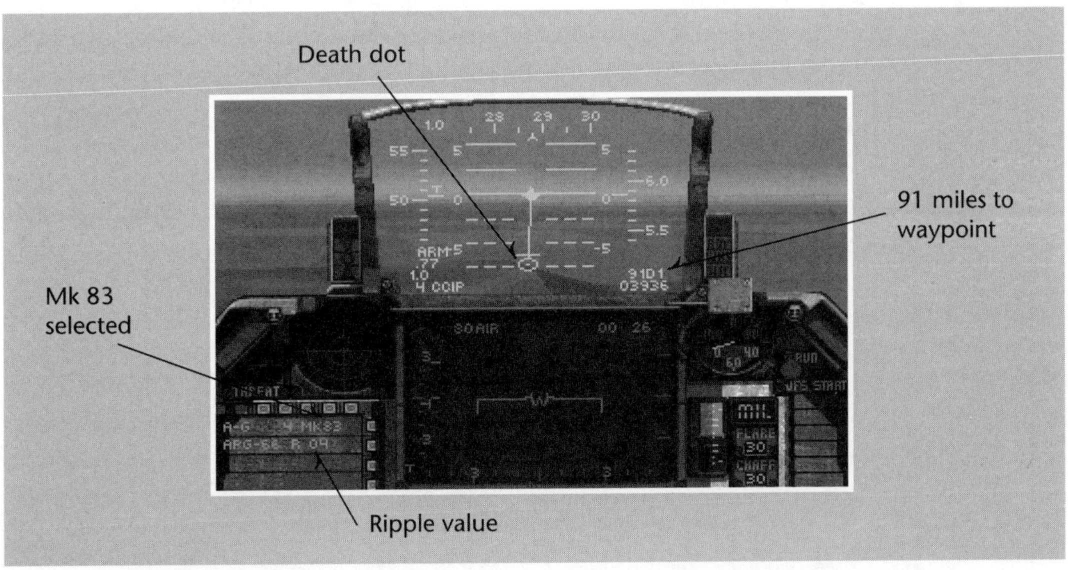

Figure 9-42 Initial Cockpit

Notice the stores panel in Figure 9-42. The ripple value in the figure has been set to 4, indicating that all four Mk83s will be released together. While this increases the chances of hitting a single target, it limits the attacking aircraft to only one attack. Since you have only a single target for this mission, you should increase the ripple value to 4 by pressing '.

TIP: Generally, if you are assigned only a single target, set the ripple value high — drop all of your ordnance and destroy the target on the first pass. However, if you are assigned multiple targets, you will have to use lower ripple values and conserve weapons.

You are now ready for action and should proceed directly to waypoint 1. Despite the fact that you will be attacking from a medium altitude, you should still fly at a relatively low altitude until you near the target. As you can see in Figure 9-42, waypoint 1 is over 90 miles away. You should fly at an altitude of 5,000 to 6,000 feet until you are within 20 miles of the target. Doing so decreases the risks of being detected by enemy radars.

Closing on Primary Target

As you approach the target, two contacts will appear on your REO. Lock and interrogate using the sequence of T, Z, and N. You should hear the IFF tone indicating friendly aircraft; they are the F-16s of flight 2. Remember, the F-16s are here to help you; they need to attack the target before you arrive, or else they accomplish nothing. Be sure to keep your speed under 500 knots to ensure that flight 2 arrives on target before you. Break the radar lock and proceed toward your target.

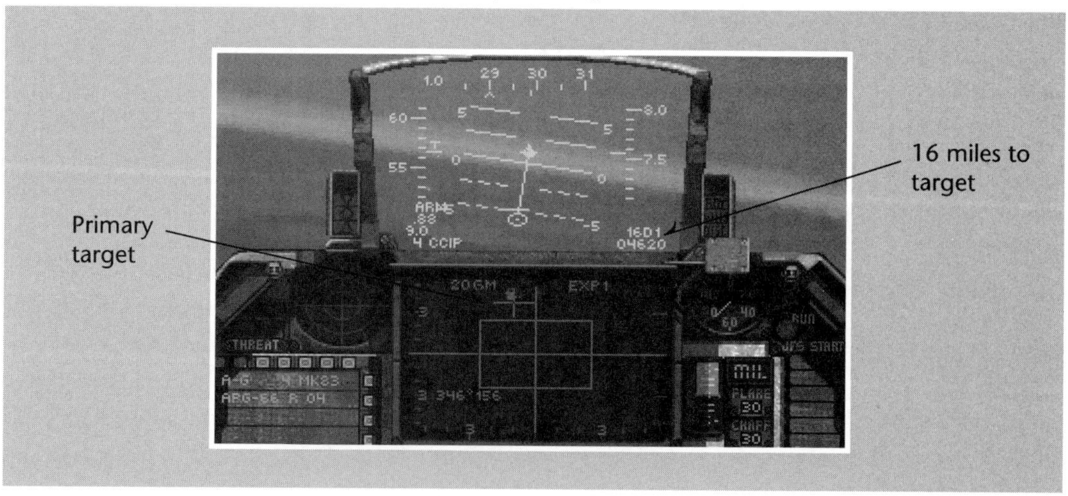

Figure 9-43 Primary Target Visible with GM Radar

When the range to the target decreases to 20 miles, switch from NAM radar to GM radar by pressing F7. As you recall from Operation Iron Breaker, when using GM radar, the primary target will be designated with a bright crosshair on the REO. Figure 9-43 illustrates how your screen should look. Since you are now within 20 miles of the target, apply full power and climb steeply to about 20,000 feet AGL. When you are seven miles from the target, you should begin your attack dive. Figure 9-44 shows how your screen should now appear.

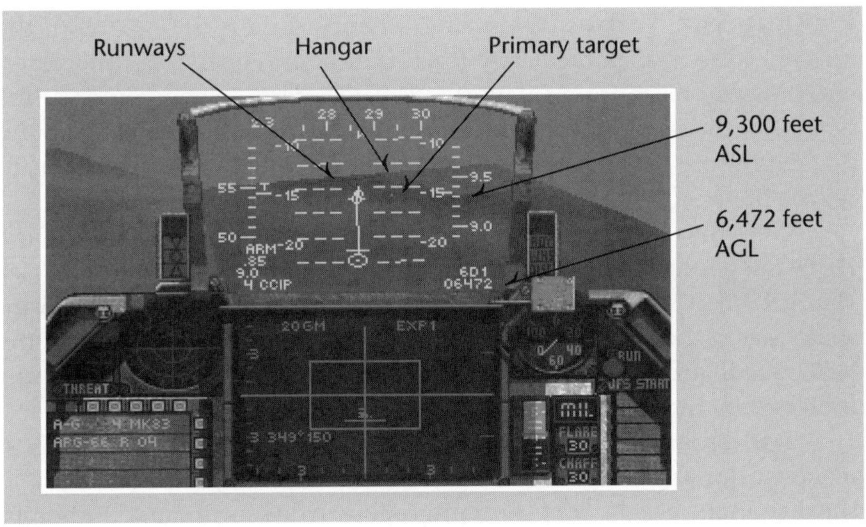

Figure 9-44 Beginning the Attack Dive Too Low

In Figure 9-44, the F-16 is in a shallow, 15° dive. The airbase is visible in the HUD; the runways and hangars are easily identifiable, while the communications building can just be recognized. However, Figure 9-44 illustrates a common error that must be avoided. While the aircraft's altitude is over 9,000 feet ASL, due to the terrain the F-16 is only about 6,400 feet AGL. This F-16 has begun the attack dive too low. Not only is it well within the 12,000 feet limit of the SA-7 SAM, it is dangerously close to the ground considering the aircraft must remain in this dive for several more seconds.

WARNING: When flying air-to-ground sorties, always monitor your AGL altitude, not your ASL altitude. When the AGL altitude goes to zero, you crash, regardless of your current altitude ASL.

The Death-Dot: Aiming the Mk83

Whether or not free-fall bombs hit the intended target depends solely on the death-dot at the bottom of your HUD. During your dive, you must steer the F-16 so that the death-dot is positioned exactly over the desired target. You may need to reduce throttle or apply speed brakes to allow sufficient time to accomplish this, especially in low-altitude attacks. Once the dot is superimposed exactly over the desired object, you must tell the F-16's computer to begin CCIP computations by pickling the target.

Pickling the Target Normally, when you press the SPACEBAR, the selected weapon is immediately fired. Iron bombs operate a little differently. As you recall from Chapter 5, *Using Weapons,* when you press the SPACEBAR, the F-16 flight computer interpolates the position on the ground marked by the death-dot. The flight computer then calculates when to release the weapons based on your current approach.

Once the target is pickled, the death-dot remains at the bottom of the HUD, but a long, vertical bar appears through the center of the HUD (see Figure 9-45). A small horizontal bar moves down this vertical line toward the center of the HUD. When the horizontal bar reaches the center of the HUD, the flight computer automatically releases the number of weapons indicated by the ripple value.

It is absolutely critical that once the target has been pickled the F-16 makes no deviations in course or attitude. The wings must be kept level, and the dive angle must be kept constant. Failure to do so will cause the bombs to miss their targets.

Overriding the Pickle and Making Corrections Sometimes, after you've pickled the target, you realize that the death-dot was not perfectly superimposed over the target. If you allow the computer to release the weapons automatically, the bombs are certain to miss. You may abort the CCIP sequence at any time by pressing the X key. The X key not only breaks radar locks in air-to-air modes, it also breaks CCIP locks in air-to-ground modes. You may then make course corrections and repeat the pickling process.

Sometimes, you may want to release the bombs immediately. Perhaps the F-16 has entered a slight roll or turn after the target was pickled, but the target is so close you don't have enough time to re-pickle. Maybe ground units have opened fire and you just want to dump your weapons and hope for the best. Other times you may simply want to test your reflexes and release the ordnance manually. In these circumstances, after the target has been pickled, pressing (SPACEBAR) a second time will immediately release the selected ordnance.

> **NOTE:** Pressing (SPACEBAR) once pickles a target; when it is pressed a second time, the selected weapon immediately releases.

Executing the Attack

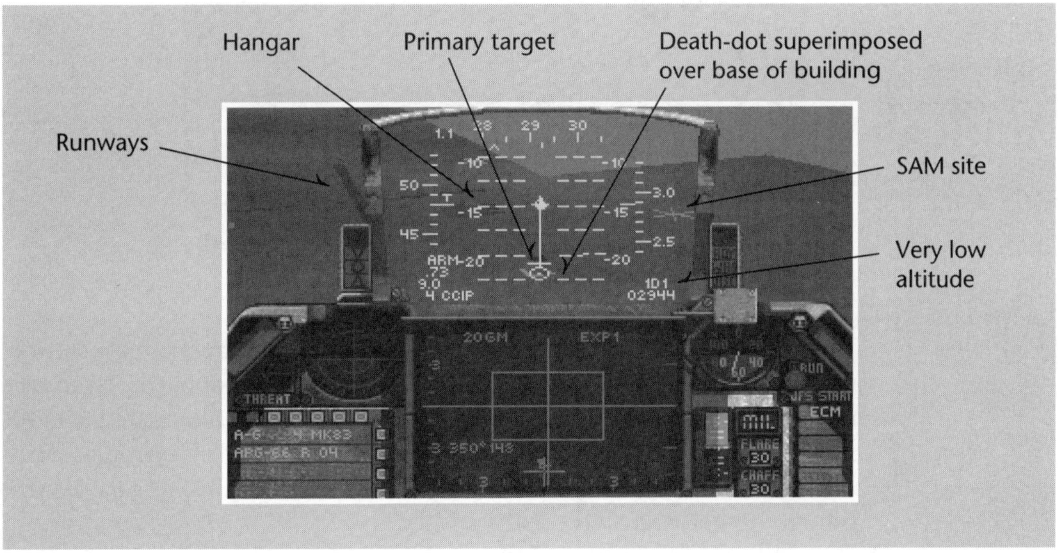

Figure 9-45 A Perfect Pickle, But Too Low

Figure 9-45 shows a clear view of the enemy airbase, and the communication HQ building is clearly visible along the bottom of the HUD. Notice the position of the death-dot: perfectly placed over the base of the building. The F-16's wings are exactly level and the target is directly in front of the aircraft; this is a perfect setup for the pickle. Steer your F-16 until the death-dot is similarly placed over the building and press (SPACEBAR) to pickle the target.

Despite the perfect pickle setup, Figure 9-45 shows the result of beginning the attack dive too low. The example F-16 is not even 3,000 feet above the ground! Not only is the F-16 well within range of all surface-to-air weapons, it is in dire danger of crashing before the weapons can be released. Even if the weapons are released on time, it is highly likely that the F-16 will take damage from the explosions. At this point in your attack run, your altitude should be above 10,000 feet.

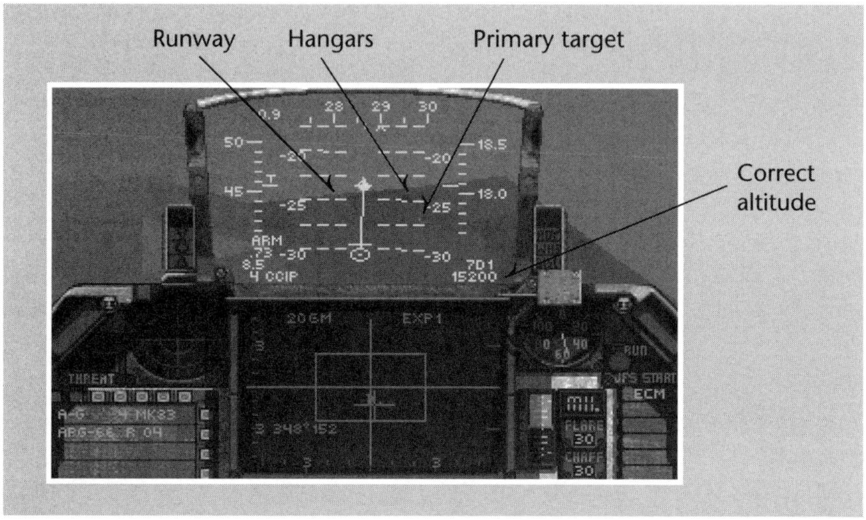

Figure 9-46 A Correct Pickle and Altitude

The Correct Approach Figure 9-46 shows a correct approach from medium altitude. In the example, the death-dot has not been placed over the target yet, but the F-16 is still over 15,000 feet AGL (compared to 6,400 AGL in Figure 9-44). Note that while the target is still seven miles away, visibility is still good. Three key features (the runways, the hangars, and the primary target) can all be distinguished.

Figure 9-46 shows the view from an F-16 which has placed the death-dot directly over the target and has pickled the target by pressing (SPACEBAR). The vertical bar indicating the pickle has been set is visible in the center of the HUD, and the release timer bars can also be seen. The upper bar will slowly move downward, toward the lower bar. When the two bars converge, the bombs will be dropped automatically. You may immediately level off and depart the area.

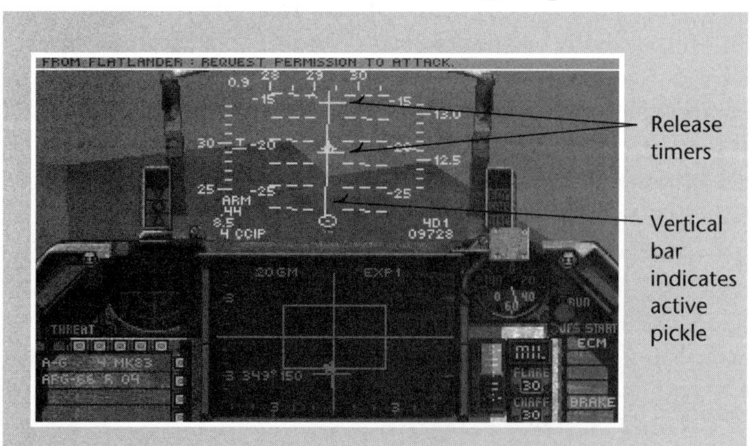

Figure 9-47 The Release Timers

Mission Debriefing

Figure 9-48 shows the result of a direct hit on the communications building. Note that while the black region on the building indicates a hit, there are three marks indicating misses beside the building. At least three of the four bombs failed to hit the target. Had the ripple value been set lower, it is likely that the building would have been missed altogether.

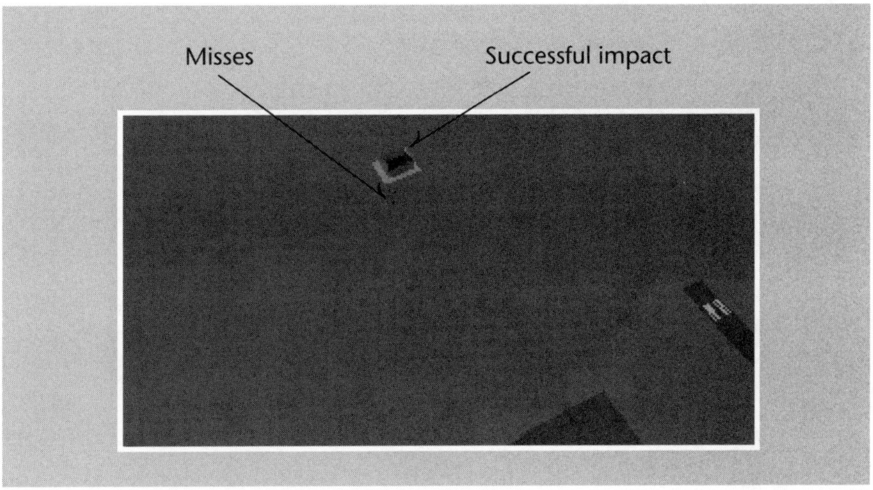

Figure 9-48 A Perfect Hit

How did you fare? You may consider the mission a success only if the primary target was destroyed. If the primary target was destroyed, proceed to the next mission.

If you failed, what went wrong?

- Were you shot down? If so, chalk this up to bad luck. Other than executing evasive maneuvers and engaging ECM, you have little control over this. Try the mission again.
- Did you crash? This is a result of starting the attack too low and taking too long in the dive. Repeat the mission, making sure to start the dive at a higher altitude. Also, know when to give up. If you cross 10,000 feet and have not already pickled the target, break off the attack. It's better to return with a functional aircraft than to push a bad situation and become a wet spot on the desert.
- Did you survive, but fail to hit the target? The hardest part of CCIP bombing is placing the death-dot precisely over the target. Skill in this area comes only with practice. Repeat the mission. Try using the

brakes to slow your descent. At speeds under 300 knots, you can use the rudder controls, [and] keys, to help point the F-16's nose.

Mission 7: Operation Sky Sentry

Prohibit Enemy Aircraft from Fleeing

ZNR CCCCC
I 18 0930Z JAN 92
FM RED FLAG HQ DIV//GEN WAITE//
TO 386TH FSFORUM SQU CMDR//COL BASHAM//

BT
S E C R E T
REF: DAILY ATO: OP: SKY SENTRY (S)
(S) OP: FALLING SKY CONSIDERED SUCCESSFUL. ENEMY COMMUNICATIONS NETWORK DISRUPTED. ENEMY FORCES ARE IN FULL RETREAT.

ENEMY AIRCRAFT ARE ATTEMPTING TO FLEE THE COUNTRY. ENEMY PILOTS ARE ATTEMPTING TO FLY TO MEXICO AND REQUEST ASYLUM. EFFECTIVE IMMEDIATELY, NO AIRCRAFT IS PERMITTED TO ENTER MEXICO. YOUR SQUADRON IS ORDERED TO MAINTAIN CONTINUOUS CAP ALONG THE U.S. - MEXICO BORDER. YOU ARE ORDERED TO DESTROY ALL ENEMY AIRCRAFT ENCOUNTERED.

ET

Nellis AFB, NV—0930 HRS

It's been two days since Operation Falling Sky. It appears that the enemy president was not present when the communications building was destroyed, but that his two sons were. One was killed, the other seriously injured. Predictably, radical nations and organizations around the world are condemning the attack, calling it, "a blatant and illegal attempt to assassinate the rightful leader of a sovereign nation."

The destruction of the comms center has had a profound effect. Enemy forces in the field appear to be completely isolated from their central command and are operating under the independent direction of individual division commanders. Amid rumors that the enemy president has gone into hiding, three different enemy generals have declared themselves in charge. A power struggle has begun, and further rumors report the enemy president will go into exile, if not voluntarily, then by force.

Allied casualties continue to be light. In the past two days, an F-111 failed to return from a deep strike, and two F-4s fell victim to enemy SAMs. Enemy air resistance has been light; few enemy fighters takeoff, and most of the ones that do attempt to fly to Mexico.

Mission Briefing

"Today, this squadron has been ordered to fly continuous combat air patrols along the border between the U.S. and Mexico," The Red Flag instructor begins. "You are ordered to engage all enemy aircraft encountered and to intercept any aircraft, military or civilian, attempting to cross into Mexico. Be warned, however, there are many friendly aircraft operating in the area; avoid friendly casualties at all costs."

The Task: Aerial Blockade

"Your aircraft will execute an aerial blockade of Mexico. No aircraft will be allowed to cross into Mexican airspace. Two flights each composed of two F-16s will execute this mission. The two flights will patrol adjacent areas; if one flight becomes overwhelmed during combat, they should maneuver toward the other flight for assistance.

"Flight 1 will carry four AIM-120 AMRAAMs, four AIM-9M Sidewinders, and an ALQ-131 ECM pod. Flight 2 will carry two AIM-120 AMRAAMs, four AIM-9M Sidewinders, and an ALQ-131 ECM pod. Each flight should continue its patrol until fuel or weapons status becomes prohibitive.

"You are fully versed in usage of these weapons, air-to-air combat maneuvering, and defensive tactics. You're ready to fight. Dismissed."

Mission Analysis

This mission emphasizes a single element: continuous combat air patrols. Frequently in Falcon 3.0 campaigns, you'll have a specific area to defend instead of a specific target to attack. You will be assigned an area or border to patrol and you will be expected to stop any aircraft attempting to cross that line.

Continuous CAP missions require expertise in two skills: using radar to detect, track, and target enemy aircraft, and air-to-air combat maneuvering. The prior training missions, both in this chapter and Chapter 5, *Using Weapons,* provided the necessary training in these two areas. As an individual pilot, you are ready to execute this mission.

Teamwork: The Key to Success

As you are already aware, teamwork between you and your wingman is an absolute must if you are to survive a mission. You also know that coordination between multiple flights of aircraft attacking multiple targets can overwhelm and defeat enemy defenses. In this particular mission, however, two independent flights of aircraft will be executing the same mission in adjacent airspace. This gives you an additional option: luring the enemy aircraft into an area supported by other friendly aircraft.

For example, your flight of two F-16s may engage a group of four or more enemy aircraft. Depending upon various factors such as enemy pilot skill, aircraft type, and weapons availability, this could easily be an unwinnable situation for you and your wingman. Your options are to retreat altogether and allow the enemies to pass, or to maneuver toward the other patrolling aircraft, thus drawing them into the fight.

You Are the Bait

Using yourself as bait, you can execute defensive maneuvers in the direction of the other flight of F-16s. This is a dangerous tactic, and should be used only when you and your wingmen are unable to obtain an offensive position. When you are already forced into a strictly defensive situation, you have nothing to lose.

This requires you to have intimate knowledge of the other F-16's flight plan. You must know where to find them at all times. Normally, you will adjust both your and their waypoints so that your flight paths intersect at one waypoint. Using the SHIFT-B and SHIFT-V keys to select waypoints during flight, you will always know exactly how far you are from the rendezvous position.

Other F-16s May Be Preoccupied

Be warned, however, that arriving at the rendezvous does not guarantee support; the other F-16s may be engaged in a battle somewhere else along their flight path, low on fuel and returning to base, or simply patrolling another portion of their flight path and unaware of your situation.

You can protect against this somewhat by designating small areas for each CAP flight to patrol, such as 60 or less miles. If you have a long border to patrol, this approach requires more aircraft, but it has numerous advantages. First, each flight is situated closer to the neighboring flights, increasing the availability of mutual support. Second, because the APG-66 has an 80 mile range, the patrolling F-16s can cover the entire area between their current positions and the edge of their patrol zone at all times. Third, the patrolling aircraft will reverse course more often when patrolling a smaller zone, thereby reducing the likelihood that enemy aircraft can sneak by while the F16's back is turned.

> **NOTE:** Additionally, you may want to actually overlap the flight paths of the patrolling F-16s to ensure that there are no holes for enemy fighters to slip through.

Mission Walk-Through: Preflight

Preflight preparations for this mission focus more on the actions and locations of your own forces than of the enemy. During a typical CAP mission, attacks are usually expected from a given direction, but the nature of the attack (when, strength, type of aircraft, etc.) is unknown. In such missions, you simply fly around the sky and wait for an adversary to show up. As stated in the above Mission Analysis, you may need to give or receive support to or from other CAP groups; therefore, you must be familiar with their positions.

To avoid engaging friendly forces by mistake, you should also gather all available information on other friendly aircraft in the area. During Red Flag training missions, the flight paths of all friendly pilots are available to you. However, during actual campaigns, you will receive little, if any, information on other friendly aircraft. Flight plans for aircraft in your squadron are always available; however, unless you are ordered to escort some other aircraft group, you will rarely be told they exist.

> **NOTE:** The Allied Waypoints screen in Red Flag mode and the Set Waypoints screen in campaign mode will always be the most detailed information source on other allied aircraft. Although the Set Waypoints screen will rarely be complete, there is no other source of this information while in campaign mode.

Allied Waypoints

If you haven't already done so, select a squadron and enter Red Flag. Proceed to the Allied Waypoints screen by pressing the NELLIS COMMAND button, then the ALLIED AIRCRAFT button, and finally the ALLIED WAYPOINTS button.

Notice the FLIGHT # display indicates there are three flights of allied aircraft. Initially, you can see on the map that your flight, flight 1, consists of two F-16s flying an east-west CAP mission bounded by waypoints 1 and 2. By pressing the FLIGHT # button, you can see that the next flight is composed of C-130s making their way northward to Nellis — don't shoot at these guys! Another press of the FLIGHT # button shows that the remaining flight is your companion CAP flight.

The other CAP flight is of particular interest. Notice that the patrol region between their starting and first waypoints extends between your start position and Nellis. These aircraft are positioned for double duty: first, they provide CAP coverage in airspace adjacent to your patrol zone; second, they are positioned between you and Nellis, thus also performing the reception escort role. If you run out of fuel or weapons with bandits on your tail, you can head for home and let the other F-16s clear your six o'clock position.

Also note that the two CAPs intersect near your first waypoint. If you become entangled in a difficult situation and require help, your best bet is to press SHIFT-V until the waypoint indicators on the HUD point to waypoint 1, and head for help.

Waypoint Design Considerations

When designing CAP flight paths on your own, follow a few simple guides:

- Always place waypoints that define the edges of the CAP within 60 to 70 miles of each other. Since the F-16's APG-66 radar has a maximum range of 80 miles, the patrolling aircraft can monitor the entire route from any point along that route. This reduces the opportunity for enemy aircraft to slip past the patrolling F-16.

- When assigning multiple CAP flights, always overlap the ends of the patrol routes. This ensures that no holes exist between CAP routes and places each flight within range to assist the adjacent flight(s).

- When patrolling particularly critical routes, double your CAP assignments. If you must prevent enemy strike aircraft from attacking your home airbase, assign two groups of CAP aircraft to patrol the same area.

- Always take as many of the best air-to-air weapons as you can get. No matter how many missiles you carry, you will probably need more.

Using these techniques and some forethought, you should have no problem engineering effective CAP zones. By reverse analyzing these techniques, you can also derive methods for defeating enemy CAP patrols, such as: using large numbers of aircraft to *surge attack* a single point along an enemy CAP route, and attempting to penetrate at the least covered positions along an enemy CAP. The latter is more difficult to accomplish and requires you to locate and monitor enemy positions while searching for weak spots.

Mission Walk-Through: The Flight Line

Since you are nearing graduation from the Advanced Flight School, the flight line walk-through of this mission will be considerably smaller than in previous missions. By this time, you should be completely familiar with the operation and usage of the HFR, your offensive weapons, and defensive counter-measures. You should be fully versed in missile avoidance techniques and ACM tactics. If you are not completely familiar with any of these topics, you are not ready to graduate from the Advanced Flight School, and should repeat the appropriate training missions. Otherwise, select your pilot and make your way to the cockpit.

Environmental Awareness

Your CAP has been defined between your first and second waypoints. While you are flying between these two points waiting for bad guys to show up, you should mark the positions of friendly aircraft you encounter. Once you've ascertained that a contact is friendly, you should immediately note its heading, altitude, and airspeed, as well as your own, for future reference. Since you are traveling between at least two points, at some time you will have to break contact with the friendly while you travel in the other direction. When you return to the previous course, you will regain contact. By comparing the flight data from the previous contact, you can usually determine if this is the same friendly or a new contact.

> **TIP:** In crowded airspace, keeping track of all other friendly aircraft can be a difficult task. To ease this burden, try keeping a notepad and pen near your computer. During flight, use this pad to record notes

(*Continued*)

about other aircraft encountered. Many pilot supply stores sell small clipboards called *kneepads*. Kneepads can be strapped to your thigh allowing you quick access to your notepad. Real pilots use kneepads for exactly this purpose during actual flights.

Alternatively, place a piece of clear plastic over one of the maps included in the Falcon 3.0 package. Using non-permanent markers, mark the known positions and routes of aircraft on the plastic prior to flight. During the mission, mark the positions and flight data of contacts on the plastic. This gives you a quick reference between the flight plan and the actual contacts.

Patrol Guidelines

- Always keep track of other friendly aircraft. When you have several contacts on your REO, it is inefficient and often impractical to lock every contact and interrogate its IFF. You need the ability to eliminate some contacts solely by their position.
- Don't fixate on a single hostile contact. While you focus your attention on one bandit, a larger group may pass by you unnoticed.
- Use your radar intelligently. Until you actually decide to attack a bandit, constantly turn your aircraft in various directions, thus widening your field of view. When an engagement is unavoidable, then focus and fixate on your target.
- Don't stray too far from your assigned course. The bandits may be trying to lure you away so bombers or strike aircraft can slip by. Even if you down the bandits, you will be unable to stop the attack aircraft if you are too far out of position.
- Watch out for enemy ECM use. Your long range AMRAAMs may be rendered useless by enemies toting ECM gear. In such cases, you will be unable to maintain a radar lock on the bandit, and many spurious radar contacts will be displayed on your REO.

TIP: When encountering heavy, enemy ECM usage, your only recourse is to fly directly toward the spurious blips until they are within 10 miles. Then switch to the padlock view by pressing the 8 key and shut the APG-66 off by pressing R. ECM has no effect on visual abilities, so padlock will still acquire and track bandits once they are within visual range (5 miles). You can then use padlock to maneuver the bandit in front of you and fire either a heat-seeking AIM-9 Sidewinder (unaffected by ECM) or the 20mm cannon.

Remember, in this mission, the enemy aircraft are trying to fly south, past you. You can assume that most bandit contacts will be north of your position, flying south. Fly your route and engage any and all bandits that attempt to cross it. Don't waste fuel or ordnance, every bullet and every drop of fuel counts! When you've finished the mission, proceed to the debriefing.

Mission Debriefing

You may consider this mission a success only if:

- You survive the mission, and
- You downed at least two enemy fighters, and
- Either you or your wingman downed an An-12 cargo plane.

Did you succeed? If so, congratulations, you're ready to proceed to the final exam. If not, analyze what went wrong.

- Did you get shot down? You are outnumbered on this mission, and it will take some skill in aerial combat to succeed. However, this mission is no more difficult than any standard campaign mission. Practice air-to-air combat maneuvers and repeat the mission.
- Did you fail to shoot down the An-12? The enemy fighters in this mission are trying to occupy you so that the An-12 can slip by unnoticed. Repeat the mission, and patrol the area more thoroughly. Make sure you know who is in the sky with you before you concentrate on a specific target.
- Did you run out of fuel or weapons? Knowing when to leave a fight is as important as knowing how to fight. Always keep a close watch on your fuel and weapons status. When you get low, start looking for opportunities to disengage. Repeat the mission.

> **TIP:** Disengaging from air-to-air combat is like marriage; it takes the consent of both parties involved to work. Just because you are low on fuel, your enemy will not graciously allow you to leave. It may take some time before the opportunity to disengage presents itself. To avoid additional difficulty, start looking for the chance to bug out before you need it.

Mission 8: Operation Final Exam

Apply Principles Learned

ZNR CCCCC
I 20 0730Z JAN 92
FM RED FLAG HQ DIV//GEN WAITE//
TO 386TH FSFORUM SQU CMDR//COL BASHAM//

BT
S E C R E T
REF: DAILY ATO: OP: FINAL EXAM (S)
(S) ALLIED FORCES HAVE SECURED THE CRASH SITE OF THE AN-12 DOWNED DURING OP: SKY SENTRY. ANALYSIS OF THE WRECKAGE HAS CONFIRMED THE ENEMY PRESIDENT WAS ON BOARD AND WAS KILLED.

THE ENEMY GOVERNMENT IS IN SHAMBLES. MULTIPLE GOVERNMENT AND MILITARY OFFICIALS ARE CLAIMING THE PRESIDENCY. THE MOST INFLUENTIAL OF THESE RIVALS, A GENERAL FORMERLY IN CHARGE OF THE WAR EFFORT, IS ADVOCATING CONTINUED HOSTILITIES AGAINST THE U.S. AND HAS FORMED HIS OWN MILITARY GOVERNMENT AT THE ENEMY AIRBASE. MOST OF THE FORCES LOYAL TO THIS GENERAL HAVE POSITIONED THEMSELVES AROUND THE AIRBASE.

DESTRUCTION OF THE RUNWAYS AT THIS AIRBASE DEEMED CRITICAL. THIS WILL ISOLATE THE ROGUE GENERAL. THE 386TH SQUADRON IS ORDERED TO ATTACK AND DESTROY THE RUNWAYS AT THIS AIRBASE IMMEDIATELY.
ET

Nellis AFB, NV—1045 HRS

As it turns out, the enemy president was onboard the An-12 you shot down during Operation Sky Sentry. Without a coherent leader, the enemy army's command structure collapsed. Several high ranking generals and government ministers have declared themselves each to be the new president. Military forces are divided, each unit loyal to one of the would-be presidents. The most influential of the rival presidents is the general who formerly controlled the war effort against the U.S.

This general has formed his own military government at the enemy airbase due west of Nellis. Due to the destruction of the communications building at this airbase, this general must use inbound and outbound aircraft to receive supplies and news, and to communicate with loyal subordinates.

For all practical purposes, the war is over. Enemy forces poised on the brink of civil war would have a difficult time organizing a car pool, let alone an organized strike against the U.S. However, the U.S. President is not willing to quietly sweep this matter under the carpet. The President wants a formal declaration of surrender from the enemy forces clearly indicating the end of hostilities. It is believed that isolating the rogue general from the remaining enemy forces will topple his ad-hoc government and allow a more moderate person to take charge.

Despite the imminent end of the war, this mission will be your most difficult. This is your final exam. You must now take full leadership of the 386th squadron and apply your training on your own. If you succeed in this mission, you will truly be ready for deployment to the campaigns!

Mission Briefing

"Congratulations," begins the Red Flag Instructor, "This is your final mission. Completion of this mission will fulfill all graduation requirements. You've learned the necessary skills, now it's time for you to apply those skills. Unlike previous missions, Operation Final Exam will have no mission walk-through. Once you have been briefed, it will be up to you to devise an attack strategy, assign the aircraft and pilots, and to choose the appropriate ordnance. If this mission succeeds, you graduate and will be assigned a campaign. However, if you fail, you will be ordered to repeat various portions of the Advanced Flight School training program."

Mission Parameters

"Your goal for this mission is the destruction of the runways at the enemy airbase. To this end, eight F-16s organized in four two-plane groups are standing by. All pilots in your squadron are available, and a wide variety of ordnance is at your disposal.

"Runway destruction requires a special weapon, the BLU-107B Durandal runway cratering device. The Durandal is a free-fall bomb with sequenced detonations. The first explosion creates a hole in the runway into which the rest of the weapon falls. Then, the rest of the weapon detonates beneath the runway's surface creating a huge crater. Note that the Durandal needs to be dropped near the center of the runway to maximize effectiveness. In cases where runways intersect, the Durandal should be dropped on that intersection point to cripple both runways.

"The Durandal is a simple, iron bomb requiring standard CCIP bombing techniques to deliver. Based on the available intelligence information, you will have to decide for yourself whether to approach from high, medium, or low altitudes."

Additional Resources

"You have a total of eight F-16s available for this mission. Assuming you use two for the actual attack on the runway, this leaves six for additional support roles. Due to the high probability of SAMs and AAA, you will probably want to assign two F-16s to defense suppression roles. Many enemy fighters have been spotted operating from the airbase, so you will probably need two F-16s assigned to CAP duties. Assign the final two F-16s to additional support roles as you see necessary.

"This is your final exam so take plenty of time planning the mission; don't cut yourself short. Use the principles you've learned so far to assign and arm your aircraft effectively. Given the proper tactics, this mission isn't too difficult. You may fly any role you want, you don't have to personally attack the runways. This exam tests your ability to engineer effective, multi-plane attacks more than it tests your proficiency at weapons delivery. Good luck, dismissed."

Mission Analysis

This mission emphasizes two elements:

- Runway destruction techniques using the Durandal anti-runway bomb.
- Applying the skills you've learned previously under your own initiative.

Runway Denial

Because airpower plays such an integral part of modern warfare, enemy runways are always high priority targets. Despite the advances in air-to-air combat systems, the most effective way to keep enemy aircraft out of the sky is to keep them from ever taking off. Even though runway repair techniques exist, repairs take time and cost valuable resources. Few things can cripple an enemy as quickly as destroying his runways.

The Durandal anti-runway bomb was specifically designed for this task. It is highly effective at damaging runways, but has little or no effect against other structures. The Durandal uses multiple, sequenced detonations to penetrate beneath the runway, then destroy it from below. Because a runway must be built on solid ground, weakening the ground beneath the runway increases the amount of repair work required.

Runways are extremely long structures, and Durandals can only damage a relatively small portion of them. For example, the F-15 requires approximately 900 to 1,200 feet to take off, and close to 2,500 feet to land. A typical runway may be 3,500 or more feet long. Therefore, to disable the runway, the Durandal hits must be placed so that no undamaged length of runway is 900 feet long. Anything longer will allow enemy aircraft to takeoff, although they may have to land at another airbase. Once the enemy aircraft are unable to take off, follow-up strikes against the hangars can destroy them on the ground.

If there are multiple, intersecting runways, dropping the Durandals at the intersection point usually cripples both runways with a single pass. However, if the runways are extremely long, the undamaged portions may be long enough to permit flight operations. Since you need a precise hit to cripple the runway, you should use high ripple values. The more bombs you drop at one time, the more likely it is that one will hit the required spot. Figure 9-49 shows an F-16 dropping Durandals with a high ripple value.

TIP: In general, aim anti-runway devices for the center of undamaged sections of runway, thus cutting the usable runway length in half. Using multiple attack strikes, a single runway can be divided into three or four short, useless sections.

Figure 9-49
F-16 Dropping Durandals

Applying Your Knowledge

The rest of the mission is up to you. You know the available information and intelligence gathering tools; use them to their fullest. Make sure you know everything there is to know about the enemy prior to attacking. You know the various attack strategies, their strengths, and their weaknesses. Based on the intelligence you gather, determine how to best assign your aircraft and what approach method maximizes both safety and effectiveness. You know the weapons available to you and their abilities; arm your aircraft appropriately for their missions.

There is no walk-through for this mission. You are completely on your own. If you succeed on this mission, you are truly ready for the Falcon 3.0 campaigns. If you fail, however, you do not graduate from the Advanced Flight School. Figure 9-50 shows a properly cratered runway. Good luck!

Figure 9-50 A Direct Hit Using a Durandal.

Mission Debriefing

How did the mission go? You may consider it a success if:

- The runway was successfully hit, and
- You successfully landed back at Nellis, and
- Less than three friendly aircraft were shot down.

Did you succeed? If so, congratulations, you are definitely among the best of the best. You have completed all of the Advanced Flight School graduation requirements. You are ready for a Falcon 3.0 campaign in any part of the world. If the mission failed, analyze what went wrong:

- Did the bombs miss the runway? This could indicate several problems. If you personally flew the runway attack sortie, this indicates you need additional practice in CCIP bombing and approach tactics. Repeat Operation Iron Breaker and Operation Falling Sky, then repeat the final exam.

  If you did not fly the attack mission, this indicates that the pilots you assigned were not sufficiently skilled. Remember to always check the skills of your pilots before assigning them to a mission. Repeat the final exam giving more attention to pilot assignment.

- Were you shot down and how? The debriefing at the end of the mission should indicate what type of weapon hit you; repeat any previous missions dealing with that particular threat, then repeat the final exam.

- Were too many friendly aircraft shot down by SAMs and AAA? If so, this indicates that you either didn't distribute ECM gear widely enough, or didn't assign enough defense suppression aircraft. Repeat Operation Lights Out and Operation Falling Sky, then repeat the final exam.

- Were too many friendly aircraft shot down by enemy fighters? This indicates you need more CAP and escorting fighters. Repeat Operation Ground Shaker, Operation Fence Post, and Operation Sky Sentry, then repeat the final exam.

10

The Campaigns: Tactics and Military Doctrine

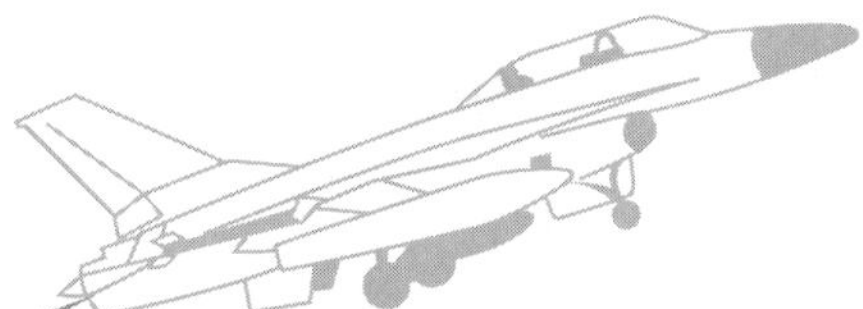

Introduction to Campaigns

Wars are not won by single aircraft. Wars are won by the coordinated efforts of hundreds (even thousands) of aircraft. By careful execution of organized strikes, the odds of each aircraft achieving its primary mission increase and friendly aircraft can be positioned to defend each other. This increases the odds of all platforms returning home to fight another day. Such strategies led to the Coalition victory over Iraqi forces in the 1991 Gulf War.

Falcon 3.0 campaigns are no exception. Falcon 3.0 campaigns depart from the traditional "one pilot against the world" style so often presented in other flight simulators, substituting a global, overall view of the war instead. Many of the tasks assigned to your squadron will support other units. It won't always be your job to fly over Baghdad and bomb the presidential palace. Instead, you may be ordered to destroy a defensive column of tanks so that friendly ground forces can roll into town and capture said palace. Your job isn't to single-handedly win the war, but to be part of the war-winning team effort.

This chapter discusses (in order): how campaign mode works, how victory is determined, your role as squadron commanding officer, considerations when assigning pilots, considerations when allocating aircraft, waypoint strategies, emergency airfields, and unauthorized missions. The following text assumes that you have read (and are familiar with) terms, phrases, and instructions presented in previous chapters and have executed the Advance Flight School training missions in Chapter 9, *Red Flag: Advanced Flight School.*

How the Campaigns Work

Falcon 3.0 campaigns are complex scenarios with many dynamic elements and events. Forces, both allied and enemy, are constantly in motion seeking to achieve predetermined goals. Many detailed factors, such as resupply routes and production capacities, are taken into account.

Strategic Objectives

In every combat zone, military leaders assess the strategic value of cities, factories, bases, airfields, oil wells, bridges, etc. Friendly supply routes are defined, and enemy supply routes are estimated. Military *choke points,* locations from which access to other militarily significant locations can be controlled, are identified. Military leaders on each side of the conflict generate a list of sites to control, sites to deny enemy access, and sites to destroy. Sites included on this list are called *strategic objectives.* In theory, once the majority of the strategic objectives are achieved, the enemy will no longer be capable of waging war. Falcon 3.0 uses this same logic.

Theater Nodes

Each Falcon 3.0 theater map includes about 80 fixed structures (airfields, towns, bridges, etc.), an unspecified amount of mobile forces (armor units, infantry, aircraft, etc.), and topographical features (rivers, mountains, beaches, etc.). Each fixed structure is called a *node.* Mobile forces move in and around the topographical features to defend and capture nodes. Each node within a theater is visible from the STRAT view on the theater map (see Chapter 7, *Introduction to the Campaigns,* for details on the theater map). Nodes are the key to campaign victory.

The Front Lines Nodes owned by opposing forces that are next to each other are called *adjacent nodes.* Adjacent nodes form the front lines of the battle. These areas are where the ground units will fight and advance. Territorial advances are marked by the seizure of enemy nodes.

Only adjacent nodes can be seized by an opposing force. There are no infiltration missions in Falcon 3.0; no special forces parachute behind enemy lines to seize strategic sites. Once a node controlled by an opposing force is captured, all opposing nodes next to it become adjacent nodes and the front penetrates deeper into enemy territory.

> **NOTE:** Nodes owned by opposite sides but located next to one another are called adjacent nodes. Ground combat occurs between adjacent nodes.

Supply Routes Nodes are not independent entities. Nodes are interlinked through a dynamic network to other nodes owned by the same army. For example, all nodes controlled by blue forces are dynamically interlinked. Adjacent nodes, however, have no links between them. Nodes linked to one another are called *connected nodes*.

Each node has at least one connected node, possibly more, forming supply routes. Additional troops and weapons are supplied to a node only from a connected node. Figure 10-1 shows a possible network of nodes.

In Figure 10-1, square nodes represent allied forces, round nodes represent enemy forces. Nodes B2 and R5 are, therefore, adjacent nodes, as are B4 and R3, and B5 and R4. These six adjacent nodes form the front line of the battle. Nodes connected by a solid line are connected nodes, such as B1 and B2.

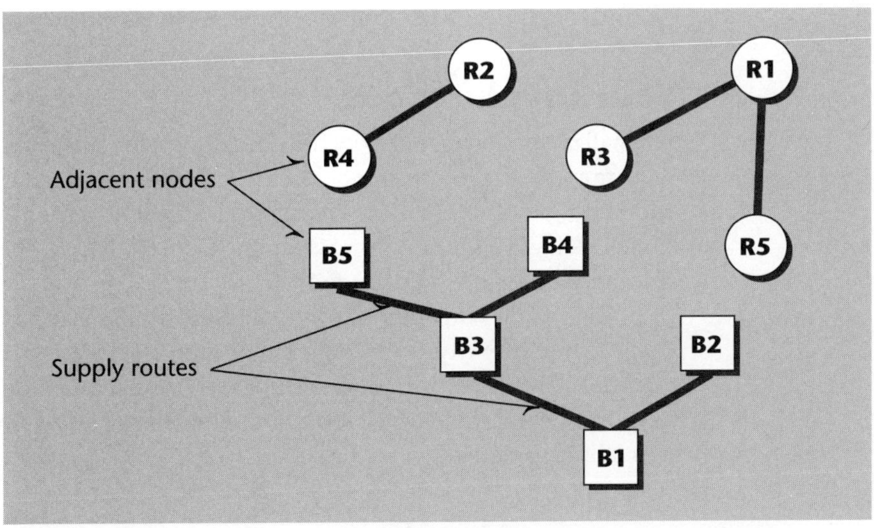

Figure 10-1 Sample Network of Campaign Nodes

In this example, node B1 is not an adjacent node; therefore, it could be bombed by opposing aircraft, but it can't be captured by opposing ground forces. B1 forms the base of a supply line that feeds all other B nodes. If, however, forces from R5 captured node B2, node B2 would become an R node, R6. In that case, the now R6 (previously B2) and B1 would be adjacent. If forces from R6 captured B1, the complete supply structure for all other B nodes would collapse.

In this example, node B1 could be a major airbase where supplies for the given theater are delivered, or it could be the only bridge spanning a major river. At any rate, capture of B1 by opposing forces would devastate all B nodes dependent upon it.

Theater Commander

Your computer plays the role of theater commander for both red (hostile) and blue (friendly) forces. At the start of a campaign and before you fly a single mission, each theater commander will determine, for both sides of the conflict, how nodes are interlinked and what the strategic objectives are. Each theater commander will constantly assess the strengths and weaknesses of the opposing force and assign missions to all forces under its command accordingly.

Referring back to Figure 10-1, if the theater command determines that the capture of node R5 will reinforce the strength of the B supply line and lead to the capture of nodes R3 and R4, you may be assigned to attack enemy ground forces near R5 so friendly forces from B2 have a numeric advantage.

Your Involvement

You will probably never know how the nodes, for either side, are connected. You are a squadron commander in a Falcon 3.0 campaign, and supply routes and strategic objectives are planned at a much higher level. You will be concerned with much more specific *tactical objectives* that the theater commander assigns your squadron.

Each time you successfully complete an assigned mission, the more likely other friendly units dependent upon you are to succeed in their missions. Each additional node captured brings your side once step closer to victory; each node lost strengthens the enemy and brings your side one step closer to defeat.

Victory Conditions: Winning the War

Total campaign victory hinges on the performance of your squadron. Yours is the best squadron in the theater and, therefore, assigned the toughest, most pivotal missions. All other friendly forces depend upon you — your success or failure directly impacts their subsequent results. Falcon 3.0 campaigns measure victory on three levels: individual mission success, daily mission success, and total campaign victory. The first two are measured against the performance of your squadron, the last is measured against the achievement of strategic objectives by the forces your squadron supports.

Individual Mission Success

Your squadron will be assigned four missions to execute every day of the campaign. Each mission will begin with a briefing, during which the purpose of the mission will be described. After each mission, you will be presented with a debriefing that reports the results and classifies the mission as a success or failure. Success or failure for a given mission is defined differently for each mission type. There are nine different types of missions, identified by specific phrases during the mission. The mission types, purposes, and success requirements follow.

> **NOTE:** The following parameters all apply to version Falcon 3.0D. Prior versions used slightly different requirements. Those versions are obsolete and information on them is not available.

1. Air Superiority

- Key Phrase: "...deny enemy air activity..."
- Purpose: Patrol an area and attack enemy aircraft found.
- Success Requirements: Destroy three or more enemy aircraft in the assigned area. Anything else will be defined as a failure.

2. Bomb Run

- Key Phrase: "...bomb <target name>..."
- Purpose: Destroy a fixed structured, such as a factory or bridge.

- Success Requirements: The named target must be destroyed. If the target is hit, but not destroyed, the mission will be defined as a failure. You must make sure to attack with an appropriate weapon that is capable of destroying the target.

3. Close Air Support (CAS)

- Key Phrase: "...command ALO has requested TAC AIR..."
- Purpose: Support ground troops.
- Success Requirements: In the specified target area, more enemy units must be destroyed than friendly units. If your pilots destroy seven enemy tanks, but the enemy ground forces destroy eight friendly tanks, the mission will be defined as a failure.

4. Combat Air Patrol (CAP)

- Key Phrase: "...fly CAP..."
- Purpose: Patrol an area and destroy inbound enemy aircraft.
- Success Requirements: Destroy any incoming enemy aircraft. If your pilots fail to down any aircraft, the mission will be defined as a failure.

5. Escort Bombers

- Key Phrase: "...escort B-52s..."
- Purpose: Ensure safety of B-52 bombers.
- Success Requirements: Your aircraft must reach the bombers, target zone. You are not responsible for the bombers actually hitting their target zone.

6. Escort Strike Aircraft

- Key Phrase: "...escort strike aircraft..."
- Purpose: Ensure safety of strike aircraft, such as F-111s and A-10s.
- Success Requirements: All strike aircraft must be functional and operational at the end of the mission. If any of the strike aircraft you were assigned to escort are shot down, the mission will be defined as a failure.

7. Escort Transports

- Key Phrase: "...milk run..."
- Purpose: Ensure that two C-130 cargo aircraft carrying supplies and ammunition arrive safely.
- Success Requirements: Both C-130s must be fully operational at the end of the mission. If either C-130 is shot down, the mission will be defined as a failure.

8. Recon in Force

- Key Phrase: "...armed reconnaissance..."
- Purpose: Search and destroy enemy ground units.
- Success Requirements: At least seven enemy ground units must be destroyed. All enemy ground units, including those encountered while flying to/from the target area are acceptable targets. If less than seven enemy ground units are destroyed, the mission will defined as a failure.

9. Scramble

- Key Phrase: "...<list of incoming aircraft> are headed for..."
- Purpose: Intercept enemy aircraft headed to attack a friendly node.
- Success Requirements: Your pilots must down at least three enemy aircraft. Less than seven friendly ground units can be destroyed by the incoming aircraft. No enemy bombers can penetrate through to your home base. If any of these three requirements are not met, the mission will be defined as a failure.

Daily Mission Success

Each side of the war begins with an initial offensive strength. This value changes daily during the campaign based on the success of individual missions. The aggressiveness of computer controlled forces (both friendly and enemy) will depend upon the magnitude of that side's current offensive strength. Offensive strength is reevaluated at the end of each campaign day.

Your squadron directly controls the changes in the offensive strength of your side. In a given campaign day, if your squadron successfully completes three or more of the four assigned missions, the allied forces' offensive strength will increase. If, however, your squadron completes less than three missions successfully, the allied offensive strength decreases. Since your squadron is considered the best in the theater, failure on your part hinders the progress of most other units in the theater.

Sustained failures will erode allied offensive strength, causing subsequent mission failures by other friendly forces. As friendly forces fail to achieve strategic objectives, enemy forces will advance, thereby increasing their offensive strength. This, in turn, causes the enemies to be more aggressive, achieve more of their strategic objectives, further increasing their offensive strength. The result is a vicious, downward spiral for friendly forces. If your side begins with a much higher initial offensive strength, the loss of a single day will have little effect on the war. If, however, your side begins evenly matched with the enemy, the loss of a single day can be devastating.

Total Campaign Victory

A campaign lasts a minimum of seven game days, sometimes slightly longer. When the time limit for the campaign expires, both theater commanders analyze the results of their attacks. An assessment of territorial gains and losses determines the results of the overall campaign.

Victory Nodes Before the campaign starts, each theater commander identifies a list of strategic objectives that must be accomplished to win the war. These objectives list nodes that must be destroyed in order to cripple the enemy, and nodes that must be captured to control the enemy, called *victory nodes*. Control of victory nodes at the end of the campaign decides the final outcome.

Three Possible Campaign Endings The campaign has three possible outcomes: Allied Victory, Enemy Victory, and Stalemate. There won't always be a single winner and a single loser. If neither side gained significant territorial advances, neither side is declared a victor.

- Allied Victory — For the allies to win, they must control at least 70% of the nodes the allied theater commander identified as victory nodes. The allies cannot win the war if they do not control at least 70% of their victory nodes.

- Enemy Victory — For the enemy to win, they must control at least 70% of their victory nodes at the end of the campaign. If less than 70% of the nodes are controlled, the enemy cannot be declared the winner.

- Stalemate — If, at the end of the war, neither side controls 70% of their respective victory nodes, then neither side is declared a winner and the war is listed as a stalemate. Allied forces, however, should still consider this a failure.

Conclusions

Complete victory depends upon allied ground forces seizing and holding key nodes. Units requiring air support prior to making critical advances depend upon your squadron. Failure by your squadron to complete an individual mission hinders the advance of that particular unit. Failure by your squadron to successfully complete three missions per day causes general morale to drop, and decreases the effectiveness of all allied forces in the theater. To ensure victory, your squadron must complete three successful missions per day. Anything less sends the allied forces down the road to defeat.

Commanding a Squadron

You are the military equivalent of middle management; you are a squadron commanding officer (CO). Higher ranking officers at theater command will define the strategic plan for the entire theater, including your squadron. Theater command will issue daily lists of goals which it expects your squadron to achieve. These goals, unique to your squadron, are called *tactical objectives*. The theater commander expects you to use the resources available to you to achieve tactical objectives using your own judgment and discretion. Once the tactical objectives are supplied to you, your only restricting factor is the resupply schedule. As squadron commander, it is your job to manage the resources available to you. This requires you to:

1. Develop tactical battle plans. This includes devising attack procedures, assigning aircraft, allocating *ordnance* (weapons), and assigning pilots.

2. Nurture the growth of the pilots in your command. Depending on how effectively you assign the pilots in your squadron, they will either improve their individual skills and become outstanding pilots, or they will be shot down and lost forever.

3. Manage and ration limited supplies of weapons, fuel, and other stores.

4. Fly missions alongside the pilots in your squadron. The CO does not sit behind a desk all day; the CO risks his life along with those in his squadron. A good CO never asks his pilots to do anything he is unwilling to do himself.

Assigning Pilots

At first glance, assigning pilots may sound like a simple task that is quickly completed. However, proper utilization of each pilot that maximizes the effectiveness of that pilot is a complicated procedure that directly impacts your individual mission success rate. Pilot assignment should not be taken lightly.

The Right Pilot for the Right Job

You have 30 pilots with varying abilities and skills in dogfighting, bombing accuracy, flying ability, and fatigue. When viewing pilot statistics from the Pilot Information screen, each pilot has four attributes:

1. Dogfighting—The air-to-air combat skill of the pilot. This value accounts for pilot intelligence, pilot skill, intuition, combat experience, and coolness under fire.
2. Bombing Accuracy—The skill the pilot has at bombing. Accounts for the pilot's ability to hit both stationary and moving targets, time weapons release to maximize destructive effect, and ability to distinguish between friendly and enemy forces.
3. Flying Ability—The general flying ability of the pilot. Includes tactics in radar avoidance, SAM evasion, and low altitude flying.
4. Fatigue—The current health of the pilot. Fatigue points are lost by flying missions, but gained by resting. The more often a pilot flies, the more fatigue points he will lose. As the pilot's fatigue value decreases, the other three attributes are adversely affected, also.

For each attribute, the higher the value, the better the pilot is in that area. Each attribute has two values separated by a "/." The right-hand number is the maximum level of that pilot and the left-hand number is the current level based on fatigue and number of missions flown. When the pilot flies, he will perform according to his respective current values, not the maximum values. A pilot with a maximum dogfighting skill of 100 and a current value of 45 will be no more effective than a pilot with a maximum dogfighting skill of 45. Current values will usually be equal to the maximum values for well-rested pilots.

TIP: When assigning pilots, be sure to assign pilots with high dogfighting skills to CAP, ESCORT, and SCRAMBLE missions; assign pilots with high bombing accuracy for ground attack missions.

Fatigue

A pilot loses fatigue points every time he flies a mission. The more stressful the mission, the more fatigue points the pilot loses. If the pilot's aircraft was shot and the pilot was wounded, the pilot will lose more fatigue points. If the pilot was forced to eject and took further injuries, even more fatigue points are lost. Fatigue points are recovered by not flying missions. For every mission that the pilot "sits out," the pilot is considered to be resting and regains fatigue points.

Generally, a pilot can fly one mission every 24 game hours and remain at peak fatigue levels. If the pilot flies more than one mission in a given 24 hour period, he will probably not be fully recovered for the second mission. This will decrease that pilot's fatigue value even further. The pilot will now probably require more than 24 hours to recover fully. Eventually, as the fatigue value decreases, the other attributes decrease also. The maximum values don't change, but the current values do.

Pilot Rotation

Your first tendency may be to pick the eight best dogfighting pilots and send them on every mission. However, you'll soon see their fatigue ratings drop and then their current scores will decrement as well. The most skilled pilot in the world still requires sleep. Soon, your best pilots become less effective than even the worst pilot in the squadron. Eventually, they will be shot down and their skill lost forever. There's only one way to avoid this: rotate your pilots. Fly the well rested, rest the well flown.

No discussion on pilot rotation would be complete without first studying the lessons learned from World War II. A quick analysis of the kill records of top pilots from the Axis powers and the U.S. will reveal a startling disparity. Leading Axis aces were credited with hundreds of kills, whereas top U.S. aces averaged between 20 and 40. There's a very straightforward reason behind this.

During WW II, as U.S. pilots began to achieve 30 or so kills, they were rotated completely out of the action and returned home where they trained the next wave of fighter pilot cadets. Here, the actual lessons learned in combat by the aces could be taught to the new pilots in the safety of training missions. When the new pilots were deployed to combat zones, they were much more prepared and effective.

Top Axis fighter pilots continued to fight in front line battles, however, until they were inevitably shot down. New pilots had no opportunity to learn the hard facts of combat before being thrust head first into battle. No matter how good a pilot is, he will eventually encounter bad luck. Maybe the aircraft malfunctions, a weapon misfires, or the enemy greatly outnumbers him. Eventually, both Germany and Japan suffered from a serious deficiency of experienced pilots. Many WW II scholars agree that the advances made by allied forces against the Japanese near the end of the war were a direct result of the lack of experienced Japanese fighter pilots. The Axis overused, and subsequently lost, their finest pilots.

Rotation: Your Responsibility

The model of WW II differs slightly from the problem facing you in Falcon 3.0. Then, leaders were faced with the question of keeping pilots in combat or sending them home. Your decision is slightly different: do you keep an individual pilot in the cockpit, or do you allow him time to rest between missions? The lesson learned from WW II still applies to your particular dilemma.

> **Bottom line:** If you want to win the campaign, you have to rotate your pilots.

The burden of assigning pilots is planted squarely on your shoulders. Falcon 3.0 assigns default pilots, but makes no effort to match skill levels with the assigned missions. You have to make the decisions; you have to assign the pilots. When you view your squadron's records, not only are you responsible for every kill listed next to your name, but also for every kill and award won by the other pilots in the squadron. However, you are also responsible for every KIA and MIA listed next to a pilot's name. You share in the glory and sorrow of every pilot in the squadron.

Familiar Pilot Names and Callsigns

There are some tricks you can use, however, to help you in this role. Falcon 3.0 allows you to change the name and callsign for every pilot in the squadron. The default names are obscure and unrecognizable. Immediately after forming a new squadron, you should rename all 30 pilots with familiar names and callsigns. See Chapter 2, *Introduction to Falcon 3.0*, for more information on how to create and edit a squadron.

How should you select names and callsigns for your pilots? Begin by avoiding cliché names, such as "Viper" and "Slayer." Such names may give your squadron a fearsome image; however, managing pilots with names so similar will become difficult and confusing. Unless you have an excellent memory, you will most likely lose track of which pilot is which during combat.

There are many excellent ways to name your pilots. Using familiar names and nicknames is probably the most efficient. Name your pilots after your friends, family, pets, neighbors, or anyone or anything familiar to you. Think about the names you assign, then apply actual nicknames as their callsigns. Pick nicknames that are easy for you to remember; always know your pilots' names and callsigns by heart. The more familiar you are with your pilots the more effectively you will utilize them.

Also, think about the personalities of the people you select. If your best friend flew fighter aircraft, would that person prefer air-to-air missions or ground attack missions? Assign that name to a pilot who has the appropriate skill. This gives you a familiar and intimate relationship with the pilots under your command.

Using familiar names helps you in three ways:

1. You choose a pilot with appropriate skills for the given mission.
2. It will be much easier to remember how often a familiar pilot has flown.
3. When you receive radio messages during combat, you will know what mission that pilot is flying.

Managing Rotation

Once you realize the need to rotate pilots and have modified your squadron with familiar names, the execution is a simple routine. Prior to each flight, you first determine how many aircraft will fly each mission type. Then, you view the information on the pilots in your squadron, choose pilots with appropriate skills and high fatigue values, and then assign them to the aircraft.

Typically, you should assign the pilots with the best related skill value and highest fatigue value to lead flights. Assign pilots with high fatigue, but low skill values as wingmen. This will increase the overall strength of your squadron. Poor pilots can only improve through flying and combat experience. An equal rotation of the roster will give all 30 pilots a chance to improve their skills.

Roster Management Utility

A freeware utility entitled, Falcnr, is included on the floppy disk that comes with this book. Falcnr is an editing tool that allows you to edit and print Falcon 3.0 squadron rosters much more easily than can be done from within Falcon 3.0. Falcnr also allows you to delete unwanted pilots and revive pilots that have been court-martialed, or declared MIA or KIA. Falcnr has many other functions as well. Refer to Appendix C for complete details on this tool.

Assigning Aircraft

When you read the briefing at the beginning of a campaign mission, you will usually be told something like, "Go do..., X F-16s are standing by," or "You have been assigned to lead Y aircraft...." You should consider the values of X and Y to specify, at best, the *minimum* number of aircraft required to execute the mission. In most cases, the number of assigned aircraft will be insufficient to complete the mission.

Available Aircraft

The mission briefing (see Chapter 7, *Introduction to the Campaigns*, for details) tells you how many aircraft have been assigned to the mission, and the maximum number of aircraft available for the mission. The maximum number represents how many aircraft your squadron has ready to fly, remaining aircraft are undergoing maintenance, refueling, etc. The total value may be as high as eight, but averages six. In our first example, we'll assume eight aircraft are available.

Target Considerations

How strong is the target? How big is the target? How much ordnance is required to destroy it? How many aircraft are required to carry that amount of ordnance? A single F-16 can carry four 2,000 pound MK-84 bombs. If the target is a large structure, like a refinery or a factory, that should be sufficient ordnance to bury it for all time.

You may be ordered to attack an armored column. Such columns often have more than 30 trucks, tanks, armored personnel carriers (APV), and SAM launchers. AGM-65 Maverick missiles are much more effective against armored vehicles than MK-84 bombs. A single F-16 can carry six Mavericks. That's hardly enough to do significant damage to a large convoy.

Before you allocate other aircraft for support purposes like CAP, or SAM suppression, be sure you allocate enough aircraft to achieve the primary objective. Be warned, you'll probably never have enough aircraft available to feel completely confident about the mission. Begin by allocating aircraft for the main strike, then analyze what support roles are required. You can change your mind until the point you go to the cockpit.

Target Defenses

Once you know how many aircraft it takes to destroy the target, consider how well defended it is. Select a STRAT mode for the campaign menu map.

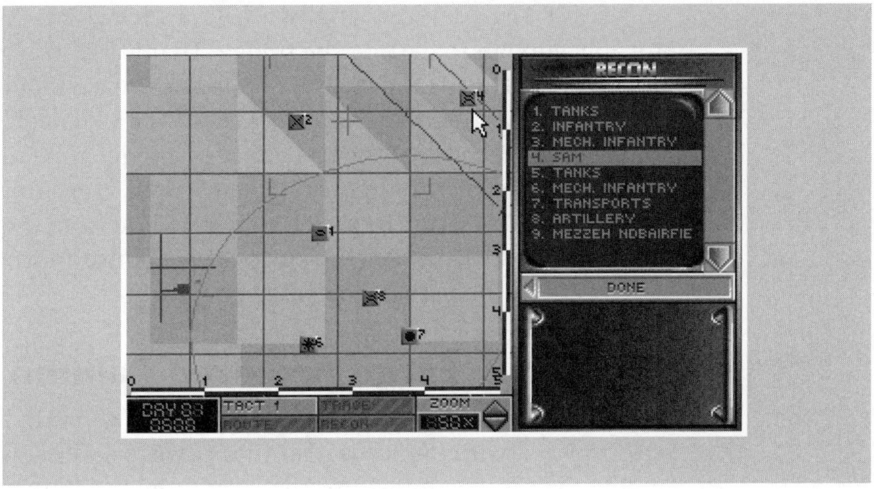

Figure 10-2 The Recon View

Are there any enemy airfields nearby? If so, you'll probably encounter enemy aircraft. How many other enemy nodes are near your target? The greater the concentration of enemy forces, the greater the concentration of enemy surface-to-air defenses.

Your target may be a moving convoy, or it may be a fixed structure at one of the enemy nodes. If your target is located at a node, you can use the RECON view from the Set Waypoints screen to get a closeup view of the target. RECON effectively shows you the latest intelligence photos available of fixed targets. Look for SAM launchers or AAA cannons, as illustrated in Figure 10-2.

If there is a high probability of enemy fighter activity, you will want to allocate a second section of aircraft armed with air-to-air weapons to patrol the area. If there are a lot of SAMs and AAA, you will want to assign a section of aircraft with HARM and SHRIKE anti-radiation missiles to clear the area before the main strike aircraft arrive. Two possible missions, attacking a heavily defended bridge and attacking a large armored column, demonstrate deployment issues.

Example 1: A Heavily Defended Bridge

Suppose you're attacking a critical bridge spanning the Tigris River in Southern Iraq. The bridge is located at an enemy node that also contains two factories, half a dozen SAM launchers, and a few AAA cannons. Two enemy airbases are within a 75 mile radius. You have eight aircraft available.

Two F-16s, each carrying two GBU-15 television-guided bombs, are probably enough to destroy the bridge. That leaves you with six F-16s for support roles. The site is heavily defended by surface-to-air weapons, so two F-16s carrying anti-radiation missiles should be assigned a defense suppression mission. Because of the proximity of enemy airfields, the probability of encountering enemy fighters is high. Two F-16s armed with air-to-air weapons should escort the attack aircraft to and from the target. The final two F-16s should be armed with air-to-air weapons and sent to sweep enemy fighters out of the path of the strike aircraft.

Example 2: Large Armored Column

Suppose you are assigned to attack an armored column, but only have six F-16s to work with. Suppose also that there is an enemy airbase nearby. Finally, you can usually assume that an armored column will have SA-6 and SA-8 SAM mobile SAM launchers.

This one is more difficult. To do serious damage to the armored column, you'll probably need more than two F-16s. However, because of the proximity of the enemy airbase, you should have a section of two aircraft flying cover. Because of the likelihood of surface-to-air defenses, you should have a section of two aircraft flying defense suppression. As predicted earlier, you do not have enough aircraft to adequately cover the task. A sacrifice must be made somewhere.

Choices like this are hard to make. Perhaps you allocate two aircraft for CAP and four aircraft for strike, but equip the strike aircraft with electronic counter measures (ECM) pods. The ECM pods provide adequate defense against radar-guided, surface-to-air threats. However, you may not have enough ECM pods available to equip all four strike aircraft.

Guidelines for Assigning Aircraft

When faced with the difficult decisions outlined above, try following these guidelines:

1. Always use two aircraft per flight, no more, no less. A single aircraft is too vulnerable to aerial ambush. However, wingmen simply follow the flight leader's movements. If you assign four aircraft in a single section, only the leader will be effectively fighting. The three wingmen will follow his lead. By splitting this group into a pair of 2-plane sections, you have twice the number of aircraft fighting effectively, and half the number of aircraft simply following.

2. *Always* have at least one flight flying air cover. There will always be enemy fighters, and they will always be trying to kill you. If you are personally flying the air cover role, try to station a reception escort around your airbase. When you bug out, you need somebody watching your back.

3. Long flights require additional fuel tanks. Each fuel tank loaded reduces the amount of weapons the aircraft can carry. On a short flight, a group of F-16s may be able to carry a load of Mavericks for the primary attack and a load of air-to-air missiles for self defense.

   If the flight is long and additional fuel is required, the F-16 may not be able to carry both offensive and defensive weapons. This means you may have to use fewer aircraft to attack the primary target and assign more aircraft to CAP and defense suppression roles.

4. Use ECM pods and anti-radiation missiles, even if it means carrying less ordnance to attack the primary target with. These devices are designed to save pilot lives. It's better to partially damage a target and have all your pilots come home than to destroy a target and lose three or four pilots.

5. Keep a close eye on your fuel, stores, and weapons supplies. Every aircraft you send into combat consumes fuel and uses stores. You only get additional supplies on the specified resupply dates, and even then you're not guaranteed to get what you need. You may be out of ECM pods and the C-130's may bring you a load of AIM-120 AMRAAM missiles. Don't waste ammo or fuel. If you don't absolutely, positively need that extra flight of two F-16s, don't send them up; conserve your fuel supply, instead.

Waypoints: Design Strategies

At the start of every mission, the computer will generate default waypoints. Rarely will these waypoints be sufficient for actual flight operations. Default waypoints usually follow a simple-minded, straight-up-the-middle, forget-about-enemy-defenses approach that will get you and your pilots shot down.

This section presents a series of attack strategies to use when designing waypoints. This section details individual attack theories, their advantages, and their disadvantages. The following section combines these theories into useful, complete waypoint constructs, complete with detailed illustrations.

What Flight Should You Fly?

The following tips and strategies require multiple flights of aircraft, and mainly apply to computer-controlled flights. While the strategies are valid for both human and computer controlled flights, you can make snap judgments and decide to deviate or change specified plans at any time. Computer-controlled aircraft will follow the specified orders to the letter. The following strategies are defined in terms that allow you to apply them to inflexible, computer-controlled flights.

This brings up an interesting question: which mission do you fly? You always fly the lead aircraft in flight #1, but what mission do you assign to that flight? Two factors should be considered when making this decision:

- What role do you most enjoy executing?
- What role is most critical, possibly requiring spur-of-the-moment decisions and plan alterations?

Definitely, you want to focus on tasks that are the most enjoyable to you. If you hate flying air-to-air combat, fly bombing missions instead. However, keep in mind that computer- controlled aircraft are simpleminded. They will execute the defined plan, and that is it. If you anticipate a role requiring reevaluation after the mission begins, you should probably fly that role.

> **NOTE:** This topic will be discussed in greater detail later in this chapter in the section entitled, "Vigilante Warfare," but the reader should always keep in mind: attacking targets other than those designated in the mission briefing will have no effect on the overall campaign.

Coordinating Strikes

It will do little good to assign a flight of aircraft to destroy enemy SAMs if the main strike force arrives at the target before it does. It will do little good to assign a fighter sweep if it doesn't reach the target ahead of the main strike. You must coordinate the main strike with the support aircraft.

Use two tricks when trying to coordinate flights: adjust the speed of the individual flights and add additional waypoints. Make sure that the speed of support aircraft (CAP flights, defense suppression flights) is set about 75 knots higher than that of the main body. This will let the support aircraft arrive at the target shortly before the main body. Be careful, however. If the main body arrives too long after the support aircraft, enemy defenses will be fully alerted and waiting. Ideally, you want your support aircraft to surprise the enemy, execute the forward attack, and then have the main strike force attack while the enemy is still confused.

You can also add additional waypoints to the path of the main strike that will cause it to fly a longer route. This will consume additional time and ensure that it arrives after the support aircraft have executed the preliminary attack. However, this technique also consumes additional fuel. On long flights, this may not be an option.

Attack Strategies in Falcon 3.0

There's no bravery in exposing your pilots to unnecessary risks, only increased chances that they will be shot down. One of the greatest weapons you can utilize is deceit. Fool the enemy into expecting an attack that will never come. Then, while his attention is focused elsewhere, attack where he least suspects. There are several tactics you can use to fool the enemy. Defining waypoints and the actions that may be assigned them is discussed in Chapter 6, *Introduction to Red Flag*, and Chapter 7, *Introduction to the Campaigns*. Once you understand the basic attack strategies, you can utilize the following series of sample waypoint constructs.

Avoid Contact The most obvious attack strategy is also the most simple: avoid enemy defenses. Use the STRAT mode on the campaign map, as well as the TRACE function (described in Chapter 7), to locate enemy force concentrations. Then, plot your waypoints to fly around these sites. Never expose your pilots to unnecessary attacks.

Pop-Up Attacks Usually, aircraft flying at altitudes below 2,000 feet can use features of the surrounding terrain to block the beams of enemy search radars. The lower the altitude the aircraft flies, the harder it is to detect. This type of flying is called *Nape of the Earth* (NOE) flying.

However, NOE flying does present difficulties when firing weapons. At low altitudes, the ordnance strikes the ground quickly and the firing aircraft may not be far enough away to evade the blast. In other cases, weapons require a complicated attack run that includes locating the primary target up to 15 miles away. At low altitude, it is usually impossible to locate a target at that range.

Therefore, the *pop-up* attack, illustrated in Figure 10-3, was devised. Aircraft fly at low altitudes during ingress (approach), then climb sharply before reaching the target. The aircraft delivers its weapons, then dives steeply and again flies NOE during *egress* (departure). Pop-up attacks are an excellent method of evading enemy defenses.

Decoys Decoys, illustrated in Figure 10-4, are one of the most ancient, but effective, tricks used in combat. Specify one section to be a decoy. Set

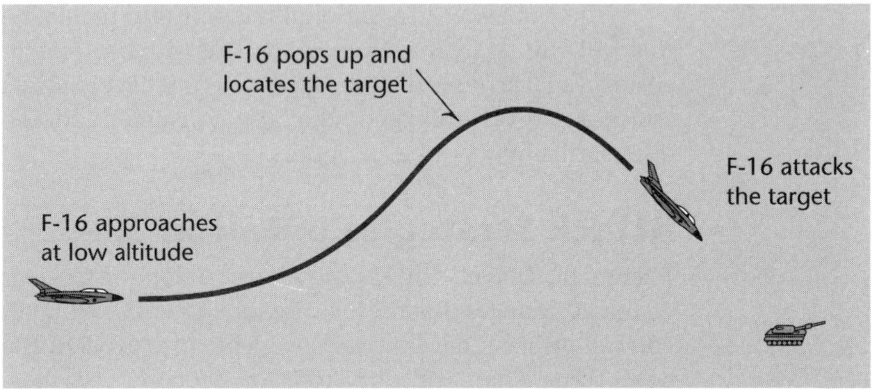

Figure 10-3 The Pop-Up Attack

its speed to 550 knots and its altitude to 10,000 feet for all waypoints. Define its waypoints to form a path that comes close to the primary objective, but then turns away. Enemy fighters will pursue the decoy away from the target zone. Meanwhile, the main strike executes a pop-up attack, as defined in the previous section. The main force should approach the target from the side opposite the decoy.

The mission must be carefully timed to succeed. Once the strike force pops up, enemy defenses will target it. Fighters pursuing the decoy are likely to reverse and attempt to intercept the strike force. Decoys should endeavor to draw enemy fighters as far from the target as possible, and strike aircraft should execute their attacks and depart the area quickly. It may be useful to have an additional CAP patrol move in to cover the retreating strike aircraft.

Multi-Directional Attacks Always keep the enemy guessing. When multiple flights of aircraft are attacking the same area, have them ingress from and egress to different directions. For example, if you have a flight of defense suppression aircraft assigned to destroy SAMs followed by the main strike, bring the SAM busters in from the East, attack, and turn North. Bring the main strike in from the West, deliver its weapons, and turn South. Never fly predictable patterns; the enemy will quickly recognize a pattern and exploit it.

Combat Air Patrols (CAP)

Combat Air Patrols must follow two rules: never leave their patrol while the aircraft they are assigned to protect are still threatened, and never hang around in enemy airspace too long. At first glance, these two rules may seem

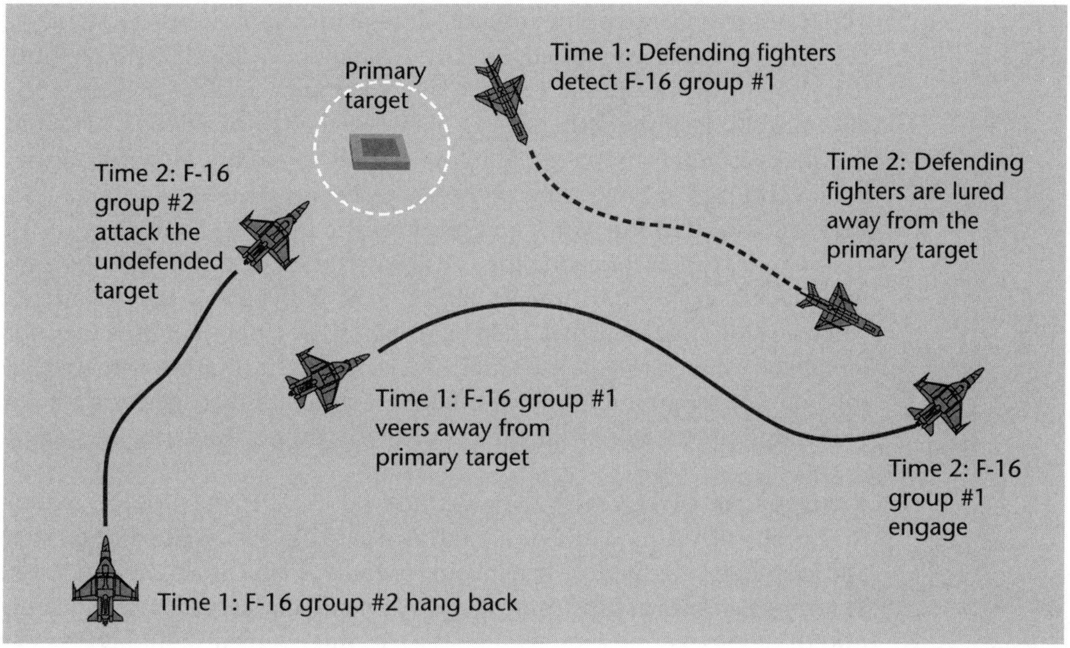

Figure 10-4 The Decoy

contradictory. In actuality, they emphasize the need for *just in time defense*, or remaining on their assigned patrol for the exact amount of time required, no longer, no less. CAP flights, therefore, also require careful consideration and precise timing. There are two forms of CAP, and each requires separate consideration.

Standard CAP Standard CAPs normally patrol the border between friendly and enemy airspace. They do not hunt down and attack enemy aircraft, rather they maintain a vigil that denies enemy aircraft access to friendly airspace. A CAP may intercept enemy strike aircraft attempting to infiltrate friendly airspace, or it may intercept enemy fighters pursuing friendly aircraft returning to base.

CAPs, therefore, focus on the first rule, never abandon their post early. The second rule has little bearing on CAPs since they rarely penetrate enemy airspace. Their waypoints, therefore, should be defined to keep them *on station* (maintain their patrol) as long as possible. This is easily accomplished in Falcon 3.0 by using the waypoint actions CAP and LOITER.

Suppose you want the CAP to patrol an area 100 miles long until it runs out of fuel or weapons. Then, and only then, may it return to base. Define a string of waypoints so the aircraft will patrol the desired area. Set the

ACTION of each waypoint to CAP, except for the last; set its action to LOITER. Computer-controlled pilots fly through the string of CAP waypoints, first. When they reach the LOITER waypoint, they analyze their fuel and weapons status. If they still have air-to-air weapons, and enough fuel, they will make another complete circuit of the CAP waypoints. However, if they are low on fuel or have gone *winchester* (have no air-to-air weapons left), they will abandon the patrol and head for the next waypoint.

The waypoint following the LOITER waypoint does not have to be the final, LAND waypoint. However, any other activities you assign for aircraft will consume additional fuel, thereby reducing the amount of time they will remain on CAP. Normally, it is best to dedicate aircraft completely to the CAP role; do not assign aircraft to first bomb a structure then perform a CAP. Dedicating aircraft to CAP maximizes their effectiveness and time on station.

Target CAP (TARCAP) The second type of CAP is called Target Combat Air Patrol, or TARCAP. TARCAP aircraft fly a patrol over a specified target zone and keep enemy fighters from harassing friendly aircraft attacking said target. This role, also known as *point defense*, is a difficult role, at best. It falls squarely into the contradiction presented by the two rules of combat air patrols.

On one hand, TARCAP aircraft must remain on station near the target long enough to allow the strike aircraft to attack and escape. On the other hand, TARCAP aircraft have limited fuel and weapons. Staying in enemy airspace too long will doom them. Even if TARCAP aircraft leave in time, there's no assurance the trip home will be easy. Enemy fighters may be waiting to ambush them as they head for home. TARCAP aircraft must depart their station while they have enough fuel and weapons to make it back to base, and fight if need be.

For this role, the simple series of CAP and LOITER waypoints is insufficient. That technique has no foresight, and doesn't allow for an ambush during egress. The strike aircraft may be back home sitting on the tarmac, but the TARCAP aircraft are still patrolling the target, exposing themselves to unnecessary risks, simply because they have sufficient fuel to do so.

A better tactic, although definitely more complex to define, is to create a series of CAP waypoints that circle the primary target once or twice, then takes them back to base. Timing becomes more critical, however. Strike aircraft cannot loiter, or they will be left unprotected when the TARCAP flight heads home. You must be careful when assigning the CAP waypoints to ensure that the TARCAP aircraft remain on station around the target for a sufficient length of time. The exact amount of time varies per mission, but as a general rule of thumb: the more strike aircraft involved, the longer the TARCAP must remain on station.

Escort Missions

Escort missions are typically the toughest tasks performed by fighter pilots. For complete details regarding escort missions, please refer to Mission 3: Operation Ground Shaker in Chapter 9, *Red Flag: Advanced Flight School.* No discussion on waypoint strategies would be complete without mentioning escort missions.

A fully engineered escort mission, as defined in Operation Ground Shaker, requires a large number of aircraft. Typically, you will never have enough aircraft to execute all of the required roles. In general terms, close escort is adequately performed by a flight with waypoint actions set to ESCORT, and the waypoints placed exactly along the flight path of the escorted aircraft. Wide escort normally is executed by assigning a flight a series of ESCORT waypoints, but placing those waypoints 30 or 40 miles from the path of the escorted aircraft. The forward escort task maps almost directly to the INTERCEPT waypoint action; place waypoints with INTERCEPT action directly ahead of the escorted aircraft. Lastly, reception escort is identical to the CAP/TARCAP mission.

Conclusion

Although planning waypoints is a difficult and time-consuming task, the survival of you and your pilots, as well as your mission success rate, depends upon proper waypoint definition. If you charge enemy forces head on, simply throwing aircraft and pilots at them, your aircraft will be shot down, your pilots will die, and you will lose the war. On the other hand, careful planning of attack strategies and supporting missions, in conjunction with management of fuel and weapons supplies, will put your squadron on the road to victory. Don't cut corners when planning missions, victory depends upon you.

Waypoint Construct Library

Effectively engineering waypoints for coordinated groups of aircraft is much more an art than a science. All of the tips and guidelines in the world are no substitute for experience. When devising a series of waypoints, don't be afraid to experiment. Try new and radical approaches, constantly adjusting your techniques and tactics. Don't be discouraged if your tactics fail, instead observe what went wrong and compensate accordingly in future missions. Refer to Chapter 6, *Introduction to Red Flag,* and Chapter 7, *Introduction to the Campaigns,* for details on creating and tailoring waypoints.

Figures 10-5 through 10-8 illustrate four basic waypoint constructs. Use these constructs as basic building blocks when defining your own waypoints. As you adjust individual elements and combine constructs to meet your individual needs, you will eventually build a substantial library of attack and approach tactics.

Returning to Base: Avoiding an Ambush

Bandits know that most aircraft returning to base are low on fuel, low on weapons, or low on both fuel and weapons. Your best pilot may destroy the primary target, but if the enemy kills your best pilot on his way home, you may receive a success for the individual mission, but your squadron strength erodes. Figure 10-5 illustrates a simple tactic that protects egressing aircraft from pursuing fighters.

Figure 10-5 shows three flights of aircraft: flight #1, the primary strike force represented by the dashed line; flight #2, the defensive reception escort represented by the thin solid line; and an enemy fighter patrol, represented by the thick solid line. Flight #1 executes a typical pop-up approach at waypoint #1, attacks the target at waypoint #2, then dives for the deck at waypoint #3 and heads for home base. Flight #2 has a cylical CAP

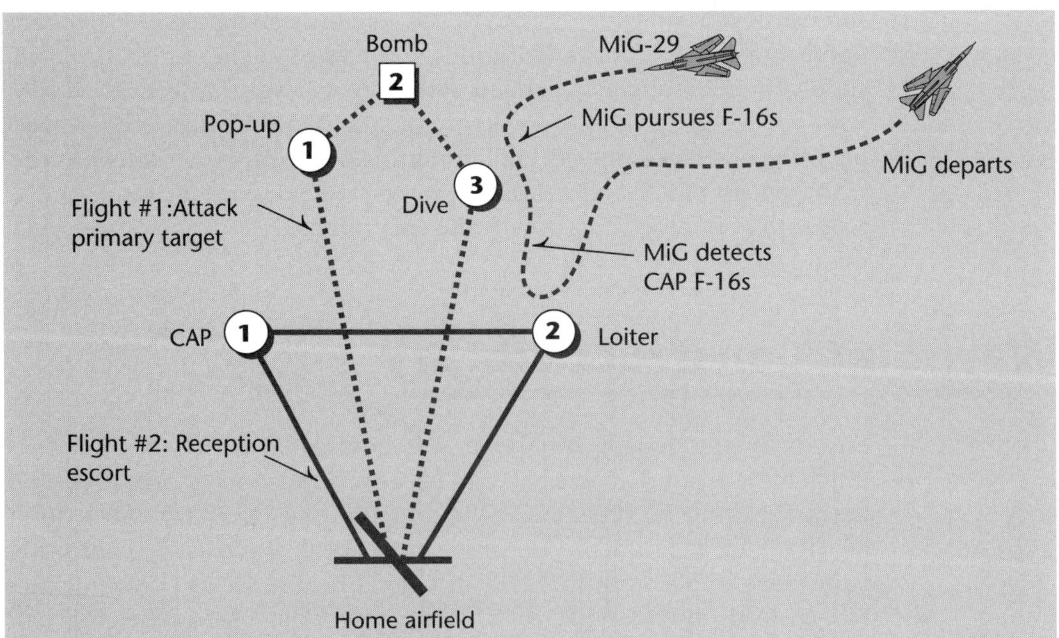

Figure 10-5 Defensive Use of CAP Aircraft

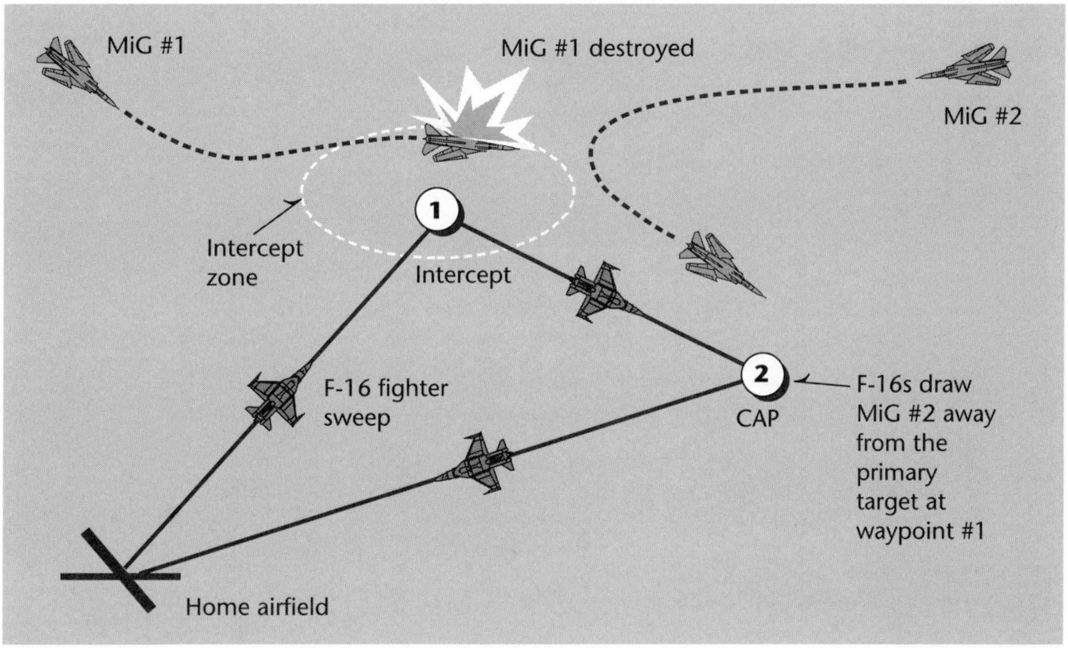

Figure 10-6 Fighter Sweep

route between its waypoints #1 and #2. Flight #1 (and any pursuing enemy aircraft) must cross through flight #2's CAP zone. As Figure 10-5 illustrates, enemy fighters must either engage the fully fueled and armed reception escort, or abandon the pursuit.

Forward Sweep: Clearing the Road

If there is a high likelihood of enemy fighter activity near the primary target, assign an initial group of F-16s to sweep them from the area. Figure 10-6 illustrates.

The primary target is at or near waypoint #1. The bandit group called MiG #1 is on CAP, patrolling the area around the target. The bandit group called MiG #2 is on a similar patrol some distance away. The F-16 group proceeds to waypoint #1 and executes an INTERCEPT action, attacking any detected bandits within the dashed ellipse. After destroying MiG #1, the area around the target is clear; however, MiG #2 is vectored to counterattack. The F-16 group moves away from the primary target, drawing MiG #2 with it. The zone around the primary target is clear of enemy aircraft, and ready for attack by the main strike force.

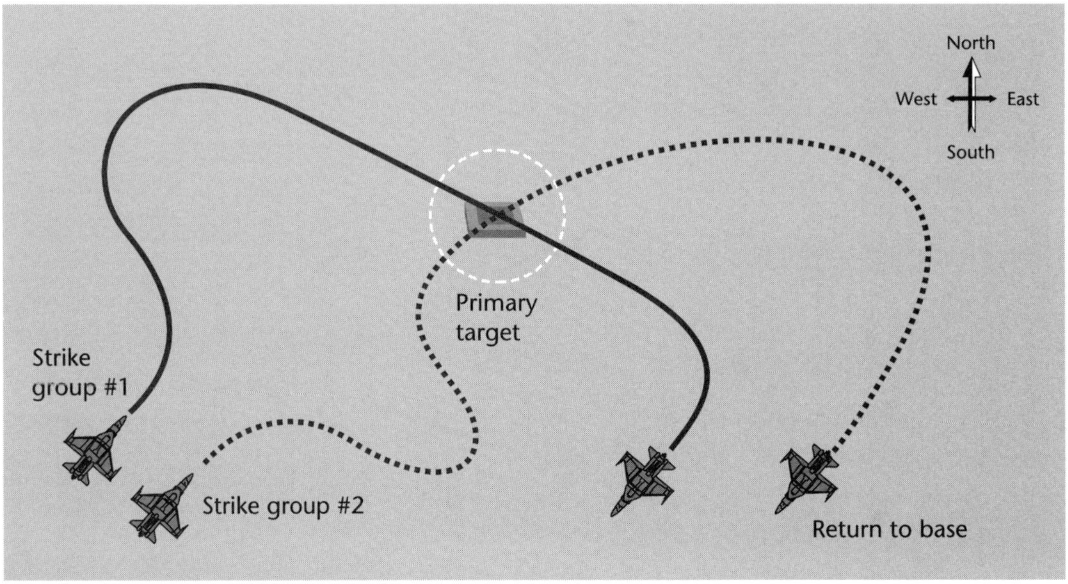

Figure 10-7 Multiple Ingress/Egress Routes

Coordinated Strike

Sometimes, multiple groups of strike aircraft may be required to ensure destruction of the primary target. In such cases, it is unwise to send all attack aircraft along the same flight path. Splitting the attack force into smaller elements reduces that chance that all strike aircraft will be detected and attacked enroute to the target. Instead, the attacking groups should approach and depart the target from unique directions. Figure 10-7 illustrates.

Figure 10-7 shows two strike groups about to attack a single target. The two groups fly in formation until they near the target. The first group breaks north, then turns and flies southeast over the target. The second group, meanwhile, deviates from its course before flying northeast over the target. Both flights then turn south and return to base. This tactic will confuse enemy defenses and increase the likelihood of all aircraft surviving the mission.

Avoiding Enemy Defenses

As the old saying goes, sometimes the best defense is a strong offense. However, often the best defense is to simply avoid the enemy altogether. Avoiding enemy positions not only decreases the amount of hostile fire your pilots are exposed to, but also decreases the likelihood of enemy forces detecting your aircraft. The result: a surprise attack by a strong, un-attrited strike force. Figure 10-8 illustrates.

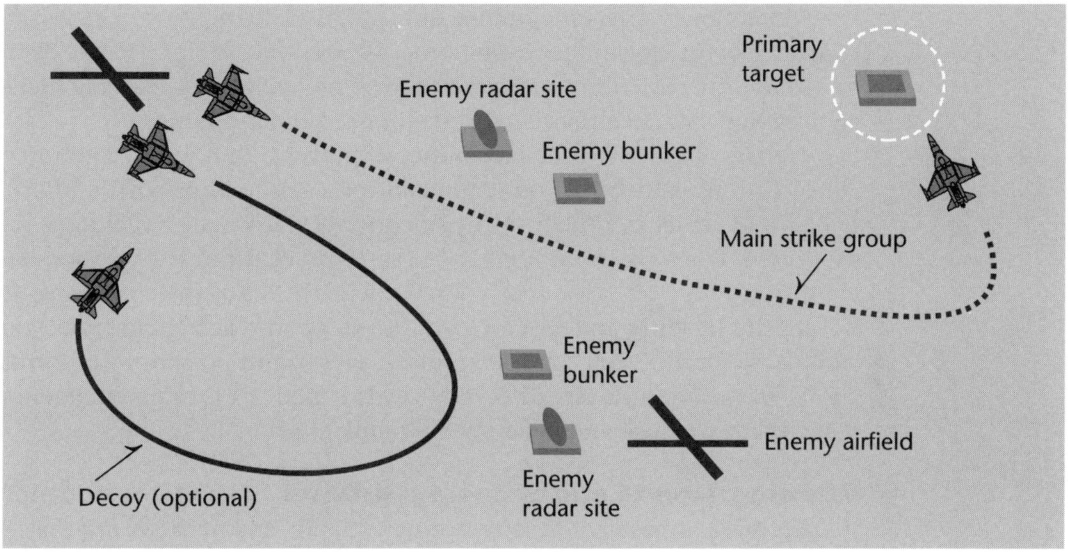

Figure 10-8 Avoid Enemy Positions

In Figure 10-8, the main strike force diverts around enemy positions rather than flying a direct route from the home base to the target, avoiding unnecessary risks and detection. Optionally, you may want to assign a second flight as a decoy. As the decoy flight is detected by enemy forces, bandits will be dispatched to attack the decoy rather than the primary strike force.

Additional Topics

There are several tactics which are not directly supported by Falcon 3.0, but that you may find useful. These tactics, discussed below, often require you to bend the rules. But then again, who ever said war was fair?

Emergency Airfields

During normal flight operations, military aircraft almost always have a secondary landing site, called either a *bingo field* or a *divert airbase,* for emergency landings. Sometimes aircraft, usually belonging to the U.S. Navy, operate in such remote areas that no other airfield is within fuel range. This condition, termed *blue water operations* by the Navy, will never occur in Falcon 3.0; friendly airbases are dispersed throughout all theaters.

Sometimes, after an intense and lengthy dogfight, you may find yourself low on fuel and far from home. Other times, your F-16 may be hit by ground fire which ruptures your fuel system; you'll begin losing fuel at an alarming rate. In either case, you will need to land fast!

As the old saying goes, "An ounce of prevention is worth a pound of cure." In the real world, you could call for a rendezvous with a KC-135 tanker and refuel in midair. As of Falcon 3.0D, air-to-air refueling is not supported. You have no cure; you need some prevention. The solution is to identify friendly airbases near your flight path. Mark their positions by noting the heading and distance you must fly to reach them from your various waypoints. You could even insert a waypoint prior to your normal LAND waypoint, and place it over a likely bingo field. In an emergency, select that waypoint and head for the hangar.

Warning: Don't Land at Enemy Airbases Make sure you identify the alternate airbase before attempting to land. Enemy bases are easy to distinguish on the campaign mode map; they are red. During flight, however, enemy bases are not color coded. They look identical to any other group of buildings with runways in the theater. If you misidentify a hostile runway as your bingo field and land there, you will spend the rest of the war in an enemy prison!

Caveats As of Falcon 3.0D, you cannot specify the waypoint action of LAND at any friendly node other than the node from which the flight originated. The Falcon 3.0 manual states that you can specify LAND at any waypoint, but in actuality, the simulation does not allow it. Therefore, you, and only you, will benefit from a bingo field. Computer-controlled pilots will not attempt to use the divert airbase, instead they will make a vain attempt to return to their home base. Hopefully, future versions of Falcon 3.0 will correct this.

Vigilante Warfare

The theater commander controls the strategic objectives and assigns your squadron to certain missions in order to achieve those objectives. However, sometimes the leaders at the top lose sight of the tactical considerations. Often times, rules of combat, called *Rules of Engagement* (ROE), restrict the soldiers in the trenches from fighting effectively. Targets are ruled off limits, attacks are restricted to certain grids on a map, or certain supplies are not made available to those who need them most. Squadron COs are faced with complying with orders dictated from on high, while at the same time maintaining the morale of disgruntled pilots.

For example, maybe there is an enemy airbase located less than 100 miles from your home base. Every time your squadron launches, fighters from this base are waiting to pounce on the fully laden and lumbering F-16s. If after several days of combat the theater commander has yet to order a strike on the enemy base, you may become frustrated and want to take matters into your own hands. If you are assigned eight aircraft to execute a task that only requires four, you may be tempted to assign the remaining four aircraft to attack another target, such as a critical airfield or bridge.

Don't bother. All territorial gains made by either side are a direct result of your squadron's mission success rate. Use of critical nodes, such as bridges and airfields, does not account for how damaged those nodes may be, but only *who owns that node*. Modern armies have specialized, mobile bridge laying equipment, and effective runway repair techniques. You may destroy a bridge, but if the enemy still owns it, Falcon 3.0 assumes he has the capability to rapidly repair it and continue using it.

Aircraft you assign to unauthorized missions will be exposed to unnecessary risk with no chance of affecting the outcome of the campaign. Eventually, a more complex campaign system may be developed for Falcon 3.0 which allows such vigilante actions to affect the war; however, nothing is expected in the near term.

Bottom line: Sending aircraft on vigilante missions accomplishes nothing except exposing those aircraft to enemy fire. Doing so simply wastes aircraft and pilots.

Questions: Special Techniques

1. Name five guidelines for assigning aircraft.
2. How many missions must your squadron successfully complete per day to increase allied offensive strength?
3. What defines the front line of combat in a Falcon 3.0 campaign?
4. What are your responsibilities as a Squadron Commander?
5. What is a "pop-up" attack?
6. What is the difference between CAP and TARCAP?

Answers

1. Use multiple, two-aircraft sections; always have air cover; use additional fuel tanks only when necessary; use ECM gear generously; and monitor fuel and supplies usage closely.
2. Three.
3. Adjacent nodes.
4. Developing battle plans, managing pilots, managing stores usage, and flying missions.
5. Approaching a target at extremely low altitude, then quickly climbing and attacking the target.
6. TARCAP specifically refers to executing standard CAP activities over a target.

11

Secrets and Tactics of the Enemy

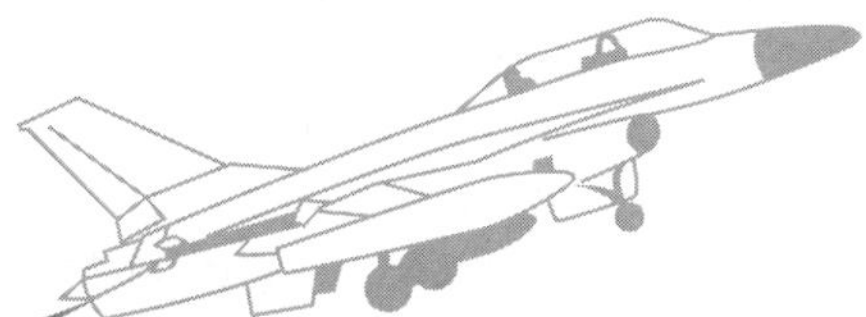

So, now you are an elite, best-of-the-best pilot. You have honed your skills in aerial combat, mission planning, and resource allocation. However, expertise in your own procedures and operations is not sufficient to wage a war. You must also know your enemy: his tactics, his capabilities, and his weaknesses. This chapter focuses on the enemy.

The Configuration Menu

You should fully understand the ramifications of selecting various options on the configuration menu. Some options affect only the performance of your particular aircraft, while others affect only the enemy. You need to fully understand the environment you are fighting in.

The Intelligence of the Enemy

The ENEMY LOGIC LEVEL on the configuration screen controls how intelligently enemy units operate. All types of enemy units, from bomber pilots to fighter pilots to ground forces, operate according to the value you choose for the ENEMY LOGIC LEVEL. Enemy units use skill values (ranging from 1 to 100) exactly like friendly pilots. As with the pilots in your squadron, the higher the skill value, the better the enemy is at that action.

Pilots at any of the four experience levels have the knowledge to execute all maneuvers, including those in the vertical plane. However, lower ability skills and lower experience levels make an enemy pilot reluctant to use advanced techniques, less aware of his environment, and slower to react. The lower the pilot's skill level, the less likely he is to utilize complex techniques, such as an Immelmann maneuver, instead making a simple break turn in the horizontal plane only.

Trainee As the name implies, this is the simplest level of enemy intelligence. Ability scores range from a minimum value of 0 to a maximum value of 25. Enemy pilots only maneuver in the horizontal plane; they do not execute maneuvers in the vertical plane, and they never exceed six Gs during maneuvering. Trainee pilots fly simple formations and are easily frightened. Trainee pilots flying ground attack missions jettison their ordnance and retreat at full speed when you radar lock them. Ground force leaders make poor choices and many errors during combat. Enemy aircraft groups usually remain bunched together, or with slight horizontal separation.

Cadet Cadet is the next higher level of enemy intelligence. At cadet level, enemy skill values range from a minimum of 25 to a maximum of 50. Enemy pilots occasionally pull slightly higher G-loads of seven Gs and begin to make basic vertical maneuvers. Pilots are still easily frightened, however. Pilots flying ground attack missions quickly jettison their loads and retreat.

Cadet fighter pilots still make many errors. They overreact when they detect that they've been locked on to; they panic quickly and maneuver sharply, breaking any radar locks they may have had on friendly aircraft. Their panic can cause enemy radar-guided missiles to go awry. Enemy pilots do not coordinate their attack efforts, and they may fire several missiles at the closest target, while ignoring all other friendly aircraft. Groups of enemy aircraft distance themselves horizontally to form a *combat spread*, but not vertically. Cadet pilots often waste missiles by firing them as soon as they radar lock a target, even if the missile has a poor chance of hitting the target.

Often, cadet fighter pilots *eyeball* or fixate on aircraft that they are attacking, following the target aircraft down to ensure that it is destroyed. They focus their entire attention on the single target they are tracking to the point of ignoring all other aircraft. Once a cadet enemy pilot has engaged a friendly fighter, it is quite easy to sneak up behind him if you temporarily shut off your radar. You can then turn your radar back on, obtain a quick radar lock, and send a missile blazing up his exhaust nozzle.

Veteran Veteran logic raises the stakes. Enemy pilot abilities range from a minimum of 50 to a maximum of 75. Enemy pilots can perform all vertical maneuvers, and sometimes pull as many as nine Gs. Ground units always use the best strategies initially, but still make tactical errors during combat.

Enemy bomber pilots no longer jettison their loads at the first sign of danger. They attempt to avoid friendly fighters, but still try to attack their targets. Enemy fighter pilots are less likely to eyeball their kills. They attempt to coordinate their attacks, and they will spread their missiles to engage multiple friendly aircraft with maximum effectiveness. Also, enemy pilots will employ vertical separation, along with horizontal separation, while flying in formation, and they begin to use multiple plane tactics.

Ace Ace pilots are the best the enemy has to offer. Pilot abilities range from a minimum of 75 to a maximum of 100. Enemy pilots often pull nine Gs while maneuvering in both the horizontal and vertical planes. Enemy fighter pilots coordinate their attacks and fire missiles at multiple friendly aircraft to disrupt friendly aircraft formations. Enemy fighters do not eyeball their kills, and do not panic when friendly aircraft radar lock them. They effectively use multiple aircraft maneuvers and wait for optimum firing conditions before launching missiles.

Ace pilots employ radar intelligently, sometimes deactivating radar to avoid giving their position away on your TWI. Enemy bomber pilots turn to avoid friendly fighters without jettisoning ordnance, then make further attempts to reach the primary target. Enemy ground units always use the best strategies and rarely make mistakes during combat.

Ace fighter pilots often coordinate multiple flights of CAP aircraft and use sucker tactics against you. Often, a group of powerful MiG-29s will fly tight circles 40 or 50 miles in front of you, seemingly unaware of you. However, as you close on what appears to be sitting ducks, a pair of lowly MiG-19s approach from the blind spot directly behind and below you and open fire!

SAMs and AAA

The SAMs-AAA setting modifies only the enemy SAMs and AAA. Friendly SAMs and AAA are unaffected by the value you select for this option. There are five possible settings.

None This setting completely turns all enemy ground fire off. No enemy SAMs or AAA fire, ever.

Recruits This is the most basic level of SAM and AAA activity. Ground units rarely fire, and when they do, their accuracy is poor.

Reserves SAMs and AAA begin to fire with regularity. Accuracy is average, and units respond slowly. Units do not coordinate their attacks against multiple friendly aircraft; all units may simply attack the first target they detect.

Regulars SAMs and AAA fire heavily with very good accuracy. After friendly aircraft have been detected, SAM and AAA units respond quickly. They engage multiple targets, but do not attack at maximum range.

Elite These are the best. SAM and AAA units respond very quickly to incoming aircraft, coordinate their attacks against multiple targets, and are very accurate. SAMs and AAA attack at the maximum ranges of their weapons and with heavy fire.

Other Options

Enemy forces are not affected in any way by the remaining settings. Enemy forces always use "LOW" weapons effectiveness, "COMPLEX" flight model, limited fuel, limited armament, limited chaff and flares, and limited intelligence. In other words, enemy forces always use the most realistic values for these options.

Enemy Air-to-Air Weapons

The enemy has a variety of radar and weapons systems. While not every system fielded in the real world is modeled in Falcon 3.0, those that are included in the simulation conform to real world performance specifications. Most of the necessary information on ranges and capabilities is included in Appendix D, Reference, of the Falcon 3.0 manual. However, there are a few additional points you should be aware of.

Radar-Guided Missiles

Friendly forces carry the AIM-120 AMRAAM radar-guided missile. Enemy forces have two radar-guided, air-to-air missiles, the Matra Super 530 and the AA-7 Apex. The Falcon 3.0 manual incorrectly identifies the Matra and Apex as active radar homing missiles.

> **NOTE:** When any of these three radar-guided missiles are fired at a friendly pilot, that pilot will announce, "Magic! Magic!"

Active and Semi-Active Radar Homing However, of the three missiles, only the friendly AIM-120 is an active radar-guided missile. Both the Matra Super 530 and the AA-7 Apex use semi-active radar homing (SARH).

Active radar missiles, such as the AIM-120, have an onboard radar system. The launching aircraft must first lock the target using the aircraft's radar. Once the missile is airborne, though, it uses only its own radar to track the target. The launching aircraft can break lock and pursue another target without affecting the missile.

SARH missiles, on the other hand, do not have a radar transmitter; they simply receive the reflections of the radar from the launching aircraft as it bounces off of the target. For this reason, the launching aircraft must maintain a radar lock on the target until the SARH missile hits it. If the radar lock is broken, the SARH missile simply flies harmlessly away. Both the Matra Super 530 and the AA-7 are SARH missiles, and perform accordingly in Falcon 3.0, despite the statements in the manual.

Missile Performance The Matra Super 530 is a French-built missile, carried only by the various Mirage aircraft. Despite the SARH restriction, this missile has respectable performance characteristics. Capable of speeds over mach 4, it has a range in excess of 20 miles and can reach altitudes greater than 80,000 feet. The missile can pull up to 20 Gs during flight, making it a most difficult adversary to evade.

The AA-7 Apex is a product of the former Soviet Union and is carried by most Soviet-built fighters you encounter in Falcon 3.0. Despite being more widely distributed, it is somewhat less effective than the Matra Super 530. It has a long range of 25 miles, but has serious performance limitations. The Apex is severely limited in altitude performance and is effective only at low and medium altitudes. The missile is also slower, with a maximum speed of mach 3.5. The AA-7 has one distinct advantage, however. It has an 88 pound warhead, compared to the 66 pound warhead of the Matra.

Evasion Tips Besides the normal evasive maneuvering and use of chaff to escape enemy missiles, you can also use the missiles' performance weaknesses listed above to increase your chances of survival. When your MISSILE and LOCK warning lights come on, and the TWI shows a diamond indicating an air-to-air radar, keep the following in mind:

- Always remember that both the Matra Super 530 and the AA-7 are SARH missiles. If you can break the radar lock the enemy has on you, the missile will fall harmlessly to the ground.
- The AA-7 is less effective at high altitudes. If you know the launching platform is not a Mirage, you can be fairly certain the inbound missile is an AA-7. Climbing to altitudes above 30,000 feet may place your aircraft outside the missile's performance envelope.

When an enemy aircraft locks on to you, there are three ways to break that lock: extend out of range, maneuver out of radar coverage, and convince the enemy to break the lock for you.

Extend Out of Range Missiles are propelled toward their target by powerful rocket engines. However, these engines are not active during the entire time the missile is in flight. Missile bodies have a limited amount of space to store the seeker, the warhead, the engine, and the fuel. To reduce the amount of fuel required, missile engines fire for only about half of the missile's flight, accelerating the projectile to speeds of mach 3 and above. For the remaining portion of the flight, the missile simply coasts. Therefore, if a missile is fired at you at long range, you have two advantages to exploit:

- By the time the missile reaches you it will probably be out of fuel, meaning it will have no thrust to attempt to counter evasive maneuvers.
- The missile's maximum range is measured from the point where the missile is fired. If that point is 20 or more miles away from your current position, you only have to travel 5 or 10 miles to escape the missile's range. In the time it takes the missile to accelerate and travel 20 miles, you only have to travel one fourth of that distance.

When the enemy has locked on to you, check his position on your TWI. The TWI displays a 30 mile range. If the offending radar is displayed near the edge of the TWI, you are probably outside of missile range. Immediately turn your aircraft so that the bandit is directly behind you. Increase your speed and extend from the bandit.

A missile will continue toward you until it runs out of fuel, so don't be alarmed if it seems to follow your escape for a long time. If, however, the missile continues to close and appears to be overtaking you, increase throttle to full afterburner and point the nose of your F-16 straight up, pulling maximum Gs in the process. At long range, the missile is probably gliding and will be unable to chase your F-16 in a climb. Figure 11-1 illustrates.

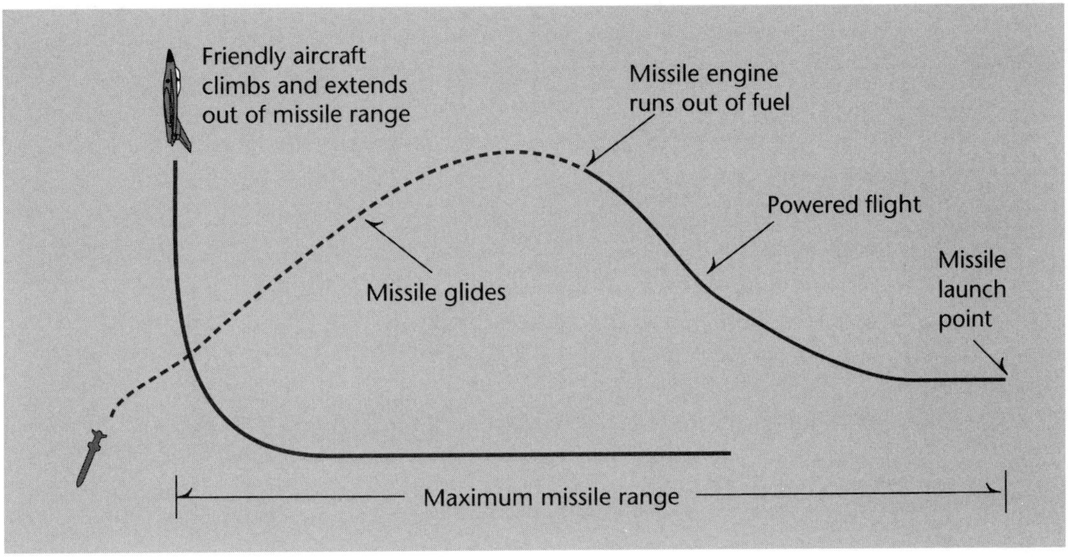

Figure 11-1 Extending Beyond a Missile's Range

Breaking Radar Lock by Maneuvering As you recall from Chapter 8, *Using High Fidelity Radar*, radar waves emit as a cone from the antenna, with the point of the cone touching the antenna. The size of the base of the cone determines how much area the radar is covering. At short ranges, it may be possible to make a sharp, high-G turn and escape the area being scanned by the enemy's radar, thereby breaking the lock-on. Figure 11-2 illustrates.

As shown in figure 11-2, remember that the farther the range of the radar, the greater the area the cone covers. At long range, it may be impractical or impossible to escape the enemy radar cone. This tactic, therefore, is best reserved for short range situations where the area being scanned by the hostile radar is much smaller.

Persuading the Enemy to Break a Radar Lock The third method of breaking a radar lock is to persuade the enemy to do it for you. The enemy pilot may have to maintain a radar lock on you for his missile to track you; but using the AMRAAM, you are under no such obligation. The contest of nerves begins when you are approaching a bandit head-to-head. Assuming the bandit is using the AA-7, when the range between you decreases to 20 or so miles he should get a radar lock on you, and will quite probably fire a missile at you.

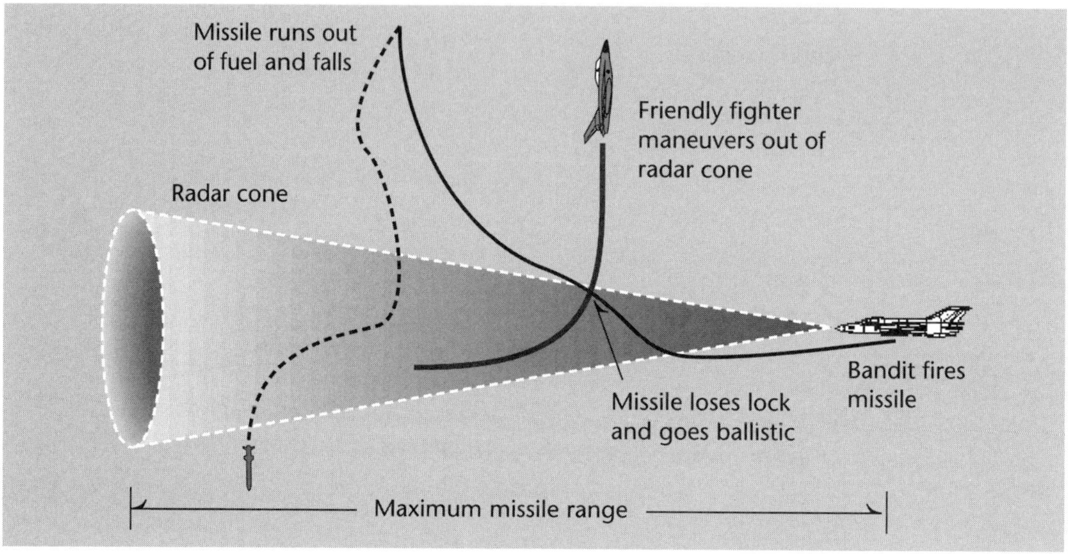

Figure 11-2 Maneuvering Against a Radar Lock

For the moment, you are at a distinct disadvantage. Your AMRAAM won't acquire the bandit until the range decreases to less than 17 miles. Lower your speed slightly (to reduce closure rate) and continue directly toward the bandit. The enemy missile will be speeding toward you, but don't panic.

When the range decreases to 15 to 17 miles, your AMRAAM should acquire the bandit. Immediately fire the missile at the enemy fighter. Just as your TWI detects the inbound missile, the enemy's TWI will report your missile headed toward the bandit. The pilot will panic and make a hard maneuver to attempt to lose your missile, thereby breaking his radar lock. The enemy missile will go ballistic and your AMRAAM will continue toward the bandit. The AMRAAM may not hit the bandit, but it gives you a few seconds to press the advantage and secure a better firing position.

Veteran and Ace Pilots However, this tactic is only effective with trainee and cadet enemy pilots. Remember that during the time you take to close to AMRAAM range, the enemy missile is quickly accelerating to maximum speed and closing on your aircraft. Your missile, when fired, takes a finite amount of time to accelerate to maximum speed, while the enemy missile continues toward you at its full speed. At certain ranges, the enemy missile collides with your aircraft several seconds before your missile collides with the bandit aircraft. Ace and veteran pilots realize this and utilize these seconds wisely.

Top quality enemy pilots wait coolly, maintaining their radar lock on you, as long as possible. At the last possible second, the enemy pilot breaks hard to evade your missile; but because of his level of poise, the enemy missile may have already destroyed your aircraft. When the enemy pilot maneuvers to evade your AMRAAM, he may no longer be concerned with maintaining a radar lock.

Infrared (IR) Homing Missiles

IR homing missiles complement radar-guided missiles, rather than replace them. IR homing missiles do not transmit any active signals; instead, they track the heat being emitted by the target's engine(s). Therefore, unlike radar-guided missiles, IR homing missiles do not announce their presence on the target's TWI. However, due to the difficulties in sensing heat emissions, IR homing missiles have a much shorter range, usually below ten nautical miles.

> NOTE: When a friendly pilot detects an inbound heat-seeking missile, he announces, "Atoll!" or, "Magic!" on the radio.

AA-2 Atoll The AA-2 Atoll is the rough equivalent of the AIM-9P. The Atoll has a very short range of 5nm. The Atoll is a rear-aspect missile and must remain directly behind the target aircraft where it has an unobstructed view of the target's exhaust. This missile is carried by Soviet-built aircraft. If a friendly pilot spots one of these missiles, he then calls, "Atoll! Atoll!" over the radio.

AA-8 Aphid The AA-8 Aphid is an advancement of the AA-2. While still having only a 5nm range, the Aphid is an all-aspect missile, meaning it can track heat emissions from any angle, even head on, to the target. This missile is carried by Soviet-built aircraft. If a friendly pilot spots one of these missiles, he calls, "Magic! Magic!" over the radio.

R.550 Magic The French-built R.550 Magic is an all-aspect missile sporting a 6nm range. This missile is carried by the Mirage III, the Mirage V, and the Mirage F1 aircraft. When a friendly pilot spots one of these missiles, he calls, "Magic! Magic!" over the radio.

Evasion Techniques Like radar-guided missiles, you can often extend out of the missile's range if the missile has been launched at long range. As the missile approaches, hard maneuvering in conjunction with dispensing flares may fool the missile. Unlike radar-guided missiles, breaking the radar lock the launching aircraft has on you does nothing.

Breaking Contact Heat-seeking missiles, both rear- and all-aspect, require a direct, unobstructed view of the heat source. Clouds effectively block this necessary view. If you are aware of an inbound IR missile and there are nearby clouds, turn towards and enter the cloud. Unless the missile is very close, it will lose you.

The Sun IR missiles often stop tracking a target if another, brighter, hotter target appears between the missile and the original target. Flares use this principle and generate extremely hot flashes designed to fool the missile. However, during daylight battles, pilots have the hottest heat source within 200 million miles to contend with: the sun. The sun generates so much heat that IR missiles often track it, running out of fuel long before reaching it, and falling harmlessly to the ground.

Figure 11-3 illustrates using the sun as a decoy. Turn your aircraft directly toward the sun, causing your aircraft to temporarily obstruct the missile's view of the sun. This gives the missile an unobstructed view of your exhaust. Then, make a hard maneuver toward the missile. Turning toward the missile causes the fuselage of your aircraft to block the missile's view of your exhaust and presents and unobstructed view of the sun. Normally, the missile will forsake your aircraft in favor of the sun.

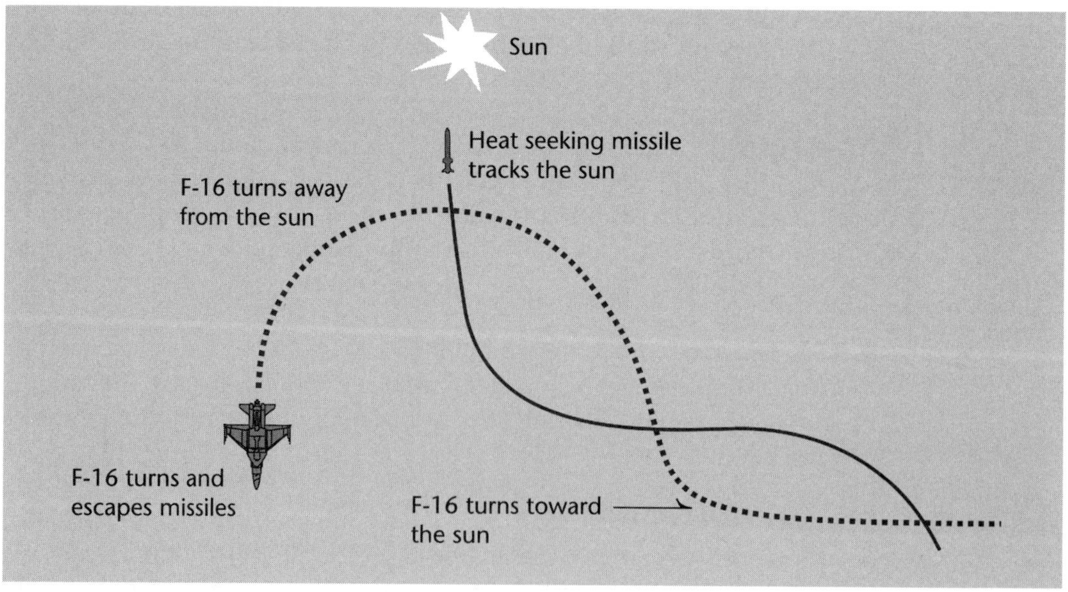

Figure 11-3 Using the Sun as a Decoy

Enemy Radar and Radar Detection Systems

Like you, the enemy pilots depend upon radar, TWI, and IFF systems to locate, track, and identify other aircraft. Most different aircraft use different radar systems. It is imperative that you know the capabilities of the enemy's electronic eyes and ears. Your APG-66 can outperform many radar systems fielded by the enemy, but not all of them. You must know when the enemy can electronically see you and when he can't. This section first discusses enemy countermeasures and warning systems, then lists radar data for every enemy aircraft that carries radar.

Enemy Electronic Countermeasures

As of version Falcon 3.0D, enemy pilots have the capability of using ECM gear. ECM gear is loaded on a random number of aircraft during each mission. Depending upon the skill of that particular pilot, he may make effective use of the ECM gear, or not use it at all. If the enemy activates ECM, it probably will break any radar lock on him and display additional ghost images on your REO. If friendly AWACS detect enemy ECM usage, they inform you. This at least warns you that enemy aircraft are nearby.

Enemy Threat Warning Indicators

Like you, the enemy has TWI radar detectors. Soviet-built aircraft carry either the Sirena II or Sirena III radar warning systems. While little is known publicly about these systems, it is speculated that each version covers different frequency ranges because larger aircraft (such as Tu-16 Badgers and Tu-95 Bears) are known to carry both systems. Similar to your own TWI, ranges of the Sirena systems are both estimated to be 30nm.

> **NOTE:** Your APG-66 can locate and track targets at ranges as distant as 80nm. Therefore, if you have locked a target at a range greater than 30nm, that target will not be able to detect your radar lock.

Enemy Radar Systems

The following tables list each radar-carrying type of enemy aircraft, alphabetized by manufacturer and designation. The tables list each radar's name, its type, how it registers on your TWI, its range, and various associated notes.

IL-76 "Mainstay"

Radar Name	Type	Range	Note
SU-AWACS	Airborne Early Warning. Appears as 6 on TWI.	Unknown	First photographed in 1987–few details known.

Designated the Soviet Union AWACS (SUAWACS), few details are known of this aircraft's full capabilities. It was designed to operate in conjunction with MiG-29, MiG-31, and Su-27 fighter/interceptor aircraft in order to increase their already formidable air-to-air capabilities.

MiG-19 "Farmer"

Radar Name	Type	Range	Note
High Fix	Continuous Wave (CW). Displayed as 3 on TWI	5 nm	Obsolete by modern standards

Appendix D of the Falcon 3.0 manual states that the MiG-19 has no onboard radar. This, however, is incorrect. The MiG-19 actually was the first production Soviet aircraft to carry a limited functionality (by today's standards), onboard, air-to-air radar. You will discover this fact when you first meet a MiG-19 in combat.

The MiG-19 carries a short-range, continuous-wave (CW) radar called the High Fix, used to conduct air-to-air searches. As you will recall from Chapter 9, *Advanced Flight School*, CW radars constantly emit radar energy and appear as a 3 on your TWI. Because the High Fix radar has such a limited range, a MiG-19 generally requires other search aircraft, such as the IL-76 Mainstay, to vector it toward targets. Once it closes within 10nm, it activates its radar and attempts to obtain an exact *fix* on the target. It then closes to within one to two nautical miles and attacks the target with a 30mm cannon. The MiG-19 can also carry the AA-2 Atoll, a rear-aspect, infrared homing, air-to-air missile.

Because the High Fix is not a Doppler radar, ground clutter renders it useless against targets at lower altitudes than the MiG-19.

MiG-21 "Fishbed"

Radar Name	Type	Range	Note
Jay Bird	Pulse-Doppler, with limited Look-Down, Shoot-Down capability. Displayed as a 2 on TWI.	43 nm	Former Warsaw Pact nations known to be upgrading and improving MiG-21 radar systems.

This aircraft, which was allegedly built in greater numbers than any other fighter aircraft in history, carries the Sirena III warning system and the Jay Bird search-and-track radar system. Many reports on the capabilities of the Jay Bird radar conflict with one another. Range has been estimated as high as 31nm, but is probably no greater than 20nm. Being a CW radar, it appears as a 3 on the TWI.

Because the Jay Bird is a not a Doppler radar, ground clutter renders it useless against targets at lower altitudes than the MiG-21.

MiG-23 "Flogger"

Radar Name	Type	Range	Note
High Lark	Pulse-Doppler, with limited look-down, shoot-down capability. Displayed as a 2 on TWI.	43 nm	Believed to be derived from AWG-10 from F-4s shot down over Vietnam.

The first pulse-Doppler radar fielded by the Soviet Union, it is widely believed that it was based upon AWG-10 radars recovered from F-4 Phantoms shot down over North Vietnam. This radar has a moderate range of 43nm, giving the MiG-23 the ability to detect targets before they get within weapons firing range. Because this is a Doppler-based radar, ground clutter is not a problem. Thus, the MiG-23 has the ability to track and fire on targets flying at altitudes lower than its own (look-down, shoot-down capability).

The 43nm range of the High Lark radar is greater than the 30nm range of the F-16 TWI. That means that MiG-23s can locate your aircraft at a range not displayed by your TWI.

MiG-25 "Foxbat"

Radar Name	Type	Range	Note
Fox Fire	Pulse-Doppler, with continuous wave. Displayed as a 2 on TWI.	60 nm	Uses both Doppler and CW modes.

The Fox Fire radar apparently uses a pulse-Doppler system for target acquisition and tracking, but then illuminates the target with CW radar while guiding SARH missiles toward the target.

MiG-29 "Fulcrum"

Radar Name	Type	Range	Note
Slot Back	Pulse-Doppler, with limited look-down, shoot-down capabilities. Displayed as a 1 on TWI.	54 nm	Full details unavailable.

Modern Soviet combat aircraft carry highly capable air-to-air radar. While full details of the Slot Back radar are not known, it is widely believed that the Slot Back radar system is comparable to the APG-66 used in the F-16. This pulse-Doppler radar is fully capable of locating and tracking targets below the MiG-29. The range of this radar allows the MiG-29 to conduct aerial searches without the assistance of AWACS aircraft such as the IL-76 Mainstay. The MiG-29, equipped with this radar, is a dangerous adversary.

Mirage III, Mirage V, and Mirage F1

Radar Name	Type	Range	Note
Various	Pulse-Doppler, displayed as a 4 on TWI.	50 nm	None.

The various Mirage aircraft are equipped with multiple types of radar. However, all three types are displayed as a 4 on the TWI. No other enemy radars are displayed as such. If, during combat, you detect a 4 on your TWI, you can be assured that it is one of the Mirage series.

Su-27 "Flanker"

Radar Name	Type	Range	Note
Unknown	Pulse-Doppler, with full look-down, shoot-down capability. Displayed as a 1 on TWI.	Reported in excess of 100 nm.	None.

The most formidable radar system fielded by the enemy, few details are currently available. It is widely believed to be far superior to the APG-66 used by the F-16. Although it is designed to operate in conjunction with the IL-76 Mainstay, the SU-27's reported radar range of over 100nm gives it considerable standalone capability.

Aerial Combat Maneuvering (ACM)

The enemy is fully trained in ACM; to defeat him you must also be. Chapter 6, *Introduction to Red Flag*, presented three basic maneuvers: the scissors, the high Yo-Yo, and the Immelmann. Additional tactics, some based on the previous three, follow.

The following tactics are designed for one-on-one combat situations, something you will rarely encounter. Many of the tactics require planning and setup time, time that may not be available in a many-versus-many dogfight. Fixation on a single target often leaves you open to attack from his wingman. You should familiarize yourself with the following tactics, then create Red Flag missions and practice them.

Proaction Versus Reaction

In actual combat, you usually execute sequences of maneuvers and fire at targets when the opportunity happens to arise, rather than track a single target for an extended period of time. There are two approaches to ACM:

learning to maneuver against another aircraft, and learning how to maneuver your aircraft to a particular position. At first glance, the difference between the two may seem subtle, but they are quite different.

The first approach is purely reactive; you observe the enemy's movements, then respond. You learn that when the enemy makes a certain move, you counter with a different tactic. This forces you to play a perpetual catching-up game, even when you are in an offensive position. Using this approach, if the enemy makes a radical, unexpected maneuver, you will often lose him.

With the second approach, you learn how each maneuver works, and how your aircraft is positioned at the end of the maneuver. You don't respond to the enemy, you position your aircraft to maximize the effectiveness of your weapons, regardless of the enemy's position. You then have the flexibility of offensively and creatively maneuvering your aircraft. You take proactive steps to kill your enemy. This is the proper way to learn ACM.

Assuming an Offensive Position

There's an old saying among fighter pilots, *"Fancy flying never killed an enemy yet."* All the clever maneuvers in the world can not down your enemy; it takes a missile or a bullet to do that. You must *always* be attempting to gain a firing position while maneuvering, even when the enemy is on your six.

> TIP: Until you put the enemy on the defensive he will keep firing at you. The more bullets the enemy fires at you, the greater the likelihood one will hit you.

The Danger Zone Figure 11-4 illustrates the danger zone. The danger zone is the best area from which to attack the target. The danger zone extends behind the target +/– 30° right, left, above, and below the target. Attacking from within a target's danger zone presents an aspect angle of not more than 30°. As you recall from the discussion on aspect angle from Chapter 9, *Advanced Flight School*, air-to-air weapons perform better when fired at low-aspect angles.

> NOTE: Gaining access to an opponent's danger zone, while denying him access to your own is the basic premise of ACM.

Corner Speed Always keep your speed high. The F-16 turns best at a speed of 450 knots. This speed is called the *corner speed*. Your F-16 maneuvers best at the corner speed, pulling maximum G loads with a minimum turn radius. It is easy to lose speed while maneuvering. Below 350 knots, the performance of your F-16 is seriously degraded.

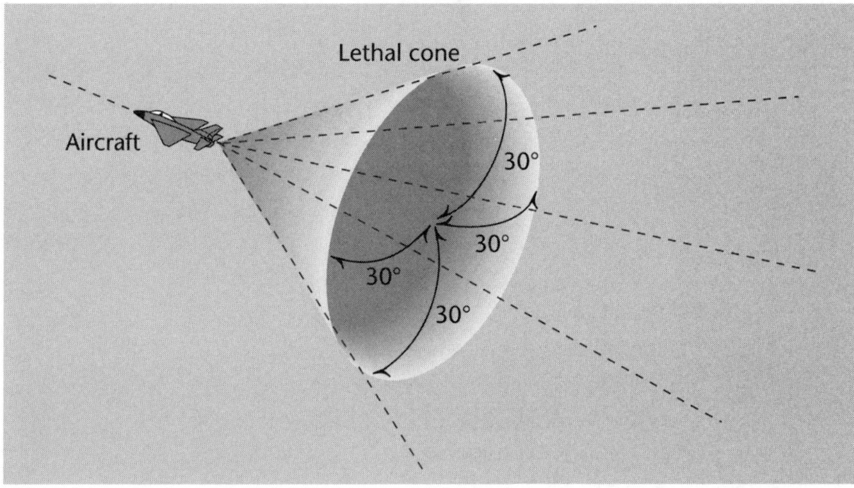

Figure 11-4 Radar Zone

Energy Management Always remember: there are two types of energy: kinetic and potential. Speed is kinetic energy, altitude is potential energy. If you are flying fast at low altitude, you have high kinetic energy. If you are flying slow at high altitude, you have high potential energy. Maneuvering and pulling high G-loads requires high speed. *You must maintain high kinetic energy to perform combat maneuvers.*

Kinetic energy and potential energy can be exchanged. If you are flying fast (high kinetic energy) you can climb. Your speed will drop, but your altitude increases (increasing your potential energy). If you are at a high altitude (high potential energy), you can dive. Your altitude decreases, but your speed increases (increasing kinetic energy).

The trick is to maintain energy. Try not to slow down without climbing. If you slow down, but you do not gain altitude, the energy you lose simply goes away. If you use a climb to slow down, however, you trade your kinetic energy for potential energy. You can then dive and convert the potential energy back into kinetic energy (speed). Pilots have a saying regarding energy, *"Out of airspeed, altitude, and ideas."* If you lose too much speed at low altitude, you have no energy to maneuver with and are an easy target.

The Break Turn

Usually referred to simply as a *break*, the Break Turn is the root of all combat maneuvers and the most commonly executed maneuver. The most common communication between wingmen is a frantic order to break either left or right. Figure 11-5 illustrates.

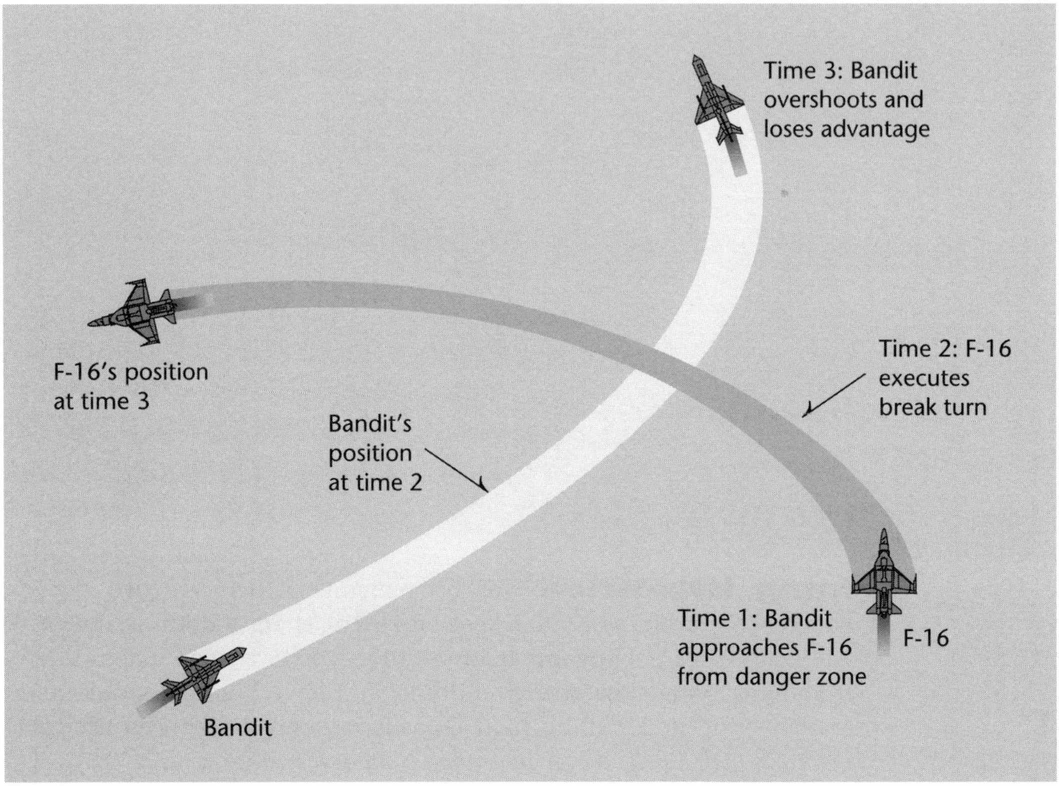

Figure 11-5 The Break Turn

The situation begins when a pilot discovers a bandit within his own danger zone. The fighter makes a hard turn (breaks) *toward* the bandit, pulling a high G-load and quickly creating a high aspect angle. In Figure 11-5, the F-16 sees the bandit at approximately a seven o'clock position. The F-16 breaks to the left, quickly increasing the aspect angle, making it difficult for the bandit to fire.

Additionally, the F-16 loses speed as it pulls high G-loads. If the bandit aircraft's turn performance is inferior to the F-16, as the F-16 slows, the bandit may be unable to turn with the F-16 and *overshoot*. When the bandit overshoots, he passes past the F-16 and is no longer in firing position. Figure 11-5 shows an overshoot at time 2. At time 2, the F-16 could *reverse* (turn the opposite direction) and begin scissoring with the bandit.

TIP: The break turn must not be sustained for long periods of time! Sustained high-G turns bleed speed, leaving you low on energy.

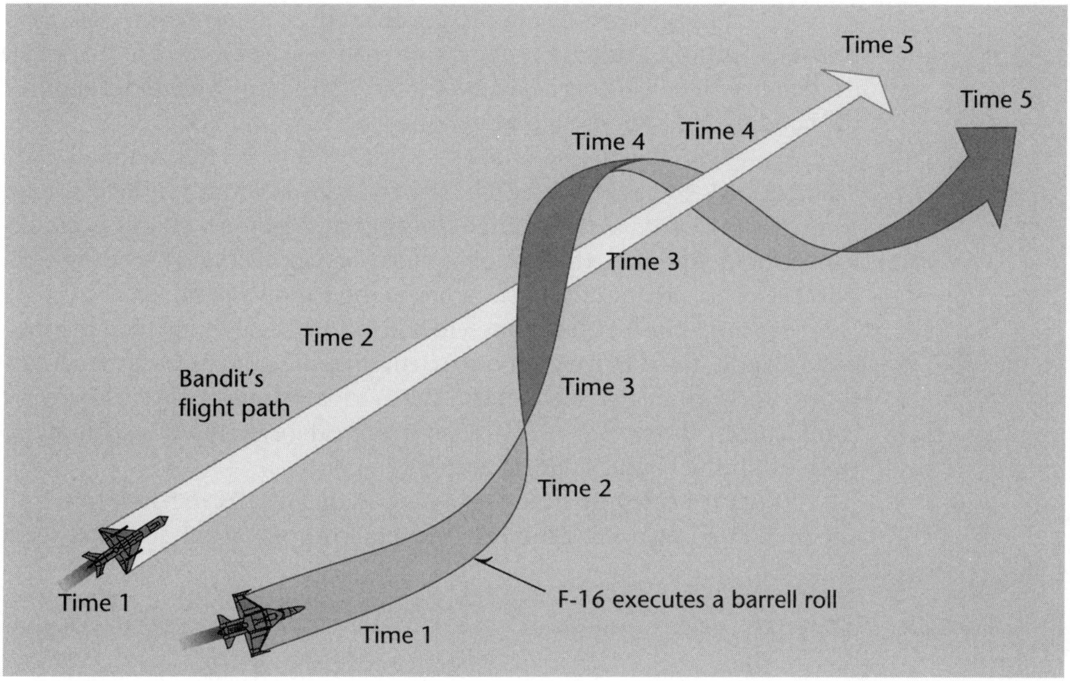

Figure 11-6 Preventing an Overshoot with a Barrel Roll

The Barrel Roll

The barrel roll, used during both offensive and defensive maneuvering, is one of the oldest ACM tactics. The barrel roll uses the vertical plane, converting speed to altitude, and allowing the pilot to maneuver inside his opponent. Figure 11-6 illustrates the basic barrel roll from an offensive position.

At time 1, the F-16 is a comfortable distance behind and well within the danger zone of a slow moving bandit. At time 2, it is evident that the F-16 is moving considerably faster than the bandit and will soon overshoot. At time 3, the F-16 pilot pulls the stick back and to the left, causing the F-16 to roll left as it climbs. At time 4, the F-16 is inverted above the bandit. Because the F-16 slowed during the climb, the bandit has moved away from it. The F-16 pilot continues his roll, and by time 5 has circumscribed a circle around the flight path of the bandit. At time 5, the F-16 is again behind the bandit, but with increased separation. The F-16 has converted its newly gained altitude back into speed and is again rapidly approaching the bandit.

By lengthening the time span between time 3 and time 4, the F-16 could gain additional separation. The longer the F-16 climbs, the more it will slow, and the farther the bandit will move away. This may be necessary to execute a missile attack against the bandit. At time 2, the F-16 may be too close to fire a missile. The F-16 extends the climb (the span between times 3 and 4) so that the bandit will pull farther away. When the F-16 completes the roll at time 5, the bandit will be far enough away for a missile attack.

Figure 11-7 illustrates the defensive use of the barrel roll. At time 1 in this example, an F-16 has a bandit off its right wing, well within the F-16's danger zone. The F-16 just executed a right break turn, and the bandit is beginning to overshoot. At time 2, the F-16 pilot pulls the stick back and to the right. The F-16 begins to circumscribe a circle about the bandit's path.

At time 3, the F-16 has completed the climb. Depending upon the speed of the bandit, the F-16 may choose to lengthen the span between time 2 and time 3 to gain greater separation. The F-16 continues its roll downward, completing it at time 4. The F-16 is now comfortably behind the bandit, and well within the bandit's danger zone.

You must carefully time the execution of a defensive barrel roll. If the enemy is more than a few hundred feet behind you, he will see you execute

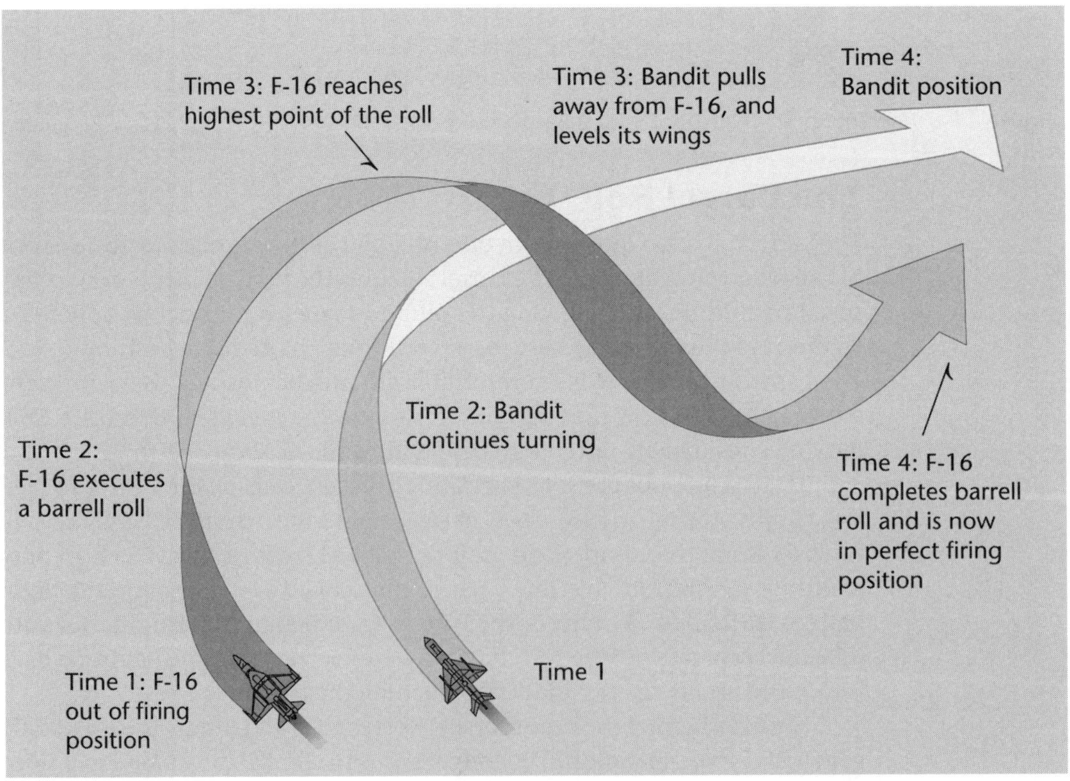

Figure 11-7 Using the Barrel Roll to Convert from Defense to Offense

the roll and follow you. You must lure the enemy to extremely close range, possibly by extending speed brakes, then execute the barrel roll quickly.

Rolling Scissors

The barrel roll combined with the scissors provides an additional option called the rolling scissors. Figure 11-8 illustrates. Like normal, flat scissors, the opponents during rolling scissors are attempting to turn behind each other. However, during rolling scissors, the opponents are executing a series of barrel rolls around each other's flight paths. Rather than simply trying to out-turn each other (as in flat scissors), the opponents are using the vertical plane as well.

Zoom Climb

The Zoom Climb exploits the strengths of modern, high-thrust jet engines over older, less capable ones. The zoom climb is used when one opponent enjoys either a huge kinetic energy (speed) or thrust advantage over the other. Figure 11-9 shows the zoom climb. At time 1, an F-16 approaches a MiG-19 head-on. The F-16 is moving faster than the MiG-19, and has a more powerful engine. Both fighters enter steep climbs as they approach each other. At time

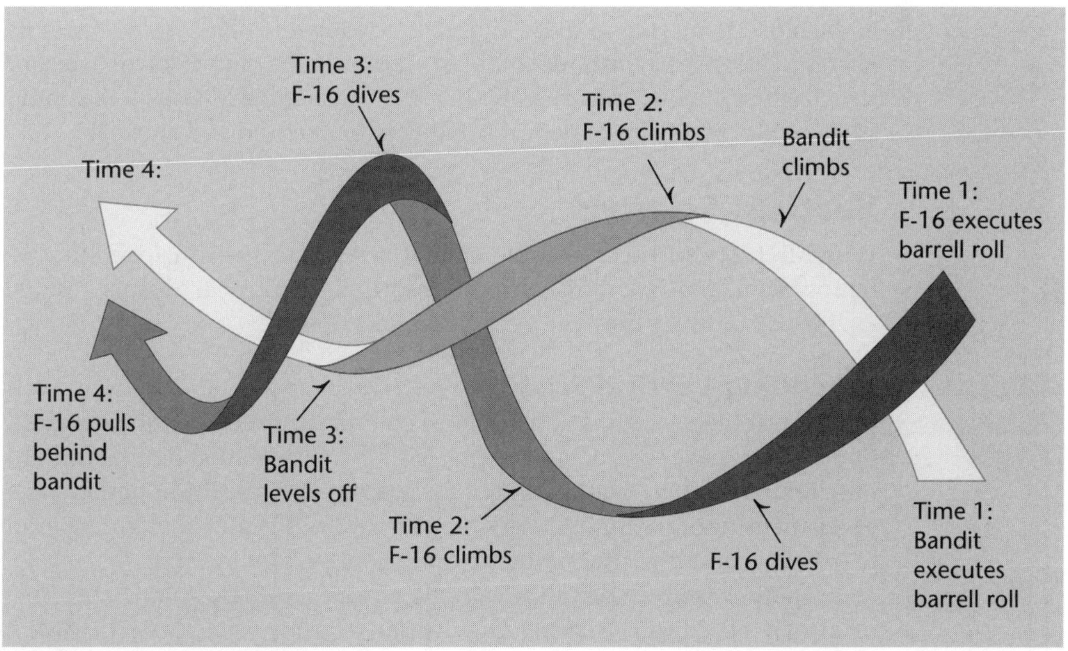

Figure 11-8 Rolling Scissors

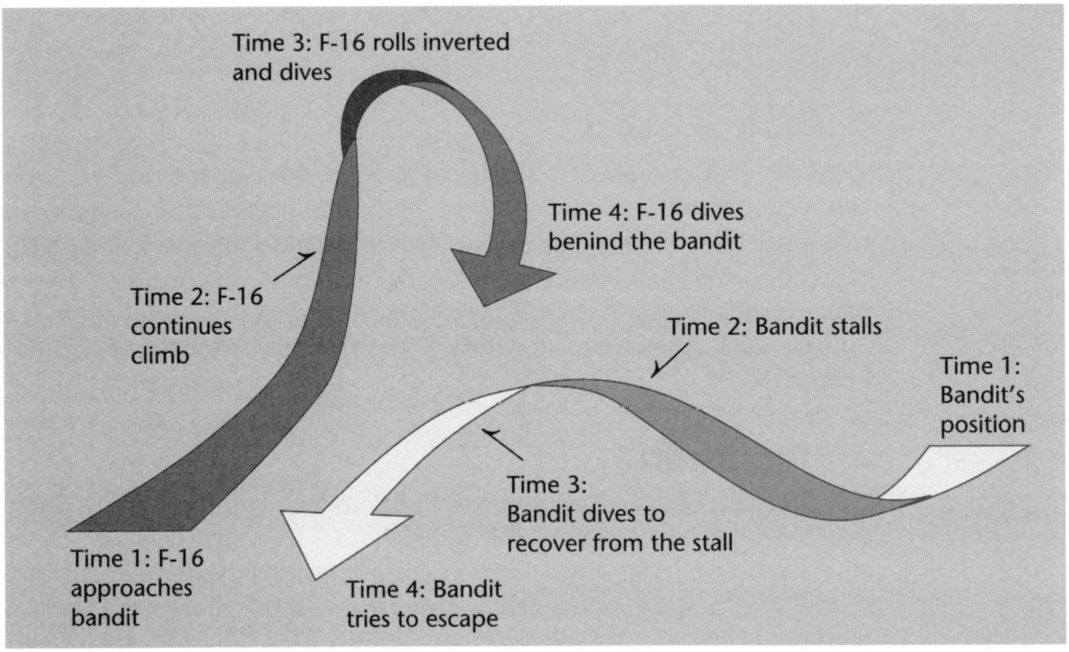

Figure 11-9 The Zoom Climb

2, the MiG-19 runs out of speed and stalls, forcing it to dive. The F-16 uses its energy advantage to continue climbing. At time 3, the MiG-19 dives to regain speed, while the F-16 rolls and also dives. At time 4, the MiG-19 is regaining speed while the F-16 is in perfect firing position behind and above it.

Vertical Scissors

When fighters with comparable energy levels and thrust capabilities attempt zoom climbs, a third form of scissoring, the vertical scissors, results. Figure 11-10 shows how the vertical scissors operate.

Ascending Vertical Scissors An F-16 and a MiG-19 approach, both traveling at high speeds. At time 1, both commit to a zoom climb. At time 2, both fighters have considerable energy left. However, neither fighter wants to out-climb the other. If either fighter rockets skyward, the lower fighter has a excellent firing opportunity. Therefore, at time 2, both fighters execute aileron rolls while climbing, attempting to force the adversary in front.

Neither fighter gains an advantage, and by time 3 the MiG-19 has bled off all of its speed and is stalling. Gravity pulls the nose of the MiG-19 toward the ground, making it unable to shoot at the F-16. The F-16, meanwhile,

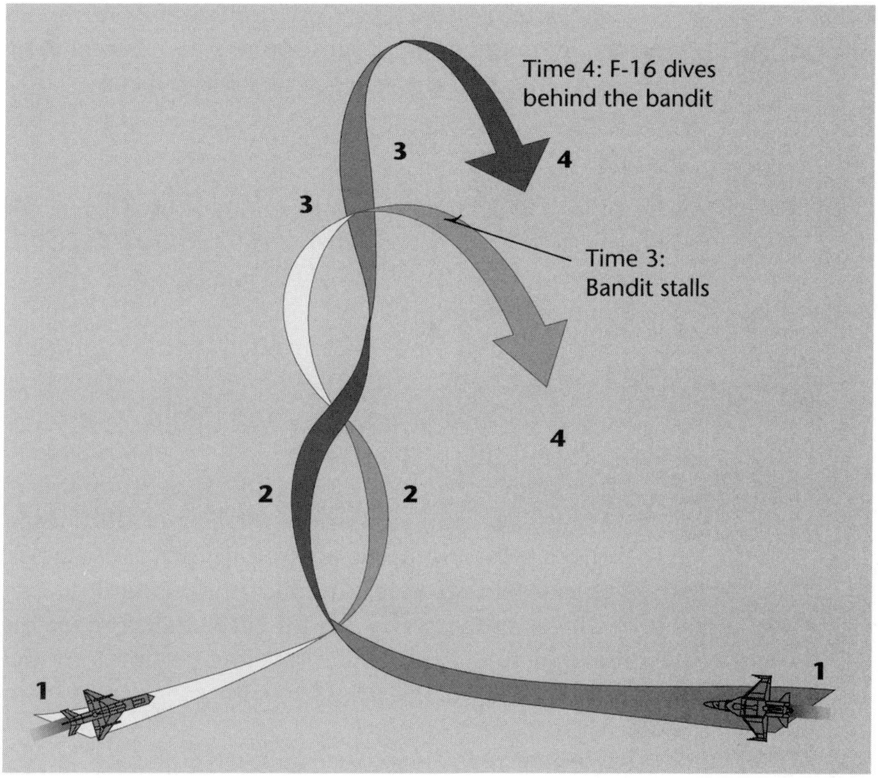

Figure 11-10 The Vertical Scissors

continues to climb for slightly longer, then rolls over and dives toward the MiG-19. At time 4, the MiG-19 is picking up speed, but the F-16 is already in perfect firing position behind it.

> **NOTE:** Veteran and ace level enemy pilots often execute vertical scissors.

During vertical scissors, you must carefully control your climb rate. Climb too fast and you'll present a clear view of your exhaust to your enemy. Climb too slow and you'll stall, allowing your enemy to roll behind you.

Descending Vertical Scissors Vertical scissors can also be executed during dives. Each fighter attempts to slow its descent and force the opponent in front. In descending vertical scissors, the fighter with the most kinetic energy is at a distinct disadvantage; the fighter that can slow itself quickest has the advantage.

The ground also plays an important role in descending vertical scissors. By maintaining a position slightly above the enemy, he may be forced to remain in the scissors too long and crash.

Split-S

The split-S, illustrated in Figure 11-11, is used primarily to escape other maneuvers, especially the flat scissors. At time 1 in Figure 11-11, an F-16 is pursuing a MiG-21. The MiG-21 has just executed a break turn and the F-16 is about to overshoot.

The pilot rolls the aircraft inverted at time 2 and pulls back hard on the stick at time 3. The pilot continues to pull back on the stick as the aircraft dives. As the aircraft dives, the pilot reduces throttle to avoid gaining too much speed. The aircraft completes a half loop by time 4 and at time 5, it is flying straight and level, but at a heading 180° offset from the original heading.

The split-S requires at least 7,000 feet of altitude above ground level. Executing a split-S from a lower altitude increases the risk of colliding with the ground. Furthermore, the pilot must carefully control the aircraft's speed between times 3 and 4. If the speed increases too much, the pilot will require more time to pull out of the dive at time 4. At lower altitudes, high dive speeds increase the risk of crashing.

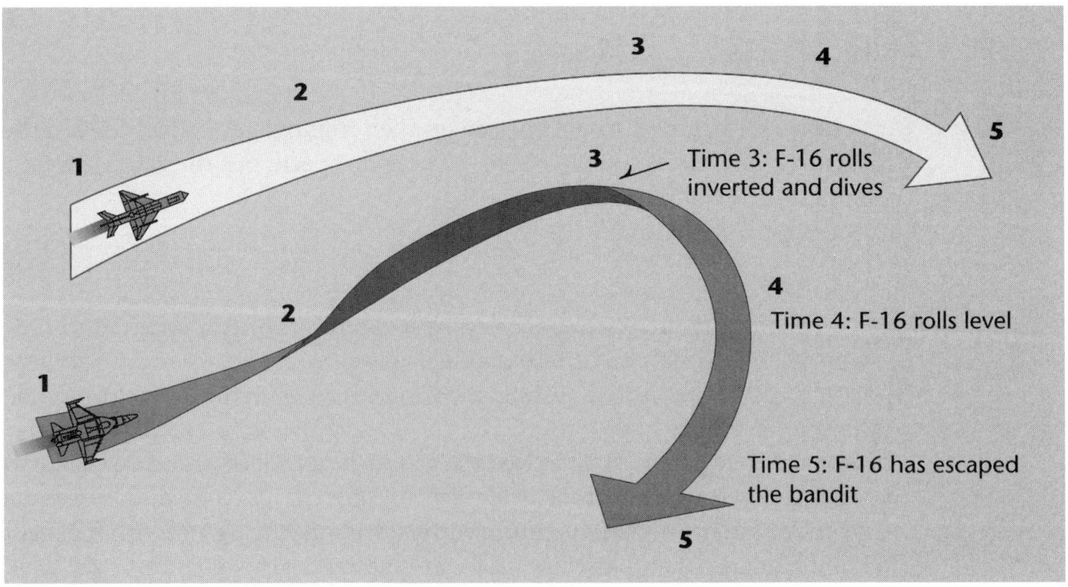

Figure 11-11 The Split-S

The split-S should never be executed when there is an enemy within your danger zone. An enemy can easily follow you through a split-S, and maintain a position in your danger zone at time 5. Only execute a split-S when your opponent is not behind you.

Lead Pursuit Turn

Most combat engagements eventually degrade to a turning battle between the opponents. In many turning battles, you gain a position behind the enemy, but are out of missiles and too far away for a gun attack. The high G-loads you pull during the turn bleed additional speed and you are unable to close on the bandit. The lead pursuit turn, illustrated in Figure 11-12, presents one possible solution to this dilemma.

At time 1 in Figure 11-12, the F-16 is tucked comfortably behind the MiG, easily matching the MiG's turn. However, the F-16 is too far behind the MiG to execute a gun attack and is losing speed in the turn. The F-16 pilot pulls back on the stick, tightening the turn and pointing the F-16's nose in front of the bandit. The F-16 turns inside the bandit and closes the gap between the two aircraft.

However, the tighter turn of the F-16 causes it to bleed even more speed. The F-16 closes on the bandit, but quickly depletes its energy. If the attack fails, the bandit's superior speed will quickly extend it out of range again. The lead pursuit turn is a one-shot-only tactic; if you miss, the bandit will escape.

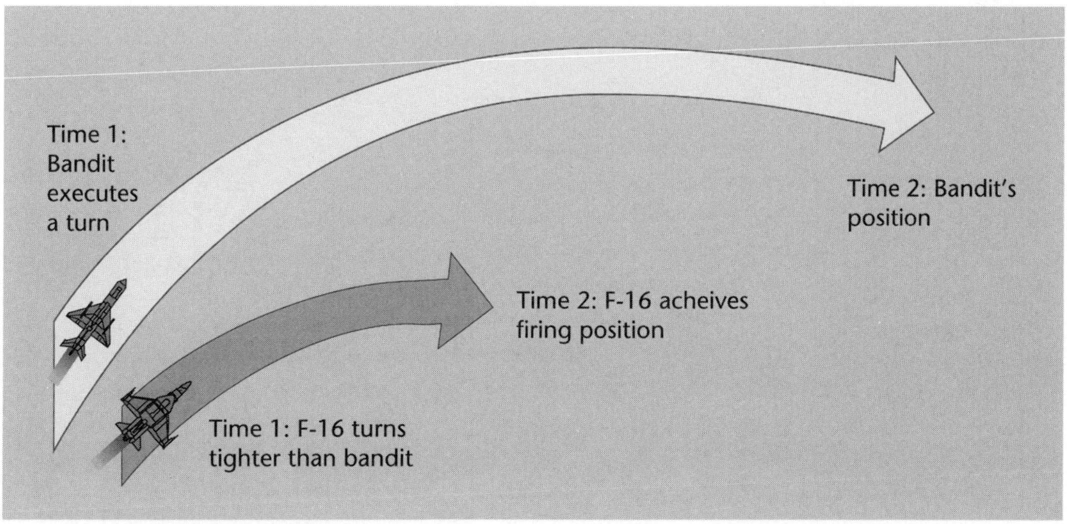

Figure 11-12 Lead Pursuit Turn

Lag Pursuit Turn

Aircraft turn performance is defined by two measures: the number of degrees turned per second, called the *turn rate*, and the turn radius. Figure 11-13 illustrates turn performance data for the F-16 and MiG-21 at a speed of Mach .85 and an altitude of 20,000 feet. The turn radius in feet and turn rate in degrees turned per second are shown for both aircraft.

As shown in Figure 11-13, the MiG-21 has a turn rate of 15.2° degrees per second at a turn radius of 2,250 feet. The F-16 has a superior turn rate of 28.4 degrees per second and a tighter turn radius of 1,200 feet. These values vary for every speed at every altitude, but clearly show the F-16 has a distinct advantage over the MiG-21.

Matching Turn Rate, Not Turn Radius Intuitively, most pilots attempt to match the bandit's turn radius during combat, thus maintaining a position within the bandit's danger zone. However, if the speed between the two aircraft differs greatly, the bandit may enjoy a tighter turn radius, but an inferior turn rate. In such cases, you can maintain a position behind the bandit by matching his turn rate rather than his turn radius. This is called a lag pursuit turn, and is illustrated in Figure 11-14.

In Figure 11-14, the bandit is traveling slower than the F-16 and is, therefore, enjoying a turn radius advantage. The faster traveling F-16 cannot match the bandit's turn without reducing speed. However, the

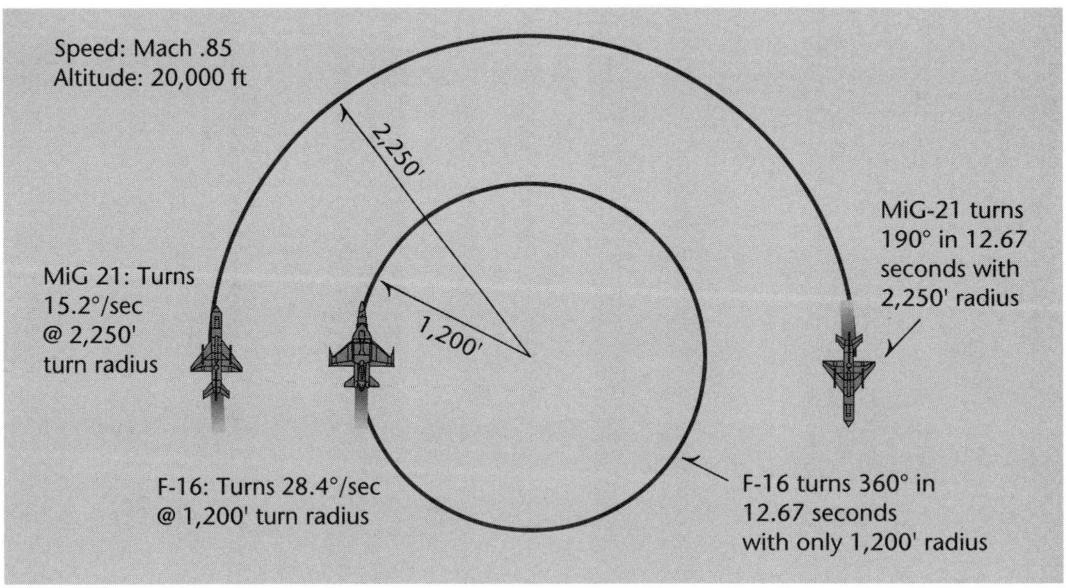

Figure 11-13 Turn Radius Versus Turn Rate

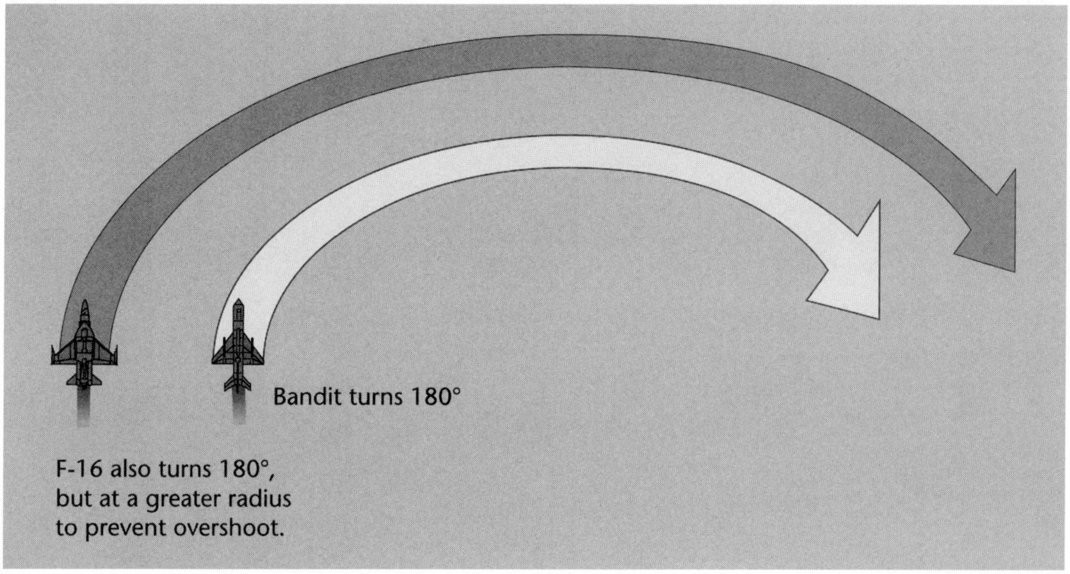

Figure 11-14 Lag Pursuit Turn.

slower moving bandit cannot match the F-16's turn rate. The F-16, without losing energy, can match the bandit's turn, following a parallel arc outside of the bandit's turn. At time 2, both aircraft are traveling at the same speeds as time 1, and the F-16 has maintained its position behind the bandit.

The lag pursuit turn has one disadvantage. The nose of the F-16 never points at the bandit during the turn. Despite remaining behind the bandit, the F-16 is never in a firing position. The lag pursuit turn, however, does place the F-16 in a situation similar to time 1 in Figure 11-7. You can then execute the barrel roll described in Figure 11-7 to achieve a firing position.

TIP: The lag pursuit turn should be used when you are in the bandit's danger zone, but about to overshoot. The lag pursuit turn does not present a firing position, but maintains your position behind the bandit. You should subsequently use another maneuver, such as the barrel roll, to achieve a firing position.

Lag Displacement Rolls

The lag displacement roll is a complex maneuver, combining both the barrel roll and the lag pursuit turn. The lag displacement roll is difficult to practice and difficult to execute. It should be used as a spur-of-the-moment maneuver, used to gain a firing position quickly. Figure 11-15 illustrates the lag displacement roll.

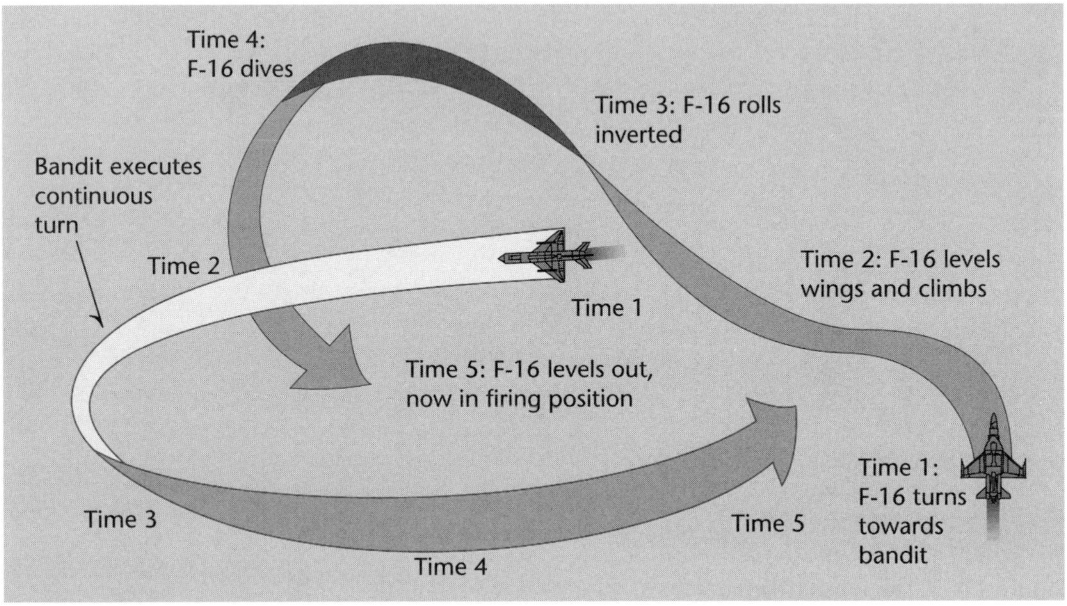

Figure 11-15 The Lag Displacement Roll

The lag displacement roll begins at time 1 when the F-16 follows a turning bandit at close range. The range between the F-16 and the bandit is too low to attempt a missile shot, but the F-16 doesn't have sufficient energy to execute a lead pursuit turn. While the bandit is executing a sustained break turn at time 2, the F-16 pilot levels the wings and pulls back on the stick. At time 3, during the climb, the F-16 pilot rolls the aircraft inverted while still pulling back on the stick.

During the climb, the F-16 pilot exchanges speed for altitude. The pilot times the climb to allow the bandit to turn 80° to 90°. At time 4, the F-16 begins an inverted dive, similar to a split-S. The pilot controls the F-16's speed during the dive to allow the bandit to turn another 80° to 90°. At time 5, the F-16 has reversed its course 180°, while allowing the bandit to turn in front of the F-16's new heading.

Timing the Lag Displacement Roll If the climb (the time span between times 2 and 3) is not sustained long enough, or the F-16 pulls out of the dive (time 5) too soon, the bandit will have insufficient time to complete its turn. The F-16 will still be pointing towards the bandit at time 5, but at a high aspect angle. The aspect angle may be high enough to thwart a missile attack.

By carefully controlling the span between times 2 and 5, you can force the bandit to present a low-aspect, rear-quarter view of itself. This places you in perfect firing position behind the bandit. While the lag displacement roll is difficult to master, if executed properly, it is difficult for the bandit to counter.

Countering Maneuvers Countering the lag displacement roll requires the defending pilot to know that the maneuver is being executed against him. If the defender fails to recognize the lag displacement roll, he has little hope of countering it. The defender is already at a disadvantage because the attacker is behind him. To counter, the defending pilot must maneuver into the vertical plane, attempting to remove the attacking pilot's advantage.

First, referring to Figure 11-16, the bandit could execute a zoom climb at time 2 or time 3, while the F-16 is still climbing. The zoom climb could terminate normally when one fighter runs out of energy and stalls. If both fighters have comparable energy levels, they may enter vertical rolling scissors. In any case, the original advantage of the F-16 is neutralized, and the bandit has an opportunity to take the offensive.

Second, referring to Figure 11-17, the bandit could execute a split-S at time 4. The bandit should roll slightly during the dive so that it is approaching the F-16 head-on at time 5. The bandit has failed to seize the offensive, but has neutralized the F-16's previous advantage.

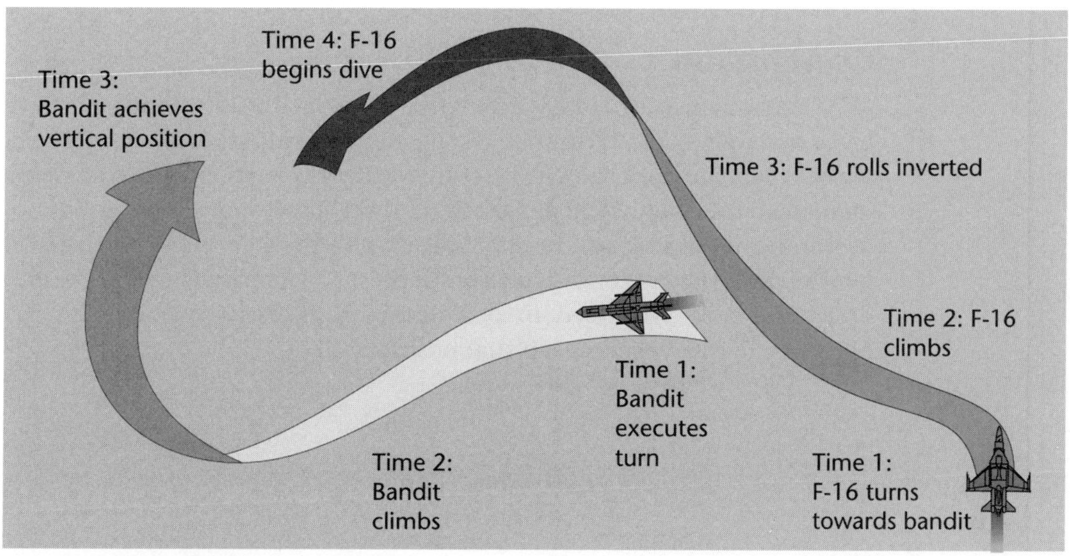

Figure 11-16 Countering the Lag Displacement Roll — Method 1

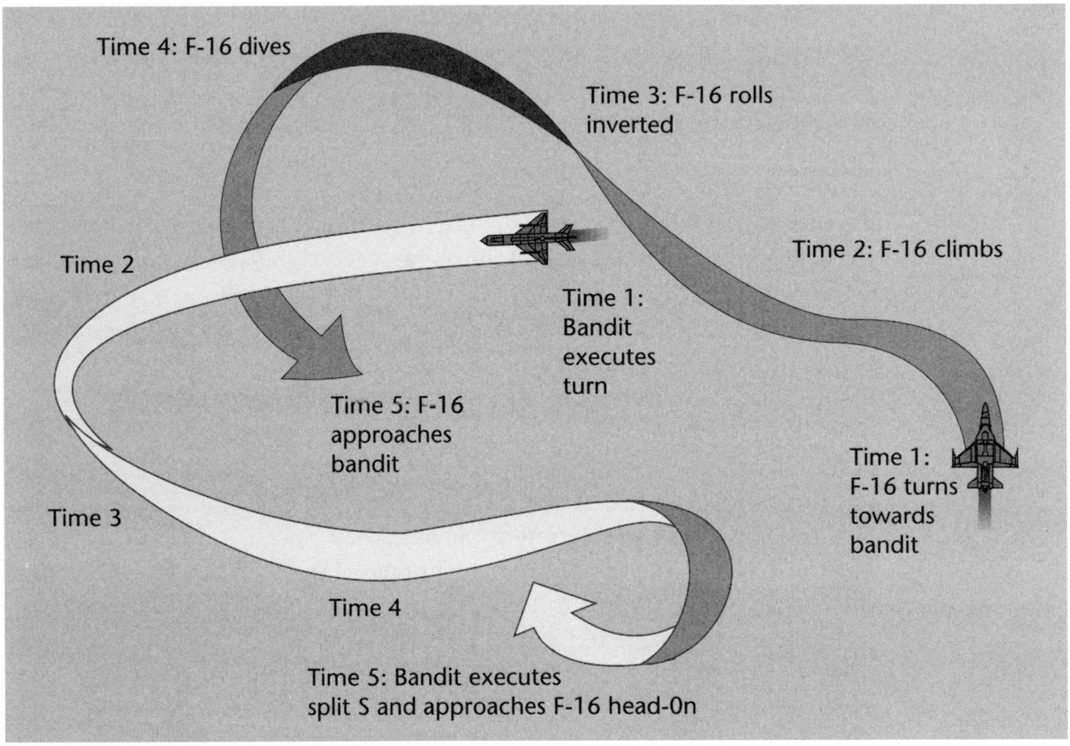

Figure 11-17 Countering the Lab Displacement Roll — Method 2

Conclusion

ACM is as much an art as a science. While many tactics and maneuvers have been developed, most combat engagements result in seat-of-the-pants, shoot-when-the-opportunity-arises flying. If you consistently use the same maneuver, the enemy will detect this and act accordingly. As stated at the beginning of this section, you should learn how the above maneuvers affect your aircraft. During combat, do not simply pick a maneuver to execute, but determine how you need to position your aircraft, then execute the necessary maneuvers to reach that position.

Questions: How Does the Enemy Fight?

1. What are the different levels of pilot skill and how do they differ?
2. What does the acronym SARH stand for?
3. True or false: Heat-seeking missiles are fooled by flares, but not by the sun.
4. What is the maximum radar range for the MiG-19, MiG-21, MiG-23, MiG-25, and MiG-29?

Answers

1. Trainee, Cadet, Veteran, and Ace.
2. Semi-Active Radar Homing
3. False. Heat-seeking missiles are fooled by both the sun and flares.
4. 5nm, 20nm, 43nm, 60nm, and 54nm, respectively.

12

Operation Fighting Tiger

The Best Gets Better

Spectrum Holobyte continues to improve a good thing. Besides the original three theaters of conflict (Israel, Kuwait, and Panama), Spectrum Holobyte has created an add-on campaign entitled Operation: Fighting Tiger, abbreviated as O:FT. Operation: Fighting Tiger introduces three new theaters of conflict as well as new aircraft, weapons, ships, and missions.

Besides the three new theaters, Operation: Fighting Tiger comes with a new version of the Falcon program itself, entitled Falcon 3.01. Previously, each new version of Falcon 3.0 appended a letter to the name, such as Falcon 3.0a, Falcon 3.0c, and Falcon 3.0d. The new program included with Operation: Fighting Tiger includes not only all fixes from the previous versions, but many additional enhancements. Some of these enhancements are available only within the new Operation: Fighting Tiger theaters, others are globally available to all theaters. Falcon 3.01 is not simply a new version of Falcon 3.0, but an entirely new program. The new program is significantly different enough to warrant a more distinct name.

The Operation: Fighting Tiger package includes two components. First, an upgraded Falcon program, named Falcon 3.01. Second, add-on data files for three new theaters of operation for use with the updated program. All functionality from previous Falcon 3.0 versions is incorportated in Falcon 3.01. You may continue to wage campaigns in the original three theaters. You must already own Falcon 3.0 in order to upgrade to Operation: Fighting Tiger. Operation: Fighting Tiger should be available at your local software store.

> Spectrum Holobyte is expected to release a Falcon 3.0 upgrade, called Falcon 3.0E. Falcon 3.0E is expected to be a free upgrade to all owners of Falcon 3.0, which will incorporate bug fixes from Falcon 3.01, but none of the Falcon 3.01 new features. See Appendix E for information on receiving Falcon 3.0 upgrades.

Installation of Operation: Fighting Tiger updates your version of Falcon 3.0 to Falcon 3.01 and installs the new theaters. It is not necessary to maintain separate Falcon 3.0 and Falcon 3.01 directories.

This chapter discusses the changes and additions associated with Falcon 3.01. The developments are presented in the same order as the material through the earlier chapters. For example, topics dealing with basic flight are presented first, then discussion of new radar types, followed by listings of new aircraft, ships, and weapons.

Basic Flight Changes

Falcon 3.01 incorporates three major changes to basic flight: night missions, improved Instrument Landing Systems (ILS), and VASI runway approach lights. These three changes do not radically alter how an F-16 flies, but they do change how you use your cockpit instrumentation.

Improved ILS

As described in Chapter 3, *Learning to Fly*, the Instrument Landing System (ILS) is designed to direct an aircraft on final approach to a runway. Two lines, one vertical and one horizontal, move across the HUD to indicate which way you should turn, climb, or dive in order to make a perfect landing. When the lines are perfectly centered both horizontally and vertically you are making a perfect approach.

Flight Path Deviation Indicator The Falcon 3.0 HUD, however, operates oncorrectly . The vertical line, indicating flight path deviation, fails to guide you to the runway. Instead, it acts like a non-directional beacon, perfectly aligning in the center of the HUD anytime your aircraft is pointed at the runway, regardless of your heading and the runway's orientation.

Falcon 3.01 has corrected this problem by providing two separate ILS options. The original ILS system is still activated by pressing \ and is referred to as the *beacon mode ILS*. Additionally, a new, correct ILS system is activated by pressing SHIFT-\, known as the *deviation mode ILS*. The runway heading indicator in the lower right corner of the HUD is now suffixed by either the letter "B" to indicate beacon mode, or the letter "D" to indicate deviation mode. Figure 12-1 illustrates this.

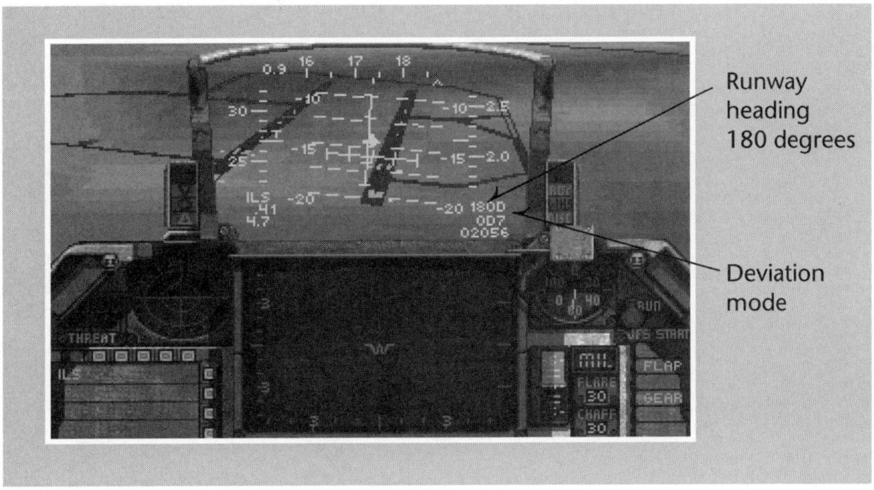

Figure 12-1 Runway Heading Indicator

View Shift In Falcon 3.0, lowering the landing gear or engaging the beacon mode ILS also caused an often disorienting shift in the forward view. Your point of view raises 5°, which causes you to look through the HUD at an odd angle. When flying level, the -5° pitch line on the flight path ladder (instead of the 0° pitch line) is aligned with the horizon. While this awards a better view over the nose of the F-16, it often causes disorientation and increases the difficulty of landings.

A new option to disable this view shift has been added. When the ILS is engaged (in either mode) or the landing gear is lowered, the view shift still occurs. Then, you can return to the normal view angle by pressing SHIFT-SCROLL LOCK. Your forward view will immediately revert to its normal perspective.

> **NOTE:** The view shift is engaged automatically every time you engage the ILS or lower the landing gear. You will have to manually disable the view shift each time unless you use F3MAPS to permanently disable it. See Appendix C for details on using F3MAPS.

VASI Runway Lights

Many runways at major airports have an additional landing aid known as the *Vertical Approach Slope Indicator,* or VASI, system. Most runways added in Operation: Fighting Tiger have two dual-color lights placed approximately 50 feet apart near the approach end of the runway. Because of their orientation, the further light appears "above" the closer light. These lights change between red and white to indicate if your approach is too low, thus helping you avoid crashing just short of the runway. Figure 12-2 shows a VASI lighting system.

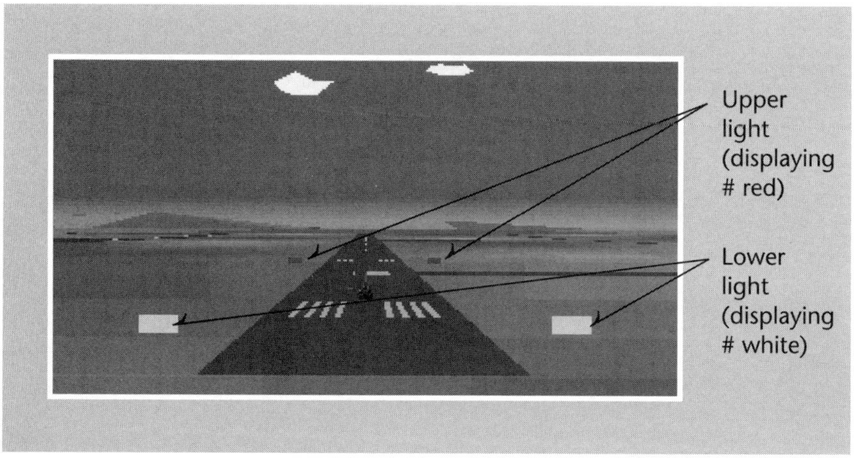

Figure 12-2 VASI Lighting System

As you approach a VASI-equipped runway, one light will be white, the other red. Depending upon which light is red, your approach is either acceptable, or too low. Pilots are taught a simple rhyme to describe the meaning of the lights, *red over white, you're alright, white over red, you're dead.* This rhyme states: if the upper (further) light is red, and the lower (closer) light is white, your approach is either on or above the appropriate glidescope or descent path. You might touch down in the middle of the runway instead of on the end, but you won't crash before reaching it. In the other case, where the upper light is white and the lower light is red, you are too low and need to slow your descent.

NOTE: VASI approach systems are not available at all runways. Only one end of selected runways within the Operation: Fighting Tiger new theaters (Kurile Islands, Pakistan, and Korea) are equipped VASI systems. Runways in the original Falcon 3.0 theaters (Kuwait, Israel, and Panama) do not have VASI systems.

VASI systems are especially useful at night or when your HUD has been damaged in combat. In either case, it may be difficult to properly approach the runway. Using the VASI system to correct your approach may save your simulated life.

Night Missions

In Falcon 3.0, campaign missions were flown at four times during a given day: morning at 0600 hours, midday at 1200 hours, evening at 1800 hours, and dusk at 2100 hours. Falcon 3.01 has removed the dusk missions flown at 2100 hours and replaced them with night missions flown at 2300 hours. Your new mission times are 0600, 1200, 1800, and 2300.

At 2300 hours, the world is a black place. Without the sun to illuminate them, the sky, sea, and landscape all appear as dark expanses. The sky and sea become deep blue and the land becomes contoured shades of black and dark blue. Bright stars fill the sky, city lights and roads illuminate brief patches of the countryside, and occasional ships appear as bright dots on the water. Aircraft sometimes activate navigation lights, and can be seen as white dots streaking across the sky.

The War Must Go On Other items on the ground, such as soldiers, tanks, bunkers, and trucks use the night to hide them from your preying F-16. Ground units avoid lighting themselves. Given the extreme darkness of the night, items such as tanks and trucks remain completely invisible until you are only a few hundred feet away from them. Even then, they appear only as slight shadows and are difficult to discern. For all intents and purposes, they can't be seen by your naked eyes.

But, like the U.S. Mail, neither rain, nor snow, nor gloom of night shall stop you. Your superiors will still order air-to-air and air-to-ground sorties on night missions, and they fully expect you to complete them. This means that you must learn to fight like you never have before. You must learn to rely on your instruments and your HUD to guide you through the dark.

Navigational Data You will have only the navigational data of your waypoints to get you to your target and back. You won't be able to fly to the approximate area, then circle and search for the exact target. If you misplace a waypoint while planning a mission, you will never find your target. Extra care must be taken during mission planning to ensure finding the target and your way home!

Instrument Flying Ground features, such as hills and mountains, now are black voids which meet an equally dark sky, making them almost impossible to distinguish. Low-level flying becomes extremely hazardous. Enemy radars, however, penetrate night and day with equal ease. If you are assigned a ground strike at night, you still need to fly extremely low and let the ground mask you from enemy defenses.

As you know, your HUD is equipped with a radar altimeter showing the exact distance your aircraft is above the ground, regardless of how high above sea level it is. In almost all cases, hills and mountains have long, gradual slopes that gently climb into the sky. During your low-level flight, pay close attention to the radar altimeter in the lower right corner of the HUD (shown in Figure 12-3). The radar altimeter will indicate any changes in your height as the altitude of the terrain increases and decreases, allowing you to compensate appropriately. Unless you are flying over water (where the surface is always flat), you must pay particular attention to your radar altimeter, lest you collide with a nearby hill.

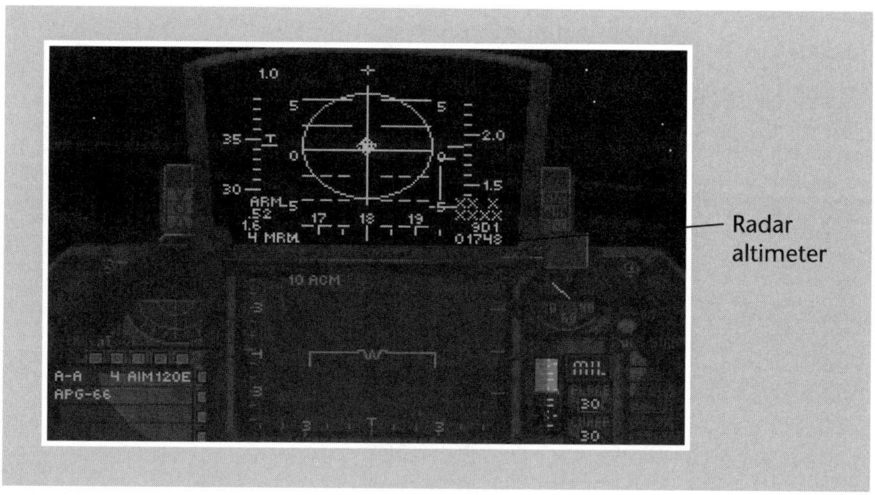

Figure 12-3 The Radar Altimeter

Some mountains have extremely steep slopes that increase in altitude rapidly. In such cases, your radar altimeter may not indicate the severity of the situation until it is too late to compensate. Your best approach is to fly over the same terrain during daylight and familiarize yourself with its features before attempting low-level night flights.

Vertigo Equally dangerous during night flights is the loss of balance, or sensation of *vertigo*. Vertigo occurs when you lose all visual references indicating which way is up, down, and level. Pitch blackness (where no visual cues exist at all) can definately cause vertigo, but so can semi-blackness. In semi-black conditions, scattered lights and changes of hue combine to form obscure shadows and create a false sense of perspective.

In either case, when your brain loses its sense of balance, it compensates by creating a false one. That is, your brain picks a direction, and you "feel" or perceive that direction to be "up." This feeling, however, rarely coincides with the data presented by your cockpit instruments. Many pilots rely more heavily on visual cues than on their flight instruments and make inappropriate flight adjustments based on their incorrect perceptions.

Semi-black conditions are actually more dangerous than pitch black conditions. Pitch black conditions have no visual cues whatsoever, so the pilot knows that his senses have no frame of reference. Semi-black conditions, which you will often encounter in Falcon 3.01, have some slight visual references, which your brain will try to reconcile. Under such conditions, regardless of what you "feel," you must rely solely on your instruments. Your senses can be fooled, but your instruments never lie.

Attacking Ground Targets at Night Locating ground targets at night is extremely difficult. Blending into the darkness, ground units (tanks, trucks, etc.) are impossible to see until you are practically on top of them. By this time, they are well aware of your presence and are prepared to return fire. Figure 12-4 shows a typical view of a tank at night.

Figure 12-4 A T-80 in the Dark

For night CAS and strike missions, forget about using unguided, CCIP style bombs, such as the Mk 82. You'll never find your target until you are too close to engineer your attack run. Mk 82HD Snakeye bombs are somewhat useful because they are delivered from low altitudes directly over the target; however, you still have the difficult task of locating your target.

Your most effective weapon for night strikes is the AGM-65D Maverick. This version of the Maverick uses an infrared imaging seeker rather than the television system used by the AGM-65B. The infrared seeker of the Maverick-D especially suits it for night combat. Because the Maverick automatically aquires targets, it can do the dirty job of locating a target for you.

Ingress at low altitude, flying directly toward the target waypoint. The waypoint indicator is the only navigational aid available, so be extremely careful not to deviate from the assigned flight path. When you close within 15 miles of the target, climb to about 7,000 feet AGL. At this altitude, enemy search radars will easily detect you, so be prepared to act quickly and escape. Point your nose back down toward the target. If there are enemy units there, your Maverick will detect them and lock onto one.

At this point, things start getting hectic. After ordering your wingman to engage, fire your missile, then press T to select another target. Continue selecting new targets until you've exhausted your supply of Mavericks. As you pass over the target, dive to low altitude, order your wingman to disengage, and head for home.

> TIP: Making multiple passes over a target is almost always a bad idea. Because of your pop-up approach tactics, multiple passes over targets at night is almost always fatal. Make only one pass at the target, fire all of your weapons, and return to base.

If you don't fire all of your Mavericks on the first pass, don't worry, just take them back to base with you. You may be tempted to make another low-altitude pass since you know the exact location of the enemy units, but because of your previous high altitude, every enemy fighter in the vicinity knows you are there. Once you start firing, you can bet they're going to come after you. It is far better to return home and fight again some other day than to die.

Air-to-air Missions at Night You may be assigned air-to-air missions at night, such as bomber intercepts, fighter sweeps, and escort missions. Like ground units, aircraft are extremely difficult to see at night. The padlock view, which normally has a four mile range, is greatly reduced at night. Air combat relying on visual methods is virtually impossible. Instead, you will have to rely solely on your REO and your HUD to find, identify, and persecute enemy aircraft. Fortunately, the F-16's powerful APG-66 radar is custom made for this task.

Missile Range Combat Combat at missile ranges (from 2nm up to 24nm, depending upon the missile type) aren't too difficult. Using the data from the REO, you can monitor the bandit's flight. Using the data from the HUD, including the target designator box and aspect angle indicator, you can maneuver into a firing position as easily at night as during the day. For full details on using the radar in air-to-air combat, refer to Chapter 8, *Using Hi-Fidelity Radar* and Chapter 9, *Red Flag: Advanced Flight School.*

Knife Fights Close range dogfights, called *knife fights*, where the range to the target is less than 1nm are a different story. At these close ranges, combat relies on visual abilities. Sudden maneuvers by a bandit can often break a radar lock when fighting at such close ranges, requiring you to maintain visual contact with the target until radar contact can be reestablished.

Under such conditions, it is strongly recommended that you avoid knife fights. Instead, use high-speed, quick-pass, hit-and-run tactics against your opponent. Try to fire a missile at the bandit from long range. Come in close to your target only long enough to fire a single volley of 20mm shells, then increase to full throttle and extend away. Attempt to gain sufficient range to allow a missile shot, then turn back toward the bandit, acquire a radar lock, and attack. If you are unable to get a missile to track the target, fire another burst of 20mm rounds at the bandit as you speed by. Extend in the opposite direction and repeat the process.

> **WARNING**: Avoid direct head-to-head passes with bandits. When you open fire with your cannon, they will return fire with theirs. Instead, approach the target from an aspect angle of 10 ° to 15 °. This will limit the bandit's ability to return cannon fire.

If you do become entangled in a knife fight, watch for your opportunity to escape. Don't press the attack from a weak or marginal position. If the opportunity for escape arises, *take it*. After extending and gaining some separation, reassess the situation. If you have sufficient fuel and missile supplies, begin the hit-and-run tactic. If, however, your supplies are low, head for home.

Wingman Commands

Three new wingman commands have been added in Falcon 3.01: *tighten formation, widen formation,* and *return to base.*

- Tighten Formation, SHIFT-F This command orders your wingmen to move in closer to you during flight. As your flight group gets closer, it will become difficult for enemy radars to determine exactly how many aircraft are in your group. Each time you order your wingmen to tighten, they move closer to you. When tightening further risks a collision, they respectfully decline your order.

- Widen Formation, SHIFT-G This command orders your wingmen to move farther apart. Use this command to widen formations during air intercepts, thus allowing your flight to encircle the enemy. Each time you order your wingmen to widen, they will move farther apart, until doing so would restrict visual contact with you. At that point, they respectfully decline your order.
- Return to base, SHIFT-H This command orders your wingmen to immediately abort the mission and return to base. Once this command is given, wingmen will ignore all subsequent orders from you. Use this command only when you wish to immediately abort the mission.

Radar and ECM System Changes

Falcon 3.01 introduces new radar modes for both your F-16 and enemy forces. These additions supplement the previous radar systems described in Chapter 8, Using Hi-Fidelity Radar, and Chapter 9, Red Flag: Advanced Flight School. Their use can improve your combat performance, but in no way invalidates the information presented in previous chapters.

New ACM Scan Mode

The ACM mode of the Hi-Fidelity Radar has been expanded. The real APG-66 radar has two different scan modes in ACM mode. The first scan patter covers an area 20° wide by 20° high, which centered 6° degrees below the aircraft. The depressed center of the 20° x20° scan is designed for use against targets below the F-16. The second pattern covers an area 10° wide 40° high, centered 20° above the aircraft. The raised center of the 10°x40° scan is designed for use against targets above the F-16. In Falcon 3.0, ACM mode only implemented 20°x20° scan patterns. Falcon 3.01 introduces the 10°x40° scan pattern.

NOTE: ACM radar mode is only available to HFR users. Please refer to Chapter 8, *Using Hi-Fidelity Radar*, for details.

Scan Pattern Toggle To select the new scan pattern, first engage ACM mode by pressing F6. ACM will initialize with the 20°x20° pattern. Press SHIFT-F6 to toggle between 20°x20° and 10°x40° scans. When the

10°x40° scan is selected, a vertical line will appear in the center of the HUD, as shown in Figure 12-5.

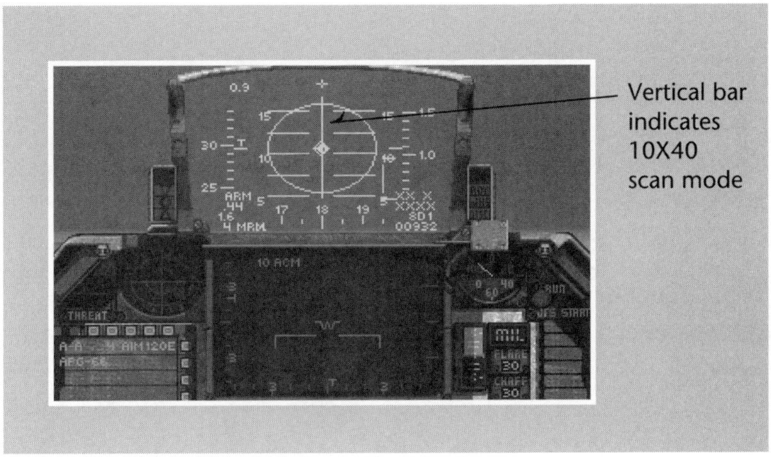

Figure 12-5 10°x40° Scan Mode

Using 10°x40° Scans Since the 20°x20° scan is depressed 6°, the radar actually scans +/- 10° on either side of the aircraft. Vertically, it scans +14° above the F-16 and -26° degrees below. The 10°x40° scans +/- 5° on either side of the F-16, +60° above, and -20° below. The two scan patterns are illustrated in Figure 12-6.

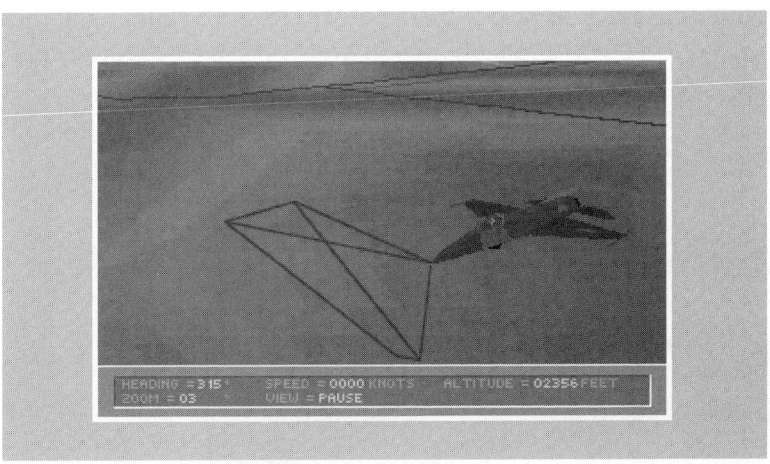

Figure 12-6 ACM Scan Modes

The 20°x20° pattern is a general purpose scan, for use when the bandit's flight path is aligned with yours, but it is not centered in front of your aircraft. Figure 12-7 shows a pilot's view of the 20°x20° scan, and targets it is effective against. Note that targets may be below the F-16 and, therefore, not visible in the figure. Since the 20°x20° scan is depressed 6°, it can still acquire that target.

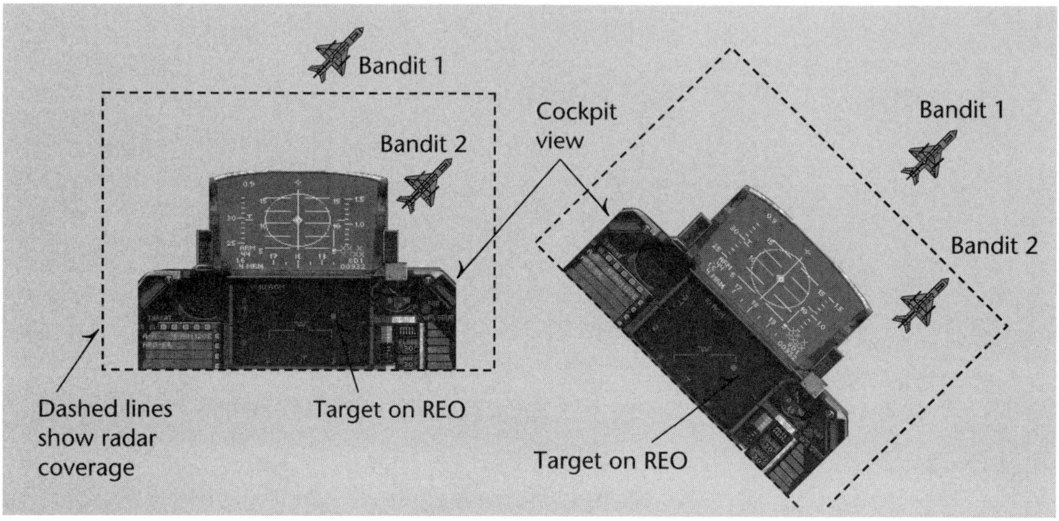

Figure 12-7 Employing 20°x20° Scan Mode

The 10°x40° mode is tailored for turning battles where the enemy aircraft is directly ahead, but on a tighter arc, as shown in Figure 12-8. As you can see in Figure 12-7, using 20°x20° mode, you need to turn tighter than your opponent in order to place him directly in front of your aircraft and obtain a radar lock. This probably means you will have to reduce speed

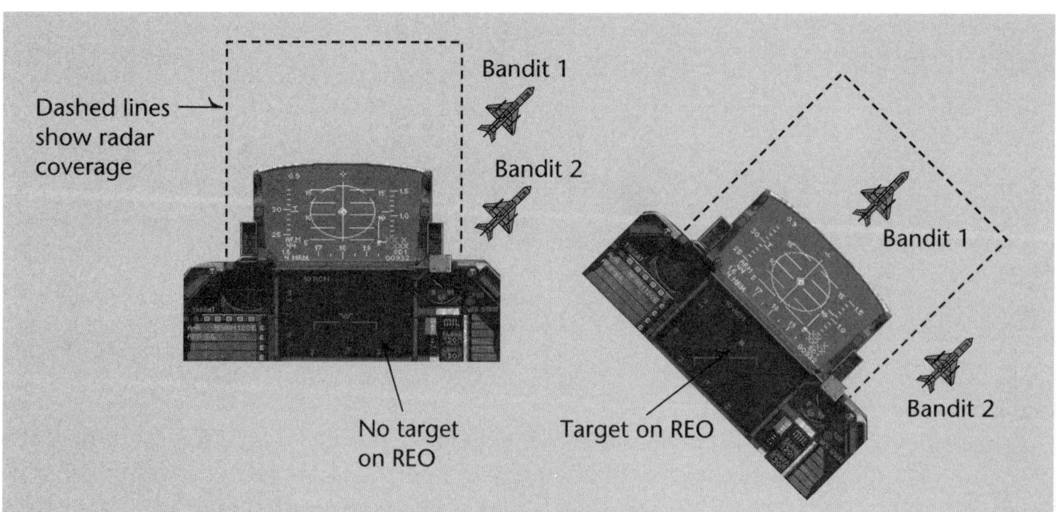

Figure 12-8 Employing 10°x40° Scan Mode

(never a good thing to do in combat) or pull high-G loads (and risk blacking out). Using the 10°x40° mode, however, simply banking the F-16 aligns the F-16 with the bandit's plane of travel, and places it within the radar scan.

> **TIP:** In general, during initial moments of combat, use the 20°x20° scan to locate targets anywhere in front of you, especially below you. Once you've singled out a target, continue to use the 20°x20° scan if he is making erratic maneuvers in both the vertical and horizontal planes. If the target is making hard break turns in an attempt to out turn you, switch to the 10°x40° scan and break toward the bandit.

New SEA Radar Mode

Because of the addition of anti-shipping missions in the Kurile Islands theater, an additional radar mode is required. The new SEA radar mode, selected by pressing F4, is custom designed for employing the Harpoon missile against ships. The SEA radar mode is also activated any time the Harpoon missile is selected. This mode is available only when flying the new FSX fighter (see notes on new aircraft later in this chapter).

Configuring SEA Radar SEA radar is usable only against ships and cannot be used against ground targets. SEA radar has four search ranges (10nm, 20nm, 40nm, and 80nm), selected by pressing F8, just like Hi-Fidelity Radar. As with other radar modes, pressing SHIFT-F8 reverses the selection order.

The distance the radar energy can travel is limited by the curvature of the Earth. The lower you fly, the quicker the curve of the earth will block your radar's view. Figure 12-9 shows the minimum altitudes required for each SEA radar range. Note that these numbers are relevant only to the simulation, and not accurate in the real world.

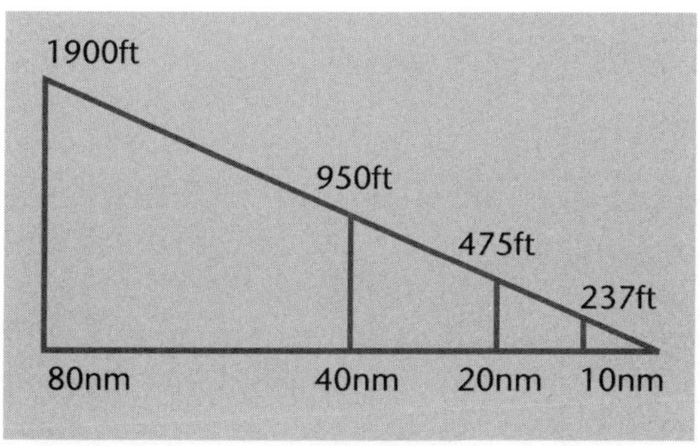

Figure 12-9 Minimum Altitudes Required Per SEA Radar Range Setting

Additionally, SEA radar has two magnification settings, 1x and 4x. Use F1 to increase magnification, use F2 to reduce magnification. The magnification level is displayed in the upper right corner of the REO, as shown in Figure 12-10.

SEA Radar REO SEA radar displays ships using three shades of green on the REO based on the amount of water the target ship displaces. Small ships displacing less than 20,000

tons are displayed in dim green. Medium sized ships displacing 20,000 to 40,000 tons are displayed in medium green. Large ships displacing over 40,000 tons are displayed in bright green. Before executing an anti-shipping mission, check the displacement of the target ship.

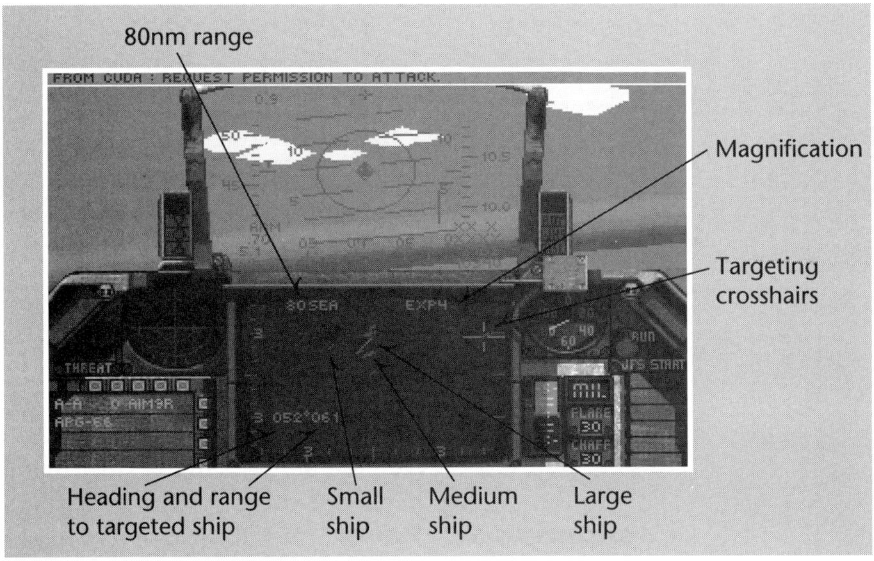

Figure 12-10 SEA Radar REO

Figure 12-10 shows a typical SEA radar display. The target ship is selected by pressing (T). The crosshairs will step through each contact as you press (T), then repeat. The data in the lower left corner of the REO is the heading and range to the target ship. Once a target is selected, SEA radar passes navigational information to your Harpoon missiles. Once the missile is fired, it relies solely on that data to find its target. Complete instructions on using the Harpoon missile are listed later in this chapter.

New Enemy Radar Threats

You are not the only one to receive new radar modes in Falcon 3.01. The Russian Navy, introduced in the Kurile Islands theater, brings several new early warning and missile guidance radars to the simulation. Tactics for defeating these new radars and associated surface-to-air missiles do not change from Falcon 3.0 to Falcon 3.01. Information displayed on your TWI, and the ranges at which these new systems can harass you, have changed. You will have to take into account longer-ranged radars (and the greater threat they present) when planning missions and understand the new radar codes displayed on your TWI during combat. New weapons and threats are discussed in the section titled New Weapons and Technology.

Threat-Warning Indicators

The operation of the TWI has changed in Falcon 3.01. While the TWI shows the approximate bearing to the enemy radar, it no longer gives accurate range information. Stronger signals are displayed closer to the center of the TWI, while weaker radars are displayed toward the outer edge. A strong SAM guidance radar 25 nautical miles away will be displayed closer to the center of the TWI than a weak air-to-air radar only 10 nautical miles away!

Campaign Mode Changes

New Theaters

Operation: Fighting Tiger introduces three new theaters of combat: Kurile Islands, Pakistan, and Korea. Each of these theaters includes only limited support from the U.S.—namely, your squadron. Unlike the Kuwaiti theater where you are a small part in a large U.S. military movement, your squadron is the lone American involvement in Operation: Fighting Tiger.

In all three new theaters, your squadron has been deployed to an unstable region to protect U.S. interests there. In each case, lack of domestic support for military intervention has been weighed against the value of political alliances with the warring factions. In all three theaters, massive military intervention has been ruled out in favor of a token, show-of-arms deployment. Because of your squadron's quality, it is believed that your squadron can provide the most military strength for the least military presence.

Limited Warfare So, in Operation: Fighting Tiger Campaigns, your squadron will fight alongside the local forces involved in the conflict without support from the massive U.S. war machine. Your missions will range from simply guarding U.S. and local civilian assets, to escorting local military forces and protecting them from their enemies, to actually executing strikes against key enemy installations.

Fight Smart Since you only have your 30 pilots and 18 F-16s to wage war, it is unlikely that you will be able to overwhelm the enemy simply by shear force. Although you do possess technologically advanced weapons, the introduction of the Russians in Operation: Fighting Tiger and their technology nullifies this advantage. Rather than projecting brute force, you must employ tactics learned in Chapter 9, *Red Flag: Advanced Flight School* and Chapter 10, *The Campaigns: Tactics and Military Doctrine.*

Campaign Difficulty

The difficulty of a Falcon 3.0 campaign was a fixed quantity. You could control the intelligence level of enemy forces from the Configuration screen, but nothing else. Falcon 3.01 has revised the way campaign difficulty is determined. You now have three difficulty options available on the Configuration screen: ESY (easy), STD (standard), and HRD (hard). The harder the campaign, the less often you will receive additional supplies. Additionally, enemy forces will make better use of their air assets, assigning aircraft to protect mobile forces and to defend high-value targets. The STD difficulty level in Falcon 3.01 is less difficult than an original Falcon 3.0 campaign.

> **NOTE:** The new difficulty option on the Configuration screen affects the original Falcon 3.0 theaters as well as the new Falcon 3.01 theaters.

Kurile Islands Specifics

By far, the majority of new features Falcon 3.01 introduces are specific to the Kurile Islands theater. The Kurile Islands theater deviates substantially from the other five theaters. Alongside the Kuwaiti theater (which is the only theater to offer widespread combat by a massive U.S. force), the Kurile Islands theater is probably the most interesting of the lot. During all missions in the Kurile Islands, you will fly the new FSX fighter rather than a standard F-16. For details on the FSX, see the section on new aircraft in this chapter.

Rules of Engagement The introduction of Rules of Engagment (ROE) sets the Kurile Islands theater apart from all others. All other theaters operate in a state of open warfare; any enemy detected can be fired upon. In the Kurile Islands, tensions between the U.S. and Russia and the threat of the conflict expanding from a simple Japanese-Russian tussle to a full blown super-power conflict preclude the use of unrestricted warfare. ROE are divided into three levels:

- Avoid Combat: Avoid combat with hostile forces at all cost. You may not fire upon hostile forces, even if they fire upon you first. Until AWACS issues clearance for you to engage enemy units, you may not fire, or return fire, *under any circumstances*. Your AWACS controller will inform you if clearance to engage enemy forces is received.
- Self defense: You may not initiate hostilites, but once fired upon, you may freely return fire. You may also fire upon enemy forces if you see them attack other friendly units.
- Weapons Free: You may attack all enemy units at your discretion.

There are three types of enemy forces in the Kurile theater: ground forces, naval forces, and air forces. Different ROE levels will be applied to the three ground forces. For example, you may be told you can freely attack any enemy ship encountered, but can only attack enemy aircraft if they fire upon you first. You may be told that you can attack enemy ground forces freely, but must avoid enemy aircraft at all costs. The ROE for each mission is listed in the mission briefing. Once the "weapons free" order is issued during a briefing, no ROE will be listed in subsequent briefings.

Violating ROE Computer pilots on both sides of the conflict, based on their flying and dogfighting ability, are susceptible to losing their nerve and opening fire under inappropriate circumstances. The higher the pilot's skill levels, the less likely he is to erroneously engage enemy units. When operating under restrictive ROE, be sure to assign your best dogfighting pilots.

Violating ROE can bring about serious consequences. Depending upon the nature of the violation, the offense may be overlooked, or the offending pilot may be court martialed and kicked out of the Air Force. If the offending pilot opened fire under tense situations, the violation may be ignored. If the offending pilot opened fire against a totally unsuspecting adversary, he will probably be severely punished.

> **NOTE:** Using the FALCONER utility included on the Falcon 3.0 Flight Disk, you can revoke court martials and reinstate offending pilots to flight status. You may also deal your own punishment using FALCNR, stripping offending pilots of rank and awards.

Not all consequences of ROE violations are distributed from your commanders. Enemy leaders may alter their attitudes toward U.S. forces according to the violation. Enemy pilots may become more likely to open fire on U.S. aircraft following an ROE violation, or enemy leaders may issue orders to freely attack U.S. fighters on sight. Violations by either side escalate the tension levels until eventually a state of open warfare exists.

Open warfare places your squadron at a disadvantage. Your 30 pilots and 18 aircraft are the only U.S. forces supplementing a Japanese contingent facing a numerically superior, and technologically equivalent Russian force. If the situation dissolves to unrestricted warfare, your squadron is greatly outnumbered. *It is in your best interest to avoid open warfare with the Russians in the Kurile Islands theater.*

War of Nerves Some missions may require you to repel enemy fighters without firing on them. This requires you to scare them away by maneuvering into a firing position on the bandit's six o'clock and obtaining a radar lock. Pilots with low flying and dogfighting abilities will easily be frightened away. More intelligent computer pilots will attempt to call your bluff. They will attempt to maneuver behind *you* and obtain a lock on *you* in order to scare *you* away.

That's where the danger comes in. When you have a perfect firing position behind a Su-27, the temptation to fire a Sidewinder up its tailpipe may be too great for you to resist. Likewise, computer pilots, based upon their skill levels, may be unable to overcome the same temptation. They may only *intend* to scare you away, but may decide to launch a missile at you when they obtain a good firing position. Pilots that lose their nerve may not turn to run, either. They may, instead, decide to open fire on you in (what they believe to be) self-defense.

When you are assigned a mission to repel enemy aircraft without firing on them, be ready for anything. Most times, the enemy aircraft will return home without incident. Other times they may attempt to radar lock you, just to call your bluff, then return home without incident. At other times, they may open fire without warning, or your own wingmen may lose nerve and start firing without permission. When this happens, all combatants will subsequently open fire, and missiles will fly in every direction!

> **WARNING:** During such tense missions, do not allow a bandit to remain on your six with a radar lock on you. The enemy pilot may only be trying to scare you, or he may be preparing to send a missile up your exhaust.

Interesting Missions These restricted combat missions are some of the most interesting Falcon 3.01 has to offer. You may fly the exact same mission to repel bandits over and over again, but the actions of the pilots, based on their skill levels, will vary each time. The same mission has potentially hundreds of different outcomes.

Anti-Shipping Strikes The introduction of the Russian fleet in the Kurile Islands brings another type of attack to your squadron, *anti-shipping strikes*. Anti-shipping strikes range from attacking small amphibious landing boats to attacking heavily armed *Kirov* class cruisers to attacking mighty *Kustenov* class aircraft carriers.

You use different types of weapons against ships based on your mission objectives. You can use Maverick missiles against small ships, or close range attacks on larger ships. It will take many Mavericks, though, to sink a *Kirov* class cruiser. You will sometimes use anti-radiation missiles (AGM-45 Shrike and AGM-88 HARM) to destroy ship based radars. Other times, you will use the new AGM-84 Harpoon missile to destroy large combat ships. By far, the Harpoon is your most effective weapon against ships, its 500 pound, penetrating warhead being large enough to sink even the mighty *Kustenov* class aircraft carriers.

How the Harpoon Works When a target is selected using the SEA radar, navigational data is passed to the missile before it is launched. Once launched, the Harpoon missile follows the navigation information for most of its flight. The missile dives and skims above the surface of the water until it closes within a few miles of the target. It then activates its onboard targeting radar and searches +/- 45° either side of its flight path for the target ship. If the ship has moved, or the navigational input was in error, and the target cannot be located, the missile begins a predetermined search pattern. Once the target is acquired the missile executes a pop-up attack, first climbing steeply, then diving on the target.

Firing the Harpoon Missile The AGM-84A Harpoon missile is an extremely easy, fire-and-forget weapon. It is completely dependent upon the SEA radar mode for initial targeting and navigational information, but the Harpoon requires (and accepts) no additional information from the launching aircraft once it has been fired. To fire, press BACKSPACE until the Harpoon is selected, which will also automatically select the SEA radar mode. Using the T key, designate the desired target, then press SPACEBAR or the joystick button to fire the weapon. The missile will fly to its target without additional intervention from you.

Standoff Attacks Using the Harpoon There's more to a successful attack than simply launching a weapon, though. The Harpoon missile is designed as a *standoff attack* weapon. It has a maximum range of 57 nautical miles, allowing you to attack ships from standoff ranges where the threat of counterattack by enemy SAMs is greatly reduced. Standoff attacks allow you to retreat after firing the weapon before enemy defenses can counterattack.

No SAM missile in Falcon 3.01 has a range equal to the Harpoon, but combat ships always operate in groups. Your target may be the *Kustenov* carrier 55 miles away, but an accompanying *Kirov* cruiser may be only 40 miles away. You are safely out of range from the *Kustenov*, but the *Kirov* may still launch SAMs at you. Also, enemy fighters will be vectored toward you once the incoming missile is detected.

> **TIP:** When executing a standoff attack, release the weapon (in this case, the Harpoon) and withdraw immediately, before enemy forces can counter.

Wingmen and Harpoons Wingmen will request your permission before firing Harpoon missiles. Once they are within range of the target, your wingman will repeatedly request permission to fire. Once you issue the SHIFT-E engagement order, he will fire all available Harpoons at the specified target. He will notify you over the radio each time he fires a Harpoon.

Designing a Standoff Attack To maximize effectiveness and your chances of survival, design your ingress flight path carefully. Place your first waypoint about 65 miles away from the target at an altitude under 2,000 feet. This will help you evade enemy search radars as you approach the target. Place your second waypoint at 10,000 to 15,000 feet about 50 miles from the target. Your third waypoint should direct you back toward your base at a low altitude of 2,000 feet. Place your fourth waypoint back at your base and land.

You will execute a steep climb between the first and second waypoints. Enemy forces will detect your presence, but you are already within weapons range. When you reach the second waypoint, select the Harpoon by pressing BACKSPACE and select an 80nm range for the SEA radar by pressing F8. Fire the weapon quickly, and press SHIFT-B to select the third waypoint. Dive quickly to evade incoming fighters and head for home.

Harpoon Weaknesses The Harpoon is not a magical, always successful weapon. The Harpoon can be defeated by enemy defenses. Once the missile activates its targeting radar, it is susceptible to jamming and chaff, just like any other radar-guided missile. Also, most warships carry *point defense guns*, sometimes called *Close In Weapons Systems* (CIWS). CIWS link rapid-fire guns capable of firing 3,000 (or more) 20mm (or larger) rounds per minute with a fire control radar. The radar system tracks the incoming Harpoon and creates a barrier of lead to destroy the inbound missile. Additionally, large cruisers and aircraft carriers may require up to four Harpoon hits to sink them. A single FSX can carry only two Harpoon missiles, thus requiring large numbers of dedicated aircraft to sink a large ship.

To ensure the destruction of the target, attempt to overwhelm enemy defenses. CIWS fire control radars use multiple antennas positioned along the ship. Each antenna can only track a fixed number of targets at one time. If many missiles approach the ship from one side, the CIWS' fire control radar may become overwhelmed. *Attempt to overwhelm CIWS fire control radars by firing large numbers of Harpoon missiles at once.*

Each CIWS gun has only a limited number of rounds. Multiple waves of incoming Harpoon missiles may deplete the CIWS ammunition supply, allowing subsquent waves to attack the ship unimpeded. If you have at least four FSX aircraft available for the attack, *attempt to overwhelm CIWS guns by firing large numbers of missiles in waves.*

Mission Success Parameters

The types of missions available in a campaign and their success requirements have been changed in Falcon 3.01. Many new missions have been added. The information presented in Chapter 10, *The Campaigns: Tactics and Military Doctrine*, remains valid for Falcon 3.0 campaigns, only. New success parameters for Falcon 3.01 missions are listed here.

1. Air Superiority

Key Phrase: "...sweep enemy airspace..."

Purpose: Clear an area of enemy aircraft.

Success Requirements: Destroy at least one enemy aircraft. You must destroy more enemy aircraft than you lose, and at least one of your fighters must survive.

2. Amphibious Landing CAP

Key Phrase: "Provide air cover for LSTs landing..."

Purpose: Protect troops making an amphibious landing from enemy strike aircraft.

Success Requirements: Remain on station for at least ten minutes. At least 50% of the Allied ground forces must survive.

3. Anti-Shipping Strike

Key Phrase: "Attack the Russian fleet. Your target is..."

Purpose: Damage enemy naval vessels.

Success Requirements: Score at least one hit on one ship of the target class.

4. Bombing Run

Key Phrase: "...bomb <target>..." or "...strike <target>..."

Purpose: Bomb the specified target.

Success Requirements: Destroy the target listed in the TARGET display on the Waypoint Setup screen. You may change the specified target at that location, but you may not move the waypoint to a new location.

5. Close Air Support

Key Phrase: "...ALO has request Tac air to..."

Purpose: Support ground troops.

Success Requirements: At the specified target, more enemy units must be destroyed than friendly units. If your pilots destroy seven enemy tanks, but enemy forces destroy eight friendly tanks, the mission will be a failure.

6. Combat Air Patrol (CAP)

Key Phrase: "...fly CAP..."

Purpose: Patrol an area and destroy inbound enemy aircraft.

Success Requirements: Stay on patrol for at least ten minutes. You must also destroy any enemy aircraft attacking friendly forces before they inflict allied casualties. At least one of your aircraft must survive.

7. Escort — Rendezvous

Key Phrase: "We have just received an SOS from..."

Purpose: Rendezvous with allied aircraft under attack and cover their retreat.

Success Requirements: At least one of the endangered allied aircraft must survive, and at least one of your aircraft must survive.

8. Escort — Strike or Bomber Aircraft

Key Phrase: "...escort <name of strike aircraft> on a strike against..."

Purpose: Ensure safety of attacking aircraft from enemy fighters and SAMs.
Success Requirements: You must fly within 10nm of the target waypoint. The strike aircraft must return without losing a single aircraft. At least one of your aircraft must survive the mission.

9. Escort — Trains

Key Phrase: "...troops are moving by train to..."
Purpose: Protect troops moving by railroad.
Success Requirements: The train must reach its destination without being damaged.

10. Escort — Transports

Key Phrase: "...milk run..."
Purpose: Ensure that cargo aircraft reach their destination.
Success Requirements: All of the transport aircraft must reach their destination and at least one of your aircraft must survive the mission.

11. Front Line Screen

Key Phrase: "Lead a flight of... on a defensive screen..."
Purpose: Destroy any enemy aircraft encountered in the specified zone.
Success Requirements: You must remain on patrol for at least 10 minutes. You must destroy any enemy aircraft encountered before they attack any allied positions. At least one of your aircraft must survive the mission.

12. Ground Strike

Key Phrase: "...destroy as many enemy units as possible."
Purpose: Strike enemy mobile ground forces.
Success Requirements: Destroy 20% of the enemy units at the target area.

13. High Asset Value CAP (HAVCAP)

Key Phrase: "Rendezvous with the E-3 AWACS at..."
Purpose: Protect the valuable E-3 from enemy fighters.
Success Requirements: Maintain the patrol for at least 10 minutes. The E-3 and at least one of your aircraft must survive the mission.

14. Interdiction — Airborne Assault

Key Phrase: "Intercept and eliminate the An-12s carrying the assault force."
Purpose: Stop enemy paratroopers from deploying.
Success Requirements: Shoot down an An-12 or prevent 75% of the paratroopers from landing.

15. Interdiction — Enemy Train

Key Phrase: "Do not allow the train to reach its destination."

Purpose: Stop an enemy train.

Success Requirements: Score at least one bomb or missile hit on the enemy train.

16. Scramble

Key Phrase: "AWACS has detected... enemy aircraft approaching..."

Purpose: Get airborne and intercept inbound hostile aircraft.

Success Requirements: Destroy all enemy aircraft listed in the briefing before they bomb allied positions. At least one of your aircaft must survive the mission.

17. Supply CAP

Key Phrase: "A helicopter force is ferrying supplies..."

Purpose: Protect resupply helicopters.

Success Requirements: At least two helicopters must deliver supplies and return to their base. You must remain on patrol for at least 10 minutes, and at least one of your aircraft must survive the mission.

18. Suppression of Enemy Air Defenses (SEAD) — Naval Forces

Key Phrase: "...strike against the Russian fleet and destroy at least one SAM or AAA system..."

Purpose: Disable enemy naval air defense systems.

Success Requirements: Destroy at least one naval anti-aircraft weapon. Using anti-radiation missiles to destroy radar systems is acceptable.

19. Suppression of Enemy Air Defenses (SEAD) — Ground Forces

Key Phrase: "Destroy as many anti-aircraft weapons..."

Purpose: Disable enemy land-based air defense systems.

Success Requirements: Destroy at least 33% of enemy anti-aircraft weapons at the specified target. Using anti-radiation missiles, as well as Maverick missiles or bombs is acceptable.

20. Recon in Force (Tactical Recon)

Key Phrase: "Fly to waypoint X, then return to base."

Purpose: Reconnoiter the specified region, destroying as many enemy units as possible.

Success Requirements: You must fly within 10nm of the specified destination, and at least one of your aircraft must survive the mission.

New Weapons and Technology

Both Allies and enemies receive new weapons and new technology. This section discusses the new additions, and their impact on your flight operations.

New Air-to-air Weapons

Both Allied and enemy forces receive new weapons in Falcon 3.01, although not all of them are available in every theater. The U.S. gains improved versions of the AMRAAM and Sidewinder, while the enemy forces gain three completely new missiles.

Allied Weapons

AIM-120E AMRAAM
Type: Active radar guidance
User: U.S. and Allies
Theaters: Kurile Islands only

The AIM-120E AMRAAM is an improved version of the standard AIM-120. Although the AIM-120 has a specified range of 25nm, it will never lock on to a target more than 15nm away. The new AIM-120E will lock and track targets at the maximum range of 25nm.

AIM-9R Sidewinder
Type: All-aspect heat-seeking
User: U.S. and Allies
Theaters: Kurile Islands only

This upgraded AIM-9P introduces very little new functionality. Its range has not been increased. Like the other versions of the Sidewinder, the AIM-9R will not lock a target farther than 5nm away, despite the stated 10nm range. The AIM-9R uses a larger acquisition circle on the HUD than the AIM-9P, making it easier to lock targets. However, the -9R seeker head does not scan the HUD like the -9M does. Therefore, the -9M is still easier to use in combat than the -9R. The Operation: Fighting Tiger manual states that the -9R should have a better hit-to-miss ratio than the -9M, though. In actual combat tests, little difference has been found between -9M and -9R performance.

Enemy Weapons

AA-9 Amos

Type: Midcourse SARH, terminal active-radar guidance
User: Russia only
Theaters: Kurile Islands only

This is a long-range, standoff intercept missile used by the MiG-31. This missile combines both SARH and active radar guidance. The launching aircraft locks onto the target aircraft and launches the missile. The missile flies to within 15nm of the target using SARH guidance from the launching aircraft (refer to Chapter 11, *Secrets and Tactics of the Enemy* for a discussion on SARH missiles). Then, the missile activates an onboard, active radar. For the remainder of the flight, the missile relies on its own guidance to destroy the target. See the section on missile evasion tips below for details on avoiding AA-9 missiles.

The AA-9 has an extremely long range. It is estimated to be effective from 45nm to 85nm, although, in actual combat, its usable range is probably much less. Like your missiles, Russian missiles suffer performance degradation under real-world circumstances.

AA-10 Alamo

Type: Both all-aspect heat-seeking and SARH versions exist.
User: Russia
Theaters: Kurile Islands only

The AA-10 has two versions, one with an all-aspect, heat-seeking tracking system, the other with an SARH guidance system. The heat-seeking version of the missile has a stated range of 5nm, but is probably only usable at ranges under 3nm in combat. The SARH version has a stated range of 18nm.

The SARH version will appear on your TWI, just like the Matra Super 530 and the AA-7 Apex. Normal evasion techniques presented in Chapter 11, Secrets and Tactics of the Enemy are usable against the SARH version of the AA-10. The heat-seeking version, like all other heat-seeking missiles, will not appear on your TWI. Use normal heat-seeking missile evasion techniques (also discussed in Chapter 11) to evade heat-seeking AA-10s.

AA-11 Archer
Type: All aspect heat-seeking
User: Russia
Theaters: Kurile Islands only

The AA-11 is the most advanced heat-seeking missile in the Russian arsenal. It can only be carried by the MiG-29, MiG-31, and Su-27. Its performance is extremely simliar to the AIM-9M, but it has a slightly shorter specified range of 8nm. In actuality, the AA-11 is rarely effective at ranges over 5 miles.

Missile Evasion Tips

The AA-10 and AA-11 missiles introduce no new technology, and normal procedures for evading heat-seeking missiles are effective against them. The AA-9, however, introduces active radar guidance, a serious threat to your aircraft.

For most of its flight, the AA-9 uses normal SARH guidance, and normal evasion tactics discussed in Chapter 11, *Secrets and Tactics of the Enemy* are effective against it. When the missile comes within 15nm of its target, however, it uses its own onboard radar to pursue the target. At this point, the launching aircraft no longer needs to maintain a lock on your aircraft, and renders the tactic of forcing the enemy to break radar lock ineffective.

The AA-9 still flies like a normal missile, though. It has the same weaknesses: it has a limited range that you may be able to escape, it has limited fuel and cannot maneuver near the end of its range, it has performance limits and hard evasive maneuvers may lose it, and it is susceptible to chaff and ECM.

To defeat this missile, you will still use the same techniques used against the AA-7 Apex, but you must use them at different times. The AA-9 has an extremely long range of 85nm. If fired from this range, the missile will operate in SARH mode for over 80% of its flight. If you can break the launching aircraft's lock on you, the AA-9 will spiral helplessly to the ground. At such long ranges, though, the launching aircraft is out of your AIM-120's range. You will have to rely on maneuvering, rather than counterattacking, to break the lock. If the missile is fired from long range, your best action is to turn, increase to full throttle, and run away from the missile. Even though it is extremely fast (mach 4.5+), if fired at maximum range, you should have no problems extending out of its range.

Once the AA-9 has closed to within 15nm, you have two choices: extend out of its range, or rely on maneuvers, chaff, and ECM. Once the missile closes to this range, successfully extending out of its range is highly unlikely, especially if the missile was fired less than 40nm away. Use chaff, ECM, and missile avoidance maneuvers to escape the AA-9 under most circumstances.

New Aircraft

Both the Allied and enemy forces receive new aircraft in Falcon 3.01, although not all of them are available in every theater. The new aircraft and their radar systems are listed below using the same table format used in Chapter 11, *Secrets and Tactics of the Enemy.*

F-5E Tiger II

Radar Name	Type	Range	Notes
APQ-159	I/J Band Continuous Wave. Appears as a 3 on TWI.	40nm	Maximum search range of 40nm, 12nm lock-on range.

As of 1992, 1,640 F-5A and F-5E variants remain in service in 31 countries. Being cheap, but extremely limited in capabilities, the F-5 never received much attention in the U.S., but quickly became a hit with smaller, limited-budget nations. The U.S. T-38 trainer is the only variant of the F-5 actively used by U.S. Forces. In Falcon 3.01, only friendly air forces fly F-5s.

J-7 Airguard

Radar Name	Type	Range	Notes
DARIN	Ground attack radar only. Appears as a 5 on TWI.	8nm	Provides air-to-air ranging information only.

The J-7, the Chinese version of the MiG-21, has an extremely limited air-to-air radar which can only provide bearing and range information to the target. No tracking lock-on capability exists. DARIN is designed for use with short range, heat-seeking air-to-air missiles.

Jaguar

Radar Name	Type	Range	Notes
Agave	Ground attack with limited air-to-air search capabilities. Appears as a 5 on TWI.	22nm	None

When the Jaguar was orginally designed in the mid 1960s, it incorporated the latest, state-of-the-art technologies. It was one of the most advanced aircraft of its day. It is now outdated and only produced (under license) by HAL of India.

MiG-31 "Foxhound"

Radar Name	Type	Range	Notes
Flash Dance	Pulse-Doppler. Displayed as a 1 on TWI.	Search: 165nm; tracking: 145nm	Can target four to six targets simultaneously.

The MiG-31 is a heavily modified, more capable version of the MiG-25. It can carry up to eight air-to-air missiles, including the AA-9 Amos which has a reported range of 85nm. This means the MiG-31 can radar lock and fire missiles at you while still outside of your radar range. Reports vary, but it can attack at least four targets simultaneously, and possibly as many as six.

Mirage 2000

Radar Name	Type	Range	Notes
None	Pulse-Doppler. Displayed as a 1 on TWI.	54nm	Uses U.S. technology.

The French-built Mirage 2000 has been sold to many nations hostile to the U.S. The radar is a joint U.S./French design and is significantly inferior to the F-16's APG-66. The Mirage 2000 employs a modern airframe, though, and outperforms the F-16 in certain regards such as a faster top speed, and a slower stall speed.

Mistubishi F-1

Radar Name	Type	Range	Notes
None	Multi-mode, ground attack system. Displayed as a 5 on TWI.	Unknown	Not designed for air-to-air combat.

The F-1 is a redesigned Jaguar ground attack fighter, with poor air-to-air abilities. The F-1 can carry Sidewinder missiles, but is ill-suited for aerial combat.

Unmanned Fighter (UMF)

Radar Name	Type	Range	Notes
Unknown	Unknown	Unknown	None

The UMF is a fictitious creation of Falcon 3.01 and has no counterpart in the real world at this time. The sparsely provided performance data in the Operation: Fighting Tiger manual is all that is known about this aircraft.

Q-5 Fantan

Radar Name	Type	Range	Notes
Unknown	Ground attack system. Displayed as a 5 on TWI.	Unknown	Not designed for air-to-air combat.

The Q-5 began development in 1958 as a follow-up to the MiG-19/J6 aircraft. The Chinese have upgraded this aircraft over the years, and the latest variants carry a digital avionics suite complete with a ground attack radar system. The Operation: Fighting Tiger manual incorrectly reports the Q-5 as a copy of the MiG-19. The MiG-19 is a single engine fighter while the Q-5 is a dual engine, ground attack aircraft.

New Ground Threats

In Falcon 3.0, there were only two types of ground-based radars: continuous wave and pulse-Doppler. In Falcon 3.01, this list has been expaned to six.

Table 12-1 lists the different radar types, how they appear on your TWI, and ranges of associated SAMs.

TWI Code	Radar Type	Usage
1	Continuous Wave	SAM guidance
2	Pulse-Doppler	Short-range SAM guidance
3	Continuous Wave	AAA fire control
4	Pulse-Doppler	Long-range SAM guidance
5	Pulse	Long-range search
6	Chirp	Long-range search and track

Table 12-1 TWI Codes and Associated Radars

The most revolutionary new radar type is the *chirp*. Normally, on pulse radars, a second pulse cannot be transmitted until the first pulse has returned, else the radar unit loses track of which return is associated with which pulse. Since pulses take a finite amount of time to travel, pulse radars must either limit their range or the rate of pulses. Limiting range has the obvious disadvantage, limiting the rate of pulses allows objects to move farther between pulses, possibly breaking contact.

Chirp radars vary the phase and frequency of transmitted pulses so that each return is easily associated with a transmitted pulse. Chirp radars can then transmit pulses at a high repitition rate (allowing better coverage of contacts) while travelling long ranges (allowing detection of more targets).

Conclusion

Operation: Fighting Tiger is more than an add-on module to Falcon 3.0; it is an advancement. Although Falcon 3.01 does not fix all bugs (most notably, it does not fix the HFR auto-range/elevation scan bug), it does solve most problems encountered in Falcon 3.0.

Appendix A
The Falcon 3 Flight Disk

Falcon 3: The Complete Handbook includes a disk, the Falcon 3.0 Flight Disk, that contains a demonstration version of Falcon 3.0, a host of mission files, and two utility programs that enhance Falcon 3.0. We have separated the contents of the Falcon 3 Flight Disk into four self-extracting compressed files. You can load one of the sections individually or load all four files at one time.

This appendix provides the instructions for loading each of the individual sections, along with a list of the extracted files. In the case of the mission files, we have provided a brief description of each mission and the chapter and section of the book where you use it.

The Falcon 3.0 Demonstration

The DEMO.BAT file calls a self-extracting archive file (RES001.EXE) which contains the Falcon 3.0 demonstration released by Spectrum Holobyte. This demonstration is a limited version of the full Falcon 3.0 package. The demonstration provides a challenge and shows the *look and feel* of the software. The demonstration files require 1.2 meg of free disk space.

> **WARNING:** Do not install the demonstration to the drive and directory where Falcon 3.0 resides (if installed). Doing so will overwrite critical files in the directory. Neither the demo nor the full version will operate properly in this case. If this happens, reinstall the full version.

Installing the Falcon 3.0 Demonstration

To install the demonstration:

- Place the companion disk in your 3.5-inch disk drive.
- Change to the flight disk drive by typing the appropriate drive letter (**A:** or **B:**) and press ENTER.

- To install the demonstration files, type **DEMO x:\subdir** and press ENTER, where x:\subdir is the drive and directory specification. Normally, this is C:\FALDEMO.

A message should appear to indicate the installation is taking place. The installation will take several seconds.

Checking the Demonstration Files

The following is a list of Falcon 3.0 demonstration files (filename and size) that are installed from the flight disk. To check the files, change to the drive you installed the files to by typing the drive letter (for example, C:) and press ENTER. Change to the install directory by typing **`CD \subdir`**, where subdir is the directory in which you installed the demonstration. Type **DIR** and press ENTER to see the directory.

Falcon 3.0 Demonstration Files

Filename		Size	Filename		Size
FALCON3	EXE	395684	ABOUT		51558
RESTART	004	56	TITLE		46460
FALCON3	DOC	22641	DEMOOBJ		16306
INS		1600	ANIMBACK		44157
MISSION	MIS	1544	TAXI	ANM	129445
DEMOALT		7680	DEMOMAP		1296
WAIT		5009	&FLARE		3840
INSTALL	EXE	2712	&GUNS1		3056
FLYBY		7168	&BIGBANG		8544
FALCON3	VOI	96441	COCKPIT		171255
OBJECTS		105270	&WITCH	NEW	154
TEXT		4329	&OCKON	NEW	802
INSTRUCT		52460	&3-MISSI	NEW	3706
FALCON3	MUS	20493	FALCON3	SND	1111

If you have a printer you can get more information about the demonstration by typing TYPE FALCON3.DOC > PRN: at the demonstration subdirectory.

Starting the Demonstration

Once the Falcon 3.0 demonstration has been installed, you can start the demo by performing the following:

- Change to the subdirectory in which you installed the demo (for example **`CD\FALDEMO`**).

- Type **FALCON3** and press ENTER.

The demonstration begins. You can get more information on using the Falcon 3.0 demonstration in Chapter 1, *The Falcon 3.0 Demonstration.*

The Red Flag Mission Files

The MISSION.BAT file calls a self-extracting archive file (RES002.EXE) which contains Red Flag Mission files. The mission files are used with lessons and exercises throughout the book. The mission files require approximately 60K of free disk space.

> **WARNING:** If you have created any missions that have the same filename as those that are included on the flight disk, you will be asked if you want to overwrite the file during installation. Answering Y will result in the loss of your original mission file. You can rename your mission files to prevent this.

Installing the Red Flag Mission Files

To install the mission files:

- Place the flight disk in your 3.5-inch disk drive.
- Change to the drive by typing the appropriate drive letter (A: or B:) and press ENTER.
- To install the Red Flag mission files, type **MISSION x:\subdir** and press ENTER, where x:\subdir is the Falcon 3.0 drive and directory specification. Normally, this is C:\FALCON3.

A message should appear to indicate the installation is taking place. The installation takes several seconds.

Checking the Mission Files

The following is a list of the Falcon 3.0 mission files along with the chapter and lesson that they are used in and a short description of the mission file.

Filename	Used in	Description
TAKEOFF RFM	Chapter 3 — Lesson 1	Learn the takeoff procedure
GFORCE RFM	Chapter 3 — Lesson 2	Effects of G-forces on flight
VIEWS RFM	Chapter 3 — Lesson 3	Learn the view keys
WAYPOINT RFM	Chapter 3 — Lesson 4	Learn how to follow waypoints
LANDING1 RFM	Chapter 3 — Lesson 5	Learn how to land — straight-in

Filename	Used in	Description
LANDING2 RFM	Chapter 3 — Lesson 5	Learn how to land — military
MANEUVER RFM	Chapter 3 — Lesson 6	Learn advanced maneuvers
NORTHWST RFM	Chapter 3 — Exercise 1	Flight exercise
LONGFLGT RFM	Chapter 3 — Exercise 2	Flight exercise
CANYON RFM	Chapter 3 — Exercise 3	Flight exercise
PADLOCK RFM	Chapter 4 — Lesson 1	Learn to use padlock view
SAD RFM	Chapter 4 — Lesson 2	Learn SAD mode radar
SAM RFM	Chapter 4 — Lesson 3	Learn SAM mode radar
TWI1 RFM	Chapter 4 — Lesson 4	Learn to use the TWI (aircraft)
TWI2 RFM	Chapter 4 — Lesson 4	Learn to use the TWI (SAM)
AVOID1 RFM	Chapter 4 — Lesson 5	Learn rear-aspect A-A avoidance
AVOID2 RFM	Chapter 4 — Lesson 5	Learn all-aspect A-A avoidance
AVOID3 RFM	Chapter 4 — Lesson 5	Learn SAM missile avoidance
GMRADAR RFM	Chapter 4 — Lesson 6	Learn to use GM radar mode
TARGETS RFM	Chapter 4 — Exercise 1	Radar exercise
AVOID4 RFM	Chapter 4 — Exercise 2	Radar exercise
GMSEARCH RFM	Chapter 4 — Exercise 3	Radar exercise
AIM120F RFM	Chapter 5 — Lesson 1	Learn to fire AIM120 A-A — head-on
AIM120R RFM	Chapter 5 — Lesson 1	Learn to fire AIM120 A-A — rear
AIM9M RFM	Chapter 5 — Lesson 2	Learn to fire AIM-9M A-A missile
AIM9P RFM	Chapter 5 — Lesson 3	Learn to fire AIM-9P A-A missile
MAVRICK1 RFM	Chapter 5 — Lesson 4	Learn to fire AGM-65B A-G missile
MAVRICK2 RFM	Chapter 5 — Lesson 4	Learn to fire AGM-65D A-G missile
ANTIRAD RFM	Chapter 5 — Lesson 5	Learn to fire AGM-88/AGM-45 A-G
LAUSTRAF RFM	Chapter 5 — Lesson 6	Learn to use Rocket Launcher/Cannon
MK82BOMB RFM	Chapter 5 — Lesson 7	Learn to use free-fall bombs
MK82DBMB RFM	Chapter 5 — Lesson 7	Learn to use free-fall bombs
MK83BOMB RFM	Chapter 5 — Lesson 7	Learn to use free-fall bombs
MK84BOMB RFM	Chapter 5 — Lesson 7	Learn to use free-fall bombs
GUIDED RFM	Chapter 5 — Lesson 8	Learn to use guided bombs (GBU-15s)
DURANDAL RFM	Chapter 5 — Lesson 9	Learn to use Durandals (BLU-107s)
CLUSTER RFM	Chapter 5 — Lesson 10	Learn to use cluster bombs (CBU-?)
WEAPON1 RFM	Chapter 5 — Exercise 1	Weapons exercise
WEAPON2 RFM	Chapter 5 — Exercise 2	Weapons exercise
WEAPON3 RFM	Chapter 5 — Exercise 3	Weapons exercise
CHAP8EX1 RFM	Chapter 8 — Exercise 1	Learn to use High Fidelity Radar
CHAP8EX2 RFM	Chapter 8 — Exercise 2	Learn to use High Fidelity Radar
LITEOUT RFM	Chapter 9 — Mission 1	Advanced Red Flag mission
IRONBRKR RFM	Chapter 9 — Mission 2	Advanced Red Flag mission
GRNDSHKR RFM	Chapter 9 — Mission 3	Advanced Red Flag mission
SNDBLSTR RFM	Chapter 9 — Mission 4	Advanced Red Flag mission
FNCEPOST RFM	Chapter 9 — Mission 5	Advanced Red Flag mission
FALNGSKY RFM	Chapter 9 — Mission 6	Advanced Red Flag mission
SKYSNTRY RFM	Chapter 9 — Mission 7	Advanced Red Flag mission
FNLEXAM1 RFM	Chapter 9 — Mission 8	Advanced Red Flag mission

Using the Red Flag Missions

You can load any of the above Red Flag missions using LOAD MISSION at the Red Flag control screen. Refer to the appropriate chapter for details on each mission.

Falcnr — Falcon Squadron Utility

The FALCNR.BAT file calls a self-extracting archive file (RES003.EXE) which contains the program files for the Falcnr squadron utility. The utility files require 215K of free disk space.

Installing the Falcnr Utility Files

To install the Falcnr files:

- Place the companion disk in your 3.5-inch disk drive.
- Change to the drive by typing the appropriate drive letter (A: or B:) and press ENTER.
- To install the Falcnr utility files, type **FALCNR x:\subdir** and press ENTER, where x:\subdir is the Falcon 3.0 drive and directory specification. Normally, this is C:\FALCON3.

A message should appear to indicate the installation is taking place. The installation takes several seconds.

Checking the Falcnr Files

The following is a list of the Falcnr files. The files will be intermixed with Falcon 3.0 program files. To verify a particular file is present, type **DIR** and the exact filename and press ENTER.

FALCNR	EXE	183624
FALCNR	DOC	19450
README	NOW	3219
F3	PAL	2779
F3	BAT	46
386TH	F3S	1980
387TH	F3S	1980
FSFORUM	SQN	252

The FALCNR.DOC and README.NOW files contain more information on the Falcnr squadron utility. Also, you can refer to Appendix C for more Falcnr information.

F3MAPS — Falcon 3.0 Customization

The F3MAPS.BAT file calls a self-extracting archive file (RES004.EXE) which contains the program files for the F3MAPS utility. The utility files require a minimum of 145K of free disk space.

Installing the F3MAPS Utility Files

To install the F3MAPS files:

- Place the flight disk in your 3.5-inch disk drive.
- Change to the drive by typing the appropriate drive letter (A: or B:) and press ENTER.
- To install the F3MAPS utility files, type **F3MAPS x:\subdir** and press ENTER, where x:\subdir is the Falcon 3.0 drive and directory specification. Normally, this is C:\FALCON3.

A message should appear to indicate the installation is taking place. The installation takes a few seconds.

Checking the F3MAPS Files

The following is a list of the F3MAPS files. The files will be intermixed with Falcon 3.0 program files. To verify a particular file is present, type **DIR** and the exact filename and press ENTER.

F3MAPS	EXE	117280
F3MAPS	DOC	20434
README	F3M	6085

The F3MAPS.DOC and README.F3M files contain more information on the F3MAPS utility. Also, you can refer to Appendix C for more F3MAPS information.

Appendix B
AIRCRAFT AND GROUND FORCES OF FALCON 3.0

This appendix breaks down all of the allied and enemy aircraft and ground forces in Falcon 3.0. Each aircraft or ground unit is shown as it appears in a Falcon 3.0 mission. We have listed the Threat Warning Indicator signature when applicable. The entries also provide the type of the aircraft or ground force unit.

Allied Aircraft

F-16 Fighting Falcon

Type : Fighter
TWI Signature: 2
Ceiling: 60,000 ft
Manufacturer: General Dynamics
Range: 2,415 nm
Crew: 1

FSX*

*This aircraft is available on the Operation: Fighting Tiger campaign disk

Type : Fighter
TWI Signature: 2
Ceiling: 60,000 ft
Manufacturer: General Dynamics
Range: 2,415 nm
Crew: 1

F-15 Eagle

Type : Fighter
TWI Signature: 1
Ceiling: 60,000 ft
Manufacturer: McDonnell Douglas
Range: 2,500 nm
Crew: 1

F-5E Tiger II*

*This aircraft is available on the Operation: Fighting Tiger campaign disk

Type: Fighter
TWI Signature: 3
Ceiling: 51,000 feet
Manufacturer: Northrop
Range: 1,300 nm
Crew: 1

F-14 Tomcat

Type : Fighter
TWI Signature: 1
Ceiling: 56,000 ft
Manufacturer: Grumman
Range: 1,750 nm
Crew: 2

FA-18 Hornet

Type: Fighter
TWI Signature: 1
Ceiling: 50,000 feet
Manufacturer: McDonnell Douglas
Range: 2,000 nm
Crew: 1

Mitsubishi F-1*

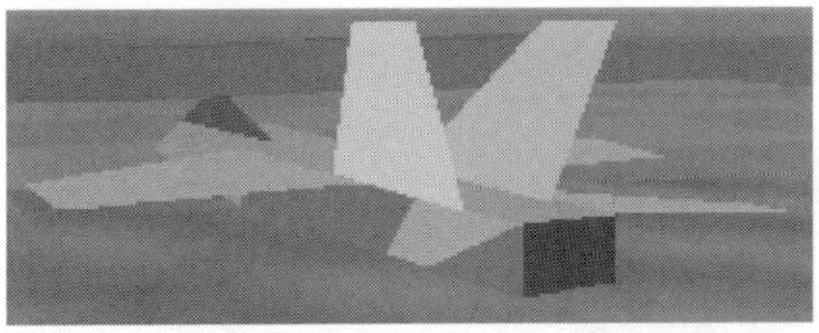

*This aircraft is available on the Operation: Fighting Tiger campaign disk

Type: Attack
TWI Signature: 5
Ceiling: 50,000 feet
Manufacturer: Mitsubishi
Range: 750 nm
Crew: 1

Tornado

Type: Strike
TWI Signature: 1
Ceiling: 70,000 feet
Manufacturer: Panavia
Range: 2,100 nm
Crew: 2

Kfir-C7

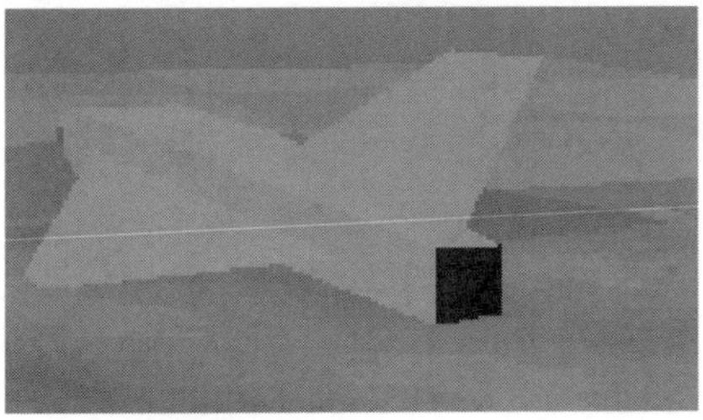

Type: Fighter
TWI Signature: 4
Ceiling: 58,000 feet
Manufacturer: Israel Aircraft Industries
Range: 1,600 nm
Crew: 1

A-4 Skyhawk

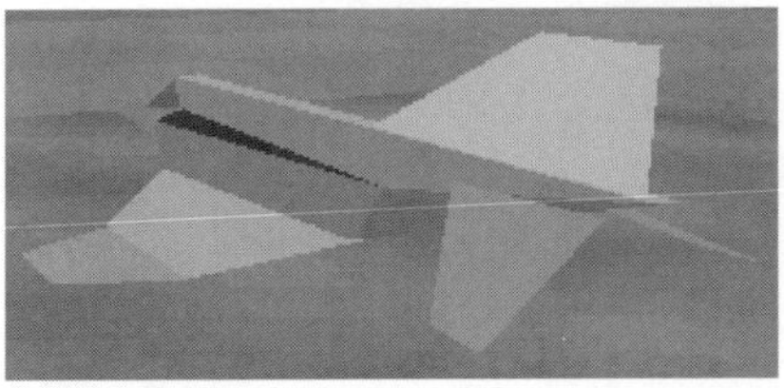

Type: Attack
TWI Signature: N/A
Ceiling: 42,000 feet
Manufacturer: McDonnell Douglas
Range: 800 nm
Crew: 1

F-111 Aardvark

Type: Bomber
TWI Signature: 2
Ceiling: 57,000 feet
Manufacturer: General Dynamics
Range: 3,000 nm
Crew: 2

A-10 Thunderbolt

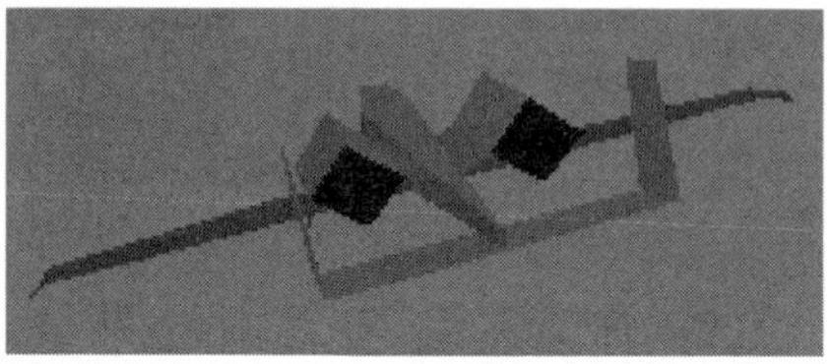

Type: Close Air Support
TWI Signature: N/A
Ceiling: 45,000 feet
Manufacturer: Fairchild
Range: 2,240 nm
Crew: 1

F-117A Stealth Fighter

Type: Bomber
TWI Signature: N/A
Ceiling: N/A
Manufacturer: Lockheed
Range: N/A
Crew: 1

AH-64 Apache

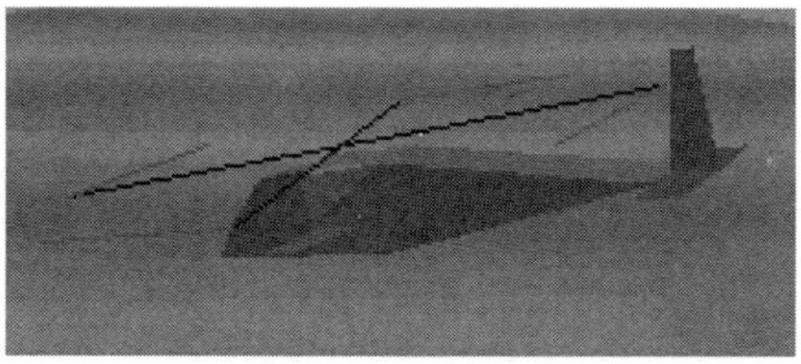

Type: Helicopter
TWI Signature: N/A
Ceiling: 21,000 feet
Manufacturer: McDonnell Douglas
Range: 1,100 nm
Crew: 2

UH-60 Black Hawk

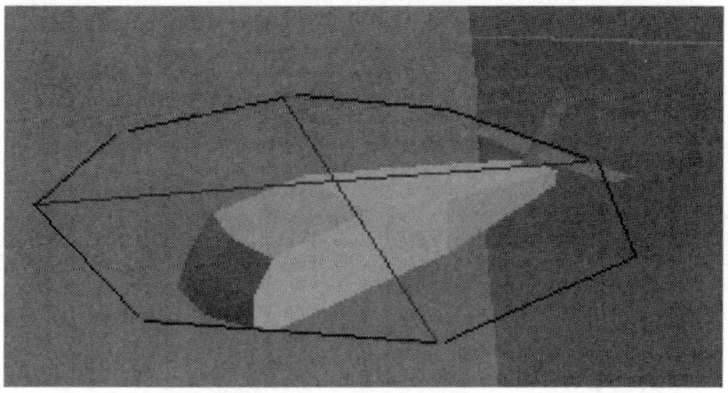

Type: Helicopter
TWI Signature: N/A
Ceiling: 19,000 feet
Manufacturer: Sikorsky
Range: 325 nm
Crew: 3

C-130 Hercules

Type: Transport
TWI Signature: N/A
Ceiling: 33,000 feet
Manufacturer: Lockheed
Range: 4,200 nm
Crew: 12

B-52 Stratofortress

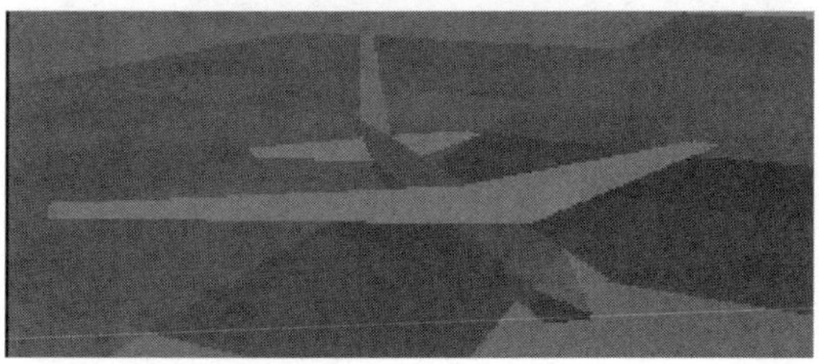

Type: Bomber
TWI Signature: 4
Ceiling: 55,000 feet
Manufacturer: Boeing
Range: 8,800 nm
Crew: 6

E-3

Type: AWACS
TWI Signature: 6
Ceiling: 30,000 feet
Manufacturer: Boeing
Range: 3,700 nm
Crew: 20

Allied Ground Forces

M1 Abrams

TWI Signature: N/A
Type: Tank

M2 Bradley

TWI Signature: N/A
Type: Mechanized Infantry

Allied Ground Troops

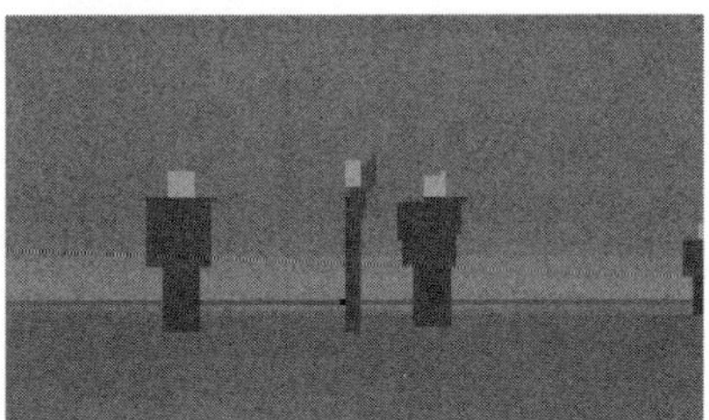

TWI Signature: N/A
Type: Infantry

Allied Truck

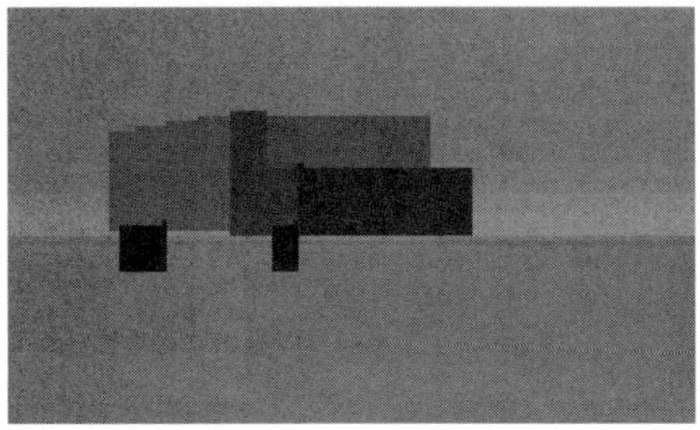

TWI Signature: N/A
Type: Transports

M163

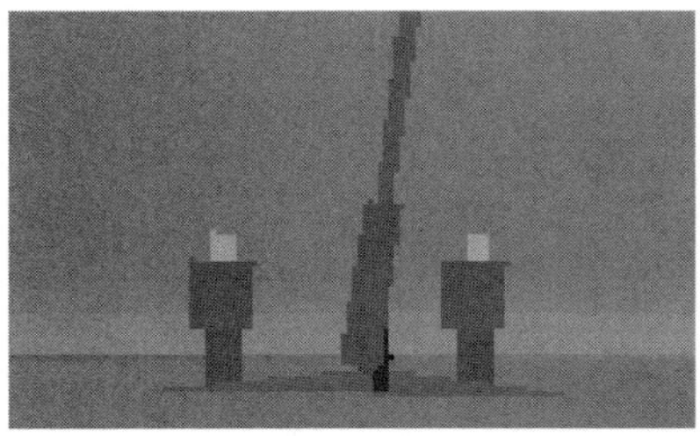

TWI Signature: N/A
Type: Artillery

Shahine

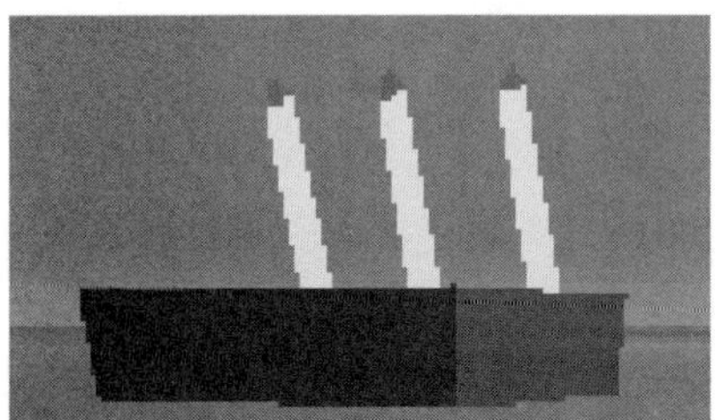

TWI Signature: 1
Type: SAM

Wildcat

TWI Signature: 1
Type: AAA

Enemy Aircraft

MiG-29 Fulcrum

Type: Fighter
TWI Signature: 1
Ceiling: 60,000 feet
Manufacturer: Mikoyan Gurevich
Range: 1,400 nm
Crew: 1

SU-27 Flanker

Type: Fighter
TWI Signature: 1
Ceiling: 60,000 feet
Manufacturer: Sukhoi
Range: 2,000 nm
Crew: 1

Mirage F1

Type: Fighter
TWI Signature: 4
Ceiling: 65,000 feet
Manufacturer: Dassault-Breguet
Range: 1,000 nm
Crew: 1

MiG-23 Flogger

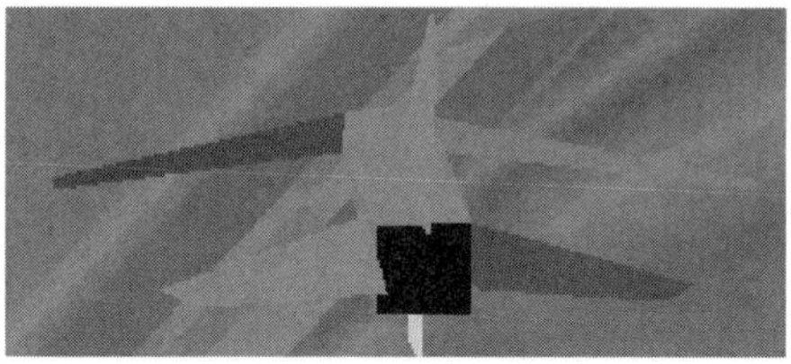

Type: Fighter
TWI Signature: 2
Ceiling: 60,000 feet
Manufacturer: Mikoyan Gurevich
Range 1,400 nm
Crew: 1

MiG-21 Fishbed

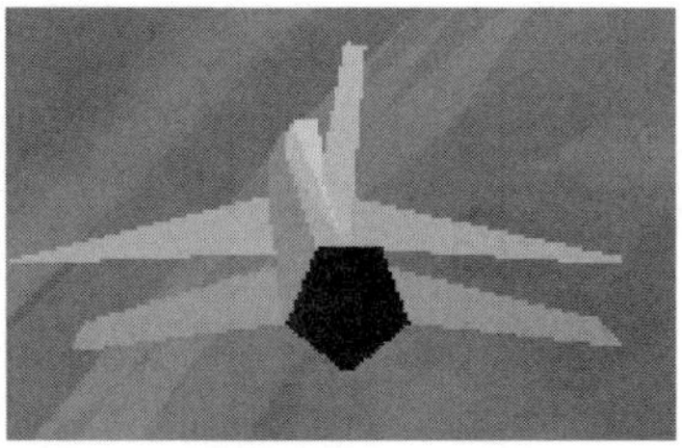

Type: Fighter
TWI Signature: 3
Ceiling: 59,000 feet
Manufacturer: Mikoyan Gurevich
Range: 1,500 nm
Crew: 1

Mirage 5

Type: Fighter
TWI Signature: 4
Ceiling: 55,000 feet
Manufacturer: Dassault-Breguet
Range: 1,400 nm
Crew: 1

SU-24 Fencer

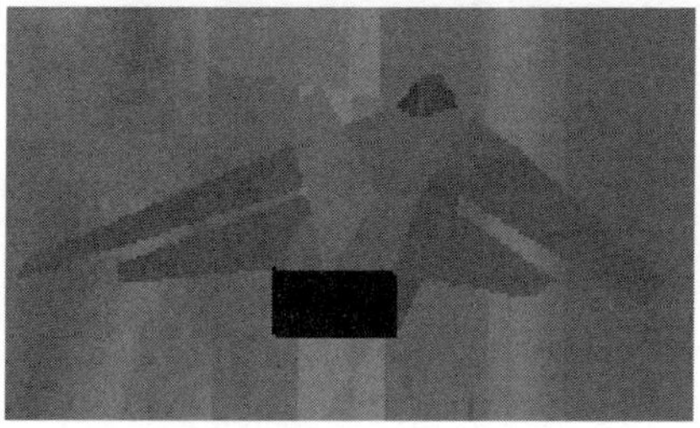

Type: Bomber
TWI Signature: 5
Ceiling: 57,000 feet
Manufacturer: Sukhoi
Range: 2,000 nm
Crew: 2

SA-342 Gazelle

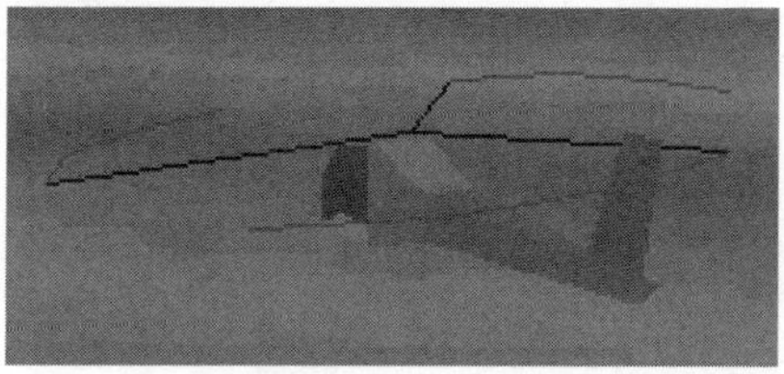

Type: Helicopter
TWI Signature: N/A
Ceiling: 13,500 feet
Manufacturer: Aérospatiale/Westland
Range: 360 nm
Crew: 2

MiG-27 Flogger

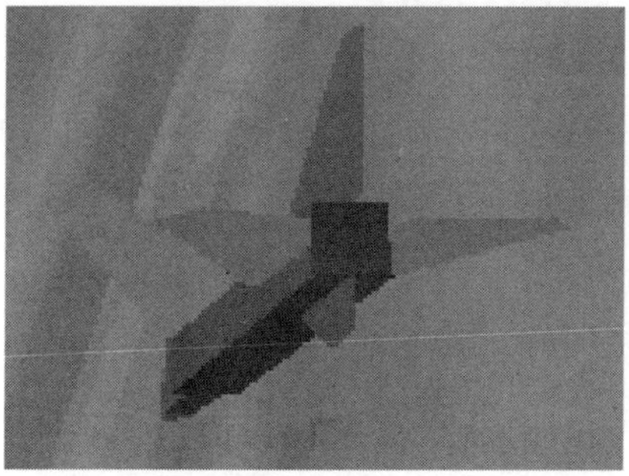

Type: Fighter
TWI Signature: 2
Ceiling: 55,000 feet
Manufacturer: Mikoyan Gurevich
Range: 1,350 nm
Crew: 1

J7 Airguard*

*This aircraft is available on the Operation: Fighting Tiger campaign disk

Type: Fighter
TWI Signature: 3
Ceiling: 60,000 feet
Manufacturer: Chengdu
Range: 1200 nm
Crew: 1

Q5 Fantan*

*This aircraft is available on the Operation: Fighting Tiger campaign disk

Type: Attack
TWI Signature: 5
Ceiling: 52,000 feet
Manufacturer: Nanchang
Range: 1080 nm
Crew: 1

AN-12 Cub

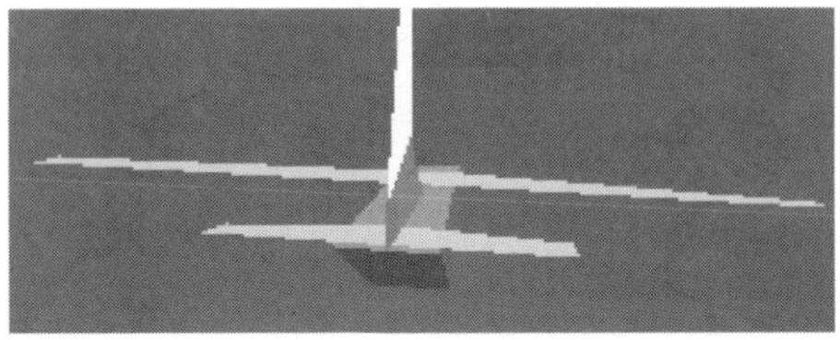

Type: Transport
TWI Signature: N/A
Ceiling: 33,000 feet
Manufacturer: Antonov
Range: 3,000 nm
Crew: 10

TU-22 Blinder

Type: Bomber
TWI Signature: N/A
Ceiling: 60,000 feet
Manufacturer: Tupolev
Range: N/A
Crew: 3

IL-76 Mainstay

Type: AWACS
TWI Signature: 6
Ceiling: 50,000 feet
Manufacturer: Ilyushin
Range: 3,500 nm
Crew: 15

Enemy Ground Forces

T-72

TWI Signature: N/A
Type: Tank

Enemy Truck

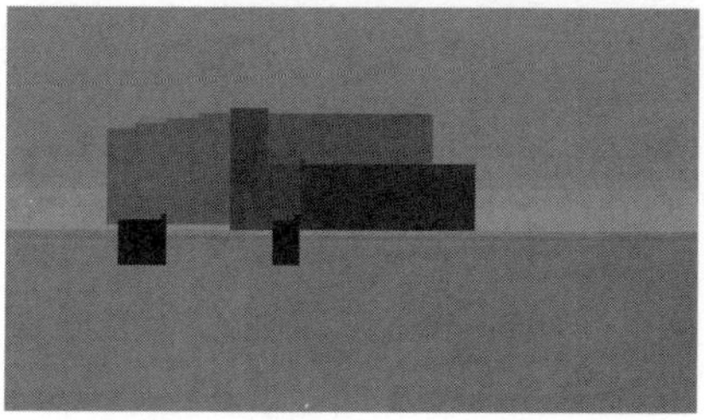

TWI Signature: N/A
Type: Transports

BMP-1

TWI Signature: N/A
Type: Mechanized Infantry

D-30

TWI Signature: N/A
Type: Artillery

SA-7 Squad

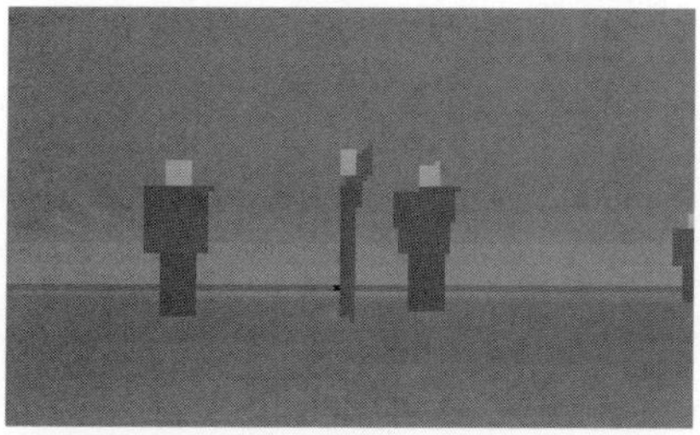

TWI Signature: N/A
Type: Infantry

SA-6

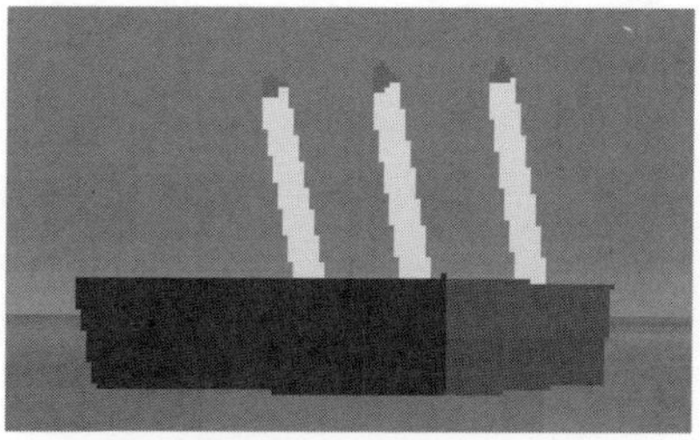

TWI Signature: 1
Type: SAM

ZSU-23-4

TWI Signature: 1
Type: AAA

Appendix C
Skunk Works' Utilities

As the old saying goes, you can't please everyone. Although the creators of Falcon 3.0 strove to meet both the functional and ergonomic requirements of most players, Falcon 3.0 pilots inevitably requested additional capabilities. Fortunately, dedicated members of CompuServe's FSFORUM, a forum devoted to PC flight simulators, decided to do something about these additional requests. Affectionately known as the FSFORUM Skunk Works (a reference to the Lockheed Skunk Works division, designer of numerous super-secret aircraft), this group developed several utilities to aid Falcon 3.0 pilots.

Many Falcon 3.0 tools are available from CompuServe's FSFORUM. Two of those utilities are included on the enclosed floppy disk. These are not demonstration programs; they are fully functional, intact versions. Each will be briefly discussed, then information on receiving upgrades and other utilities from CompuServe will be presented.

> **NOTE:** The tools on the included floppy disk require version Falcon 3.0D in order to execute. If you do not have Falcon 3.0D, please refer to Appendix E, *Falcon 3.0 Upgrades* for instructions on upgrading.

Falcnr: The Campaign Falconer

Falcnr, short for "Falconer," edits Falcon 3.0 squadron rosters and much more. Authored by Rob "Orinoco" Heittman, Falcnr includes the following features:

- Complete roster management—You can change the name, callsign, flying abilities, rank, fatigue value, and status of any pilot in any squadron.
- Printer interface—You can print a squadron roster showing each pilot's rank, name, callsign, fatigue value, and flying abilities.

- Auto-perfect option—You can set all pilots' attributes to 100 (maximum) with a single command.
- Auto-unfatigue—You can refresh all fatigued pilots with a single command.
- Awards and medals—Edit medals and awards pilots have received; you can give pilots additional awards, or remove unwarranted ones.
- Add your own picture to Falcon 3.0—Using a scanned picture of yourself you can assign your picture to any Falcon 3.0 pilot.
- Campaign stores management—You can adjust the number of weapons, the amount of fuel, and the number of aircraft available to your squadron, *any time during a campaign!*

Installing Falcnr

The Falcnr package consists of four files: FALCNR.EXE, FALCNR.DOC, README.FAL, and F3.PAL. These four files have been compressed, Refer to Appendix A for FALCNR installation instructions.

NOTE: Falcnr must be installed in the same directory as Falcon 3.0.

Not all of the Falcnr files are required at runtime. If you are stressed for space on your hard disk, you may want to print and delete the documentation files. If you need them again, you can extract them from the enclosed floppy. A brief description of each file follows:

- FALCNR.EXE—This is the executable file. Start Falcnr by executing this file.
- README.NOW—This is a simple text file containing important, last minute notes. Read this file using your favorite text editor.
- FALCNR.DOC—This is a simple text file containing complete instructions and notes regarding Falcnr. *It is highly recommended you read this file!*
- F3.PAL—This is a binary file containing data on the color palette used by Falcon 3.0. Falcnr needs this file when inserting additional faces into a Falcon 3.0 squadron.

Executing Falcnr

Execute Falcnr by running the executable file:

```
C:\FALCON3> FALCNR
```

The first time Falcnr is run, it displays the following message:

```
FALCONER will make a duplicate of your PILOT.BIN file in a file named PILOT.ABK.
This file must exist for FALCONER to run, since FALCONER permanently modifies
PILOT.BIN when adding new pilot faces. To restore the stock pilot faces, you may
copy PILOT.ABK back over PILOT.BIN.
        The duplicate file will be made and FALCONER will terminate. Run
FALCONER again to begin editing squadrons and campaigns.
```

Execute Falcnr again to begin editing squadrons and campaigns.

Pull-Down Menu Interface

Falcnr uses a standard, pull-down menu interface with both mouse and keyboard access. Mouse users need only to click on the desired actions; keyboard users access functions through a system of *hot keys*. Each menu item has one capitalized, yellow letter. Pressing ALT plus that letter executes that function. There are four main menus: *File, Edit, Reports,* and *Campaign.*

- File—This menu allows you to open a squadron, save a squadron, and exit the program. *You must open a squadron to begin editing, and you must save it after editing to preserve your changes.*
- Edit—This menu allows interactive editing of individual pilots, assignment of replacement pilots, and several single-step editing commands.
- Reports—This menu allows you to print squadron rosters.
- Campaign—This menu allows you to edit campaign data, such as the number of available aircraft, amount of fuel remaining, and the number of weapons available.

Using Falcnr

Falcnr lets you effectively name and manage your pilots, as well as reverse the effects of critical mistakes. For example, if your three best pilots were killed on a mission, you can use Falcnr to resurrect them, replace their destroyed aircraft, and replace the lost ordnance to your supply depot.

Falcon 3.0 automatically assigns awards and court-martials pilots. Falcnr allows you, the squadron commanding officer, to also do these tasks. You can give awards to any pilot you feel deserved them, revoke awards automatically given by Falcon 3.0, court-martial pilots who perform poorly, or revoke court-martials allocated by Falcon 3.0.

You can easily transfer pilots between squadrons. Falcnr allows you to *export* the data regarding a single pilot to an external file, then *import* that data into a different squadron. Lastly, if you have a scanned picture of yourself in PCX format, Falcnr can import your picture into Falcon 3.0!

Conclusion

Falcnr is an excellent utility allowing you versatile control over your squadron. With Falcnr in your arsenal, you are truly a squadron commander, with the ability to edit and manage your pilots and campaigns. The author of this excellent tool, Rob "Orinoco" Heittman, can be contacted at CompuServe userid: 72700,1067.

F3maps — Control Your Environment

F3maps, authored by Greg Prete, configures Falcon 3.0 to suit your individual tastes. F3maps actually patches the Falcon 3.0 code, allowing you to adjust features to your individual tastes. F3maps has the following features:

- Change maps used for Red Flag and Instant Action missions—Normally, all Red Flag missions occur at Nellis AFB, and all Instant Action missions occur in the Kuwaiti theater. Using F3maps, you can select any available theater for use with Red Flag or Instant Action.

- Decode Red Flag missions—View the data within Red Flag missions as text, allowing you to explore Red Flag missions without starting Falcon 3.0.

- HUD declutter option—Numerous static displays are placed on the HUD in an attempt to clarify the meanings of HUD symbols. F3maps turns these static displays off, allowing greater visual clarity.

- Disable ILS view shift—Whenever the ILS is engaged, Falcon 3.0 automatically (and disturbingly) alters the forward viewing angle. If you find this view shift disorienting, F3maps will disable the view shift. This feature was developed by Steve Kramp and incorporated into F3maps by Greg Prete.

- Adjust default view magnification—Falcon 3.0 always resets the view magnification to 2X at the start of each mission, requiring you to manually change it during every mission. F3maps will adjust the default magnification factor to 1X, 2X, 4X, or 8X.

- Automatic Red Flag mission generator—F3maps will automatically create completely random Red Flag missions (in the currently selected theater) to maximize your training and hone your combat skills.

> **NOTE:** All of these options are completely user selectable and can be reversed at any time. While F3maps does patch the Falcon 3.0 code, all changes are reversible by F3maps.

Installing F3maps

The F3maps package consists of three files: F3MAPS.EXE, F3MAPS.DOC, and README.F3M. Like Falcnr, refer to Appendix A for F3MAPS installation instructions.

To run properly, F3maps must be installed in the same directory as Falcon 3.0. F3maps installs the following files in your Falcon 3.0 directory:

- F3MAPS.EXE—The executable file. Execute this file to start F3maps.
- README.F3M—This is a simple text file containing last-minute, important release notes.
- F3MAPS.DOC—This is a simple text file containing complete F3maps documentation. *It is strongly recommended you read this file prior to executing F3maps.*

Executing F3maps

Execute F3maps by the following command:

```
C:\FALCON3>  F3MAPS
```

F3maps displays an initial banner, then you may begin editing.

Pull-down Menu Interface

F3maps also uses a standard pull-down menu interface with both mouse and keyboard access. Mouse users need only to click on the desired menu action. Each menu item has a capitalized, red letter. Keyboard users access menu functions by pressing ALT in conjunction with the highlighted letter. F3maps has four main menus, *File, Utilities, Windows,* and *Help.*

- File—This menu allows you to view a text file, change the current directory, execute Falcnr without exiting F3maps, and exit.
- Utilities—This menu is the heart of F3maps. All of F3maps' functions

are accessed from this group.

- Windows—This menu allows basic control over F3maps windows.
- Help—This menu allows you to read F3maps' documentation file and information banner.

Conclusion

F3maps configures Falcon 3.0 to *your* specifications! Adjust view magnification, HUD options, and view shifting to meet your individual requirements. F3maps allows you to tailor Falcon 3.0 and maximize your flying abilities! Greg Prete, the author of F3maps, can be reached at CompuServe userid: 70720,2566.

> **NOTE:** Both Falcnr and F3maps are packaged with The Waite Group's *Falcon 3.0: The Complete Handbook* with the full consent of the authors. Both of these programs are provided as freeware; you may freely distribute these tools, but not for profit.

Other Falcon 3.0 Utilities

Many other excellent Falcon 3.0 utilities can be obtained through CompuServe. If you have a CompuServe account, type **GO FSFORUM** at any prompt, then check out section eight, Modern Air Combat. Section eight is dedicated to flight simulators modeling modern combat aircraft. You'll find many Falcon 3.0 utilities in the associated section eight library.

Operation: Fighting Tiger

The versions of Falcnr and F3maps supplied on the Falcon 3.0 Flight Disk are incompatible with Operation: Fighting Tiger. Upgraded versions of these utilities are not available at the time of this writing. In the event that new versions become available, you can obtain them from Lib 8: Modern Air Combat in CompuServe's FSFORUM. Use the instructions supplied with your CompuServe account and your telecommunications program to download programs from CompuServe.

Appendix D
Combat Data Tables

The information in this section will provide you with information you need in battle. The combat reference tables summarize basic enemy aircraft information. It is designed to provide data on enemy aircraft performance and weapons ranges at a glance based on two key attributes: aircraft type and onboard radar type. Next, the threat warning table summarizes TWI threat codes from ground radars and matches them to missile systems. Finally, the fuel calculation table helps you determine how much fuel is required to complete your mission.

Using The Combat Reference Table

When an enemy radar source is first detected on your TWI, look down the Threat Number column of the following table to determine the various types of aircraft this threat could be. Then read the various rows from left to right to see a summary of that aircraft's offensive and defensive capabilities.

When you have visually identified an enemy aircraft, look down the Aircraft column until you find the entry for that aircraft. Then read that row from left to right to see a summary of that aircraft's offensive and defensive capabilities.

Attribute Summary

The meaning of each attribute and the possible values follow:

- **Aircraft**—The name and NATO designation for each enemy aircraft.
- **Threat Number**—The number displayed on your TWI when that particular aircraft activates its radar. "—" means this aircraft does not have radar.
- **Type**—The type of aircraft. Fighters are divided into two classes, Fighter A and Fighter B. Fighter A aircraft equal or exceed the capabilities of your F-16. Fighter B aircraft are inferior to your F-16.
- **RH missile**—The type and range of radar-homing, air-to-air missiles carried by that aircraft. SARH means semi-active radar homing. "—" means that aircraft cannot carry radar-guided, air-to-air missiles.
- **IR missile**—The type and range of heat-seeking, air-to-air missiles carried by that aircraft. Missiles are classified as all- or rear-aspect, followed by maximum range. "—" means that aircraft cannot carry heat-seeking, air-to-air missiles.
- **Gun**—If that type of aircraft carries a gun, the maximum range of that gun is given. Tail mounted guns are noted. A "—" indicates that aircraft does not have a gun.
- **Max Spd**—The maximum speed of that aircraft. Supersonic aircraft are listed in *Mach numbers* (the aircraft's top speed divided by the speed of sound), subsonic aircraft are listed in miles-per-hour.

Aircraft	Threat Number	Type	RH Missile	IR Missile	Gun	Max Spd
AN-12 "Cub"	—	Transport	—	—	Two tail mounted; 1 mile range	480mph
IL-76 "Mainstay"	6	AWACS	—	—	—	530mph
J-7 "Airguard"	3	Fighter B	—	All-aspect; 5 miles	1.5 miles	Mach 2.05
Jaguar	5	Ground Attack	—	All-aspect; 10 miles	1.5 miles	Mach 1.6
Mi-24 "Hind"	—	Attack helicopter	—	—	Multiple cannons	210mph
MiG-19 "Farmer"	3	Fighter B	—	Rear-aspect; 5 miles	1.5 miles	Mach 1.45
MiG-21 "Fishbed"	3	Fighter B	SARH 25 miles	All-aspect; 5 miles	1.5 miles	Mach 2.1
MiG-23 "Flogger-B"	2	Fighter B	SARH 25 miles	All-aspect; 5 miles	1.5 miles	Mach 2.35
MiG-25 "Foxbat"	2	Fighter B	SARH 25 miles	All-aspect; 5 miles	—	Mach 2.82
MiG-27 "Flogger - D and -J"	2	Ground Attack	—	Rear-aspect; 5 miles	1.5 miles	Mach 1.75
MiG-29 "Fulcrum"	1	Fighter A	SARH 25 miles	All-aspect; 5 miles	1.5 miles	Mach 2.3

Table D-1 The Combat Reference Table (*continued*)

Aircraft	Threat Number	Type	RH Missile	IR Missile	Gun	Max Spd
MiG-31 "Fox-hound"	1	Fighter A	SARH 85 miles	All-aspect; 8 miles	1.5 miles	Mach 2.4
Mirage III	4	Fighter B	SARH 22 miles	All-aspect; 6 miles	1.5 miles	Mach 2.2
Mirage V	4	Fighter B	SARH 22 miles	All-aspect; 6 miles	1.5 miles	Mach 2.2
Mirage F1	4	Fighter A	SARH 22 miles	All-aspect; 6 miles	1.5 miles	Mach 2.2
Mirage 2000	1	Fighter A	SARH 22 miles	All-aspect; 6 miles	1.5 miles	Mach 2.35
Q-5 "Fantan"	5	Ground Attack	—	—	1.5 miles	Mach 1.5
Sa-342 "Gazelle"	—	Helicopter	—	—	1.5 miles	174 mph
Su-24 "Fencer"	5	Ground Attack	—	—	1.5 miles	Mach 2.2
Su-25 "Frogfoot"	—	Ground Attack	—	All-aspect; 5 miles	1.5 miles	Mach 0.8
Su-27 "Flanker"	1	Fighter A	SARH 25 miles	All-aspect; 5 miles	1.5 miles	Mach 2.3
Tu-22 "Blinder"	—	Bomber	—	—	Rear mounted 1.5 miles	Mach 1.4
Unmanned Fighter "UMF"	1	Fighter A	May not be allowed	All-aspect; 8 miles	1.5 miles	Unknown

Table D-1 The Combat Reference Table

Threat Warning Table

Table D-2, the threat warning table summarizes all ground based radars used in Falcon 3.1. This table has little application in Falcon 3.0 since Falcon 3.0 uses only two types of ground radars for all weapon systems. Those two radar types have not changed in Falcon 3.1, but three additional radars have been added.

For each entry, the radar type, name, and associated surface-to-air weapons are listed. In cases where multiple radar names use the same TWI code, the table includes a separate entry for each radar. Radar types are listed as CW (continuous wave), Pulse (pulse-Doppler) or Chirp.

TWI Code	Radar Type	Radar Name	Weapon System	Missile Range altitude in Feet	Max Missile	Missile Speed	Notes
1	CW	Straight Flush	SA-6	30nm	47,000	Mach 2.5	Mobile land based
2	Pulse	Land Roll	SA-8	10nm	20,000	Mach 2.0	Mobile land based
2	Pulse	Pop Group	SA-N-4	8nm	39,000	Mach 3.0	Ship based
2	Pulse	Cross Swords	SA-N-9	8nm	39,000	Mach 2.0	Ship based
3	CW	Bass Tilt	AAA Fire Control	1nm	2,000 I	—	Mobile and and ship based
4	Pulse	Pet Hand	SA-4	44nm	80,000	Mach 2.5	Fixed land bases
4	Pulse	Top Pair/Steer /Dome	SA-N-6	54nm	100,000	Mach 6	Kirov class cruisers
5	Pulse	Long Track	—	—	—	—	Search Radar
5	Pulse	Strut Pair	—	—	—	—	Search Radar
6	Chirp	Sky Watch	—	—	—	—	Used for long range detection

Table D-2 The Threat Warning Table

Fuel Usage Tables

The following fuel usage tables are derived from the Operation: Fighting Tiger manual and lists the maximum range of an F-16 carrying different amounts of fuel at different drag values. The drag values are specified on the Load Armaments Screen inside the program. These values are only valid for Complex and High Fidelity flight models. The Moderate flight model increases fuel range by 15%, the Simple flight model increases fuel range by 25%.

The additional tables explain how fuel range is modified dependant upon the altitude and speed you fly at. Please note that these values are approximate. Based on fuel consumption during flight, releasing weapons, and varying speed, actual mileage may vary.

Calculating Fuel Requirements

The fuel usage table specifies the base amount of fuel required to fly a mission at a speed of 450 knots and an altitude of 8,000 feet. Since this profile will rarely meet your needs, and since flying at different speeds and altitudes cause fuel requirements to change, you must first determine your *Corrected Flight Range* (CFR) based upon your planned flight profile. Your CFR is the distance that your engine actually thinks it must fly based upon the amount of fuel it is consuming. You must equip your aircraft with enough fuel to fly the CFR, regardless of what the actual distance to the target is.

Airspeed Modification Table

Table D-3 lists the modification of fuel range based upon the speed you fly. High speeds markedly increase your range.

Modification Factor	350kts	450kts	550kts	630kts
	1.05	1	0.91	.83

Table D-3 Airspeed Modification Table

Altitude Modification Table

Altitude also effects fuel usage, as shown in table D-4. Flying at high altitude greatly increases the amount of fuel consumed.

Modification Factor	500ft	8,000ft	20,000ft	30,000ft	40,000ft
	0.83	1.0	1.67	2.5	3.33

Table D-4 Altitude Modification Table

Calculating CFR

Using the STRAT mode of the Edit Waypoints screen, determine the approximate distance to the target. Determine the average speed at which you will fly. Determine what altitude you will spend the most time flying at. This your planned flight profile.

Multiply the planned flight range to the target by the altitude and airspeed modification values. This produces your the CFR, number which indicates your flight distance taking modifications into account. For example, suppose you are going to fly 400nm at 550kts and 20,000 feet with a gross weight of 24,000 pounds and a drag factor of 101. This configuration yields an CFR of 607.88nm. Even though you are only flying 400nm, because of your flight profile, your engine will require 607.88nm worth of fuel. Now, refer to Table D-5, The Fuel Usage Table on the next page.

Fuel Usage Table

This table specifies the F-16's fuel radius based upon the weight and drag factor per available fuel options. Check your weight and drag factors on the Load Armament screen. Find the weight and drag combination in Table D-5, The Fuel Usage Table that closest matches your configuration. Read across the appropriate weight/drag row until you find the first range that *exceeds the CFR value* previously calculated.

Drag and Weight	Internal only	Internal + Centerline & Wing	Internal + Wing	Internal, Centerline,
Drag = 22 @ 20,113 lbs	450nm	575nm	—	—
Drag = 100 @ 23,500 lbs	420nm	540 nm	710nm	—
Drag = 200 @ 26,000 lbs	370nm	475nm	625nm	730nm
Drag = 400 @ 31,500 lbs	290nm	370nm	490nm	575nm

Table D-5 Fuel UsageTtable

In the example, we calcuated a CFR of 607.88nm. Supposing we have a weight of 24,000 lbs at a drag factor of 101, the second row of the table is the closest match. Moving across the table, the third entry has a range of 710nm using wing tanks in addition to internal fuel. This means, for our example, to complete the mission you will require wing tanks in addition to your combat load.

> **NOTE:** If you are flying using the Simple flight model, increase the range values in the Fuel Usage Table by 25%. If you are flying using the Moderate flight model, increase the range values in the Fuel Usage table by 15%.

Appendix E
Falcon 3.0 Upgrade Information

Falcon 3.0 Upgrades

With the arrival Operation: Fighting Tiger, there are three versions of the Falcon 3.0 program file which are compatible with this book: 3.0D, 3.0E, and 3.01. Using prior versions of Falcon 3.0 may produce results inconsistent with the text of this book.

Fixes incorporated in Falcon 3.0D resolve most of the critical, playblocking Falcon 3.0 bugs. Falcon 3.0E contains minor bug fixes not addressed in Falcon 3.0D. Falcon 3.01 includes all the previous bug fixes and adds new, unique features not found in either Falcon 3.0D or Falcon 3.0E; it is the program file provided with Spectrum Holobyte's Operation: Fighting Tiger upgrade, described in Chapter 12. Upgrading to Falcon 3.0D or Falcon 3.0E can be accomplished by registered Falcon 3.0 owners without charge. Falcon 3.01 is only available commercially as part of the Operation: Fighting Tiger package.

Determining What Version You Have

If you purchased your copy of Falcon 3.0 prior to June 1992, you probably do not have Falcon 3.0D. Falcon 3.0E should be available after September 1992. You can determine which version you have by checking the version display on the Credits screen.

When Falcon 3.0 initializes, after the opening animation, you see an image of a MiG-29 with an F-16 tucked closely behind as the names of the developers are displayed. This is the Credits screen. In the lower right-hand corner, the version number is displayed as Falcon 3.0, Falcon 3.0A, Falcon 3.0C, Falcon 3.0D, or Falcon 3.0E. If you do not have Falcon 3.0D or later, you should upgrade.

WARNING: Falcon 3.0B is a bogus version distributed on bulletin board systems that contains a virus. Falcon 3.0B is not an official product of Spectrum Holobyte and should be avoided.

Obtaining the Falcon 3.0 Upgrade

There is no charge associated with upgrading to Falcon 3.0d or Falcon 3.0E. Spectrum Holobyte distributes the Falcon 3.0D upgrade to registered users free of charge. Three ways to obtain the upgrade are listed below according to response time; the first method listed is the slowest, the last method listed is the fastest.

- Spectrum Holobyte will notify all registered users by mail and explain the upgrade procedures.
- You can contact Spectrum Holobyte's Customer Service department directly. The first page of the Falcon 3.0 manual lists the Customer Service department's phone number. Additionally, Spectrum Holobyte can be reached via electronic mail on several popular computer networks (CompuServe, Internet, Prodigy, etc.). The email addresses for these networks are also listed on the first page of the Falcon 3.0 manual.
- If you have a CompuServe account, you can download Falcon 3.0 upgrades from the Game Publishers' Forum. Enter GO GAMEPUB at any CompuServe prompt. Section 5 of the Game Publishers' Forum is dedicated to Spectrum Holobyte. Their Customer Service representatives place Falcon 3.0 upgrades in the associated Library 5 in a single, compressed, archive file.

Use the instructions supplied with your CompuServe account and your telecommunications program to download the compressed file to your computer. Then, you must use the PKUNZIP utility to extract the individual upgrade files from the compressed archive file. Follow the directions in the file PATCH.DOC to install the upgrade.

NOTE: To use option 3, you must have a CompuServe account, you must know how to download files to your computer, you must have the PKUNZIP decompression utility, and you must follow the directions provided in the PATCH.DOC file.

Falcon 3.0d Notes

Version Falcon 3.0D varies substantially from its predecessors. In addition to fixing fatal errors and critical bugs, several game enhancements are also included. These enhancements are

- Improved artificial intelligence — Computer controlled aircraft (both friendly and hostile) act much more aggressively and intelligently.
- Improved Electronic Countermeasures — ECM pods and chaff act realistically. Computer controlled aircraft make much better use of countermeasures.
- Improved Campaign Structure — Many revisions have gone into the campaign system. Ordnance and weapons stockpiles are correctly managed. Mission debriefings are greatly improved.
- Aircraft avoid the ground — B-52s (and other aircraft) no longer crash into the ground for no reason.
- Pilot Skills Advancements are improved — Red Flag missions now properly increment the skills of squadron pilots.
- Padlock view improved — The padlock view will now track incoming missiles.
- Communications Mode Improved — Two player and multiple player modes are more reliable.

Additionally, many bugs causing problems with sounds, graphics, and crashes have been repaired. Falcon 3.0E is a more recent upgrade which fixes known problems with Falcon 3.0D. It should be available through the same channels as previous upgrades sometime after September 1992. In summary, upgrading is well worth the time it takes to obtain and install the program file.

Index

WAITE GROUP PRESS™

FRACTAL CREATIONS

Explore the Magic of Fractals on Your PC

by Timothy Wegner and Mark Peterson

Over 40,000 computer enthusiasts who've purchased this book/software package are creating and exploring the fascinating world of fractals on their computers. **Fractal Creations** includes a full-color fractal-art poster, 3-D glasses, and *Fractint*, the revolutionary software that makes fractals accessible to anyone with a PC. *Fractint* lets you zoom in on any part of a fractal image, rotate it, do color-cycle animation, and even choose accompanying sound effects and a 3-D mode. PC Magazine said "**Fractal Creations**...is a magical ride...guaranteed to blow your eyes out." Winner of the 1991 Computer Press Association Award for "Best Non-Fiction Computer Book." For MS/PC DOS machines; best with a VGA video board and a 286/386 processor.

ISBN 1-878739-05-0, 315 pp., 1 5.25" disk, color poster, 3-D glasses, $34.95 US/$44.95 Can., Available now

VIRTUAL REALITY PLAYHOUSE

by Nick Lavroff

Jack-in to the world of Virtual Reality with this playful new book and disk package. Virtual Reality is a new interactive technology which creates the convincing illusion that you are completely immersed in worlds existing only inside your computer. **Virtual Reality Playhouse** lets you enter those worlds and even create your own personal digital dimension. Expand the parameters of your mind as you move rapidly from an introduction of virtual reality's basic concepts to visual explorations illustrating real-life applications. Demo programs include a 3-D simulation that puts you inside a robot which travels through a computer-generated city. Or, you can play a game in a 3-D room that can be tilted, spun, and twisted in near impossible ways. Put on the enclosed 3-D glasses and jump right into any one of 8 startling VR simulations. There are even plans for building your own LCD shuttering VR glasses and power glove to manipulate objects in a VR world. For MS/PC DOS machines.

ISBN 1-878739-19 -0, 146 pp., 1 3.5" disk, 3-D glasses, $22.95 US/$29.95 Can., Available June 1992

RAY TRACING CREATIONS

Create 3-D Photorealistic Images on the PC

by Drew Wells

With the **Ray Tracing Creations** book/disk combination, you can immediately begin rendering perfect graphic objects like the ones in computer movies. Using the bundled powerful shareware *POV-Ray* program, you'll learn to control the location, shape, light, shading, and surface texture of all kinds of 3-D objects. *POV-Ray's* C-like language is used to describe simple objects, planes, spheres, and more complex polygons. Over 100 incredible pre-built scenes are included that can be generated, studied, and modified any way you choose. This book provides a complete course in the fundamentals of ray tracing that will challenge and entice you. Contains 386 and 286 versions of *POV-Ray*; VGA display required. For MS/PC DOS machines.

ISBN 1-878739-27-1, 400 pp., 1 HD 3.5" disk, 3-D glasses, $39.95 US/$49.95 Can., Available December 1992

Send for our unique catalog to get more information about these books, as well as our outstanding and award-winning programming titles, including:

Master C: Let the PC Teach You C and **Master C++:** Let the PC Teach You Object-Oriented Programming. Both are book/disk software packages that turn your computer into an infinitely patient C and C++ professor.

Workout C: Hundreds of C projects and exercises and a full-featured C compiler make this an unbeatable training program and value.

C++ Primer Plus: Written by Stephen Prata in the same style as his C Primer Plus, which won the Computer Press Association's coveted "Best How-To Computer Book" award and sold over 400,000 copies.

Object Oriented Programming in Turbo C++: Robert Lafore, master teacher of the programming art, takes the prospective C++ programmer from the basics to the most complex concepts, and provides anyone with C++ programming experience a comprehensive reference.

Windows API Bible: The only comprehensive guide to the 800 instructions and messages in the Windows Application Programming Interface.

Visual Basic How-To and **Visual Basic Super Bible.** Both books cover the unique Microsoft language that makes Windows programming much more accessible. **How-To** covers tricks, tips, and traps of VB programming. **Super Bible** is the ultimate compendium of reference information on VB.

Turbo Pascal How-To: Everything you need to know to begin writing professional Turbo Pascal programs.

WAITE GROUP PRESS™

MULTIMEDIA CREATIONS

Hands-On Workshop for Exploring Animation

by Philip Shaddock

Contemplating the jump into multimedia? Do it with **Multimedia Creations** and its powerful bundled *GRASP* program. Whether novice or programmer, you can create your own animated interactive audio-visual programs: from concept through post production, renderings to video tape. After a brief primer on PC video systems and animation fundamentals, you can start working with *GRASP*, creating everything from educational programs to your own multimedia cartoons. Work through the entire book/disk package to learn tricks like windowing, color cycling, sprite animation, delta compression techniques, and classical flipbook-style animation. And there are advanced chapters with in-depth coverage and reference sources for power users. Accompanying shareware programs provide you with the basic tools for creating complete multimedia presentations on the PC. For MS/PC DOS machines.

ISBN 1-878739-26-3, 450 pp, 2 5.25" disks, $44.95 US/$56.95 Can., Available October 1992

FRACTALS FOR WINDOWS

The Magic of Fractals Becomes Even More Accessible

by Tim Wegner, Mark Peterson, Bert Tyler, and Pieter Branderhorst

This is a perfect companion to **Fractal Creations**, but it probes deeper. It is bundled with *WINFRACT*, a powerful Windows program which enables you to play with over 80 fractals, or create totally new fractals, controlling your experiments simply with a zoom box, buttons, dialog boxes, menus, and a mouse. And because *WINFRACT*'s core technology is the latest version 18 of *FRACTINT* for DOS, it's faster than lightning at computing fractals. Plus you can generate fractals in the background! If you don't have any programming experience, that's ok. We've designed this package so you can still climb on board. But if you are a programmer, you'll love this rich resource of spectacular images you can use with other Windows programs.

ISBN 1-878739-25-5, 350 pp, 1 HD 3.5" disk, color section, 3-D glasses, $34.95 US/$44.95 Can., Available December 1992

TO ORDER TOLL FREE CALL 1-800-368-9369

TELEPHONE 415-924-2575 • FAX 415-924-2576

SEND ORDER FORM BELOW TO: WAITE GROUP PRESS, 200 TAMAL PLAZA, CORTE MADERA, CA 94925

Qty	Book	US/Can Price	Total
____	C++ Primer Plus	$26.95/34.95	______
____	Fractal Creations ❏ 3.5" ❏ 5.25" disk	$34.95/44.95	______
____	Fractals For Windows	$34.95/44.95	______
____	Master C ❏ 3.5" ❏ 5.25" disks	$44.95/56.95	______
____	Master C++ ❏ 3.5" ❏ 5.25" disks	$39.95/49.95	______
____	Multimedia Creations	$44.95/56.95	______
____	OOP in Turbo C++	$29.95/32.95	______
____	Ray Tracing Creations	$39.95/49.95	______
____	Turbo Pascal How-To	$24.95/32.95	______
____	Virtual Reality Playhouse	$22.95/29.95	______
____	Visual Basic How-To	$34.95/44.95	______
____	Visual Basic Super Bible	$39.95/49.95	______
____	Windows API Bible	$39.95/49.95	______
____	Workout C	$39.95/49.95	______
Calif. residents add 7.25% Sales Tax			______
Shipping			
UPS ($5 first book/$1 each add'l)			______
UPS Two Day ($10/$2)			______
Canada ($10/$4)			______
		TOTAL	______

Ship to

Name ______________________________

Company ______________________________

Address ______________________________

City, State, Zip ______________________________

Phone ______________________________

Payment Method

❏ Check Enclosed ❏ VISA ❏ MasterCard

Card# ______________________ Exp. Date ________

Signature ______________________________

SATISFACTION GUARANTEED
OR YOUR MONEY BACK.
NO QUESTIONS ASKED.

Environmental Awareness

Books have a substantial influence on the destruction of the forests of the Earth. For example, it takes 17 trees to produce one ton of paper. A first printing of 30,000 copies of a typical 480 page book consumes 108,000 pounds of paper which will require 918 trees!

Waite Group Press™ is against the clear-cutting of forests and supports reforestation of the Pacific Northwest of the United States and Canada, where most of this paper comes from. As a publisher with several hundred thousand books sold each year, we feel an obligation to give back to the planet. We will therefore support and contribute a percentage of our proceeds to organizations which seek to preserve the forests of planet Earth.

This is a legal agreement between you, the end user and purchaser, and The Waite Group®, Inc., and the authors of the shareware programs contained in the disk. By opening the sealed disk package, you are agreeing to be bound by the terms of this Agreement. If you do not agree with the terms of this Agreement, promptly return the unopened disk package and the accompanying items (including the related book and other written material) to the place you obtained them for a refund.

SOFTWARE LICENSE

1. The Waite Group, Inc. grants you the right to use one copy of the enclosed software programs (the programs) on a single computer system (whether a single CPU, part of a licensed network, or a terminal connected to a single CPU). Each concurrent user of the program must have exclusive use of the related Waite Group, Inc. written materials.

2. Each of the programs, including the copyrights in each program, is owned by the respective author and the copyright in the entire work is owned by The Waite Group, Inc. and they are therefore protected under the copyright laws of the United States and other nations, under international treaties. You may make only one copy of the disk containing the programs exclusively for backup or archival purposes, or you may transfer the programs to one hard disk drive, using the original for backup or archival purposes. You may make no other copies of the programs, and you may make no copies of all or any part of the related Waite Group, Inc. written materials.

3. You may not rent or lease the programs, but you may transfer ownership of the programs and related written materials (including any and all updates and earlier versions) if you keep no copies of either, and if you make sure the transferee agrees to the terms of this license.

4. You may not decompile, reverse engineer, disassemble, copy, create a derivative work, or otherwise use the programs except as stated in this Agreement.

GOVERNING LAW

This Agreement is governed by the laws of the State of California.

Please fill out this card if you wish to know of future updates to *Falcon 3: Complete Handbook*, or to receive our catalog.

Satisfaction Report Card

Company Name: ____________________

Division/Department ____________________ **Mail Stop:** ____________________

Last Name: ____________________ **First Name:** ____________________ **Middle Initial:** ______

Street Address: ____________________

City: ____________________ **State:** ____________________ **Zip:** ______

Daytime telephone: (   ) ____________________

Date product was acquired: Month ______ **Day** ______ **Year** ______ **Your Occupation:** ____________________

Overall, how would you rate *The Waite Group's Falcon 3*

- ☐ Excellent ☐ Very Good ☐ Good
- ☐ Fair ☐ Below Average ☐ Poor

What did you like MOST about this product? ____________________

What did you like LEAST about this product? ____________________

Please describe any problems you may have encountered with installing or using Image Lab: ____________________

How do you use this book (tutorial, reference, problem-solver...)? ____________________

How did you find the pace of this book? ____________________

What computer languages are you familiar with? ____________________

What is your level of computer expertise?

- ☐ New ☐ Dabbler ☐ Hacker
- ☐ Power User ☐ Programmer ☐ Experienced professional

Is there any program or subject you would like to see The Waite Group cover in a similar approach? ____________________

Please describe your computer hardware:

Computer ______________ Hard disk ______________

5.25" disk drives ______________ 3.5" disk drives ______________

Video card ______________ Monitor ______________

Printer ______________ Peripherals ______________

Where did you buy this book?

- ☐ Bookstore (name: ______________)
- ☐ Discount store (name: ______________)
- ☐ Computer store (name: ______________)
- ☐ Catalog (name: ______________)
- ☐ Direct from WGP ☐ Other ______________

What price did you pay for this book? ______________

What influenced your purchase of this book?

- ☐ Recommendation ☐ Advertisement
- ☐ Magazine review ☐ Store display
- ☐ Mailing ☐ Book's format
- ☐ Reputation of The Waite Group ☐ Topic

How many computer books do you buy each year? ______________

How many other Waite Group books do you own? ______________

What is your favorite Waite Group book? ______________

Additional comments? ______________

☐ **Check here for a free Waite Group Press catalog**

NO POSTAGE
NECESSARY
IF MAILED
IN THE
UNITED STATES

BUSINESS REPLY MAIL

FIRST CLASS MAIL PERMIT NO. 9 CORTE MADERA, CA

POSTAGE WILL BE PAID BY ADDRESSEE

Waite Group Press, Inc.
Attention: *Falcon 3: The Complete Handbook*
200 Tamal Plaza
Corte Madera, CA 94925

FOLD HERE

LIMITED WARRANTY

The following warranties shall be effective for 90 days from the date of purchase: (i) The Waite Group, Inc. warrants the enclosed disk to be free of defects in materials and workmanship under normal use; and (ii) The Waite Group, Inc. warrants that the programs, unless modified by the purchaser, will substantially perform the functions described in the documentation provided by The Waite Group, Inc. when operated on the designated hardware and operating system. The Waite Group, Inc. does not warrant that the programs will meet purchaser's requirements or that operation of a program will be uninterrupted or error-free. The program warranty does not cover any program that has been altered or changed in any way by anyone other than The Waite Group, Inc. The Waite Group, Inc. is not responsible for problems caused by changes in the operating characteristics of computer hardware or computer operating systems that are made after the release of the programs, nor for problems in the interaction of the programs with each other or other software.

THESE WARRANTIES ARE EXCLUSIVE AND IN LIEU OF ALL OTHER WARRANTIES OF MERCHANTABILITY OR FITNESS FOR A PARTICULAR PURPOSE OR OF ANY OTHER WARRANTY, WHETHER EXPRESS OR IMPLIED.

EXCLUSIVE REMEDY

The Waite Group, Inc. will replace any defective disk without charge if the defective disk is returned to The Waite Group, Inc. within 90 days from date of purchase.

This is Purchaser's sole and exclusive remedy for any breach of warranty or claim for contract, tort, or damages.

LIMITATION OF LIABILITY

THE WAITE GROUP, INC. AND THE AUTHORS OF THE PROGRAMS SHALL NOT IN ANY CASE BE LIABLE FOR SPECIAL, INCIDENTAL, CONSEQUENTIAL, INDIRECT, OR OTHER SIMILAR DAMAGES ARISING FROM ANY BREACH OF THESE WARRANTIES EVEN IF THE WAITE GROUP, INC. OR ITS AGENT HAS BEEN ADVISED OF THE POSSIBILITY OF SUCH DAMAGES.

THE LIABILITY FOR DAMAGES OF THE WAITE GROUP, INC. AND THE AUTHORS OF THE PROGRAMS UNDER THIS AGREEMENT SHALL IN NO EVENT EXCEED THE PURCHASE PRICE PAID.

COMPLETE AGREEMENT

This Agreement constitutes the complete agreement between The Waite Group, Inc. and the authors of the programs, and you, the purchaser.

Some states do not allow the exclusion or limitation of implied warranties or liability for incidental or consequential damages, so the above exclusions or limitations may not apply to you. This limited warranty gives you specific legal rights; you may have others, which vary from state to state.